WRITING OUT OF PLACE

Writing out of Place

Regionalism, Women, and American Literary Culture

JUDITH FETTERLEY AND
MARJORIE PRYSE

UNIVERSITY OF ILLINOIS PRESS
URBANA AND CHICAGO

∞ This book is printed on acid-free paper.

The Library of Congress cataloged the cloth edition as follows:
Fetterley, Judith, 1938–
Writing out of place : regionalism, women, and American literary culture / Judith Fetterley and Marjorie Pryse.
p. cm.
Includes bibliographical references and index.
ISBN 0-252-02767-1 (acid-free paper)
1. American literature—Women authors—History and criticism.
2. Feminism and literature—United States. 3. Women and literature—United States. 4. Place (Philosophy) in literature. 5. Regionalism in literature. 6. Setting (Literature) I. Pryse, Marjorie, 1948– . II. Title.
PS147.F48 2003
810.9'9287—dc21 2002002828

PAPERBACK ISBN 978-0-252-07258-1

CONTENTS

ACKNOWLEDGMENTS

We would like to thank our students at the University at Albany, State University of New York, and colleagues at other institutions who have shared our interest in reading and talking about American literary regionalism and the mostly women writers who created it. We also want to thank the members of the Northeast Nineteenth-Century American Women Writers Study Group and the Society for the Study of American Women Writers for numerous discussions of nineteenth-century U.S. literary history and culture, some quite germane to this project. Several persons have shared their own knowledge with us and have been particularly helpful in the writing of this book. We acknowledge in particular Paula Bennett, Joanne Dobson, Frances Smith Foster, Sharon Harris, Susan Harris, Joan Hedrick, Gregory Jay, Charles Johanningsmeier, Karen Kilcup, Paul Lauter, Susanne Opfermann, Sarah Way Sherman, Catherine Sustana, Beth Weatherby, and Sandra Zagarell.

We also acknowledge and thank the various editors who, at one point or another, have played significant roles in helping us develop our work: John Benedict, late of W. W. Norton and Company, and Julia Reidhead, W. W. Norton, our editors for *American Women Regionalists, 1850–1910: A Norton Anthology* (1992); Leslie Mitchener of Rutgers University Press, who served as editor for the *American Women Writers Series,* a series that made available the first contemporary reprints of several regionalist writers; and most recently, Joan Catapano, earlier an editor for each of us individually at Indiana University Press, and now our editor at University of Illinois Press. We would also like to thank our copy editor at Illinois, Carol Betts, for her hard work on our behalf.

CHAPTER 1

Redefinitions

Now if anybody gets this book before the hundred years dont burn it, so the young woman can have the benefit of what is intended for her.

—Sarah Orne Jewett, "Diary" (1867)

Sarah Orne Jewett began a diary September 7, 1867, the week she celebrated her eighteenth birthday. As part of the entry for September 29, she invents an imaginary reader named Phebe and decides to keep a journal "with a view to your getting some improving information young woman!" In order to begin to write, Jewett first creates a relationship "a hundred years from now" with "some girl like me," and she implies that an attempt to pass along to Phebe "the benefit of what is intended for her" will ensure that no one will burn her book. Although we will not construct a "Phebe," a figure who drops out of sight early in the diaries to be replaced with the names of Jewett's real friends,[1] the impulse to write in order to pass on what Jewett and other nineteenth-century American regionalist writers valued to readers a century later informs our own desire in writing this book. *Writing out of Place* begins with our sense that Jewett addresses us in her diary; that we, in a conscious use of the historical present tense, address readers who may also live a hundred years from now; and that the act of reading regionalism, then writing about our reading, involves us in a process that makes a difference in the way we "read" the culture in which we live—and, we hope, in which readers a hundred years from now will also read. In so doing we echo Willa Cather, who closed her "Preface" to *The Best Stories of Sarah Orne Jewett* by predicting a "long, joyous future" for *The Country of the Pointed Firs*, yet located the onset of that future "in far distant years to come." She wrote: "I like to think with what pleasure, with what a sense of rich discovery, the young student of American literature in far distant years to come will take up this book and say, 'A masterpiece!' as proudly as if he himself had made it. It will be a message to the future" (11).

Introducing the Writers

In *Writing out of Place* we examine a collection of American literary texts from the late nineteenth and early twentieth centuries that we believe speak to readers in a variety of ways. By "locating" these texts that have seemed for so long to be "out of place" in American literary culture, we are not trying to establish regionalism as a fixed literary category, but rather to understand it as the site of a dialogical critical conversation. However the writers of these texts would have articulated their concerns had they written in forms other than sketches and fictions, it remains the case that readers now find in their work issues that have increasingly occupied our attention at the turn of our own century. Regionalist texts call into question numerous cultural assumptions about literary history, poetics, thematics, genres, and reading strategies that their authors probably would recognize and that this book in effect argues they anticipated. In addition, some of the texts also raise questions for theory that the writers might not recognize, or might pose differently. Some of these questions will involve us in discussions of epistemology, of race and class, and of queer theory. Many of the texts of regionalism contradict ideas of the "American" and of American literature that were in their formative stages after the Civil War, became crystallized in the political philosophy of the Theodore Roosevelt era, and in the twentieth century served U.S. imperialism.

From our earliest discussions about regionalism almost two decades ago, we agreed that our first goal ought to be to make the texts of regionalism available to readers. To this end, Fetterley coedited the American Women Writers series for Rutgers University Press, which has brought back into print numerous nineteenth- and early-twentieth-century writers including the regionalists Alice Cary, Rose Terry Cooke, and Mary Austin.[2] Together we coedited *American Women Regionalists, 1850–1910: A Norton Anthology,* which we view as the first of a two-part effort (the second being *Writing out of Place*) to create a community of readers for regionalism and to generate critical conversation about a movement that American literary history has not yet made visible.[3] As we debated our selections for *American Women Regionalists,* we became aware that the texts themselves "define" regionalism. We also realized that we were not trying to recover authors so much as texts. We are proposing and claiming as regionalist a certain group of prose texts by writers whose larger literary production may be at variance with the principles of regionalism they themselves demonstrate. Our interests are more critical and theoretical than they are biographical and historical; we are intrigued by the aggregate effects of regionalist materials across differences of geography, generation, race, and class.

It seems appropriate, therefore, to begin *Writing out of Place* by introducing the texts we have previously collected, even though we will be discussing additional texts and writers, for these texts represent the tradition we will be seeking to identify in this chapter and throughout this book. *American Women Regionalists* includes sketches and short fictions generally published between 1850 and 1910, with the exception of the opening sketch by Harriet Beecher Stowe, "Uncle Lot" (1834), and the closing story by Cather, "Old Mrs. Harris" (1932). As we will discuss in more detail in chapter 3, "Uncle Lot" stands as one of the preliminary texts that allow us to understand the origins of regionalism. "Uncle Lot" derives its energy, first, from its title character, thereby initiating regionalism as a fiction that privileges character over plot, and second, by engaging in a literary and critical dialogue with some of the assumptions of early American fiction as Washington Irving delineated these in "Rip Van Winkle" and "The Legend of Sleepy Hollow," thereby associating regionalism with an element of critique. As we will discuss in chapter 2, Cather's "Old Mrs. Harris" serves as a postscript to the collection, marking the limits of the development of nineteenth-century regionalism. Although she dedicated her first novel, *O Pioneers!* to Sarah Orne Jewett as a way of recognizing her indebtedness to the older woman who had mentored her writing in the year before her own death, Cather primarily chose to write novels that engaged in other conversations than those of her regionalist predecessors. In "Old Mrs. Harris," however, written near the end of her career, she takes up the question of her relation to regionalism, writing in effect an elegy for a mode of writing and a generation of writers no longer useful for her. These two texts thus serve to frame the anthology and the tradition, even though they may not be representative of other work by Stowe and Cather.

Within this frame, we included in *American Women Regionalists,* in chronological order of first regional publication, texts by the following writers, only some of whose names may be familiar even to scholars of American literature: Alice Cary, Rose Terry Cooke, Celia Thaxter, Sarah Orne Jewett, Mary Noailles Murfree, Mary E. Wilkins Freeman, Grace Elizabeth King, Kate Chopin, Alice Dunbar-Nelson, Sui Sin Far, Zitkala-Ša, and Mary Austin. Reading this list of names in this order raises several issues that we will begin to address in this introduction. First, there are names missing from this list that are often associated with the categories of regional writing or local-color fiction, an absence that invites us to clarify the difference between these two and to define how we are using the term "regionalism." Second, we chose to organize the anthology chronologically rather than by region, a decision that raises additional questions of how we understand the relation of region to regionalism and the relation of regionalism to place, as well as the critical problem Jewett poses for a tradition literary history has constituted as minor. Third, the anthology includes only women writers, which marks for discussion the relationship between gender and regionalism and perhaps highlights the chronological period within which these women wrote. Fourth, this list includes writers identified as racially "other," thus directing attention to how and whether race emerges as a concern within a movement defined primarily by gender as well as to whether "white" itself constitutes a racial marking in regionalism, thus requiring us to think about the relation of gender as a category of analysis to other categories of analysis such as race. Finally, in its move across the nineteenth and into the twentieth century, the list raises questions concerning how the meaning of "region" changes over time; implicates the critical study of regionalism in changing concepts of nation that, by the end of the nineteenth and the beginning of the twentieth century, involve questions of imperialism; and invites us to reflect on contemporary manipulations of regions and regional people, especially women workers, in postcolonial variations on imperialism in our own time. Introducing regionalist texts and writers involves addressing these issues, and as we take them up in turn, we will do so primarily as they allow us to address the critical and theoretical concerns that will occupy us in *Writing out of Place.*

The Question of the Category

The first issue our list of regionalist writers raises concerns the category of regionalism itself. As we will discuss at length in chapter 2, historians have minimized, ignored, and disparaged these writers, either relegating them to the category of "local color" or describing them as a subset of realism by the phrase "regional realists." Our choice of the identifying term "regionalism" to refer to the tradition we wish to bring into visibility removes these writers from that subset, turns the modifier into a noun, and locates regionalism alongside realism and naturalism as a parallel tradition of narrative prose written roughly in the second half of the nineteenth century and at the turn into the twentieth (to cite a useful locution by Elizabeth Ammons in *Conflicting Stories*). While regionalism shares certain features of mode and subject matter with realism, it does not share the ideological underpinnings of the more familiar category. Indeed, as we will discuss in chapter 7, regionalism poses both a critique of and a resistance to the cultural ideologies that realism naturalizes. Readers may also associate the term "regionalism" with the Southern Agrarians of the 1930s who chose it in order to avoid the contentiousness of the nineteenth-century word "sectionalism" while still arguing for a Southern "regionalist" renaissance in literature.[4] While the Agrarians gave us some of our most provocative twentieth-century critics and writers, including Cleanth Brooks and Robert Penn Warren, their use of the term "regionalism" bears little relation to our own, as it is based on conservative values rooted in the ownership of land and its cultivation, naturalizes physical geography to define regions, and in particular seeks to justify the South's continuing cultural and economic autonomy.

Furthermore, while those writers we have termed regionalist are often interested in features of the physical landscape, they are not nature writers; on the contrary, even Thaxter and Austin, whose work privileges the natural world, focus on the relationship between that world and human consciousness. Regions, for these writers, have boundaries, but those boundaries that separate regional from urban or metropolitan life highlight relations of ruling rooted in economic history and the material requirements for everyday livelihood rather than in physical and "natural" borders. These writers both in their fictions and in their own biographies frequently move back and forth between urban and rural/"regional" places; while cosmopolitan attitudes might assume clear barriers between the modernizing life of the cities and the presumptively premodern world of the regions, for the writers themselves and in their regionalist texts, these barriers become permeable and transitive.[5]

Significantly, the etymology of the word "region" does not suggest any connection to "natural" or geographical boundaries. To be ruled is to be *regional* (the word deriving from the Latin *regere*); to rule is to become the king of the *realm* (also from *regere*). But he who rules is the *rex*, and the territory of the realm is the *real* (all related etymologically). Thus a region is an area ruled by a more powerful entity, earlier a king, in modern times the state or nation, and increasingly at present global economic interests. The very words "region" and "regionalism" therefore convey political relations of subordination. However, these relations are far from fixed. As Frank Davey suggests, writing within a Canadian context in which regionalism has become a political strategy as well as a literary movement, we need to re-understand regionalism in terms of institutions and processes such as the nation-state, colonialism, and globalization (1–2). Although there are intriguing differences between regionalism as it operates politically in Canada and in the United States, the theoretical analysis that emerges from Davey's examination of present-day regional politics in Canada articulates the dynamics of the tensions between local color and regionalism that we wish to explore. Indeed, Davey's complex understanding of regionalism helps explain the marginalization of those particular regional texts that make visible rather than conceal the presence of ideology.

Davey argues that it is the role of the critic to denaturalize what it means to claim a regionalist identity, either for someone who inhabits a specific geography or for a literary text that takes place within an identifiable region. "Far from being a geographical manifestation, a regionalism is a discourse. . . . As a discourse, it represents a general social or political strategy for resisting meanings generated by others in a nation-state, particularly those generated in geographic areas which can be constructed by the regionalism as central or powerful" (4). Davey makes a distinction here between regionalism as a political strategy of resistance and regionalism as a commodity production of the nation-state that serves its political interests while pretending to be nonideological. For example, the idea of geographical determinism, used to contain the development of regional and transregional political power, "is popularly concealed beneath touristic images of landscape and inarticulately authentic individuals," and so "there appears to be no ideology" in such representations (5).[6] When regionalist texts challenge these touristic images and allow regional persons to insert articulations of their own understanding of region, they disrupt this popular conception, reveal regions themselves to be discursive constructions, and ultimately critique the commodification of regions in local color as a destructive form of cultural entertainment that reifies not only the subordinate status of regions but also hierarchical structures of gender, race, class, and nation. In effect, literary regionalism uncovers the ideology of local color and reintroduces an awareness of ideology into discussions of regionalist politics.

For Davey, one aspect of the ideology contained in the regionalism produced by the nation-state is the naturalizing illusion that "while the nation-state is an abstract concept, with exchangeable citizenships and shiftable borders, regionalism has a concrete ground in the geography that it invokes as its region" (4). What a geographical grounding for regionalism obscures are "the politically oppositional aspects of regionalism: that regionalism is cultural rather than geographic, and represents not geography itself but a strategically resistant mapping of geography in which historic and economic factors play large but largely unacknowledged parts" (4). In Davey's understanding of regionalism as a "strategically resistant mapping of geography" that can make visible "historic and economic factors" we can begin to sketch the connections between literary regionalism in the United States as a site for critical analysis and the emerging interest of critical theorists in the effects of regionalization on a global scale. Regionalism as a strategy operates within larger power relations that include the politics of literary recovery and canonicity as well as the politics of contemporary industrial nation-states.[7] As both a literary and a political discourse, regionalism thus also becomes the site of contestation over the meaning of region, one that reveals the ideological underpinnings of regionalization.

Our choice of the term "regionalism" to mark the category of texts that exist in this site of contestation results from the ironically fortuitous way in which literary historians have casually designated nineteenth-century works set in geographical regions outside urban centers as "local color." Even feminist critics have, until recently, accepted this term and used it to refer to any nineteenth-century regional writer.[8] Not even in the Southern Agrarians' use of the term to invoke a cultural sectionalism have critics chosen to mark the elements of critique and resistance in certain regional texts. Thus the term becomes available for redefinition, and in adopting it to refer to those texts that mark such elements, we also understand that regions are never fully ruled. It is only from the perspective of the *rex* or the *realm,* or from cosmopolitans who have much to gain by "regionalizing" and thereby containing the power of certain groups of people, that regions seem to be both "natural" and "separate." Sandra Zagarell has recently identified this perspective in writing of Freeman. She suggests that "Freeman's work endeavors to undo regionalism's habitual casting of rural New England as separated from the rest of the nation" ("Introduction" xx) and observes that "Freeman occasionally took open exception to the regionalist premise that New England villages were the preserves of richly traditional cultures" (xxi). The "regionalist premise" she is underscoring here and arguing that Freeman works against is in effect a "regionalizing premise," the cosmopolitan view that to "regionalize" is to contain and dismiss any resistance a region might make to its very regionalization.

In articulating regionalism as an "open exception" to this premise, and in tracing this "exception" across a range of texts by predominantly women writers, we are conscious of being influenced by Michel Foucault's understanding of resistance. In his analysis of power in *The History of Sexuality, Vol. I* as "strictly relational," Foucault describes resistance as a "multiplicity of points" and he argues that "[t]hese points of resistance are present everywhere in the power network" (95). He writes further that resistances

> are distributed in irregular fashion: the points, knots, or focuses of resistance are spread over time and space at varying densities, at times mobilizing groups or individuals in a definitive way. . . . Are there no great radical ruptures, massive binary divisions, then? Occasionally, yes. But more often one is dealing with mobile and transitory points of resistance, producing cleavages in a society that shift about, fracturing unities and effecting regroupings, furrowing across individuals themselves, cutting them up and remolding them, marking off irreducible regions in them, in their bodies and minds. (96)

It is significant that Foucault uses the language of regions to describe the fracturing effects of points of resistance on individual unities for it associates regionalism with an understanding of resistance that is not always "passive, doomed to perpetual defeat" (96). It is as if regions can generate points of resistance, but in "irregular fashion." Writers of and from regions who locate fictions as points of resistance rather than as commodified "local coloring" offer a set of textual sites where the process of "fracturing unities and effecting regroupings" is given place, character, and regional voice.

We use the term "regionalism," then, to articulate the perspective from ruled places that includes the perception that "regionalization" is not natural; it is not a feature of geography, though topography may play some part in changing economic conditions. Rather, regionalism asserts that the regionalizing premise concerns the consolidation and maintenance of power through ideology and is therefore a discourse, as Davey explains above, rather than a place. In constructing the literary category of regionalism, in effect, by studying writing that already recognizes itself to be "out of place" even in its relation to place, we are thereby adding a discursive marker to certain texts and inviting readers to immerse themselves in the "open exception" regionalists take to the very power structure that has "regionalized" their characters and their writing. We make a distinction between those writers who accept the assumptions of the regionalizing premise and those who take exception to these assumptions. Those writers or texts that take such exception also mark themselves as "out of place" in their culture. Although it would be too much to claim that to read these latter texts as regionalist discourse, as resistant voices from the regionalized, can "overrule" the power structures of the political and cultural construction of regions themselves, we will demonstrate in *Writing out of Place* that learning to recognize the discursive marker that differentiates regionalism not only from local color but also from literary realism has the potential to change the way readers see regional worlds.

Questions of literary categories are not unique to our project; they continue to characterize efforts by editors and critics to come to terms with regional writers. Although editors early in the twentieth century as well as our own contemporaries have blurred the distinctions between regionalism and local color, the texts that we call regionalist are also those that seem the most unstable in terms of their categorization. The most recent collections, *The Portable American Realism Reader* edited by James Nagel and Tom Quirk in 1997, and *American Local Color Writing, 1880–1920* edited by Elizabeth Ammons and Valerie Rohy in 1998, are typical of earlier collections in the way they conflate regionalism and local color and, in the case of Nagel and Quirk's title, bring the categories of regionalism, local color, and naturalism under the umbrella of realism.[9] Both of these collections are useful in implicitly raising questions of category and both make available to readers texts that are difficult to find. If we examine the contents of these two collections together with *American Women Regionalists,* we discover that the boundaries between categories almost entirely dissolve, with the possible exception of naturalism; in this category there are no texts by women and the only naturalist writers who occupy more than one category for Nagel and Quirk are Stephen Crane and Hamlin Garland, whom they also call realists.

The Portable American Realism Reader contains three parts—"Regionalism and Local Color," "Realism," and "Naturalism." "Regionalism and Local Color" includes primarily writers we have called regionalist and will, throughout this book, differentiate from local color: Stowe, Jewett, Freeman, Cooke, King, Chopin, and Dunbar-Nelson. The only writers Nagel and Quirk add to this category are Mark Twain, Bret Harte, George Washington Cable, and Constance Fenimore Woolson. However, Ammons and Rohy omit Twain, Cable, and Woolson from their collection of local-color writing and curiously add Jack London, a naturalist according to Nagel and Quirk. The category Nagel and Quirk term "Realism" seems even harder to pin down as it also includes Jewett, Freeman, Chopin, and Dunbar-Nelson, as well as Zitkala-Ša, Austin, and Sui Sin Far, writers termed regionalists in *AWR.* Joel Chandler Harris, Charles Chesnutt, Hamlin Garland, and Abraham Cahan, claimed as local-color writers by Ammons and Rohy, are realists for Nagel and Quirk, though Garland is also a naturalist. In addition to Ambrose Bierce, Harold Frederic, Charlotte Perkins Gilman, Madelene Yale Wynne, and Zona Gale, whom neither of the other collections include, Nagel and Quirk have remaining as the core of their "Realism" category Henry James, Edith Wharton, William Dean Howells, and Stephen Crane, also a naturalist.

To complicate the problem of definition even further, Ammons and Rohy use "local color" in their title, but then in the first sentence of their introduction refer to the category their collection represents as "literary regionalism" (vii). They write, alluding to the question of category, "There was never a single local color or regionalist tradition, as suggested by today's debate about which term best names the tradition" (vii). In attempting to extricate the writers included in *AWR* from any simple conflation with the categories of local color or realism, we are seeking to highlight how questions of category and the ways particular writers and texts fit neatly into or challenge categories also become questions of ideology. In *Vested Interests,* Marjorie Garber calls the transvestite character in Western culture the "third term" that creates a "category crisis" for the binary male/female. As she writes, "The 'third' is that which questions binary thinking and introduces crisis" (11). Although realism and local color are not binaries in the same way that male and female are considered to be, the fact that the writers we have designated regionalist cannot be contained in either category, as evidenced in part by the instability of their assignment in contemporary anthologies, posits regionalism as a crisis-creating "third" that makes visible the ideological implications of American literary history. As we will indicate throughout *Writing out of Place,* regionalist texts create more than one kind of "category crisis."

Questions of Chronology and Place

While it would be reasonable to assume that an anthology of regionalist writers would foreground region as a principle of organization, we chose to organize our anthology chronologically rather than by region. We did so for a variety of reasons and in spite of our recognition of the limitations of chronological organization, indeed of the ways in which such organization can be misleading. Chronological organization, for example, implies that regionalism is a literary tradition with a beginning, middle, and end, and to a certain extent, the "story" we tell about the origins of regionalism in chapter 3 as well as our assertion earlier in this introduction that Cather's "Old Mrs. Harris" marks its limits would suggest that we are thinking about regionalism in this way. Without question there is evidence of literary influence that would establish prior and subsequent texts; for example, Jewett acknowledged Stowe's novel *The Pearl of Orr's Island* (1862) as one of her own formative texts; later, Jewett read and mentored Cather's early work. Although we have not found any evidence that Cary and Stowe knew each other when they were both living in or near Cincinnati, Cary would have had access to Stowe's earliest regional sketches and might have been encouraged to write regionalist fiction by her example. Years after

Cary's death, her close friend Mary Louise Booth served as Freeman's editor at *Harper's Bazar*, and we have speculated that the young Mary E. Wilkins, on one of her visits to Booth's home in New York City, might have inquired about the portrait of Alice Cary which Booth hung in her library and might have read the earlier writer's work. Paul Dunbar, in a letter to the young Alice Ruth Moore (later Dunbar-Nelson), associated her sketches with the work of Grace King, and Kate Chopin claimed that Freeman was a "great genius" and that she knew of "no one better than Miss Jewett to study for technique and nicety of construction" (Seyersted 52).

We did not, however, choose to organize our anthology chronologically in order to propose regionalism as a tradition characterized by a linear model of development, for such a proposal would in fact be misleading. Moreover, we are aware that the linear model implicit in chronological organization frequently translates into assertions of hierarchy and dominance that are also inaccurate as descriptors of regionalism. For example, Mark Twain critics often examine the way Twain's humor grows out of the humorists of the Old Southwest (a group of writers we will examine in chapter 3) but present Twain as realizing the possibilities of this humor in ways the earlier writers could not have done. Of course, for Mark Twain critics, humorist writing after Twain is inevitably a falling away. Similarly, the literary historian Van Wyck Brooks described the early nineteenth-century male writers as "the flowering of New England"; by implication, writers from New England after midcentury, most notably Stowe, Cooke, Freeman, and Jewett, represented whatever was left after the "flowering."[10] It would be inaccurate, however, to think of regionalism as a tradition that leads up to, then falls away from, one or two great writers. While Jewett might in many ways constitute regionalism's "Mark Twain" since *The Country of the Pointed Firs* (1896) remains the most widely known regionalist fiction, it would be misleading to describe those writers who preceded her as mere precursors or to describe those who succeeded her as diminished versions of her achievement. Indeed, were we to compare any other writer in the tradition with Jewett, we would find ways in which that writer exceeded Jewett's achievement. Literary regionalism is not in fact a tradition characterized by the model of development implicit in chronological organization. Early regionalist fictions are as good as late regionalist fictions, and the issues regionalist writers address as well as their strategies for writing do not change significantly over time, though their concerns reflect different historical and political issues. The issue of chronology and the question of Jewett became particularly significant in the 1990s, with a series of critical works that tend to conflate Jewett with regionalism.[11] While both of us have published articles on Jewett and admire her work, we do not propose Jewett as model, standard, or apex for the larger movement. Rather, we understand the disproportionate attention to Jewett as reflecting the pressures and politics of literary study and the need to create "canonical" authors. While in some ways Jewett's work makes the best case for her canonical status as at least a "major minor" writer, we are not writing a book about or in defense of Jewett. Although we find Jewett central to our thinking in several of the chapters that follow (particularly in chapters 7 and 11) and frequently take issue with some of the arguments critics have made about her work since they constitute the primary site of the current conversation about regionalism, we do not seek to reinscribe Jewett's preeminence. Rather, we seek to disrupt any move to suggest that once one has read Jewett one has read regionalism. Indeed, we hope to stimulate a much broader interest in this literary tradition and to complicate the reading of Jewett by placing her in the context of this larger tradition in which she was a participant but not the "queen."

Despite its limitations, chronological organization remains preferable to geography as a way of presenting regionalist texts in an anthology designed to identify the tradition, as was *AWR*, even though we have not chosen chronology as an organizing principle for the critical discussions that constitute *Writing out of Place.* Chronology enables us to establish, for example, that the tradition of regionalism actually began in and with Ohio, not New England; Stowe was living in Cincinnati when she wrote "Uncle Lot" and Cary's *Clovernook* sketches represent life in Mt. Healthy, a rural community just north of Cincinnati. In this case, the chronological organization of regionalism actually works against assertions of dominance and hierarchy implicit in geographical organization that tend to give primacy to New England and to mark it as a region different in kind from all other American regions. (We might note here that Ammons and Rohy also recognize the prevalence of this tendency by their own resistance to it, using the term "Northeast" rather than "New England" and placing the category third rather than first.)

More significant, however, we chose chronological organization because of the way we understand place in relation to regionalism. On the one hand, we understand regions as far more local and specific than the areas designated by anthologies such as Ammons and Rohy's. On the other hand, as we have discussed above, we understand region less as a term of geographical determinism and more as discourse or a mode of analysis, a vantage point within the network of power relations that provides a location for critique and resistance. Ironically, despite its organization on the basis of conventional understandings of region (the South, Midwest, Northeast, and West), *American Local Color Writing* omits any rationale for its apparently geographical organizing principle and instead reveals a commitment to alternative understandings. In their introduction, Ammons and Rohy do not address the issue of what distinguishes one region from another or how a writer gets assigned to a region, relying, it would seem, on assumptions prior to and external to their text which they do not question. While they divide writers geographically, they emphasize that "writers from each region" are "grouped together in order to illustrate how different authors have widely varied takes on the same region" (xxvii). In addition to emphasizing differences within regions, their introduction focuses on themes that link authors across geographical boundaries rather than on themes or forms that distinguish regions from each other, asserting that "links among authors . . . can be sketched using gender, sexuality, and class as organizing principles" (xxvii), an assertion with which we concur.

To the extent that regions do specify place, we would identify them as much more local than Ammons and Rohy's designations suggest. For example, Sui Sin Far's "region" is the urban Chinatown of Seattle and the West Coast—hardly the same "West" as that of Bret Harte's or Jack London's fiction (included along with Sui Sin Far in their "West"); Thaxter's is a group of islands, the only ones of their kind, off the coast of New Hampshire; Murfree's is the Tennessee mountains of Appalachia, not a region that can be consolidated into any monolithic "South"; we might say that Cary's is midwestern, to the extent that she writes about rural communities on the outskirts of Cincinnati, but when she was writing Cincinnati saw itself as the "Queen City of the West," not the Midwest; Austin writes about the sparsely populated California desert; and for Zitkala-Ša, the "West" is complicated by her identity as Dakota and her upbringing on the reservation. Chopin, King, and Dunbar-Nelson all place their fictions in Creole Louisiana, a "region" hardly metonymic for the "South"; furthermore, while King depicts the effects of dispossession on white women and Chopin is interested in the "region" of women's sexuality, for Dunbar-Nelson "region" connotes a hybrid space where to be Creole may also mean to be part African. Cooke and Freeman explore rural and village New England; Jewett's region, like Stowe's in *The Pearl of Orr's Island,* is the invaginated Maine coast and the offshore islands. Indeed, regionalist texts seem designed to create a crisis for the category of region, as when, for example, Thaxter in *Among the Isles of Shoals* not only makes distinctions between islands that to most appear indistinguishable but also identifies "regions" on Appledore, an island of less than a hundred acres, thereby raising the question of how small a place would have to be before it would no longer have regions.

While the particularity of the local sites within which regionalist fiction takes or creates place presents a problem for any attempt to locate them in larger categories of regions, at the same time it is analytic rather than geographical commonalities that construct regionalism across the borders that are presumed to divide writers. For example, Thaxter and Austin, writing from strikingly different landscapes and at opposite ends of the continent, have more in common with each other than they do with many of the writers with whom they are often grouped on the basis of geographical region. Ammons and Rohy allude to what we would call an analytics of regionalism when they write, "While some readers still take the region in regionalism at its most literal, comparing regionalist literature with environmentalism and nature writing, . . . region is more accurately a metaphor that describes differences of culture as well as geography" (xxviii). Moreover, they organize their introduction around categories of analysis "that traverse regionalist writing as a whole," categories such as "Culture,

Nation, and Empire," "Race Issues," and "Gender and Sexuality" (xxviii). Throughout *Writing out of Place* we will be exploring the meaning and implications of this understanding of region, but we can begin this exploration by turning to the third issue our list of writers raises.

Gender and Regionalism

As Pryse has discussed in more detail elsewhere ("'Distilling Essences'"), identifying as regionalist primarily texts by women writers leads us to explore the relationship between "women's culture" and regionalism and to ask whether regionalism reinforces or critiques the nineteenth-century ideology of "separate spheres." In observing that regionalism is in effect a women's literary tradition, we place regionalism, as we will discuss in more detail in chapter 2, within a feminist analytic and we associate it with a critique of gender. By further observing that many of the writers collected in our anthology did what we consider to be their best and most recoverable work within the mode of regionalism, we implicitly argue that such a critique constitutes a significant element of regionalism's continuing interest for twenty-first-century readers. In so doing, we follow the line of thought set forth by Cecelia Tichi: "Under cover of regionalism, however, these women writers explored the territory of women's lives. Their essential agenda in the era of the new woman was to map the geography of their gender. They were regionalists—but not solely in the ways critics have conventionally thought. The geography of America formed an important part of their work, but essentially they charted the regions of women's lives, regions both without and within the self" (598). Because writing regionalism allowed writers to be "free to say," a phrase we take from Cooke's "Miss Beulah's Bonnet" and whose significance we discuss in chapter 5, they were able to map a "geography of their gender" that remains vibrant and useful for our own navigations.

Feminist historians who have studied the American nineteenth century (Gerda Lerner, Carroll Smith-Rosenberg, and Linda Kerber, among others) have addressed the concepts "woman's sphere" and "women's culture." As a tradition produced by women in the second half of the nineteenth century, regionalism reflects the reality that gender was, and is, as Eve Kosofsky Sedgwick puts it, "the single most determinative diacritical mark of social organization" (*Epistemology* 87). To the degree that regionalism participates in those distinctions that characterize the ideology of separate spheres—for example, it presents itself as minor not major, regional not national, storytelling not literature, folk craft not high art, as minimally literary not replete with classical references, and requiring little talent or training to produce—it can be said at once to emerge from and to reinforce the ideology of separate spheres. Yet to the degree that it questions, troubles, and complicates these oppositions, it can be said to resist the ideology of separate spheres. Regionalism constitutes a space within which nineteenth-century women writers could critique the construction and operation of this ideology, even as they sought to promote the alternative vision women constructed within their allotted "separate sphere," a vision that was itself at once a product of the social essentialism of gender and a resistance to that essentialism. Indeed, we would argue that "region" in regionalism marks precisely that point where women's culture becomes conscious of itself as critique. In Freeman's "A Church Mouse," for example, Hetty Fifield, a homeless woman as the story opens, manages to create a space of her own and a home for herself within the public meetinghouse. Because she understands that within the ideology of "woman's sphere," "woman" and "home" are inextricably linked, she can work within her culture's assumptions about women to gain entry to the meetinghouse even though such entry also works against other assumptions about women, namely that they have no business doing the job of church sexton for which Hetty has applied and certainly no business living in the meetinghouse.[12] When she curtains off a portion of the meetinghouse with her sunflower quilt (*AWR* 348), she literally creates a region within the public space that she then constructs as her own separate "sphere." The sunflower quilt, emblematic of "women's culture," however, offers Hetty's rhetorical challenge to the ideology of separate spheres, for its very flimsiness suggests how thoroughly the private sphere of women is embedded in and a part of the public sphere of men and thus how public women's culture actually is. The instability of the border between public and private, emblematized by Hetty's quilt, receives further confirmation when the smell of her Saturday night dinner remains to greet Sunday morning worshippers, permeating the entire meetinghouse with the odor of cooked cabbage and inducing the men of the village to seek, unsuccessfully, to reinstate the boundary between home and meetinghouse.

With Freeman's story as our example, we would argue that regionalism marks that point where region becomes mobilized as a tool for critique of hierarchies based on gender as well as race, class, age, and economic resources. Here we would point to the parallels between the process of creating regions and the ideological construction of "separate spheres" for men and women. Both involve structures of dominance, draw boundaries of containment, prescribe and/or restrict political and economic power, construct cultural barriers, obstruct the perspective of persons who accept the hierarchical structures that relegate certain persons to disenfranchised status, and require strategies of translation, conversion, and internalization from those so disenfranchised. In describing the "third stage" in historians' understanding of the concept of "separate spheres," a stage propelled by "the need to break out of the restrictive dualism of an oppressive term (women's sphere) and a liberating term (women's culture)," Linda Kerber indicates that historians now take "an interactive view of social processes," seeking "to show how women's allegedly 'separate sphere' was affected by what men did, and how activities defined by women in their own sphere influenced and even set constraints and limitations on what men might choose to do—how, in short, that sphere was socially constructed both *for* and *by* women" (18). She further suggests that a "major characteristic of the current stage of understanding is that we are . . . treating the language of separate spheres itself as a rhetorical construction that responded to changing social and economic reality" (21). Similarly, we would propose that we understand "region" in regionalism not as a referential geography but rather as "a rhetorical construction" that enables understanding not only of the process of creating regions but of the process of creating other hierarchies as well. In this sense it provides that "constant analysis of language" whose purpose, according to Kerber, "is to assure that we give power no place to hide" (39).

The predominance of women among regionalist writers may also reflect the social and political ferment that roughly coincides with the chronology of the tradition itself. Although we cited 1850 and 1910 as organizing dates for *American Women Regionalists,* it would be more accurate to note the coincidence of the earliest regionalist writing by Cary with the period immediately following the 1848 Seneca Falls Convention for Women's Rights and the signing of the "Declaration of Sentiments." While references to the activists Cooke calls "the Rights Women" and to the suffrage movement itself are rare and uncharacteristic across the span of regionalist texts, the thematics of these sketches and stories overwhelmingly concern women's social and economic independence and development outside conventional roles prescribed by a "separate spheres" culture. The year 1920, then, seems a more accurate date as well to bracket the general close of the nineteenth-century tradition. Sui Sin Far published *Mrs. Spring Fragrance* in 1912, and the stories and novel of Cather that arguably come closest to being influenced by the unconventional portrayal of women in the work of her predecessors are those she wrote during the final decade of the suffrage movement, namely *The Troll Garden* (1905), some of whose stories Jewett herself read, and *The Song of the Lark* (1915).

When we consider the fiction written by the male writers that Nagel and Quirk include in the category "Regionalism and Local Color" or that Ammons and Rohy include in their anthology, we rarely find texts that recognize the ways spheres of the local and of women's place reveal ideological contradictions, and hardly ever texts that work to undermine ideologies of separateness and regionalization when these primarily affect women's lives. That is not to say that male regional writers do not write about women characters. For example, Garland begins "Mrs. Ripley's Trip" with "Mother's" announcement that she is going to make a visit to "Yaark State." For her husband, Uncle Ripley, "in this case, as in all others, the money consideration was uppermost" (183), and the story focuses on the struggle between husband and wife concerning whether or not Mrs. Ripley has enough money for her trip. Unlike Freeman's "The Revolt of 'Mother,'" roughly contemporaneous with "Mrs. Ripley's Trip," in which "Mother" decides to move her family into the new barn her husband has built in order to get him to recognize the extremity of her situation and in which her struggle occupies most of the story, the husband in "Mrs. Ripley's Trip" very early on concedes the importance of the vacation for his wife. However, Garland construes Mrs. Ripley's decision as a vacation not a "revolt," the story portrays Uncle Ripley's generosity of spirit as well as his wife's ambivalence about making the trip, and Garland's narrator stays behind with Uncle Ripley rather than following Mrs. Ripley. We see her leave; and at the end of the story we watch her return, "a queer little figure struggling along the road, . . . an old woman laden with a good half-dozen parcels" (192). All we hear about the trip is that it was "'Pretty good. But I kep' thinkin' o' Ripley an' Tukey all the time. I s'pose they have had a gay time of it' (she meant the opposite of gay)" (192–93). The only thing Mrs. Ripley seems to have learned as the result of her trip is that "'gittin' home to Ripley'" (193) is her primary goal in life. The story's last sentence makes this point: "She took up her burden again, never more thinking to lay it down" (194).

In our reading of "Mrs. Ripley's Trip," we are making a distinction between a story that resists recognizing the contradictions life as a regional wife produced for women and therefore is unable to critique the ideological operations of gender, and one that does recognize such contradictions and does engage in critique. We are suggesting that just because a story adopts a regional setting, it does not necessarily take up the question of what "region" means or how it is deployed. In Bret Harte's work, for example, the interest of the fiction actually derives from the distance between urban, Eastern reader and quaint Western character—a distance some readers find appealing, but which the regionalist writers avoided. Other male writers present more complicated situations, though the basic distinction remains. Garland often expresses sympathy for his characters (as we have described above, Uncle Ripley is quite sympathetic to his wife's desire for a vacation) but that sympathy falls short of exploring ideological contradictions. Most readers agree that *Adventures of Huckleberry Finn* expresses sympathy toward Southern blacks, though critics have been troubled for years by various aspects of the portrayal of Jim and by the way the novel finally evades the question of social responsibility for slavery. While arguably "local" and Southern, however, *Huckleberry Finn* does not explore questions of region. Nor does it problematize gender; indeed, in the famous scene in which Huck puts on a dress and impersonates a girl, gender is represented in essentialist terms as that which cannot be disguised or hidden, and cross-dressing becomes a source of humor rather than an opportunity for gender critique. Sherwood Anderson's portraits of small town life after the turn of the century are sympathetic even though the story he tells in *Winesburg, Ohio* focuses on why a young man like George cannot develop in a place like Winesburg rather than on why and how such a place might be able to nurture its own inhabitants, including George's mother. In sharing George's perception of the other inhabitants of Winesburg, the narrator models narrative distance for the reader and, despite the sympathetic portraits, the characters in *Winesburg* are explicitly described as "grotesques."

The Case for Chesnutt

Initially we had intended to include in *Writing out of Place* a chapter that would address more fully the relationship to our tradition of those male writers typically identified with nineteenth-century regional fiction—Harte, Edward Eggleston, George Washington Cable, Mark Twain, Garland, and, of course, Charles Chesnutt. We had also intended in this chapter to address the place of men as characters and, occasionally, narrators in regionalism, to explore regionalism's analysis of what King calls "the monotonous tone of [male] supremacy" ("A Drama of Three," *AWR* 384), and to articulate its project of reconstructing manhood, particularly in the context of recent work in men's studies. As we began work on this chapter, however, we came to realize that we were in effect projecting another book; and we realized as well that we had in hand a book already longer than we had initially contemplated, one that had reached the limits of what we could write, our publisher could publish, and our readers could read. We have incorporated some of the material of this projected chapter in chapter 11, but we leave the rest to be taken up in other work, whether by ourselves or by others.[13] We cannot, however, move away from this subject without some discussion of Chesnutt, for among the list of possible male candidates for inclusion in the category of regionalism, the most likely is Chesnutt, particularly in his sketches in *The Conjure Woman and Other Tales.* Indeed, in a certain sense, Chesnutt creates a "category crisis" for us as he forces us to recognize that gender does not provide an absolute determinative for regionalism. While we cannot within the limits of this book explore fully the implications of this "crisis" for our category, we do wish to share with readers some of our reflections on the relation of Chesnutt to regionalism.

In *The Conjure Woman,* Chesnutt creates a frame narrative that depicts the relationship between Uncle Julius, a black man who has developed complex strategies for survival in the post–Civil War South; John, a white Northern entrepreneur who has come South to buy an abandoned vineyard; and John's wife, Annie, whose poor health has prompted the move. Chesnutt explores the white man's "inability" to understand Uncle Julius's tales about the horrors of slavery and their relation to the problems of a Northern model of wage-capitalism. In the way Uncle Julius is able to use storytelling to create connections across differences of region, race, and gender and to interrupt the operations of power, *The Conjure Woman* becomes a regionalist text, and regionalism becomes a form of "conjure."

Numerous discursive and formal strategies link *The Conjure Woman* and the texts of regionalist writers. As we will discuss throughout this book, regionalist narratives emphasize their link to an oral tradition in part by the use of dialect but even more in the way storytelling and the relation between storyteller, story, and reader/listener become woven into these narratives. This link to an oral tradition and a storytelling relation, especially as one develops between Uncle Julius and Annie, accurately describes the frame that allows us to read *The Conjure Woman* as a coherent text rather than as a series of stories. In addition, as part of that storytelling relation, both regionalist texts and *The Conjure Woman* demonstrate their interest in teaching urban and/or white readers how to read differently. The frame narrative that runs through all of the stories in *The Conjure Woman* invites Chesnutt's own readers to choose Annie as our model for response, for John remains an unempathic reader from beginning to end. Because of the assumptions he brings with him, John views Uncle Julius's stories as merely folk tales and embellishments, the product of a former slave socialized to "entertain" his social superiors and whose imagination still bears traces of African superstition. Annie, on the other hand, "is of a very sympathetic turn of mind" and "takes a deep interest in the stories of plantation life" (45). After Julius has finished his story of "Po' Sandy," for example, Annie exclaims, "'What a system it was . . . under which such things were possible!'" (53). Chesnutt, and Julius, have taught Annie how to "read" the horrors of slavery embedded in the mode of magical fable or folk tale which Julius chooses for his own narratives. John, however, can hardly "read" at all. After hearing the tale of Po' Sandy, he responds, "'What things?' I asked, in amazement. 'Are you seriously considering the possibility of a man's being turned into a tree?'" (53). Annie's different response to Uncle Julius reveals John's "inability" to understand Julius's stories as the effect of his power—his social standpoint—as well as his prejudice.

Chesnutt also proposes, as do regionalist writers, that stories can heal, that the relationship between narrator/storyteller and reader/listener can produce real change. Thematically, the effect of stories on their readers occupies both Chesnutt and the regionalists. From John's perspective, Julius tells "plantation tales" not simply to entertain his "superiors" but also to pursue his own economic advantage through such entertainments (57); at the end of "The Goophered Grapevine," the first story in the collection and, like many of the regionalist texts, published for the first time in the *Atlantic,* in 1887, John observes that Julius's cautionary tale "doubtless" derived from his desire to continue to realize "a respectable revenue from the product of the neglected grapevines" (43). It does not occur to John that the tales, and Julius himself, have contributed to a "marked improvement" in Annie's health (82). Yet Chesnutt traces this improvement to the very closeness that has developed between Julius as teller/writer and Annie as listener/reader. In "Sis' Becky's Pickaninny," Annie's health suffers an "unexpected turn for the worse" and while John tries numerous remedies, including reading novels to her (82), she begins to recover from a serious depression only when Julius shows up with a rabbit's foot and a story to go along with it. In this story, one of several that focus on a female protagonist, when Sis' Becky is sold without her child, Aun' Peggy, the conjure woman, "'tu'nt little

Mose ter a hummin'-bird, en sont 'im off fer ter fin' his mammy'" (87).[14] By the end of the story, through a series of conjures, mother and child are reunited, Annie is on her way to "ultimate recovery" (92), and the story ends with John discovering the rabbit's foot in the pocket of Annie's dress. Because John is like the master in the tale who "'wuz one er dese yer w'ite folks w'at purten' dey doan b'liebe in cunj'in'" (91), he cannot invest the rabbit's foot with either meaning or power. He is cut off from seeing the relationship that has developed between Julius and Annie and in understanding the significance of Annie's ability, as the text progresses, to articulate her desire to hear more: "'Tell us about it, Uncle Julius,'" she says, "'a story will be a godsend to-day'" (96). Eventually, in the concluding story, "Hot-Foot Hannibal," Annie actively works with Julius, based on her "reading" of the story he has told, to help him reunite her sister Mabel with a lover, Murchison, whom she regrets she has sent away, just as Chloe, in Julius's story, regrets having caused her own lover to be sold off the plantation.

In reading the individual stories collected in *The Conjure Woman,* we can also identify Chesnutt's strategy of reworking nineteenth-century plantation literature (for example, that of Thomas Nelson Page or the Uncle Remus tales), a tradition remarkably similar in form and assumptions to what literary historians have termed "local color."[15] Although John retains presumptive authority as the first-person narrator of the frame that surrounds the individual tales, he permits and even encourages Julius to become the narrator of his own stories, and in this way Chesnutt creates a text narrated from inside the ruined plantation that, postbellum, becomes a synecdoche for a region now "ruled by" a larger Union, no longer a country in itself or even a political section. Chesnutt thereby locates his own narrative authority in a regional figure. In addition, while each individual tale has a plot and Chesnutt's relationship to plot differs from that of the regionalists, as we will discuss below, the frame narrative that teaches us how to read the text does not; the larger motive in *The Conjure Woman* appears to reside in the schooling of Annie, her coming to consciousness, her ability to learn to "read" the tales Julius tells and even, in "The Conjurer's Revenge," to criticize the telling ("'That story does not appeal to me, Uncle Julius, and it is not up to your usual mark. It isn't pathetic, it has no moral that I can discover, and I can't see why you should tell it'" [79]).[16] All of these features of *The Conjure Woman* clearly resemble regionalism's strategies and are directed to similar ends.

Like some of the regionalist writers, Chesnutt may also be understood as writing in the context of the reunification between North and South after the war, a context that foregrounds the emergence of new hierarchies facilitated by the concepts of region and nation. John's view that the possibility of marrying Annie's Northern sister to a Southerner in "Hot-Foot Hannibal" offers "another link binding me to the kindly Southern people among whom I had not long before taken up my residence" (108) allows Chesnutt to locate his text apparently as part of this national project. However, Chesnutt recognizes that this national project typically presents itself as an interaction between white men and takes place in a landscape which, due to the failure of Reconstruction, has been evacuated of the presence of black men as significant players in the economic, social, and cultural reshaping of the late nineteenth-century South. When John and Annie first arrive at the "place" John intends to buy, there is no one in the "yard"; but when Annie complains of weariness, they return to the yard "where a pine log, lying under a spreading elm afforded a shady though somewhat hard seat. One end of the log was already occupied by a venerable-looking colored man" (34). Aware of John's intention, since he has come alone to look over the place several times before, Julius avoids the direct confrontation of greeting them upon arrival, yet carefully positions himself as someone already there. The landscape that initially appears empty and thus available for John's uncomplicated habitation and possession proves already peopled, and John and Annie, like the tourists who flock to New England in the post-bellum summers, are entering someone else's world.

The opening of "The Goophered Grapevine" brings the reader into Julius's world with the same deliberateness Thaxter uses in *Among the Isles of Shoals* (1873). When John first brings Annie to look at the old plantation he intends to buy, they drive "out of town over a long wooden bridge," pass the "county fairground," and enter "a road so sandy that the horse's feet sank to the fetlocks." They drive up hill and down, "past cultivated farms, and then by abandoned fields," once or twice through "virgin forest," become confused at a crossroads, ask directions of a "little negro girl," and eventually drive between a "pair of decayed gateposts . . . and up a straight sandy lane . . . to the open space where a dwelling-house had once stood, evidently a spacious mansion" (33). In introducing his narrative, Chesnutt brings John, Annie, and his readers closer and closer to a place that cannot be seen at a distance and can only be reached by means of "local" directions; even a small child who lives in the place knows more than its new owner. Uncle Julius's presence on the log in the yard, as we have noted, further undermines the dominant narrative of the project of national reunification. While to John, the plantation represents a real-estate transaction, and while to Northern editors and readers, the story, like the local-color tradition, invites readers to "regionalize" the once-threatening South and to view it as a source of the quaint and the colorful, Chesnutt presents a third perspective in the person of Uncle Julius.

In "Hot-Foot Hannibal" Annie prompts the telling of the tale by asking Uncle Julius, as if he and she have learned to speak in code across the social proscriptions that separate them, "'And why does Chloe's haunt walk?'" Julius answers, "'It's all in de tale, ma'm . . . It's all in de tale'" (110). John, who has by now at least developed a rationale to cover his own unacknowledged interest in Julius's tales, exclaims, "'Tell us the tale,'" for "I was willing to humor the old man's fancy. He had not told us a story for some time" (110). In order to enter Julius's world, the reader, like Annie and John, must pay attention to the tale, for the tale itself contains the meaning of Julius's presence as much as does Chesnutt's frame. Chesnutt thereby proposes a kind of "close" or relational reading as a way of understanding how frames and tales intersect in *The Conjure Woman.* As we will end by developing in chapter 11, such reading also characterizes the work of the women regionalists. For both Chesnutt and the women, reading relationally brings narrator and listener, text and reader into "close" contact; both frame and tale invite the reader into a world inhabited by persons who become visible for the first time to the (urban, white, Northern) reader by means of an "inside" narrative. Carpetbaggers like John, who represent for Chesnutt Northern capitalism, commodity production, and the nation-state, carry the values of "white economic power" that "has seized control and relegated the people to wage slavery [in the postbellum South]" (Hovet 88). "The Goophered Grapevine" and other tales in *The Conjure Woman* become narratives of encounter between the values Julius represents and the incursions of "white economic power." In bringing his reader "close" to Uncle Julius and the others who people his world, Chesnutt seeks to "conjure" such an encounter in fiction and to use that "conjure" to position the values of local place against those of John's economic imperialism.

Annie becomes the mediating figure between Julius and Chesnutt's reader. When Annie puts the rabbit's foot in the pocket of her dress in "Hot-Foot Hannibal," she moves still further into Julius's world, beyond her concern for his practical affairs and into his world of conjure. But because John is such a bad reader, he cannot detect how much Julius's tales have moved her to sympathy. Even though John hints that Julius may have intentions he cannot fathom—"nor do I know exactly what motive influenced the old man's exertions in the matter" (119)—the ending of the story, and of the *Conjure Woman* itself, is one of domestic harmony as John narrates it: "It is certain that a most excellent understanding existed between [Julius] and Murchison after the reconciliation, and that when the young people set up housekeeping over at the old Murchison place, Julius had an opportunity to enter their service. For some reason or other, however, he preferred to remain with us. The mare, I might add, was never known to balk again" (120). Neither, presumably, does Annie suffer any further difficulty with depression, or give John any further concern. If "it's all in de tale" and in the detail, as it also is in regionalist narratives, then we can read Chesnutt as inscribing the limits of the story he can tell in those last two sentences. For the "close" reader, the ending of "Hot-Foot Hannibal" invites attention to the phrase "for some reason or other." While the frame narrative "contains" Uncle Julius, and while Julius's narrations "contain" a critique of slavery that his folkloristic representation at the same time manages to ameliorate for readers like John, the story Chesnutt cannot tell would involve exploring the nature of the alliance Annie and Julius form by the end of the text.

Not at all folkloristic, the suggestion of erotic connection between the white woman and the black man, carried in the detail of Annie's putting the rabbit's foot Julius gives her into her dress pocket, adds a note of realism to *The Conjure Woman,* in which Julius himself is "not entirely black," and consequently, racially mixed. Even John, upon meeting Julius in "The Goophered Grapevine," notes that the "quality of his hair . . . suggested a slight strain of other than negro blood" (34). Cross-racial relationships, a social phenomenon suppressed by American history but embodied in Chesnutt's narrative from the beginning, certainly included white women as well as white men; John, however, is incapable of imagining that a white woman might become attracted to a black man, especially one whom he consistently describes as "old," and therefore, while he does not understand Julius's decision to "remain with us," he does not suspect—nor necessarily would other white readers who were Chesnutt's contemporaries, even in the North—that "some reason or other" might be more "other."[17] The name Hannibal, of course, alludes to the Carthaginian general in the Punic Wars who managed to guide elephants and thousands of men across the Apennine Alps, a border considered almost impassable. By the 1890s, white Southerners' fear of miscegenation had replaced their fear of slave revolt, and thus to contemplate such a relationship between a black man and a white woman, if Julius and Chesnutt do so, becomes the social equivalent of Hannibal's crossing the Alps with elephants: it cannot be imagined. Yet in the context of "Hot-Foot Hannibal," in which Annie ultimately conspires with Julius and Mabel so that Mabel's lover Murchison will not, like Chloe's in Julius's narrative, be sent away, there is a third relationship as well and an implication—again, for the "close" and relational reader—that Julius makes himself useful to John so that he, too, will not be sent away. The real "conjure" in *The Conjure Woman* is thus to take up the question of miscegenation, but to do so almost invisibly, as just the faint taste of roots and herbs a cook might add to okra soup, as Aunt Peggy instructs Solomon in "Mars Jeems's Nightmare" (60), or in a pinch of language, just a phrase, something added to the text, "some reason or other." The relationship between Uncle Julius and Annie can serve as a point of access for Northern readers who might be willing to read past conventional assumptions about black men, black dialect in literature, the South, and white women—but only for those readers capable of entertaining real social reconstruction.

While we understand regionalism's efforts as a sustained exploration of the power of narrative to "conjure" readers, to teach them to see as Julius sees, Chesnutt does differ from regionalism in his move into the supernatural world, one that John associates with black people. Although John mires himself in contradiction by pointing out that the rabbit's-foot story takes place "before this curious superstition had attained its present jocular popularity among white people" (83)—thereby suggesting that superstition is not only the domain of blacks—he tells Julius, "half to him and half to my wife, 'your people will never rise in the world until they throw off these childish superstitions and learn to live by the light of reason and common sense'" (83). Indeed, there are very few legends or superstitions in the work of regionalist writers, and while those that exist emerge from regional characters, the dominant mode of regionalism is realistic, not magical or fabulist. Quite the contrary is the case in Julius's tales, all of which move into some realm of the supernatural, as if the very plantation world is a form of "conjure"—"what a system it was . . . under which such things were possible"—and only a counter-magic can reverse its effects.

Chesnutt also differs from the regionalists in the way *The Conjure Woman* foregrounds the issue of property. Julius has known what it is like to be property as a former slave, and John has come South in the first place to acquire land for a vineyard. In his attempt to understand the "simplicity of a life that had kept [Julius] close to nature" (55), John tells us,

> Toward my tract of land and the things that were on it—the creeks, the swamps, the hills, the meadows, the stones, the trees—he maintained a peculiar personal attitude, that might be called predial rather than proprietary. He had been accustomed, until long after middle life, to look upon himself as the property of another. When this relation was no longer possible, owing to the war, and to his master's death and the dispersion of the family, he had been unable to break off entirely the mental habits of a lifetime, but had attached himself to the old plantation, of which he seemed to consider himself an appurtenance. (55)

John's view of Julius's relation to land that John owns but Julius still occupies clearly serves his interests. Chesnutt, however, makes it quite clear that Julius's relation to the land is not defined by romantic reveries over creeks and swamps and hills, and that he understands the "things that were on it" to be physical structures and produce that can be used and sold. Indeed, Julius's relationship to "John's" land is proprietary, and the tensions between Julius and John derive in good part from struggles over what ownership of property means. This emphasis distinguishes Chesnutt from the women regionalists, who not only root their images in the natural rather than the supernatural world, but whose characters also have a different relation to property.

In *Resisting Novels,* Lennard Davis suggests that whereas in "traditional society, such as the pre-novelistic world Georg Lukács describes in his *Theory of the Novel,* the stories were laid out in folklore and legend," and "plot in these earlier periods was part of the collective, social fabric," "belonged to the community," and "embodied the values and strains within the community," plot in the early modern period "has no relation to traditional myths or storytelling. It comes into usage in the sixteenth century, roughly the period that heralds print and early picaresque novels and tales. The origin of the word 'plot' is related first to a plot of land, and subsequently to the describing of that bit of land—that is, plotting its dimensions. So, rather than coming out of myth or pre-established stories, 'plot' in English seems related to property" (201). Pursuing this argument, he proceeds to demonstrate the "early recognition of literature as property" with the founding of copyright laws as well as the way narratives have become viewed as "properties," and suggests that plot has thus become central to the "commodification of narrative" (201–2). Citing Walter Benjamin, Davis argues that "the decline of storytelling is linked to the rise of the novel" and that "the realistic plot mimes the real world to convince us that its existence is more real than the folktale" (203). While we will take up questions of form in other chapters, particularly chapter 6, we want to observe here that plot in the novelistic sense is largely absent in regionalism and that plot in Chesnutt resides in the folktale, so that, in a sense, both Chesnutt and the regionalists are trying to find some way of storytelling not linked to property.

However, *The Conjure Woman* does have plot—the literal plot of land on which the original plantation and vineyard stood as well as the plot that involves ongoing if understated conflict between Julius and John concerning who will claim "ownership" of this land. In the passage we quoted above, in which John and Annie return to the yard to find a black man sitting on a log, Chesnutt allows John to define the relationship between the two men as one that involves property: "'Don't let us disturb you,' I said. 'There is plenty of room for us all'" (34). Of course, there is *not* "plenty of room" for both John and Julius to claim ownership of the plantation. While John negotiates any anxiety he may feel over Julius's claims by defining his relationship as "predial"—Julius's attachment to the land rendered as "attached to the land," thus making him an attachment of the land and like the buildings on it part of what John owns—Julius continues to press his claims for occupancy if not ownership, primarily through his relationship to Annie, whose empathic response frequently leads her to intervene between Julius and John in ways that serve Julius's economic and personal interests.

Abolitionist discourse of the early nineteenth century gained much of its rhetorical power from emphasizing the moral impossibility of treating a man as a thing to be owned like other property. To the extent that the Civil War was fought and won to make it possible for black men to own both themselves *and* property—as witness the Reconstruction slogan, "Forty acres and a mule"—Uncle Julius inhabits a world where the issue of who and what he owns is of paramount importance. In addition, while the postwar amendments to the Constitution ensured the right of former slaves to vote if they were men, both white and black women remained in disenfranchised positions. Struggles for social and legal equality at the end of the nineteenth century took place between men. While by the end of the nineteenth century women could hold real property in their own names, in terms of their freedom of self-determination, if they chose to marry (hardly a choice for most women) in a substantial sense they became the property of one man or another. In *The Conjure Woman* Chesnutt does not imagine that Aunt Peggy could have the same relationship to John and Annie that Uncle Julius does, or become involved in the same struggle over the ownership of property. For Uncle Julius, however, "conjure," in the form of the tales he tells, is a power used to establish his relationship to property, and thus it reflects the power property has for him. For both Julius and Chesnutt, then, "conjure" becomes associated with "properties" in Davis's sense. It is this emphasis on property, and on male identity as linked with the ownership of land and with conflicts over that ownership, that differentiates Chesnutt from the writers included in *American Women Regionalists,* whose relation to place is not bounded by property lines or ownership and whose sense of identity is not dependent on concepts of ownership.[18]

However, Chesnutt also distinguishes between Julius's and John's relation to ownership. When Annie prefers hearing Julius's tales to John's novels, Chesnutt reclaims property—both real and literary—from its commodification. Or rather, Chesnutt proposes competing perspectives on property ownership: does it mean legal individualistic ownership involving copyright as well as the right to mime "the real world to convince us that its existence is more real than the folktale"; or does it mean locating "collective" ownership of story and tale in a specific vineyard, landscape, or region without acceding to the individualistic and imperialistic values of "white economic power"? While these are questions the women regionalists might have asked, they do not; their preference for the sketch form over the novel, which we will discuss in chapter 6, precisely because it enabled them to avoid the problems of plot, displaces property as the central dispute, though for the women questions of the "minor" and its literary reception become property, if not plot, questions in Davis's sense. If Julius can have a relationship with Annie, then Chesnutt further questions John's ability to sustain white male ownership as "exclusive." In so doing, Chesnutt also calls attention to gender differences between his work and that of the women regionalists, for none of whom "ownership" of other women becomes even implied as an issue.

Clearly, the case of Chesnutt involves much more than the question of a single male writer's inclusion (or not) in the category of regionalism. By providing what appears to be a counterexample—a man who seems to have written regionalism—Chesnutt leads us to question as well the relationship between regionalism and the folktale. One way of understanding *The Conjure Woman* is to see Chesnutt standing in the same relation to the plantation tradition of writing about slavery that the regionalist writers do to the local-color representations of regional and especially women's lives, thereby allowing us to conclude that there are more similarities than differences between Chesnutt and the women regionalists. To the extent that *The Conjure Woman* reflects the formal and thematic concerns of regionalism, the relevant question becomes to what extent regionalism creates a bridge between white and African American literary texts. In their sustained exploration of a "close" relationship with readers, regionalist narrators rely on storytelling as a form of "conjure" in many of the same ways that Chesnutt does. Thus we understand a "close" analysis of regionalism as one way for critical readers to explore the textual strategies African American writers also use, developed in the long trajectory of connections between folk narrative in the nineteenth century and the "magical realism" of Toni Morrison a century later. *The Conjure Woman* becomes the text that reveals points of intersection and points of difference between regionalism and African American writing, but we would not have recognized either intersection or difference without our attention to gender as a category and method of analysis.

Race and Regionalism

Although initially our recognition of regionalism as primarily a women's tradition of writing led us to omit Chesnutt, the extent to which race emerges as a concern within a tradition defined primarily by gender and the degree to which gender as a category of analysis facilitates or obstructs a critique of hierarchies based on race has led us to complicate our understanding of the interweaving of gender and race in the discourse of region and nation. While we take up these questions more fully in chapter 9, we offer here some introductory observations.

The extent to which African American writers found regionalism a congenial mode of writing, one that could be used to articulate their own specific standpoint, cannot, we believe, be fully measured until scholars undertake a comprehensive analysis of the content of those post–Civil War African American newspapers that have survived.[19] The emergence of African American newspapers in the period of Reconstruction and beyond provided African American women writers in particular with the publication opportunities offered earlier generations of white women by the explosion of magazines and annuals.[20] While what Frank Luther Mott has labeled a "mania" for creating new magazines continued in the post–Civil War period, providing writers with "a relatively easy and profitable outlet for their wares" in "a country . . . crying for regional materials, particularly local-color stories" (Nagel and Quirk xvii, xxiii), racial prejudice on the part of editors and readers created obvious barriers for women of color seeking outlets for their "wares." Indeed, one might read Dunbar-Nelson's "The Praline Woman" as an analysis of precisely these difficulties. Until we know how many African American writers entered the world of print through writing dialect, local color, or regionalist fictions for local African American papers, we will not know the extent to which African American women in the latter part of the nineteenth century found these modes congenial and useful or whether the distinctions we make in the print world of white women between those who wrote local color and those who wrote regionalism obtain to the same degree. What we do know is that both Dunbar-Nelson and Chesnutt specifically acknowledged Grace King's work, thereby providing some basis for further inquiry into the potential usefulness of regional modes for African American writers.

We might speculate that African American writers would have found it difficult to adapt the conventions of local color to their purposes, given its reliance on racialist distinctions for its meaning (even the term "local color" has a racialist cast, suggesting that the "local" against which the national defines itself is also the "colored") and given its equal reliance on dialect, often racially coded, as a source of humor at the expense of those speaking it. As the publication history of *Paul Marchand, F.M.C.* suggests, Chesnutt himself was unsuccessful in publishing fiction that directly addressed questions of color within the rubric of the regional.[21] Furthermore, because regionalist writers did not explicitly theorize the distinction between regionalism and local color, it would have been difficult for African American writers to make such a distinction or to locate in some of what was called local color a regionalist mode of writing not only less "white" but potentially antiracist. Fictions such as Gertrude Dorsey Brown's "Scrambled Eggs" and Pauline Hopkins's "Talma Gordon," both included in Ammons and Rohy's *American Local Color Writing,* employ the thematic of "amalgamation" and so expose, as they confound, the premises of racial prejudice. However, save for the presence in Brown's story of black characters who speak dialect, neither story contains features usually associated with local color. Nor do they locate authority in a regionalist voice or in local folk culture, as does Chesnutt's *The Conjure Woman.* While these examples might suggest that African American women in the latter part of the nineteenth and the early part of the twentieth century found local color to be a mode of limited value, our speculations are intended primarily to mark these questions as an area for further study, recognizing as well that similar investigations need to be undertaken for women writers who come from communities of color other than African American.

At least three women writers of color, however, found in regionalism a viable and powerful mode of writing, one capable of representing their own particular standpoint. As we shall demonstrate throughout *Writing out of Place,* the fictions of Dunbar-Nelson, Sui Sin Far, and Zitkala-Ša do not constitute a separate category; indeed, their texts are central to our definition and understanding of regionalism, complicating and problematizing many of its key features. Moreover, their work provides a richer context for exploring race in the fictions of white women regionalists, in particular for understanding texts such as King's "A Crippled Hope" and Jewett's "The Foreigner" that problematize white women's attitudes toward race. At the same time, their work addresses differences other than race as well, in particular questions of class that we explore in chapter 9 and of the queer that become our concern in chapter 10. Regionalism becomes a site where questions of race and questions of gender find mutual and dynamic articulation for both white writers and writers of color.

In addition, we would speculate that the work of regionalism may also make a contribution to "whiteness" studies. Regionalism as a discursive strategy as well as a literary mode makes regions themselves visible as already marked sites of both gendered interrogation and white critique. For example, Ammons and Rohy trace a connection between turn-of-the-century anxieties over racial reproduction and regionalist writing. Pointing out that "the marked decline in birthrates among white middle- and upper-class women . . . produced enormous cultural anxiety around the turn of the century," they observe that "between 1905 and 1910, this anxiety took shape in the antifeminist and racist rhetoric of 'race suicide,' which cited the growing numbers of nonwhite and immigrant Americans as reason for privileged white women not to shirk their reproductive duties, lest they commit, as President Theodore Roosevelt wrote in 1911, the 'racial crime' of 'willful sterility'" (xxi). Drawing on the work of Caroline Gebhard, they further observe that "at the turn of the century, regionalist writing was portrayed by its detractors as an unhealthy genre in specifically gendered terms" (xxiii), as regionalism became associated with the figure of the spinster and hence with deviance and sterility. Fictions written by spinsters about spinsters were charged not only with being a literary "dead end," but also with the "'reproduction of eccentricities, oddities, peculiarities'" (xxiii).[22] As Ammons and Rohy note, the language used by James Herbert Morse in 1883 is hardly accidental in its linking of anxieties about literary production with anxieties about national reproduction. As Lawrence Oliver has shown, for Theodore Roosevelt, the architect of an American imperialism understood as an explicitly racial enterprise, "the literary and the political were inextricably linked" (93), and in numerous instances Roosevelt used his political power to make appointments and support projects that would promote a specifically white male canon of American literature dedicated to promoting "the ideology of 'true Americanism,' a 'manly' ideology that the Rough Rider repeatedly set in contrast to the 'over-civilized, over-sensitive, over-refined' culture of the Eastern establishment" (95) and one that was explicitly racialized as Anglo-Saxon.

In this context we might understand the refusal of white women regionalists to place their fiction in the service of reproducing "true Americanism" or white Anglo-Saxon masculinity as a form of antiracist work, a form of white critique. Moreover, this context marks the impossibility of separating issues of gender from issues of race; and if the one is always imbricated in the other, then questions of race, whether foregrounded or not, are always present in questions of gender. The recognition of this analytic potential, powerfully realized in the work of Dunbar-Nelson, Sui Sin Far, and Zitkala-Ša, as well as in the work of several white regionalist writers, creates the context for our own work in *Writing out of Place.*

Regionalism as Critique

To the extent that white male critics have adopted the rubric of "whiteness" studies for their own analysis of the social constructedness of race, "whiteness" may provide a theoretical link between questions of race in regionalism and questions of gender in nation.[23] This is particularly evident in the ways in which white masculinity at the turn of the twentieth century constructed imperialism itself as an extension of a white male nation, marginalizing regionalism and regional things as female and even, for Theodore Roosevelt, unpatriotic. Thus to the extent that regionalism engages in white and male critique as a critique of nation, it also challenges turn-of-the-twentieth-century U.S. imperialism. Theodore Roosevelt exhorted Americans in 1905 to "grasp the points of vantage which will enable us to have our say in deciding the destiny of the oceans of the East and the West" (*The Strenuous Life* 28). We will take up regionalist critique of such "points of vantage" in chapter 8 in a discussion of feminist standpoint epistemology. Here, we want to underscore the ways in which imperialist discourse at the turn of the twentieth century attempted to disarm regionalist critique as a potential threat.

Roosevelt both engendered and reflected turn-of-the-twentieth-century ideologies that defined regionalism as dangerous to the nation, articulated masculinity as the model for a nation's "strenuous life," and viewed the role of the United States in Hawaii, Cuba, Puerto Rico, and the Philippines as doing "our share of the world's work, by bringing order out of chaos in the great, fair tropic islands from which the valor of our soldiers and sailors has driven the Spanish flag" (24).[24] A decade before he spoke these words, in an 1894 speech delivered fairly early in his rise to national prominence, Roosevelt associated regionalism with unpatriotic and anti-American sentiment. He wrote: "In the first place we wish to be broadly American and national, as opposed to being local or sectional. We do not wish, in politics, in literature, or in art, to develop that unwholesome parochial spirit, that over-exaltation of the little community at the expense of the great nation, which produces what has been described as the patriotism of the village, the patriotism of the belfry" ("True Americanism" 51–52). As we trace regionalism's interest in anti-imperialism in various ways throughout this book, and particularly in chapter 7, Roosevelt's warning suggests that what more than a century later critics have perceived as the quiet, nostalgic, and nonideological writing of the regionalists actually seemed to him to threaten the "great nation." We might even speculate that in order for imperialism to win the hearts of Americans, regionalism had to be discredited. At the very least, Roosevelt's warning lends credence to our own revision and redefinition of regionalism and its effects. As we will describe in detail in chapter 2, the construction of American literature as a field of study in the early twentieth century seems to have set itself the task of removing any "over-exaltation of the little community" in order to create a literature of the "great nation" by marginalizing, neglecting, or disparaging regional and regionalist writers. While regionalist writers made no explicit antiwar pronouncements, the meaning of their different approach to others—which we will demonstrate in different ways in chapters 4, 5, and 6—takes on further significance in light of the fact that Roosevelt took the attitudes they represented in their texts quite seriously.

In making the distinction between local color and regionalism that we will explore in more detail in chapter 3, we wish to distinguish between the literary uses of regional persons that reinforced their representation as strange, exotic, or queer, and those texts that approach regions without predetermining what narrators or readers might find there. Such texts recognize that any significant analysis of region must begin with what Clifford Geertz has called "local knowledge" and with what he describes as "a continuous dialectical tacking between the most local of local detail and the most global of global structure in such a way as to bring them into simultaneous view" (*Local Knowledge* 69). While the cultural attitudes reflected in local color may be understood as conducive to the political imperialism of the Theodore Roosevelt era, the critique of those attitudes apparent in an analysis of regionalist texts offered readers an opportunity to think in ways radically different from those of the local colorists. Regionalist texts register the challenges to the values of village life from the combined strengthening of the nation-state, its association with aggressive masculinity (exemplified by Roosevelt's formulation of the "strenuous life"), and the disjunctions of everyday life industrialization had already begun to produce. Above all, regionalist texts offer a place from which twenty-first-century readers can think again about the consequences of creating regions for either cultural or economic exploitation. Naming the work the regionalist writers have produced as critique removes it from conventional associations between women, village life, and nostalgia, enabling us to understand both the regionalization of women writers in American literary history and the feminization of regions in the U.S. move toward imperialism.

Regionalism as Cultural Healing

As we will indicate throughout this book, one of the most intriguing aspects of regionalism is the way registers of critique and alternative visions coexist. Regionalism offers unconventional, noncanonical, and counterhegemonic stories of female (and male) development across the life cycle; and because these stories are so rich in the texts of regionalism and so absent from the texts generally understood as "American literature," regionalism calls attention to the paucity of cultural locations in which women and nonwhite and nondominant men might find affirmation. Canonical American literature and culture almost exclusively tell the stories of boys growing up; bonding between young men (sometimes across racial lines); men's travels, interests, obsessions, hopes, and dreams for America; and men's images of what women want and what the "American girl" should become. While these stories have created much of what we understand as American, we believe that American culture is impoverished by the imbalance, even the surfeit of "heroic" stories about men and boys, and that the texts of regionalism provide an alternative vision of what American culture might look like if the stories we chose to pass on to the next generation of readers reflected a broader spectrum of values. Indeed, male characters in regionalism, while rarely the center of critical attention, offer readers a vision of the possibility that masculinities themselves might become more various and fluid than they are in the official story. As we will discuss in chapters 3 and 11, this was certainly Stowe's interest in her first New England sketch, "Uncle Lot"; and Jewett's Elijah Tilley from *The Country of the Pointed Firs,* Chopin's Ozème in "Ozème's Holiday," and Dunbar-Nelson's M'sieu Fortier among others all provide models of men who share some of the values the nineteenth century assigned to women.

Unlike either a nostalgic regionalism or one constructed by the nation-state to serve its own interests, a critical and discursive regionalism has the potential to transform the study of American literature and culture. In its combination of the critical and the visionary, its potential for redressing the imbalance between women's and men's stories in representations of the American, and its offer of alternative understandings of what U.S. culture both has been and might still become, regionalism also creates the possibility for healing, in particular a healing connection between text and reader, and a revisionary understanding of "close" or relational reading, as we will explore in chapter 11. Regionalist writers across decades, regions, and color lines create cultural medicine women and herbalist-healers not as marginal freaks but as central to the narratives and to the different perspective regionalism offers.[25] The New England women Stowe describes as women of "faculty" provide early prototypes of the regional figure as cultural healer; in *The Pearl of Orr's Island,* Stowe calls Aunts Roxy and Ruey "cunning women" as well as women of "faculty," referring to the word's biblical use (*AWR* 26; see Jeremiah 9:17). Jewett creates Mrs. Todd, in *The Country of the Pointed Firs,* as a healer with communal and spiritual powers. Chesnutt's "conjure woman," Dunbar-Nelson's "wizened one" in "The Goodness of Saint Rocque," and Austin's basket maker all serve to extend the concept of healer in regionalism across racial lines. Women of "faculty" and "conjure woman" may be terms that emerge from different regions with different cultural origins, but in the texts of regionalism, these women offer a transgeographical vision of critique that emerges from and combines with empathy.

Some Notes on Form

We will conclude this introduction with a few comments about our own form. Rather than write a literary history or organize our work by essays on individual authors or literary works, we have chosen a set of critical and theoretical problems that the texts of regionalism considered as a group pose for and beyond literary study. Some of these problems—such as those we take up in the chapters on analytics (2), origins (3), poetics (4), thematics (5), and form (6)—recognizably raise questions common to literary inquiry. However, other chapters take up more theoretical and cultural questions, such as those on the American (7), epistemology (8), race and class (9), and queer theory (10). We will conclude by taking up questions of "close" or relational reading, empathy, and models of emotional development, including further discussion of men in regionalism (11). Although the more conventional literary questions dominate the first half of the book, we do not insist on sequence as a mode of organization.

Readers interested in any particular topic or problem will be able to enter the discussion elsewhere than at the beginning. Neither are we implying a hierarchy between the more literary readings and the more theoretical discussions, though it makes sense to us that readers less familiar with the texts of regionalism might need us to privilege the literary from time to time. We also understand the numerous articles we have each previously published on regionalist writers and texts as contributing to this discussion, but except for part of chapter 3, we have not revised them for republication here. However, we do view them as this book's hypertext, if you will, and we treat them as "attachments" that in many cases provide more extended critical readings than we have space to include here.

We have not chosen a different approach in chapters 1 and 11 as "introductory" or "concluding" chapters from that which we take in other chapters because we cannot either "introduce" or "conclude" the book without engaging in textual analysis. The form this chapter has taken, including a section on a single text, *The Conjure Woman,* as part of a more general topic, generally describes the form of all subsequent chapters, including the last, in which textual analysis and references to what most readers understand as theory mutually inform each other. Indeed, in a certain sense, we have tried to write this book as itself a form of storytelling.

As storytellers often do, we also find ourselves relating only parts of the critical "story" about any particular text in any given chapter, coming back to that same text from different perspectives in other chapters. While this book includes readings of texts, we do not attempt to create a comprehensive reading of any particular text, and neither do we limit discussion of a text to one chapter if it also has something to add in another. Our own readers interested in following a particular text may trace the various sequences of critical commentary by referring to the index, or by following the occasional cross-references we have provided as a guide. Over the course of the book, some texts will seem more singular than others, but it has been as a group that these texts have variously entered for a time, then reentered, our discussions. Inevitably such a method has produced some repetition, but we have lived with this group of texts for a long time and they have seemed to move in and out of our chapters with something of a will of their own.

In this way, we view our own form in *Writing out of Place* as having an effect on the reader similar to that of the approach Thaxter creates in *Among the Isles of Shoals.* Thaxter's narrative disrupts expectations concerning what a book-length narrative will include, and we hope *Writing out of Place* will similarly challenge the conventions of a critical book. Thaxter's narrative also sets up self-consciousness about "approach"—to the islands themselves, to their own particular relationship to history, to their nonhuman inhabitants—as a central aspect of its story. Thaxter presents the bird, plant, rock, and marine life on the Shoals as different from human life and writes a narrative in which "readers" of the Shoals and readers of the *Shoals* must develop "ears made delicate by listening" in order to "hear" the different sounds, or rotes, of the waves as they strike different islands, and, indeed, to approach any aspect of the islands and their narrative with understanding. Delicacy, listening, respect, the ability to move in slowly or not at all in observing, a willingness to see with another's eyes rather than to *look at* the "other," all characterize Thaxter's text (and the texts of regionalism in general) and, we would argue, articulate an alternative to imperialism and exploitation as an attitude toward cultural difference. While we have chosen to be more discursive than Thaxter, we have tried to place our own readers "among" the problems regionalism raises, as if these literary, critical, and theoretical problems form a coherent grouping but, like the islands of Thaxter's text, also sketch their own particularities just as the individual regionalist texts differentiate themselves within the category.

Lines near the opening of Thaxter's narrative describe this process of differentiation. Thaxter writes, "sailing out from Portsmouth Harbor with a fair wind from the northwest, the Isles of Shoals lie straight before you, nine miles away,—ill-defined and cloudy shapes, faintly discernible in the distance," but that "as you approach they separate, and show each its own peculiar characteristics" (*AWR* 157). *Among the Isles of Shoals* has taught us to take a different "approach" to reading the literary texts in our study as well (see Fetterley's essay on Thaxter, "Theorizing Regionalism"). The texts of regionalism, like Thaxter's islands, "separate, and show each its own peculiar characteristics," for regionalism takes up the question of the "peculiar" and the particular rather than what is "universal" or even what is "American." Thaxter's interest in her own readers' "approach" to the islands epitomizes the care with which the narrators of regionalist texts prepare their own readers to approach regional subjects. While in a certain sense this book contains an unfolding argument, any particular chapter also stands alone, just as Thaxter's islands do. Like the sound of the waves at different points on the shores of the islands, the combined voices of two critics, a variety of interpretive and theoretical registers, and the varied texts of more than a dozen writers give each chapter its own particular "rote." Unlike Thaxter's *Shoals,* however, where the few inhabitants "troubl[e] themselves but little about what State they belong to" (*AWR* 159), and where "the faint echoes from the far-off world . . . 'Winfield Scott and Santa Ana!' 'The war in Mexico!' 'The famine in Ireland!' . . . all meant nothing to us" (176), we want this book to create readers who do trouble themselves "about what State they belong to," and who wish to locate themselves among the literary, critical, and theoretical problems regionalism raises. Above all, we want this book to help readers find in regionalism the echoes, not so faint, of a world not so far off.

CHAPTER 2

Locating Regionalism in American Literary History

To understand the fashion of any life, one must know the land it is lived in.

—Mary Austin, "The Basket Maker"

If certain experiences are never spoken about, if certain people or issues are seldom heard from, it is supposed that silence has been chosen.

—Catharine MacKinnon, *Feminism Unmodified*

While we began the project that has eventuated in this book out of an interest in nineteenth-century American women writers, we did not set out to discover regionalism, for nothing in the frames available to us then could have made visible a tradition of women's writing that preceded the Civil War, that linked together women writers across decades and geographies, and that self-consciously distinguished itself from local color. While gender as a category of analysis created the conditions that made possible our recovery of this tradition—that is, our decision to read systematically in the work of nineteenth-century women writers enabled us to locate regionalism—we were attracted to this particular body of women's writing because it is also a tradition of feminist writing. What intrigued us then, and continues to intrigue us so many years later, are the connections between a literature associated with place and a feminist analytic. As we seek in the next few pages to explore the nature of these connections, we are also seeking to understand why it was women who predominantly wrote regionalist fiction. What was there in the discourses that located region and that were located in region that allowed regionalism to serve as the site for the articulation of a feminist analysis of the situation of women?

"The Relatively Narrow Interests of Regionalism"

We begin our exploration with some reflections on a comment we encountered in the introduction to a recent collection of the fiction of Dorothy Canfield

Fisher, an early twentieth-century writer who expressed a sense of connection to nineteenth-century regionalist fiction: "In the tradition of Harriet Beecher Stowe and Mary E. Wilkins Freeman, Fisher showcases her command of dialect in each story. Yet, like the best work of those writers and the well-wrought Maine tales of Sarah Orne Jewett, Fisher's Vermont stories transcend the relatively narrow interests of regionalism or 'local color'" (Madigan 4). In this comment we can observe an instinctive, almost automatic reflex by which an editor seeks to recover a writer who could be labeled regionalist by disassociating her from the very category that presumably serves as the basis of his interest in her work. This discourse not only locates regionalism as inevitably representing "narrow interests"; it also locates aesthetic value in those aspects of a text that can be read as transcending its local context, indeed in a text's capacity to be de-localized, stripped of its "geography," and removed from any sense of "situatedness." We might observe a similar phenomenon in the work of Hamlin Garland. As a series of essays written by the man most closely associated with regional writing, *Crumbling Idols* (1894) is frequently invoked as theorizing and thus legitimating the local-color movement. While Garland claimed the term "local color" to describe his own writing and argued that "it is the differences which interest us" (*Crumbling Idols* 49), he concludes that "local color means national character" (53), curiously conflating the local with the national. Perhaps because he could not reconcile what he perceived as a potential source of inspiration in the "local" with his desire to be taken seriously by Eastern audiences as a "national" writer, he developed a theory of the "local" that enabled rather than critiqued the concept of nation. As Stephanie Foote notes, Garland "promises that the democratization of literature will help usher in the movement of cultural and economic capital from the East to the West" and makes "the argument for the public, even national, necessity of local color" (57).[1] Ironically, then, Garland's work participates in the discourse that posits the local as valuable only if it can serve the interests of something larger than itself, only if it can be seen to transcend its own "relatively narrow interests."

We may observe similar moves in discourses that invoke the category of "women" in contexts that recognize the category as a product of systematic structural hierarchies—locutions such as Sandra Harding's "the new sciences are not to be *only* for women" or "[a]fter all, we want to change the world—not only women" (*Whose Science* 5, 274). Such discursive moves are almost as automatic as Madigan's comment on Fisher and serve a similar function—namely, to attach value to the specific subject by removing it from the marked category, to avoid the appearance of pleading "special interests," and to deflect the hostility that inevitably greets any discourse that draws attention to structural injustice. In effect, such locutions identify the significance of "geography" through their very need to transcend it. For when we actually reflect on what such locutions might mean, we discover the absurdity of a proposition that through the tag of "not only" claims the interests of over half the population to be narrow, limited, and self-interested. We can further discover that women, no matter how large a percentage of the population they represent, are always understood to be a subset of a larger category labeled "people" or "humans" or "the world" and are thus in effect conceptually regionalized—situated, located, accorded geography. As MacKinnon puts it, "There is a belief that this is a society in which women and men are basically equals. . . . In such a world, if . . . a person has an experience there are words for it. When they speak and say it, they are listened to. If they write about it, they will be published. . . . Feminism is the discovery that women do not live in this world" (*Feminism Unmodified* 168). Rather, women inhabit a region, and the moment one speaks as a woman who recognizes this fact one becomes regionalized. Because dominant discourses similarly locate "women" and "region," we can imagine how regionalism might become the location of feminist analysis. We can elaborate this connection if we return for a moment to the distinction we introduced in chapter 1 between regionalism and local color, a distinction that can be summarized as the difference between "looking with" and "looking at." If a text looks "with" regional characters, location becomes marked rather than transcended and the text retains its "geography." When a text looks "at" the region, however, geography and location characterize only one aspect of the text while the perspective of the one who looks is framed as universal and transcendent.

We may further illuminate the connections we are making here between regionalism and feminism as discourses of self-conscious location by drawing on the work of Linda Alcoff. Alcoff attempts to define "woman" in a way that neither grounds that definition in biology (the "cultural feminist essentialized subject") nor argues that woman is solely a discursive construct that renders the category "fundamentally undecidable" (340) and by deconstructing the female subject threatens "to wipe out feminism itself" (339). In so doing, she suggests that we understand "woman" as defined by a particular position and that we understand gendered identity as a product of "positionality" (349). The positional definition, she argues, makes a woman's identity "relative to a constantly shifting context, to a situation that includes a network of elements involving others, the objective economic conditions, cultural and political institutions and ideologies, and so on. . . . The position of women is relative and not innate, and yet neither is it 'undecidable'" (349), and we would add, neither is it unlocatable.

While Alcoff's definition avoids the problem of essentialism, she is quick to assert that neither does it "imply that the concept of 'woman' is determined solely by external elements and that the woman herself is merely a passive recipient of an identity created by these forces" (349), the pitfall toward which poststructuralist thought inevitably moves. Rather she argues, drawing on Teresa de Lauretis, "the identity of a woman is the product of her own interpretation and reconstruction of her history, as mediated through the cultural discursive context to which she has access" (349). Therefore, the concept of positionality includes the recognition "that the position that women find themselves in can be actively utilized (rather than transcended) as a location for the construction of meaning, a place from where meaning is constructed, rather than simply the place where meaning can be *discovered* (the meaning of femaleness). The concept of woman as positionality shows how women use the positional perspective as a place from which values are interpreted and constructed rather than as a locus of an already determined set of values" (349). Alcoff's theory helps explain the emergence of feminist consciousness and analysis, as well as its "uneven developments"[2]—why some women become feminists and others don't—as she points out that "when women become feminists the crucial thing that has occurred is not that they have learned any new facts about the world but that they have come to view those facts from a different position, from their own position as subjects" (349–50). To put this in terms of our own discussion, we might say that regionalism represents that point where women recognize their locatedness within the dominant discourse, accept the concept of location, and use it to critique received meanings and construct new ones.

To summarize, we may observe that as "woman" and "region" share similar locations within dominant discourses, are each the "marked" case, women become in effect regionalized and regions become in effect feminized, and it is difficult to center either woman or region without encountering the charge of seeking to represent "relatively narrow interests." Writing that accepts its location, draws attention to its geography, and is also by, about, and in a certain sense for women becomes doubly regionalized and doubly feminized. Such writing, however, allows for the emergence of a feminist analytic. Regionalist writers draw attention to location in order to analyze situatedness; they utilize a regionalist positionality to interpret the discursive systems that create the concept of region and to construct alternative meanings. As we understand it, regionalism is a body of fiction that exists in tension with the definition of itself as "regional." As we shall discuss at various locations throughout this book, regionalism is inherently dialogic; it engages the assertion that it represents narrow interests and is in some sense "crazy," a word that appears often in regionalist texts and is applied to those who challenge the dominant discursive structures. In a certain sense, then, for a text to be "regionalist" almost any place will do since, to recast the epigraph from Austin with which we opened this chapter, the "land" such a text explores is a conceptual framework and the life it fashions is a subject position constructed by this framework. While regionalist writers obviously invest in and commit to the specificity of place, they do not do so in a way that reifies or essentializes place, for place is also always a discursive location, an analytic, a subject position from which meaning can be constructed rather than discovered. Regionalist characters occupy positions that others, not themselves, view as crazy, queer, exotic, or local, and the knowledge they construct emerges from the experience of occupying a position defined by others as "regional."

Regionalist writers adopt an analytic of positionality in order to articulate the perspective that emerges when, in Alcoff's words, "the point of departure, the point from which all things are measured, has changed" (350).

Regionalism as a Feminist Analytic

The two writers included in *American Women Regionalists* with the clearest claim to theorizing regionalism in the way they focus on the relation between positional perspective and topography, between identity and the land, are Thaxter (in *Among the Isles of Shoals,* 1873) and Austin (in *The Land of Little Rain,* 1903). Yet ironically both Thaxter and Austin construct landscapes notable for their sparseness, desolation, and the apparent absence of both social inscription and any sustenance at all for human life, landscapes that might well be considered blanks, offering no sense of any meaning to be discovered. As landscapes of deprivation and blankness, they could be read as emblematic of the situation of women in patriarchal culture and particularly of those women who find themselves most at odds with the identity scripted by such a culture for them. As such, a feminist reader might read the landscapes themselves as a form of critique. Yet the point of both Thaxter's and Austin's meticulous, loving, even obsessive observations of their respective topographies is to demonstrate how meaning can be constructed rather than discovered, how in environments of such apparent desolation a woman can in fact find a way not just to survive but to flourish. Indeed, both writers suggest that the more remote, the more marginalized, the more written off as a blank space and seen as a silence that has been chosen, the more likely a region is to provide a space for the construction of meaning, for both writers seize on the very desolateness of the landscapes, their apparent social vacantness, to create a space outside the law that sentences women and regions to narrow interests that do not really matter. As Austin writes at the beginning of *The Land of Little Rain,* "Not the law, but the land sets the limit" (*AWR* 567), and in this "country of lost borders" the desert becomes metonymic for the woman herself outside the law. Although Thaxter and Austin inhabit and write about very different landscapes, they both call into question "the point from which all things are measured," the conceptual framework that would locate them and their texts as marginal, local, and regional and would reserve the terms "central," "universal," and "national" for that which they are not. It is the similarity of their critiques despite the radical separation of their geographies that establishes regionalism as an analytic, one that links regions rather than using landscape only to mark sectional and textual differences.

Fictions by Cary and Freeman further demonstrate how regionalist writers use the location of region to foreground a critique of the location of women. In her preface to the first volume of *Clovernook* sketches, Cary claims to be writing about a region of the country unfamiliar to many of her readers, "the inhabitants of cities, where, however much there may be of pity there is surely little of sympathy for the poor and humble," except as it is constructed through a political rhetoric that from time to time invokes "Ohio" for purposes that have little to do with the people who actually live there and to whom, as she puts it, the praise sounds "peculiar" (*AWR* 60–61). Thus at the outset Cary understands "region" as a concept constructed by a variety of dominant discourses and situated in relation to the positions of those who "live in what is called the world" (60). In locating her sketches as the attempt to describe Ohio regional life from the perspective of an insider, she makes a connection between the consciousness of her narrator and "the interior of my native state, which was a wilderness when first my father went to it, and is now crowned with a dense and prosperous population" (60). In equating region with a positional consciousness developed in opposition to dominant discourses, and in making that consciousness identifiably female—"Without a thought of making a book, I began to recall some shadows and sunbeams that fell about me as I came up to womanhood" (60)—Cary indicates how the location of place reflects the situatedness of women and specifically of a young woman who refers to her life as "little" and "noiseless." With such locutions the narrator of the *Clovernook* sketches recognizes her own position as constructed by dominant discourses in precisely the same way as the position of her native state is constructed.

In the story "Uncle Christopher's" from *Clovernook* (1853), Cary launches a powerful critique of those discourses of dominance that construct her narrator's and her region's situation, and demonstrates the way regionalism both creates and is illuminated by a feminist analytic. The story opens on an intensely cold night as the narrator sits comfortably inside by the fire while her father looks out, commenting on the sleds moving past the window. "It was not often," the narrator tells us, "that we had such a deep snow as this, and it carried the thoughts of my father away back to his boyhood, for he had lived among the mountains then, and been used to the hardy winters which keep their empire nearly half the year" (*AWR* 62). The conventional reference to the New England winters that "keep their empire nearly half the year" invokes the sign of "nation," the center against which all else is measured and in terms of which Ohio is found wanting. The narrator writes that "the snow and I were never good friends" and is thus herself found wanting; indeed, she must be nudged several times before she offers the response her father expects when he proposes to take the carriage on a visit to Uncle Christopher's. Forcing a smile to her lips as they set off, she overhears her father telling the servant that he himself would just as soon stay home but "'my daughter has taken a fancy to a ride, and so I must oblige her'" (62).

Arriving at the farmhouse of Uncle Christopher after a long drive culminating in a difficult walk through drifts of snow, she encounters Uncle Christopher himself:

> Uncle Christopher was a tall muscular man of sixty or thereabouts, dressed in what might be termed stylish homespun coat, trowsers and waistcoat, of snuff-colored cloth. His cravat was of red-and-white-checked gingham, but it was quite hidden under his long grizzly beard, which he wore in full, this peculiarity being a part of his religion. His hair was of the same color, combed straight from his forehead, and turned over in one even curl on the back of the neck. Heavy gray eyebrows met over a hooked nose, and deep in his head twinkled two little blue eyes, which seemed to say, "I am delighted with myself and, of course, you are with me." Between his knees he held a stout hickory stick, on which, occasionally, when he had settled something beyond the shadow of doubt, he rested his chin for a moment, and enjoyed the triumph. (*AWR* 65)

As this unnerving portrait makes clear, Uncle Christopher assumes himself to be the center of the universe and expects everyone, but particularly women and children, to define themselves in relation to him. Indeed, Uncle Christopher's wife and daughters are subordinate to the point of caricature and their portrait reveals their location within a discourse that understands "woman" as "the place where meaning can be *discovered*":

> the women so closely resembled each other, that one could not tell them apart; not even the mother from the daughters. . . . all had dark complexions, black eyes, low foreheads, straight noses, and projecting teeth; and all were dressed precisely alike, in gowns of brown flannel and coarse leather boots, with blue woollen stockings, and small capes, of red and yellow calico. . . . By one corner of the great fireplace they huddled together, each busy with knitting, and all occupied with long blue stockings, advanced in nearly similar degrees toward completion. Now and then they said "Yes, ma'm," or "no ma'm," when I spoke to them, but never or very rarely anything more. (64)

While the narrator remains at Uncle Christopher's, she witnesses what it means to be subjected to his rule. Delivered over to him, just as she has been, is a little boy, his grandson, whose father has sent him to Uncle Christopher's so that "'grandfather would straighten me'" (74). Mark has discovered a kitten in the barn and has tried unsuccessfully to hide it inside the house. For this act of defiance, he must take the kitten out and drown it in the well. But instead, the following day, it is Mark who drowns trying once again to save his kitten who has survived being dropped in the well. Since Uncle Christopher commands the discourses of dominance and is supported by the economic, political, and ideological systems of power they represent, no law will touch him for his treatment of Mark and it is unlikely that he will undergo any permanent change of heart. Mark has been marked as a "simpleton" for his empathy toward the kitten and as dangerous for his insubordination in proposing that attention be directed to something other than Uncle Christopher himself. Those so marked must be either eliminated or brought back under rule. Thus when his wife actually dares to express some sympathy for Mark, Uncle Christopher bangs his book on the table and yells, "'Woman, fret not thy gizzard!'" His text has the desired effect; "the old expression of obsequious servility was back, and she resumed her seat and her knitting" (72).

The narrator, however, recognizing how she too is marked by Uncle Christopher, uses her position to articulate a protest and to construct an alternate meaning for the events she witnesses. She characterizes Mark's story as "instructive to those straight and ungenial natures which see no beauty in childhood, and would drive before its time all childishness from life" (80). While her "book" may not have the weight of Uncle Christopher's Bible and patriarchal law, it brings into being an alternative discourse that functions as a critique of him and all he represents. Although at the beginning of the story the narrator feels powerless to speak on her own behalf, by the end she achieves a positional perspective that allows her to express the marked subjectivity that is at once the region's, her own, and Mark's, and to resist being herself "straightened," turned into yet another indistinguishable daughter.

While in Cary's pre–Civil War Ohio farmhouses, memories of boyhood where winters that "keep their empire nearly half the year" conflate New England with the nation, Freeman in "A New England Nun" identifies post–Civil War New England as a region and associates the region with the production of a particular female subjectivity through the doubly, even trebly regionalized connotations in her title. She evokes the specificity of New England with a few quick strokes—dust, currants, best china, stone walls, haying. But while such specificity matters, what matters more, as for Cary, is the drama of the discourse of nation and region as this drama is played out in the lives of individual men and women. Joe Dagget believes he must leave his village and his sweetheart to seek his fortune in Australia—somewhere in "what is called the world," to recall Cary's phrase. From Joe's perspective, once he leaves the region it ceases to exist; that is, while he himself may change, he assumes that what he leaves behind will be exactly the same when he returns. Joe is no Uncle Christopher, yet the assumptions of the two men are remarkably similar.

But something does happen in and to the region of Louisa Ellis during Joe's absence. Joe can believe that Louisa will be waiting, unchanged, upon his return because he assumes that she has accepted the dominant script; Freeman writes, "gently acquiescing with and falling into the natural drift of girlhood," Louisa "had seen marriage ahead as a reasonable feature and a probable desirability of life. She had listened with calm docility to her mother's views upon the subject" (*AWR* 359–60). In his absence, however, Louisa constructs a different script, one that radically challenges Joe's assumptions. In essence (and Louisa is fond of "distilling essences"), Louisa discovers the pleasure of being, as Freeman puts it, "a veritable guest to her own self," of referring only to her own interests and pleasures and desires. She discovers the pleasure of occupying the subject position habitually assumed by those who are aligned with nation rather than region; she discovers the pleasure of a life lived without reference to its usefulness to someone else but simply for its own purposes. When Louisa contemplates marrying Joe Dagget, she has "visions, so startling that she half repudiated them as indelicate, of coarse masculine belongings strewn about in endless litter; of dust and disorder arising necessarily from a coarse masculine presence in the midst of all this delicate harmony" (361). If Louisa marries, she will lose both region and self; she will lose the location from which she can construct rather than receive meaning. Escaping marriage she feels like a "queen who, after fearing lest her domain be wrested away from her, sees it firmly insured in her possession" (365).

In a way that critics have seen as quiet, "A New England Nun" keeps pressing the question, why shouldn't Louisa do things the way she wishes? Why shouldn't the album be under the gift book if that's the way she wants it? And why should we call her a fussy old maid and assume that Joe ought to be able to put the books any way he wants and also set free the old dog Caesar whom she has kept chained ever since he once bit a neighbor? Most crucially, why should Louisa have to leave her home, her region, and move to Joe's house where his way of doing things will take precedence and where she will become the place where meaning is discovered rather than the place from which it is generated? The answer that hums beneath the surface like the "busy harvest of men and birds and bees" in the "fervid summer afternoon" of the story's end is—no reason, except that the combined discourses of nation and masculinity would have it so and that is really no reason at all. At the end of her story, Freeman comments, "If Louisa Ellis had sold her birthright she did not know it, the taste of the pottage was so delicious, and had been her sole satisfaction for so long" (365). If birthright here means the right to participate in systems that locate "woman" as the place where meaning can be discovered rather than constructed, then Louisa has done well to sell it. If, however, birthright means the right to "actively utilize" rather than "transcend" one's position (Alcoff 349), then perhaps Louisa has actually reclaimed her birthright. In this context, we might define regionalism as the act of claiming women's birthright to a feminist analytic and, in the spirit of Louisa Ellis, we might define our effort to locate regionalism as the act of articulating this birthright.

The Politics of Gender and Genre

In "The Spinster in the House of American Criticism," Caroline Gebhard traces the process whereby the local-color movement, so dominant in the last decades of the nineteenth century, came to be understood not only as "timid and old-fashioned, a product of antiquated femininity, but also out of keeping with modern nationalism" (79). "There is," she argues, "perhaps no better case study in the politics of gender and genre than that afforded by the feminization and marginalization of local color in American literature"; and she observes that "volumes have been devoted to the rise of realism and the development of naturalism in nineteenth-century America, while critics have largely dismissed that vast, uneven, and sprawling body of fiction known as local color—even though it comprises a vital popular tradition in which both men and women wrote—simply because of its association with women" (82). She writes further that "the connection between local color and effeminacy is so well-fixed in critics' minds that when they wish to reclaim particular writers for more serious treatment, they often adopt the strategy of arguing that the writer is not a local colorist after all" (83), a strategy we have seen in Madigan's comments on Fisher. Another strategy "is to divide local color itself into its masculine and feminine practitioners" (83) so that certain writers can be redeemed from the general stigma and the literary historian can acknowledge the existence of local color without having to compromise the masculinist and nationalist narrative of American literature.

The masculinist bias evident in even the earliest of American literary histories ensured that the dominant categories of American literature would derive from the work of men. Thus realism, since it could be seen as theorized by Howells and practiced by Mark Twain and James as well as by Howells himself, achieved status as a major mode of late nineteenth-century writing, and many of the writers and texts that we consider regionalist survived in literary history by being subsumed under the category of realism. Similarly, local color, though stigmatized in relation to realism, could be rescued for history to the degree that it could be associated with the work of men. Within this framing, women practitioners of local color are read in terms of their dependence on and imitation of male precursors, relations among women writers are ignored, and the possibility that a male writer might have modeled his work upon a female precursor is nonexistent. From our perspective, this history is one of suppression and distortion, the history of a silence that has not been chosen. Because realism and local color are really different from regionalism as we understand it, many of the writers whom we consider central to our tradition could not be made to fit into these categories and hence have "disappeared." Similarly, those writers, however stigmatized and marginalized, who did survive because they could be somehow made to fit within these categories suffered major distortion in the process. Moreover, because their texts were never deemed truly representative of the categories within which they were included, they became in effect examples of failed or second-rate local color and of a very minor mode of realism. Not only has their claim to aesthetic success and literary status been successfully checked; their role as originators of an alternate tradition has been suppressed and the complex web of their interrelations with each other obliterated. Literary historians have told a very different story from the one we wish to tell and we will attempt to summarize their story in the following narrative.

Cambridge History of American Literature

Since the inception of American literature as a teaching field in the early twentieth century, three literary histories emerging from three different historical and political moments have attempted to construct narratives of the development and organization of nineteenth-century writing.[3] The first major effort to produce a comprehensive, encyclopedic history that would include the perspectives of many literary historians was the four-volume *Cambridge History of American Literature* (1917–21).[4] David Shumway describes *CHAL* as "the first major cooperative project in American literature to be undertaken within the academy" (87) but proposes that we consider it as "a predecessor to, rather than the beginning of, American literature as a discipline" since "the boundaries it assumed for American literature failed to become the boundaries of the discipline" (89). He observes that "'literature' is a broadly inclusive term in the *Cambridge History,* and no serious genre of writing on any subject falls outside of its purview" (89), including articles on travel writing, political writing, children's literature, humorists, annuals, and others that would quickly fall out of the definition of the field. However, when Shumway examines *CHAL* from the perspective of African American and women writers, he finds it quite exclusive and in these exclusions to have indeed assumed the boundaries that will define the field. Noting that "American literature could have been conceived as multilingual and multiethnic as early as 1920" (93), he refers to the ideology informing *CHAL* as "overtly racist" and "somewhat more covertly, sexist" (91). The contradiction between the general inclusiveness of *CHAL* and its exclusions on the basis of race and gender points to the unacknowledged ideology at work in its formation and underscores the significance of the editors' statement of purpose in compiling this history: "Acquaintance with the written record of these two centuries should enlarge the spirit of American literary criticism and render it more energetic and masculine" (*CHAL* 1:x).

In addition to the "masculinism" that, as Shumway observes, "would become even more pronounced in the decades to come," and the "racism at the root of what would become the canon of American literature" (95), there is an additional animating spirit at work in *CHAL.* Despite their occasional reliance on region as a principle of organization, the editors of *CHAL* seek to distance and distinguish their history from those earlier efforts that succumbed to the temptation "to magnify the achievements of one's own parish at the expense of the rest of the country" (*CHAL* 1:v). While recognizing that such "local pride" was and is "a useful passion" in a country as diverse as the United States and that it has indeed "stimulated the production of our innumerable 'local colorists,'" giving rise to many "entertaining books and articles on the New England School, the Knickerbocker School, the Southern School, the Hoosier School, and the rest," they nevertheless declare that "it is not conducive to the production of a quite unbiased history of American literature" (1:v–vi). While the editors of *CHAL* equally reject the overt chauvinism consequent upon succumbing "to the temptation of national pride," Shumway can summarize their work as representing "a declaration of the independence of American literary history, for in it American literature, however flawed and ill-defined, is treated as a separate national literature to be judged on its own merits" (93). The spirit of nation and nationalism animates *CHAL* and ensures that region will be considered subordinate. Thus *CHAL* does not include "regionalism" as a literary category (the term appears nowhere in any of its indices) nor does it include a chapter on those innumerable local colorists whose work has produced so many "entertaining" books and articles. To avoid any association with the merely entertaining and, we might add, the merely regional, *CHAL* disperses the material that might have appeared in a chapter on the local-color movement into two adjacent chapters entitled "Dialect Writers" and "The Short Story." Nevertheless, these two chapters establish certain key features of the story that our literary histories tell about regionalism and local color.

C. Alphonso Smith, author of the chapter titled "Dialect Writers," introduces his observations on "dialects of the whites" with the following comment: "Why dialect should have been so sparingly used by American writers before the Civil War and why it should have become so constituent a part of American fiction immediately after the Civil War are questions not easily answered" (*CHAL* 2:360). Because his "partial" explanation represents one of the most prevalent stories told about local color and regionalist writing, we quote it at length:

> A partial explanation would seem to lie in the increasing sectionalism from 1830 to 1860 which, culminating in 1865, gave place not only to an increasing sense of national solidarity but to a keener interest in how the other half lived. Sectionalism meant indifference and ignorance; union means reciprocal interest and understanding. There can at least be no doubt that the American short story has been the chief vehicle of dialect since the Civil War, and the American short story, by its fidelity to local usages, has done more during these years to acquaint or reacquaint the North with the South and the East with the West than any other type of literature. (2:360)

Smith's "explanation" situates local color as a post–Civil War phenomenon, a location that, as we shall see, allows it to begin with the work of male writers and to be fathered rather than mothered. Such a move effectively eliminates from the history the work of Cary and the prewar writings of Cooke and Stowe. Smith also constructs regional writing as the literary consequence of union and as serving the interests of union since it promotes "reciprocal interest and understanding" and thus links "the far separated sections of the United States into closer bonds of union and fellowship" (2:361). Smith further associates the local-color or regional impulse with the form of the short story, observing that "excellence in dialect and excellence in the short story have been almost synonymous in American literature since the Civil War" (2:360). Implicit in this narrative, then, is an ideology of form as well. While the short story can do valuable work to "acquaint or re-acquaint" the regions of a nation with each other, it cannot presumably do the work of representing the nation as a whole. Such a project requires a larger form, and just as the nation is more important than any of its regions, so this larger form, implicitly understood as the novel whose "federalizing plot," in the words of James Cox, "tends always to subordinate the parts to the whole" ("Regionalism: A Diminished Thing" 781), is more valuable than those short fictions appropriate to the representation of regions.

In his chapter on "The Short Story," Fred Lewis Pattee reinforces the connection between the short story form, the regional impulse, and the post–Civil War period. While he surveys the appearance of the short story in American literature from its beginnings to the present moment and notes that "the tremendous influence of Irving" is responsible for the fact that "the unit of measure in American fiction is a short one," he reserves a special emphasis for Bret Harte, whose "'The Luck of Roaring Camp,' whatever one may think of its merits, must be admitted to be the most influential short story ever written in America" as it "stampeded America and for two decades set the style in short fiction" (*CHAL* 2:369, 377). With Harte, who according to Pattee came to the short story "by way of Irving," Pattee introduces the term "local color" and repeats the story told in the previous chapter of *CHAL:* "And yet Harte was an effect rather than a cause. America was ready for local colour. The Civil War had liberated America from provincialism. . . . The new emphasis was now upon the nation rather than upon the state or section. . . . The era following the war was an era of self-discovery" (2:378, 379). Once American literature has Harte, Pattee's narrative can explain all subsequent writers and texts, including, among others, Constance Fenimore Woolson, Murfree, George Washington Cable, Freeman, King, and Chopin, who produced a veritable "tide of short fiction the chief characteristic of which was its fidelity to local conditions" (2:388–89).

In writing of Jewett, however, Pattee recognizes a tradition "affected not at all by Harte, but by Mrs. Stowe and Rose Terry Cooke" (2:382). Earlier he has credited Cooke with being "the first significant figure" in the transition of the short story in the fifties and sixties toward "the dawning of definiteness, of localized reality" (2:372), and because of her capacity to continue to grow and change she became "the pioneer and leader not only of the group of depicters of New England life, but of the whole later school of makers of localized short fiction realistically rendered" (2:373). However, in contrast to his positioning of Harte as an intervention of extraordinary force, Pattee views Cooke as a writer who "came gradually, an evolution, without noise or sensation" (2:373). A similar minoritizing quietism pervades his treatment of Jewett as well, whose artistry he acknowledges but whose aesthetic achievement he links to the slightness of her materials and her investment in "recording the fading glories of an old regime" (2:383). Here we can see evidence for Gebhard's assertion that in treating local color, literary historians have distinguished between male and female practitioners of the mode and while treating both as relatively minor have found the women to be still more minor. Despite his occasional enthusiasm, Pattee ends his chapter with a narrative of the minority of the short story, calling it "the natural device of a young nation just emerging from its adolescence" and asserting that "on the whole the short story episode in American literary history has been a symptom not of strength but of weakness" (2:394). Like the other features of *CHAL*'s narrative of the regional, this one remains entrenched in later histories of American literature, serving to contain the challenge that regionalist fiction poses to the dominant narratives of American literature and to ensure that its alternative possibilities for the story of writing in the United States will remain unrealized.

The contradictions in *CHAL* between the impulse toward inclusiveness and the exclusions necessary to create the fiction of a national literature are highlighted by the final chapter of its last volume. For those of us impressed by Werner Sollors's efforts to recover the literatures of the United States written in languages other than English,[5] it may come as a surprise to discover that the final two chapters of *CHAL* are devoted to "Non-English Writings." For those of us who have come to think of the inclusion of Native American literature as a relatively recent phenomenon, a product of the social movements of the 60s and 70s, it may be equally shocking to discover that the final chapter, "Non-English Writings II," takes up what its author, Mary Austin, refers to as "Amerind literature" (612).[6] While Austin may appear to have the last word, so to speak, her influence on the future development of American literature "seems to have been," as Shumway puts it, "nil" (92). In considering Austin's chapter we can perhaps understand why Shumway positions *CHAL* "as a predecessor to, rather than the beginning of, American literature" (89), since it appears at a moment before the consolidation of the discipline, and, while it contains the elements that will shape that consolidation, perhaps most important the conviction "that there is something to be studied," it also contains "unrealized possibilities" that could have resulted in American literature's becoming "something quite other than what it became" (93). In the final chapter of *CHAL,* while Austin's discussion seems to subsume America's "aboriginal literature" into the "revelation of the power of the American landscape to influence form" (*CHAL* 4:633), thereby minimizing the genocide of the people by reclaiming their poetry and song, it also keeps open the possibility that American literature might have taken an alternative direction, one that would include the local and the regional. Expressing the hope that a contemplation of "Amerind literature" will help us "to rid ourselves of the incubus of European influence and the ever-present obsession of New York," Austin concludes that "there is no quarter of our land that has not spoken with a distinct and equal voice, none that is not able, without outside influence, to produce in its people an adequate and characteristic literary medium and form" (4:634). As Shumway writes, Austin's inclusion of Native American literature within the larger category of American literature "illustrates that the object of study was not the inevitable one" (92). Austin's interest in region kept open the possibility that American literature would not "inevitably" become exclusive.

What kept these possibilities from being realized, however, was the consolidation of a conception of American literature "as the reflection of the nation, rather than any of its regions" (137), achieved through the founding in 1921 of the American Literature Group within the Modern Language Association. As early as its third meeting, the ALG, according to Shumway, expressed "nationalist sentiments" and recorded its preference for "'presenting American literature as expression of national (historical) consciousness and not as aesthetic offshoot of English literature'" (133). As American literature began to develop as a field, it was predominantly the ALG members who defined the discipline. This group excluded "most women and others not properly connected" (149) from leadership, as well as from scholarship. While the earliest issues of *American Literature,* formed by ALG members in 1929, included several articles on minor writers, the only woman included in the early years of the journal was Emily Dickinson (182). "In the first ten years of its existence, *American Literature* published 24 full articles (as distinct from Notes and Queries or Reviews) by women scholars out of a total of 208" (Lauter 29), and an article taking an African American writer as its subject would not appear until more than forty years later.[7] In addition, under the leadership of Norman Foerster, the ALG established the categories in terms of which American literature would be understood and read. Not surprisingly, these categories did not include regionalism.

Literary History of the United States

The second cooperative history of American literature, *Literary History of the United States,* though first formally proposed at a meeting of the American Literature Group in 1938 (Shumway 302), was not published until 1948.[8] According to its general editor, Robert Spiller, "*LHUS* shared, of course, in the impulse of radical nationalism, social ferment, and reassessment of the native tradition that has followed every successful American war . . . and in the argument that political independence and world power should be followed by cultural independence and a position as one of the world's literatures."[9] The agenda of what was to become "the definitive history of American literature for at least the next 40 years" (Shumway 305) was thus explicitly nationalist. Perhaps not surprisingly then, the editors acknowledge that, even as such a collaborative project runs the "risk of differences of perspective or opinion," their goal has been to produce "a coherent narrative" (*LHUS* 1:vii, viii). The editors acknowledge as well that many of the individual chapters "have been substantially revised in order to fit them into the larger plan," and parts of some chapters "have been lifted and incorporated elsewhere"; additionally "the editors have themselves written many chapters and have supplied necessary links" in the interests of ensuring a coherent narrative (1:viii).

While geography serves as an organizing principle throughout *LHUS,* the phrase "regionalism and local color" appears in the index as a reference to Carlos Baker's chapter titled "Delineations of Life and Character." While for Baker this movement is primarily a post–Civil War event, as it was for the authors of the *Cambridge History,* he sets it in relation to a "democratic regionalist tradition" that had begun in both the North and the South before the war (*LHUS* 2:844). It is this vision of regionalism as an expression of the "democratic" that informs Baker's approach and makes him sympathetic to the women writers he discusses. Indeed, Baker's chapter lacks the misogyny whose prevalence elsewhere in *LHUS* suggests that one goal of this generation's history was the desire to associate the American with the masculine in order to make the profession of reading, teaching, and writing about American literature an appropriate one for men to engage in; the desire, in effect, to realize the stated aim of *CHAL* to "enlarge the spirit of American literary criticism and render it more energetic and masculine."

Baker's chapter, however, deals only with the North and the South, for *LHUS* follows the strategy identified by Gebhard of dividing "local color itself into its masculine and feminine practitioners" in order to rescue the movement from the general stigma of the feminine. Thus the chapter that follows Baker's, written by Wallace Stegner, takes up the writing of the West and Midwest and constructs a tradition that can be read as entirely masculine and thus valued accordingly. In this story democracy means the discovery of "Pike," "the basic American, the common man," and "when Pikes began *writing* books, we had for the first time a literature that mass America could feel in its bones" (*LHUS* 2:864, 865). A tradition replete with paternities—like Pattee, Stegner credits the author of "The Luck of Roaring Camp" with being "the father of all Western local color" (2:867)—its achievements are valued to the degree that they display masculine vigor. Within this narrative the handful of women writers Stegner mentions can be presented as mere imitators and rather ineffective ones at that. Thus he asserts that "in the wake of Harte and [Joaquin] Miller—especially of Harte—came a whole generation of lesser local colorists mainly female. They are worth a summary statement, hardly more" (2:868).

Baker, who takes up only New England and the South, begins his story with Stowe, whose "return from the intersectional triumph of *Uncle Tom's Cabin* to her true literary ground, the delineation of New England life and character," was hailed by James Russell Lowell because she alone was "capable of perpetuating, through the medium of prose fiction, the fast vanishing essence of Yankeeism"

(2:843). In contrast to Pattee's and Stegner's treatment of Harte as an originary figure marking a major intervention in American literature, Baker constructs Stowe as the heir to a tradition that "had begun to take form and amass substance" long before her return and that provided "ready to her hand" all the elements she would employ (2:844). However, not only is he careful not to accord Stowe too much originary power; he also quickly goes on record as aware of both "her own limitations as a writer" and the "limitations . . . of the literary movement to which her name thus early lent prestige," weaknesses to which she also "fell heir" (2:844). Thus Baker demonstrates the pattern Gebhard has identified in which enthusiasm for regionalism is possible when the tradition can be understood as male but critical distance becomes necessary when the tradition is understood to include women. For Baker, regionalism, though democratic in its impulses, is full of flaws, a movement with its heart in the right place but lacking a certain critical intelligence. Nevertheless, Baker does write appreciatively and positively of Cooke, Thaxter, Freeman, and Jewett as writers who "proved that in the proper hands the democratic regionalist tradition was still capable of development" (2:844). He treats Jewett with respect, reads her carefully, and declares her career to be the "most distinguished . . . among all the writers of regional fiction" and *The Country of the Pointed Firs* to be "the best piece of regionalist fiction to have come out of nineteenth-century America" (2:845).

Significantly, Baker introduces the theme of the reading public's "insatiable interest" in regions only in his comments about the South and New Orleans. In introducing his discussion of the South, for example, he states: "When the reading public discovered, somewhat belatedly, an insatiable interest in prewar planters and country gentlemen, poor whites of mountain, piedmont, tidewater, and bayou, and the plantation Negro, whether enslaved or emancipated, the writers were ready to supply the demand" (2:848). In discussing Murfree, he writes, "the Southern poor white, described here and there by earlier writers, began to look like a subject for exploitation" (2:850). This asymmetry, though subtle, suggests that for Baker New England constitutes a different kind of region than the South and New Orleans, one that exists in a different relation to the "nation" and is indeed potentially synonymous with "the reading public" so insatiably interested in the South. Implicit as well is the suggestion that the New England writers have a different relation to their material than do the writers of other regions, a difference that we might frame as the distinction between regionalism and local color. Baker seems to recognize here the different possibilities present in fiction that approaches the region from the perspective of inhabitant and advocate rather than from that of the outsider and exploiter. Intuitively, and in contrast to Stegner, he associates the insider perspective with the work of the women regionalists of New England.

In summarizing the achievement of the regional movement in the East and the South, Baker returns to an awareness of its limitations. Like the authors of

CHAL, Baker identifies the tradition of regional writing with the form of the short story and sketch; and like them, he associates the limitations of the tradition with the limitations of its form. Yet for Baker that limitation figures primarily as its writers' "refusal or failure to compress the sprawling sketch into the tighter limits of the bona fide short story" (2:860). Thus, while capable of intuitively recognizing certain differences within the tradition he discusses, Baker apparently cannot imagine the possibility that the sketch might not be a failed short story but a form in its own right. Still, in concluding, Baker returns to his association of regionalism with democracy, seeing in regionalism not merely the work of cultural preservation but also the creation of "a usable past" capable of challenging "the monster bulk of America" (2:860).

Columbia Literary History of the United States

Although Austin contributed to *CHAL* and Jewett achieves some prominence in *LHUS,* it is clearly only the renewed attention to women writers, the efforts to recover and reprint "lost" nineteenth-century writers, and in particular the attention to the writers we call regionalist, that leads the third and most recent collaborative literary history, *Columbia Literary History of the United States* (1988),[10] to address for the first time the question of regionalism and the differences between realism, regionalism, and local color. In their "General Introduction" to *CLHUS,* the editors acknowledge changes in the understanding of what constitutes each of the terms of their title, "literary," "history," and "United States." Thus, in contrast to the 1948 *LHUS,* the editors of *CLHUS* "have made no attempt to tell a 'single, unified story' with a 'coherent narrative'" (*CLHUS* xxi); rather they wish to foreground the tension between the desire to unify and "to provide coherence and organization to our literary heritage" and the desire "to challenge existing orders" (xxiii). As a result we find in *CLHUS* a privileging of stories over story and thus not surprisingly the volume offers more than one story of the origins, function, and value of regionalism; indeed, in *CHLUS* there are four writers who take up the question of regionalism.

We will address Neil Schmitz's essay "Forms of Regional Humor" in chapter 3, but we would note here that his "story" is, first, a narrative of Southern regional humor, and second, intensely gendered; indeed, it is a version of the Civil War understood as a gender war enacted through text and form. In his tale of two regions, New England and the South, Schmitz creates the South as the region fighting for its life in the works of the humorists of the Old Southwest against a seriousness represented by New England women and particularly Stowe, whose *Uncle Tom's Cabin* in 1852 "takes the sweetness of the patrician Southern sensibility, that benign, ironic quality, and slowly, carefully, empties it" (*CLHUS* 310). According to Schmitz, Southern regional humor had a distinctive form—the tall tale—and through this form, a conversation by, about, and among men of different classes, the South sought to work out its relation to itself. Stowe disrupts this conversation as she enters the "space" of Southern writing, "appropriates its speech, its locales, rewrites its characters" and in the process "thoroughly wrecks its composure" (310).[11] As a result, regional writing after *Uncle Tom's Cabin* is "contentious" and the tall tale is replaced by the "Southern rage" of George Washington Harris's Sut Lovingood (310).

The term "regionalism" as distinguished from regional writing makes its first official appearance in the three literary histories of the United States in an essay by Eric Sundquist in *CLHUS* titled "Realism and Regionalism." Although Sundquist acknowledges that the hierarchy which constructs realism as a larger concept than regionalism and which often views regionalism as a subset of realism reflects disparities in economic and political power rather than absolute aesthetic judgments, he does not himself take on the issue of challenging this hierarchy but writes essentially within its terms, defining regionalism as a subset of and a lesser form of realism—for example, he writes that "all these elements raise the novel [*The Grandissimes*] above sheer regional interest" (*CLHUS* 515). Neither does Sundquist distinguish between regionalism and local color, terms he uses interchangeably. Like Smith and Pattee in *CHAL* and Baker in *LHUS*, Sundquist generally locates local color as a post–Civil War phenomenon and within this frame he casts regional fiction as pervaded by "a sense of crisis or loss," a lament for a vanishing way of life, "a literature of memory" as "the sparsely populated, flawlessly sketched landscapes of the local colorists came to seem a lost world" (508–9). Not surprisingly, this lost world "is often lodged in the vestiges of a world of female domesticity" (509). Sundquist's initial presentation of regionalism as a literature of memory and thus predominantly the work of women leads him curiously to include Murfree in the same section in which he discusses Jewett and Freeman, writing that "Murfree's fiction, along with Jewett's, offers a window into secluded territory receding into a past paradoxically contemporaneous with the urban worlds of Howells and Crane" (510). Here Sundquist implicitly demonstrates how gender as a category of analysis can rearrange the definition of region.

Although Sundquist begins his discussion of regionalism with New England, a move virtually de rigeur by this point in the writing of American literary history, he gives New England relatively little space and indeed seems unwilling to accord it the attention that its role as first region would imply. Having identified New England regionalism with the work of women writers, he seems anxious to move as quickly as possible to regions where male writers can be seen as playing a more prominent role, namely, the South and the West. While he is careful to mention the occasional woman writer in his lengthy treatment of these regions, his inclusion of Murfree in his brief discussion of New England is symptomatic of the gender interests that shape his narrative as he in effect removes her from consideration as a Southern writer, contains her critique of the encroaching institutions of anthropology, medicine, law, and the mining corporation on the Appalachian mountain communities of Tennessee (see Pryse,

"Exploring Contact"), and relegates her to the "minor" genre of (New England) regionalism written by women. Not surprisingly, then, Sundquist's discussion of the South and the West focuses on male writers and his narrative contains the familiar patterns of paternity and precedence. Cable emerges as "the most notable of the New Orleans writers," Harte "initiated the vogue of Western 'local color,'" Hamlin Garland's "achievement . . . crowned the Midwestern realist tradition," and Edward Eggleston figures as "the father of us all" because Garland says he is (514, 516, 518).

In describing the work of the local colorists and particularly those of New England, Sundquist engages as well in the familiar practice of miniaturizing. Referring to Jewett's "exquisite craft" and quoting Howells, "who wrote [to] her, 'your voice is like a thrush's in the din of all the literary noises that stun us so'" (509), he portrays regionalism as a tradition in which considerable talent is exercised upon very little content, making possible the production of those "flawlessly sketched landscapes." As a tradition having little to say no matter how well it says it, the very artistry that might claim for regionalism a significant place in American letters becomes a sign of its essential insignificance. When Sundquist turns to the South, however, he also discovers a literature of memory but one that, instead of producing flawless sketches, returns as "magnificent dreams probed with both tragic sympathy and devastating irony by such writers as Mark Twain, William Faulkner, and Robert Penn Warren" (511). In its first appearance in the omnibus American literary histories, "regionalism" is marked by gender, but it is only those regions that can be gendered male that receive significant attention and are understood to have produced a theory of regionalism and an enduring "aesthetic" (517). Indeed, one might read Sundquist's chapter as a response to the climate that has required him to name regionalism at all and as an effort to redirect the recovery of regionalism away from a tradition of women's writing, to gender it male by identifying it with the male writers of the South and West, and to accord it aesthetic status by associating it with the work of major male novelists and in particular Faulkner. The subtext of Sundquist's essay might be said to be the construction of Faulkner as the greatest of all American writers. Needless to say, in such a context even Jewett's chances for recovery as a major American writer are remarkably diminished.

The third writer to take up the story of regionalism in *CLHUS* is James Cox in an essay titled "Regionalism: A Diminished Thing." Cox asserts that his subtitle[12] refers to the fact that after the Civil War, regions "displaced the fierce sectionalism that had led to the national conflict" and that "regions, in this post–Civil War sense, are sections that have lost not merely national political power but the political power to be nations" (*CLHUS* 763). While Cox's essay deals primarily with the regionalism of early to mid-twentieth-century American literature, he introduces his narrative with a discussion of a New England that "even as its literary power was waning, remained the dominant region in American literature until 1900" (768). The first historian to acknowledge that regionalism began with Stowe's 1834 "A New England Sketch," he grants her not only originary power but genealogical influence as well. "The writers who contributed most to the movement were," he writes, "significantly, women. It is not too much to call them the literary daughters of Harriet Beecher Stowe" (767). Yet his assessment of these writers contains the same dismissive judgments we have seen before. While they brought to their work an artistry missing from Stowe, their fiction "is one of recessiveness, disclosing the isolate individual at the edge of eccentricity in the process of resisting change" (767). Theirs is a region "whose nature has grown thin, whose economy has grown stingy, whose society has grown small," and while it gave them "a refuge for imaginative expression, yet it was also the enclosure that kept them in their place" (767). We can see here that association of regionalism with the figure of the spinster that Gebhard has observed and we can see as well the familiar pattern of minoritizing.

Embedded in Cox's narrative is the view of regionalism as "a subordinate order of realism," an identity that gained it the support of Howells, whose ambition to make realism "the ideology of a national literature" enabled him to appreciate regionalism as a "diminished" representation of a "larger reality" (767). In his view of the relationship between realism and regionalism, Cox rehearses the accepted critical narrative even as he himself opposes the "federalizing plot" that has rendered regionalism "a diminished thing." In his treatment of the Southern women "who proved superior to their new England forbears" in realizing the "possibilities" of their region—Katherine Anne Porter, Eudora Welty, Flannery O'Connor—he honors them for their recognition that "the plotted novel" worked "against true regional space" and for their pursuit of "the classic regional form—the short story" (781). While Cox shares with other historians the association of regionalism with the form of the short story or sketch, he stands alone in according the form positive value precisely because it subverts the hierarchy of nation and region. In a reading of Faulkner that could be used to "rescue" Jewett, he argues that although "Faulkner is rightly denominated a novelist, his breakthrough involved decentering the temporal sequence of plot, displacing it with rhetoric and voice" (782). In the ultimate irony, then, Cox's essay establishes a context that might ultimately spring open the "enclosure" that has kept writers like Jewett so long "in their place."

CLHUS contains a fourth story about regionalism rather different from those told by Schmitz, Sundquist, and Cox and the first to be written by a woman. In an essay entitled "Women Writers and the New Woman," Cecelia Tichi constructs a narrative that sets itself in conscious opposition to the story of regionalism as a literature of memory and "affectionate nostalgia" (*CLHUS* 597) and instead views writers such as Jewett and Freeman as using regionalism to negotiate the issues of their own particular historical moment. Part of a group of writers "stirred" by the figure of the "new woman" to write "a fiction of iconoclasm, a scathing indictment of the status quo," they were also aware of the enormous conservatism that greeted their efforts with resistance, rejection, and "even outrage" (599, 595). Walking "a narrow line between frankness and the ostracism that frankness might incur" (597), they gained acceptance under the rubric of regionalism since regionalism could be read as merely an exercise in nostalgia and a minor one at that. Using regionalism as a cover, these writers, according to Tichi, mapped "the geography of their gender. They were regionalists—but not solely in the ways critics have conventionally thought. The geography of America formed an important part of their work, but essentially they charted the regions of women's lives, regions both without and within the self" (598). Using gender as a category of analysis informed by a specifically feminist perspective, Tichi redefines regionalism as "the territory of women's lives" and specifically of women's "consciousness" (597).

Our reading of regionalism shares many elements in common with Tichi's narrative: the contemporaneity of regionalism, the recognition that one cannot make sense of its texts without using gender as a category of analysis, the association of regionalism with feminism, and the critical view of these writers as aesthetically self-conscious. Yet Tichi's story retains some crucial features of the earlier narratives and thus diverges significantly from our own. In presenting Freeman as an "instructive case" of the "literary predicament" faced by those writers trying to walk that "narrow line," she argues that Freeman, like her characters, employs "little female weapons," and she associates this strategy with the issue of form: "The passions of the woman writer must be roused—but formally constrained lest she be judged frightfully abnormal" (599). In articulating the view of regionalism as in some sense diminutive, Tichi apparently reiterates the assessment of the short story and sketch as limited forms. Tichi's own text operates from the assumption that the major engagements of the "new women writers" took place within the canvas of the novel and that regionalism formally and thematically limited even Jewett. Thus she reads *A Country Doctor,* a novel, as Jewett's feminist manifesto and *The Country of the Pointed Firs,* a collection of linked sketches and "her acknowledged masterwork," as written in a tradition that blunts her feminist principles and makes her a "gentle iconoclast" (600). In Tichi's essay there is no sense that the thematics of regionalism could themselves be "a scathing indictment of the status quo."

Cather and Wharton

In creating *American Women Regionalists,* we chose Cather's "Old Mrs. Harris" as the concluding selection because, just as Stowe's "Uncle Lot" imagines regionalism without fully realizing its possibilities, "Old Mrs. Harris" contains within it the imagination of regionalism understood to be no longer viable. Our design proposes that fictions themselves can constitute a form of literary history and we wish to conclude our examination of the treatment of regionalism within U.S. literary history by considering two such fictions, Cather's "Old Mrs. Harris" and Edith Wharton's *Ethan Frome.*

As Marilee Lindemann notes in her discussion of Cather's relation to "the culture wars of the 1920s," Cather was fully "engaged with, in, and against the American literary history that was being invented all around her at this crucial moment in her career. Aside from her obvious professional interest in the formation of that history, Cather had personal connections to several of its important makers" (91). Describing both her editorial decisions and her preface to her edition of *The Best Stories of Sarah Orne Jewett* and the two narratives she was working on at the time, *The Professor's House* and *Death Comes for the Archbishop,* as engagements in American literary history, Lindemann reveals a Cather aware of and concerned about the effect upon her own work and reputation of various forces operating in the construction of American literature in the 1920s.[13] While Cather's early ambitions persisted throughout her career, Lindemann claims that by the 1920s those ambitions "seem tempered by the concern that differences of region and class as well as of gender might be greater impediments to success than the girl who had played at being a pope had perhaps imagined" (86). Written somewhat later than the period Lindemann discusses, "Old Mrs. Harris" (1932) articulates Cather's need to separate from the writing tradition created by an earlier generation of women even as she, unlike Wharton, also honors these writers and their work, and in so doing she tells a story about regionalism similar in many ways to the stories presented by the various literary histories we have examined.

Old Mrs. Harris has left her home in Tennessee to follow her daughter and her son-in-law west to Colorado. In this "new world" Mrs. Harris has become effectively a servant, someone who does the work of the household but who remains invisible, partitioned off into a back room in the house and rarely allowed into the parlor, a woman who provides cakes for church socials she does not herself attend. Mrs. Rosen, the next-door neighbor, and Cather's version of the regionalist narrator, struggles to get to know the "real grandmother," to make her visible so as to hear and hence to be able to tell her story. She tries to care for and comfort grandmother, bringing her treats of food designed to tell her that she, Mrs. Rosen, finds grandmother far more interesting and valuable than her daughter, Mrs. Templeton, or her granddaughter Vicki. But old Mrs. Harris resists all her efforts, refusing in effect to become a subject of regionalist fiction.

Unlike Mrs. Rosen, Cather's narrator locates her story elsewhere—in Victoria Templeton's refusal of a domestic role and her rage at the biological constraints of repeated pregnancy; in granddaughter Vicki's self-centered struggle to find a way to leave home and go to college, to move out of a community of women and into the world of the University of Michigan and coeducation. For Vicki "home" is not a source of comfort and support but rather a site of intense competition for scarce resources of time, attention, and money, and her response to the news that Mrs. Harris is sick is "bitter"—"Wasn't it just like them all to go and get sick, when she had now only two weeks to get ready for school, and no trunk and no clothes or anything?" (*AWR* 636). Cather does not fault Vicki for her self-centered response for she recognizes that Vicki's future lies elsewhere than in the regionalism of old Mrs. Harris and that her development requires different values from those represented by this regionalism. In contrast to Jewett's model of departure and return, which we will discuss more fully in chapter 11, Cather presents generational imperatives that make the needs of the young, the middle-aged, and the old distinctly different and inevitably incompatible. While this model does not allow or produce the rhythm of separating while staying connected, she tempers the bitterness and frustration inherent in her modernist vision with a theory of archival consciousness, suggesting that when Victoria and Vicki "are old, they will come closer and closer to Grandma Harris" and they "will regret that they heeded her so little" (637–38). This regret will not make them bitter toward the young and more appreciative of the old; rather it will activate their sympathies for the young because they will be able to remember what they themselves once felt: "They will say to themselves: 'I was heartless, because I was young and strong and wanted things so much. But now I know'" (637–38). In contrast to regionalism that posits "now I know" as the source of story and the repository of that wisdom and those values that can and should be taken out of the place and passed on and down, and unlike Jewett's positioning of Mrs. Todd that leads to multiple identifications across generations, Cather's "now I know" expresses the irrelevance of one generation's knowledge and values for another. For Cather, story will always reside with the young because those who are older have the archival consciousness that makes them capable of understanding the young and of reading their stories—"'We are only young once, and trouble comes soon enough'" (617)—but those who are young do not yet know enough to read the stories of the old.

No longer the source of story, regionalism in Cather's "history" is reduced to simply offering comfort; dying, old Mrs. Harris comforts herself with "remembering the old place at home" (637). While regionalism, "the old place at home," once provided Mrs. Harris with status and agency, allowing her to live in her own house, order life to her "own taste," and rule her world "jealously" (617), it did not provide her with a story capable of resisting the "young" narrative of her son-in-law's desire to better himself by going west. Instead regionalism becomes a comforting memory. Through a carefully constructed fiction, Mrs. Rosen manages to provide comfort for Grandma Harris in the form of an old sweater, left behind by Mrs. Rosen's visiting nephew and accepted by Mrs. Harris because, as Mrs. Rosen says, "'The yarn might be good for your darning'" (604). Mrs. Harris calls this sweater "her little comforter" and she turns to it in the early morning hours when she is awakened by the discomfort of "the hard slats under her, and the heaviness of the old home-made quilts, with weight but little warmth, on top of her" (604). Gift of the would-be regionalist narrator, this little sweater comes to stand for the comfort of that other, older way and only this "spot" of regionalism can be counted on to warm the ache in her chest:

> On winter nights, and even on summer nights after the cocks began to crow, Mrs. Harris often felt cold and lonely about the chest. Sometimes her cat, Blue Boy, would creep in beside her and warm that aching spot. But on spring and summer nights he was likely to be abroad skylarking, and this little sweater had become the dearest of Grandmother's few possessions. It was kinder to her, she used to think, as she wrapped it about her middle, than any of her own children had been. She had married at eighteen and had had eight children; but some died, and some were, as she said, scattered. (604)

Unlike Wharton, Cather views regionalism without hostility; her model insulates her from the possibility that regionalism could exert any coercive influence on her, and it prevents her as well from lapsing into nostalgia. By reducing regionalism to comfort and making it the place to which Grandma turns when all else has failed, Cather underscores the limitations of regionalism for a modernizing culture committed to separating from its past. While the image of Grandma clutching her sweater for comfort is poignant, it is not compelling. Through her portrait of old Mrs. Harris, Cather encourages her own reader to separate from regionalism. Indeed, in Cather's hands, the regionalist impulse becomes "scattered." Her story suggests that Mrs. Rosen's efforts to tell Grandma's story should be undone, her "fiction" in fact realized, and the sweater unraveled to become pieces of yarn stitched into other stories, just as Cather herself has done in "Old Mrs. Harris."

We concluded *American Women Regionalists* with Cather's "Old Mrs. Harris" and her proposition that regionalism can no longer serve the purposes of an ambitious girl from the "provinces" who seeks to be a major American (not woman) writer because her treatment of regionalism is sympathetic; even as she separates herself from the tradition of her predecessors she honors that tradition and mourns the loss of the connection. Wharton figures as another ambitious woman, this time from the metropole, who regards "regionalism" as the sign of her predecessors' limitations and who seeks, through her own construction of its narrowness, to dissociate herself from these foremothers so that she may join the company of American (not women) writers. Unlike Cather, however, Wharton treats regionalism with extreme hostility and even fear. Her earlier *Ethan Frome* (1911) constitutes Wharton's contribution to the treatment of regionalism in American literary history. In *A Backward Glance*, Wharton acknowledges that "[f]or years I had wanted to draw life as it really was in the derelict mountain villages of New England, a life even in my time, and thousandfold more a generation earlier, utterly unlike that seen through the rose-coloured spectacles of my predecessors, Mary Wilkins and Sarah Orne Jewett"

(293). As Donna Campbell writes in her study of the turn-of-the-century reaction against regionalism, "The task Wharton sets for herself in writing *Ethan Frome* is, quite simply, to confront the genre of local color fiction on its own terms, and, using the same local color settings and characters as her predecessors, particularly those of Sarah Orne Jewett's *Country of the Pointed Firs,* to disrupt and transform its narrative conventions, the assumptions underlying its iconographic and symbolic structures such as storytelling, preserving, and healing, and its insistence on the value of self-denial" (*Resisting Regionalism* 162).

When Wharton's narrator first encounters Ethan Frome and seeks an explanation for the look on his face, "'as if he was dead and in hell now'" (*Ethan Frome* 6), Herman Gow offers the following: "'Guess he's been in Starkfield too many winters. Most of the smart ones get away'" (6). In *Ethan Frome* those who live in the region see it as a trap, the enemy, a force that will crush, break, and cripple you if you can't figure out how to escape it. Finding the struggle to survive so daunting, those who stay in the region become incapable of making meaningful connections with each other. Wharton's Starkfield seems virtually uninhabited and the absence of human figures aggravates the starkness of the landscape. In contrast to Jewett's narrator in *The Country of the Pointed Firs,* who seems to meet everyone in Dunnet Landing, Wharton's narrator meets almost no one, as if no one really lives there, as if Starkfield does not encourage visits; no "golden chain of love and dependence" links "far island" and "scattered farms" (*The Country of the Pointed Firs* 90). Rather, Wharton's characters struggle in isolation to survive overwhelmingly assaultive forces where links become tethers "checking each step like the jerk of a chain" (*Ethan Frome* 3) and where sympathy takes the form of wishing one's friend had not survived the "smash-up" (4).

Wharton records the negative effects of the region as well through her charge that it turns its inhabitants into versions of the same. When the narrator enters Frome's house, he hears "a woman's voice droning querulously" which "ceased as I entered Frome's kitchen, and of the two women sitting there I could not tell which had been the speaker" (25, 173). The droning force of the region defies human efforts to individuate, for even Ethan uncannily resembles his wife and his former lover, who initially seemed so different from each other. Ironically, Wharton also charges the region with rendering its inhabitants inarticulate, as if the struggle to survive severe winters has left them no energy for talk. Terrified by his mother's silence, Ethan marries the first voice he hears only to discover that she too falls silent and that when she does speak, he wishes her droning would cease. In Starkfield, those who are voluble offer only a meaningless drone while the speech of those who might have something to say, like the younger Mrs. Hale, is broken, fragmentary, and incomplete, the verbal equivalent of Ethan's lameness that checks every step "like the jerk of a chain." In her introduction Wharton postulates that there might have been a village gossip "who would have poured out the whole affair" of Ethan's life to the narrator "in a breath" (ix), but she insists that such a story would be worthless given the "deep-rooted reticence and inarticulateness of the people I was trying to draw" (ix). By definition, then, life "as it really was" in the region can never be articulated by those who live there, and any attempt to do so will inevitably be false, "rose-coloured."

Wharton not only charges her predecessors with a false representation of region; she also charges them with failing to present human life as it "really" is. By failing to engage the issue of sexuality, regionalism, according to Wharton, ironically produces the "rose-coloured" perspective conventionally associated with romance or with sentimentalism. Evading sexuality, Wharton suggests, limits the range of emotions one can depict, the moral issues one can engage, and hence the scope of one's work; for Wharton, we might say, it defines the limits of regionalism and relegates it to the status of minor literature. *Ethan Frome* proposes the potential of sexual passion to destroy human lives as a reality that can occur anywhere; when writers and texts engage this passion they move from the merely regional to the universal, from the minor to the major. In so obviously echoing *The Scarlet Letter* in her own text, Wharton reminds us that, while the particular form Ethan's sexuality takes can perhaps be attributed to the region and that while such passion has the potential to rip apart human lives, it can also force our confrontation with the moral law and teach us who we are. Moreover she suggests that any body of fiction that fails to engage these passions will itself be without either ethical complexity or self-knowledge and thus will be minor, not major.

When Herman Gow blames the region for Ethan's arrested development, claiming that the smart ones get away, he implicitly genders the smart ones as male and the region as female. Although Elizabeth Ammons has argued that in this text the force of the region bears equally on men and women (see *Edith Wharton's Argument with America* 69–72), it requires effort not to see the entrapping region as female and the entrapped subject as male. While the figure of Ethan elicits the narrator's sympathy and by his account that of other villagers as well, Zeena and Mattie are aligned with the forces of region and elicit the same fear, loathing, and primitive terror that Starkfield does. Indeed, when the narrator enters Ethan's kitchen we finally learn what makes the region and by extension regionalism so terrifying. Suffocatingly claustrophobic; utterly regressive; filled with the meaningless whining drone of the voices of women incapable of development (soon after his marriage "Ethan learned the impossibility of transplanting" Zeena for "she could not have lived in a place which looked down on her" [*Ethan Frome* 71]), who therefore perversely thrive in an environment that destroys a man like Ethan and parasitically feed off of him—this is the kitchen, the region, and regionalism as seen by Wharton's narrator and it is hell, now understood and located.

In the virulence of its critique of regionalism's fundamental values, *Ethan Frome* becomes Wharton's effort to undo the work of her predecessors and to substitute her version of reality for theirs. As Donna Campbell observes, "Considered as the corrective rewriting of what Wharton saw as the bleak rural landscapes, grotesquely extended love affairs, excessive preserving, and incredible renunciations and self-denial of local-color fiction, *Ethan Frome* almost becomes Wharton's blackly comic joke, a vision of the genre so extreme as to border on private parody" (172). In order to parody, one must know the original, and *Ethan Frome* contains considerable parody. For example, in the perverse relation of Zeena and Mattie, Wharton parodies the regionalist thematic of female friendship with its potential for community and advocacy and for eliciting stories and voice. Zeena herself parodies Jewett's Mrs. Todd, for like Mrs. Todd, Zeena has knowledge of herbs and medicines and presents herself as a healer. Yet her interest in "healing" derives from her utter self-absorption ("her skill as a nurse had been acquired by the absorbed observation of her own symptoms" [72]) and she manufactures "sickness" as a tool to control, manipulate, and punish others. In Wharton's text the woman of faculty becomes a figure of terror whose capacities emerge only in situations that maim and cripple others.

Perhaps the most striking feature of *Ethan Frome* in comparison with the texts of Wharton's "predecessors" lies in its use of a male narrator to tell a man's story. Here we can read Wharton's "determination to contrast her own modern (masculine) perspective with that of the local color 'authoresses' who used female interpreters" (Campbell 163). In this context Wharton's objection to the "rose-coloured spectacles" of Jewett and Freeman appears to have to do less with their presenting a too genial view of New England and more with their construction of region as a place in which women can thrive, find voice, and tell their stories, and with their use of regionalism to create sympathy for women and to present alternative feminist values. In *Ethan Frome* Wharton substitutes sympathy for the man for sympathy for the woman or, to put it slightly differently, she substitutes the man's story for the woman's story. In distancing herself from her female predecessors Wharton aligns herself with her male predecessors, particularly Hawthorne, as we have noted above. As Carol Singley observes, Wharton "herself invited comparison of her writing with his." She responded to criticism about her other New England novel, *Summer* (1917), by "rail[ing] against readers" who compared her work to that of "authoresses" and failed to measure it against the example of Hawthorne (112). By evoking *The Scarlet Letter* in writing *Ethan Frome*, Wharton implicitly claims the right to be read and judged in the context set by Hawthorne, not that set by Freeman and Jewett. We may, however, still register surprise at the vehemence of Wharton's implicit assertion that to be taken seriously as an American writer she would not simply have to dissociate herself from those despised female predecessors; she would as well have to disavow a literary tradition sympathetic to women, indeed undo it by overwriting it with a story that renders women as the enemy, the spaces they occupy as hell, and men as the victims of women's oppression. As we will discuss in more detail in chapter 7, regionalism constitutes a "category crisis" not only for Wharton but for American literature, revealing the deeply disturbing foundations of the field.

In choosing to end her novella with Mrs. Hale's comment that she doesn't see much difference between "'the Fromes up at the farm and the Fromes down in the graveyard; 'cept that down there they're all quiet, and the women have to hold their tongues'" (*Ethan Frome* 181), Wharton suggests that regionalism was written by women who ought to have had to hold their tongues. Unlike Cather, whose "Old Mrs. Harris" reads regionalism as simply no longer useful to someone like herself, Wharton seems to view regionalism as lethal and *Ethan Frome* becomes her attempt to bury it. Given the content of *Ethan Frome,* we can extrapolate the source of her terror. The claustrophobic, regressive world of the kitchen/region evokes the non-nurturant mother who seeks to freeze her child in a state of permanently arrested development and to substitute the seductions of the easy and the safe for the child's desire to develop: "The story suggests both Wharton's fear of entrapment within an unnecessarily limited tradition and her apprehension that a radical break could destroy her promising career" (Campbell 171). Wolff identifies the seduction and the terror regionalism posed for Wharton:

> If we remove the accidents from the work of a writer like Sarah Orne Jewett (even one with such mastery), what will we find? What is the subject of her loving attention? In social terms, we must speak of a diminished world where all pleasure, all hope, all energy have been focused into the simplest acts of subsistence. . . . The disruptions in such a world are few (and they often come as unwelcome invasions from the world outside), but peace has been purchased at the price of passion. There is no rage, and the climax of sexual fulfillment has been indefinitely suspended. It is a twilight world; perhaps a world of senescence, but more probably an evocation of childhood. . . . And if by some terrible chance we should achieve the world of that dream—a world where our entire energies are focused into the acts of eating and sleeping and being taken care of, a world devoid of emotions powerful enough to change it or disrupt it, a world where man's deep harmony with nature makes his life virtually indistinguishable from the lives of simple animals . . .—if we should sink into the oblivion of such a world, we would go mad. Taken seriously, the beckoning vision of the New England regionalists becomes a nightmare. (182–83)

In this context regionalism comes to figure as a regressive "mother," a mode of writing hopelessly locked in the backwater of the minor, yet seductive in its promise that success will attend one's acceptance of and comfort with such status. Wharton might well have registered the implications of Jewett's association of Mrs. Todd with *tod,* the German word for death, and interpreted it as a version of the siren call ("I knew well enough what songs those sirens sang" [Introduction, *Ethan Frome* vii]) to the ambitious woman writer to give up the struggle to escape the limitations of her gender.

According to Cather, Jewett "once laughingly told me that her head was full of dear old houses and dear old women, and that when an old house and an old woman came together in her brain with a click, she knew that a story was under way" ("Preface" 9). In *Ethan Frome* an old house and an "old" woman come together with a click that signals danger and the story that gets underway sets about confronting and mastering that danger by undoing the work of "dear old" Jewett. Undoing the work of "dear old" Jewett could serve to summarize the dominant treatment of regionalism in official and unofficial U.S. literary history. In her 1972 essay "The Literature of Impoverishment," Ann Douglas Wood claims that for the writers we have termed regionalist, "writing offered an exercise in nostalgia or a release for despair" (13), and she describes these writers as "depressed" (17) observers of "the plight of American women of their own status or sensibility, unwilling or unable to change their way of life although it barely afforded them a sustenance" (18). Echoing Wharton's charges, she argues that for these writers "the country village is a kind of concentration camp filled with the feminine relics of the past" (19) and the "house" that constitutes their characters' identity "is no longer a garden of delights, but a bed of weeds; it is not rampantly fertile, but barren, and even poisonous" (22). Although they "had only limited use for [the] sentimentalism" of their predecessors, "they had nothing to put in its place but its negation" (17). In a rhetorical register of rising intensity, Wood concludes her essay with the charge that these writers were "witches" who "seemed to sense that they were sucking artistic life from the nearby [*sic*] moribund body of the provincial society about which they wrote" and whose "only message is a curse against the society which has denied [them] a place" (28). Gebhard comments that such "harsh treatment of the female local colorists remains disturbing" (87), particularly in the way Wood joins male critics in associating the woman writer in America with an "artistically sterile" spinsterhood (85), but Richard Brodhead has demonstrated the continuing currency of the power of such "harsh treatment" of "female authorship in America" in *Cultures of Letters.* Clearly regionalism as an American literary tradition elicits passionate and divergent responses that could be characterized as doing and undoing the work of "dear old" Jewett—Howells's enthusiasm met by the modernists' contempt; Wood's fear and loathing countered by Josephine Donovan's adulation; the feminist recovery project overturned by Brodhead's reading of regionalism as easy, complicit, and corrupt. Above all, it constitutes a past and present site of contestation in American literary history over the meaning of the American, of the literary, and of history.

Geographics

Our point here in retelling the stories that the three omnibus literary histories of the United States and the texts by Cather and Wharton construct with respect to regionalism is to indicate the role certain assumptions, including those about gender, have played in the construction of these narratives, rendering the tradition we seek to recover invisible or, if dimly seen, insignificant. As we have indicated in the preceding summary, American literary history has viewed regionalism through frames derived from either a nationalist agenda or from models established with male writers as the central points of reference. The effect of these frames has been to diminish, disperse, and dismiss regionalism and to make it inaccessible to critical view. Our goal in this book is to re-frame or re-locate regionalism so as to open what Freeman in "A Mistaken Charity" calls "chinks" (*AWR* 319) in the apparently seamless narrative of diminution and dismissal. Our argument starts from a different location than that of any of these literary histories and enables us to ask whether the "interests" of regionalism consistently dismissed as narrow might not be better labeled "different" or even "oppositional" as they challenge the interests represented by the dominant discourse and threaten to reveal those interests as equally "narrow." We begin precisely with those "narrow" interests of regionalism that reveal the connection between regionalism and feminism as we struggle to effect new understandings of what Gregory Jay has reconceived as "writing in the United States" (264).

In addition, as the preceding discussion indicates, we situate *Writing out of Place* within the larger feminist project of the recovery of women writers, a project that Elaine Showalter has labeled "gynocriticism."[14] Gender as a category of analysis made the tradition of regionalism visible to us and, as we have also indicated, we have used what we call a feminist analytic to interpret the meaning and significance of this tradition. In concluding her introduction to *Mappings: Feminism and the Cultural Geographies of Encounter*, Susan Friedman describes her approach as "text-centered" and declares, "I have turned to these texts with a frankly instrumentalist intent—for what they have to teach academic feminism, their potential interventions in the great debates of the day, and for their collective wisdom and pleasure. The stories they tell matter. So do the stories we tell about them" (13). We would similarly position our work for we believe as well that the stories we have to tell in this book "matter." Having observed throughout our analysis of the treatment of regionalism in American literary history the different ways in which the power to name matters, we seek to appropriate this power to ourselves and our project. Gender as a category of analysis made possible the discovery of this tradition; feminist politics has inspired its recovery; a feminist analytic enables and informs our reading it; but naming it allows us and others to talk and write about it.

In *Mappings* Friedman attempts to develop a mode of feminist criticism that goes beyond previous models, and she indicates her intent by titling her first chapter "'Beyond' Gender: The New Geography of Identity and the Future of Feminist Criticism." Despite her astute analysis of the political dangers of her proposal to go beyond gender, an awareness she conveys by placing "beyond" in quotation marks, she argues that there are compelling reasons to do so. "Gynocriticism," she writes, "however revitalized, retains gender as the assumed foundation of feminist critical practice and thus remains out of step with locational discourses of identity and subjectivity" (25). Nevertheless, she recognizes that "there are still compelling reasons—both epistemological and political—to do a kind of feminist work rooted in gynocriticism and gynesis" and that because the historical conditions still exist that gave rise to this work such "projects have continued legitimacy and urgency" (31, 32). Proposing in effect a pattern of "uneven developments" in the feminist intervention into the field of literary studies, she offers a model of multiple and flexible strategies.

While in many ways, as we have indicated, our project remains "rooted in gynocriticism and gynesis," Friedman's development of a feminist critical practice based on a privileging of positionality or situatedness, on what she terms discourses of "geographics" (19), has particular resonance for our work:

> Like relational discourses, situational approaches assume that identity resists fixity, but they particularly stress how it shifts fluidly from setting to setting. Geographic allegorization, in other words, is not merely a figure of speech, but a central constituent of identity. Each situation presumes a certain setting as site for the interplay of different axes of power and powerlessness. One situation might make a person's gender most significant; another, the person's race; another, sexuality or religion or class. So while the person's identity is the product of multiple subject positions, these axes of identity are not equally foregrounded in every situation. Change the scene, and different, relevant constituents of identity come into play. (23)

Friedman's emphasis on "setting as site for the interplay of different axes of power and powerlessness" evokes our understanding of region as a location that makes visible the cultural situatedness of women, and her understanding of identity as "the product of multiple subject positions" evokes our recognition that the subjects of regionalist fiction, be they women or men, are multiply located along "axes of identity" that include not only gender and region but race, class, economic status, physical ability, age, and their relation to what their society considers the "normal," and that in different fictional settings different axes become the focus of the text. While gender and region remain the primary terms grounding the feminist analytic of *Writing out of Place,* we share Friedman's view of "geographics" as unsettling the fixities of gynocriticism and as discouraging "the grand narratives . . . to which gynocriticism tends" (28). Friedman concludes her discussion of reading "'beyond' gender" by calling for a criticism that will be "locational" but remain feminist. Although different of course from Friedman's, in this book we too seek to practice a locational feminist criticism.

CHAPTER 3

Origins: The History of an Impulse

Without a thought of making a book, I began to recall some shadows and sunbeams that fell about me as I came up to womanhood, incidents for the most part of so little apparent moment or significance that they who live in what is called the world would scarcely have marked them had they been detained with me while they were passing, and before I was aware, the record of my memories grew to all I now have printed.

—Alice Cary, "Preface" to *Clovernook*

Origin Texts: Mitford, Edgeworth, Neal, and Paulding

When Alice Cary, "without a thought of making a book," sat down to write of those "shadows and sunbeams that fell about me as I came up to womanhood" (*AWR* 60) and called the result *Clovernook; or, Recollections of Our Neighborhood in the West,* she in fact drew upon a well-established tradition, one that associated the form of the sketch with a specific regionally inflected location and that included a substantial number of works by women writers. A brief look at some of the titles published in the decades between Cary's birth in 1820 and the appearance of *Clovernook* in 1852 will give readers a sense of this context. In 1820, for example, Harriet Cheney published *The Sunday School, or Village Sketches;* in 1822 Catharine Sedgwick's *A New England Tale* appeared, followed in 1824 by Lydia Huntley Sigourney's *Sketch of Connecticut;* and the decade closed with Sarah Josepha Hale's *Sketches of American Character* and William Leggett's *Tales and Sketches. By A Country Schoolmaster* in 1829. The decade of the 30s opened with Mary Griffith's *Our Neighborhood* and John Greenleaf Whittier's *Legends of New England,* both in 1831; in 1832 James Hall published *Legends of the West,* followed in 1833 by William Cox's *Crayon Sketches* and Eliza Leslie's *Pencil Sketches* and in 1834 by Albert Pike's *Prose Sketches and Poems,*

Written in the Western Country; Augustus Baldwin Longstreet published *Georgia Scenes* in 1835, and in 1836 Griffith published a second volume, *Camperdown; or, News from Our Neighborhood;* 1838 produced Eliza Lee's *Sketches of a New England Village,* Eliza Cabot Follen's *Sketches of Married Life,* Benjamin Drake's *Tales and Sketches from the Queen City,* and Joseph Neal's *Charcoal Sketches or Scenes in a Metropolis;* and in 1839 Caroline Kirkland's *A New Home—Who'll Follow? or, Glimpses of Western Life* appeared. In the 1840s we have N. S. Dodge's *Sketches of New England; or, Memories of the Country* (1842); Harriet Beecher Stowe's *The Mayflower; or Sketches of Scenes and Characters among the Descendants of the Pilgrims* (1843); William Tappan Thompson's *Chronicles of Pineville* (1845); Elizabeth Allen's *Sketches of Green Mountain Life* (1846); T. B. Thorpe's *The Mysteries of the Backwoods; or Sketches of the Southwest* (1846); John Robb's *Streaks of Squatter Life, and Far-West Scenes* (1847); and Fanny Forester's *Alderbrook* (1847). Moreover, as Lawrence Buell has noted, "Owing to the precedents of Irving and Mitford, from the 1820s on a standard item in the repertoire of antebellum literary magazines and annuals was the short local tale or sketch" (*New England* 294), often later collected and published as books. Sandra Zagarell observes that "in the 1820s and 1830s, in the village sketch, a new kind of fictional narrative . . . proliferated in the magazines, annuals, and gift books of the era and took the form of book-length works like Lydia Sigourney's *Sketch of Connecticut, Forty Years Since* (1824)" ("'America'" 143).

In *Stories of American Life* (1830) and *Lights and Shadows of American Life* (1832), according to Clarence Gohdes the "first general anthology of American short stories" and "a major document in the earliest annals of the discipline now called 'American Civilization' or 'American Studies'" ("Foreword" iii), Mary Russell Mitford identified the short story or sketch as a specifically American art form and indicated that a collection of such fictions was the best way to communicate to an English audience the essence of American culture and character. In the preface to her *Stories,* Mitford explains that her "principal aim has been to keep the book as national and characteristic as possible," an aim that, interestingly enough, justifies her exclusion of Irving as "essentially European" (v, iv). Ironically, Mitford herself was best known for her own collection of sketches, *Our Village* (1824–32), in which, according to Zagarell, she "adapted the sketch form Washington Irving had used in his *Sketch Book* (London, 1819–20) and replaced his peripatetic 'alienated observer' narrator with an empathetic woman deeply involved in her own village" ("Narrative" 501). Josephine Donovan writes that *Our Village* "pioneered the village sketch tradition" and invented "a form of fiction which later women writers found congenial" (*New England* 23), and Zagarell sees Mitford as providing the "format" for later U.S. village-sketch narratives ("'America'" 146). In devoting herself to a "form of fiction" she identifies as peculiarly American to present the essence of "local life in a provincial English town" (Donovan 23), we can imagine Mitford as in fact thinking more regionally than nationally, as viewing both the United States and England as regions of some larger Anglo-American entity and as themselves composed of regions. As we examine the relation of the national to the development of the sketch in the United States, we would do well to keep this point in mind, as it suggests that the sketch form through its association with the regional complicates and even destabilizes the concept of nation. Moreover, the instance of Mitford reminds us that gender produces an additional complication in the relation of the sketch to the national as Mitford originates a tradition of women's writing that she associates with the American—we might note here that the dog who plays so large a part in these sketches is named Mayflower—but that she uses to portray an English village. Despite these complexities, *Our Village* underscores the intimate connection between the sketch form, the regional location, and the woman writer. What it lacks, however, is any sense that this combination could be used to create a space of critique. For the articulation of this possibility, we must turn to another, even earlier text, Maria Edgeworth's *Castle Rackrent.*

George Watson writes that Maria Edgeworth's "*Castle Rackrent* (1800) is the first regional novel in English, and perhaps in all Europe" (vii). Edgeworth's critics have noted her influence on Sir Walter Scott and the historical novel; on the development, even the invention, of children's literature; and on early nineteenth-century American women readers and writers in general.[1] Indeed, Catharine Sedgwick dedicated *A New England Tale* (1822) to Maria Edgeworth "as a slight expression of the writer's sense of her eminent services in the great cause of human virtue and improvement" (7) and Edgeworth reviewed *A New England Tale* and, later, Sedgwick's *Redwood* (1824). Stowe apparently recalled hearing Edgeworth's "Frank" as a child (Wilson, *Crusader in Crinoline* 39); though we have been unable to confirm that Cary read Edgeworth's fiction for children, she may very well have done so because both parents were readers and apparently acquired "the works of the standard English poets" (Pulsifer 11); and Nan Prince in Jewett's *A Country Doctor* reads Edgeworth's *The Parent's Assistant; or, Stories for Children* (87).

Marilyn Butler attributes Edgeworth's success in her stories for children in part to her "handling of setting" (162). She writes that "the tales of *The Parent's Assistant* [1796] do manage to give the impression of being 'placed' within a landscape, or inside a house. . . . The stories convey a few everyday objects with the clarity which characterizes certain selective childhood memories" (162–63). Edgeworth took care to "place" her child readers in a fictional landscape that established her as the first writer who wrote directly for children rather than for their parents; "what mattered most was making them direct enough to please the child" (163). We would speculate that even in their encounters with Edgeworth as child readers, the young Harriet Beecher, Cary, and perhaps Jewett would have responded to the power of Edgeworth's fiction to place the reader in an identifiable setting. In *Castle Rackrent,* Edgeworth extended her "handling of setting" to regional fiction for adults. Walter Allen describes the "new territory" Edgeworth occupied with the publication of *Castle Rackrent:*

> Maria Edgeworth gave fiction a local habitation and a name. And she did more than this: she perceived the relation between the local habitation and the people who dwell in it. She invented, in other words, the regional novel, in which the very nature of the novelist's characters is conditioned, receives its bias and expression, from the fact that they live in a countryside differentiated by a traditional way of life from other countrysides.
>
> The region she discovered was Ireland, and, with Ireland, the Irish peasant. (108)

There are numerous elements of *Castle Rackrent* that make it of continuing interest to readers today and further identify it as a stunning origin text for regionalism, as well as for that larger category, "regional fiction." Most significantly, of course, *Castle Rackrent* is set in a particular place, indeed, is the first Irish fiction. While Sedgwick's dedication accurately characterizes most of Edgeworth's fiction as service in the cause of human improvement, didactic both in intent and execution, *Castle Rackrent* does not possess explicit didactic purpose. Rather, the didactic requirement is replaced by, and somehow met in, the text's sympathetic depiction of Irish peasant life. Additionally, though Watson and other critics term *Castle Rackrent* a novel, the work is at best novella-length and is actually comprised of two separable sketches, the second apparently written two years later than the first (Watson 123). The form Edgeworth chose for *Castle Rackrent* is unlike the form she chose for any other work; even *The Absentee* (1812), generally considered her next best fiction, contains regional elements (two-thirds of the book is set in Ireland and concerns Irish identity) but takes the form of the novel of manners. While *Castle Rackrent* may have influenced Scott and the history of the English novel, only regional writers following Edgeworth adapted its form.

Further, the narrator of *Castle Rackrent* is a disenfranchised person, a family retainer who tells the Rackrent family history "in his own language, which, though naturally a literary version, is close enough to Irish peasant speech to retain the illusion of authenticity" (Allen 109). Yet Edgeworth has no interest in a local-color treatment of either her narrator, Thady Quirk, or the characters in the family saga itself. Rather, her sympathetic portrait makes possible a critique of the abuses of economic power by the Irish gentry. As Thady writes of one of his masters, Sir Murtagh, "he taught 'em all, as he said, to know the law of landlord and tenant" (*Castle Rackrent* 15). Above all else, *Castle Rackrent* tells the story of abuses committed in the defense of money, property, and class, including the imprisonment of the Jewish Lady Rackrent for seven years by her husband, Sir Kit, because she would not turn over to him the diamond cross for which he married her.

A preoccupation with hierarchies characterizes Edgeworth's other fiction as well as *Castle Rackrent.* Elizabeth Harden writes that "*The Popular Tales* (1804) . . . were written for the middle and lower classes. . . . They stand apart from the current fiction of the time by treating the average middle-class man and woman with dignity and respect" (40–41). Women characters abound in Edgeworth's fiction; many of her novels center around heroines and include memorable female characters from servant as well as landed classes (Mrs. Petito in *The Absentee* offers one example of such a servant character). Edgeworth's father believed in women's education and women's abilities and encouraged her to write. In an early and little-known feminist essay, *Letters for Literary Ladies* (1795), Edgeworth refutes the argument that women cannot become literary without ceasing to be women and advocates for women to learn science as well as literature. When Rachel Mordecai, an American Jewish woman, wrote Edgeworth in 1815 "to complain of the derogatory manner in which she had depicted Jews" in earlier fiction, Edgeworth responded by writing *Harrington* (1817), "to counteract 'the illiberality with which the Jewish nation had been treated' in some of her works" ("Preface" to *Harrington,* qtd. in Harden 88). And in at least one other tale, "The Grateful Negro" (*Popular Tales,* 1804), Edgeworth expresses her concern for the plight of the slaves on the island of Jamaica. Although this tale ends by identifying one "good" planter, Mr. Edwards, who merits the allegiance of his slaves, it also depicts the abuses of slavery and argues for the end of the slave trade to British colonies. Sustained interest in the categories of gender, class, and race thus characterizes much of Edgeworth's fiction. But only in *Castle Rackrent,* where she integrates social critique with the depiction of region, does she produce, we would propose, a text that remains compelling across almost two centuries.

Writing about Ireland for an English audience historically engaged in the extermination of the Irish as if they were of a different race, Edgeworth adopts a position of advocacy. Although Edgeworth herself did not settle in Ireland until she was fourteen (her father had been an "absentee" Anglo-Irish landlord who returned to Ireland to manage his estate), she entered the region disposed to see it and its people on their own terms. Technically a possession of England even before the Irish Parliament passed the Act of Union in 1800, and suffering from the enforcement of barbarous laws against Catholics, Ireland, by the middle of the eighteenth century, contained a populace four-fifths of whom were poor, "rackrented," and engaged in local rebellions (Flanagan 14). Edgeworth's awareness both of the historical subordination of Ireland and of the inherent contrast between the English view of the Irish and the Irish view of themselves resembles Cary's awareness of the subordination of rural Western culture to the urban pretensions of New York and her region's resistance to this subordination. Edgeworth and Cary share a sense of advocacy for overlooked and maligned persons, connected to regions with distinctive cultures, unable to emerge from stereotypes. Moreover, *Castle Rackrent* derives its interest not from plot but from character. The text consists of the history of Castle Rackrent as told by Thady Quirk, the faithful retainer whose empathy extends to the owners who rack as well as to the tenants who are racked. Although Thady's critique is indirect—he is himself unflaggingly loyal to his various masters—he is by no means stupid and his consciousness provides the controlling force of the narrative.

Finally, Edgeworth placed her fiction in an historical context but she focuses on private and domestic life rather than history. In her own "Preface" to *Castle Rackrent,* she writes, "We cannot judge either of the feelings or of the characters of men with perfect accuracy from their actions or their appearance in public; it is from their careless conversations, their half finished sentences, that we may hope with the greatest probability of success to discover their real characters" (1). For this reason, she claims to be justified in collecting "the most minute facts relative to the domestic lives, not only of the great and good, but even of the worthless and insignificant" (2). Similarly, Cary declared in her "Preface" to *Clovernook* (1852) that "there is surely as much in the simple manners, and in the little histories every day revealed, to interest us in humanity, as there *can* be in those old empires where the press of tyrannous laws and the deadening influence of hereditary acquiescence necessarily destroy the best life of society" (*AWR* 60). The "careless conversations" and "half finished sentences" that interest Edgeworth aptly describe Cary's sketches, and Cary's avowed purpose in her own writing might be inserted without notice as part of Edgeworth's preface. Our interest in Edgeworth, however, lies primarily in her demonstration of the possible connections between the sketch form, the regional location, the emphasis on character, the woman writer, and the critique of imperialism.

In placing her emphasis on character rather than plot, Edgeworth makes a connection between the regional character and the ability to convey an alternative point of view. In her review of *Redwood,* Edgeworth wrote of Sedgwick's character Aunt Debby that "it is to America what Scott's characters are to Scotland, valuable as original pictures, with enough of individual peculiarity to be interesting, and to give the feeling of reality and life as portraits, with sufficient also of general characteristics to give them the philosophical merit of portraying a class" (qtd. in E. Foster 68). Edgeworth's comments have the effect of establishing America as a region bearing a relation to England similar to that of Scotland. As we explore the origins of regionalism, we might do well to consider the emphasis on character in some of the texts of the young Republic as it sought to establish its own alternative point of view and its distinctiveness. In the pre-texts that constitute the context for the tradition of regionalism, the cultural work of American literature can be understood in part as the creation of identifiable characters who, while regional within the United States, can also be deployed to represent "America" as a region in relation to England. Significantly, however, this project depended upon the association of the American character with the specifically masculine.

In the period that serves as the seedbed for regionalism, the period from 1820 to 1850, scholars have agreed on the preeminence in American culture and texts of two specific characters, the Yankee and the Kentuckian, the peddler and the frontiersman, the lion of the east and the lion of the west. According to Daniel Hoffman, "Along the northeastern seaboard a well-defined type, the Yankee, developed early in folklore and, by the 1830s, appears in popular culture to have displaced the undifferentiated American of the Franklin and Crèvecoeur variety. A parallel development along the frontier brought the character of the Backwoodsman into folktales, almanacs, popular fiction, theatricals, and, in the person of Davy Crockett, into national political prominence" (34).

Since the time of Royall Tyler's *The Contrast* (1787), the Yankee character formed a staple item in popular drama, fiction, and culture. As an instance, we might mention John Neal's *Brother Jonathan, or, the New Englanders* (1825). Writing in response to Sydney Smith's 1820 sneer, "who reads an American book," Neal sought to produce not only a book written by an American that would capture the English reading public but also a book flamboyantly American, an "American" American book. Although Neal's novel has served later scholars "as a regional source book on Yankee dialect and folklore" (Sears 73), it was distinctly unsuccessful as a novel, suggesting perhaps by its failure the difficulties of connecting this particular cultural project with the form of the novel. In a similar vein, but more influential in terms of popularity and impact, were Seba Smith's Jack Downing letters, which began appearing in 1829 and were collected in book form in 1833. Smith's letters, widely reprinted and imitated, gave considerable vogue to a particular version of the Yankee as a specifically American character. Portrayed in the political cartoons of the 1830s and 1840s "in top hat, tailed coat, and striped trousers" (Rickels and Rickels 139), Jack Downing served as the prototype for the figure of Uncle Sam.

Despite Jack's popularity, it was the figure of the peddler who embodied his nation's restlessness and its obsession with improvement that proved to be the primary character associated with the "Yankee nation." Irving, who would permanently insert this figure into American literary history, rehearsed his construction of Ichabod Crane in his earlier *Knickerbocker's History of New York* (1809) as he described "that singular race of people inhabiting the country eastward" of the New Netherlands and the "peculiar habits which rendered them exceedingly annoying to our ever-honored Dutch ancestors," including "a certain rambling propensity . . . so that a Yankee farmer is in a constant state of migration; *tarrying* occasionally here and there" (212). With a concern for economy that often verged on stinginess, this figure also had the reputation of being a hard bargainer and a somewhat shifty dealer in goods. Moreover he often won his arguments through specific verbal strategies designed to throw his opponent off guard—to wit, the habit of always answering one question by asking another. It is this figure whom Stowe seeks to "convert" in "Uncle Lot" in an effort to destabilize the rapidly solidifying connection between the region, the American, and the specifically masculine.

In choosing the title *The Lion of the East* for an ephemeral play of 1835 based on the character of Jack Downing, the authors were hoping to capitalize at once on the popularity of Smith's creation and on the popularity of James Kirke Paulding's *The Lion of the West,* first produced in 1831. According to Smith's biographers, "Both characters are projects in the search for the distinctive American character" (Rickels and Rickels 139). We can use this bit of ephemera, however, to draw attention to the similarity of these apparently different lions and to the role of gender in the construction of the distinctive American; those candidates brought forward most frequently and aggressively to meet the need for the identifiably American displayed behaviors, patterns of speech, and values as distinctively masculine as they were American. Nimrod Wildfire, for example, the lion of Paulding's play, drew on the popularity of figures like Mike Fink, who first appeared in print in James Hall's *Western Souvenir* (1829) and shortly thereafter in a second sketch in Timothy Flint's *Western Monthly Review* (July 1829), and Davy Crockett, who became the subject of countless tales, almanacs, and narratives after entering Congress in 1828. Paulding himself had already published a collection of sketches, *Letters from the South* (1817), that were, according to Henry B. Wonham, "the first to connect the genre [of the tall tale] with native character types, like the hunter and the boatman" (292). Characterized by what Hoffman calls "rhetorical" or "cockalorum braggadocio," Colonel Wildfire takes the stage with the specific task of subduing one Mrs. Wollope who has come to America "to ameliorate the barbarism of manners in America" and specifically to improve the condition of women: "the women here like those of Turkey are treated as domestic slaves. Now my system is to raise my own sex to its proper dignity, to give them the command and so refine the men" (Paulding 31; also qtd. in Hoffman 68). Based obviously on Frances Trollope, whose *Domestic Manners of the Americans,* published in March 1832, caused an enraged response from certain portions of America, a response still active in the 1880s when Mark Twain attacked her in *Life on the Mississippi,* Mrs. Wollope registers particular disgust with Colonel Wildfire's insistence on various masculine prerogatives, as illustrated in her sketch of him in his "favorite position, rocking in a chair with his legs out of the window" (Paulding 41). Thus his triumph over her has not only the effect of gendering America male in contrast to a feminized "mother" country; it has the effect as well, no matter how contextualized by other elements of the play, of staking out America as a region in which the right of boys to be boys will be vigorously and aggressively defended.

One of the charges leveled most frequently against the historical Frances Trollope, and parodied extensively in Paulding's play, was her gullibility. In reflecting on the origins of the tall tale as a specifically American narrative form, Norris

Yates refers to the "view that the tall tale originated in an attempt to fool the newcomer" (147). When this newcomer was a foreigner and specifically British, determined to discover and publish the "truth" about the region of America, feeding him or her a tall tale would have had the added delight of making a fool of one's "mother." The tall tale, cockalorum braggadocio as narrative form, has long been recognized as distinctly masculine. More recently, however, critics have come to understand it as functioning not simply to enable masculine expression but also to exclude and denigrate women, and thus to disable their claims to citizenship and narrativity. As Wonham points out, not only are the content and the teller of these tales distinctively masculine, so also is the privileged audience, those imagined as getting the joke. Moreover, the action of such tales typically involves the humiliation of a naive outsider frequently figured as female whose "victimization," as in the case of Mrs. Wollope, "becomes a patriotic victory for American wit" (Wonham 297). The tall tale serves an audience of "boys" whose enjoyment depends upon the exclusionary practices of an "inside joke" (303, 305). Growing up just a few miles north of Cincinnati, Cary would most certainly have been aware of Mrs. Trollope (who resided in Cincinnati in the years preceding publication of *Domestic Manners*), Mike Fink, the tall tale, the regional sketch, and the issues raised by this cultural mix—who gets to tell stories, what kinds of stories can be told, who is the privileged audience and what is the point of the telling, and, still further, what relation exists between region, nation, and gender.

Women Writers: Sigourney, Kirkland, and Sedgwick

In *New England Local Color Literature,* Donovan traces the origins of what she calls "a woman's tradition" in "the earliest novels by women in the eighteenth century," the expression of a "women's literary realism" that "grew out of the bourgeois critique of the romance" but that contained "an awareness and concern about female characters and female roles which the male writers' critiques did not" (11). She concludes her brief survey of British origins with an emphasis on Edgeworth, whose *Castle Rackrent* she identifies as "one of the first examples of dialect use in English literature" and a text to which Scott, who "popularized" the use of dialect in his Waverly novels, acknowledged himself indebted. For Donovan, Edgeworth's significance lies equally in the fact of her feminist perspective; her texts include a critique of patriarchy and, referring to *The Absentee* (1812), Donovan writes, "For the first time we have the suggestion that women's freedom from the social oppression of the urban marriage market rituals lies in a return to the local world of the provinces" (23). This is one reason why, according to Donovan, Edgeworth "carries forward the traditions of women's literary realism and articulates the world-view that is inherited most directly by the American school" (23).

In examining the American origins of New England local color, Donovan identifies a tradition of "realism . . . that existed side by side with the much more visible and popular sentimentalist tradition," and she includes as an example Hale's *Northwood* (1827), "perhaps the first work to include real details of the New England locale" (31). Donovan also includes Kirkland as an early American writer who influenced both Stowe and Cooke (35) and who self-consciously associated her work with Mitford's, though "Kirkland carried the village sketch tradition far beyond its genteel origins and paved the way for the growth of a genuine women's realism" (36). Donovan mentions Cary as a writer who continued the village-sketch tradition but dismisses her as lacking "a precise descriptive sense of local detail" and as tending "toward sentimentalism in character and plot" (34). Stowe's *The Mayflower* (1843) provides the "culmination of this early tradition of village sketches" and "was the first work in the tradition of local color realism" (34). Despite the sketchiness of her treatment of texts and despite the idiosyncrasy of some of her positions (on Sedgwick, for example), Donovan has made the only attempt so far to identify the origins in British and American women's writing of a tradition that includes many of the writers we identify as regionalists.

Zagarell's work on antebellum village sketches also offers a useful context for considering the origins of regionalism. For Zagarell the key to contemporary interest in the literature of the antebellum village sketch lies in its relation to America; she writes that this literature "is more than the source of a group of quaint, enduring cultural motifs; it constitutes one important site of an ongoing debate about the composition and character of America—a dispute about the place of difference and diversity in this nation" ("'America'" 143). According to Zagarell, village sketch literature can be divided "into two strains—one in which 'America' is tantamount to a homogeneous village community, another that proclaims the Americanism of diversity and features communities with diverse populations" (144). Using the example of Lawrence Buell's *New England Literary Culture,* Zagarell argues that in existing treatments of village-sketch literature, only the first "strain" receives attention and recognition. She further argues that the paradigm derived from an analysis of this strain "casts little light on the other strain of village-sketch literature" (145), which is in effect a tradition of women's writing. For, as Zagarell observes of the tradition she seeks to recognize and attend to, "Most strikingly—and arguably of key importance for these and other shared characteristics—the authors of all of these works were women" (145). While regionalist writers do not evince the explicit concern over the definition of America that informs these narratives, many of their features characterize regionalist texts as well, suggesting an impulse toward regionalism in texts that preceded it. Among these features we might note an emphasis on the "relational, inclusive, and generally empathic" (145); a capacity for "accentuating . . . diversity" (146); a quality of "polyphony" that derives from allowing diverse voices to speak; a narrative form that is "loose and open-ended" and that capitalizes "on the capacity of the sketch . . . to accommodate synchronicity and resist closure" (147); and a narrator who "mediate[s] between the voices of community members and the language of a readership living elsewhere" (147).

In considering Zagarell's examples of early village-sketch narratives, however, certain differences emerge between this tradition and that of regionalism, including the location and status of the narrator, her relation to her material, and the purpose of her narration. In Sigourney's *Sketch of Connecticut, Forty Years Since,* the narrator, relatively unspecified and uninflected, is presumably herself an inhabitant of N——, yet she so totally identifies with Madam L——, the aristocratic though benevolent "ruler" of N——, that she does not provide an independent voice. Indeed *Sketch of Connecticut* presents itself primarily as an act of hagiography and its purpose would seem to be that of offering Sigourney the opportunity to make a public statement of her gratitude to her former patron, Madam Lathrop of Norwich. While we may applaud Sigourney's proposal of Madam L—— as the example of who in the new Republic should be invested with economic, social, and political power, especially when we consider who actually had such power at the time, we cannot avoid recognizing the hierarchical nature of her model for community. In N—— all the inhabitants turn to Madam L—— for moral instruction, economic support, and personal validation. Zagarell observes that *Sketch of Connecticut* creates space for the narratives of numerous marginalized groups—native Americans, African Americans, revolutionary soldiers abandoned by the government, single white women, farmers. However, the content of the stories they tell seems determined by Sigourney's need to construct Madam L—— as a model of aristocratic wisdom and benevolence. Rather than providing an opening into the world of the other, the stories present an opportunity for Madam L—— to dispense instruction and charity, both of spirit and purse, and to demonstrate her antislavery convictions and her patriotism. Adopting Zagarell's description of these texts in general, we might say that "the narrator alone appears to decide what is relayed to the reader" ("'America'" 148) and that the construction of Madam L—— controls this decision.

We might make a similar point with respect to Kirkland's *A New Home, Who'll Follow?* (1839) where the narrator clearly occupies the position of "outsider" despite her efforts to acclimate. As Mrs. Clavers follows her husband to the "wilds" of Michigan where he hopes to find the economic and personal success that eluded him in western New York, she never forgets that she comes from the "east." Her text takes the form of letters to friends left behind in her old "home," and in these letters she describes to them her experiences as she encounters a culture and country almost foreign. Perhaps because Clavers so clearly retains her status as an outsider, Kirkland can create more space than Sigourney for the voices and stories of others that seem more authentic because not so obviously controlled by what the narrator wants to hear. Moreover, Clavers presents herself not as simply listening to these voices and stories but as affected by them; she engages in complex internal negotiations around her own biases and prejudices, seeking to reconstruct herself in accord with the values and necessities of her new home, yet seeking as well to reconstruct it in accord with the values she has brought with her. However, despite her repeated presentation of herself as "wandering"—"I have departed from all rule and precedent in these wandering sketches of mine. . . . But I think I have discovered that the bent of my genius is altogether towards digression. Association leads me like a Will-o'-the-wisp" (*A New Home* 177)—Clavers never relinquishes control over her narrative or its meaning. Interpreting that meaning, Zagarell writes:

> Suggesting that community will continue to take shape through the vital, often difficult, always absorbing process of cultural interchange and re-formation, *A New Home* also passes on to its readers the burden of participating in this process with a new self-awareness. Still, this move, although educational, also represents a reconfiguration of the narrative's alliance with these readers: it instructs them in how to prevail. *A New Home* thereby closes with a final assertion that the values of Clavers's, and Kirkland's, own class and region should predominate in the new kind of community and culture that it depicts with such freshness. ("'America'" 155–56)

Zagarell's comments suggest the connection between the project of reconstructing America and the need for narrative control, and indicate that a focus on "America" produces a homogenizing effect even in narratives self-consciously seeking to represent diversity. In disengaging from the ambitions of reconstructing America, in choosing to focus instead on what Buell calls "one of the consolations of village life"—namely, "the symbolic importance of small forms of dissent" (*New England* 318)—regionalism creates a space for the presentation of narratives from within the region not controlled by a narrator's desire to hear only what she wants to hear, or by her need to convince readers that the Wolverine in the Michigan wilds must be civilized, or by her ambition to create a hegemonic model for community in America.

Addressing the issue of the origins of village-sketch literature, Zagarell writes, "I do not develop a single explanatory model for this literature. To do so would entail forcing it into a distorting mold, for the narratives in this group are not simply about diversity, they themselves are diverse" ("'America'" 145). In thinking about the origins of regionalism, we too do not offer "a single explanatory model." Rather, in surveying certain aspects of the literary landscape that preceded and was therefore available to regionalist writers and that shaped their sense of what they could do, we are in effect tracing the history of an impulse. In her discussion of narrative of community, a mode of writing that emerged after the Civil War and that, anticipated by women's experiments with village-sketch literature, "was often self-consciously regional" ("'America'" 158), Zagarell writes, "The concept of narrative of community, then, brings to light a cultural impulse that was not, until now, sufficiently clear and makes visible structures and purposes shared by works that have not been grouped together, many of which have been troublesome to those seeking to fit them within prevailing generic categories" ("Narrative" 502). Zagarell's description of her work on narratives of community describes our work on regionalism as well, but we find the phrase "cultural impulse" particularly compelling. While regionalist texts clearly differ from both village-sketch literature and narratives of community (and we might note here that Zagarell does not include Cary's *Clovernook* in either category), we nevertheless view regionalism as developing a cultural impulse present in a variety of texts that preceded it.

In concluding this section of our treatment of origins, we wish to take note of a text by Sedgwick, who, as one of the best known early American women writers, arguably influenced regionalism. *Redwood* (1824) dramatizes Sedgwick's recognition of the possibilities of regionalism and her recognition that both the novel form and the project of reconstructing America prevent the full realization of these possibilities. A novel Buell describes as undertaking an "ambitious social analysis by bringing together a group of figures who comprise in microcosm the contrasts between New England, the Middle Atlantic States, and the South" (*New England* 295–96) and which he sees as the logical outgrowth of *A New England Tale* (1822), the first in "a tradition of attempts at the Great American novel, New England style" (295), *Redwood* opens with a carriage accident that thrusts a southern gentleman and his daughter on the mercies of a New England farmer and his family. Although Sedgwick acknowledges that "Mr. Lenox, as master of the family, was entitled to precedence in our description" (*Redwood* 32), Lenox himself voluntarily confounds this hierarchy by issuing the command, once he realizes bones have been broken, to "call Debby," who is "'as skilful as the run of doctors'" and "'a nat'ral bone-setter'" (27). Before the first chapter has fairly begun and before anyone else in the Lenox family has been "introduced," the reader encounters Debby, a six-foot-one "Amazon" of some fifty years whose "stature and . . . weatherbeaten skin would have led one to suspect that her feminine dress was a vain attempt at disguise" (32, 31). Debby enters the scene "muttering something about the boys, boy-fashion, having left out the old mare" (27). From Debby's perspective boys should not be allowed to be "boys" if that means overlooking their cruelty to animals, particularly animals who, like Debby herself, are female, old, and unattractive; it is, she declares, "'a shame for the boys to neglect her because she grows a little old and unsightly'" (27). So "imbued with the independent spirit of the times," Debby has, at the close of the Revolutionary War, refused an offer of marriage for "she would not then consent to the surrender of any of her rights, and there was no tradition in the family that her maidenly pride had suffered a second solicitation" (32). Called in to deal with the consequences of the accident, Debby, in keeping with her independent spirit, immediately takes control of the situation despite the evident aversion and distrust of her patient, Mr. Redwood.

Although Sedgwick presents Debby here and elsewhere as somewhat "monstrous" (31) and grotesque, perhaps reflecting her anxiety over creating a figure who overturns not only the rules of precedence but the norms of gender, her desire to "call Debby" so immediately to the stage suggests that part of the value of the novel for her lay in its capacity to create a space, a region within it, for the creation of such a character even as it carefully confined that character to a subtext. Situating her novel within the context of creating an American literature that will promote an appropriate and legitimate American nationalism and engaging as well in the project of reconstructing America, Sedgwick defines her text as extending beyond the merely regional. But to the extent that *Redwood* is nevertheless and still "a New England tale"—the action of the novel involves the conversion of the Southern to the Northern in the figure of Mr. Redwood and, when such conversion fails, the expulsion of the Southern from the Republic as his unreconstructable daughter Caroline marries a British officer, removes to the West Indies, and dies—its regionalism allows Sedgwick to create and introduce a figure decidedly different from the heroines her dominant tale requires. In *Redwood,* then, we find, as we will later in Stowe's *The Pearl of Orr's Island,* the association of the regional with the creation of a space for female difference, for women who are competent, independent, old, unsightly, and queer. While Sedgwick could not imagine such a woman as the primary subject of a novel, any more than Stowe could several decades later, the urgency of her desire to "call Debby" and her decision to give Debby the last word reflects her recognition of the value of this figure. "Call Debby," then, can be read as the legacy she passes on to those who will come after her, a command, in effect, to future women writers to create regionalism. In concluding her preface, Sedgwick writes, "The future is in the present. What we are we owe to our ancestors, and what our posterity will be, they will owe to us" (xi). Although we may not be able to establish a direct connection between Sedgwick's *Redwood* and any given regionalist writer or text, it remains a crucial document in our effort to trace the history of an impulse. The command to "call Debby" made its appearance in a variety of ways and in various texts that preceded regionalism; the particular genius of regionalism lay in answering that call.

Irving, Stowe, and Longstreet

"Probably the single most important American prose work in teaching native writers to exploit regional material for literary purposes was Washington Irving's *Sketch-Book* (1819–1820)" (Buell, *New England* 294). We have already noted Mitford's use of Irving in creating *Our Village,* itself an acknowledged source of two traditions of U.S. women's writing cognate with regionalism. Our interest in Irving, however, comes by way of Stowe's "A New England Sketch" (1834), which adopts Irving's sketch form and regional focus but challenges the uses to which this form and focus are put. A crucial origin for the tradition of regionalism, Stowe's text passes on to regionalist writers an Irving contested and revised. It is to the story of Irving and Stowe, a story enriched by reference to Augustus Baldwin Longstreet's *Georgia Scenes* (1835), that we now turn.

When Rip Van Winkle comes down from the mountain and finds his new place in his post-Revolutionary village as a "chronicle of the old times 'before the war'" ("Rip Van Winkle" 40), Washington Irving creates a vocation for the American artist. At the beginning of the tale Rip has "an insuperable aversion to all kinds of profitable labour" (30), preferring instead to spend his time telling ghost stories to children, but he awakens from his twenty-year sleep to discover that the storyteller, in the new Republic, has an important role to play. Irving further suggests that the American story will have a different content than English narrative; like the image of George Washington on the sign in front of the Union Hotel, American fiction may derive from English and European models but it is also "singularly metamorphosed" (37). However, despite Rip's altered state by the end of the tale, Irving makes it clear that certain things have not changed. George is still a George, not a Dame; Irving allows Rip a "drop of comfort" when he discovers that he has survived two wars at once, the American Revolution and the tyranny of "petticoat government," for Dame Van Winkle is dead. And Irving spares Rip any complicity in her death; she has broken a blood vessel "in a fit of passion at a New-England pedlar" (39). Angry women do not survive to tell the story of the "old times 'before the war'"; Dame Van Winkle cannot be a candidate for the American artist for this would be a singular metamorphosis indeed. For Irving, the American storyteller, like the American hero, must be male.

By granting the post-Revolutionary American artist a cultural role with secular rather than divine authority—George Washington replaces King George—Irving asserts the separation of literature from theology as the ground for an American story. Irving's tales reveal the gender anxiety that this shift created for early nineteenth-century male American writers. In their separation from Puritanism as a cultural base, turning away from the writing of sermons and towards the writing of fiction, Irving's male contemporaries split off that anxiety, which Irving figures in the image of the headless horseman as a form of psychocultural castration; they projected "headlessness" onto women writers and asserted masculinity itself as evidence of cultural authority. Irving's narrator thus fiercely refuses to take women, the already "castrated," seriously. Just in case his readers remain insufficiently convinced that Dame Van Winkle is dead and worry that she might return to haunt them or pose a threat to Rip's post-Revolutionary authority, Irving resurrects her in a literary way as Ichabod Crane in "The Legend of Sleepy Hollow," then frightens "her" out of town, not needing the Freudian and Lacanian theories of the twentieth century to make the point that gender anxiety for men signifies the fear of absence, castration, headlessness.

In "The Legend of Sleepy Hollow," Irving removes the undesirable qualities that characterized Dame Van Winkle from his portraits of the Dutch wives and projects them instead onto the character of Ichabod Crane. During Ichabod's reign over his "little literary realm" (283), the schoolroom, the pedagogue uses "a ferule, that sceptre of despotic power" and "the birch of justice reposed on three nails" (238) to enforce his limited government. Like Dame Van Winkle, Ichabod Crane in the schoolroom becomes someone to escape, and Irving describes the scholars' early dismissal as "emancipation" (284). However, outside the schoolroom, Ichabod undergoes a transformation and becomes the embodiment of Rip rather than Dame. He has a "soft and foolish heart towards the [female] sex" like his counterpart in Irving's earlier tale. He becomes the playmate of his own charges and the congenial companion of their mothers; he would often "sit with a child on one knee, and rock a cradle with his foot, for whole hours together" (276). He seems initially content to become one of the region's "native inhabitants" (273), deriving pleasure from visiting, "snugly cuddling in the chimney corner" (278), filling the role of "travelling gazette" (276), and expressing his desire for the "comforts of the cupboard" (275). Within the "female circle," he enjoys the position of "man of letters" (276). Yet Irving does not grant him Rip's place as American artist; the extracts from Cotton Mather that Ichabod contributes to the storytelling at Van Tassel's "quilting frolick" (284) do not appear to be successful in competing with the ghost stories Brom Bones tells.

Ichabod Crane will not serve as Irving's image of the American artist; neither will he provide a model for the American hero. Irving reveals him to be a fraud—not a real contender for the love of Katrina Van Tassel but instead a glutton whose desire for Katrina derives from greed and gorging. Most startling of all, Ichabod turns out to be no settler after all but rather to have fantasies of sacking the "sleepy region" in order to invest "in immense tracts of wild land, and shingle palaces in the wilderness," toward which he would set, Katrina and the children on top of a wagon and "himself bestriding a pacing mare" (280). Too much a member of the "female circle," as Irving defines women's culture, to bring off this quintessentially masculine vision, Ichabod becomes by the end of the tale merely a debased version of it, an unsuccessful suitor, an "affrighted pedagogue" (292), an "unskilful rider" (294). Reminding us that women had produced "more than a third of the fiction published in America before 1820," Lloyd Daigrepont suggests that Irving "instilled in Ichabod Crane the characteristics of those writers who dominated the American literary scene" in the early days of the Republic—what he calls a "burgeoning popular taste for the excessive emotionalism of the sentimental tale, the novel of sensibility, and the Gothic romance"—and that in the conclusion of "The Legend of Sleepy Hollow," Irving "symbolically portrayed their defeat" (69–70).

Irving creates Brom Bones instead as Crane's triumphant adversary and as an image of American manhood. "Brom Bones . . . was the hero of the scene," a man who has tamed Daredevil, a man "in fact noted for preferring vicious animals, . . . for he held a tractable well broken horse as unworthy of a lad of spirit" ("Legend" 287). As Hoffman observes, Brom Bones "is a Catskill Mike Fink, a Ring-Tailed Roarer from Kinderhook" (89). Brom Bones above all represents masculinity, a quality absent in Irving's characterizations of both Rip Van Winkle and Ichabod Crane, and this masculinity gives him authority over Ichabod. The "burley, roaring, roystering blade" has a "bluff, but not unpleasant countenance," "more mischief than ill-will in his composition," and "with all his overbearing roughness, there was a strong dash of waggish good humour at bottom" ("Legend" 281). The excesses of the "female circle" may threaten the cultural order with "petticoat government," but the excesses of masculinity contribute to our national health; we all have a good laugh at Ichabod Crane's cowardice, incompetence, and basic cultural impotence. "The Legend of Sleepy Hollow" turns the folk tale into a tall tale and identifies the tall tale as the best way to tell the American story of winning and losing. Indeed, in his postscript to this story Irving suggests that the quintessential American story will be a tall tale circulated among men for the purpose of establishing dominance. The good reader is the one who gets the joke; the bad reader is the one who doesn't get it or refuses to find it funny, perhaps because the joke is on her or him; and telling stories about winning and losing becomes itself an act of winning and losing, of inclusion and exclusion, with character, teller, and listener all invited to identify with one another and against someone else, everyone becoming a Brom Bones getting rid of an Ichabod Crane.

In selecting the opening paragraphs of "A New England Sketch" as his example of "the village as icon" in New England literary culture, Buell claims that, though Stowe had much to do with the perpetuation of "the cult of the New England village," "there is no question of originality here" (*New England* 305). Moreover, as Zagarell notes, Buell defines the tradition Stowe perpetuates but does not originate as essentially conservative, one that "actively repudiates changes afoot in the nation" by portraying the village as homogeneous, static, and pastoral ("'America'" 144). Although Buell later refers to a "metafictional dimension" to Stowe's sketch because her description of the village of Newbury "calls attention to itself as a fantasy construct" and through "playfully exaggerated, tall-tale" passages suggests "that what is being imagined is not the village itself but the cosmopolitan visitor's sense of the town as peculiarly stable," he reads this as evidence of a "split allegiance" (*New England* 310). Stowe is "charmed by the village ideal" but has "outgrown it and belong[s] to a larger world" (310). We read Stowe's sketch rather differently and while we also find in it a "metafictional dimension," we associate it with Stowe's awareness of an emerging American fiction and her attempts to redirect that fiction by revising Irving.

Stowe begins "Uncle Lot" (the title she later chose for "A New England Sketch"—after collecting it first as "Uncle Tim" in 1843 for *The Mayflower*—and by which it has since been known) by reworking Irving's "The Legend of Sleepy Hollow." Many other writers in the 1830s also built upon Irving's tale. As Hennig Cohen and William B. Dillingham observe, however, these writers most frequently found in Irving the "ingredients of a typical sketch of Southwestern humor: the physically awkward, ugly, and avaricious Ichabod; the good-natured but rowdy Brom Bones and his friends, who love a practical joke; the desirable plum, Katrina Van Tassel" (xii). Cohen and Dillingham report, "It would be difficult to estimate the number of Southern tales directly influenced by 'Sleepy Hollow,'" and they cite some examples: Joseph B. Cobb's "The Legend of Black Creek," William Tappan Thompson's "The Runaway Match" and "Adventures of a Sabbath-Breaker," and Francis James Robinson's "The Frightened Serenaders" (xii). Thus Stowe was not alone in modeling a work of fiction on "The Legend of Sleepy Hollow." However, Stowe's text critiques Irving, thereby establishing that the context for regionalism includes an approach to the representation of regional people and values that involves respect and empathy and grants voice to regional characters in the work, an approach that differs markedly from that of the "humorists" who created such characters as objects of derision rather than as subjects of their own agency.

Stowe's text specifically reveals similarities between her village of Newbury, "one of those out-of-the-way places where nobody ever came unless they came on purpose: a green little hollow" (*AWR* 4), and Irving's "little valley, or rather lap of land among high hills, which is one of the quietest places in the whole world," a "green, sheltered, fertile nook" ("Legend" 272, 279). Stowe notes the "unchangeability" of Newbury, particularly in its "manners, morals, arts, and sciences" (4–5); Irving describes the "population, manners, and customs" of his "sleepy region" as "fixed" (274). Both authors introduce their characters as representatives of the larger citizenry. Irving's Ichabod Crane "was a native of Connecticut, a state which supplies the Union with pioneers for the mind as well as for the forest" (274), and Stowe describes James Benton as "one of those whole-hearted, energetic Yankees" who possessed a "characteristic national trait" (5). Like Ichabod Crane, James Benton is a newcomer to the village of Newbury and he appears on the scene "with all his worldly effects tied in a blue cotton pocket-handkerchief" (6), just as Ichabod moves from house to house within the neighborhood "with all his worldly effects tied up in a pocket handkerchief" (333). Like Ichabod, James "figured as schoolmaster all the week, and as chorister on Sundays" (6), he makes himself at home "in all the chimney-corners of the region" (6), devouring "doughnuts and pumpkin pies with most flattering appetite" (6), and he generally "kept the sunny side of the old ladies" (7). James Benton holds what Stowe describes as "an uncommonly comfortable opinion of himself" (5); Irving's Ichabod believes that in his performance as chorister "he completely carried away the palm from the parson" (276). Both tell stories; and both have the predisposition to fall "in love with everything in feminine shape" (7). There is thus considerable evidence to suggest that Stowe in writing "Uncle Lot" seeks to evoke in readers a recollection of Irving's "The Legend of Sleepy Hollow." Stowe imitates, however, in order to revise, and this revision includes not only the reconstruction of Ichabod Crane as hero and not only the redefinition of what constitutes a story; it includes as well a challenge to Irving's understanding of who shall have narrative authority and of the relation between teller and audience.

Although Stowe presents her story as centering on the romance between James Benton and Uncle Lot's daughter Grace, content appropriate to female writers, she uses this convention to authorize herself to tell a different story. In a gesture that we might call "metafictional," Stowe indicates that the romance between James and Grace is a story that really does not need to be told:

> "Come, Grace, you know what I mean," said James, looking steadfastly at the top of the apple-tree.
>
> "Well, I wish, then, you would understand what I mean without my saying any more about it," said Grace.
>
> "Oh, to be sure I will!" said our hero, looking up with a very intelligent air; and so, as Aunt Sally would say, the matter was settled, with "no words about it." (14)

Stowe's words, like her interests, lie elsewhere—in the processes by which male characters become converted or transformed in various ways and in particular in the figure of Uncle Lot, whom she places at the thematic center of her text.

Stowe describes Uncle Lot as a "chestnut burr, abounding with briers without and with substantial goodness within" (8) but "'the *settest* crittur in his way that ever you saw'" (11). Initially Uncle Lot expresses an aversion to the young hero James Benton, so that in order to "win" Grace's favors, James must first elicit Uncle Lot's recognition of liking him. James tries to reach Uncle Lot behind the defenses he has created and to convert him into a person capable of expressing feeling, that "substantial goodness within." In the scene which depicts this "conversion," James Benton arrives for an unannounced visit at Uncle Lot's house with the ostensible goal of winning Uncle Lot's affection. Stowe writes: "James also had one natural accomplishment, more courtier-like than all the diplomacy in Europe, and that was the gift of feeling a *real* interest for anybody in five minutes; so that, if he began to please in jest, he generally ended in earnest. With great simplicity of mind, he had a natural tact for seeing into others, and watched their motions with the same delight with which a child gazes at the wheels and springs of a watch, to 'see what it will do'" (13–14). James wishes to open up the "chestnut burr" that characterizes Uncle Lot's defenses against feeling, and he uses the power of empathy—his "natural tact for seeing into others"—to help Uncle Lot recognize and reveal the "latent kindness" he holds within his "rough exterior" (14). For though he outwardly refuses each request his wife and daughter make, he always concludes by doing just as they have asked. Evidently, Uncle Lot cannot bear to *appear* kind or to be thought of as influenced by the desires of others, particularly those others who are female. Gender creates his dilemma as he is forced to deny his own desires in order to appear independent.

This dilemma, however, takes on a spiritual dimension after the death of his son George, when he cannot bear that God's will should overtake his own: "'I shall never get to heaven if I feel as I do now,' said the old man. 'I cannot have it so'" (22). In her sketch, Stowe links the issue of theological grace to the issue of gender, just as Cooke would later do in "Freedom Wheeler's Controversy with Providence" (included in *AWR*); she recognizes that a rigid adherence to codes of gender may very well keep a man from getting to heaven. Far more is at stake, then, in James's conversion of Uncle Lot than simply winning Grace; at stake is winning grace, both for James and for Uncle Lot, and when at the end of the tale Uncle Lot finds himself willing to admit that "'There's a great deal that's worth having in this 'ere life after all . . . if we'd only take it when the Lord lays it in our way'" (24), we can infer that both he and James have indeed found grace. Thus conversion replaces courtship, or seduction, as Stowe's organizing principle in the narrative and gives her narrative its direction. Not only is Uncle Lot converted; James also achieves his own spiritual conversion, and conversion to the ministry, by falling in love with Grace's minister brother George, then, upon young George's untimely death, replacing him within the family as Uncle Lot's "son" and using this position to achieve Uncle Lot's own spiritual conversion. Marriage with Grace effectively ritualizes this relationship and certifies its primacy.

The radical ambition Stowe reveals in revising Irving's definition of hero, story and narrative dynamic, as well as his representation of America and the American, may, however, have produced a compensatory conservatism. Although Stowe presents Grace as her heroine and provides an opening structure that suggests narrative interest will be equally shared between hero and heroine, in fact she pays little attention to Grace. "Like most Yankee damsels," Stowe writes, Grace "had a longing after the tree of knowledge, and, having exhausted the literary fountains of a district school, she fell to reading whatsoever came in her way. True, she had but little to read; but what she perused she had her own thoughts upon. So that a person of information, in talking with her, would feel a constant wondering pleasure to find that she had so much more to say of this, that, and the other thing than he expected" (9). Grace, however, remains silent throughout most of the sketch and readers experience no "wondering pleasure" in connection with her. As her name indicates, Grace begins the story already "converted"; she possesses from the outset the moral character to which the men in Stowe's sketch must aspire in order to demonstrate their own spiritual conversion. Grace requires no development and her development forms no part of the sketch's plot. As a result she has neither words nor story and while at the end she can declare, "'Come, come, father, I have authority in these days . . . so no disrespectful speeches,'" she gains this authority by virtue of her marriage to James (24).

"Uncle Lot" clearly demonstrates the limitations of the romance plot and the project of reconstructing America for undertaking the cultural work of writing women's lives. While Stowe displaces this plot with the narrative of male conversion to values associated with women and women's culture, she does not go further to create a space for women to tell their own stories. Nevertheless, in proposing for our consideration a hero converted from prankish boyishness into a man of deep feeling who becomes more like a woman as the sketch progresses, in presenting conversion as a model for narrative form as well as a transformative theme, and in emphasizing James's empathy, his "gift of feeling a *real* interest" in everybody and his "natural tact for seeing into others," she anticipates regionalism and can be seen as a significant point in its developmental line. Moreover, by attempting in her earliest published sketch to transform the direction of American fiction, Stowe equally attempts to convert her readers to the possibility that women might "have [narrative] authority in these days." Recognizing that for women to achieve authority in American literature would require a cultural change of heart and the conversion of men, especially of those men who, like Washington Irving, were already producing an American fiction, Stowe seeks to convert an emerging American reading public and an evolving American literature and to change its interests and direction, not by aggressive confrontation, the developmental dead end of Uncle Lot (and Brom Bones), but by the subtle, persuasive, affectional process of eliciting inner change.

Without Stowe's own later work, "Uncle Lot" might not assume the significance it does, but Stowe further elaborated the themes of "Uncle Lot" in her subsequent fiction. In particular, in such works as *Oldtown Folks* (1869) and *Sam Lawson's Oldtown Fireside Stories* (1872), Stowe continues to propose regionalism as a direction for American fiction. Sam Lawson, a character in *Oldtown Folks* and narrator in *Oldtown Fireside Stories,* is a more successful and benign version of Rip Van Winkle. For example, in "The Village Do-Nothing" from *Oldtown Folks,* first-person narrator Horace Holyoke invokes the "do-nothing" as a "soft-hearted old body" always ready to gossip with the boys because he never felt compelled by "work, thrift, and industry," unlike the rest of the village who operate by the "incessant steam-power of Yankee life" (*AWR* 40, 39). Sam is "a man who won't be hurried, and won't work, and will take his ease in his own way, in spite of the whole protest of his neighborhood to the contrary" (39). Still, Stowe portrays Sam as useful; in this chapter, as the only adult who cares about children, he comforts Horace on the death of Horace's father. For Sam, like Rip, has a "softly easy temper" that "caused him to have a warm corner in most of the households" (43), is "endowed with no end of idle accomplishments" (43), is an "acceptable watcher" at sick- and death-beds, and is also "an expert in psalmody, having in his youth been the pride of the village singing-school" (44). While these are all details that Irving uses to characterize both Rip and Ichabod, as we have demonstrated, in Stowe's hands Sam becomes a regionalist character, a man who anticipates the conversion in many regionalist texts of men to soft-heartedness (as we will discuss in more detail in chapter 11), and "queer" in his own way, a "character."

Similarly, instead of presenting Hepsy Lawson as a termagant, Stowe portrays her as a model of tolerance who yet has a right to complain. Thus Hepsy, while still a scold like Dame, elicits the reader's sympathy. Stowe writes, "Poor Hepsy was herself quite as essentially a do-something,—an early-rising, bustling, driving, neat, efficient, capable little body,—who contrived, by going out to day's works,—washing, scrubbing, cleaning,—by making vests for the tailor, or closing and binding shoes for the shoemaker, by hoeing corn and potatoes in the garden at most unseasonable hours, actually to find bread to put into the mouths of the six young ravens aforesaid, and to clothe them decently" (42). It is only when Sam makes "the small degree of decency and prosperity" Hepsy has achieved for the family a "text on which to preach resignation, cheerfulness, and submission" that Hepsy's "last cobweb of patience gave out, and she often became, for the moment, really dangerous" (42–43). She tells Sam, "'for my part, I think charity ought to begin at home'" (46) as she leads him away, "unresisting" and "captive" at the end of the chapter (46). In rewriting the relationship between Rip and Dame Van Winkle, Stowe suggests that neither Sam's yielding softness nor Hepsy's "never-ceasing" (42) attempts to change his ways are likely to produce a different Sam. Yet in then making Sam her narrator in "The Minister's Housekeeper" (included in *AWR*) and the other *Oldtown Fireside Stories,* Stowe suggests that the "do-nothing" does have a certain usefulness, as a chronicle not of the "old times 'before the war,'" as in "Rip Van Winkle," but of New England domestic life.[2]

While "Uncle Lot" suggests that the question of whether American fiction would follow lines laid out by the emerging ideology of "separate spheres" remained still open in the 1830s, Stowe's awareness of the relation of gender to narrative equally suggests the potential for the development of "separate genres." Indeed, we would propose that "Uncle Lot" initiates what might be called the "Ichabod Crane school" of American narrative as Stowe attempts to convert American readers to the value of what Irving had termed, albeit disparagingly, the "female circle" and the "sleepy region," and in the process creates the possibility for literary regionalism. What might be termed the "Brom Bones school" of American literature took its inspiration from Irving and emerged through the work of Longstreet in *Georgia Scenes* (1835) and in the 1840s and 1850s in the fiction of the humorists of the Old Southwest, who answered the question of the relation of gender to narrative either by making women characters the object of sexual humor or by omitting women from their tales altogether. While American literary history has recorded the "school" of tall tale fiction inspired by Brom Bones, "Uncle Lot" and regionalism have, like Ichabod Crane, simply disappeared, swallowed up in the vagaries of the "sleepy region."

In receiving her call to write "A New England Sketch" ("Uncle Lot")—"And so I am to write a story—but of what, and where?" (*AWR* 4)—from the members of the Semi-Colon Club, Stowe had the good fortune to attract the attention of James Hall, editor of the *Western Monthly Magazine.* One of Stowe's biographers, in describing Hall's influence, writes that he advocated "cheerfulness, morality, and regionalism" as a literary aesthetic, was "a chivalrous admirer of women writers," and encouraged payment for contributors to American periodicals (Adams 35–36). In awarding his fiction prize to Harriet Beecher's first New England sketch, he was also implicitly urging her to counter the portrait of American life that the frontier, as he knew very well, appeared to encourage. In *Letters from the West,* Hall had recorded the telling of yarns by an old keelboatman named "Pappy" whom he had encountered while traveling down the Ohio on a flatboat (Blair 70); and as editor of *The Western Souvenir,* issued in Cincinnati in 1828, "the first of American gift books from beyond the Alleghenies" (Thompson 95–96), Hall achieved the distinction of having been the first editor to publish a lengthy account of the career of the legendary Mike Fink (Blair 81–82). Like Irving, Hall appears to have been interested very early in the tall tale; but unlike Irving, he would choose, as editor of the *Western Monthly Magazine,* to encourage his contributors, especially women, to write about other regional material than the portraits of frontier life that would survive in American literary history as the humor of the Old Southwest.

Hall contrasts sharply with his contemporary, William T. Porter, whose sporting magazine, the *Spirit of the Times,* first published in 1831, provided gentlemen interested in the leisure pursuits of horse racing, hunting, and listening to tall tales with a way of gratifying their fantasies of upper-class superiority and of ratifying their belief in masculine values and male dominance. Unlike Hall, whose interest in developing Western literature inspired his work, Porter was a commercialist, interested more in the culture of the sporting world. He initially catered "to the wealthy slaveholding sportsmen and their friends and allies, who 'ruled' racing" (Yates 17). With the decline of horse racing by the end of the 1830s, Porter began to include the early local-color fiction that literary historians term the "humor of the Old Southwest." As Norris Yates observes, "the bulk of [Porter's] later readers belong to a new and larger economic and social class—a class which may have shared the values and interests but not the economic resources of the old" (21). The values and interests of the slaveholding sportsmen and their allies contrast decidedly with the values and interests of the audience for and contributors to Hall's *Western Monthly Magazine.* The readers who allowed the *Spirit of the Times* to flourish for more than thirty years may not have been able to prevent women from speaking out in public meetings, but by excluding women's voices from the province of humor they effectively defined storytelling as a masculine occupation. The writers who contributed to William T. Porter's sporting magazine continued to develop American literature as a masculine enterprise.

When Augustus Baldwin Longstreet graduated from Yale University in 1813, he entered law school in Litchfield, Connecticut, where he attended sermons by the Reverend Lyman Beecher. According to his biographer, Kimball King, "His first practice as a raconteur began during the Connecticut years," when he "found time to visit Miss Pierce's School for Young Ladies, where he frequently regaled the young women with his droll accounts of rural Georgia in his 'country boy' pose" (King 12). He may have "practiced" his craft as well during visits he made to the Beecher home; and while the young Harriet would most likely not have been part of his audience (she would have been hardly three years old), Longstreet's residence in Litchfield establishes within the Beecher household a mode of storytelling Stowe would have been aware of when she began to write.

Longstreet and his colleague on the Augusta *Sentinel,* William Tappan Thompson, both of whom published their sketches in the 1830s, were, according to Blair, the only Old Southwest humorists to treat female characters in their fiction (Blair 74). Of these two, Longstreet in *Georgia Scenes* had the greater influence. *Georgia Scenes* is an important text to examine in establishing gender consciousness as a feature of early American fiction, for while it hints at a lingering fluidity in the relationship between gender and genre in the 1830s, it also reaffirms Irving's perspective and suggests that Old Southwest humor evolved in part from a desire to suppress the possibility of female literary authority. In Longstreet's preface to *Georgia Scenes* he tells us that when he first wrote and published the sketches which went into the volume, "I was extremely desirous of concealing the author, and the more effectually to do so, I wrote under two signatures. . . . *Hall* is the writer of those sketches in which *men* appear as the principal actors, and *Baldwin* of those in which *women* are the prominent figures" (Longstreet 2). In this preface Longstreet in effect announces the bifurcation of American sketch literature along gender lines. Although he presents himself as capable of writing in both genders—and indeed several of the sketches included in *Georgia Scenes* could have appeared as the efforts of a woman writer in a contemporary publication such as *Godey's Lady's Book*—by distinguishing between stories featuring men as "actors" and women as "figures" and by claiming that such distinctions produce a need for different narrators, he suggests as well that these distinctions involve different understandings of what constitutes both story and storytelling. James Meriwether writes that "the dominant figure of the book is Hall; . . . Baldwin simply serves as a foil to the ultimately much more masculine and successful Lyman Hall" (Meriwether 359). In Baldwin's sketches, the narrator becomes a moralist who stands back from the action, contrasting "country girls" with their urban counterparts and condemning women who become "charming" creatures and lead their husbands to early graves. By contrast, in Hall's sketches, Hall participates in the action, proves himself to be a crack shot, and establishes himself as a man's man. A third character who appears in the sketches, Ned Brace of "A Sage Conversation," establishes storytelling as one of many contests, like gander pulling, horse swapping, or horse racing, in which boys or men may prove their masculinity.

Nevertheless, Longstreet evidences certain tensions in the relation of writing to gender. In "Georgia Theatrics," he suggests that what appears to be masculine violence is often mere posturing and moreover that written narratives work best when they recount a mock fight; indeed, "The Fight," a sketch that portrays a real fight, bears out this perception by its own relative failure to interest. "The Horse Swap," long considered one of his best stories and frequently anthologized, conveys Longstreet's ambivalence even more clearly. In this story in which two men try to outsmart and thereby humiliate each other, and in which male braggadocio and aggressive rivalry feature prominently, the climax occurs when Peter pulls the blanket off of Bullet's back, revealing a sore "'that seemed to have defied all medical skill. It measured six full inches in length, and four in breadth; and had as many features as Bullet had motions. My heart sickened at the sight; and I felt that the brute who had been riding him in that situation, deserved the halter'" (Longstreet 28). In drawing back from this revelation, Hall distances himself from the festering sore of a hypermasculine culture, suggesting his own equally secret identification with the feminine. And in creating this sketch Longstreet proposes that if writing involves exposing the sore on Bullet's back, it also carries a feminine marker.

However, if writing requires Longstreet to distance himself from male culture, this does not lead him to accord women narrative authority. In his treatment of Baldwin and in the content of the sketches for which Baldwin serves as narrator, Longstreet mocks the feminine and denies both women and effeminate men any efficacy as storytellers. Like Irving in his portrait of Ichabod Crane, Longstreet links Baldwin to the world of women that he simultaneously mocks. The "country girls" of "The Dance" are so "wholly ignorant" of urban fashion that "consequently, they looked, for all the world, like human beings" (9); thus Longstreet manages to make fun of both country and urban "girls" in the same jest. In "The Song," piano player Miss Aurelia Emma Theodosia Augusta Crump has hands that engage in conflict at the keyboard, and "anyone, or rather no one, can imagine what kind of noises the piano gave forth" as a result (76). Longstreet's portraits of women characters, primarily in Baldwin's sketches, led his biographer to remark, "It is hard to understand how a man who appears to have had close, satisfying relationships with his wife and daughters, all sensible, intelligent women who led exemplary lives, could portray their sex so unflatteringly, unless his bias were actually a pose, a part of his writer's mask" (King 80). However, we can read Longstreet's misogyny as part of his struggle with the relation of gender to writing, a struggle that finally leads him to "renounce" writing. He concludes *Georgia Scenes* with "The Shooting Match," a story that reinforces the association of masculinity with "theatrics," as Hall, by sheer accident, proves his marksmanship and thereby earns the votes of the country people who promise to support him if "'ever you come out for any thing'" (248). Meriwether writes that "Longstreet makes it clear that the judgment of these people is to be respected and if Hall will accept such responsibilities he will be an able and successful public official" (361), such as Longstreet himself later became in his career as a judge, preacher, and college president.

If the gender complications of writing force Longstreet into problematic "poses," he nevertheless seems determined to reserve storytelling in its oral form as an arena for masculine performance. "A Sage Conversation," Baldwin's most powerful sketch, opens with his assertion that "I love the aged matrons of our land. As a class they are the most pious, the most benevolent, the most useful, and the most harmless of the human family" (Longstreet 216). Harmless they most certainly are in the area of storytelling, for while the three aged matrons, whose hospitality Baldwin and his companion, Ned Brace, have taken advantage of, talk endlessly to each other, they do not succeed in either contriving or telling stories. In particular, they cannot construct a narrative that will solve the riddle of Ned Brace's reference to "'two most excellent men, who became so much attached to each other that they actually got married'" and "'raised a lovely parcel of children'" (218). Ned Brace stakes out a position for male narrative outside the morality that constrains Baldwin and even Hall; he tells this story just before retiring to bed so that he and Baldwin can amuse themselves by listening to their hostesses' futile attempts to make sense of his comment and thus prove to themselves that these women are indeed "harmless." Although the women may act like men as they light their pipes and sit around the fire until late in the night, they lack the imagination that would enable them to make a story of how two men in love could also have and raise children. The best they can do is to repeat at regular intervals, "'I can't study it out nohow,'" and to resolve to ask Ned for an explanation in the morning: "'They were both widowers before they fell in love with each other and got married.' 'The lack-a-day! I wonder none of us thought o' that'" (228).

If these women can make nothing of the material Ned gives them, neither can they make anything of the material of their own lives. Their talk never rises above the level of what one of them calls "an old woman's chat" (228). They miss the humorous potential of their own material; they prove themselves incapable of sustaining the line of a narrative longer than a brief comment or two; they suggest that their only expertise lies in the realm of herbal remedies; and throughout, they demonstrate the general inability of women to be storytellers. While the humorists of the Old Southwest would follow the line of development indicated by Ned Brace, later regionalist writers would take up the challenge presented by Longstreet as they worked to redefine old women, female culture, and the nature of storytelling, seeking to prove themselves something other than harmless.

With the publication of "A New England Sketch," Stowe joined an emerging group of women who had begun to publish in magazines—Lydia Maria

Child, Sedgwick, and Sigourney, among others. Stowe certainly knew Sedgwick's *A New England Tale* (1822), the novel Nina Baym credits with inaugurating the genre of woman's fiction; it had created controversy within the Beecher family, and Catharine in particular had attacked Sedgwick, a convert to Unitarianism, as having betrayed both her social position and the Calvinist tradition (Sklar 44–45). It was perhaps in recognition of Sedgwick that Stowe originally called her story "A New England Sketch," just as she may later have changed the title to "Uncle Lot" in an attempt to distance herself from Sedgwick. Baym suggests that Stowe "perceived both slavery and religion as issues transcending gender, and treated them accordingly," and that this "set her apart from the other American women writing fiction in her day" (*Woman's Fiction* 15). If Stowe chose not to model her long fictions on Sedgwick, in some of her sketches she chose as well to raise questions of region that Sedgwick, despite the regional flavor of her title, does not address.

In *The Pearl of Orr's Island* (1862), Stowe demonstrates that she also knew Sigourney's *Sketch of Connecticut*, published in Hartford the same year thirteen-year-old Harriet Beecher moved there to become a student at her sister Catharine's Hartford Female Seminary. In *Sketch of Connecticut*, Madam L—— tells Farmer Larkin, a regional character who makes a brief appearance, that she doesn't recollect the names of his children. He replies, "'It's no wonder that ye don't Ma'am, there's such a neest on 'em. They're as thick as hops round the fire this winter. There's Roxey and Reuey, they're next to Tim, and look like twins. They pick the wool, and card tow, and wind quills, and knit stockins and mittins for the fokes in the house; and I've brought some down with me to day, to see if they'll buy 'em to the marchants' shops, and let 'em have a couple o' leetle small shawls'" (Sigourney 113). It seems likely that Stowe names her own characters Roxy and Ruey in *The Pearl of Orr's Island* after the daughters of Farmer Larkin, just as she may have named Lady Lothrop of *Oldtown Folks* after Sigourney's Madam L——. The model Sigourney created in her New England farmer with his Connecticut speech rhythms also served to influence Stowe's portrait of Uncle Lot, the one character in her first sketch who speaks in dialect. Thus while Stowe responds to Irving in "Uncle Lot," she also responds to her female contemporaries.

Unlike *A New England Tale*, "Uncle Lot" does not inaugurate a genre. However, Stowe's interests in "Uncle Lot" suggest that as early as 1834 there existed the possibility that women would create not a single major tradition but two—woman's fiction and regionalism—that would develop independent of each other, yet share some common themes, concerns, and influences. Regionalism, in contrast to woman's fiction, begins inchoately, reflecting uncertainty on the part of both male and female writers in the 1830s concerning the ways in which the gender of the author might affect the formal concerns of the work. For by the 1830s the direction of critical judgment concerning women writers, though clearly forming, was not yet set. Stowe's vision of Uncle Lot as the "settest crittur you ever saw" and the challenge she sets her hero to convert Uncle Lot to the expression of feeling establishes her perspicacity in implicitly predicting that gender itself would remain a "chestnut burr" within American culture. Reading "Uncle Lot" in its various contexts also opens up the "chestnut burr" of narrative traditions in American fiction as her sketch kept alive the possibility that her female successors might develop a mode of writing that would do the cultural work of creating a form for women's narrative voice.

Humor of the Old Southwest and *Alderbrook*

In *Authorship and Audience,* Stephen Railton makes a case for the role gender played in the development of narrative traditions in the decades immediately preceding the Civil War. In making this case, Railton argues that his "decision to give gender such a decisive role in categorizing significant reading publics follows the line that analysts of Victorian American culture have long taken, from Santayana to Fred Patee [*sic*] to Ann Douglas: that Americans at mid-century tended to make increasingly sharp distinctions between male and female realms of experience, that for those Americans gender tended to be a category that took precedence over such other accidentals as age or region or class" (11). While Railton hastens to add that he does not offer gender "as a definitive way to make sense of the vast, and vastly different, number of actual people who made up 'the reading public' at the time," it does enable him to "gain access to [some] minds"—namely, the minds "of male readers in a 'feminized' culture" (11, 90).

To claim that the humor of the Old Southwest was designed to reach "a national audience of men" (91) is not simply the retrospective statement of a criticism informed by the insights of second wave feminism. Writing in 1964, Cohen and Dillingham make the same distinction, though they do so in different terms. Claiming that "the gap between the genteel literature which was being enjoyed by pale young ladies in New England drawing rooms and the masculine humor which filled the pages of the *Spirit of the Times* was immense" (xi), they argue that one of the differences between these writers and the later local colorists, whose roots can be traced to the humor of the Old Southwest, was the humorists' "lack of respect for delicate sensibilities" (xiv). However stereotyped Cohen and Dillingham's construction of the woman reader of the time might seem, their presentation of Old Southwest humor as characterized by practical jokes, misogyny, cruelty to animals, and a certain amorality, and as designed for and appealing to men, anticipates Railton's analysis. While Railton finally proposes that this humor's "ultimate consequence was to reconcile readers to the place convention marked out for them to aspire to" (105), he recognizes that in the process a different kind of cultural work occurred as well:

> Drunkenness, rage, violence, cruelty, greed, selfishness: the aboriginal pleasure-seeking self was allowed to come out of hiding. But it remained always behind

> the intricate barriers that the conventions and assumptions of the genre interposed between it and the gentleman's public identity, and not only because the right to look down on these "peasants" was the one clear privilege that their sacrifices at the altar of propriety had gained them. . . . By keeping the tales' poor white "neutral territory" so remote from the circles in which they and their readers moved, they could attack such values as religion, matrimony, chivalry, and "honour"—for although those values defined their conscious allegiance, they could not win their unconscious consent. What runs amuck in the genre is the unrepression of instinct, dressed in motley and let loose upon the circumscribed landscape of the tales. (105)

Although the texts of the humorists of the Old Southwest have largely disappeared from contemporary anthologies of American literature, as they often reflect gross racist and sexist attitudes and editors have made decisions to cut them in order to make room for previously unread texts by white women and African American writers, we find it useful to "recall" them because of the role they played in shaping the literary landscape out of which regionalism emerged and because of the importance they were accorded in the founding of American literature during the 1940s, 50s, and 60s. In *Native American Humor,* for example, Walter Blair departs from his usual reportorial tone to exclaim that out of the material of the frontier "a boisterous band of humorists produced a body of amusing narrative unsurpassed by any group in American literature" (62), and Yates claims that the *Spirit of the Times* "drew most of its readers and reputation from the geographical areas and social groups which have often been regarded, rightly or wrongly, as those most distinctly American" (4). Indeed, an unintended consequence of the "suppression" of these texts has been the loss of a certain historical grounding for both local color and regionalism and in particular the loss of regionalism's contrastive edge.

Critics have long noted the similarities between "The Legend of Sleepy Hollow" and the tales produced by the humorists of the Old Southwest, and from the evidence provided by Cohen and Dillingham, among others, it seems clear that "The Legend of Sleepy Hollow" directly influenced the development of this narrative tradition. Virtually all commentators on the humor of the Old Southwest agree as well on the hypermasculinity of its content. Both through subjects that it features—hunts, fights, gambling, swindling, drinking, politicking, horse races, and gander pulling—and those it ignores, through the characters it foregrounds and the settings in which it is located, Old Southwest humor constructs itself as a literary equivalent of male-only space and clearly writes over its door "no girls allowed." As Yates puts it, "contributors were not interested in the humdrum daily routine of the pioneer woman as she spun, sewed, cooked, washed, made soap, and frequently toiled in the corn or cotton patch alongside her man" (128). And, he writes further, they warned women away from their territory by their inclusion of and approach to "off-color subjects" (128). Indeed, in introducing his own particular "lion," Yates situates Porter and his *Spirit of the Times* in the same context of gender conflict as Paulding's play: "Moreover, this paper gave an important boost to the writing of literature about just those shock-headed, one-gallused, tobacco-spitting, whisky-guzzling coonskin republicans of the back country whose lack of domestic manners horrified Mrs. Trollope. And thereby hangs our tale" (4).

Of course, the period during which the humorists of the Old Southwest flourished coincides precisely with the period during which this region came under increasing attack for the barbarism of its "domestic manners" and particularly for the barbarism of slavery. According to Blair, these writers wanted to "interpret" their region to the East (64), and he quotes Longstreet, who hoped that through his writings "'we may be seen and heard by our posterity two hundred years hence just as we are'" (66). Similarly, when Yates writes that "[a]fter an evening with the *Spirit* a southern reader could hardly help but feel that his was a way of life distinct, for better or for worse" (88), he identifies the interpretive, even defensive, nature of this literature. Cohen and Dillingham, the anthologists who give us "Cupping on the Sternum," discussed below, are more explicit still: "Accused of both crudity and cruelty, Southerners felt the need to let the world know that they were proud enough of their colorful, rustic homeland to want to write about it with the express purpose of preserving in literature its scenes and customs" (xxiii). In this context, the value attached to the explicitly masculine and the link between the explicitly masculine and the distinctively American are deployed to gain a hearing for the South's "peculiar institution."

While the writers of Old Southwest humor may have used their fictions to express "their instinctual doubts about the sacrifices that the role of gentleman in a democracy demanded of them" and while their fictions may be located not on the frontier "but rather in a kind of psychological fairyland" where "the presocial impulses that an American gentleman was forced to repress" could be acted out "without a moment's hesitation, without a twinge of regret or embarrassment" (Railton 102, 103), they never suggest that the characters who engage in such acting out should be equated with the writer himself. In analyzing this aspect of Old Southwest humor, Railton writes that

> its humor derives solely from class distinction: from the difference between a plough horse and a real thoroughbred, from the distance between the rituals of racing as "the sport of kings" and the crude way these Kentucky squatters desecrate them in their efforts to imitate their betters. . . . In most of the sketches reprinted in Porter's two anthologies . . . , the writers expect to excite laughter simply by reporting rustic traits. Often they do not even bother to exaggerate them for comic effect; the sight of a hick wearing his first suit of store-bought clothes, or seeing a piano for the first time, or trying to waltz, or fighting, or courting, or preaching, was sufficiently hilarious. (98)

In sum, he writes, "Southwestern humor was a counterattack upon the spirit of the times, a deeply motivated repudiation of the contemporary surge of democratic impulses most conveniently represented by Jacksonianism. . . . [T]he writing of these humorists valorizes bourgeois conventions, the more aristocratic the better, as the ultimate authority. Their conscious allegiance was to the old order, the restraints of law, property, caste, religion, and institutions—all of which seemed threatened by the energies and possibilities of the rawly democratic frontier" (100, 101). According to Railton the purpose of these fictions was to establish the class identity of the writer who, while not himself a member of the southern ruling class, sought to associate himself with it, and to reinforce the class identity of the reader. From this perspective "one gets a very frank sense of the class-bound ugliness that informs the genre as a whole" (97).

In one of the most provocative recent treatments of the humorists of the Old Southwest, discussed briefly in chapter 2, Neil Schmitz implicitly challenges and complicates Railton's analysis. Agreeing that this fiction "displaced to its backcountry everything that was mean, amoral, sadistic, and drew round its villainous speech a discursive containment, the relaxed, rational Addisonian voice," he nevertheless argues that "the patrician writer who depicted the poor white was imaginative enough to catch in that rough country speech the true art of bitter knowledge, could see the native speaker's sardonic grin peel the pose from the interlocutor's Addisonian stance, and so was himself uncertain, ambivalent" (317, 318). Moreover, he indicates that the writers who, "properly speaking," should be labeled Old Southwest humorists, those who succeeded Longstreet, create fictions in which "the Addisonian narrator is often a figure of inhibition, of blindness," and he notes that in Johnson Jones Hooper's *Some Adventures of Captain Simon Suggs* (1845), "Suggs's motto—IT IS GOOD TO BE SHIFTY IN A NEW COUNTRY—is unchallenged" (316). While Schmitz reads Old Southwest humor as ultimately containing "the awful message" that "*For its overweening pride, its moral blindness, the South was to suffer castration and humiliation*" (317), he directs his rage not at the South or its pride and blindness but at Stowe, whose *Uncle Tom's Cabin* "changes everything in Southern writing" (310). After Stowe, and because of her, "regional writing is adversarial" (320) and she is responsible for the violence of George Washington Harris's Sut Lovingood, whose "yarns" first appeared in the mid-1850s, in which the "Southern rage, the Southern cruelty, that Longstreet had contained in *Georgia Scenes* is here set off in a series of demolitions" (321). "Jacksonian writers," Schmitz writes, "had wanted ruins. It got them from Sut. . . . American ruins, Harris had discovered, looked like wreckage" (323).

In case the current "suppression" of the humorists of the Old Southwest might lead us to forget the role of gender in the formation of American literature and American literary history, Schmitz's essay reminds us that the "chestnut burr" of gender, intricately connected to the burrs of class and race, sticks not only to this narrative tradition but also to our literary history. In implicitly associating the conflict between the North and South with the conflict between Stowe and the male humorists of the Old Southwest, in implicitly equating the

North's wreckage of the South with Stowe's "wreckage" in *Uncle Tom's Cabin* and reading it as "castration and humiliation," Schmitz genders American history as well. His own obvious identification with the Southern position and his extensive praise of this now almost forgotten material might lead us to interpret his essay, published in the prestigious *Columbia Literary History of the United States,* as an attempt to reinstall this narrative tradition to a central place in American literary history and specifically as *the* instance of significant regional writing in the pre–Civil War period. In the light of such claims, it becomes necessary for us to examine, however briefly, some specific texts of this tradition.

In two of his Simon Suggs tales published in the 1840s, Johnson Jones Hooper focuses on the antagonism between Simon and his father but includes cruelty to Simon's black companion as an aspect of the "humor." In "How Simon Suggs 'Raised Jack,'" Simon's father, Elder Jedediah, surprises his son and a "negro boy named Bill" playing cards in the fields instead of working. In this story, Simon at first tries to convince his father that they have been playing "mumble-peg" instead, and to demonstrate the game, forces Bill to get down on his hands and knees and try to pull a peg out of the ground with his teeth, receiving in the process a blow on the seat of his pants from Elder Jedediah's hickory. In the companion story, "Simon Gets a 'Soft Snap' Out of His Daddy," Simon escapes a whipping by talking his father into a game of cards, but not before Bill is whipped mercilessly. Part of the "humor" in this story derives from the apparent "sympathy" with which Simon watches Bill's whipping, a "sympathy" with sexual overtones. "The old man Suggs made no remark to any one while he was seizing up Bill—a process which, though by no means novel to Simon, seemed to excite in him a sort of painful interest. He watched it closely, as if endeavoring to learn the precise fashion of his father's knot; and when at last Bill was swung up a-tiptoe to a limb, and the whipping commenced, Simon's eye followed every movement of his father's arm; and as each blow descended upon the bare shoulders of his sable friend, his own body writhed and 'wriggled' in involuntary sympathy" (Meine 175–76). Of course Simon himself escapes such a whipping, and the reader can be quite certain that this will happen; the racist assumption that Bill is too stupid to outwit the "old man" and therefore deserves the whipping intended for Simon produces the "humor" of Simon's "sympathy."

One of the most egregious examples of the attitudes that in general inform the humor of the Old Southwest is Henry Clay Lewis's "Cupping on the Sternum," published in the *Spirit of the Times* in 1845. The short sketch is narrated by a male medical student who has "got as far as cupping, cathartics, and castor oil" when he receives a request to "'take the large cups and scarificator, together with a large blister, up to Mr. J. and cup his Negro girl Chaney very freely over the *sternum;* after you have cupped her, apply the blister over the same, as she has inflammation of the lungs'" (Cohen and Dillingham 337). The so-called "humor" of the sketch is based on the ignorance of the medical student, who has not yet studied anatomy, and believes that the "sternum" refers to the patient's buttocks. The "humor" is intensified by the gross racism of the portrait. The narrator writes, describing Chaney, "By way of parenthesis, let me create an idea of my patient, so that you may appreciate the field of my operation. Just imagine a butcher's block five feet long and four feet through at the butt, converted into a fat bouncing Negro wench, with smaller blocks appended for limbs, and you will have a faint conception of the figure and proportion of the delectable portion of humanity upon whom my curative capabilities were to be exhibited" (338). Yet the narrator's racism does not prevent him from constructing Chaney as a sexual object. In this passage she represents for him a "delectable portion"; in subsequent passages, he watches drops of sweat "which, like ebony beads, chased each other down her gleaming neck" and he concludes that she "perspired beautifully" (338). Sexism and racism together form the basis of Lewis's "humor," for although Chaney expects to be "cupped" on the breastbone and "proceeded to divest her bosom of its concealments," the narrator insists that she turn over so that he can "cup" her on her "stern." Here is the narrator's description of the procedure: "Chaney, seeing that there was no retreat, agreed at last to the operation. Click! click! went the scarificator, and amidst the shouts of the patient and my awful solicitude for fear I might cut an artery, the 'deed was did.' But no blood flowed, nothing but grease, which trickled out slowly like molasses out of a worm hole. I saw that the cups were too in*fat*uated [*sic*] to draw blood from that quarter. I removed them and applied the blister, and I expect fly ointment was in demand about that time" (338). The sketch's "humor" in the description of the "operation" depends on a reader who will not object to describing Chaney alternately as a block of wood and as a container of grease and fat.

Yet what the story does not say about the narrator's visit to Chaney serves also to extend its appeal to "gentlemen" of a certain type. The sketch ends without filling in the details, but in the final paragraph the narrator alludes to the passage of time ("several hours"), emphasizes that the operation has "*entirely relieved*" the patient, speculates that "she used chairs mighty little for a few weeks" and that "she hated the idea of the operation so bad that she burnt up a brand new dress just because it was *bum*bazine and reminded her, by the first syllable of the *seat* of 'Cupping on the Sternum'" (339). If we read the final paragraph in light of the narrator's sexualization of Chaney early in the sketch, then the "operation" also becomes sexualized, and the reader can imagine that the white male narrator has subjected the black woman to anal rape; the only indication of how she feels about her degradation is that she burns a "brand new dress" because it is a reminder. The message the sketch offers is that women, especially if they are black, serve as the "butt" of sexual exploitation and are so stupid that they conspire in their own victimization. Its humor relies on suppressing the reader's capacity for empathic response; only without empathy for Chaney can the reader accept "Cupping on the Sternum" as merely the antic exploits of a medical schoolboy and only without empathy for Chaney can the reader accept the sexism and racism that serve as the source of the narrator's literary authority for the "gentlemen" who read *The Spirit of the Times.*

George Washington Harris's "Mrs. Yardley's Quilting" (1867) has the apparent merit of lacking the racism inherent in "Cupping on the Sternum." However, "Mrs. Yardley's Quilting" derives its humor from misogyny and the debasing of values that during the 1840s and 1850s became associated with woman's sphere. A reader interested in nineteenth-century women's culture might find that Sut Lovingood knows a great deal about quilts, and that Harris's story records valuable information: "'Yu see quilts wer wun ove her speshul gifts; she run strong on the bed-kiver question. Irish chain, star ove Texas, sun-flower, nine dimunt, saw teeth, checker board, an' shell quilts; blue, an' white, an' yaller an' black coverlids, an' callickercumfurts reigned triumphan' 'bout her hous'. They wer packed in drawers, layin in shelfs full, wer hung four dubbil on lines in the lof, packed in chists, piled on cheers, an' wer everywhar, even onto the beds, an' wer changed every bed-makin'" (Cohen and Dillingham 182). Sut, however, has no interest in quilts at all, but merely in creating an atmosphere that will allow him and his friends to have a good time. As he tells his listener, "'Es I swung my eyes over the crowd, George, I thought quiltins, managed in a morril an' sensibil way, truly am good things—good fur free drinkin, good fur free eatin, good fur free huggin, good fur free dancin, good fur free fitin, an' goodest ove all fur poperlatin a country fas'" (182). Anything that appears to take women and women's culture seriously becomes fair game for Sut, who views quiltings as opportunities for seduction and destruction; widows as the most likely and willing victims; and women in general as ridiculous creatures whose only purpose in life is to serve as objects of humor—for example, he describes Mrs. Yardley as having been "straiched" to give her her shape, with "'mos' ove the straichin cumin outen her laigs an' naik'" (181).

As part of his good time, Sut plays a practical joke on a "red-comb'd, long-spurr'd, dominecker feller, frum town," who has joined Sut and other males for the social event associated with a quilting bee. In order to eliminate the competition posed by this town male, Sut ties a line of quilts to the back of the "dominecker feller"'s horse, then hits the horse on the back just above the tail; the horse becomes tangled up in all of the lines of quilts, then runs into the house and gets the quilt Mrs. Yardley is working on tangled up with the other quilts, many of which Sut has already cut in the middle in order to tie them to the horse. As a result of Sut's "joke," Mrs. Yardley becomes ill and dies, and Harris expects his readers to find this humorous. When someone asks Sut what caused Mrs. Yardley's death, he replies, "'Nuffin, only her heart stop't beatin 'bout losin a nine dimunt quilt'" (181).

Because quilts represent women's culture to Sut, and thus serve metonymically to represent sentimentality to Harris, some readers find the sketch more a satire on literary sentimentalism than an expression of misogyny. Nevertheless,

"Mrs. Yardley's Quilting" can become humorous only within an ideology that derogates women, the work they do, and the objects they value, and that privileges boys and boys' values. It is interesting to note that in their introductory comments on Harris, Cohen and Dillingham include his fiction in the category of "lusty realism," which they suggest derives in part from the attitudes of the East Tennessee mountain people themselves, "the satisfaction they found in the fulfillment of their natural appetites, and the results—ludicrous, pathetic, and grim—of their frustrations," as well as from Harris's "hints of humanity's predilection for devilment" (156). Neither the author of "Mrs. Yardley's Quilting" nor his 1960s editors are willing to contemplate the possibility that the East Tennessee mountain people's lives might be open to alternative readings, such as those Murfree offers in her own work, specifically in "The Star in the Valley," "Over on the T'other Mounting," and "The 'Harnt' That Walks Chilhowee," collected in *AWR*, or *In the "Stranger People's" Country;* nor do they recognize that it is the interests and assumptions of both the "gentleman" readers of Harris's time and the male literary critics of the 1960s that actually determine what constitutes "natural" appetites, constructs the mountaineers' lives as "ludicrous, pathetic, and grim," and accepts the "boys will be boys" view of "humanity's predilection for devilment."

Early regionalists wrote in opposition to the values represented by "Mrs. Yardley's Quilting." In "Mrs. Wetherbe's Quilting Party" (*Clovernook, Second Series,* 1854), for example, a description of a southern Ohio quilting is embedded in a longer story that shows Cary's sympathy for and defense of a black woman, Aunt Kitty, and of a poor white woman, Jenny Mitchel. Moreover, Cary describes the city of Cincinnati as a place where "men, women, and children hurried to and fro, and all languages were heard, and all costumes were seen, as if after a thousand generations, the races were returning to be again united at Babel" (26), and when Mrs. Wetherbe's guests arrive for her quilting, it turns out that she "had not been at all exclusive, and her invitations included all, rich and poor, maid and mistress, as far as she was acquainted" (40). The women stitch one large quilt, the men chop wood, they come together at the end of the day for a party; some of the women flirt, some of the men drink too much, the men awkwardly and gallantly escort the women home, and no one is humiliated or killed.

At the same time that the humorists of the Old Southwest flourished in the *Spirit of the Times,* Emily Chubbuck [Judson] continued the village sketch tradition in what Donovan calls a "weakened but still popular form" (*New England* 34). Chubbuck began her career as a poet but financial success came with the publication of a series of children's books. Her reputation as a literary figure, however, and her access to a larger reading public dates from 1844 when, under the pseudonym of Fanny Forester, she began to contribute sketches of village life to various magazines. These sketches she later collected in two volumes published in 1847 under the title of *Alderbrook.*

We see elements in *Alderbrook* that may have influenced Cary's *Clovernook,* both in the title Cary chose for her sketches and in her decision to collect them into two volumes. However, though most of the sketches in *Alderbrook* begin with some attention to setting and convey, albeit vaguely, a sense of their location in a particular village, they reflect a didacticism that enforces conventional understandings of gender. Often they blame women for men's failings, as in "Charley Hill," where the women do not "save" Charley as they should and are therefore responsible for his drunkenness and death; or they represent women as all too willing to save men even at the cost of becoming crippled, as in "Little Molly White." Moreover, Forester's sketches contain numerous instances of that mid-nineteenth-century dialect of gender so strikingly absent from Cary's sketches. The first story of the first volume, "Grace Linden," sets the tone: "Little girls are mimic women, and Grace was a complete little girl, with all her sensibilities, the refinements, and pretty little concealments that characterize the sex" (1:21).

The second volume of *Alderbrook* more closely resembles Cary's work in its use of a consistent narrative persona, in its greater sense of storytelling, and in its self-reflexive quality. But in sketches like "Grandfather Bray," Forester romanticizes her portrait of the "comfortable old farm-house" with its "generous court-yard, broad kitchen garden and ample out houses," its "ricks of hay, raising their conical heads down in the meadow," and the "lofty well-sweep" with its "gray old bucket," revealing nothing of the dreary aspects of farming or the sense of class injury that would occupy Cary's attention (2:35). And in "Lilias Fane," a young woman forced to become a teacher because of her father's failure earns the children's love and obedience where others, all men, have failed, yet incurs the displeasure of the townspeople for her youth, inexperience, and beauty. The story has a "happy" ending when the town's eligible bachelor decides to marry her and, even though he thinks she has done well as a teacher, advises her to resign before she is fired, for, he says, "We have coarse natures here, and *you* must not come in contact with them" (2:172). Other sketches from the second volume also reflect anxiety on the subject of women's success in activities outside the home, particularly as it relates to artistic expression. Cary and Cooke take up this theme as well, but in ways that render it far more complex, as we suggest in our discussion of Cooke's "Maya, the Princess" in chapter 10. We invite readers to draw their own conclusions by reading Forester's "Dora" next to Cary's "Charlotte Ryan," and her "Ida Ravelin" next to Cooke's "Maya, the Princess."

Alderbrook also contains instances of "conversion" narratives in which an "indurated" male (the phrase is Sigourney's, taken from "The Father") is saved from the consequences of his hardness by a woman, usually much younger, who breaks through "the crust upon the heart" ("My Old Playmate," vol. 1) and enables him to acknowledge his softness. In the context of these stories, all of which depend upon accepting the premise that women inherently possess some miraculous power of grace, "Uncle Lot" looks rather radical as it makes James

Benton rather than Grace the agent of conversion. Reacting at once to the exaltation of hardness in the literary atmosphere reflected in and augmented by the humor of the Old Southwest—Schmitz describes Sut's tales as "vividly told in a mean, hard voice" and claims that "the text itself is hard" (322)—and to the illusory claims for the power of softness in texts like Forester's *Alderbrook,* regionalist writers propose a model for conversion that is complex, earned, and "tough," one that relies on structures of empathy deeply embedded in its poetics, thematics, narrative form, and conception of reading, and one that includes a critique that extends to the telling self as well as to the story being told.

Starting with Alice Cary

The story of the origins of regionalism is neither singular nor simple. We have suggested that our story might best be called "the history of an impulse" for we certainly do not claim that regionalism came into being without reference to preceding texts. We do, however, claim that while regionalism took elements, either directly or indirectly, from many previous texts, it represents a coherent tradition of women's writing in the second half of the nineteenth century that is different from anything that preceded it. It will be our project in the rest of this book to demonstrate the validity of this claim. At the outset, however, we wish to say that this tradition of women's writing is in many respects a queer one. As we indicated in chapter 1, it is not a tradition that can be framed within the familiar linear model of beginning, middle, and end; nor is it a tradition of origins and influence, with one writer developing possibilities that are passed on to the next, who can then go "beyond" the work of the earlier writer. Although the dominance of the model of linear narration and the desire for an "author" capable of canonization exerts pressure on us to mark Jewett as the culmination of our tradition, we do not, as we observed in chapter 1, give Jewett such preeminence. Instead, we view regionalism as conceptually synchronic; over a period of roughly sixty years different writers respond similarly and differently to a cluster of concerns, a set of problems, a series of possibilities.

Still, we do propose a beginning for the tradition of literary regionalism and the measure of the queerness of our project may be taken here, for has any book on American literature ever begun with the desire to understand the origins of Alice Cary's *Clovernook*? If our tradition began with Cooke, we would have a more intelligible opening, for Cooke's first published story appeared in 1855 in *Putnam's,* a magazine whose unabashed promotion of things American gave it a purchase on the national reading public; she consistently produced a substantial body of short fiction over a considerable number of years; she emerged from a well-established tradition of New England writing; and she continued to publish in the major periodicals of her day, thus suggesting that she had influence as well as origins. Our tradition, however, does not begin with Cooke; it begins with Cary and as a result it is from the start eccentric.

Cary thought of herself primarily as a poet and it was as a poet that she made her reputation and gained national visibility. Young women coming of age as poets in the days of Cary's maturity could certainly have looked to her as a model, but we can only speculate as to whether Cooke, who began to publish fiction shortly after the appearance of *Clovernook, Second Series,* would have read Cary's sketches, or whether Jewett, who began to publish regionalist fiction a few years after Cary's death, would have known of her work as she knew of Stowe's and Cooke's. Starting with Alice Cary, thus, proposes for our tradition a model of literary history in which origins and influences must be differently understood. If by midcentury certain possibilities existed for women writers that Cary was the first to realize, then later writers, whether they knew of her or not, were following in her footsteps as they attempted in their own way to realize the possibilities she was the first to mark. Still, it seems somewhat eccentric or queer—a word we will explore in more detail in chapter 10—to begin a tradition with a writer who may not have been read by any of her fellow practitioners.

If Cary's *Clovernook* sketches were not in fact widely read (and neither volume went into a second edition), we might argue that Cary redeployed the tradition of the village sketch away from the mainstream marked out by *Alderbrook,* which went through a number of editions in the years following its publication, and removed it to the margins, identifying regionalism as a minor genre, a region within the nation of literature whose primary forms, as Cary herself insisted, were poetry and the novel. In converting *Alderbrook* to *Clovernook,* Cary rejected Forester's use of the village sketch tradition as means for delivering the didactic and formulaic contrast between the innocence of the country and the sin of the city, and harnessed it instead to the purposes of regionalism. As marginal and queer, work Cary might be said to have done with her "left" hand, regionalism becomes a space for experimentation, less prescribed by conventions of form and content and less controlled by the didactics of women's writing at midcentury, a place for imaginative play. Our eccentric story, then, begins with a writer who establishes the tradition of regionalism as itself eccentric. Moreover, if one wanted to recover Cary as an American *author,* one would have to look at her poetry and her novels, for these were the genres that she herself privileged and these were the genres that at midcentury had the authority to establish one as an author. Focusing on *Clovernook* recovers Cary as a writer, not an author, and situates regionalism outside the dominant obsession with authors.

Additionally, to begin with Cary locates the impulse toward regionalism elsewhere than in New England. While region implies a minority status in relation to nation, some regions are clearly more minor than others. As we have seen in the stories told by the literary histories, New England occupies an anomalous place in the history of American regions, sometimes understood as a region but frequently equated with the nation. In the period during which Cary came up to womanhood and writerhood, this elision occurred regularly, as witness the derivation of "Uncle Sam" from Seba Smith's decidedly down-easter Jack Downing and Porter's reference in the introduction to his second collection of stories from the *Spirit* to "the universal Yankee nation" (Yates 41). As a resident of Ohio well aware of the minority status of her own region and as a writer who chose New York rather than Boston as the place from which to reflect upon her region, Cary pulls regionalism out of the orbit of New England and keeps it from being conflated with New England literary culture or with the subset of that culture Donovan refers to as "New England local color." To start with Cary and the "West" frees regionalism from the centripetal pull of New England and marks it as a mode of representing the perspective of those occupying the margins, not the center. It reminds us that regionalism involves a way of seeing that cannot be summed up as "New Englandly" and that cannot be conflated with nation. In effect, Cary makes regionalism available to New England women writers.

Finally, beginning with Cary, whose regional sketches first appeared in the late 1840s, locates regionalism as a tradition that preceded the Civil War and makes it temporally as well as geographically eccentric. Cary requires that the history of regionalism be separated from the history of local color, a tradition clearly identifiable as a product of the post–Civil War environment, and enables us to view writers like Jewett, Murfree, Freeman, and Chopin in a context other than that of local color. It suggests that regionalism begins elsewhere than local color, and that writers before, during, and after the war start from this "elsewhere" as well. When Thaxter describes how little impact the Civil War had on the inhabitants of the Isles of Shoals, she may also be describing her situation as a writer of regionalism who continued to explore the possibilities that led Cary to write sketches with her left hand in the decade before the war, possibilities perhaps less affected by war than our literary historians would have us believe.

CHAPTER 4

The Poetics of Empathic Narration

What a pity I had not listened more attentively.

—Grace King, "'One of Us'"

Running all the way to the wigwams, I halted shyly at the entrances. Sometimes I stood long moments without saying a word. It was not any fear that made me so dumb when out upon such a happy errand; nor was it that I wished to withhold the invitation, for it was all I could do to observe this very proper silence. But it was a sensing of the atmosphere, to assure myself that I should not hinder other plans.

—Zitkala-Ša, "Impressions of an Indian Childhood"

Distilling Essences

In creating *American Women Regionalists,* we asserted that the body of material collected between its covers formed a distinct tradition of American women's writing in the second half of the nineteenth century. While we will be discussing significant differences among these writers and their work, our primary focus in the next three chapters concerns how regionalism establishes its coherence in the literary and textual questions it raises, and we begin by exploring the regionalists' writing practices. Writers themselves frequently express considerable reluctance to speak in theoretical terms about their own work, either from fear that such analysis will damage the very creativity it is intended to explicate or from a conviction that the only meaningful statement of their poetics is to be found in the work itself.[1] But readers who are deeply moved by a writer's work feel drawn to theorize the writer's practice for it serves to place them inside the work as the analytic aspect of the creative faculty that produced it. The term "poetics" serves to describe the features and principles more than a dozen writers over a period of more than half a century demonstrated in common in an array of texts that crossed regional lines and that emerged from a broad range of social and cultural perspectives. The term might also serve to identify the critical practices of a reader who, in the words of Celia Thaxter, seeks to get "close to the heart of these things" (*AWR* 166) by marking and theorizing those features and principles.

We understand the poetics of regionalism as a series of narrative effects.[2] In marking such effects, we draw on Aristotle's purpose in explicating the workings of tragedy in the *Poetics* when he writes that tragedy is the *mimēsis* of an action "with incidents arousing pity and fear in such a way as to accomplish a *katharsis* of such emotions" (*Aristotle* 296). Aristotle appears to have believed that by identifying the effects of tragedy he would make the features of that genre more intelligible to its audience and thereby even more effective. Such certainly is our position, for we can reasonably assume that without a theory of regionalism's effects and how these effects are produced, readers will have less access to the workings of regionalism and the texts of regionalism will remain relatively obscure. Furthermore, when Aristotle set out to examine tragedy, he considered as art for the first time poetry that had not yet been theorized—the "art which represents by language alone . . . has not yet received a name" (292)—and he used the term "poetics" to refer to the features and principles of an artistic use of language whose distinctiveness was to him palpable. Following Aristotle, we believe that the term "poetics" best describes that initial encounter between theorizing reader and distinctive literary practice.

This use of the term "poetics" to describe that point where textual features and reading practices meet also enables us to accomplish a shift in the definition of what constitutes "theory," for we will be arguing that one of the features of regionalism lies in the way the texts may be said to theorize themselves. We have developed elsewhere (see Fetterley, "Theorizing Regionalism") some of the reasons why the women regionalists (unlike their contemporaries Garland, Howells, and James) did not produce writing that critics might more readily recognize as theoretical and how we might read as theory the texts they did produce. In this chapter we are interested in deriving the poetics of regionalism from the narratives themselves, using regionalist texts as our theoretical base to construct an analysis that will enhance the effects of regionalism for our readers. Freeman writes of her character Louisa Ellis in "A New England Nun" that "Louisa had a little still, and she used to occupy herself pleasantly in summer weather with distilling the sweet and aromatic essences from roses and peppermint and spearmint" (*AWR* 360–61). "Distilling essences" becomes our trope for the process of extraction by which we as critics seek to get "close to the heart" of the poetics of regionalist writers.

In our discussion of the origins of regionalism in chapter 3, we described Stowe's discovery in "Uncle Lot" that conversion, a process of eliciting inner change, can provide the narrative intention for a work of fiction, its design for its readers, and we alluded to the role empathy plays in this process through

James Benton's "gift of feeling a *real* interest for anybody in five minutes" and his "natural tact for seeing into others . . . with . . . delight." In the introduction to *American Women Regionalists* we used the word "empathy" to describe one of the most significant features of regionalism, suggested that the narrator's stance of careful listening fosters an affective connection between the reader of the work and the lives the work depicts, and claimed that because regionalist narrators "identify with rather than distance themselves from the material of their stories, regionalist texts allow the reader to view the regional speaker as subject and not as object and to include empathic feeling as an aspect of critical response" (*AWR* xvii). We wish now to extend our analysis of how narrative approach in regionalist fiction models empathic response for readers and instructs them in the value of that response while at the same time it devises strategies for overcoming its readers' anticipated resistance. In particular, we will be observing how the location of the narrator works to confer value on and establish empathy with the regionalist subject by writing as if looking from the inside out rather than from the outside in. When regionalist narrators locate themselves as "'One of Us,'" the title of a story by King (included in *AWR*), they do so from a position of empathy; and when they include the reader as well as "one of us," they construct their readers as also capable of empathy. As one of Sui Sin Far's characters says, "'it takes a heart to make a heart'" (505) and the heart evinced by the narrator is meant to open the heart of the reader. While we will take up more fully the relationship between narrative strategies and questions of form in chapter 6, and the relationship between text and reader in chapter 11, here we will demonstrate the ways in which regionalist texts model changes of heart and anticipate resistance from some readers to their interest in such changes. In so doing, we also wish to emphasize the constructedness of empathic response and of narrative attempts to elicit that response. Within this frame, regionalism becomes a textual space, a bookmark within the larger terrain of what critics have constructed as "American" literature, and as such, a sign that readers may choose to find alternative. Thus we conclude the chapter by exploring how empathic narrative distances regionalism from an uncritical adoption of realist representation.

Narrative Effects

Rose Terry Cooke's "Dely's Cow" provides a useful context for our discussion of regionalism's poetics. In this story, one of the earliest texts of regionalism,[3] Cooke constructs empathic response as the subject and intent of her narration as one character describes to another the effect upon him of a certain experience that opened his heart and changed his mind, and moreover made him an agent of change for others. The multiple layers of this story about change identify the effect Cooke intends her narrative to have on the reader; we not only witness the process of conversion, we also hear it discussed as such by the person converted and thus made consciously available as a model. Moreover, the process of conversion presents itself as an interaction among men, one man creating the context for the conversion of another who in turn converts a third. Finally, this conversion opens up a space for feeling within the very citadel of masculine Yankeedom, affecting even the shrewd trader who under ordinary circumstances never misses a good deal even if it involves swindling a woman.

"Dely's Cow" tells the story of the events that lead Dely to form an unusually powerful attachment to her cow, Biddy. When her father dies and her mother remarries, Dely is thrust abruptly from her position as contented and valued daughter into that of penniless dependent. Her new stepfather is determined that she marry his son by a former marriage and subjects her to such harassment on the subject that "the poor girl had scarce a half hour to herself" (*"How Celia Changed Her Mind"* 182). Eloping with a young farmer whom she has come to love for his sympathy for her after her father's death, Dely leaves her mother behind. Her husband's ensuing enlistment in the war, the birth of a child, and the death of her mother-in-law leave Dely without companionship except for the cow Biddy. When her stepfather dies and her mother begs her to return to town to take care of her and the family's bakery business, Dely realizes she must sell the cow that has served as her soul mate through the long winter of her husband's absence. Worried about the fate of Biddy in hands other than hers, Dely asks Orrin Nye to find a purchaser for this cow. As the story unfolds we come to assume that Orrin Nye speaks of the matter to Aaron Stow because he "knew his man" as well as Stow later knows his.

Stow sets out in weather that "had settled down dreadful cold," and though he describes himself as "'naturally hardy,'" he declares, "'I didn't feel as though I could ha' gone ef I hadn't been sure of a good bargain'" (192). Like her predecessor Stowe (perhaps the echo here is intentional), Cooke analogizes the harshness of New England topography and climate to the hardness of Yankee character, and, like Stowe, she indicates that this hardness can become a trap sprung on the very man who sets it. To escape the consequences of his "nature" requires a "miraculous" intervention, here figured in the trope of death and rebirth. When he arrives at Dely's farm, Stow is unaware that he is "'nigh on to dead with clear cold,'" but when she invites him in "'to hev a cheer by the fire, fust I knew I didn't know nothin'" (192). The knowledge of knowing nothing prepares and enables him to be revived into a different state and as Dely rubs his hands and face with camphire and gives him hot tea, he finds himself "'warmed through an' through afore long, an' we stepped out into the shed to look at the cow'" (192). Here he finds himself warmed through in a far more significant way, for Dely's affection for Biddy and Biddy's affection for Dely and the tears in Dely's eyes as she thinks about the future of her cow bring him to the point of tears as well. Aaron buys Biddy and takes her directly to Squire Hollis, a man noted for his pride in and kindness to his livestock but also for his particularity about what kind of cows he buys. Although Aaron describes himself as feeling "'kinder meechin' . . . to be so soft about it as I be'" (191), he acts like one proud of his softness and convinced of its power, for he relies on softness to bring Squire Hollis to the point of purchase: "Aaron Stow knew his man. Squire Hollis pulled out his pocketbook, and paid seventy-five dollars on the spot for a native cow called Biddy" (194).

Several features of the narrative stance in "Dely's Cow" make it convincing even to a reader who resists the language of feeling. Aware perhaps of the preposterousness of the story she is about to tell, Cooke begins her narrative as a mystery to be solved—what has led to the presence of "a red cow, of no particular beauty or breed," in the farmyard of Squire Hollis, a connoisseur of rare breeds and specific beauties. Yet clearly this is no ordinary cow, for she comes when called, follows Pat, the farmhand, around the yard, and eats out of his hand. Duly astonished, as was intended, since "Pat had only displayed her accomplishments to astonish me" (182), the narrator seeks out the solution to the double mystery of the presence of an ordinary cow among the Squire's exotics and of the extraordinary character of this ordinary cow. To encourage a hearing for the solution to this mystery, Cooke creates an elaborate narrative structure that involves a narrative within a narrative within a narrative. Told primarily in the first person by the narrator, a close acquaintance of Squire Hollis, at a certain point "Dely's Cow" becomes Squire Hollis's story and he in turn allows it to become Aaron Stow's story. By the time we get to this point, we are prepared for the possibility of Stow's story because we have already been engaged by the miracle of Dely's relationship with Biddy. Aware that such affection "would seem utter nonsense to half, perhaps three-quarters, of the people in this unsentimental world" (189), Cooke nevertheless recognizes that the story of Dely's relation to Biddy is less preposterous than the story of Aaron Stow's response to it, given conventional assumptions about women and their capacity for feeling. Thus if she can disarm readers' resistance through a woman's narrative of a woman's feelings (we can assume the primary narrator to be a version of "Cooke"), she has prepared them to hear "the drover's account of the matter, which," as the narrator tells us, "will be better in his words than in mine" (191).

If we look more closely at the passage where this handing over of narration occurs, we realize that we cannot determine whether the "his" refers to Squire Hollis or to Aaron Stow: "Grandfather Hollis, who bought Biddy, and in whose farmyard I made her acquaintance, gave me the drover's account of the matter, which will be better in his words than mine" (191). Yet this subtle indeterminacy seems part of Cooke's strategy as it indicates how thoroughly Squire Hollis has entered into the drover's perceptions and feelings and thus how effective Stow's narrative has been. However we understand the origin of the words we read, we recognize the importance for Cooke of casting Stow's account as a first-person narrative, for by this cast she gives the narrative the authenticity she needs in order for it to be effective for readers. Described by the narrator as a man "not used to narration" (192), Stow cannot be accused, as Cooke herself might be, of embellishing facts or making things up, strategies employed by those more "used to narration" to produce a good story. More significant still, when Aaron Stow lays claim to a story of sentiment readers are more likely to accept the feeling as authentic. While Cooke's desire for the authenticity readers accord a reliable first-person narrator would suggest that she allow her narrator to get the story directly from Stow himself, we can see how her strategy works to create additional credibility for Stow's account even though it leads to indeterminacy and requires a sleight of hand to produce the illusion of first-person narration. As a man himself not likely to be swayed by feeling, Squire Hollis cannot be accused of misreporting Stow's account, or of embellishing Stow's response in order to make a point; indeed we can imagine that Squire Hollis would offer maximum resistance to being affected by Stow's narrative since such effect will hit both his pocketbook and his pride. If Stow's narrative can sway Squire Hollis, then it can presumably sway readers as well. Compelled to the unusual act of narration by the force of empathic feeling, Stow models for readers not only that and how change can occur, but the importance and pleasure of making one's change of heart public knowledge, for the multiple narrators indicate the wide circulation of his story. Empathic feeling can make someone not "used to narration" significantly articulate.

Cooke also seeks to overcome readers' resistance to the language of feeling and to the softness of a narrative of Yankee "conversion" by associating her story with the sentiment of abolition. In a series of events that recalls the storyline of abolitionist narratives—and Cooke did sell the story to the *Atlantic Monthly* during the war and in the wake of emancipation (it appeared in the June 1865 issue)—Dely's situation, like that of a slave after the death of a benevolent owner, is totally altered by the death of her father and she is subjected to the ill-will of her new "owner" and to sexual harassment from his son. When she finds she must give up Biddy, she addresses Aaron Stow in language equally charged with references to slavery: "'You won't sell her to a hard master, will you?'" (193). In the narrator's characterization of Dely as one of two sorts of people in the world, "those who love animals, and those who do not" (187), she places Dely implicitly within the abolitionist binary. "If sick or oppressed, or borne down with dreadful sympathies for a groaning nation in mortal struggle," she adds, "I should go for aid, for pity, or the relief of kindred feeling, to those I had seen touched with quick tenderness for the lower creation" (187). The narrator alludes to the Southern overseer in her description of "men or women who despise animals, and treat them as mere beasts and brutes" (187), but claims that Dely is that other "sort" of person, who has learned "God's own lesson of caring for the fallen sparrow," and reports that "the calf and the cat agreed with me" (187). Thus, to a certain extent, when Dely learns of her stepfather's death and agrees to return home to take care of her mother and the family business, Aaron Stow's conversion from shrewd trader to a man who feels a "soft" responsibility to find a good home for Dely's cow reflects the Northern abolitionist's feeling in response to slavery. Indeed, politics provides a rationale for Stow: "'an' then she let me know't George was in the army; an' thinks I, I guess I'll help the gov'ment along some: I can't fight, 'cause I'm subject to rheumatiz in my back, but I can look out for them that can: so, take the hull on't, long an' broad, why, I up an' gin her seventy-five dollars for that cow'" (193). Moreover, linking Stow's conversion to the readers' own likelihood of "dreadful sympathies for a groaning nation," Cooke gains an opening for her preposterous story, providing readers with a rationale for their own response. Hollis buys the cow but "irascibly." Yet at the same time, Cooke's story implicitly proposes the more radical possibility that the sentiment of abolition might open the hearts of the nation to include empathy for figures like Dely and Biddy, making "softness" a national norm.

Aaron Stow's description of his willingness to buy Dely's cow as a moment in which "'natur' was too much for me this time'" (193) serves, however, as a reminder that empathy is not a typical response and, when it occurs, it goes against the grain of dominant cultural discourses and reading practices. This momentary, perhaps even involuntary, movement of the heart appears in other regionalist fictions as well. In Stowe's *The Pearl of Orr's Island* (1862), a text with significant regionalist elements that served as the inspiration for Jewett's later work, the heroine, Mara, observes the preparations of her "brother" for his first fishing voyage to the Banks, a voyage that will serve as well as his initiation into an adult life from which she is excluded. As Moses struts about exclaiming on the glorious adventures he is sure to have, Mara acknowledges that she wishes she were going too. But, says Moses, "'you're a girl—and what can girls do at sea? you never like to catch fish—it always makes you cry to see 'em flop'" (*Pearl* 136). Without pausing to think how her response confirms his analysis of her worthlessness, Mara replies "'Poor fish'" (136). A similar moment occurs in King's "Pupasse" in which Madame Joubert, for reasons no one can understand, keeps her word with a girl who cannot advance in school but cannot bear to leave it, and, defying both her own superior and conventionality, becomes the girl's tutor so that she can eventually return to school. King's narrator speculates that for Madame Joubert "*It must* have been an inspiration of the moment, or a movement, a *tressaillement* of the heart" (*AWR* 406). Another such moment occurs in Murfree's "The 'Harnt' That Walks Chilhowee" when old Simon Burney makes a sudden decision to help Reuben Crabb stand his trial and then takes him home to live with him "with no possibility of a recompense" (*AWR* 303) because the "harnt" is bad-tempered and useless and his community thinks Burney a fool. In these brief instances we can observe the degree to which regionalist writers recognize that their poetics stand in opposition to dominant cultural discourses and challenge readers to occupy difficult positions that may create discomfort for them.

Resistance

King's "'One of Us'" reflects regionalism's awareness of the potential reluctance of readers to engage the poetics of empathic narration; indeed her narrator's thoughts wander as another woman tries to tell her a story, a story the reader never hears because the narrator has resisted listening to it. King's narrator models a kind of readerly distance, a reluctance to engage with a person who never succeeded at even the role of "sham attendant on sham sensations," a failed former singer of minor operatic roles, a *dugazon manquée* (*AWR* 391). The narrator does not listen in part because, "looking at her," she imagines the *dugazon* at the back of the stage, "there to pose in abject patience and awkwardness" while soprano, tenor, and baritone enact the real drama of the opera, the love triangle, the "'amour extrême'" (391). She does not expect the *dugazon* to have an interesting story to tell because she has not been part of the "real drama." It is this lack of drama, this failure to find the novelistic action of the love triangle, that may also lead readers to resist regionalist texts.

Narrating the story after the event, the narrator focuses on her own distractedness. She writes, "She was talking to me all the time, apologizing for the intrusion, explaining her mission, which involved a short story of her life, as women's intrusions and missions usually do. But my thoughts, also as usual, distracted me from listening, as so often they have distracted me from following what was perhaps more profitable" (391). Those thoughts construct the speaker as so insignificant that the opera troupe may have left town without remembering her; as a "heap of stiff, wire-strung bones . . . desiccating away in its last costume" (392); and as a figure that "had not that for display which the world has conventioned to call charms" (393). Yet as she catches a glimpse of the face "careworn, almost to desuetude" (392), King's narrator makes the same move as does Madame Joubert in "Pupasse." She experiences that "inspiration of the moment, or a movement, a *tressaillement* of the heart," and she begins to see the *dugazon* not as a singer who has failed but as a woman with another dream, "a woman dreaming of children," a woman longing to take care of the children without mothers and to mother them so that they would "'not know but what their mother was there!'" (393). In the narrator's movement toward the singer, she experiences a moment of regret on account of her own self-absorption: "Her life, her rearing, how interesting they must have been! What a pity I had not listened more attentively!" (394). But she helps create for the woman a "rôle" in an orphan asylum, one of the "poorest and neediest." "'One of Us'" is as much about the narrator's ability to move toward the woman at her door, to enter into an empathic relation with one "anybody would have recognized" as insignificant, as it is about the *dugazon* herself. It is about the way the narrator overcomes her resistance to listening to a woman the world has consigned to "dimness, dustiness, unsteadiness, and uselessness" (392).

"A New England Nun" engages the resistance of the reader in a still more complex and risky manner for Freeman characterizes Louisa in such a way as to elicit the very response she seeks to challenge and change. Presenting Louisa Ellis as domestic and feminine, a woman who likes to sew a seam or distill an essence for the mere pleasure of it, Freeman plays into stereotypes that may produce in the reader the unempathic response that Louisa is just another fussy old maid who needs to be liberated, like her dog, by a good man who will do things the right way. In "A New England Nun" Louisa is given the chance to move from her "pose in abject patience," to recall King's narrator's description of the *dugazon,* and to rejoin the world of love, even the drama of the love triangle, for Joe Dagget, despite his intention to honor his fourteen-year engagement with Louisa Ellis, has fallen in love upon his return with Lily Dyer, "good and handsome and smart" (*AWR* 363). Yet Freeman does not allow the reader the security of a love story. Instead, she asks the reader to imagine a different response to Louisa Ellis, one that recognizes the validity of her remaining as "queen" of her own "domain." Louisa remains single, but she has not been "disappointed in love," as conventional wisdom would explain her circumstances; and while outside her house "the air was filled with the sounds of the busy harvest of men and birds and bees," inside Louisa herself is "uncloistered." By eliciting the dominant perspective yet demonstrating that there remains for Louisa Ellis pleasure and desire unexplained by and not confined in marriage to Joe Dagget, the narrative invites readers to overcome their resistance to alternatives to conventional reading. Readers who do so may find themselves caught up in Louisa's choice, converted by the character's own "inclinations."

Freeman's empathic understanding of the position of the reader conditioned by dominant ideological and interpretive response is designed to move the reader to the position we have earlier described as looking from the inside out rather than from the outside in. As we observed in chapter 2, this position is also that of the regionalist narrator as Cary equates the consciousness of her narrator, her "interior," with "the interior of my native state," the region. Near the beginning of "At the 'Cadian Ball" Chopin's narrator writes, "That was the year Alcée Laballière put nine hundred acres in rice" (*AWR* 412), as if she were talking with friends intimately acquainted with place and person and event. King entitles her story "'One of Us,'" thereby postulating community among character, narrator, listeners, and readers. Moreover, in many regionalist texts no clear distinction exists between narrator and character. For example, Sui Sin Far's stories of Mrs. Spring Fragrance would seem to be part of her own character's "immortal book," and the narrator of King's "The Old Lady's Restoration" (both are included in *AWR*) is so close to the old lady herself that she can report what the old lady thinks and says even though she does not know her personally. In "The Star in the Valley," Murfree's narrator distances herself from the figure of Reginald Chevis, an upper-class man on a hunting vacation in the Tennessee woods who from his mountain camp sees a light in the valley and develops an elaborate fantasy about the girl he associates with it. Although in some ways Murfree herself does not evade the script she assigns to Chevis, in this story she dramatizes the crucial possibility that the "star" in the valley might look back at the gazer and might have a different view of things; she exposes the limitations of the perspective of local color and insists on the need to locate a different position from which to look at someone like Celia Shaw, one that does not stand outside and above and one that recognizes its own limitations. Indeed, in "The Star in the Valley," as in Chopin's "A Gentleman of Bayou Têche" and Dunbar-Nelson's "M'sieu Fortier's Violin" (all included in *AWR*), we can see how regionalist fiction engages in the work of theory, for in explicitly disparaging the local-color impulse regionalist writers also explicitly differentiate between their own work and the writing literary history has categorized as local color.

Narrative Stance

Regionalist narrators use their location inside the region to advocate for an empathic stance toward their subjects. In the preface to the first volume of *Clovernook* sketches, Cary presents herself as an advocate for those who live in her region of the country, seeking to gain for them something more than "the peculiar praise they are accustomed to receive in the resolutions of political conventions" (*AWR* 61). In "The Student," first published serially in the *National Era* and reprinted in the first volume of *Clovernook,* Cary's narrator, in reflecting on the fate of one whom she knew as they were both growing up, comments, "when I think of him . . . , I incline to his own soft interpretation, and almost believe he was ill-starred" (*Clovernook* 201). This insistence on a "soft" interpretation gains further significance if we connect it to a phrase from another story in the same volume of sketches. "Orphaned as we are," Cary writes in "The Sisters," "we have need to be kind to each other—ready, with loving and helping hands and encouraging words, for the darkness and silence are hard by where no sweet care can do us any good" (*Clovernook Sketches* 64; *Clovernook* 299). The "sweet care" of "soft interpretation" represents the empathic stance that characterizes the regionalist narrator. We find another resonant phrase in Freeman's "A Village Singer" when Candace Whitcomb, on her death bed, gives up her antagonism and reconciles with the woman who has replaced her as lead singer in the church choir, observing as she does, however, that "'you flatted a little on—soul'" (*AWR* 344). As one character comes, however belatedly, to empathize with another, yet leaves her with the reminder that she herself has not been sufficiently empathic, Freeman stresses the poetics of empathic narration and identifies regionalism as a mode of writing that seeks to avoid flatting, even a little, on soul.

Although Cooke does not position her narrator as an insider in the same way Cary does, like Cary she uses her narrative stance to provide an empathic rendering of the situations of her characters and to become an outspoken advocate for her characters. In "Freedom Wheeler's Controversy with Providence," a story Wharton must have missed, Cooke further sets her advocacy in the context of other writers' romanticization of those very lives: "Yet this is the life that was once the doom of all New England farmers' wives; the life that sent them to early graves, to mad-houses, to suicide; the life that is so beautiful in the poet's numbers, so terrible in its stony, bloomless oppressive reality" (*AWR* 101). In such passages and stories, Cooke identifies regionalist fiction as advocacy writing, designed to give voice to those who may not be able to speak for themselves and to take a position toward them far different from that which their culture afforded during their lifetime as well as from that which other contemporary texts take toward them. Once again, we can observe the self-consciousness with which regionalist writers approach their fiction and the ways in which they theorize in the process of writing that fiction.

Although regionalist narrators write as if from the inside, they also situate themselves as persons conversant with both the region and what Cary calls the "world" and as capable of negotiating relations between the two. As a result regionalist narrators often position themselves as interpreters or translators. Most often this translation takes place between the subject of the story and the imagined reader but on occasion regionalist narrators will engage in translation within the story itself, providing a model for readers whose capacity for empathy may be blocked by differences that seem threatening or that challenge their identity. Such, for example, is the case with Sui Sin Far's Mrs. Spring Fragrance. When Mrs. Spring Fragrance decides to write "an immortal book" on "these mysterious, inscrutable, incomprehensible Americans" (*AWR* 519), she determines that the "inferior woman" will be her first subject, for she is genuinely puzzled as to why her neighbor, Mrs. Carman, disapproves of the woman her son wishes to marry and places her into this category. Approaching her subject indirectly, Mrs. Spring Fragrance seeks out the views of the superior woman concerning the inferior woman and happens to overhear an impassioned defense of the latter by the former. Making sure to check what she has written down for its accuracy, she then takes the words of the superior woman to her friend Mrs. Carman, finding a way to translate the situation of the "inferior woman" into terms that make her intelligible and nonthreatening so that Mrs. Carman can accept "the inferior woman" as a daughter-in-law. In the process, she succeeds in changing Mrs. Carman's mind.

In her preface to the 1893 edition of *Deephaven,* Sarah Orne Jewett provides a classic statement of the regionalist writer's understanding of herself as an interpreter who provides the "sweet care" of "soft interpretation" when she claims that her motive in writing was "a dark fear that townspeople and country people would never understand one another, or learn to profit by their new relationship" (*Deephaven* 32). If we understand this "new relationship" as historical and material, emerging (as so many critics have now articulated) with the growth of tourism at the end of the nineteenth century, then the "translator" becomes the recorder of encounter and regionalism becomes situated in a "contact zone," to invoke Mary Louise Pratt's metaphor. Pratt identifies "contact zones" as "social spaces where disparate cultures meet, clash, and grapple with each other, often in highly asymmetrical relations of domination and subordination—like colonialism, slavery, or their aftermaths as they are lived out across the globe today" (4). In the United States, the region of Appalachia has been such a "contact zone," particularly upon the arrival of the mining companies in the late nineteenth century, and from this region's earliest sustained representation in Murfree's fiction, the "contact zone" has involved what Pratt terms "copresence, interaction, interlocking understandings and practices, often within radically asymmetrical relations of power" (4). In many of her short narratives, as well as in her novel *In the "Stranger People's" Country* (1891), Murfree's narrator "encounters" the preconceptions outsiders have toward her Appalachian mountaineers and self-critically positions herself as sympathetic even though she remains an outsider. Aware that persons outside of Appalachia view the mountain people as strange, Murfree takes up the "stranger people's" standpoint as her own and explores her own relationship, and the relationship of her reader, to that standpoint. In addition, we can read Murfree's fiction as her way of protecting the mountaineers' autonomy as she advocates keeping cultural distinctions alive through linguistic variation, protects the secrets of native people's antiquities, and argues against the intrusion of outsiders into the lives of her characters.

The need for the narrator to become a translator, yet the impossibility of doing so, forms the heart of Austin's regionalist fiction as well as her writing about Indians. Austin assumes that her material—the land, the fashion of a life lived in the land, the people born there or drawn to it—is foreign to her readers. Indeed, the desert country of Austin's sketches, evoked in her titles *The Land of Little Rain* and *Lost Borders,* constructs the land itself as a "contact zone." Here empathy cannot proceed along lines of simple identification, for the region is not simply foreign to most readers; it is threatening. The desert represents a landscape that in the eyes of the "world" conjures up images of barrenness and death, of the skeletons of those who have lost their way and died of thirst in Death Valley, and of Indians presumed by the dominant discourse to be savage and primitive. To bring her readers close to the heart of these things requires unique narrative strategies and Austin often tells her readers the story of why she cannot tell a story, as in "The Woman at the Eighteen-Mile" or "The Basket Maker." More than any other regionalist writer, Austin constructs her own narrative role as that of bringing readers face to face with what cannot be translated, with that "I don't know" that Arthur Ciaramicoli proposes as "one of empathy's most powerful statements" (38). He writes, "In the effort to understand, empathy asks questions and refuses quick answers. . . . From that admission of not having all the answers, empathy starts searching for ways to expand the picture in order to develop a broader understanding" (38). Similarly, Austin suggests that both characters and readers need to learn to approach the desert in a way that will expand understanding. In Austin, then, we might say that regionalism comes up against the limits of its own poetics of empathic narration for empathy seems beside the point in light of the borderers' struggles for physical survival in the desert. However, she does suggest that both characters and readers need to learn to read the land, to "listen" to the land, to approach the desert in a way that will allow mutuality of contact. She suggests that in order to do so, outsiders to the region must learn to shift the center of their perception away from themselves and the dominant perspective. Listening and right approach make shifting the center possible.

Approach

Regionalist fiction assumes that the region contains something of value, something worth readers' attention, and its poetics proposes a way to approach the region so that its value can be made intelligible and available to those inside and outside the region. Brodhead, whose work we will take up in more detail in chapter 7, characterizes Jewett and other regionalist writers as "carrying the good of the place *out* of the place" (*Cultures of Letters* 148). He writes of *The Country of the Pointed Firs* that "through this one-sided (and quite wishful) process of exchange, a life initially not the narrator's becomes her sympathetic possession; and when she has acquired enough of this life, it becomes strangely abstractable, generalizable, and portable" (148). Zagarell also reads the "good of the place" as "goods," arguing that for Jewett, the value of the region becomes located within a capitalist economy as its "goods" are granted "the status of souvenirs whose value paradoxically inheres in both their supposed representation of the essence of a place or culture and their availability for outsiders' purchase" ("Troubling Regionalism" 639). Referring to the "two great bunches of Deephaven cat-o'-nine-tails" (*Deephaven* 165) that the protagonists of Jewett's *Deephaven* take back with them to the city and that Jewett sketched for the cover of the first edition of the book (1877), Zagarell writes, "The cat-o'-nine-tails thus manifest an attitude characteristic of postbellum regionalism: although regional cultures were local and particular, cosmopolitans could easily possess their essence in detachable mementos—and in regionalist literature" (639).

Although she complicates her reading of *Deephaven* in interesting ways, suggesting that, for Jewett, regionalism "was at times self-divided" and describing Jewett as a "writer of multiple regionalisms" (641, 659), Zagarell, like Brodhead, would place regionalist writers in the category of those local-color "vandals" whose approach Dunbar-Nelson in "M'sieu Fortier's Violin" explicitly distinguishes from her own. We would propose that regionalist writers seek to share the good of the place and that, far from viewing this as a negative or damaging activity to either region or "world," they understand it as central to cultural transformation. To share the good of a place does not necessarily destroy the good of the place. Because Kate and Helen take "two great bunches of Deephaven cat-o'-nine-tails" back to the city does not mean that cat-o'-nine-tails cease to grow in Deephaven, nor does it necessarily mean that they have reduced Deephaven to a detachable memento. Readings such as Brodhead's and Zagarell's ignore the significance of the fact that Kate and Helen have actually lived in Deephaven in a house Kate's mother has inherited from her grandfather's sister, a house Kate has spent some time in as a child, and that Helen has often heard Kate's stories about her great-aunt and Deephaven.

In a certain sense, then, Kate *is* from Deephaven, a point underscored by the fact that the two servants she takes with her to Deephaven are "overjoyed for they come from that part of the country" (*Deephaven* 39). Moreover, Jewett complicates the question of what it means to come from a place in the first few pages of her text. Meeting Mrs. Kew on the stagecoach to Deephaven, Kate exclaims, "'Then you live in Deephaven, too?'" But though she has lived "'here the better part of my life,'" Mrs. Kew observes that "'I was raised up among the hills of Vermont, and I shall always be a real up-country woman if I live here a hundred years'" (41). Obviously one can feel "from" a place where one does not currently live, just as one can live in a place one does not feel "from." Deephaven itself may contain persons other than Mrs. Kew who, though they have lived there many years, feel less "from" it than does Kate, whose memories of the Deephaven Light, now kept by Mr. Kew, are powerful and deep. In Deephaven, the relationship between identity and place is hardly simple and there are no easy formulas for determining who is native and who is not. Indeed, one's capacity for identification seems closely connected to one's perception of the "good of the place" and it is precisely this capacity for connecting with the good of a place that makes location possible in a culture of mobility. When Kate and Helen take those "two great bunches of Deephaven cat-o'-nine-tails" back with them to the city, they do so to keep alive their sense of the good of the place which they are significantly "from" even though they are no longer living there.

Regionalism constructs an approach to place that makes available the good of a place for readers who may come to feel "from" it and that enhances rather than destroys the value of the region. Such an approach is designed to bring the "world" to the region in steps so gradual, careful, and respectful that readers will be able to make the transition from "world" to region and as a result will be able to see the "world" regionally. In the opening pages of *Among the Isles of Shoals,* Thaxter identifies the importance of approach as a central concept for regionalist fiction. In the passage we cited at the end of chapter 1 as creating a metaphor for our own form in *Writing out of Place,* Thaxter writes: "Sailing out from Portsmouth Harbor with a fair wind from the northwest, the Isles of Shoals lie straight before you, nine miles away,—ill-defined and cloudy shapes, faintly discernible in the distance. . . . As you approach they separate, and show each its own peculiar characteristics" (*AWR* 157). For Thaxter, sailing toward the islands illustrates the slow and careful approach to the regionalist subject that will allow the observer to see in a different way; it models a gradual transition from one way of being and seeing to another and sets in motion a process that continues once one has arrived. Thaxter observes that those who have lived on the islands develop an ability to discern differences utterly unimaginable to one who lives in what is called the world: "Each island, every isolated rock, has its own peculiar rote, and ears made delicate by listening, in great and frequent peril, can distinguish the bearings of each in a dense fog" (162). The phrase "ears made delicate by listening" theorizes approach as an aspect of narrative strategy, for it suggests both the kind of approach such fiction takes toward its subjects and invites the reader to take as well, and the value of such an approach, for "ears made delicate by listening" are the best resource in great and frequent peril, whether that be physical, emotional, intellectual, or spiritual. "Ears made delicate by listening" may also hear things that others miss. Zitkala-Ša writes about the "melancholy of those black days" and the "sad memories" when she was first taken away from her mother's wigwam and the reservation in Yankton, South Dakota. Hearing in herself the "moaning wind" of "her Indian nature," she writes that "however tempestuous this is within me, it comes out as the low voice of a curiously colored seashell, which is only for those ears that are bent with compassion to hear it" (*AWR* 555).

In the work of Jewett we also find attention to the question of approach. In "A White Heron," Sylvia learns the secret of the bird through her willingness to enter the bird's world, to get up before sunrise, make "the dangerous pass" from oak tree to pine tree (*AWR* 203), and climb to the very top from which she can see not only sunrise and sea but where the white heron has its nest. From her careful approach, she learns the secret of the bird, but the hunter does not learn hers, for with his whistle and his gun he enters the region in a way that shows no understanding of what it might mean to listen. Indeed, his whistle, "determined, and somewhat aggressive" (199), sets the tone for his approach; it scares away what might otherwise be available for him to notice and signals his arrival as the imposition of his perspective on the territory he is entering. Invested in the performance of self, he alters the environment with the supreme self-confidence of those who make a lot of noise, assured that they have no need for ears made delicate by listening. Sylvia's final silence, so troubling in some ways, marks at least the problematics of approach, the hunter's failure to listen her into speech, and her own commitment to listening ("and Sylvia cannot speak; she cannot tell the heron's secret and give its life away" [205]).

In "The Queen's Twin," Jewett also emphasizes the issue of approach. By worldly standards Abby Martin is a pathetic old lady whose extreme poverty, isolation, and hardship have produced the delusion that she is twin to Queen Victoria and shares a secret bond with her, one recognized by the queen as well. Yet when approached gradually and with respect, when taken on her own terms and allowed to shape her own story, Abby Martin presents a striking example of a woman who has managed to create for herself a sense of connection, community, and significance, to find meaning in her life by developing an interest that allows her to retain a sense of her own dignity. In order to realize this, however, one has to hear her story and Abby is not about to tell her story to just anyone. "'I do hope Mis' Martin'll ask you into her best room where she keeps all the Queen's pictures. . . . '[T]aint everybody she deems worthy to visit 'em, I can tell you!'" says Mrs. Todd as she and the narrator approach Abby's house (*AWR* 227). Abby herself tests the narrator, "looking straight in my eyes to see if I showed any genuine interest," and when satisfied that the interest is there, "she . . . smiled as she had not smiled before" and "Mrs. Todd gave a satisfied nod and glance, as if to say that things were going on as well as possible in this anxious moment" (229). When the visit is completed and the narrator has successfully listened Abby into speech, she has not only heard a story very few are privileged to hear; she has come to understand that in approaching Abby as she has, she has also managed to find meaning, community, and dignity for herself—she has come to share something of Mrs. Todd's "great soul" (199).

In "The Basket Maker," Austin foregrounds the issue of approach as she also encounters someone from whom she recognizes she has much to learn but who will not share her knowledge with just anyone and certainly not with someone who does not understand the significance of approach. The difficulty of figuring out the right approach is aggravated in this instance by the far greater cultural differences separating Austin from Seyavi, the Paiute basket maker, than those between Abby Martin and Jewett's narrator, and Austin understands how strange and even indecent she may appear to Seyavi in her hunger for the woman's knowledge: "But it was not often she would say so much, never understanding the keen hunger I had for bits of lore and the 'fool talk' of her people" (*AWR* 575). In recognizing, just as does Murfree in "The Star in the Valley," that Seyavi looks back at her just as she looks at Seyavi and that each has a perspective on the other ("'What good will your dead get, Seyavi, of the baskets you burn?' said I, coveting them for my own collection. Thus Seyavi, 'As much good as yours of the flowers you strew,'" [575]), Austin signals her narrator's possession of that empathy and respect needed to ensure the right approach, particularly with women who have seen the "influx of overlording whites" and become the "game of the conquerors" (573). Like King's balcony sitters, who recognize that if you want to hear a story you have to sit still and listen, Austin records her own willingness to sit by the hour in the afternoon sun with the old women of the campoodie, for "then, if they have your speech or you theirs, and have an hour to spare, there are things to be learned of life not set down in any books" (576). Austin gently reminds her own reader that, since the chance of the Paiutes having the reader's language is slim, it will be part of the respectful reader's approach to learn another language as well. But whether "they have your speech or you theirs," "suppose you find Seyavi retired into the privacy of her blanket, you will get nothing for that day" (577). Although Austin is honest enough to recognize in herself a bit of the gold digger or pocket hunter, "coveting" Seyavi's baskets "for my own collection," in leaving us with this image of Seyavi wrapped in the privacy of her blanket she acknowledges both the regional subject who does not want to be approached and also the approach that is no approach at all as sometimes best.

If one has the right approach, the outcome of contact is unpredictable, for letting go of preconceptions in order to achieve "ears made delicate by listening" means that what they will hear is out of their control. If the stance of the regionalist narrator toward her material is one of empathy, and if that stance imputes value to the regional subject and material, then it becomes possible for regionalist fiction to alter the reader's way of seeing the world, to bring the reader to see as Clovernook sees and not as "the world" sees. The right approach is central to this process because it can listen the regional subject into speech and thus make an alternative perspective available. But right approach is only the first step in a more complicated narrative strategy, one that involves shifting the center of perception. Sui Sin Far expresses the self-consciousness at the heart of regionalist fiction's transformative designs. As Mrs. Spring Fragrance puts it, "'Yesterday, O Great Man, I was a caterpillar'" (*AWR* 516).

Shifting the Center

When Thaxter claims that ears made delicate by listening can distinguish one rock from another in the North Atlantic coastal ocean by the sound the waves make when they hit the rock's surface, she registers the extraordinary change in perception produced by feeling, seeing, and thinking from the region, for to those who live in what is called the world, to register the existence of the Isles of Shoals at all might seem a sufficient sign of attention and to register such distinctions as Thaxter makes would be inconceivable.[4] When Cary makes us care about an incident that, if articulated outside the framework of regionalism, would seem utterly trivial and insignificant—for example, a young woman's inability to go to a party because she has ripped her only good apron on a vinegar barrel ("About the Tompkinses," included in *Clovernook Sketches*)—she registers an equally significant shift in perspective. By adopting an approach that begins with empathy and respect, regionalist fiction creates the conditions for what Pratt terms "autoethnography." Pratt describes autoethnography as narrative that emerges from indigenous or regional subjects and that is in dialogue with readers' preconceptions about those subjects. As Pratt writes, "if ethnographic texts are a means by which Europeans represent to themselves their (usually subjugated) others, autoethnographic texts are those the others construct in response to or in dialogue with those metropolitan representations" (7). Regionalist writers create texts that can be read as autoethnographies by writing from the inside out; they create narrators who empathically identify with the regionalist perspective even as they understand how regions are perceived by the "world"; and frequently these narrators create space for characters to tell their own stories. In Pratt's terms, ethnography yields to autoethnography. In this process, which we explore as shifting the center, the narrator accords authority to the regional voice and what that voice has to say becomes a center of value in the text. The precise nature of that value will be the subject of chapter 5, but here we wish to focus on the ways regionalist fiction makes possible a shift in the center of perception that can accompany a character's or reader's empathic response, King's *tressaillement* or moment of feeling that allows one to imagine, however briefly, that there might be a way of seeing things differently than one's own.

Several of the texts we have already discussed in this chapter demonstrate the possibility that the gazed upon might gaze back and offer a view of the region quite different from that which outsiders may bring with them into the region. Murfree's "The Star in the Valley," Austin's "The Basket Maker," and Sui Sin Far's "Mrs. Spring Fragrance" all propose that the "foreign" is a matter of perspective. In other texts, shifting the center of perception entirely reconfigures the reader's sense of foreground and background, turning inside out the possibilities of story inherent in the narrative, rearranging the reader's focus from the gazer to the subject of the gaze and then showing us what that subject sees and feels. We have seen this reconfiguration in King's "'One of Us'" where the narrator acknowledges that she misses much of what the woman in front of her is saying because she cannot get over her astonishment at the fact that this most insignificant of the insignificant, by definition always in the background, is actually in the foreground and speaking. Through her narrator's astonishment, King dramatizes the dislocation that occurs to one's sense of the insignificant when the regional subject begins to speak. When her narrator finally shifts her center of perception from her own preconceptions to the speaker's self-presentation, she discovers a far different story from what she had expected and comes to see quite differently.

Similarly, in Dunbar-Nelson's "Sister Josepha," a young woman on the verge of entering a convent looks up from her rosary on "fête day" "to encounter a pair of youthful brown eyes gazing pityingly upon her" (*AWR* 478). Although most stories would follow the brown eyes in their military uniform as they "marched away with the rest of the rear guard," or would tell the story of the young woman's elopement with the soldier, Dunbar-Nelson detains us with the "little sister," inviting us to imagine the consequences of this gaze: "Perchance, had Sister Josepha been in the world, the eyes would have been an incident. But in this home of self-repression and retrospection, it was a life-story. The eyes had gone their way, doubtless forgetting the little sister they pitied; but the little sister?" (478). When Sister Josepha, who longs at one point in the story "to see as much of the world as she could" (477), and who makes a plan to escape the convent, realizes that an orphan with "no nationality," no family, no friends, and considerable physical beauty would have no way of surviving in the world beyond the implied fate of prostitution, she recognizes "the complete submerging of her hopes of another life" (479). In the closing lines of the story as her opportunity comes to pass outside the convent gate, she pauses at the entrance, "then, with a gulping sob, followed the rest, and vanished behind the heavy door" (480). Sister Josepha, or Camille as she is also called, recognizes that, whether in the "pronounced leers and admiration" that led her to choose the novitiate over adoption by a man who "made her feel creepy" (476), or whether in the way Father Ray lingers over his blessing "when his hands pressed her silky black hair" (476), or whether in the gaze of the "tender, pitying brown eyes" (478), the world is not willing to see her as autonomous and self-creating. "Sister Josepha" represents the "self-repression" of the object of the gaze of the dominant discourse; Camille can find no listener for her autoethnography. By shifting the center of perception from world to region, Dunbar-Nelson enables us to understand the meaning of "Sister Josepha" from inside that location.

Jewett's "The Circus at Denby," a chapter from *Deephaven* included in *AWR*, offers a still more powerful articulation of what we call shifting the center of perception and at the same time reflects the self-consciousness with which the regionalist text accomplishes this shift. Placing this chapter at the precise middle of her text, Jewett emphasizes how central to her work, and by extension to regionalism in general, is the process dramatized within it. In "The Circus at Denby," Kate and Helen, spending the summer in Deephaven in the house Kate's mother has inherited, attend a circus with their friend, Mrs. Kew. At the end of the day, as they leave the big tent, the three women pass the sideshows and while Kate and Helen are reluctant to go in, Mrs. Kew looks so wistfully at the picture of the Kentucky giantess that they accede to her desire, especially when she confesses that "she never heard of such a thing as a woman's weighing six hundred and fifty pounds" (*AWR* 193). Almost immediately Kate and Helen are "ashamed of ourselves for being there" (193) and they move beyond the woman who is sitting in two chairs on a stage to look at the cage of monkeys that forms an added attraction to this particular sideshow. When they turn to see if Mrs. Kew is ready to leave, they are surprised to find their friend engaged in conversation with the giantess, who turns out to be someone Mrs. Kew used to know, a neighbor from the place where she grew up.

In a quiet but revolutionary shift in perspective, the sideshow freak turns out to be "somebody's neighbor" with a story and a perspective of her own.[5] Mrs. Kew's recognition of the woman—"'I thought your face looked natural the moment I set foot inside the door'" (193)—elicits Marilly's story, and as Mrs. Kew listens, the experience of the sideshow changes dramatically; as she tells the giantess, "'you've—altered some since I saw you, and I couldn't place you till I heard you speak'" (193). Initially a space in which people are invited to gaze at someone who cannot look back and to create the category of freak in order to reaffirm their own normalcy, the sideshow in *Deephaven* gets reconfigured as that moment when one can recognize the consequences of the gaze as well as find a way to place the speaking regional voice. Demonstrating that even the regionalist perspective can contain the same hierarchies against which it struggles, Jewett further reminds us that the process of shifting the center must be an ongoing one; in a text and a place that has been regionalized, there exists no perspective free from internalized re-regionalization, no place that guarantees one immunity from becoming a maker of freaks. Indeed, Jewett quickly demonstrates how easy it would be to reinscribe the dominant perspective she seeks to dismantle. In the second half of "The Circus at Denby" she describes another "show" that Kate and Helen attend that summer, an evening lecture on "The Elements of True Manhood" given by a visiting lecturer. Jewett's use of the term "show" to describe both circus and lecture alerts us to the connection between these events. When we see the spatial arrangement of the lecture we are reminded of the sideshow and we begin to wonder which is more strange—a "giantess" who does not speak but simply is there to be looked at and talked about, or a lecturer who goes on and on saying nothing of value to his audience and never imagining that they might have anything to say themselves.

Through the lecture's title Jewett invokes the figure of Ralph Waldo Emerson and the assumptions he represents. The young white man who delivers the lecture clearly shares Emerson's assumption of his own universality, for he assumes that in talking of and effectively to himself he addresses everyone. Yet in the context of Deephaven his lecture could easily be seen as the real freak show, for it was, as the narrator observes, "directed entirely towards young men and there was not a young man there" (196). What kind of person, Jewett implicitly asks, would deliver a lecture on the elements of true manhood to an audience composed entirely of women, children, and old men? What kind of person would fail to see his actual audience and presume those not there to be more important than those who are? Only a freak? Yet Jewett carefully refuses the move of simple reversal, for the object of her critique is not the young man but the culture that has created him. Young white men do not represent the majority of the population in Deephaven or anywhere else, and a culture that provides such a lecture to people so hungry for intellectual stimulation that they will come out on a dismal night and even pay for it must be complicit in assumptions of entitlement. From the perspective of the region and of women, those assumptions appear at minimum out of touch with reality and possibly even malicious in intent. For Jewett the real "freak" is the category itself, and she concludes her chapter with Kate and Helen expressing a certain degree of sympathy for the young man and his dreary lecture and even agreeing to contribute to the cost of attending it.

Revolution

Shifting the center of perception sets up the conditions for seeing differently, as if from the perspective of another. Although social theorists might not associate empathy with revolution, to the extent that empathy creates shifts or "chinks" in the social it becomes potentially disruptive and transgressive. Recognizing the potential power of seeing differently to produce social change gives Candace Whitcomb in Freeman's "A Village Singer" the inner fire of revolution: "'I'd like to know where the Christianity comes in. I'd like to know if it wouldn't be more to the credit of folks in a church to keep an old singer an' an old minister, if they didn't sing an' hold forth quite so smart as they used to, ruther than turn 'em off an' hurt their feelin's'" (*AWR* 338). When Candace's congregation retires her as their soloist without her knowledge and against her will and replaces her with a younger singer, and when she retaliates by playing her own organ on Sunday mornings and singing to drown out the voice of her rival (for she lives in a cottage "close to the south side of the church" [334]), Freeman describes her as "resistant" (337). When the minister pays her a call to ask her not to sing so loudly, she tells him in detail how betrayed and rejected she feels. Freeman describes the minister as uncomprehending; "his eyes were fastened upon a point straight ahead" and he "was incapable of understanding a woman like this, who had lived as quietly as he, and all the time held within herself the elements of revolution. He could not account for such violence, such extremes, except in a loss of reason. . . . Candace Whitcomb had been a quiet woman, so delicately resolute that the quality had been scarcely noticed in her, and her ambition had been unsuspected. Now the resolution and the ambition appeared raging over her whole self" (339). Candace's bid for empathy fails here; it cannot succeed with a man who has trod "with heavy precision his one track for over forty years" (339). However, Freeman shifts the reader's center of perception from the minister to Candace, thus aligning her story and her choice to write regionalism with elements of disruption, resistance, and revolution.

As we discussed in chapter 1, when Foucault defines points of resistance, he makes it clear that these points "are present everywhere in the power network. Hence there is no single locus of great Refusal, no soul of revolt, source of all rebellions, or pure law of the revolutionary" (Foucault 95–96). Points of resistance exist but cannot be easily or exactly located; they become part of the "strictly relational character of power relationships" (95) and are "distributed in irregular fashion" (96). Foucault's analysis describes Candace Whitcomb very well: in her "unsuspected" ambition, her demeanor as a "quiet woman," she manifests points of resistance to the gendered relations of power in her community. When she chooses to use the photograph album given to her as a gift upon her enforced retirement as a "footstool"—"'It's all it's good for, 'cording to my way of thinkin'. An' I ain't been particular to get the dust off my shoes before I used it neither'" (*AWR* 339)—she demonstrates how points of resistance can flare up and intensify in "irregular fashion" as part of the "strictly relational character of power relationships." Freeman writes that the minister "was aghast and bewildered at this outbreak, which was tropical, and more than tropical, for a New England nature has a floodgate, and the power which it releases is an accumulation" (339). Given its "nature," Candace's resistance collapses almost as quickly as it flares up, for her floodgate has not released the "source of all rebellions, or pure law of the revolutionary." Yet in the way the poetics of regionalism produces texts that "detain" the reader in empathic response, even as the narrative voice also sympathizes with the reader's bewilderment, regionalism becomes a mode of resistance to dominant reading practices. It does so in part by refusing to accept as "natural" the minister's response to Candace.

With "no single locus of great Refusal" but rather with points of resistance "distributed in irregular fashion," regionalism becomes in effect a literature of "miracle," the term Chopin uses in "A Little Country Girl" (included in *AWR*) to describe the change of heart that enables Ninette's grandparents to allow her to go to the circus. For who can say why at any given moment a heart will open or a mind change, at what point empathy will elicit social revolution? Although regionalist fiction can model the process and record the phenomenon, it finally cannot explain, no more than Foucault, how it happens, why a Madame Joubert or a Simon Burney acts in a particular manner. King's narrator gropes for explanation—"I think it was her eyes"—but she does not really know why at a certain moment she begins to hear the story the woman before her is trying to tell. We call these moments of inexplicable response "chinks," the word an elderly blind woman uses in Freeman's "A Mistaken Charity" to describe those moments when she has glimpses of light. Although in "A Mistaken Charity" these moments come about as a result of her rebellion against a particular set of power relations (the well-meaning but "mistaken" charity of the woman of benevolence who moves Charlotte Shattuck and her sister Harriét out of their dilapidated home into a "Home" for old ladies) and her truant embrace of those things that give her deepest satisfaction—a dinner collected from her own garden, returning to her own home—she can neither predict them nor control them nor produce them at will, and so they appear as a kind of miracle, a word that may express the subjective recognition on Charlotte's part of the way Foucault's points of resistance are "distributed in irregular fashion." When the two runaways manage to escape both the Home and Mrs. Simonds's "benevolence," the "chinks" in Charlotte's blindness seem signs of the triumph of resistance: "'O Lord, Harriét,' sobbed Charlotte, 'thar is so many chinks that they air all runnin' together!'" (*AWR* 323). Yet of course Freeman is not asking her own readers to see what Charlotte "sees"; the "chink" does not serve as a representational sign but rather indicates the denaturalizing of the old women's powerlessness. If we empathize with the sisters, then we "see" their social and economic powerlessness differently; and then Freeman's story challenges conventional depictions of such old women.

In "A Church Mouse," as we noted in chapter 1, Freeman makes even clearer her own understanding that "chinks" identify those gaps in hegemonic ideological systems that enable persons defined as marginal and insignificant to find ways to move to the foreground and claim their right to live on their own terms. When Hetty Fifield confronts deacon Caleb Gale with her desire to be appointed sexton of the church, Deacon Gale is astonished and appalled, but to every opposition he raises Hetty has an answer that reveals the contradictions in his position. Hetty finds a way to locate herself in the Deacon's ideological gaps: "'There's one thing you ain't thought of.' 'What's that?' 'Where'd you live? All old Sowen got for bein' saxton was twenty dollar a year, an' we couldn't pay a woman so much as that. You wouldn't have enough to pay for your livin' anywheres.' 'Where am I goin' to live whether I'm saxton or not?'" (*AWR* 345). Because Caleb cannot answer the question of where she is going to live and because his "little settlement of narrow-minded, prosperous farmers" would prove unwilling, as Freeman puts it, to "turn an old woman out into the fields and highways to seek for food as they would a Jersey cow" (349), Hetty accomplishes her goal of moving into the very heart of the community and taking up residence in the meetinghouse. As we will discuss further in chapter 8, Freeman expresses Hetty's resistance and triumph in epistemological terms: "When one is hard pressed, one, however simple, gets wisdom as to vantage-points" (349). For persons "hard pressed," the discovery of gaps in dominant ideological systems and the discovery of one's own ability to take advantage of them appear as a kind of miracle. Hetty's utter and complete satisfaction with her new home and with herself for getting it allows her to construct her life in terms of miracle, and she bursts forth in an explosion of celebration, covering the meetinghouse with her woolen art work, keeping it immaculately clean, and tolling the bell with an energy that to some seems like "delirium."

However, despite Hetty's success in finding gaps in an ideology that renders her poor, homeless, and disadvantaged, the villagers never relinquish their own desire to find an occasion that will allow them to close the gaps and reassert their own sense of normalcy. Thus when the showdown finally comes it takes another "miracle" for Hetty to maintain her place. Determined to evict her by force if necessary, the entire village gathers before the meetinghouse. As the deacons put a crowbar to the door Hetty has locked from the inside, she appears at a window to plead her case before the town. Just why Mrs. Gale experiences a change of heart at this moment—"'Of course you can stay in the meetin'-house. . . . I should laugh if you couldn't'" (355)—and just why the rest of the village takes its lead from her is inexplicable. Freeman implies that perhaps Mrs. Gale has found a way to reassert her own point of resistance; when she begins to intervene, "'Don't you let them break that door down, father,'" Freeman writes that Caleb Gale "moved away a little; his wife's voice had been drowned out lately by a masculine clamor" (354). It may matter to Mrs. Gale that her own adolescent daughter is standing watching with one of her friends as her husband proposes using a crowbar to force entrance into the meetinghouse, evoking an image of rape. Still, there is no origin of resistance, merely a "swarm of points of resistance" that "traverses social stratifications and individual unities" (Foucault 96). While we could view the "miracle" of Mrs. Gale's intervention as a consequence of "A Church Mouse" being written to the formula of the Christmas story (the story ends with Hetty, secure in her meetinghouse home, tolling the bells on Christmas morning), this would be misleading for there are "chinks" in other regionalist fictions as well—a figure who seeks an opening, a gap, and a heart capable of opening in response, with the effect of "fracturing unities and effecting regroupings" (96).

"A Church Mouse" emphasizes Hetty's ability to elicit empathic response in Mrs. Gale, thus foregrounding the shifting center of one woman's perception rather than the material desperation of the other. But if we focus on Hetty, we may also read empathy as strategy. Finding herself in the position she occupies precisely because the community in which she lives has denied her the opportunity to make a living, in order to survive she must find "chinks" both in the Deacon's reason and in his wife's emotion and must insert her own narrative just at those points. Similarly, the regionalist narrator who attempts to elicit empathy in an urban reader engages in a strategy for survival just as much as the characters we have invoked in this discussion do. Regionalist writers need readers for their sketches and stories but, like Hetty Fifield, are not willing to compromise their sense of entitlement in order to attract markets; like Cary, they believe that the "farming class" is indeed "entitled" to much more than "that peculiar praise they are accustomed to receive in the resolutions of political conventions" (*AWR* 61) when politicians are trying to earn their votes. Empathy provides the strategy for securing both markets and entitlement, for taking up residence in the meetinghouse of American literature, for asserting that they are "free to say" even if their narratives appear to challenge dominant ideologies of gender, race, class, and region. Regionalism gambles on its ability to interest readers in precisely those perspectives they may initially resist and that may severely dislocate them by offering points of resistance to their accepted narratives of the social. Thus while empathy involves "miracle," it also implies the strategy of a social transaction, and it is this particular feature of empathy that Dunbar-Nelson explores in "The Praline Woman."

In this brief but brilliant sketch (*AWR* 480–81),[6] consisting almost entirely of the talk of the woman selling pralines, Tante Marie finds a way in her interactions with passersby and potential customers to insert her story in the gaps created by their own comments: "'Mais non, what's dat you say? She's daid. Ah, m'sieu, 'tis my little gal what died long year ago. Misère, misère.'" For the praline woman empathy is at once a stance she adopts in relation to others and a strategy to shape the response of others toward her. She inserts empathic response into her dealings with her customers, opening her heart to their joy and pain and enlisting their ears to hear her own story in return. Yet these transactions are also commercial and are connected to the praline woman's economic survival. There are only two sentences in the story that the praline woman herself does not speak. In the first, "The praline woman sits by the side of the Archbishop's quaint little old chapel on Royal Street, and slowly waves her latanier fan over the pink and brown wares," the narrator positions the street vendor to attract business. In the second, "Ding-dong, ding-dong, ding-dong chimes the Cathedral bell across Jackson Square, and the praline woman crosses herself," the narrator identifies her as one who prays. In the context of the praline woman's monologue, we may surmise that she is "praying" for customers, for their spiritual salvation and for their benevolence, and at the same time for her own spiritual salvation as well as for her success in selling her pralines. Her pralines become her "pray-lines" and her "prey-lines," that which she gives and that with which she snares and attracts, her mode of connection and her strategy for survival.

Dunbar-Nelson suggests the connection between the two when, unsuccessful in getting her listener to move from opening her heart to opening her purse, she offers a mild curse: "'You tak' none? No husban' fo' you den!'" Like Freeman's homeless Hetty Fifield, the praline woman occupies a "foothold as propounder" (*AWR* 349) of the basic question of her own survival and of the contradictions inherent in a society in which people pray when the cathedral bell chimes but make no provisions except some "mistaken charity" to sustain the poor or to ensure their opportunities for empowerment. In adopting empathy as a strategy for survival, the praline woman offers points of resistance to the dominant ideologies that render her silent and invisible.

Informing this brief and fragmented story is the central "miracle" of the praline woman's having found after the death of both of her children a homeless little girl to adopt who now makes the pralines for her to sell, keeps house for her, and at night sings "'my heart is yours.'" However, as in Chopin's "A Little Country Girl," "miracle" in "The Praline Woman" appears in a context of devastation as Dunbar-Nelson further complicates the "miracle" of empathy. "The Praline Woman" ends with a big rain: "'Down h'it come! H'it fall in de Meesseesip, an' fill up—up—so, clean to de levee, den we have big crivasse, an' po' Tante Marie float away.'" In this allusion to the biblical flood and the end of the world, we read Tante Marie's tenuous grasp on material survival. Without her adoption of Didele, she would have nothing to sell; without empathy, she would probably be less successful as a street merchant and would certainly not find openings to tell her story; yet even so, both her business and the business of survival remain quite uncertain for her.

Dunbar-Nelson's task in this story is to draw the reader in at the end to such an extent that the praline woman's strategy for survival can begin to change the way the reader views the world of the street vendor and thus the ways in which the praline woman's world and the reader's world are interdependent. That is to say, the reader must not only open her heart but also open her purse. Understanding characters such as Hetty Fifield and the praline woman as entitled to more than survival will require a real shift in ideology, not merely the continued search for gaps or "chinks." Shifting the center of perception becomes at minimum a strategy for survival; but in its most miraculous form, it becomes a bid for change in what large social groups perceive to be the needs and aspirations of the collective. To what are characters like Hetty Fifield and the praline woman ultimately entitled? To the extent that empathy in regionalism underscores the difficulty disenfranchised persons have in ensuring their material survival, shifting the center of perception to such persons discomfits the reader who may believe that his or her own well-being is all that becomes necessary for the social welfare.

The "big crivasse" at the end of this very short story, the crack in the levee that portends the destruction of the praline woman's world, reminds the reader that dependency on public relief, largesse, or benevolence does not constitute genuine well-being, either for the praline woman or for her customers. Dunbar-Nelson, unlike Freeman, does not end her story with the formulaic ringing of Christmas bells, but rather with the portent of the end of the praline woman's world. Thus "The Praline Woman" opens more than a gap into ideology—it opens a "big crivasse." The fragility of Tante Marie's hold on the attention of her listeners is signaled by the vision of her floating away on the flood let loose by a break in the levee, but Dunbar-Nelson suggests that something larger than Tante Marie herself is at stake, for even Tante Marie is implicated in dominant ideology. While Dunbar-Nelson racializes the praline woman, implying that she is the same color as her "pink and brown wares," the praline woman also speaks invidiously against others and exhibits racist attitudes. At the same time that she is busy eliciting her own listeners' (and readers') empathy, she is also making certain that the Holy Father gets "'dat w'ite'" praline and criticizing her competitors—Tonita, "'dat lazy Indien squaw,'" and "'dat lazy I'ishman down de strit.'" We might read Dunbar-Nelson as suggesting here that revolution will require more than simply inverting the current structures of power, for who knows whether such a change will produce the "miracle" of opening hearts, whether eliciting empathy as a strategy for survival will produce a subject capable of empathizing with others. Yet when dominant ideologies completely give way, neither can we predict the outcome of such a break—the biggest "crivasse" of all. When Foucault asks, "Are there no great radical ruptures, massive binary divisions, then?" he answers, "Occasionally, yes" (96). The "big crivasse" at the end of "The Praline Woman" serves as Dunbar-Nelson's reminder to the reader that although her street vendor (along with Tonita and the Irishman) may not in and of herself signify revolution, and while the end of Tante Marie's economic world is always just a flood away, resistances do accumulate and there are occasionally "great radical ruptures."

Dunbar-Nelson published *The Goodness of St. Rocque and Other Stories* in 1899, the same year Charles Chesnutt published *The Conjure Woman.* When he later wrote *Paul Marchand, F.M.C.,*[7] he returned to Dunbar-Nelson's praline woman and gave her a central role in this novel. We read Chesnutt's inclusion and expansion of the character as his recognition of the potentially revolutionary nature of the "big crivasse" at the end of Dunbar-Nelson's story.[8] In *Paul Marchand, F.M.C.,* the praline woman appears as "old Zabet Philosophe," a historical figure Grace King documented in 1895 in *New Orleans: The Place and the People* (341). While we will discuss King's interest in this figure and in racial hierarchies in New Orleans in general in more detail in chapter 9, we are intrigued here by Chesnutt's apparent acknowledgment of Dunbar-Nelson as well as of King.

Chesnutt writes:

> One day in the spring of 1821, about ten o'clock in the morning an old colored woman entered the *vieux carré,* or old square, with a large basket upon her head, and took up her stand in front of the porch of the Cabildo or Hotel de Ville or City Hall. . . . She placed her basket on the pavement, removed the clean white cotton cloth which covered it, and disposed for exhibition the contents, consisting of *pralines,* or little crisp sweet cakes, a popular Creole delicacy. She then pulled out from behind one of the columns of the porch a three-legged wooden stool, hers by right of property or prescription, and took her seat upon it by the basket.
>
> "*Pralines!* Fresh and sweet! *Pralines, messieurs! Pralines, mesdames! Pralines, mes enfants!*" (*Paul Marchand* 7)

Chesnutt informs his reader that the praline vendor has "lived the greater part of her life in the houses of the rich and cultured, first in San Domingo, from which she had fled, with her master's children, during the insurrection of 1793, and later in New Orleans, where in recognition of her loyalty, she had for half a century enjoyed the privileges of a free woman" (9–10). In her link with the Haitian revolution as well as in her possession of racial knowledge capable of overturning hierarchies of inheritance in the powerful white Beaurepas family, Chesnutt's praline woman indeed has the power to make a "big crivasse."[9] At the same time that Chesnutt's reading of Dunbar-Nelson's praline woman continues to mark a connection between his work and that of the women regionalists, it seems as well to underscore the political potential of fictional representation. For both Chesnutt and Dunbar-Nelson, fictional representation is a form of conjure, one that underscores the role of language itself. While conjure may make only a brief appearance in Dunbar-Nelson (in the practices of the Wizened One in "The Goodness of St. Rocque"), the ending of "The Praline Woman" reminds us of the power of linguistic signs to evade the limitations of realism by taking on the potential resistance of conjure.

The Regionalist Sign

Because the narrator takes a minimalist role in "The Praline Woman," serving only to identify place and time, Dunbar-Nelson in effect equates the praline woman's world, and her resistance, with language. Tante Marie exists in place and in time only as a speaking voice; when she ceases to speak, she floats away. Her final words, "Pralines! Pralines!," seem to come from a distance as she fades from view. The removal of any narrator but the praline woman herself from this sketch creates an almost absolute equation of character with text. In what amounts to a monologue, the text does not exist without the speaker, but neither does the speaker exist without her text. In Dunbar-Nelson's emphasis on this mutual dependence, she calls the reader's attention to the regionalist sign as a linguistic construction and offers resistance to its being read as simply representational. Royal Street and New Orleans become referential in the sketch but the "praline woman" exists only to the extent that she makes words, and these words at best ambivalently exist outside the text, and then only to the extent that they garner readers. Indeed, it is difficult to determine exactly how many customers appear in the sketch, what the gender of the child Didele is, or how seriously to take Tante Marie's prediction at the end of her narrative. What seems almost certain is that she opens the text to her own reader in the last line: "'Bonjour, madame, you come again? Pralines! Pralines!'" In thereby implicating the reader's agency in giving life to her text, she calls our attention to her own artifice. In this way she makes a connection between readerly empathy and textual power.

In his discussion of post-structuralist theory, Terry Eagleton writes: "the realist or representational sign, then, is . . . essentially unhealthy. It effaces its own status as a sign, in order to foster the illusion that we are perceiving reality without its intervention. The sign as 'reflection,' 'expression' or 'representation' denies the *productive* character of language: it suppresses the fact that we only have a 'world' at all because we have language to signify it, and that what we count as 'real' is bound up with what alterable structures of signification we live within" (136). Despite Dunbar-Nelson's interest in Tante Marie's economic survival, "The Praline Woman" is not a work of realism. Above all, Charlotte Shattuck's "chinks," Hetty Fifield's "vantage-points," and the praline woman's "big crivasse" resist naturalizing poverty and powerlessness. At the same time they refrain from making excessive claims for their own political power. Rather, these signs that resist the ideological structures of realism call into question the sense of normalcy that Mrs. Simonds in "A Mistaken Charity," Deacon Gale in "A Church Mouse," or the Holy Father in "The Praline Woman" invoke. They do so by emphasizing the constructedness of "reality," thereby disputing the features of realist representation that are apparently unchangeable because they are "natural." Rather than suppressing the way language works, Dunbar-Nelson indicates that the praline woman's world exists only to the extent that she has "language to signify it"; the "alterable structures of signification" in which her "pray-lines" become indistinguishable from her "prey-lines" produce the "big crivasse" in the text, the crack in the realist levee that marks the emergence of regionalist poetics.

Eagleton writes further that "the 'healthy' sign, for Barthes, is one which draws attention to its own arbitrariness—which does not try to palm itself off as 'natural' but which, in the very moment of conveying a meaning, communicates something of its own relative, artificial status as well" (135). As art, regionalism must communicate "something of its own relative, artificial status" to avoid becoming just as "unhealthy" as the realist sign under which critics have conventionally assumed it to be written. As Austin writes in "The Basket Maker," "Every Indian woman is an artist,—sees, feels, creates, but does not philosophize about her processes. Seyavi's bowls are wonders of technical precision, inside and out, the palm finds no fault with them, but the subtlest appeal is in the sense that warns us of humanness in the way the design spreads into the flare of the bowl" (*AWR* 547). We can read the "humanness" of Austin's characterization of Seyavi's art as the sign by which regionalist fiction warns us of its own "relative, artificial status," for, as we have come to understand more than a century later, humanness and humanism may be the supreme fictions. When we frame certain phrases in regionalist fiction in such a way as to make them serve as theory ("ears made delicate by listening," "if you was me you would know there was chinks"), we seek as well to de-realize regionalism and point readers to the "humanness," artifice, and constructedness of its poetics.

Empathic response is regionalism's "pray-line," its hope to elicit the reader's engagement with Austin's humanness; but it is also a "prey-line" with its own economic and cultural survival at stake. Thus even as it problematizes the attraction of the outsider to the region, it also involves a come-on to the "stranger." In the words of Dunbar-Nelson's praline woman, "'I know you étrangér. You don' look lak dese New Orleans peop'. You lak' dose Yankee dat come down 'fo' de war'" (*AWR* 480). There is no guarantee that the regionalist sign, by denaturalizing the representation of regional people, will produce either Foucault's "strategic codification of points of resistance" or the "miracle" of empathic reading; on the contrary, it may open up the region to exploitation. At the end of Chopin's "The Gentleman of Bayou Têche," the Cajun character finally consents to have his picture made, and the artist promises to use the story's title as the picture's caption (*AWR* 426). However, since Evariste cannot read, he will never know whether the outsider keeps his promise, or whether his picture will be framed in such a way as to ironize its caption. Nor can Chopin be sure that she has sufficiently disrupted dominant reading practices to prevent her characters from being subject to the predation of readers wanting reassurance that their own reality is the "natural" one. All the regionalist text can do is to offer a design that "warns us of humanness" in its recognition of "the *productive* character of language" and the relation of the "real" to "alterable structures of signification." While we may be unable to ascertain whether the regionalist text changes any reader's mind or opens any reader's heart, we can examine the art of the regionalist text and see the way in which it hopes to accomplish such change. Ultimately this is the only point of resistance a text can have, its "design" on the reader that, like Seyavi's art, "spreads into the flare of the bowl."

In regionalism's unwillingness to "'naturalize' social reality," in Eagleton's terms, it "draws attention to its own arbitrariness," reminding us as critics that while empathic response may create resistance to dominant reading practices, it is nevertheless a "miracle" indeed whenever such response actually works toward what Foucault describes as "the strategic codification of these points of resistance" (96). The regionalist text thus sets itself up, like a mirage in the desert, to point to where water should be. Aware of its own constructedness, and of empathy as a learned approach, and at the same time proposing empathy as a solution for survival in a world of difference, the regionalist text serves as a reminder, like a mirage, that what the reader needs to find—or to make for herself—is water. As Austin writes, "that is as good a pointer as any if you go waterless in the country of Lost Borders: where you find cattle dropped, skeleton or skin dried, the heads almost invariably will be turned toward the places where water-holes should be" (*AWR* 591).

The poetics of regionalism identifies the "places where water-holes should be"; it provides no guarantee of safe passage beyond the boundaries of either "natural," geographical, cultural, or critical laws but rather marks the necessity of the construction of empathy, and it comes to reside in the reader whether or not she or he will find "water" there. Regionalism requires an active reader, one who is willing to get "close to the heart of these things"; its poetics can show readers what empathic response looks like and how it works, but it cannot guarantee that readers will believe it. So it asserts only that the mirage in the desert may become a reader's water-hole if she or he knows how to read closely. As Austin writes, "There are many areas in the desert where drinkable water lies within a few feet of the surface. . . . It is related that the final breakdown of that hapless party that gave Death Valley its forbidding name occurred in a locality where shallow wells would have saved them. But how were they to know that?" (*AWR* 568). Regionalism attempts to properly equip travelers "to go safely across that ghastly sink" (569) but it cannot make them "know that."

Awareness of the artifice of regionalism does not, however, necessarily lessen its effects; indeed, we find ourselves moved by these texts into a literary region that rewrites critical borders. Yet we recognize that, despite regionalism's anticipation of readers' resistance, our own readers may remain as resistant to our critical narrative as the narrator of King's "'One of Us'" initially is to the story of the woman before her. Locating regionalism, then, involves dislocating our own readers; as Austin puts it, "Out there where the borders of conscience break down, where there is no convention, and behavior is of little account except as it gets you your desire, almost anything might happen; does happen, in fact, though [we] shall have trouble making you believe it" (589).

CHAPTER 5

"Free to Say": Thematics

"I thought you was dead, an' thar you was a-settin'."

—Mary E. Wilkins Freeman, "On the Walpole Road"

Identification of themes is a necessary condition for an emotional response to a literary work and its poetic world.

—Menachem Brinker, "Theme and Interpretation"

Thematics and American Literature

In *Manhood and the American Renaissance,* David Leverenz recounts an incident in which he experienced a definitive "shock of recognition." During a meeting of instructors for a required sophomore course in close reading, a rather heated discussion occurred over an assignment for *Adventures of Huckleberry Finn,* with his colleagues in British literature arguing for one that would focus students' attention on Mark Twain's ironic narration while he proposed one that would ask them to think about Twain's treatment of the theme of authority. Leverenz recalls that the discussion concluded with his colleague in eighteenth-century British literature "airily" waving his hand and exclaiming dismissively, "Have it your way. . . . The dumb ones will write about themes, and the smart ones will write about narration" (173). What Leverenz and his colleagues in American literature discovered from this interchange is, as he puts it, that "Americanists tend to be theme people" (173), though one suspects he also discovered in a rather visceral way the usually unarticulated hierarchy governing many English departments and the contempt for American literature and Americanists that often accompanies this hierarchy. (In recent years, of course, new hierarchies privileging theory over literary texts, or replacing literature with cultural studies, have complicated and perhaps obscured the animosities previously reserved for Americanists.) Indeed, there is a rather direct connection between the contempt evident in this interchange and the conclusion that Americanists tend to be theme people, for thematics has historically provided the most powerful tool for responding to the intellectual assumptions underlying this contempt—namely, that there really is no such thing as American literature and that what is called American literature is better understood as a subset, and a rather inferior one at that, of the larger field of British literature.

To put it most simply, the problem facing those who seek to identify and create a distinctively American literature, whether it be in 1830 or 1890 or 1920 or 1950, or now, is definitional—how to establish such an entity in the absence of the obvious unifying features of language (written in American—*what* is that), geography (written in America—*where* is that), and historical origin (*when* can America be said to have begun). Thematics provides a solution to this problem—American literature is made up of those texts that take up distinctively American themes. However, while thematic criticism may create the illusion of a field, it accomplishes this sleight of hand by deferring the problem of definition to a prior question. In discussing *The Education of Henry Adams,* Leo Marx comments: "If the tendency toward an abstract or a dialectical view of life is a distinctive characteristic of American culture, then *The Education of Henry Adams* is one of the most American of books" (347). Indeed *if* "we" could agree on the distinctive characteristics of American culture, one might make a case for constructing the field of American literature as that body of texts which addresses these distinctive characteristics. Yet this is a very big "if" and as Leo Marx acknowledges at the end of *The Machine in the Garden,* a book recognized as foundational in the post–World War II construction of American literature, the determination of the distinctive characteristics of American culture "ultimately belongs not to art but to politics" (365). Thus, if "American" literature is or has been defined by thematics, thematics itself is a creature of politics, as contemporary feminist, African American, Marxist, lesbian and gay, and "New Americanist" critics in the 1970s, 80s, and 90s have increasingly made clear.

For several decades now feminist critics in particular have worked to uncover and analyze the politics informing the construction of the field of American literature, though they have also challenged the distinction between art and politics proposed by Leo Marx. In her 1981 essay "Melodramas of Beset Manhood," for example, Nina Baym analyzes the gender implications of the role of thematics in the construction of American literature. Arguing that from the start theories of American literature begin "with the hypothesis that American literature is to be judged less by its form than its content" (*Feminism* 5) and that inevitably this content included some quality of "Americanness," she points out how "Americanness" itself came to constitute literary excellence. "Inevitably, perhaps, it came to seem that the quality of Americanness, whatever it might be, *constituted* literary excellence for American authors. Beginning as a nationalistic enterprise, American literary criticism and theory has retained a nationalist orientation to this day" (Baym 5). Emerging from such a nationalist orientation, "before he is through, the critic has had to insist that some works in America are much more American than others, and he is as busy excluding certain writers as 'un-American' as he is including others. Such a proceeding in the political arena would be extremely suspect, but in criticism it has been the method of choice" (6).

If thematic content forms the basis for determining what is *American* literature, as much critical energy will need to be devoted to showing why some writers and texts are "un-American" as to showing why others are American. As Baym observes, "it is odd indeed to argue that only a handful of American works are really American" (7). The construction of American literature appears to have required that some group or groups of potentially American writers had to be available to be constructed as un-American in order to make the case for the Americanness of those different from them, and women writers emerged as the most likely candidates for the role of the un-American. As Baym points out, while there is nothing inherent in the notion of the American to gender it male, the presence of women writers and their works "is acknowledged in literary theory and history as an impediment and obstacle, that which the essential American literature had to criticize as its chief task" (9). As part of the nationalist enterprise of the construction of American literature, critics seeking a foundationalist concept of the American have drawn on the energies and even the erotics of various exclusionary hierarchies, including but not limited to sexism, to locate their rhetorical authority.

Indeed, we need look no farther than the anecdote David Leverenz recounts to see how this works. Acknowledging that his colleague's response "was a superb put down, of course," Leverenz orchestrates his own. He attacks the classism of his British literature colleague's distinction between smart and dumb by invoking homophobia, confirming Baym's point that American criticism has reflected "melodramas of beset manhood" (10). Leverenz renders his colleague effeminate through attributing to him the quintessential "fag" gesture of the airily waving hand and by implication constructs himself and the other Americanists as real men concerned with such masculine issues as authority; by so doing he also, of course, constructs classism itself as a form of effeminacy peculiar perhaps to the British. In miniature he replays the dynamics through which Americanists have distinguished the American from the British for years as they have sought to take the positive energy associated with manliness and attach it to the American. An inevitable part of this critical erotics has been the construction of women, as writers, subjects, and persons, as un-American. To turn to Leo Marx again, how do we know that Hawthorne is a great American writer, one who embodies the essence of what it means to be American? Because he has caught so perfectly "the sickly sweet, credulous tone of sentimental pastoralism" characteristic of "the ladies' books for which he often wrote" and has undercut it through his ironic and tragic recognition of what would actually be required to fulfill the genuine "pastoral hope" (275). Marx *knows* who our serious writers are, those who have been capable of discovering the meaning inherent in their culture's contradictions, because he has available for comparison a category of writers who presumably missed these contradictions. As Lora Romero writes, "the 'feminization' of early nineteenth-century cultural production and consumption is one of the most basic assumptions made by critics about the period, even in the face of dubious literary historical evidence. Representing the masses as feminine obscures the way in which constructions of countercultural authorship maintain not just male authority but also the cultural authority of a small number of male authors in the face of increasing cultural access to literacy across a range of antebellum populations" (107). In the mid-twentieth-century construction of the field of American literature, then, it was highly unlikely that a woman would be perceived as an American writer. Of course, in this construction, midcentury critics implied that women writers could not be understood as contributing to the nationalist enterprise, an assumption that critics in the 1980s and 90s ironically worked hard to demonstrate is not necessarily accurate.

In this context one can understand why thematics has fallen out of favor as a method of approach for those persons interested in the reconstruction of American literature. In recent approaches to American literature, there is an apparent distrust of thematics understood as not only nationalist but also hegemonically white, male, and heterosexist as a basis for constructing a field called American literature. In his introduction to a collection entitled *The Return of Thematic Criticism,* Werner Sollors, tracing the "widespread, yet undeclared 'thematic' practice" in contemporary criticism, notes that "few scholars now seem to be willing to approach methodological issues of thematic criticism, or to look at their own works in the context of thematics" (xiii). He connects his general observations specifically to the field of American literature, observing further that "though key works in American Studies may be considered exemplary of the thematic method, few Americanists today seem to understand or define their work in the context of thematics" (xiv). In addition, he points out that in a recent MLA bibliography "there are only a very small number of entries under the heading 'Theme,' not a single one of which refers to studies of literature of the United States" (xii). Yet thematics remains a powerful tool for those interested in the work of recovery. As Thomas Pavel indicates in "Thematics and Historical Evidence," his contribution to Sollors's collection, thematic criticism has been taken up and "revived" by "a coalition of critics politically committed to feminism, Afro-American culture, ethnic and sexual minorities, and the post-colonial Third World" (124) because thematics has the capacity for "transforming a hermeneutic activity into a cultural revolution" (125).

In a similar vein, Nancy Armstrong, in an essay in the same collection, traces the "genealogy" of theme to the "long-standing opposition between what a text refers to [its theme] and what it is in and of itself [its form]" (39). She argues that while Foucault seems to offer a "way around this opposition by inviting us to consider what a text *does,*" she reads *Discipline and Punish* as "the story of a theme, or how discipline transformed itself from a residual cultural formation into the master theme of modern culture" (39). Modernism itself depends on "the elevation of discipline over all other methods of organizing cultural information. For what is modernism's privileged object, if not a self-enclosed and internally coherent system of relationships capable of containing any kind of cultural theme by such devices as paradox, contradiction, ambiguity, irony, negation, and so forth?" (41). Within modernism, "themes that ordinarily cut across a wide range of media and genres were suddenly contained and subordinated by the specialized aesthetic themes called form," and "certain themes, like discipline itself, renounced the status of theme and claimed to be forms" (41). For Armstrong, the "various formalisms that developed within linguistics, literature, biology, the human sciences, and economics during the early decades of the twentieth century" served as "respecializations of discipline" that "reproduced the classificatory behavior of dominant culture as Foucault describes it. The implications for contemporary literary criticism are clear. This brief genealogy of discipline reveals that what we call 'form' is simply the dominant theme of a given moment. In turn, what we call 'theme' identifies certain residual and undervalued terms, potentially capable of becoming new cultural forms, much as discipline once did" (45). Armstrong's reflections on theme at once suggest the prevalence of thematic criticism in what might appear to be quite otherwise, indicate the difficulty of separating theme from form, and offer thematics as the location of Foucaultian points of resistance, as the discursive location of alternative or oppositional values. In part perhaps because of such associations, Sollors writes, "thematics may be an approach to literature that dares not speak its name" (*Return* xiv).

As we seek to explain to readers the conceptual coherence that allows us to designate regionalism as a tradition of American writing, and as we seek as well to explain our own attraction to and investment in this tradition, we find ourselves drawn to the frame of thematics, yet also somewhat afraid to speak its name. Indeed, regionalist fiction first caught our attention because we found in it thematic content quite different from what we had been trained to register as distinctively American; we found in it an alternative, even oppositional, thematics. While we might propose that the thematics we associate with regionalism offers an alternative point of departure for the definition of the "Americanness" of American literature, we believe such a move would be at once counterproductive to our larger purposes and antithetical to what we value in regionalism, for such a move would simply reinscribe the hegemonic construction of the field of American literature that has served in the past to exclude regionalism from it. The situation is further complicated by the fact that as a group regionalist writers showed little interest in the "question of the American" and did not position themselves as seeking to write a distinctively *American* literature. We find ourselves, therefore, confronting a paradox: our project depends upon the existence of something that can be called American literature for it is the frame provided by this field that has enabled us to "see" the tradition we call regionalism; yet we wish to speak outside the frame of the "American" and "un-American," we wish to be free not to say either "American" or "un-American." Additionally, we recognize the politically problematic role that thematics has played in the construction of American literature, yet we want to avail ourselves of the very power that thematics possesses, a power that enabled it to accomplish the construction of a field.

Acknowledging such paradoxes, however, can serve ends that are politically repressive by entangling those who would challenge dominant paradigms in critiques that expose their complicity in the very paradigms they seek to challenge. Paralysis, silence, the inability to speak one's name frequently result from such entanglements and so the issue becomes one of freedom of speech. Already minoritized and regionalized by our advocacy on behalf of a group of women writers who lived in the geographical United States before women were citizens, we seek to become "free to say" thematics and to offer a reading of regionalism that posits its primary thematic as that of "free to say," thus re-placing regionalism as a meta-critique of the problem of thematics in the field of American literature.

Freedom of Speech and Interpretive Desire

In her impassioned discussion of the relation between feminism, pornography, and the First Amendment, Catharine MacKinnon underscores the significance of framing regionalist thematics under the aegis of "free to say." In MacKinnon's analysis, the First Amendment guarantee of freedom of speech was intended to preserve a right that elite white men already possessed; it was not created in order to bring into speech those whose silence was presumed to be a natural or necessary social and political fact. "By contrast with those who wrote the First Amendment so they could keep what they had, those who didn't have it didn't get it. Those whose speech was silenced prior to law, prior to any operation of the state's prohibition of it, were not secured freedom of speech. Their speech was not regarded as something that had to be . . . affirmatively guaranteed" (*Feminism Unmodified* 207). Furthermore, according to MacKinnon, First Amendment law has worked to protect systems of discourse designed specifically to reinforce and continue the silence of those groups whom the framers of the Constitution never intended to empower but who might mistakenly think they were so included. While MacKinnon herself specifically targets the discourse of pornography, many other discourses prevalent in a patriarchal culture have the same effect that she ascribes to pornography: "the point is . . . that the assumptions the law of the First Amendment makes about adults—that adults are autonomous, self-defining, freely acting, equal individuals—are exactly those qualities that pornography systematically denies and undermines for women" (181). In other words, according to MacKinnon, the free speech of men silences the free speech of women and "any system of freedom of expression that does not address a problem where the free speech of men silences the free speech of women, a real conflict between speech interests as well as between people, is not serious about securing freedom of expression in this country" (193).

MacKinnon's analysis establishes a context within which it is possible to understand the emotional and cognitive energy of a thematics of "free to say" for a tradition of women's writing. However, as MacKinnon indicates, in order for women's freedom of speech to mean anything substantive it must be understood as part of a dialogue with others who seek to suppress it or who derive pleasure from exerting power over it. Women cannot afford the illusion that speaking only to "oneself" constitutes genuine freedom. Dunbar-Nelson's "The Praline Woman" offers one instance of a text that foregrounds this perception and articulates the significance of dialogue to issues of freedom of speech. It would be easy to read this story as simply a monologue in which the kind of person the First Amendment never intended to bring into speech finally has a chance to speak without interruption. In a certain sense, as we have indicated previously, this story offers an example of the way regionalist fiction "listens" such persons into speech and serves as a form of "mother." In this context the praline woman's vision of her own death at the end of her "monologue" suggests the relation of speech to life; with the end of speech comes a vision of the "deluge," as other discourses overwhelm the voices of the characters regionalism has "listened" into life. Yet this apparent monologue can be seen as a dialogue, for, as we observed in chapter 4, if we read closely we realize that the praline woman speaks in response to someone else or to elicit a response from someone else. By constructing an apparent monologue as in fact a dialogue, Dunbar-Nelson dramatizes the necessarily relational nature of regionalist fiction, its recognition that to be "free to say" its speech must exist in dialogue with other discourses. In this context, we could read the fiction's definition of death as equivalent to speech that has become genuinely monologic; Tante Marie's final fantasy contains only the memory of former interactions and is disconnected from any context of present response. She is rescued from this "deluge" only by the appearance of one final potential customer, or by the ongoing dialogue of readers with her text.

Regionalism's emphasis on the dialogic underscores its recognition that its thematics, what it desires to be free to say, are alternative not dominant. By building resistance into their texts and incorporating the discourse of the "deluge," regionalist writers signal their awareness that the thematics readers bring with them are not necessarily those of regionalism and that their texts must do a certain kind of work on and with readers if these thematics are to be heard. In this context, Pavel's understanding of thematics becomes useful. Pavel argues that a text is a system of signs designed to make readers care about certain things and not others: "a text rather looks like a maze of lures, baits, and snares, each competing for a glimpse of attention, each trying to make us care about things we may or may not have noticed before" (130). He defines themes as those "topics a text is built to make us care about. In the act of reading, our attention, shaped by its own cares, looks for topics it cannot bear to ignore. But the text we read is designed to force us to notice certain other topics and make us care about *them*" (130). While he intends his essay as a cautionary tale against what he sees as the misreadings of excessively "political" criticism in which readers allow what they care about to obscure what the text cares about, we can adapt his model as a way to understand regionalism's engagement with its readers and use it to map part of the dialogics of regionalist fiction whose texts are designed "to make us care about things we may or may not have noticed before" or cared about before.

Pavel recognizes that the reading transaction includes not only the desire of texts to make readers care about certain topics but also the desire of readers to make texts care about certain topics. This recognition provides a context within which to consider the experience of those readers, the object of Pavel's scolding, who already care about the topics regionalist texts desire us to notice. Pavel focuses on the encounter between a text's desire and what he calls "the full force of our interpretive desire" (122) in order to warn against the dangers of "political" criticism, describing "the full force of [the] interpretive desire" of "political" critics as equivalent to the touch of King Midas making "every text they lay their hands on channel the same message: the message they want to hear" (121). But in those instances in which the desires of texts and the desires of readers are complementary rather than oppositional, the case presumably of the canonical reader and the canonical text, interpretive desire takes on a different valence, particularly when both desire and theme are noncanonical. In the case of regionalist fiction, then, we could argue that its thematics validates the interpretive desire of the silenced and disenfranchised, and we could postulate that such readers are drawn to these texts precisely because their thematics meet the "full force of our interpretive desire," providing such readers with the experience Pavel takes for granted in the canonical reading of the canonical text. In this context we can understand somewhat differently the appeal of thematic criticism for that "coalition of critics politically committed to feminism, Afro-American culture, ethnic and sexual minorities, and the post-colonial Third World" (124), an appeal that for Pavel derives from thematic criticism's usefulness in allowing texts to be "divided into friendly and inimical" on the basis of criteria that are "simple and compelling" and thus allows "teaching literature . . . to become a political weapon" (124, 125).

While Pavel's approach to thematics could be seen in one sense as modeling empathy, in that he urges readers to listen to what the text has to say rather than what they want it to say, the context within which he delivers his message gives it a decidedly different effect. Indeed, we might see here an instance of what Ciaramicoli refers to as "the dark side of empathy" (113) as Pavel invokes the power of empathy to coerce those toward whom the dominant culture is decidedly unempathic to blame themselves for not attending appropriately to its texts and for seeking alternative fictions. When Pavel writes, "it could happen that, carried away by commitment to their own concerns, critics will have neglected the text's own effort to mold their attention and lead their gaze," and when he asks "whether our attention always needs to seek what we care about, preempting other interests" (131), we experience a form of pressure familiar to women in patriarchal culture as he, in effect, demands, however gently, that the noncanonical reader abandon her effort to find textual representation of those "narrow" topics that her attention, shaped by its own cares, "cannot bear to ignore" and to give herself over to those topics that the canonical text "is designed to force us to notice." Pavel does not include in his analysis the scene of a canonical reading of a canonical text nor does he take up the scene of canonical critics reading the noncanonical text and perhaps equally neglecting "the text's own effort to mold their attention and lead their gaze." Of even less interest to Pavel, we might assume, and even less culturally imaginable is the scene of the noncanonical critic reading the noncanonical text, the scene that perhaps best represents our own position in this book. For when we acknowledge that we first located our interpretive desire in the texts of regionalism, we are in a sense taking on a "queer" critical position, that of noncanonical critics engaged in caring connection with noncanonical texts—a position as readily discounted, or perhaps as stigmatized, in critical discourse as that of the homosexual in that moment in 1870 when, according to Foucault, homosexuality came to identify not a behavior but a new category or "species" of persons (43). Seeking for ourselves the privilege Pavel implicitly accords the canonical reader of the canonical text, that luxury of finding represented in a text those topics one "cannot bear to ignore," and resisting the voices that would have us do otherwise, we became interested in regionalism precisely because the full force of our interpretive desire found in regionalism the "friendly" rather than the "inimical."

Pavel's model of readers' relations to texts, clearly intended to disempower the noncanonical or "political" reader, evokes Foucault's description of the interconnections of power and pleasure that accompany the new "regime of discourses" (27) which he traces to the late nineteenth century. Foucault describes the scenes of examination and confession that produce the pleasures of power under the new regime: "The pleasure that comes of exercising a power that questions, monitors, watches, spies, searches out, palpates, brings to light; and on the other hand, the pleasure that kindles at having to evade this power, flee from it, fool it, or travesty it" (45). Above all, he sees the objects of examination as "fixed by a gaze, isolated and animated by the attention they received" (45). If we replace the human objects of examination by narrative texts, Foucault's analysis would construct the text's desire as one that flees, fools, or travesties the reader's "gaze," yet is also animated by that "gaze." In such a model, the act of criticism becomes a process of searching out, bringing to light, and exercising power over the text. But what if we were to imagine a model of reading that starts from someplace other than the pleasures of power as Foucault understands them? What if we were to imagine the act of reading as emerging from a desire for a kind of connection different from that which attends such pleasures? As MacKinnon writes about the persons to whom she has addressed her analysis of pornography, "Audiences constantly expressed their desire for sexual connection undominated by dominance, unimplicated in the inequality of the sexes, a sexuality of one's own yet with another. . . . Meaning in relation is understood to require much more than a scenario of sensation; pleasure is easy compared with connection, which is hard" (*Feminism Unmodified* 217). Given an interpretive desire that seeks "connection undominated by dominance," we propose regionalism's thematics, its "topics," its *topos,* as that place in the text where such readers may locate their desire.

When we each separately began reading regionalist fictions in the late 1970s, then began reading them together in 1980, we discovered that these texts were designed to make readers care about what we also cared about, and that is why we became interested in recovering them. We also believed that the noncanonical status of these texts was related to its thematic content, to the definition of its topics as "the narrow interests of regionalism." Thus we share Pavel's interpretive concern but from a different critical standpoint, and we locate the interpretive struggle elsewhere, not in the efforts of the canonical text to resist the noncanonical reader but in the noncanonical text's recognition, as it emerges dialogically in characters like the praline woman, that many of its readers do not enter the text caring about those topics it seeks to make us care about. Indeed, we read regionalist fiction as a body of texts designed to make us care about characters and concerns considered minor, deviant, queer, or crazy by the dominant culture. In this sense, regionalist fiction occupies the same position as feminist discourse and like it, can be said, as Catharine MacKinnon puts it, to be "the art of the impossible": "In feminist terms, it is difficult to be narrow if you truly are talking about the situation of 53% of the population, but it is almost impossible to survive if you do—which makes these one and the same challenge" (*Feminism Unmodified* 10). It is within this context that we seek to formulate the meaning of the title we have given to this chapter, "free to say," for we see regionalism as carving out a discursive space in which it is possible to say things that do not conform to the dominant culture and still survive, and we equally see regionalism as carving out a discursive space in which we too are free to say that this is what it says.

"Miss Beulah's Bonnet"

We take the phrase "free to say" and the title of this chapter from an 1880 story by Cooke, "Miss Beulah's Bonnet," a story whose subversive content so diverges from the cultural norm that it elicits strong negative reactions in our students and indeed gives us pause. For while asserting that we ourselves are also "free to say" in this book, we are aware of the limits of an acceptable feminist critical discourse even at the beginning of the twenty-first century.

Although Cooke opens her story with Miss Beulah's visit to her milliner to refurbish a bonnet that she has worn her entire adult life (even older than Miss Beulah, it was "'mother's weddin' bunnit,'" [*AWR* 122]), we begin our story with the sentence Miss Beulah utters later on, after what Cooke's narrator calls "this tale of woe about her bonnet" (125) is well underway, for it is this sentence that creates consternation and defensiveness among male and female students alike: "'I'm free to say I never did like boys'" (130). While being "free" is one of the characteristic ways Miss Beulah Larkin identifies herself (when the bonnet is finally delivered, she says "'I'm free to own it suits me,'" 125), the particular discursive freedom she claims for herself with respect to boys recalls the First Amendment in both form and content and positions Miss Beulah as seeking for herself those rights the constitution never intended to give her. We read Cooke's story as an exploration of why being "free to say I never did like boys" provides an appropriate rhetoric for such a challenge, given a context in which the expression "boys will be boys" seems a formula constructed to silence radical speech about certain male behavior, in which girls and women are denied the same linguistic and discursive freedom boys and men take for granted, and in which misogyny and the mistreatment of girls evoke little consternation.

That Cooke was aware of writing a challenge to the privileging of boys in her culture seems quite clear. She published "Miss Beulah's Bonnet" in 1880 in the midst of the craze for "bad boy" books, four years after Mark Twain's *The Adventures of Tom Sawyer* (1876) and four years before *Adventures of Huckleberry Finn* (1884), at the end of the decade that began with Thomas Bailey Aldrich's *The Story of a Bad Boy* (1870) and during the decade that witnessed the flourishing of George W. Peck's bad boy stories (the first collection, *Peck's Bad Boy and His Pa,* appeared in 1883).[1] Cooke's fiction is filled with characters who expostulate on the general nastiness of boys; indeed one might read such references in their aggregate as Cooke's response to the "bad boy" craze.[2] But when Miss Beulah declares "'I'm free to say I never did like boys,'" her comment resonates far differently from those of characters in other stories, for "Miss Beulah's Bonnet" revolves around the issue of how much attention a boy deserves and how readers feel about his decision to revenge himself on Beulah for her failure to give him that attention. Even further, in a major shift of values and perspectives, Beulah's story indicates that a woman's bonnet may occupy a position of cultural importance far more significant than that occupied by a boy's injured ego. Indeed, the bonnet itself becomes a sign that the deacons in the church find themselves unable to read but which they sense contains a meaning they would like to understand. Beulah's freedom to say "I never did like boys" creates an opening for Cooke to articulate the significance of bonnets.

The story is easily summarized. Beulah Larkin, a single woman who lives with

Nanny Starks, a "little maid she had taken to bring up," in a large house she has inherited from her grandfather, but whose income is based on a "small amount of money carefully invested" and is therefore precarious, agrees to take in her widowed and impoverished niece and her niece's three children for an extended visit (*AWR* 123). Although the niece, Eliza, is a "woman of resource" and sees the visit as a way to be spared the expense of board and lodging for her family during a period when her older daughter, Sarah, is saving to get married, Miss Beulah is pleased to welcome her family into the "clean, large, cool chambers that were such a contrast to the hot rooms, small and dingy, of their city home" (124). However, she has not counted on Jack, an eight-year-old boy, and his influence over three-year-old Janey, a child who very soon becomes, "in spite of her naughtiness, mistress of Aunt Beulah's very soul" (125). Jack's mischief is of a different order and seems intended to torment all living creatures and especially his aunt. Jealous of Beulah's attentions to Janey, he takes revenge on Miss Beulah the day the treasured bonnet is returned from the milliner. Enlisting Janey to actually carry out the plan so that he can "honestly" claim "'I hain't touched your old bonnet'" (127), he hides the bonnet under the seat cushion of a "large rocking-chair, well stuffed under its chintz cover, and holding a plump soft feather cushion so big it fairly overflowed the seat" (126). The bonnet is first flattened when, later in the day, the minister's wife pays a call and sits on the chair, and then soaked when later in the week Janey spills a pitcher of milk on the chair, and the combination of these events renders it entirely worthless. Although Beulah goes back to Mary Jane Beers, the milliner, to choose a new bonnet, and although she finds one she likes, she also discovers that her investments have not paid any dividend "owing to damage by flood and fire, as well as a general disturbance of business all over the country" (133), and that because she has promised most of her meager income to Sarah for her wedding, and the rest to her church's "home missions," she cannot afford to buy a new bonnet.

With no bonnet other than one that no longer seems respectable, she feels she cannot attend Sunday services though she keeps up her attendance at her church's prayer meetings and, for a while, the sewing circle. After two months pass, the church deacons, "mightily scandalized," call on Miss Beulah to ask why she has stopped attending. When they press her for her reason, she replies, "'Well, if you must know, I hain't got no bunnit'" (135). When they ask "'Why not?'" she replies, "'Cause Miss Blake sot on it'" (135). The deacons do not know how to respond to the news that the minister's wife has sat on Miss Beulah's bonnet. "The strife of tongues, however, did not spare Aunt Beulah, if the deacons did," and when Mary Jane Beers returns in September from a visit to her sister and attends the first fall meeting of the sewing circle, "[I]t was then and there she heard the scorn and jeers and unfounded stories come on like a tidal wave to overwhelm her friend's character" (135). But Miss Beers is the only one outside Beulah's family who knows what actually happened. To defend her friend, she tells the story of Jack, the minister's wife, the milk, and the bonnet, as well as the truth of Miss Beulah's economic situation. "Touched" by Miss Beers's "warm and generous vindication," the sewing circle proposes to buy Miss Beulah a bonnet (136). There is no need to do so, however, for Sarah, now married and working as a milliner, has already sent her great-aunt a bonnet she has made to replace the one that was destroyed. Beulah returns to church, and "Jack did not say anything about it, nor did the congregation, though on more than one female face beamed a furtive congratulatory smile; and Deacon Flint looked at Deacon Morse across the aisle" (137).

While Cooke's story takes Miss Beulah, her need for a bonnet, and her judgment of Jack and the deacons quite seriously, it otherwise earns its humor in quite conventional ways. On one level the saga of the bonnet is approached with the irreverence characteristic of the humorists of the Old Southwest. The minister's wife's extended visit, while the reader knows she is sitting on the bonnet, creates a thoroughly irreverent moment, and the narrator draws out the humor of the scene as "Mrs. Blake removed her bonnet, and sank down on that inviting cushion with all her weight, glad enough to rest, and ignorant of the momentous consequences" (127). Cooke has no problem making fun of Mrs. Blake's weight; when Miss Beulah finally discovers the crushed, wet bonnet, the narrator writes, "Mrs. Blake's two hundred pounds of solid flesh had reduced bonnet and cushion alike to unusual flatness" (128). Other characters in the story see humor in the situation, including a neighbor who is present when the bonnet is discovered, "flattened out almost beyond recognition, and broken wherever it was bent, its lavender ribbons soaked with milk" (129), even though Miss Beulah "witheringly" stifles their mirth. Moreover, while the story ends, the humor apparently does not; the narrator writes, "If there is any moral to this story, as no doubt there should be, it lies in the fact that Mrs. Blake never again sat down in a chair without first lifting the cushion" (137). Furthermore, though the narrator does not directly earn the story's humor at Miss Beulah's expense, the fact that she is an "old maid" puts her in the category of persons about whom her society feels "free to say" just about anything.

By employing the conventions of a humor gained at women's expense, Cooke lets her readers know that she is fully aware of the dimensions of her own discursive freedom. For, just as we argued in chapter 3 that Stowe rewrites Dame Van Winkle, Cooke in "Miss Beulah's Bonnet" rewrites the story of Tom Sawyer and Aunt Polly and dares to suggest that Aunt Polly is justified in her attitude toward Tom. Cooke's narrator makes it clear that Miss Beulah's attitude is not based on prejudice but on provocation: "Jack was a born nuisance: Miss Beulah could hardly endure him, he did so controvert all the orders and manners of her neat house" (124). He breaks up the hens' nests, makes the cat's life "a burden to her in a hundred ways," never gives Nanny Starks any peace, "felt a certain right" to torment Aunt Beulah "that would not have been considered a right, had he felt instead any shame for abusing her kindness" (125), disembowels one of Janey's new dolls, and threatens his three-year-old sister with bears and guns if she tells where the bonnet is. By all objective report, Miss Beulah is justified in saying that "'of all the boys that ever was sent into this world for any purpose, I do believe he is the hatefulest'" (130).

Yet every group of students with whom we have read this story defends Jack against Miss Beulah and reads her as a boy- and man-hater, probably (they suggest) *because* she is an "old maid." In effect, they side with the deacons, who see "sister Larkin" as "a leetle contumacious," a woman with no good reason either for her own attitudes about boys or for needing a bonnet to attend church. Clearly dialogic as it includes the discourse of the deacons and elicits resistance in readers, Cooke's story engages as well in dialogue with the deacons' discourse. Although the deacons feel entitled to speak without having to draw attention to the fact that they are "free to say," they are, as Miss Beulah observes, liars. Even though Deacon Morse is a "'hero at prayer, and gives heaps to the s'cieties,'" and even though he "'don't read no novels nor play no cards'" (131), she reminds him that "'stayin' at home from meetin' wa'n't no worse'n sandin' sugar an' waterin' rum; and I never heerd you was dealt with for them things'" (134). While the truth of her accusations strikes Deacon Morse dumb, "Deacon Flint took up the discourse," suggesting "'we didn't know but what you was troubled in your mind'" (135). Although the deacons propose that if Miss Beulah "'had a good reason'" she would be willing to tell it, when she does tell the truth neither they, nor apparently some of her readers, know what to do with it: "Here was a pitfall. Was it proper, dignified, possible, to investigate this truly feminine tangle? They were dying to enter into particulars, but ashamed to do so: nothing was left but retreat" (135). Miss Beulah's story creates an "emergency" for the deacons who are reduced to adding an "accent of reprobation" to their goodbyes and who leave "in deep doubt as to what they should report to the church" (135). She creates a similar "emergency" for those readers who cannot imagine how to "report" on a story that does not privilege boys. At the same time, in describing the deacons as dying to enter into particulars but ashamed to do so, Cooke indicates the discursive limits patriarchal culture imposes on men who have no resources for reporting a story that challenges their assumptions and their dominance. She further suggests that part of the cultural work of regionalism involves converting "deacons" from boys who take pleasure in destroying bonnets into men who are not ashamed of their interest in women's lives and are free to enter into the particulars. In constructing the male readers of her fiction as men who are able, unlike the deacons, actually to hear women's stories, Cooke enacts such a conversion and in the process makes it clear that men's interest in women's stories is essential to the larger cultural project of making bonnets as important as boys.

"Miss Beulah's Bonnet" places the thematics of regionalism in the discursive freedom Cooke allows her narrator and Miss Beulah. The regionalist writer is "free" to prefer to write stories about bonnets to stories that make heroes out of bad boys, and to write stories about a character who, when asked by Deacon

Morse to free her mind "'for the good of the church,'" recognizes that "'mabbe 'twouldn't be altogether to your likin', deacon, if I did free my mind'" (134). Indeed, the bonnet itself becomes a trope for regionalism in this story. When the bonnet arrives from the milliner's, Miss Beulah wears it in front of the mirror, "turning it from side to side, and, in short, behaving exactly as younger and prettier women do over a new hat, even when it is a miracle of art from Paris, instead of a revamped Leghorn from a country shop" (126). At the end of the story, when Miss Beers comes to Beulah's defense at the sewing circle, she describes her as "'a real home-made kind of a saint. I know she don't look it; but she doos it, and that's a sight better'" (136). Her own bonnet, and Cooke's story, is no "miracle of art from Paris," but is rather "home-made," a "revamped Leghorn from a country shop." While the bonnet itself, originally owned by Miss Beulah's mother, gets crushed and soaked and must be replaced—for, contrary to the view of regionalism literary historians have recounted and we have discussed in chapter 2, regionalism does not equate to nostalgia for a vanishing way of life—the story about it continues to circulate its alternative thematics. Miss Beers's story about Miss Beulah and her bonnet (a retelling of Cooke's own story) not only creates a "warm and generous vindication" that "touched many a feminine heart, which could appreciate Miss Beulah's self-sacrifice better than the deacons could" (136), but also creates a sense of collective empowerment that enables the "furtive congratulatory smile" these women share on the Sunday Miss Beulah returns to church; and they share it within the place and under the very gaze of the deacons whose own "discourse" (135) has attempted to crush Miss Beulah just as Mrs. Blake crushed her bonnet. Thanks to her bonnet, however, Miss Beulah has been "free to say," and therefore so have we.

In our reading of Cooke's story, "Miss Beulah's Bonnet" becomes, in the words of Pavel, a text "designed to force us to notice certain other topics" than those most readers enter the text caring about and to "make us care about *them*." However, if we return for a moment to "The Circus at Denby" and recall how Jewett's narrator suggests the ludicrousness—dare we say narrowness—of a lecture on "The Elements of True Manhood" delivered to an audience made up entirely of women, children, and old men, we might argue that, just as regionalism recognizes that some readers may not enter its texts caring about what it cares about, so it also recognizes the needs of those readers whom the dominant discourse excludes as its audience, who seek textual representation of those topics they "cannot bear to ignore," and presents itself as intended precisely for such persons. Written in part for such persons and designed to pay attention to them, regionalist fiction promotes inclusivity as a cultural value over exclusivity. Even a partial list of the subjects that regionalism seeks to gain attention for and to make us care about is impressive in its range of inclusion. Above and beyond the large categories of women, children, and old men—women being a focus of attention in virtually all of regionalist fiction, while children are central to the work of Cary and old men gain attention in the work of Jewett—

Cooke and Murfree write sympathetically about characters who are weak and have difficulty surviving; Jewett, Thaxter, and Austin promote respect for animals; Freeman's and King's characters include poor, elderly, homeless, lower-class, and "dispossessed" women, as well as women others might deem "crazy"; Chopin portrays Cajun characters and women's sexuality; Dunbar-Nelson writes about characters of mixed racial origins; Zitkala-Ša addresses Indian tribal survival and autonomy; and Sui Sin Far dares to write sympathetically about Chinese immigrants during the era of the Chinese exclusion laws.

Are There Any Lives of Women?

As MacKinnon writes, "Women have been deprived not only of terms of our own in which to express our lives, but of lives of our own to live. The damage of sexism would be trivial if this were not the case" (*Feminism Unmodified* 15). And as Carolyn G. Heilbrun writes: "What matters is that lives do not serve as models; only stories do that. And it is a hard thing to make up stories to live by. We can only retell and live by the stories we have read or heard. We live our lives through texts. They may be read, or chanted, or experienced electronically, or come to us, like the murmurings of our mothers, telling us what conventions demand. Whatever their form or medium, these stories have formed us all; they are what we must use to make new fictions, new narratives" (37). In Stowe's *The Pearl of Orr's Island,* Mara Lincoln, believing herself to be excluded from her "brother's" schooling but intensely interested in the intellectual adventures he is about to have, listens eagerly as his tutor describes the next book Moses will be given to read:

> "It is called Plutarch's 'Lives,'" said the minister; "it has more particular accounts of the men you read about in history."
>
> "Are there any lives of women?" said Mara.
>
> "No, my dear," said Mr. Sewell; "in the old times women did not get their lives written, though I don't doubt many of them were much better worth writing than the men's." (165)

As a tradition of writing, regionalism—anticipating MacKinnon and Heilbrun—provides an affirmative answer to Mara's question. Recognizing that "free to say" is meaningless if women are deprived of lives to live and recognizing as well that lives to live depend upon stories to tell, regionalism postulates a different understanding of "lives" than Plutarch's. To represent women in "history," regionalism moves outside the master narrative that informs Plutarch's *Lives* and attends instead to anecdotal moments, to, as Cary puts it, those "little histories every day revealed" that have more "to interest us in humanity" than "there *can* be in those old empires" (*AWR* 60).

Perhaps more crucial still, regionalism proposes that women have the desire to speak, the desire to tell the stories of their lives and so to have lives to live. In one of her earliest fictions, "Dreams and Tokens" (*Clovernook Sketches*), Cary suggests that women are natural storytellers with an endless fund of anecdotes from which to spin and weave their tales. Sent on an errand to the local tailoress, Cary's narrator discovers that cutting clothes and spinning yarns are connected. The narrator's arrival makes only a brief interruption in the flow of storytelling that occurs as one woman cuts and another woman knits. By associating the domestic work of women as they cut and knit and sew with the activity of storytelling, Cary implies that the one leads inevitably to the other and thus that women find storytelling natural and easy. More interesting still, these stories, in which the tellers figure prominently, delight their listeners, both male and female, young and old. Missing a tale her housekeeper wished to tell her because she was too impatient to listen becomes the narrator's greatest misfortune in "The Wildermings" (*Clovernook Sketches*).

Being "free to say" means, then, that women have the discursive freedom to fulfill their desire to tell stories. In "The Balcony" (1892), the preface to her first collection of regional sketches, King associates women's stories with "summer nights on balconies" where women sit "in their vague, loose, white garments, . . . their sleeping children within easy hearing" (*AWR* 380). Women talking on balconies—"men are not balcony sitters"—tell "experiences, reminiscences, episodes, picked up as only women know how to pick them up from other women's lives, . . . and told as only women know how to relate them" (380). Their children safely asleep on summer nights in "long-moon countries," each woman "has a different way of picking up and relating her stories" (381). King writes of the storyteller, "each story is different, or appears so to her; each has some unique and peculiar pathos in it. And so she dramatizes and inflects it, trying to make the point visible to her apparent also to her hearers. Sometimes the pathos and interest to the hearers lie only in this—that the relater has observed it, and gathered it, and finds it worth telling. For do we not gather what we have not, and is not our own lacking our one motive?" (381).

In identifying telling and listening as motivated by "lacking," King suggests that the "relater" and her "hearers" form a relationship based on mutual need, and furthermore that the storyteller, as she "dramatizes and inflects" her story, tries to share the meaning of her observations with her listeners in ways that fill the lack in both teller and listener. King suggests as well that in this women's culture, of mothers at hand but relaxing their vigilance, the very identity of children takes form. She writes, "And the children inside, waking to go from one sleep into another, hear the low, soft mother-voices on the balcony . . . and it seems to them, hovering a moment in wakefulness, that there is no end of the world or time, or of the mother-knowledge; but, illimitable as it is, the mother-voices and the mother-love and protection fill it all,—with their mother's hand in theirs, children are not afraid even of God" (380). For King, storytelling becomes associated with filling a lack and with "mother-knowledge" in particular. Children supposed to be asleep may actually be awake, listening to the stories, or, instead, looking across the "dim forms on the balcony" to the "heavens beyond." Women who are mothers may try to inflect their own stories, but from the child's perspective they become "dim forms on the balcony." Regionalist fiction takes up the thematic of "mother" as "dim forms." It is more than "other women's destinies" that these balcony-sitters are trying to create; it is the very concept of "mother-knowledge" itself.

In "The Trial Path" (1901), Zitkala-Ša also suggests that women are storytellers and that they often design their stories specifically for other women. In this sketch, Zitkala-Ša portrays a grandmother telling stories to her granddaughter in an effort to pass on and hence keep alive the histories, traditions, and sacred knowledge of her tribe. Unlike "The Balcony," however, in which the children move in and out of sleep soothed and secure in the mother-knowledge articulated as story, the child in "The Trial Path" falls asleep at the very point for which the story has but served as prelude: "My grandchild, I have scarce ever breathed the sacred knowledge in my heart. To-night I must tell you one of them. Surely you are old enough to understand" (*AWR* 562). In this passage Zitkala-Ša signals the enormous rift that has opened up between the generations of her people, making the sacred knowledge so central to the grandmother of so little interest to the granddaughter that, once what she mistakenly thinks of as the real story is over, she falls asleep. In relating the grandmother's need to preface what she really wants to say with the conventionally romantic story of her own young love, Zitkala-Ša acknowledges as well her own difficult position as an Indian storyteller seeking to communicate with a predominantly white audience, struggling to create the context and conditions within which she can be heard. Implicitly dialogic, "The Trial Path" leaves suspended not simply the question of who will listen to the grandmother's knowledge but more significantly what else she has to say since this is merely "one of them." Regionalist writers ponder the questions these sketches pose: if mothers and grandmothers, with their "mother-knowledge" and "sacred knowledge," cannot really control the circumstances of their stories' own reception, cannot control whether the children are asleep or awake, and what the children make of the "dim forms" that call themselves "mother," then is "mother" itself a knowledge that can be passed down, or is it instead a concept that children construct out of their own "lacking," and if so, how does the concept of "mother" function when actual mothers, like so many in regionalist fiction, are as evanescent as the "pretty reflections" and the "fragile soap bubbles" that color the dreams of the children of the balcony-sitters?

If women can be storytellers and if they recognize that telling stories is a way to fill their lack, then "mother-knowledge" and "sacred knowledge" become their own constructions, their own equivalents for the actual "dim forms" in which half-awake children and sleeping grandchildren find comfort. Regionalism itself functions as a retelling of sacred knowledge, and the form this thematic takes involves the insoluble contradiction between the invocation of "mother" as a sign of and for comfort, filling the "lacking," and a perennial and even universal disappointment, a deep sadness that underscores regionalist narratives; for one of the curious features of regionalism is that, though the narratives frequently invoke "mother" in various ways, they also construct this connecting thematic against the loss, death, or absence of biological mothers. In theory, "mother" consoles; in practice, "she" exists as "dim forms," fabrications of the imagination, stories told, or "gathered." The granddaughter in "The Trial Path" fails to see the urgency of staying awake to hear what her grandmother wishes to tell her, for it has not yet occurred to her that the knowledge her grandmother wishes to pass on is not only valuable but is almost already gone, or never existed *except* in story.[3]

In their self-consciousness concerning the surrogacy of story as a metonym for "mother" who exists only *as* "story," and in the tension they express between this knowledge and the desire to believe in "mother-knowledge," many regionalist texts take place, not through either realistic or sentimental depictions of mother, but rather through difficulties with "mother" as a thematic. Thus, in the midst of narratives that appear to find consolation in constructing stories about mothers, we find regionalist fictions that are motivated by motherlessness and tell stories of characters whose lives—King's "structures or ruins of life" (*AWR* 381)—are marred and marked by biological mothers who have become ill and died, have been neglectful or abusive, become estranged, or have been complicit in socializing daughters in ways that constrain their development. Indeed, some of the fictions that seem most strongly to affirm the consolations of mother-love rely on various surrogacies, real mothers being nonexistent or peripheral to the construction of the thematic.

Some of the narratives that concern themselves most explicitly with a need for solace ironically also envision a deeply and essentially motherless universe. A quick review of a few of the narratives included in *American Women Regionalists* marks this contradiction. *The Pearl of Orr's Island* (excerpted in *AWR*) begins with not one but two scenes that create orphans—Mara Lincoln's mother dies in childbirth after watching her husband's ship sink before he can safely return to harbor; Moses Pennel's mother drowns after another shipwreck but manages to entwine her child in her dead arms and to deliver him safely to shore where he is rescued and brought up by surrogate parents. Yet Stowe's novel constructs God "not so much like a father as like a dear and tender mother" (*Pearl* 348).[4] In Cary's "Uncle Christopher's," marked by the narrator's empathy for the motherless Mark who has been abandoned by his father to the "straightening" of his grandfather, the narrator is herself apparently motherless and equally abandoned by her father, against her will and beyond her control, to "Uncle" Christopher. The narrator consoles herself, and little Mark, by emphasizing the surrogacy of acts of mothering: another child in the household, Andrew, becomes Mark's protector; Mark dies in an attempt to rescue the kitten he has been forced to throw into the well; and the narrator herself tells her story as a way of questioning abusive parents, fathers like Uncle Christopher (or even her own) and mothers like Christopher's wife who do not intervene. Similarly, in "Freedom Wheeler's Controversy with Providence," Cooke constructs her truth about fathers in the words of the child Marah, who refuses to say the Lord's Prayer, "'Me don't want Father in heaven: fathers is awful cross'" (*AWR* 113). However, in this story a mother dies in childbirth, leaving the children she loves in the hands of the man whose desire for a son has been the cause of her death. Lowly, this aptly named woman, seems to incarnate mother-love with her "affluent mother-heart" as she cares for her babies with "the surest joy that earth knows" (101); but the acts of "mother" must be carried out by the childless aunts, Huldah and Hannah, who become after her death surrogate mothers for Lowly's daughters, the children whom their father rejects because they are girls.

Numerous stories focus on motherless or surrogately mothered children—Jewett's "A White Heron" and *A Country Doctor,* King's "Pupasse," Chopin's "Odalie Misses Mass" and "A Little Country Girl," Dunbar-Nelson's "Sister Josepha"; in other narratives, one character adopts or takes care of a child or, often, an abandoned or disabled adult—Murfree's "The 'Harnt' That Walks Chilhowee," King's "'One of Us,'" Chopin's "Ozème's Holiday," Dunbar-Nelson's "The Praline Woman"; in others, daughters and mothers are estranged, as in Chopin's "Lilacs," Zitkala-Ša's "Impressions of an Indian Childhood" and "School Days of an Indian Girl," and Cather's "Old Mrs. Harris." It is as if regionalist writers have discovered a gap in the ideological construction of nineteenth-century concepts of motherhood. Anticipating the modernist thematic of the death of God, regionalist writers in the previous century already recognized that, in spite of their culture's obeisance to the concept, mother is dead. Or, to express it slightly differently, they recognize that "mother" is in fact a cultural construct, presumed to serve the function of nurturing the kinds of adults who, as in MacKinnon's description of the subject of First Amendment rights, become "autonomous, self-defining, freely acting, equal individuals" (*Feminism Unmodified* 181). However, since a mother by definition cannot be such an individual and since girls are raised to become mothers, the presumption of "mother" does not exist for girls, nor does "mother" in fact exist for all boys. While caring and the nurturing of both autonomy and human connection are values that pervade regionalist fiction, and while the process of listening characters into speech serves a kind of "mothering" function, regionalist texts also suggest that the mothering necessary to human development is not easy to find and bears no certain relationship to biological mother. In the language of Austin, regionalist characters exist in a "land of little rain"; like cattle who have died trying to cross the desert, "[their] heads almost invariably will be turned toward the places where water-holes should be" (*AWR* 591).

Implicit in Austin's description of "places where water-holes should be," even so, is a gentleness toward either person or beast who sets out across the desert. Or, to recall Cary's phrase from "The Sisters," "Orphaned as we are, we have need to be kind to each other—ready with loving and helping hands and encouraging words, for the darkness and the silence are hard by where no sweet care can do us any good" (*Clovernook Sketches* 64). In turning its head to the place where "mother" should be, the human child and, later, the longing and "orphaned" adult learn how much in excess of actual satisfaction is the "lacking" King identifies as the "one motive" for observing, gathering, and telling every story that "*is* different, or appears so" (*AWR* 381). The thematics of regionalism thus construct "mother" in a different way than conventional understandings of the word. "Mother" is not dead but lives whenever a character in regionalist fiction recognizes another's need for kindness, help, and a human connection that takes place in part through storytelling itself.

That such a recognition emerges from the perception of being orphaned, whether in a material or metaphysical sense, serves to underscore that "mother" is socially constructed. Yet regionalist texts do not offer "father" as a better alternative. Indeed, in a moment as startling to the contemporary reader as Miss Beulah's statement "'I'm free to say I never did like boys,'" in "Freedom Wheeler's Controversy with Providence" Cooke's narrator writes, "it would have been painful to see how 'father' was a dreadful word, instead of a synonym for loving protection and wise guidance" (*AWR* 113). As noted above, she allows Marah, one of Freedom's daughters, to be free to shock Freedom's Aunt Hannah by refusing to say the Lord's Prayer and to be free to reject "father in heaven": "'Me won't! Me don't want Father in heaven: fathers is awful cross. Me won't say it, aunty'" (113). Regionalist characters consistently choose "mother" over "Father" (whether on earth or in heaven), but what they choose is a concept of "mother" that the texts of regionalism thematically work out and reimagine across decades, writers, and regions. In the next section, we will explore the ways in which regionalist texts recognize that mother may be dead but that "mother" lives, and that storytelling can stand in for the various functions of the work of mothering—namely, the work of providing mirroring, nurturing, comfort, models for human connection, and images of the world that can become the child's legacy. We will use the word "mother" in this chapter from this point forward to indicate a sign that marks the site where "water-holes should be," and under which regionalist texts construct an alternative discourse for lack, it appears, of any better word.

"Mother" Lives

Freeman's "On the Walpole Road" explores the way the concept of "mother" offers an opportunity for storytelling that provides comfort, a source of connection, and implicitly social acceptance for a woman who might need it, but indirectly, in a way that, as Mis' Green, who tells the story, admits, has "'gone round to the northeast'" (*AWR* 314). Returning home from the Walpole market on a summer afternoon, two women travel a particular road and both the road and the threat of a storm provide occasion for a story that, as we later learn, is so important to its listener that she seems likely to have chosen the "road not much traveled" (307) simply in order to elicit the story again. According to her younger companion, Almira, about forty and the driver of the open, horse-drawn carriage, the seventy-year-old narrator, Mis' Green, should have been a minister. Such a comment frames the older woman's story as a form of sacred knowledge, as a kind of gospel, good spell, good story. Although Mis' Green acknowledges that she would have been a minister "'ef I had been a man'" (308), her "scripture" is decidedly unorthodox. Expressing her view that Gabriel's trumpet is not going to be "frightful" but that "'it's goin' to come kinder like the robins an' the flowers do in the spring, kinder meltin' right into everything else,'" elicits her younger companion's response, "'That ain't accordin' to Scripture,' said Almira, stoutly" (307). Mis' Green replies, "'It's accordin' to my Scripture. I tell you what 'tis, Almiry, I've found out one thing a-livin' so long, an' that is, thar ain't so much difference in things on this airth as thar is in the folks that see 'em. It's me a-seein' the Scripturs, and it's you a-seein' the Scripturs, Almiry, an' you see one thing an' I another, an' I dare say we both see crooked mostly, with maybe a little straight mixed up with it'" (308). Mis' Green then begins to tell a story that she thinks will keep them both from "'getting aggervated at the horse,'" who does not share their sense of urgency at the impending storm and "jogged along undisturbed" (308).

In this story, Mis' Green tells of how she was called one day to a funeral and "'when we'd got halfway thar or so, thar come up an awful thundershower from the northwest, jest as it's doin' today'" (309). Believing that it is her Aunt Rebecca who lived "'on this very road'" who has died, Mis' Green declares, "'I couldn't ha' felt much worse ef it had been my mother,'" for Aunt Rebecca had come to nurse her through a fever "'the year after mother died'" (308). Mis' Green continues, "'I allers knew I should ha' died ef it hadn't been for her'" (308). When she arrives at the funeral and finds that it is Uncle Enos who is dead and not Aunt Rebecca, she breaks out in hysterical laughter, laughing "'till the tears was running down my cheeks'" because, as she tells her living aunt, "'I thought you was dead, an' thar you was a-settin'" (310). We might translate this as regionalism's discursive freedom to announce the resurrection of "mother," or, more radically, to declare that "father" is dead but "mother" lives. Mis' Green recognizes that she is behaving inappropriately since many of Uncle Enos's relatives who have gathered for the funeral "'looked at me as ef they thought I was crazy. But seein' them look only sot me off again'" (310). Her hysterical laughter acknowledges that she knows she is violating custom, breaking a taboo, announcing a radically different thematic, but she continues to "speak" anyway, setting her announcement of the resurrection of "mother" in dialogue with those who consider it unspeakable.

At the end of the story, Almira admits that she has heard the story before, "'the last time I took you to Walpole.'" What readers realize, then, is that both women have an unspoken agreement to tell and hear this story again and again, but to treat each telling as if it were "news." Telling and hearing this story has ongoing significance in the lives of these women for the story of "'mother' lives" serves as an alternative Scripture, one that some readers may find "crooked mostly," but one which offers Almira consolation for some unspoken lack, loss, or grief which we may infer. For "mother" in this story does not depend on biological relationship; Aunt Rebecca is "like" a mother to Mis' Green and Mis' Green's entire narrative may be read as serving several "mothering" functions to her younger companion. Aunt Rebecca's biological mother has in fact been the agent of her daughter's oppression, the reason why she married a man she did not love and missed marrying the one she did. Furthermore, Mis' Green does not believe that Aunt Rebecca "'was ever really happy or contented'" (312), and when Uncle Enos's death frees her at last to marry the man she had been forced to reject, Mis' Green expresses the opinion that "'sometimes I used to think they wa'n't so happy after all'" (313).

Although the story does not explicitly identify Almira as a single woman, the lack of any reference to family or children at home marks her as a candidate for the pity the world gives the "old maid." Through Mis' Green's "crooked mostly" way of seeing, she implicitly tells Almira that marriage does not necessarily provide consolation, even though she reports that "'ef Aunt Rebecca didn't find anything just as she thought it was goin' to be, she never let on she was disapp'inted'" (314). Mis' Green's story "mothers" Almira against the world's pity and rejection of single women and in the process provides at least her own story as an alternative "mother" for the younger woman, a way of recognizing her value. Mis' Green offers Almira consolation, esteem, and connection—gifts that biological mothers are supposed to but often are unable or choose not to provide. Most important, she provides her with the knowledge that "mother" is a concept amenable to surrogacy and thus multiply located. While some regionalist fiction does celebrate the love of daughters for biological mothers, perhaps most notably Jewett's *The Country of the Pointed Firs* in the relationship of Mrs. Todd to her mother, Mrs. Blackett, and to Green Island, "where mother lives" (*The Country of the Pointed Firs* 30), the significance of regionalist fiction lies in its dissociation of mothering from biological mother and in its modeling the possibility of women receiving mothering from a variety of sources. In regionalism, then, the recognition that "mother" is a construction, rather than necessarily producing a sense of ontological abandonment, instead offers daughters the opportunity to be free to say "mother" does indeed live. In a sense we might say that regionalism represents the art of finding "mother" in a culture profoundly uninterested in mothering daughters and even hostile to such a possibility.

As we suggested in our brief analysis of Thaxter and Austin in chapter 2, among regionalist writers they are the two who most clearly foreground a sense of place, for whom topography is the primary subject and the land a major character. Although their landscapes stand at opposite ends of the continent and differ strikingly from each other, extraordinary parallels in their work suggest that for regionalist writers the landscape itself may also provide a mothering function. In *Among the Isles of Shoals,* among other things the story of the birth of a poet, Thaxter links her ability to act on the desire growing ever more powerful within her "to *speak* these things that made life so sweet," a desire previously held in check by her sense of her own inadequacy, to her ability to transpose the biological mother whom she so deeply associated with her island home to the landscape itself and to recover from "nature" that sense of mirroring and connection, of relation, that one hopes to get from "mother." Austin, whose life was literally saved by eating the grapes that grew near her desert home, writes in her third-person autobiography, *Earth Horizon,* that she was able to find in the desert the sustaining "mother" she never had and thus to construct herself as a source of power and knowledge and story (*AWR* 564–65). While few other regionalist writers foreground place to the extent that Thaxter and Austin do, their work provides a frame for understanding a key operation of regionalist fiction, one that marks a clear distinction between regionalism and local color. In regionalist fiction "mother" lives in the landscape and landscape becomes one of several sources to which the orphaned or inadequately mothered may turn for sustenance, even in a "land of little rain." In constructing the landscape as mother and mirror, regionalist fiction understands place as the location of the "same" rather than as the location of the exoticized other who is different from the self. Regionalist characters find themselves mirrored in the landscape and regionalist writers see in their characters, whether persons or places, something that is "like" themselves. This recovery of the self becomes a form of mothering important to those who are themselves viewed as "different" in "what is called the world" (*AWR* 60). The "minor" or "marginal" place regionalist fiction has been granted in American literary history calls attention to its difference; indeed, regionalist fiction itself has proved a "sideshow" for those critics and literary historians who find the woman writer "free to say" to be a kind of freak. In this reading of regionalism in which writers recognize their similarity to regional characters rather than using narrative to contain the difference of "others," place serves to support the writer's freedom to assert her own difference by providing a mirror and a "mother" that reflects and supports that difference. Far from being an exercise in nostalgia for a vitality long gone, regionalism associates place with the most vital power imaginable, that of "mother-love," what Cooke describes in "Freedom Wheeler's Controversy with Providence" as "the only love that never fails among all earthly passions" (*AWR* 103), a love available to be discovered, recovered, or constructed whether or not it is present in biological mothers.

Jewett articulates the thematic of "'mother' lives" in "A White Heron," where the countryside serves as a child's source of mothering. Nine-year-old Sylvia is rescued by her grandmother from town and its attendant terrors—"the great red-faced boy who used to chase and frighten her" (*AWR* 199)—and brought to the country to live: "Everybody said that it was a good change for a little maid who had tried to grow for eight years in a crowded manufacturing town, but, as for Sylvia herself, it seemed as if she never had been alive at all before she came to live at the farm" (198). Sylvia, whom her grandmother describes as "afraid of folks" and whom she has chosen "from her daughter's houseful of children" (198), finds companionship in the cow and in all the wild creatures of the forest, particularly the birds. Indeed it is the very absence of "folks" that enables Sylvia to flourish because "folks" are not interested in mothering this girl and in a world of folks she can find nothing that nourishes her: "She thought often with wistful compassion of a wretched dry geranium that belonged to a town neighbor" (198). We might recall here that the landscapes of Thaxter and Austin are similarly devoid of "folks" and their institutions, and we might recognize as well the connection between this absence of folks and the regionalist writer's ability to find "mother," for when, as Austin puts it, "not the law, but the land sets the limit" (*AWR* 567), it is possible for those whom the law does not serve and whom the First Amendment does not protect to find nourishment and support, identity and agency in the land. The "mothering" Sylvia gets from the region enables her to deny the desire of the hunter, an older and more acceptable version of the great red-faced boy, to refuse to tell him where he may find the nest of the heron and so kill and stuff the bird, and thus implicitly to resist the desire of "folks" to kill and stuff her as well. So mothered, she becomes "free" not to give the ornithologist what he wants and is willing to pay for and "free" to assert her own difference against the combined pressure of her grandmother and the attractive male stranger.

Much of the power of "A White Heron" comes from Jewett's dialogic recognition of the extent to which her story of this "lonely country child" (205) differs from the narratives her readers find more familiar. To get her story heard she must construct it as a self-conscious counterthematic, one that is aware of what it opposes and of taking the "road not much traveled." Thus, like Freeman in "A New England Nun," she includes within her story traces of the dominant thematic of heterosexual romantic love as Sylvia recognizes her "loving admiration" for the young sportsman even though she "would have liked him vastly better without his gun; she could not understand why he killed the very birds he seemed to like so much" (201). Jewett writes that "the woman's heart, asleep in the child, was vaguely thrilled by a dream of love" (201), and even at the end of the story, after the guest has gone away disappointed, Jewett acknowledges Sylvia's own potential to "have served and followed him and loved him as a dog loves" (205). In doing so she elicits the response that would read Sylvia's fear of the red-faced boy and her later rejection of the hunter as a sign of sexual repression that relegates her to permanent adolescence and deprives her of (hetero)sexuality. Yet Jewett elicits this response in order to challenge it; she asks what it is "that suddenly forbids her and makes her dumb," why just at the point "when the great world for the first time puts out a hand to her, must she thrust it aside for a bird's sake?" (204). In the narrator's final invocation to "woodlands and summertime" to "remember" and "bring your gifts and graces and tell your secrets to this lonely country child" (205), Jewett re-articulates the "mothering" Sylvia derives from the landscape and constructs regionalist fiction as itself a form of mothering absent in the responses of those who would see in Sylvia only a fear of growing up and would understand growing up to mean a heterosexuality of "pretty feathers stained and wet with blood" (205). In the choice between seizing the "splendid moment" as the young man "waits to hear the story she can tell" (204) and reading beyond the "young man's kind appealing eyes" to see there an image of selling, and selling out, the region's "rare bird" (201), she listens to the very "mother" she herself has discovered in the heron in its nest, which is after all nothing other than her desire that her own difference from that "great world" find support and nurturing. In constructing the region as a "mother," regionalism engages in the cultural work of raising girls differently despite a "great world" that shares Freedom Wheeler's view that "'gals ain't worth namin' anyhow!'" (102). Regionalist writing seeks to counter the dominant narrative that, as King puts it, "the insignificant are so easily forgotten" and to construct its texts as "mothers" who do indeed care for those whom the world not only forgets but often actively seeks to kill.

As we have noted previously, the work of raising girls in a culture that either ignores them or seeks actively to de-develop them concerns Stowe in *The Pearl of Orr's Island,* a text that also constructs regionalism as a dialogue with dominant cultural narratives and embeds this dialogue in a novel that ultimately fails to sustain a regionalist vision; like so many heroines in nineteenth-century fiction by men and women writers, Mara dies a sacrificial death rather than triumphing over her own orphaning. In *The Pearl of Orr's Island,* however, Stowe introduces Aunts Roxy and Ruey as regional figures, distinguished from the normative and uninflected world of the protagonists by their speech, habits, situation, and in the case of Aunt Roxy, perspective as well. Constructed as different and marginal, Aunt Roxy can articulate a position that Stowe's narrator is not yet "free to say." In our reading, Stowe's novel thereby becomes a prior text for regionalism but not a full exemplar of the mode. Yet it is a text we find crucial to our understanding of the thematics of regionalism as it reveals more precisely just what regionalist fiction is free to say that other modes of nineteenth-century women's writing, and specifically the novel, are not. As Fetterley observes in "Only a Story, Not a Romance," Stowe's text, as well as its history of interrupted serial publication, reveals a great deal of anxiety concerning the story *The Pearl of Orr's Island* ultimately tells. In this novel, the female protagonist is orphaned when her father dies in shipwreck and her mother dies in childbirth. While the story in which Aunt Roxy and Aunt Ruey might be able to bring Mara up and to "mother" this orphaned female child is one that regionalist writers, answering Catharine Sedgwick's command to "call Debby," will develop, Stowe is compelled by her commitment to the mainstream, to the perspective of the "world" and to the form of the novel, to abandon Mara and tell a story that focuses on the conversion of men. The only way she can really "convert" Moses Pennel, the male child also orphaned at birth, washed ashore in the arms of his dead mother, raised as Mara's "brother" and educated in male entitlement, is to deprive the grownup Moses of his desire to marry Mara by writing Mara's premature death by consumption.

The Pearl of Orr's Island is, in Stowe's own words, "no great romance . . . , —only a story," because, as Fetterley reads it, it creates a "plot to bring Moses down, to dispossess him of his masculine prerogatives and his sense of superiority" ("Only a Story" 124) and in the process to write a critique of the conventions of romance and in particular their debilitating effects for girls' development. Consigning girls to the realm of romance (and consigning Mara's education to lessons in mortuary art) does not produce a healthy adult woman, according to this novel; and it is Mara's gender that not only excludes her both from Moses's Latin lessons and his sea voyage, but produces as well the narcissistic wound that Stowe implies leads to her consumption. Stowe critiques the position of inferiority in which Mara must try to grow up as best she can; at one point the minister, Reverend Sewell, recognizes that Mara's health would also benefit from a sea voyage: "'But she's a woman,' he said, with a sigh, 'and they are all alike. We can't do much for them, but let them come up as they will and make the best of it'" (*Pearl* 167). While Stowe can work out her own anger at this inferior position by at least rescuing Mara, if death is a rescue, from marriage to Moses, she cannot construct a life for Mara. In Aunt Roxy, however, Stowe does create a "mother" for Mara who tries to keep her alive when she becomes ill and who articulates an alternative perspective. On hearing that Mara has become engaged to Moses, whose education in male privilege leads him to assume that girls exist to serve men and that no matter how badly men behave girls will still and always love them, Aunt Roxy alone dissents from the dominant view of the engagement as a fortunate event that will be, in the words of Mara's grandparents, who are also Moses's adoptive parents, the "saving" of Moses. Identifying the discursive freedom available to the regionalist figure, Aunt Roxy declares, "'I a'n't one of the sort that wants to be a-usin' up girls for the salvation of fellers'" (352). Although Stowe can offer only God as an effective "mother" substitute (as when Mara says, "'God has always been to me not so much like a father as like a dear and tender mother'"), through Aunt Roxy she creates regionalism as the location of a thematics in which "mother" either as narrator or character takes an active role in advocating for the life of the "daughter," even though in this case her regionalist perspective is overruled by the "world."

Although most regionalist fictions follow the model set by Stowe and present advocacy as a position one woman takes with respect to another or to a girl child, a few stories stake out a still more radical position, that of women standing up for and mothering themselves. The relative infrequency of this version of "'mother' lives" suggests its radical nature, yet it is the logical extension of the thematic, for the ultimate goal of the cultural work of raising girls, of "mothering," is to provide daughters with enough self-esteem to advocate for themselves. In one of Cooke's last stories, "How Celia Changed Her Mind," the "changed mind" she relates moves Celia Barnes from the story's opening, in which Celia accepts the dominant attitude of her community and despises herself for being an old maid, to its conclusion, when she vows to adopt two orphaned children "'and fetch 'em up to be dyed-in-the-wool old maids'" (*AWR* 153). Celia arrives at this change ironically by deciding to marry late in life not simply to escape the despised status of old maid but to gain an advocate for herself, someone who will take her part and defend her in public. Discovering after marriage just what marriage means to most women and how far more frequently they acquire thereby an abuser rather than an advocate, she comes to recognize that she has to stand up for herself. Refusing to wear mourning when her husband dies and gleefully taking as much of his estate as she can get, because as she says she has earned it, Celia constructs an alternate institution, an old maids' Thanksgiving, dedicated to feeding herself and all the other old maids in the village and to declaring a far different view of what is good for women than the one articulated by the dominant institutions of her culture.

Expressing Desire

Like *The Pearl of Orr's Island,* Chopin's *The Awakening* embeds elements of regionalism but stops short of a full articulation of its thematics. As we will discuss further in chapter 10, Chopin's Mlle. Reisz offers the single woman artist as an alternative to Edna Pontellier's oppressive marriage, but Chopin does not develop her potential, instead joining with other characters in her own novel in portraying Reisz as "queer." In both *The Pearl of Orr's Island* and *The Awakening,* the female protagonist does not survive either her female socialization or her author's narrative. Still, the power of *The Awakening* rests in Chopin's willingness to give a woman who is herself a mother ongoing desire that the very state of motherhood has neither satisfied nor extinguished, and Chopin's other fiction also links "'mother' lives" with the thematic of a woman recognizing and believing herself entitled to her own desire. Indeed, in "The Storm," Calixta, like Edna Pontellier already a mother, continues to recognize her own desire; Chopin describes Calixta's "firm, elastic flesh" as "knowing for the first time its birthright" (*AWR* 450) when she finally consummates her desire for Alcée Laballière during a thunderstorm.

While "The Storm," like *The Awakening,* equates that desire with heterosexuality, the story "Lilacs" suggests that female sexuality may take other forms. In this story, in which we also find a Mother Superior who served as a surrogate mother to the young Adrienne before she left the convent, married, and moved to Paris, the grown and now widowed Adrienne returns to the convent once a year when the lilacs bloom. When she arrives, she takes up again an ongoing intense sensual relationship with one of the nuns, Sister Agathe, "more daring and impulsive than all" the others. Chopin writes, on describing Adrienne's annual arrival, "What embraces, in which the lilacs were crushed between them! What ardent kisses! What pink flushes of happiness mounting the cheeks of the two women!" (*AWR* 435). However, the discovery of Adrienne's affairs in Paris as well as the hint of the temptations she offers Sister Agathe lead to the convent doors being locked against her arrival at the end of the story. Her previous gifts to the convent returned to her at the door, with a letter saying "'By order of our Mother Superior'" (443), a distraught Sister Agathe kneeling by the bed "on which Adrienne had slept," and a lay sister sent out to sweep away the lilac blossoms Adrienne has let fall (444), all suggest that while it may be in part Adrienne's worldliness that has alienated the Mother Superior, it is more likely the fact that upon her departure the previous year Sister Agathe had not been "satisfied to say good-by at the portal as the others did" but had walked down the drive with Adrienne "as far as she might go" (440). Female sexuality for Chopin knows no regulation; neither the institution of marriage nor that of the Church nor that of heterosexuality constrain Chopin's critique of the strictures on women's desires. In "Lilacs," she associates these strictures with a surrogate mother's abandonment. Near the end of the story, as Adrienne is leaving the convent without having gained entrance or even caught a glimpse of Sister Agathe, Chopin writes, "There was no anger in her heart; that would doubtless possess her later, when her nimble intelligence would begin to seek out the origin of this treacherous turn. Now, there was only room for tears. She leaned her forehead against the heavy oaken panel of the door and wept with the abandonment of a little child" (444). In the scene of Adrienne's abandonment by Mother Superior, Chopin links the inability of women to achieve their desire with the absence of mothering or with abuse of its power. However, what makes "Lilacs" memorable is not the "treacherous turn" that will lead to anger but rather Adrienne's discovery of her own desire and her ability to articulate that desire—as well as Chopin's ability to imagine that women's desire can be multiply located.

Unlike Austin, who in "The Walking Woman" associates sexuality with women's independence, thereby linking adult women's desire with First Amendment rights and citizenship, Chopin seems much less interested in developing her female characters as independent beings; however, in her depictions of women who assert that they are "free to say" they experience sexual desire, she radically extends the concept of advocacy for the self to the woman who recognizes her own desire. Constructing women as desiring subjects and articulating that desire presents considerable difficulties, for it not only challenges the premises of women's passive and submissive nature and questions the most intensely managed aspect of women's socialization; it also confronts the problem of finding an adequate sign for conveying women's desire, a symbolic equivalent for the phallus. Sigmund Freud, of course, saw women as only lacking and he associated women's lack of a penis with their passivity and their lack of "a desire of one's own," as Jessica Benjamin titles her discussion of the problem. As Benjamin argues, a "theory of maternal identification" may help solve the difficulty of representing women's desire, but only if such "maternal identification" serves to rewrite "the cultural image of woman-as-sexual object." Benjamin writes, "The 'real' solution to this dilemma of woman's desire . . . has to do with the need for a mother who is articulated as a sexual subject, who is an agent, who does express desire" (89). Finally, then, a regionalist thematic of "'mother' lives" must include "mother" as more than a source of nurturance and development; "mother" must be free to articulate herself as desiring subject, as agent of desire, and she must be free to define desire, in the language of Freeman and Chopin, as her "birthright." One aspect of the thematics of "'mother' lives," then, involves the myriad ways regionalism offers for figuring women's desire—that desire so powerfully articulated by Austin in her description of the desert: "and you could not move her, no, not if you had all the earth to give, so much as one tawny hair's-breadth beyond her own desires" (*AWR* 592).

However, since expressions of female desire that can be in any way construed as sexual often serve to make women vulnerable to assault and exploitation, we are not surprised to find women adept at expressing such desire indirectly. Such indirectness particularly characterizes Cary, writing in the middle of the nineteenth century at a time when the ideology of gender explicitly proscribed women as having desire. Cary "invents" regionalism to discover, explore, and figure unauthorized desire, even though she often finds it necessary to displace the articulation of this desire onto the unauthorized wishes of a little boy:

> "I suppose you have never been to school, Pete. May-be you don't know what a school is?"
>
> "No, sir," said Peter; "I have never been to school but I know what it is, and I should like to go."
>
> "I suppose," said the uncle, "you would like a great many things."
>
> Peter said, "I would like a great many things," and the whole family laughed outright. ("Peter Harris," *Clovernook* 140–41)

Cary's articulation of the desire of women for "a great many things" is often quite indirect. For example, in "About the Tompkinses" (*Clovernook Sketches*), this desire takes the form of a young woman's yearning to attend a party and manifests itself in the creativity and energy she invests in making something to wear in the hope that she will be allowed to have her desire. In another story, "Charlotte Ryan" (*Clovernook Sketches*), when a young woman actually fulfills her desire to attend a party and finds herself the center of attention as a social success in a world far removed from her humble origins, she can only collapse in tears and cry out that she wished she had never left home, so difficult is it for women to reconcile themselves as desiring subjects with the sense of themselves as virtuous or good.

Cary solves this dilemma to some extent through the creation in many of her sketches of a narrator who expresses desire as the wish to see, to hear, and hence to know. In "My Grandfather," the opening sketch of the first volume of *Clovernook* (1852), Cary introduces her narrator as a child who possesses "an irrepressible desire to see" so strong that she pushes her way uninvited into a room where her grandfather is dying. Since this sketch documents the origin of the narrator, we come to realize that every word this narrator writes is in effect a product of that desire: "so eagerly I noted every thing, that I remember to this day, that near a trough of water, in the lane, stood a little surly looking cow, of a red color, and with a white line running along her back" (*Clovernook* 15). In a certain sense, then, the entire body of Cary's regional fiction is a manifestation of female desire; her texts are saturated with the traces of a desire we can recover if we learn to see as Clovernook sees. Ultimately, "'mother' lives" becomes an emblem for the range of expressions of women's desire, whether of Miss Beulah's for a new bonnet, Mis' Green's for a "crooked" Scripture, or Adrienne Farival's for a season of lilacs.

Indeed, even Chopin participates in the more dispersed articulations of female desire by placing it in characters and situations not readily sexualized as in "A Little Country Girl," a story that may be seen as expressing in its own way the point that, contrary to Cary's implication in "Charlotte Ryan," no danger to the universe is actually posed by a girl getting what she wants. In this story a little girl so desperately desires to go to the circus that, when she believes she will not be allowed to go, she wishes for a storm to ruin the event. When she finally does get to go and the storm she would have considered a "miracle" materializes, she believes that she is responsible for the collapse of the circus tent and the damage to her grandparents' crops (*AWR* 453, 456). In the intensity of her conviction we can read Chopin's recognition of the terror that accompanies the expression and fulfillment of desire in women, and in its absurdity we can read Chopin's critique of that fear. Fortunately for Ninette, a neighbor recognizes the extent of the child's desire, its importance for her development, and he intervenes (457).

The "Whoop" of the Heart

We might adapt a phrase from Zitkala-Ša and describe the discursive freedom of regionalist fiction as a "whoop" of the heart, an exuberant expression of women's desire that is deeply subversive. Indeed, as witness our students' response to "Miss Beulah's Bonnet," the discursive freedom of regionalism produces narratives that readers may not initially know how to read, so unaccustomed are we to recognizing women as agents of desire and to validating women's growth and development when that development challenges prescribed modes for female socialization and behavior or male privilege. Yet the thematics of regionalism become even more subversive for being so understated and dialogic. When Freeman, for example, calls a story "The Revolt of 'Mother'" (*Selected Stories*) and analogizes the act of mother's moving into the barn to the storming of Quebec, we are free to say that her language of overt resistance reveals the relatively tame nature of her text. The real revolt of regionalist fiction occurs in a frame that does not rely on the very systems of discourse it seeks to subvert and that does not call such attention to itself, for we might argue that the greatest of all the subversions of regionalism lies in proposing the survival of the women whom it presents ("mother" *lives,* after all) and the strategies of survival are not necessarily those of overt resistance. Regionalism is a fiction of resistance but it is a fiction in which resistance rarely takes the form of open revolt, often suicidal for women such as Freeman's own Candace Whitcomb in "A Village Singer" or the better-known Edna Pontellier in Chopin's *The Awakening;* the resistance of regionalist fiction more typically takes the form of understated rebellion and subversion, the "whoop" of the heart.

We take as a starting point for the final section of this chapter the description Zitkala-Ša provides of herself as a rebellious child removed from her native home and placed under the "iron routine" of the "civilizing machine" of a "paleface" school in "The School Days of an Indian Girl" (*AWR* 554). Forced one day to prepare the turnips for dinner for having violated a rule that to her seemed "needlessly binding," she handles them with such force as to break the bottom of the bowl, for the order was to "mash these turnips" and mash them she did. Later, "as I sat eating my dinner, and saw that no turnips were served, I whooped in my heart for having once asserted the rebellion within me" (552–53). Although scolded for having broken the bowl, she can hardly be punished further for simply doing what she was told. Zitkala-Ša's "I whooped in my heart" serves to capture both the feeling and the form of the various acts of resistance, rebellion, and subversion that occur in regionalist fiction.

This feeling and form can be seen in Freeman's "A New England Nun," in which Louisa Ellis without fanfare, without the language of storming the heights of Abraham, finds a way to get what she wants. As Freeman puts it, Louisa discovers when she needs it a power of which she was not previously aware and which she may never need to use again, and, though "meek of its kind" (364), it provides a sufficient weapon for her purposes. In a similar vein, Hetty Fifield in Freeman's "A Church Mouse" never openly questions the values of her community that would, if she let them, consign her to any one of a number of unpleasant alternatives. Rather she chooses simply to respond to those assertions of "common sense" that Caleb Gale assumes will silence her and to present herself as a problem she can help him solve. Hetty engages in behavior similar to Zitkala-Ša's, for she uses the very structures designed to oppress her to get what she wants—a room of her own that she can inhabit and decorate to her own heart's delight. If her village would like to treat Hetty as they treat their animals, turning her out to graze, she will take them at their word and engage in the purposeful pursuit of her own survival that we associate with nonhuman animals. As indicated by the title of her story, Freeman accords Hetty the instinct for survival of a church mouse, a desire that female socialization seeks to eliminate in women.

In "A Mistaken Charity," two old women transported against their will to the Old Ladies Home find a way to resist the consequences of their neighbor's benevolence. Leaving the insignia of their violation hanging on the bedposts as a kind of sentence—those new white lace caps they are required to wear since the Old Ladies Home insists on their being ladies—they put on their old clothes and with their heads uncovered "just as they always had done" (*AWR* 320), they return to their real home, a run-down old cottage that Freeman analogizes to the "tenement" of a squirrel. Once again Freeman uses the discourse of reduction to provide a point of resistance, for who would deny the squirrel her right to a nest? Indeed, having a home of their own makes it possible for these two old women to accomplish their act of resistance. "A Mistaken Charity," then, reveals the connection between home, "where mother lives" (Jewett, *The Country of the Pointed Firs* 30), the region, and women's capacity to resist. This connection creates a mode of resistance that can seem almost instinctive and not a matter of conscious thought. For example, in Murfree's "The 'Harnt' That Walks Chilhowee," Clarsie Giles, when told that she should stop feeding the "ghost" because it is against the law, responds by simply saying, "'I can't holp it'" (*AWR* 301). Similarly, when Sylvia in Jewett's "A White Heron" decides not to tell the secret of the bird, she does so without evidence of conscious deliberation. Indeed, if one takes Freeman's "A Village Singer" as an instance, one might argue that consciously undertaking an act of rebellion, of "revolution" (339), becomes self-destructive in regionalist fiction.

In the final analysis, the thematics of regionalism are those of resistance. Resistance occurs when women who are supposed to be silently acquiescent speak for themselves or are listened into speech; resistance occurs when characters advocate for their birthright, their own right to lives and desires of their own; resistance occurs when regionalist fictions pay attention to the insignificant, the marginalized; resistance occurs when regionalism asserts that "mother" lives and only "father" has died. We might summarize these thematics as the subversion of those assumptions the dominant discourse considers unassailable. In this context it is the hysterical laughter of Mis' Green upon finding Aunt Rebecca alive that best represents the "whoop" of the heart. We find a variant on this laughter in Sui Sin Far's "The Sing Song Woman," who is also characterized as a laughing woman. When confronted with the news that her friend is about to be forced to marry a man she does not know and whom she does not love because he is Chinese and her parents want her also to be Chinese and not American, Ah Oi laughs—"a peculiar, rippling, amused laugh" (*AWR* 503)—and then plans a trick that will subvert the conventions of her culture. This laughter, a surrogate for the language of open revolt, is deeply subversive and we can hear its echoes throughout regionalist fiction. Yet at a certain point this laughter becomes self-conscious.

Though typically understated, subtle and indirect, King's "The Old Lady's Restoration" offers a character addicted to consciousness and insistent on saying always "whatever she thought, regardless of the consequences, because she averred truth was so much more interesting than falsehood" (*AWR* 395). In particular the old lady despises the way society constructs women as "natural" liars, and "nothing annoyed her more in society than to have to listen to the compositions women make as a substitute for the original truth. It was as if, when she went to the theater to hear Shakspeare [*sic*] and Molière, the actors should try to impose upon the audience by reciting lines of their own" (395). When she finally recovers her former wealth and those "friends" who were quick to desert her in her poverty seek now to reconnect with her, she gives them a lesson in "original truth":

> "Comfort!" She opened a pot bubbling on the fire. "Bouillon! A good five-cent bouillon. Luxury!" She picked up something from a chair, a handful of new cotton chemises. . . . "And friends! My dear, look!" Opening her door, pointing to an opposite gallery, to the yard, her own gallery; to the washing, ironing, sewing women, the cobbling, chair-making, carpentering men; to the screaming, laughing, crying, quarreling, swarming children. "Friends! All friends—friends for fifteen years. Ah, yes, indeed! We are all glad—elated in fact. As you say, I am restored." (399)

Although the old lady's visiting "friends" report that she has lost her mind, King leaves her readers with a story that exposes the poverty of "those compositions women make as a substitute for original truth" and makes us realize how profoundly uninteresting such compositions are. As the old lady is "restored," so we are re-storied and this may be the ultimate subversion of regionalist fiction—it gives us such different and such interesting stories. With a strange and unauthorized "whoop" of the heart, regionalist texts, with their thematics of "'mother' lives," have the capacity to satisfy our interpretive desire. Thematics can therefore become a way to collect alternative texts; the stories that propose themselves as "free to say" that women possess the desire to live and to speak of their lives may not serve the interests of an "American" literature, but they do provide a way to construct a narrative that understands itself as a "crooked mostly" coherence.

CHAPTER 6

The Sketch Form and Conventions of Story

It was the old, old story,—the one eternal novelty that never loses its vitality, its interest, its bewitching power, nor ever will till time shall be no more.

—Rose Terry Cooke, "Dely's Cow"

The Novel and Plot

It is ironic that Jewett's *The Country of the Pointed Firs* has dominated critical discussion in recent attention to regionalism, for in terms of form *Pointed Firs* is anomalous.[1] This emphasis on *Pointed Firs,* however, provides a measure of the difficulties we encounter in trying to establish the value of a tradition that did not generate texts sufficiently long to be considered significant. It allows us to explore what we have referred to in chapter 2 as the ideology of form. Indeed, as we have seen in our review of the treatment of regionalism and local color in American literary history, the association of these traditions with the short story and the sketch has consistently served to justify their marginalization. While there are some titles in the tradition that might appear to be longer works—for example, Thaxter's *Among the Isles of Shoals,* Austin's *The Land of Little Rain,* Sui Sin Far's *Mrs. Spring Fragrance,* even Cary's first series of *Clovernook* sketches and King's *Balcony Stories*—each of these texts prioritizes the sketch form and each gains its coherence from the thematic similarities of the collected material rather than from any formal elements of a longer narrative. It is the case, then, that regionalist fiction consists primarily of short sketches and the individual sketch constitutes its essential form. Choosing a marginal form to express a thematics of "free to say" reflects regionalist writers' self-consciousness concerning their project. But why the sketch allows one to be "free to say" requires some attention to the cultural context within which these women wrote. Most of the writers we include in the tradition of regionalism wrote novels as well. However, when we look at the novels, for example, of Cary, Cooke, Murfree, Freeman, Chopin, Austin, or even Jewett, we are struck by their difference from the regionalist fiction of these writers; they appear almost as if they were the work of a different writer. This difference invites us to examine in particular the form of the novel as a way of understanding more fully the relation between "free to say" and the form of the sketch.

As a major nineteenth-century genre, the novel offered a writer the opportunity to be considered a major author of fiction, to have influence on readers, and to engage in what we now perceive as "cultural work."[2] Because of its significance, however, the novel and its author were subjected to considerable cultural scrutiny. Because the novel among literary forms appealed particularly to women readers and thus was understood to play a major role in the social construction of gender, women's novels, as Nina Baym has demonstrated in *Novels, Readers, and Reviewers,* came under even more scrutiny. Reviewers and editors constructed special requirements whose purpose "was to neutralize the threat of the woman author by setting her to work on behalf of true womanhood" (255); and in compartmentalizing authors into two categories, the "genius" (always male) and the "woman," "the most bizarre result . . . was that in writing as women, female authors were not allowed to say what they knew about their own sex . . . because their knowledge did not accord with the stereotype of the sex they were required to represent" (258). Baym concludes that "[a]ny deviation, on the part of speaking women, from an ideal of the female voice became the occasion for a generalized gender terror and called out a gender terrorism" (266). In the climate male readers and reviewers established early in the nineteenth century, women who aspired to write "what they knew about their own sex" would have to do so in forms other than the novel. If we examine the work of regionalists who chose to write both novels and shorter forms, we might conclude that women writing novels were in effect different subjects than those same women writing sketches and that this difference affected what they did or did not feel "free to say."

Nineteenth-century readers also accorded considerable significance to plot, and the novel's investment in plot provided one source of its prominence. According to Baym, plot determined whether a text would be read as a novel, and reviewers often angrily accused texts of claiming to be novels when they were nothing more than sketches. As an example, Baym cites a *Putnam's* reviewer in 1856 who claimed that *Uncle Tom's Cabin* and *Dred* were not really novels but were rather "series of sketches" (69), with the implication that "the prominence of plot made the novel superior to the more desultory sketch or tale" (70). The requirement of plot had serious implications for what women writers were free to say in novels, since they were limited by what readers expected to find. Not surprisingly, these expectations of what constituted plot and thus made a novel really a novel were culturally conservative, privileging heterosexual romance and those female characters who could be imagined as participating in such a romance—young, unmarried, but marriageable, and excessively feminine, since the sexuality that formed the essence of plot was understood as the attraction of opposites and required intense gender differentiation to be convincing to readers. The discursive limits of the novel were therefore substantial where women were concerned, and indeed the novel proved to be a difficult forum for the articulation of nineteenth-century feminist questions since its conventions worked against the possibility of writing "any lives of women."[3]

The Pearl of Orr's Island provides evidence of Stowe's recognition that dominant narrative forms made it difficult to write women's lives; it offers an example of the way gender conventions governed the plot of texts perceived to be novels and of a woman author's struggle with those conventions. Stowe began what she called her "Maine story" almost immediately after completing *Uncle Tom's Cabin,* whose original subtitle as it appeared in the *National Era*'s announcement of May 8, 1851, was "The Man Who Was a Thing," out of an impulse, we would argue, to prove that women were not "things" either and to establish the humanity of women through the writing of a woman's life. The decision to write a Maine story suggests that she also perceived a connection between regionalism and the writing of a woman's life. Yet though Stowe may have chosen to write a Maine story because of her attraction to the discursive possibilities of regionalism, when she began her novel with the birth of Mara and chose to make Mara the heroine of her book, she entered inevitably into a set of pressures that circumscribed her choices for developing Mara's "life" and story, a field of force constructed by the conventional understanding of plot. When she chose as well to introduce a male protagonist into her text at a very early stage and through a birthing scene quite comparable to Mara's, the pressure to turn her narrative into a romance became overwhelming, so synonymous for most readers is this story with the idea of story itself as Cooke reminds us in the epigraph to this chapter. While Stowe might have wished to consider the differences between growing up male and growing up female even in New England, at some point she came to realize that the form she had chosen made only one story possible and the second half of her text, the part Jewett found so disappointing, expresses her recognition of and capitulation to that fact.[4]

As we have noted, Stowe chooses to begin her text with the birth of her heroine, but immediately following this opening sequence, she introduces Aunts Roxy and Ruey, "two brisk old bodies of the feminine gender and singular number" (20).[5] The pleasure Stowe takes in describing Roxy and Ruey, who may be women but who hardly fulfill conventional expectations for the "feminine gender," suggests that the opportunity to create such characters played a large role in Stowe's motivation for writing *The Pearl of Orr's Island.* It suggests as well, as we proposed in our discussion of Sedgwick's *Redwood* in chapter 3, the connection between the regionalist impulse and the possibility of creating women characters whose behavior will deviate from the conventions of femininity. As the story progresses and the field of force exerted by the heterosexual romance plot set in motion by the "births" of heroine and hero becomes stronger and stronger, Aunt Roxy's difference becomes more and more acute; by the end of the novel, as we have indicated in the previous chapter, we find her opposing the heterosexual romance plot as inherently immoral.

In the context of the novel, however, Roxy cannot prevail; her rule is overruled, that is to say, "regionalized," and she exists in the text as a marginal figure, inhabiting a region within the realm of the text. One cannot imagine Stowe's novel with Roxy or Ruey at the center. Yet consider the opening of Freeman's "On the Walpole Road": "One summer afternoon two women were driving slowly along a road . . . in a dusty old-fashioned chaise, whose bottom was heaped up with brown-paper parcels. One woman might have been seventy, but she looked younger, she was so hale and portly. She had a double, bristling chin, her gray eyes twinkled humorously over her spectacles, and she wore a wide-flaring black straw bonnet with purple bows on the inside of the rim" (*AWR* 306). Suddenly Roxy and Ruey are at the center and everything looks different: "the other woman was younger—forty, perhaps" (*AWR* 306). Once we leave the realm of plot and enter a region of narrative form that evades the visibility of the novel, it becomes possible for a writer to begin a story with two older women who are possibly single and certainly singular. Choosing a form that escapes plot, regionalist writers are free to center character, and since the sketch does not prescribe what kind of character can be centered (its story is not *the* story), regionalist writers become free as well to focus on a whole range of persons who would inevitably be marginalized in novels.[6] Cooke articulates this freedom in her description of "Miss Lucinda" as "no tragedy in high life, no sentimental history of fashion and wealth, but only a little story about a woman who could not be a heroine" (*"How Celia Changed Her Mind"* 151).

Regionalist fictions frequently theorize their form by means of stylistic features embedded within their narratives. An exploration of form in various regionalist writers demonstrates an array of variations on the general challenge these writers chose to confront—namely, how to tell other stories than the "old, old, story," how to convince readers like the granddaughter in Zitkala-Ša's "The Trial Path" that the "real" story lies elsewhere, and how to develop alternative conventions for storytelling. As we discuss some of the writers collected in *AWR* with a focus on how they achieve a form for the sketch that allows it to carry the thematics of "free to say," we can see as well that the sketch form itself was not homogeneous. In "The Balcony," King writes that "[e]ach woman has a different way of picking up and relating her stories. . . . Each story *is* different, or appears so to her. . . . And so she dramatizes and inflects it, trying to make the point visible to her apparent also to her hearers" (*AWR* 381).

In presenting our work on regionalism, we are often asked if when we say "sketch" we don't really mean short story. In fact, we use the term "sketch" rather than short story intentionally because even though, as we have seen in our reading of Carlos Baker in chapter 2, the sketch is still lower on the scale of literary value than the short story, this term conveys the open-endedness, fragmentary nature, and indeterminacy we see as essential characteristics of regionalist fiction. With its relative lack of interest in plot and its anecdotal nature, regionalist fiction conveys the sense that here is one story but there are many others; and through its fragmentary nature, it creates a context within which beginnings, middles, and ends are relatively unimportant. In trying to answer the question we are often asked, we find ourselves describing regionalist fiction as in a certain sense antipathetic to form, relying for its ability to be "free to say" on choosing a mode of delivery that does not emphasize form. We mean of course form as readers conventionally understand it, form that readers recognize as such—a fiction that has a distinctive beginning, middle, and end and is designed to produce a single and often dramatic punch. Indeed, we might almost say that regionalist fiction rejects form since it recognizes that form tends to equate with structures designed by persons in power to tell their stories. As we try to talk about form in regionalist fiction, then, we find ourselves facing the difficulty of how to talk about form in texts that seem to be formless. One way of approaching this difficulty is to focus on regionalist writers' understanding of story, and on how their use of the sketch interrupts conventional expectations of story.

Fragment as Form in Cary

We recognize a consciousness of form when Cary embeds conventional plots and the characters associated with them in her sketches but, choosing not to center them, ruptures their claim to be the story and indicates instead that they are only one of a series of events forming the thematic content of her fiction. In "The Wildermings," for example, the narrator records her encounter with her new neighbors, a strange young man and a still stranger child whose eyes never close. As we come to realize the relation of the young man and child to the dead Mary Wildermings, who "'they say, died watching for one who never came, and the baby was watchful and sleepless from the first'" (*Clovernook Sketches* 29), we recognize the outline of the conventional story of seduction and abandonment. "The Wildermings," however, is not intended as a cautionary tale that warns the reader of a fate worse than death, for the complex connection between the narrator's desire to see and understand and the child's watchfulness even in death disrupts such a reading. In this sketch the implicit plot of seduction and abandonment becomes part of another story and is not the focus of the narrator's attention.[7] In what might well be called the inaugural gesture of regionalist fiction, Cary's "Preface" to the first series of *Clovernook* sketches locates the origin of her fiction in some place other than the "thought" that goes into making a "book"; specifically she locates the origins of her fiction in the shadows and sunbeams that fell about her, incidents unremarkable to most but associated for her with her deepest feelings of sorrow and joy. In writing of incidents so unremarkable as to be free of the shaping force of others' interpretations and thus of preconceived notions of meaning and form, Cary finds herself "free to say" a great deal. For Cary, then, being "free to say" depends upon embracing the fragment as her form.

"Uncle William's" provides an opportunity to explore the sketch as a composition of fragments. Taking the coach to visit her Uncle William, Cary's narrator hears bits of conversation that could easily form the basis for conventional stories. For example, one man points in passing to a tree, saying that "'one of my fellows hung himself there last week'" (Fetterley, ed., *Provisions* 227). A woman with a child responds angrily to the suggestion that she wrap him in her shawl: "'I am not his mother by a great sight; she's in a mad-house; they just took her this morning. It was a dreadful sight—she a raving, and the children screaming and carrying on at a dreadful rate'" (228). And a woman who behaves as women who are seduced and abandoned behave in "literature" moves in and out of the narrator's visit, leading her to note, "A year after my visit I heard, by chance, that Mrs. Hevelyn was dead, and the fragment of her life and love that I have written, is all I know" (240). The narrator embeds these fragments within a narrative that is itself fragmentary. We never learn why the narrator embarks on this visit in the first place and we are further baffled when Cousin Delia, the most likely reason for the narrator's visit, departs on the very coach that has brought the narrator to her uncle's. Neither the remaining cousin nor Uncle William will talk of Delia; indeed Uncle William never talks at all and cousin Jane will talk only of the weather, which for her is always pleasing. Life at Uncle William's barely contains even "incidents of so little moment," and were it not for a garrulous neighbor there would hardly be anything to report at all. Although framed by the narrator's journey to Uncle William's and her implied return home, Cary's sketch contains nothing that could be typically called a beginning, middle, or end. No moment is more significant than any other; material could be reordered without apparent effect for nothing happens that could be called a turning point or climax; and the division of her story into sections serves primarily to convey the sense of time passing. Moreover the narrative does not end, it simply stops; Cary's concluding reference to "the fragment of her life and love" reminds us of the fragmentary nature of her own narrative and of the fact that it could just as easily have stopped elsewhere as continued on and that it could just as easily continue on as stop. Cary's narrative in fact conveys the sense of going nowhere; it appears as aimless and random as the conversation within the coach and makes a sharp contrast to the purposiveness we assume informs such journeys. Going nowhere, however, slows us down, disrupts our expectations, rearranges our focus away from some anticipated end point and onto what is "passing"; it detains us in "Clovernook" long enough for us to learn to see as Clovernook sees, to mark the unremarkable, to discover the significance of the insignificant. What holds our interest, what makes us only too happy to be going nowhere, are the perceptions of Cary's narrator. Because of the narrator, we read with interest how the pig drover "pointed out all the places in which the hogs he had just sold had rested of nights" and how all the passengers "looked with interest at the various fields, and woods, and pens, where the drover's hogs had rested on their fatal journey toward the city" even though, as she says, "it would be hard to tell why" (224).

Cary wrote "My Grandfather" for her first series of *Clovernook* sketches and specifically as the "introduction" to that collection; in this narrative we encounter the origins of that consciousness which forms the source of our interest throughout her sketches. Although few regionalist writers would follow Cary in her use of the first person, her choice foregrounds the importance of narrative identity to regionalism. As we have discussed at length in chapter 4, this identity involves empathy, but we might extend that analysis here to suggest that regionalism also involves what we might call, following Nelle Morton's concept of a "theopoetics," a theology of narration (32).[8] Regionalist fiction posits a narrative identity that notices what others have missed; it posits the presence of that "great Listening Ear" which Morton's theopoetics imagines at the heart of the universe (55), someone like the narrator of "Uncle William's," who notices and recalls "the young women whose histories I began to mark when we were girls together in the district school" (Fetterley, ed., *Provisions* 223). The fragment is the form such a person chooses to record the histories of those too insignificant to figure in what passes for history and story in the "world."

In "My Grandfather," Cary identifies the consciousness capable of such marking as one aware of her own apparent insignificance: "What changes are to be counted, even in a little noiseless life like mine!" (*Clovernook Sketches* 9). Marking her own significance is understandably the first act of a consciousness that would wish to mark the significance of others who have also been considered insignificant. Cary sets her narrative in that time before "the shadow first came over my heart, that no subsequent sunshine has ever swept entirely away" (9), but we discover her as already shadowed, both literally and figuratively outside the circle of significance. Playing outside while the rest of her family remains within, the narrator is suddenly sad. She draws close to the window and looking within sees her mother making a ruffle that she thinks may be for her to wear to school; minutes later, however, her mother puts the ruffle on her little brother. She watches her father mending a bridle and rebuking one brother for reading foolish stories while reducing the other to tears by teasing. Yet at least her brothers are noticed; even teasing and rebuke convey significance. In the story her brother reads aloud, a wild man has been discovered who flees in terror from his pursuers, all the while screaming hideously. In her fascination with this story, Cary's narrator marks her own "wildness" and suggests that even though her life appears "noiseless" her sketches may be a form of screaming to be heard.

Relieved of fear by laughter within the house, she sits down to play with a string of brier-buds and hears in the distance the sound of an approaching horse. Horse and rider stop at her cottage with the news that her grandfather is dying. For Cary, narrative identity, the origin of her particular form of storytelling, begins with this moment of loss. But what exactly has she lost? Her grandfather has always been a "cold forbidding presence," a man whose kindness even "was uncompromising and unbending," who made no "manifestation of fondness, such as grandchildren usually receive," save once when he gave her an apple but took all pleasure from the gift by rebuking her for thanking him (14). As he is dying, she makes one last attempt to gain some recognition from him: "I stole to the door of his room in the hope that he would say something to me, but he did not, and I went nearer, close to the bed, and timidly took his hand in mine; how damp and cold it felt! yet he spoke not, and climbing upon the chair, I put back his thin locks, and kissed his forehead. 'Child, you trouble me,' he said, and these were the last words he ever spoke to me" (19).

Death removes the possibility that he will ever recognize or mark her; death requires her to acknowledge that she will never get his attention. Out of such loss, however, she develops the capacity to signify and the determination to be herself one who notices—"so eagerly I noted everything, that I remember to this day" (15). She begins by noticing herself, for she remembers that "children know more, and want more, and feel more, than people are apt to imagine" (16). If we return to that moment when the narrator first hears the sound of approaching loss, we discover her "arranging my string of brier-buds into letters that will spell some name, now my own, and now that of someone I love" (12). Writing becomes the way she notices and "spells" herself and those she loves into existence. The fragments she writes become a form of reparation for the losses inflicted by cold, forbidding grandfathers who do not notice one's existence.

Narrative Interruptions in Jewett

"A White Heron" can be read in part as Jewett's response to Stowe's *The Pearl of Orr's Island,* her analysis of the constraints that the form of the novel placed upon Stowe's ability to develop her material and her theorizing of what might be done with that material in the form of the sketch. The material of "A White Heron" is quite similar to that of *The Pearl of Orr's Island*—a young girl growing up in Maine, a young man entering her world who is only "like" a brother to her and so carries the possibility of heterosexual romance, the struggle between them over the value of a bird's life.[9] Indeed, since regionalist fiction very rarely offers a little girl as the central character,[10] we can read Jewett's choice as a signal of her intent to revise Stowe's story; and in the difficulties "A White Heron" presents to many readers we can measure the extent of the intervention required for Jewett to turn her story out of the path set in motion by "boy meets girl," out of the force field of plot, and into a different way.

We might complicate still further our understanding of "A White Heron" as an act of revision if we consider another possible origin for Jewett's story. In an 1876 letter to Annie Fields, Thaxter, who married at sixteen, was the mother of a son at the age of seventeen, and once described herself as living in "a howling wilderness of men" (*Letters of Celia Thaxter* 49–50), wrote: "Could I be 10 years old again—I would climb to my lighthouse top and set at defiance anything in the shape of man" (Rosamond Thaxter, *Sandpiper* 115). In this context we might read "A White Heron" as Jewett's effort to imagine a different story for her friend, one not determined by the conventions of plot. Recalling Nathaniel Hawthorne's description of Thaxter in *The American Notebooks* as the Miranda of the Isles of Shoals, we recognize how easily Thaxter's story could be fit into the romance plot of "The Tempest," in which a beautiful young girl isolated on an island falls in love with and marries the first man to be shipwrecked on her shore (537). Jewett's task, then, is to make a story out of a young girl's avoidance of this plot. To do so she chooses to write a sketch, and thereby makes the point that the cultural work of regionalism requires this form.

The story begins slowly with the narrator describing topography, person, and movement in a leisurely way, conveying the sense of there being "all the time there was" (*AWR* 198) for the little girl and the cow to enjoy the pleasures of an ordinary daily ritual. At a certain point, however, we realize that the narrator's voice has become a vehicle for sharing the thoughts and voices of others. From a reference to what "everybody" knows, she moves easily into what Mrs. Tilley knows, even telling us what she "said to herself" (198), and from Mrs. Tilley she moves into what Sylvia knows and thinks. Jewett's narrator constructs herself as receptive; she possesses a permeable consciousness that can curl up beside the consciousness of others so that what they know and think can seep into and speak through her own. Additionally, this narrator recognizes that Sylvia must be approached with great care, indirectly and without violence. Jewett contrasts the approach of her narrator to that of the hunter, whose entrance into Sylvia's world, signaled by the word "suddenly," disrupts the relation of narrator and character. Although Sylvia "stepped discreetly aside into the bushes," she was "just too late. The enemy had discovered her" (199). So unlike the narrator, who knows how to approach Sylvia and who constructs herself as receptive to Sylvia's consciousness, the hunter signals intrusion and a displacing of Sylvia's perceptions with his own.

Jewett's narrator underscores the contrast later in the story when Mrs. Tilley is telling the hunter about her son Dan, whose arguments with his father drove him to leave home and who has not been heard from in a long time: "The guest did not notice this hint of family sorrows in his eager interest in something else" (200). In the intimate connection between speaking and listening, who is listening shapes what gets told, and Jewett identifies her narrator as one who can "hear" Sylvia because she is not focused on "something else," on hunting and stuffing, on characters and action. Even Mrs. Tilley, who might have other stories to tell, shares the hunter's conviction that real stories lie elsewhere, in California perhaps with the son who never writes: "'There, I don't blame him, I'd ha' seen the world myself if it had been so I could'" (200). Because of his interest in "something else," the hunter misses what might be a far more interesting story than the one he is pursuing and he misses as well the story Jewett wants to tell us. If we are not to miss it, Jewett must teach us to be a different kind of reader than the hunter and to have a different understanding of story. Once we recognize her task, we can understand what might otherwise seem to be flaws in her narration—those moments in which Jewett's own voice seems to enter the story, displacing the narrative voice she has established and the relationship between her narrator's consciousness and Sylvia's. Jewett does not approach her readers directly until she has elicited our expectations of an "old, old story" and has suggested that Sylvia might yet become the heroine of a romance, writing that "as the day waned, Sylvia still watched the young man with loving admiration. She had never seen anybody so charming and delightful; the woman's heart, asleep in the child, was vaguely thrilled by a dream of love" (201). It is only in the following section that Jewett takes the risk of interrupting her story in order to speak directly to her readers and her interruptions are designed as interventions that challenge readers' expectations of story.

"A White Heron" is a story about risks and risk-taking that is itself risky. Mrs. Tilley takes a risk in removing "Sylvy" from her mother and siblings and bringing her back to an isolated farm with only herself and a cow for company, for "who can tell?" (205), she might have mistaken the child's capacity for loneliness. Sylvia herself risks the content she has found in her new home by allowing herself to "love" the hunter and she puts herself at risk, first physically and then spiritually, by climbing the tree. The "daring step" from tree to tree is itself a "dangerous pass" (203) but more dangerous still is the knowledge she acquires from taking this risk, for once she knows the location of the heron's nest she might indeed reveal it. And the hunter presents himself as one who will take any risk necessary to kill a rare bird. Jewett herself risks being dismissed as sentimental, minor, and silly in taking the chance that she can get us to see as significant, even shattering, an event that most would see as not worth reporting—a little girl chooses not to speak; indeed, as we have indicated in chapter 5, she risks misinterpretation of the meaning of Sylvia's decision. In her efforts to make her own "daring step," she takes the further risk of including those atypical interpolations so troublesome to many readers, as they seem to interrupt the narrative stance she has established at the beginning of her story, to draw too much attention to herself, and to use language that may strike us as overly emotional. When Sylvia has climbed to the top of the pine tree and is looking for the white heron's nest, the narrator interrupts: "Now look down again, Sylvia . . . ; there where you saw the white heron once you will see him again; look, look!" (204); and again, "And wait! wait! do not move a foot or a finger, little girl, do not send an arrow of light and consciousness from your two eager eyes, for the heron has perched on a pine bough not far beyond yours, and cries back to his mate on the nest, and plumes his feathers for the new day!" (204). Has she been successful?

Risks imply danger and in "A White Heron" interruption signals the presence of danger. To return to the moment in which the hunter first enters the story, Jewett writes, "Suddenly this little woods-girl is horror-stricken to hear a clear whistle not very far away. Not a bird's whistle, which would have a sort of friendliness, but a boy's whistle, determined, and somewhat aggressive" (199). Jewett "interrupts" her own text here by "suddenly" switching to the present tense, creating in us an alertness similar to Sylvia's. If interruptions signal danger, perhaps Jewett's own interruptions are designed to alert us to certain dangers. Her first such interruption occurs, we note, as Sylvia begins her journey to discover the heron's nest: "Alas, if the great wave of human interest which flooded for the first time this dull little life should sweep away the satisfaction of an existence heart to heart with nature and the dumb life of the forest!" (202). In identifying the danger to Sylvia, Jewett may also be alerting us to the dangers to herself—the possibility that she too might give in to the hunter and make her story conventional, might turn it into a romance and so seek to rescue "this dull little life" and perhaps her own reputation, might write a plot that the world would recognize as her own "great enterprise" (203), might herself fail to take a risk. Perhaps then we should read these interruptions as Jewett's way of alerting herself to the dangers that beset a writer trying to resist the seductions of plot. In this case we should not be surprised that she invokes a kind of supernatural aid for Sylvia at story's end, writing, "Were the birds better friends than their hunter might have been,—who can tell? Whatever treasures were lost to her, woodlands and summer-time, remember! Bring your gifts and graces and tell your secrets to this lonely country child!" (205). It is after all a great responsibility to write some other story than Cooke's "old, old story," a great risk both for female child and female author, and indeed who can tell how it will turn out.

Freeman's Use of Framing

If "A White Heron" can be said to interrupt readers' expectations concerning plot in order to teach us how to read the sketch, Freeman's stories emphasize the significance of "frame" to achieve the same effect. Furthermore, while Jewett's interruptions in "A White Heron" do not characterize her work in general, Freeman's use of framing is visible across her short fictions. Many of Freeman's stories begin with a paragraph written by a narrator who defines her task as purely descriptive, as simply setting the scene. Yet sentences that seem uninflected have the effect of a visual zoom into the story, bringing the reader in from a distance, implying a change in the perspective from which things are seen, and reminding us that "the point of departure, the point from which all things are measured, has changed" (Alcoff 350). Such paragraphs serve to convey Freeman's own understanding of the sketch as a form that frames its fictions.

For example, among the stories included in *AWR*, "A Mistaken Charity" opens as follows: "There were in a green field a little, low, weather-stained cottage, with a foot-path leading to it from the highway several rods distant, and two old women—one with a tin pan and old knife searching for dandelion greens among the short young grass, and the other sitting on the door-step watching her, or, rather, having the appearance of watching her" (*AWR* 314). From the beginning, the narrator reminds her readers that those who look in on a scene can draw no definitive conclusions about what they think they are seeing. It will be the function of the story to unfold what lies behind "the appearance."

Similarly, "Sister Liddy" opens with the following: "There were no trees near the almshouse; it stood in its bare, sandy lot, and there were no leaves or branches to cast shadows on its walls. It seemed like the folks whom it sheltered, out in the full glare of day, without any little kindly shade between itself and the dull, unfeeling stare of curiosity. The almshouse stood upon rising ground, so one could see it for a long distance" (*AWR* 323). The opening sentences create a scene that places the reader at "long distance," a distance the story will attempt to close. By this opening, Freeman also constructs the typical viewer, or reader, as possessing the "dull, unfeeling stare of curiosity" of those who live "a long distance" from the almshouse and for whom it is a visible sign of their own good fortune and "charity." Perhaps because in "Sister Liddy" Freeman will be asking more of her reader than in most of her work—to enter the world of Polly Moss and the other female residents of the almshouse—she takes particular care to position the almshouse with respect to the village and its town fields before she begins to narrate, "Polly Moss stood at the west window in the women's sitting-room" (323).

Again, "A New England Nun" begins with the following sequence: "It was late in the afternoon, and the light was waning. There was a difference in the look of the tree shadows out in the yard. Somewhere in the distance cows were lowing and a little bell was tinkling; now and then a farm-wagon tilted by, and the dust flew; some blue-shirted laborers with shovels over their shoulders plodded past; little swarms of flies were dancing up and down before the peoples' faces in the soft air. There seemed to be a gentle stir arising over everything for the mere sake of subsidence—a very premonition of rest and hush and night" (*AWR* 356). As Freeman brings us into her fiction, we hear cows "somewhere in the distance." Even the paragraph's concluding line adjusts our view; instead of the "gentle stir" leading to the commotion of plot, it seems to "be arising over everything for the mere sake of subsidence." What matters in this story is what settles down, not what gets stirred up.

While such scene setting may be a common feature of novels, it is unusual to find it in regionalist fiction. The only other writer included in *AWR* who uses the technique to any extent is Murfree (see, for example, the opening passages of "Over on the T'other Mounting" and "The 'Harnt' That Walks Chilhowee"). It is, however, so pronounced a feature of Freeman's fiction that we read it as her way of calling attention to regionalism itself, of marking the distance the reader must travel in order to enter the scene with respect. Freeman frames her texts to make a break between readers' expectations and the material of her fictions, to indicate to readers that they must set aside the frames they typically bring to fiction and prepare to see differently. We can understand how Freeman's use of framing works if we examine in more detail her story "A Poetess."

Like the other stories we have cited, "A Poetess" begins by creating a border or lens edge around a visual scene in which the narrator has marked an obstructed view: "The garden-patch at the right of the house was all a gay spangle with sweet-peas and red-flowering beans, and flanked with feathery asparagus. A woman in blue was moving about there. Another woman, in a black bonnet, stood at the front door of the house. She knocked and waited. She could not see from where she stood the blue-clad woman in the garden. The house was very close to the road, from which a tall evergreen hedge separated it, and the view to the side was in a measure cut off" (*AWR* 365–66). The reader enters "A Poetess" with the woman in the black bonnet; and, like hers, our "view to the side" is "in a measure cut off." Separated from the road by a tall evergreen hedge, the house and the garden are themselves framed, regionalized. Persons who come into regional worlds from outside—in this case, it is the woman in the black bonnet who has entered the yard behind the evergreen hedge—must adjust their vision, must learn to see "to the side." But this takes time. So "A Poetess" begins with the woman in the bonnet entering the house and calling for someone named Betsey, but no one hears or responds except a canary. Freeman writes, "'She ain't there,' said the woman. She turned and went out of the yard through the gap in the hedge; then she turned around. She caught sight of the blue figure in the garden. 'There she is,' said she" (366). Freeman creates her zoom effect for the reader as we follow the woman in the black bonnet, but the story itself only begins—begins in the sense that the world inside the hedge becomes animated with dialogue and action—when the woman we have been following manages to catch the attention of the other woman, who "did not notice her until she was close to her and said, 'Good-mornin', Betsey.' Then she started and turned around" (366). It is at this point that the narrator also brings the reader "close to her" and we are allowed to enter the world of the poetess with Mrs. Caxton, the woman in the black bonnet.

For years Betsey Dole has served the needs of her community by writing obituary verse. When Mrs. Caxton's little boy dies, she turns to Betsey, recognizing that, while nothing can help the rawness of the fact of death ("'nothin' amounts to anything—poetry or anything else—when he's *gone,*'" [368]), Betsey's verse will bring some comfort. Although Mrs. Caxton speaks deprecatorily of Betsey's choice, despite her poverty, to grow flowering peas and beans instead of "real" ones that she could eat (367), to prioritize the pretty over the practical, the comfort she hopes to get from a poem about little Willie depends upon the "pretty." The "pretty" in turn depends upon the concept of frame: "'I've been thinkin' . . . that it would be real pretty to have—some lines printed on some sheets of white paper with a neat black border'" (368). For Mrs. Caxton, such a frame will also establish the value of the verse and thus framed it will signify the value to her of her lost child. Indeed, when Betsey delivers the finished obituary poem, Mrs. Caxton finds it "'jest as comfortin' as it can be,'" she feels "'real obliged to you, Betsey,'" and she offers to give Betsey "'one of the printed ones when they're done'" (371). Mrs. Caxton's appreciation is intimately connected to her ability to visualize the poem as already framed, and Betsey herself recognizes the connection between framing and value. Already "flushed" with a sense of "recognized genius" when she receives her copy because it is printed and framed by a black border, she declares, "'I think it would look pretty framed'" (372). Although Betsey has "never received a cent for her poems, . . . [t]he appearance of this last in such a shape was worth more to her than its words represented in as many dollars" (372).

Frames confer value; they signal that what occurs within the frame has significance and deserves attention; they say that someone has cared enough to select what exists within the frame from everything else that might be framed. But frames themselves can be framed, as we saw with Betsey's poem, and subsequent frames can compete with previous ones. The black border confers value on Betsey's poem for Betsey and Mrs. Caxton, but when Mrs. Caxton finds out that the minister has commented that the poem is "'jest as poor as it could be, an' it was in dreadful bad taste to have it printed an' sent round that way,'" (373) his frame replaces hers. Even though Mrs. Caxton defends both the poem and the printing to Betsey—"'H'm! If anybody wants to say anything against that beautiful poetry, printed with that nice black border, they can. I don't care if it's the minister, or who it is'" (373)—neither she nor Betsey can see the poem as they had before. The minister's comment turns Betsey into "a victim whom the first blow had not killed" (373), but Betsey herself completes the act, collecting all of the poems she has ever written and burning them in the stove, then succumbing to consumption. Although the minister is a distant and shadowy figure in the story, as a man and a minister he is already framed as an authority. Moreover, he writes poetry himself and has had some "'printed in a magazine'" (373). We know that magazine publication carries a great deal of significance to Betsey, for when she first learns that Mrs. Caxton intends to print her verse, Freeman writes, "It was to her as if her poem had been approved and accepted by one of the great magazines" (372). Betsey accepts the value of the frame conferred by publication and ranks it higher than any frame she or Mrs. Caxton can bring to her work.

Writing herself for publication, though not perhaps in "one of the great magazines," Freeman realizes the power of publication to create a frame that confers value. In this story, magazine publication is associated with the minister's perspective and Freeman embeds this perspective within her story. While Betsey writes into the night to compose little Willie's poem, Freeman describes her in terms that echo the conventional view of the sentimental and devalued "poetess." She writes, "Betsey in this room, bending over her portfolio, looked like the very genius of gentle, old-fashioned, sentimental poetry. It seemed as if one, given the premises of herself and the room, could easily deduce what she would write, and read without seeing those lines wherein flowers rhymed sweetly with vernal bowers, home with beyond the tomb, and heaven with even" (369). Yet "A Poetess" does not finally share this perspective. Indeed, in this sketch Freeman seeks to use the power conferred by the frame of magazine publication to engage in a re-framing of the figure of the poetess. We can read the opening paragraphs of the story as drawing a border around Freeman's text that separates it from the frames readers might bring to it, thus removing readers from the perspective that would share the minister's evaluation of Betsey. Although "A Poetess" does not frame Betsey Dole's poetry as good, neither does it duplicate the minister's evaluation. While Betsey is not paid for her work and is not published in magazines, her poetry has value for her community and is circulated. Indeed, as Pryse has written, Betsey manages to create "an alternative immortality for the child in her poem and also manages to console the mother more deeply than the minister did" ("Afterword" 329). Despite her devaluation as "sentimental," Betsy has considerable power to confer value on little Willie. Furthermore, the moment in which Mrs. Caxton first concludes "'She ain't there,'" then discovers "'There she is,'" (*AWR* 366), recalls the theme, "'mother' lives," that we discussed in chapter 5, and aligns Betsey with the value of the living mother. Freeman allows us to see the complex network of connection within which women provide comfort for and confer value on each other. Since these connections offer an alternative to the minister's role in the community and hence challenge his authority, Freeman's approach allows us to see as well the interested nature of the minister's frame, one that not only disrupts the connections between women but also their relation to their own emotions. By calling the poem about the dead child in bad taste, the minister implicitly suggests that Mrs. Caxton's grief is in bad taste, is, as we might say, "sentimental." By contrast, Freeman frames the power of a mother's grief for a dead child, the value of the ways women turn to each other for comfort and relief, and the potential for the "sentimental" poetess to confer an immortality on little Willie that will be more enduring to Mrs. Caxton than any illusion of life after death that the minister can create.

Yet the most significant act of Freeman's reframing occurs after Mrs. Caxton has repeated the minister's comment to Betsey and Betsey is left alone. Betsey speaks aloud "as if she recognized some other presence in the room" (374). Freeman writes, "'I'd like to know if it's fair,' said she. 'I'd like to know if you think it's fair. Had I ought to have been born with the wantin' to write poetry if I couldn't write it—had I? Had I ought to have been let to write all my life, an' not know before there wa'n't any use in it? Would it be fair if that canary-bird there, that ain't never done anything but sing, should turn out not to be singin'? Would it, I'd like to know? S'pose them sweet-peas shouldn't be smellin' the right way? I ain't been dealt with as fair as they have, I'd like to know if I have'" (374). While we might read Betsey's impassioned outburst and her subsequent burning of all her poems as a capitulation to the minister's values, in this passage Freeman emphasizes Betsey's sense of injustice and injury. In her rage at a fate (or at "some other presence") that allowed her to be born wanting to write poetry yet without the ability to do so, we see a far different Betsey than the one summed up as "the very genius of gentle, old-fashioned, sentimental poetry" (369). We see instead a woman possessed of ferocious energy, a fierce desire to create, and a powerful ambition, and if this is what has inspired her verse, even though it seems formulaic and insipid, we are invited to rethink our approach to the genre. Moreover, Betsey's sense of injury and injustice implies a critique of the minister himself, as she calls into question what appears to be the immediate and inevitable superiority of his frame. Why indeed should the random opinions of this "country boy" be given such importance and why should publication in a magazine confer the attribute of "good" on anything?

Similarly we can read Betsey's dying request to the minister that he write a poem on the occasion of her death as a subtle form of revenge inspired by this very critique and the fierce ambition behind it. Although Betsey couches her request as a capitulation to the minister's frame—"'I've been thinkin' that—mebbe my—dyin' was goin' to make me—a good subject for—poetry, if I never wrote none'" (377)—her request requires him to engage in the production of the very kind of poetry he considers poor and to do so out of the context of those relations and emotions he considers to be in bad taste. He cannot refuse her dying request any more than she could refuse Mrs. Caxton, and to honor her request he will have to write her kind of poetry. In ending this way, Freeman thus draws a line around her story, framing it for our contemplation and conferring value on "a poetess."

Dialect and Dialogue in Cooke

Whether Freeman makes her formal frame explicit in the opening passages of her fiction or whether, in stories like "A Church Mouse" or "Christmas Jenny" (*Selected Stories*), she adopts the conventions of the Christmas story popular in the annuals and gift books of her era as a way of framing, her use of form creates an "evergreen hedge" (*AWR* 366) within which her characters can be "free to say"; her frame makes legible that moment when her characters finally speak but their speech typically has the rhetorical effect of monologue. In contrast, Cooke's stories frequently begin with a character speaking in dialect and in dialogue, though Cooke also often begins her stories with the kind of authorial intrusion we characterized as "interruption" in our discussion of Jewett above.[11]

As Stowe's *The Pearl of Orr's Island* lets us know, the dialect voice announces the presence of regionalism, not simply because it signals that the person speaking occupies a different position from those who speak the dominant discourse of "standard" English, but also because it blurs the distinction between the oral and the written and claims for itself the less privileged status of the oral. Regionalist texts create the illusion that we are hearing rather than reading, as if the writers themselves are telling stories on King's balcony. As we have already noted and will develop more fully in chapter 11, this emphasis on listening is central to regionalist fiction, for it is designed to accomplish "hearing one another to speech" (Morton 55); it creates a context within which those whom the dominant discourse silences can discover they have a listener and so become encouraged to speak. When Cooke begins her stories with the voice of a character, she constructs her reader as a listener, as an ear. Her form frames her fiction as an act of hearing and defines the work of her fiction as listening her characters into speech. For example, "How Celia Changed her Mind" opens with Celia declaring, "'If there's anything on the face of the earth I *do* hate, it's an old maid!'" (*AWR* 137). But it ends with her taking back "'all the sassy and disagreeable things I used to be forever flingin' at old maids'" (153), for the story has listened her into a different kind of speech.

Cooke's extensive use of dialect allows her to create the illusion of the oral and as a consequence she can propose that, while plots in novels construct "woman" and require her madness, suicide, or murder, actual living women have different stories to tell about their lives, stories that we more readily associate with oral narration. Like other regionalists, Cooke is well aware of the distinction between story and plot and well aware that she is writing or telling not the "old, old story" of boy meets girl but, as in the case of "Dely's Cow," the rather different story of girl meets cow and peddler meets girl who loves cow. Through this emphasis on the oral, Cooke constructs a fictional form that privileges stories rather than *the* story and constructs regionalist fiction as a space of sharing in which story can be set alongside story and many stories can be told. As we have observed in chapter 4, at a certain point the first-person narrator in "Dely's Cow" turns the text over to "grandfather Hollis," who "gave me the drover's account of the matter," and "grandfather" has apparently turned the storytelling over to Aaron Stow, for Cooke writes that the account "will be better in his words than mine" (*"How Celia Changed Her Mind"* 191). In the process of creating a form that allows her to share fictional space with her characters, Cooke positions her narrator as one who listens to her characters' stories and thus teaches her own readers how to be listeners.

Cooke begins storytelling, as it were, where Stowe leaves off, with Aunts Roxy and Ruey. In the process she foregrounds character and accords value to the regional voice; when she opens her story with that voice, she is telling her own readers that what her characters have to say matters. Even when she begins with the voice of a narrator, she writes in such a way as to engage us immediately with character, as her descriptions often "speak" her characters. For example, we might consider the opening of "Freedom Wheeler's Controversy with Providence": "Aunt Huldy and Aunt Hannah sat in the kitchen,—Aunt Huldah bolt upright in a straight-backed wooden chair, big silver-bowed spectacles astride her high nose, sewing carpet-rags with such energy that her eyes snapped, and her brown, wrinkled fingers flew back and forth like the spokes of a rapid wheel" (*AWR* 94). Indeed, Cooke's description of Aunt Huldah could serve as well to describe her own narrative voice, for her narrator expresses herself with an energy that makes eyes snap and fingers fly. Cooke's narrative voice reinforces the voice of her characters; though she does not herself write in dialect, her narrator shares with her characters a certain energy and outspokenness, a sense of being herself free to say. For example, in a memorable moment in "Freedom Wheeler's Controversy with Providence," Aunt Huldah takes out her frustration with Freedom's "gentle" wife, Lowly, who reminds the older woman that "'Scripter says wives must be subject to husbands'" (122), by pouncing upon the nearest hen and forcing her to sit on thirteen eggs. Cooke's narrator writes, "She [the hen] evidently represented a suffering and abject sex to Aunt Huldah, and exasperated her accordingly. Do I not know? Have not I, weakly and meekly protesting against their ways and works, also been hustled and bustled by the Rights Women?" (100). Cooke's narrator has a pronounced personality; for this reason there is little distinction between those stories in which she uses a first-person narrator and those in which she more typically uses a third-person narrator. In both instances, Cooke's narrative voice serves primarily to authenticate and reinforce the dialect voice of her characters.

Dialects in Dialogue in Murfree

In a certain sense, it is relatively easy for regionalist writers to move Roxy and Ruey to the center of their stories and to create a fiction in which Roxy is "free to say." In creating Roxy and Ruey, Stowe herself, as we discussed in chapter 3, drew on a fairly long history of literary representations of the New England "character" and Cooke is free to begin storytelling where Stowe left off because the dialect her characters speak is already familiar to readers; indeed one might argue that her stories come framed by her readers' equation of dialect with the way New Englanders speak in "literature." Moreover, as we discussed in chapter 2, New England has a history of being equated with nation; thus Cooke can create a narrator who is similar to her characters and readers will still grant such a narrator narrative authority. In effect, readers can accept a connection between narrative voice, narrative authority, and speaking New Englandly; indeed they can accept the premise that there is little distance between narrator and character. Murfree, writing about the Tennessee mountaineers, encounters a different situation. The dialect in which Murfree's characters speak is the most pronounced in all of regionalist fiction; it sounds like a foreign language and we have elsewhere described Murfree's use of dialect as a test of the reader's willingness to learn a new language in order to "enter" the region of her mountain fiction (see Pryse, "Exploring Contact"). In introducing a dialect unlike anything readers can be presumed to have heard or read before and one that readers are unlikely to associate with narrative voice, Murfree takes on the challenge of creating a context within which her readers can hear what the mountaineers have to say without concluding that they are simply queer. In presenting the greatest apparent contrast between narrative voice and dialect voice, Murfree foregrounds the issue of difference and raises the possibility that her work can be read as an effort to negotiate difference.

When the dialect voice enters a Murfree story (and she rarely begins a story in dialect), it comes as a shock; indeed we understand that shock to be intentional. Yet when we look more closely, we see that Murfree's narrative voice differs considerably from what we assume to be standard narrative English. Murfree's narrator, for example, uses words that readers are unlikely to have encountered elsewhere, words such as "amethystine" (*AWR* 276), "silver repoussé" (296), and "fulvous-tinted" (300), and her prose could be described as "purple," exaggerated, and overwrought. While Murfree's choice of narrative prose accentuates the difference between her characters' speech and her own, it does so in order to negotiate difference as something other than the queer in opposition to the normal. Eventually we come to realize that Murfree's narrative voice is itself a dialect and that in her fiction she creates a system like her beloved "mountings"—two dialects that, like the parallel ranges of the southern Alleghenies described at the beginning of "Over on the T'other Mounting," "fare along arm in arm, so to speak" (*AWR* 271). Like the mountains, the two dialects, "following the same course through several" (271) pages, produce a "parallel system of enchantment" (287). By making her narrative voice itself a dialect, Murfree suggests that narrator voice and character voice represent two ways of seeing, knowing, and speaking, neither of which is better or stranger than the other. Murfree dramatizes the enchantment of parallel systems by frequently beginning her stories with narrator and character describing the "same" scene in their own dialect. For example, consider the opening passage of "The 'Harnt' That Walks Chilhowee": "June had crossed the borders of Tennessee. Even on the summit of Chilhowee Mountain the apples in Peter Giles's orchard were beginning to redden, and his Indian corn, planted on so steep a declivity that the stalks seemed to have much ado to keep their footing, was crested with tassels and plumed with silk. . . . 'An' it air a toler'ble for'ard season. Yer wheat looks likely; an' yer gyarden truck air thrivin' powerful'" (286).

Moreover, Murfree constructs her stories in such a way as to suggest that from the perspective of her characters the narrator's way of speaking might seem just as much a dialect and just as queer as theirs might seem to her. Murfree's mountaineers have a perspective on the non-mountaineer and her fiction foregrounds the thematic of gazing back, dramatized by her rendering of Tennessee topography in the imagery of parallel mountain ranges each gazing back at the other. Indeed, we might read her story "Over on the T'other Mounting" as a critique of the approach of local color that tends to normalize one perspective and queer or demonize the other. Despite local superstitions, T'other Mounting proves not to be inhabited by witches and what happens over there is no more or less unlucky than what happens on Old Rocky Top; in truth "'*Anythink* might happen thar'" (277) or here. Despite its inhabitants' complacency, Old Rocky Top is not as peaceful or domestic or civilized as it appears; it harbors jealousy, rivalry, and murderous hate and we know that it could burn, as T'other Mounting does, despite the presence of its church. In this story Murfree makes the point that each mountain range, or subject position, provides a perspective on the other and that neither is better or more normal than the other. More important, she suggests that just as her characters can move back and forth between one mountain range and the other, readers can move back and forth between these different perspectives and in a certain sense inhabit and learn from both.

In her way of telling a story Murfree shows us this possibility for she presents her fiction as the collaborative effort of her two dialects. Murfree draws our attention to this collaboration when, for example, she follows a character's long narrative with the comment, "This story was by no means unknown to the little circle, nor did its narrator labor under a delusion that he was telling a new thing" (275). Murfree allows her character to convey information to her readers that could be more easily and less awkwardly provided by her narrator because she does not wish her narrator to be solely responsible for telling the story. However, unlike Freeman in "On the Walpole Road," she does not wish her characters to do all the storytelling either. Rather she creates fictions in which character and narrator work collaboratively, each telling certain parts of the story. In "Over on the T'other Mounting," after her characters have finished telling their version of Tony Britt's history and present circumstances, the narrator begins with her version. At a certain point the voices intermingle and we move easily from one to the other: "Little as he knew of life, he knew how hard his had been, even meted by those of the poverty-stricken wretches among whom his lot was cast. 'An' sech luck!' he said" (279). Murfree reiterates her point thematically; when one of her characters describes the argument between Tony Britt and Caleb Hoxie that forms the kernel of the story's action, he calls it "'a mighty differ'" (274), language that Tony Britt himself reinforces when he vows, "'He's got ter 'count ter me, ef he ain't ter the law; an' he'll see a mighty differ atwixt us'" (279). At such points we understand that for Murfree the real story involves the complex vision made possible by multiple perspectives and we realize as well that each dialect functions as a way of listening the other to speech.

Form as "Restoration" in King

In "The Balcony," King theorizes storytelling, making her fiction an obvious focus for our reflections on form. In the country of which she writes, "much of life" is passed on balconies where "the women love to sit and talk together of summer nights" (*AWR* 380). Women pass "much of life" telling stories about their own or other women's lives or destinies—"this is what interests women once embarked on their own lives" (380). King is careful to point out that "the embarkation takes place at marriage, or after the marriageable time" (380), and to signal that her understanding of story will differ from those fictions that always *end* in marriage (or the death of the romantic heroine) and will begin *after* the point at which most novels end. When King writes that the women's stories "seem to be furnished real and gratis, in order to save, in a languor-breeding climate, the ennui of reading and writing books" (381), she is not calling into question her storytellers' tolerance for the work of reading and writing but rather their boredom with stories about women's lives that are not "furnished real and gratis." At her own point of embarkation, King identifies "interest" as lying elsewhere than convention would locate it and suggests that her balcony stories will take us to places as much out of the way as the balcony itself, a site where a different kind of story can be told from those required by the prescriptions and proscriptions of conventional stories of women's lives. Although the relaxed pace implied by a "languor-breeding climate" may be shadowed by a lack of energy as well as "ennui," it also legitimizes a looseness in form similar to the garments the women put on when they are through with what is required to meet the day, a looseness that enables them to talk easily "about this person and that, old times, old friends, old experiences" (380) and to move imperceptibly into something that could be called a story. From such an embarkation one might expect the stories themselves to be loose and open and to convey, as do the "mother-voices" to the half-waking children, a sense that they have no end.

King also proposes that women whose behavior and desires are regulated by social institutions require a special time, place, and form—perhaps at the end of the day, in a setting removed from those institutions to which they have obligations, and with temporary license to set those obligations and prohibitions aside—if they are to articulate what really interests them, if they are to be truly "free to say." Her emphasis on "interest" suggests that in this setting and through this form women can think and feel in ways different from those required by the conventions of daily life. Indeed, King suggests that the very women who in other contexts might be figures of convention (such as those her narrator comes to scorn in "The Old Lady's Restoration") become transformed by the process of storytelling on the balcony into persons capable of sharing a "real and gratis" interest in other women's lives as they come to understand them in this out-of-the-way place and time. For King storytelling itself constructs its listeners as well as its tellers as persons who participate in an "interest" that is neither solely self-interested nor an act of prurience, exploitation, or social control. That King should identify these listeners as women is not surprising, for in a gender-stratified society, women are more likely to know how to read women's lives. King specifically claims women as the only competent readers of the stories that emerge from the balcony, "experiences, reminiscences, episodes, picked up as only women know how to pick them up from other women's lives"

(380); and she further identifies women as the only competent tellers of the stories of women's lives, for her balcony stories are told "as only women know how to relate them" (380).

In this context, we understand King's use of quotation marks in the title of her sketch "'One of Us,'" a phrase often used to exclude outsiders, to mark an as-if relation between the reader of that story and the former opera singer who arrives at the narrator's door with a story of her own. While the narrator writes that, at first, it requires a "little mental rehabilitation" (*AWR* 390) to recognize the apologetic singer when she shows up at her door, by the end of the story the title's punctuation creates a special meaning for the phrase "one of us," for the narrator has herself become "one" with the unfortunate woman, and as she tells the woman's story and the way listening to it has changed her, she brings the reader as well into that special relation, as if "one of us," as if also interested "real and gratis" in the "whilom *dugazon*" (391).

In "The Balcony," as we noted in chapter 5, King suggests that women tell stories to make up for what they lack. The teller of "The Old Lady's Restoration" proposes that what she, and by extension her listeners, most lack and therefore most need is "truth"; to the extent that their lives are denied them by the untruths of convention and conventional behavior, only the truth will give them back their lives. In this perception she has an ally in the old lady herself: "She always said whatever she thought, regardless of the consequences, because she averred truth was so much more interesting than falsehood" (*AWR* 395). In presenting her predilection for truth as an issue of "interest," the old lady appears as the ideal participant in the world of balcony stories, one who would know both how to tell and how to listen. In the close connection the sketch establishes between character and narrator, we might find evidence of Ciaramicoli's claim that "empathy's strength comes from its commitment to the truth" (148) and see in the old lady a figure of "King" as well. By the narrator's own account, the "truth" of this story has been lost. Since she presents herself as neither a participant in the events she recounts nor an intimate of the old lady, being of neither her generation nor neighborhood, her own access to the story would have to come through the accounts of those very persons whose versions she sees as inventions, revisions, embellishments. The story she tells, then, must be a story she reconstructs from what she has heard, a story she reads empathically out of the one she has been told through her capacity to identify with the old lady's perspective; hence such locutions as "the old lady must have made . . ." (396). In this way, the narrator works to accomplish a genuine "restoration."

The narrator tells the story in a leisurely fashion, as leisurely as the "promenade" the old lady makes from affluence to poverty, and her mode of telling contrasts with the rapidity ("it was which one would get to her first" [396]) and the appetitiveness of the narrations constructed by those who seek to re-member the old lady after her restoration, to return her to membership in their society and to claim her as "one of us." As indicated in "The Balcony," the languor, leisure, and relaxation of summer nights leads not to inattention but rather to a kind of alertness that misses nothing. Similarly, the old lady "traveled her road from affluence to poverty so leisurely that nothing escaped her eye or her feelings, and she signalled unhesitatingly every stage in it" (395). In connecting her balconied stories with an alertness that misses nothing, King suggests that they offer our best chance at "truth." Her narrator also signals unhesitatingly that much of what passes for narrative in the world is a tissue of self-serving lies: "'We will go to her, like children to a grandmother, etc. The others have no delicacy of sentiment, etc. And she will thus learn who really remember, really love her, etc.'" (397). When the "news" of the old lady's restoration appears, a flurry of narratives begins as people become occupied with "resuscitating their old friendships for her" (397), inventing and retelling stories about the old lady's plans: "The old residence was to be rebought, and refurnished from France; . . . the old cook was to be hired back from the club at a fabulous price; the old balls and the old dinners were to gladden the city—so said they who seemed to know" (397). Although grandmothers must be dragged out of oblivion as well to provide some semblance of veracity to these stories (395), in all this narrative activity we find little interest in the "truth."

If King's story can be read as signaling the need for truth, it also marks the difficulties that accompany trying to know the truth. For, ironically, the more the old lady comes to live outside the formulas of convention, the lies that structure the "world" ("'when I say the world I mean society,'" the old lady says [396]), the more she comes to know and the less chance she has of communicating her knowledge. As the narrator expresses this irony, the old lady's "observations, which, of course, could be made only to intimates, became fewer and fewer, unfortunately, for her circumstances were becoming such that the remarks became increasingly valuable" (396). While several "friends" might still be around to hear her remark on how little her mother "knew" about luxury and necessity—"'I assure you it is perfectly new to me to find that an opera-box is not a necessity'" (395)—by the time she comes to understand the truth about friends and Christianity ("'when I say Christianity I mean our interpretation of it'" [396]), almost no one has stayed to listen. More pointedly still, her last recorded remarks, which by the logic of King's story are the most valuable, cannot be heard at all by those who seek her out, and so they return to their world with the report "that they had found the old lady, and that she was imbecile; mind completely gone under stress of poverty and old age" (399). Since after this no more is heard from the old lady, at least by those with access to "publication," those who can tolerate "the ennui of reading and writing books" of acceptable fictions, we can only imagine what has been lost not simply to literature but to the life passed on the balcony.

For King's narrator, then, storytelling works as a mode of reparation and restoration. Although we do not know precisely how it happens, she has been able to read beyond the report of the old lady's imbecility and to reconstruct from what she has heard and from what she knows of the reporters and of the "society" they represent what the old lady actually said, or must have said. In this sense, the old lady is truly restored. More significantly, those who listen to the narrator's story are themselves restored, for while in other contexts they might be imagined as participating in the greed and self-delusion that motivates the construction of society's fictions and produces the boredom or "ennui" of falsehood, on the balcony they become persons capable of hearing the old lady's story and seeing the world from her perspective; they are restored to the values that inform the balcony as opposed to the "world."

Sui Sin Far and Language on the Border Land

In *Borderlands/La Frontera,* Gloria Anzaldúa describes the "*mestiza* consciousness" that the mixed-race person develops and characterizes the "clash of voices" that "results in mental and emotional states of perplexity" as a feature of "the mestiza's dual or multiple personality" (77–78). Anzaldúa writes: "*El choque de un alma atrapado entre el mundo del espíritu y el mundo de la técnica a veces la deja entullada.* Cradled in one culture, sandwiched between two cultures, straddling all three cultures and their value systems, *la mestiza* undergoes a struggle of flesh, a struggle of borders, an inner war" (78). Anzaldúa's technique of interweaving two languages—English and Spanish in effect "face" each other on the page—though evocative of Murfree, may most readily be seen in regionalism in the stories and sketches of Dunbar-Nelson, who inserts words in French, Cajun, and Creole into her English narration. However, it is Sui Sin Far, working "on the border land" in *Mrs. Spring Fragrance and Other Writings* (60), who most fully realizes the intent of Anzaldúa's technique, even though she rarely chooses to write a transliteration of a Chinese character's immigrant English. Like Anzaldúa, Sui Sin Far presents in her fiction the struggle of the *mestiza,* the person who experiences "the coming together of two self-consistent but habitually incompatible frames of reference" (Anzaldúa 78). Instead of juxtaposing two different languages or dialects, Sui Sin Far uses English in such a way as to represent the "coming together" of different worldviews and value systems. On those rare occasions when she attempts a transliteration of Chinese pronunciation, her characters become marked as incompetent speakers of English in a way that tends to confirm negative stereotypes about immigrants in general and Chinese immigrants in particular.[12] To avoid this problem, Sui Sin Far instead seeks to demonstrate the way multiple worldviews may be created within one language by varying the patterns of English sentence structure while remaining within acceptable grammatical and stylistic usage.

As Amy Ling and Annette White-Parks write in their "Introduction" to *Mrs. Spring Fragrance and Other Writings,* "Sui Sin Far was a writer of multilayered visions, all frequently operating at once" (6). For the characters in *Mrs. Spring Fragrance,* such "multilayered visions" create a cultural spectrum anchored at one end by a Chinese traditionalist view and at the other by an "Americanized" perspective. While writing as someone she herself described as possessing a "Eurasian mental portfolio"[13] (an expression similar to Anzaldúa's "*mestiza* consciousness") would seem to tip the balance of Sui Sin Far's own perspective toward the "Americanized" end of the spectrum, her narrator draws a line on the page which even her Americanized Chinese characters do not cross: they do not speak (and the narrator does not use when she is speaking for them) English sentence constructions that dominate and subordinate. The effect is to distance her white reader from his or her own "native" language and, in the process, to create a textual space within which that reader may come "closer" to the worldview of the Chinese immigrant; the narrator gives the reader access on the page and in the reader's own language to the world of the immigrant at the same time that she separates the reader from this way of using the English language.

Although the use of subordinate clauses in an English sentence identifies that sentence as "complex," and the sentence construction Sui Sin Far much more often uses is termed "simple," the texts of the stories and sketches included in *Mrs. Spring Fragrance* locate, in manipulating the syntactic form of the English sentence, an alternative conceptual space within which the American reader can "think" about the Chinese. Not only does the prevailing syntactic unit in Sui Sin Far's work involve simple sentences or their linking by way of coordinating conjunctions into compound sentences, but also those qualifying conjunctions that emphasize the grammatical subordination of one idea to another, conjunctions such as *however, therefore, thus, although,* or *unless,* are almost entirely absent except when these conjunctions are used adjectivally. Nonrestrictive relative clauses tend to be noun or adjective clauses, and adverbial and qualifying conjunctions and clauses are rarely used except to identify time and place and on those occasions when a white character is speaking or when the narrator is presenting the perspective of that character.

To cite an example of Sui Sin Far's preference for coordination over subordination and her use of compound rather than complex syntactical constructions, we may consider the beginning of "The Wisdom of the New" where Wou Sankwei hears stories in his Chinese village from a man who had immigrated to California during the gold rush but has returned to China a beggar. Sui Sin Far writes, "So the old man would tell stories about the winning and the losing, and the stories of the losing were even more fascinating than the stories of the winning" (*Mrs. Spring Fragrance* 43). "The Wisdom of the New" begins neither by qualifying or elaborating the narrative of this Chinese man nor by indicting Americans for their exploitation of him, but rather by presenting his stories as equally weighted since the presumptively less interesting is enhanced by a fascination that maintains a balance between the winning and the losing. The syntax Sui Sin Far chooses eschews a complex sentence construction that might have combined dominant and subordinate clauses in favor of a compound sentence construction that presents the experience as evenhanded. The effect brings the American reader up against conventional expectations that "losing" is always a subordinate experience to "winning," thereby inoculating the narrative against the implications of a "complex" syntax and replacing it with an understanding that opposites do not have to oppose each other, that each may become a part of the other. The effect is to create, through the relative symmetry of compound clauses and sentences and the relative absence of subordinating conjunctions, a sense of balance that gives Sui Sin Far control over her reader's approach to the tensions that characterized the American attitude toward Chinese immigrants at the end of the nineteenth century and ultimately allows her to write about the Chinese experience in the United States in such a way that her American readers can hear what she has to say.

The subjects Sui Sin Far treats in her fiction include the range of responses Chinese immigrants take upon their arrival in "the land beyond the sea," as Wou Sankwei characterizes America (43). Some characters become quite Americanized. For example, the title story in the collection *Mrs. Spring Fragrance* opens as follows: "When Mrs. Spring Fragrance first arrived in Seattle, she was unacquainted with even one word of the American language. Five years later her husband, speaking of her, said: 'There are no more American words for her learning.' And everyone who knew Mrs. Spring Fragrance agreed with Mr. Spring Fragrance" (17; *AWR* 505). For another example, Wou Sankwei, in "The Wisdom of the New," has preceded his wife to America by seven years, and the American friend "who had taken him under her wing shortly after his arrival in America" characterizes him as a businessman of reputation among the Chinese and says that he "'is as up to date as any young American'" (*Mrs. Spring Fragrance* 45). Among the Chinese immigrant community, there are therefore characters who move in and out both of Chinese and American social and cultural groups.

Many variations on "Americanization" occur in Sui Sin Far's stories, and each brings into relief "*un choque*, a cultural collision" (Anzaldúa 78). For example, we can consider the desire of Laura, the daughter of Mrs. Spring Fragrance's Chinese neighbors, to choose her own husband, the "American-born" Kai Tzu, instead of allowing her parents to follow "the ideals of their Chinese forefathers" and to arrange her marriage (*Mrs. Spring Fragrance* 17; *AWR* 506). There are also characters who, like Anzaldúa, are "sandwiched between two cultures," are "*mestiza.*" Mag-gee, in "The Sing Song Woman," is a "half-white girl" and resists marrying the "Chinaman" to whom her parents have betrothed her. She tells her Chinese friend Ah Oi, "'I was born in America, and I'm not Chinese in looks nor in any other way'" (126; 503). Pan, in "'Its Wavering Image,'" is also "a half-white, half-Chinese girl" (61; 526) but by the end of the story, in spite of the fact that she can pass for white, Pan puts on Chinese dress and claims the identity of a Chinese woman. White Americans on one side, and on the other the Chinese who either remain in China or return there, refusing Americanization, create Anzaldúa's "sandwich" effect for the Chinese American characters who occupy some middle space, becoming what Kate McCullough calls "borderland inhabitants" of "border locations" (228–29). Wou Sankwei's wife, Pau Lin, in "The Wisdom of the New," represents a traditional Chinese woman's response to the "land beyond the sea." Pau Lin speaks no English, punishes her son for trying to learn the language, and by the end of the story, after she has killed her child to prevent him from entering the American school, turns her back on America as she and Wou Sankwei prepare to return to China.

Mrs. Spring Fragrance takes upon herself the task, as she expresses it in the opening passage of "The Inferior Woman," of explaining the ways of one culture to another. The story opens,

> Mrs. Spring Fragrance walked through the leafy alleys of the park, admiring the flowers and listening to the birds singing. . . . As she walked along she meditated upon a book which she had some notion of writing. Many American women wrote books. Why should not a Chinese? She would write a book about Americans for her Chinese women friends. The American people were so interesting and mysterious. Something of pride and pleasure crept into Mrs. Spring Fragrance's heart as she pictured Fei and Sie and Mai Gwi Far listening to Lae-Choo reading her illuminating paragraphs. (*Mrs. Spring Fragrance* 28; *AWR* 515)

While her project proposes to disrupt vectors of dominance and submission and to establish that the gazed at can also look back, her book will have a Chinese readership only if those readers are themselves English-speaking and, like herself, at least partially Americanized. In fact, Mrs. Spring Fragrance is writing a book about Americans, about their reception of and relationships with the Chinese, as much for readers in the dominant culture as for her "Chinese women friends." McCullough cites a November 1909 column from the periodical *The Westerner* in which the editor prints a letter from Sui Sin Far, who wrote as follows: "There may be a certain literary prestige in having one's work accepted by the Eastern critics; but my stories and articles in 'The Westerner,' 'Out West,' and 'Post-Intelligencer' accomplish more the object of my life, which is not so much to put a Chinese name into American literature, as to break down prejudice, and to cause the American heart to soften and the American mind to broaden towards the Chinese people now living in America—the humble, kindly, moral, unassuming Chinese people of America" (235).

Becoming the reader's guide to understanding the "cultural collision" between immigrant Chinese and white Americans, Mrs. Spring Fragrance illuminates for her readers the ways in which the white men and women who take on the responsibility for "Americanizing" the Chinese often become an impediment to cultural understanding despite, in the words of Freeman, their "mistaken charity." For example, though Adah Charlton in "The Wisdom of the

New" develops insight into Pau Lin and expresses her concern to Wou Sankwei, Sui Sin Far points us to Adah Charlton's racial privilege as well as to her insight. She writes about Adah when she and her aunt pay a visit to Pau Lin and her husband, "The American woman could not, of course, converse with the Chinese. Secure in the difference of race, in the love of many friends, and in the happiness of her chosen work, no suspicion whatever crossed her mind that the woman whose husband was her aunt's protégé tasted everything bitter because of her" (*Mrs. Spring Fragrance* 51). Even more problematic as models for white behavior are the immigration agents, who keep recent immigrants, even infants as in "In the Land of the Free," in detention for months upon their arrival, or the ethnocentric local-color journalist Mark Carson in "'Its Wavering Image,'" who earns Pan's trust in order to sell her secrets by writing an article about the Chinese community for a white newspaper.

Sui Sin Far does create one white woman who helps her narrator accomplish her task of breaking down prejudice, of causing "the American heart to soften," but significantly this occurs as a result of this character's intervention into the lives of other white Americans. By this approach Sui Sin Far registers her concern with the efforts of white women to "Americanize" the Chinese and proposes instead that white Americans work to change white American hearts and minds. Set against characters like Adah Charlton and Mark Carson, the suffragist character Ethel Evebrook in "The Inferior Woman" provides a model for understanding across class lines that can be extended to cross-cultural and cross-racial interactions. In "The Inferior Woman," Mrs. Spring Fragrance is trying to "soften" her American neighbor's heart toward the working-class woman, Alice Winthrop, whom her son Will loves and wishes to marry. Mrs. Carman, however, is set on her son's marrying the privileged and educated Ethel Evebrook. During a conversation between Ethel Evebrook and her mother, Mrs. Spring Fragrance, unobserved by the white women, sits on a porch outside the window taking notes. What she overhears is Ethel's defense of the self-made Alice, her criticism of Mrs. Carman's attitude, and her rejection of the hierarchy of "inferior" and "superior" women.

When Mrs. Spring Fragrance later relates this story to her neighbor, Mrs. Carman, she uses the syntax of simple and compound construction: "'I listen to what is said. I apprehend, I write it down. Let me illustrate by the "Inferior Woman" subject. . . . I go to see the Superior Woman. I sit on the veranda of the Superior Woman's house. I listen to her converse with her mother about the Inferior Woman. With the speed of flames I write down all I hear. When I enter the house the Superior Woman advises me that what I write is correct. May I read to you?'" (39; *AWR* 524). When Mrs. Carman agrees, Mrs. Spring Fragrance reads what she has overheard. "'Mrs. Mary Carman,' said she, 'you are so good as to admire my husband because he is what the Americans call "a man who has made himself." Why then do you not admire the Inferior Woman who is a woman who has made herself?' 'I think I do,' said Mrs. Carman slowly" (38; 524).

Mrs. Spring Fragrance's success relies on translation—not into Chinese, but into "American" English. Sui Sin Far suggests here that in order to show people something they have not understood for themselves, in order "to cause the American heart to soften and the American mind to broaden," it is necessary to translate for them in their own language.

In contrast, in the second section of "The Inferior Woman," the only characters present are the white characters Will Carman and Alice Winthrop. The section contains numerous subordinate clauses. For example, Sui Sin Far writes, "If for a moment the small mouth quivered, the firm little chin lost its firmness, and the proud little head yielded to the pressure of a lover's arm, it was only for a moment so brief and fleeting that Will Carman had hardly become aware of it before it had passed" (32; 518). What is at stake for these lovers is indeed the conditional clause, for Alice waits for Mrs. Carman's approval. Will tells Alice, "'If you will put your hand in mine and trust to me through all the coming years, no man or woman born can come between us.'" She answers him, "'I will not be your wife unless your mother welcomes me with pride and with pleasure'" (32; 518). Although they are using the English language only to communicate with each other, Will and Alice are also revealing in their use of complex sentence constructions the role of the dominant clause in English to win at least rhetorical points.

By relying heavily on a combination of simple and compound sentences when her Chinese or Chinese "Americanized" characters are speaking or thinking, and using complex sentence constructions with embedded conditional clauses only when her white American characters are speaking or thinking, Sui Sin Far constructs English itself as a site of cultural encounter. Both the form of Mrs. Spring Fragrance's intervention and of Sui Sin Far's syntax suggest that there are truths—even ironies—to be conveyed in sympathetic action and simple sentence construction. Most of all, her sentences suggest that the character of the Chinese people is already embedded as a potential within the English language—a language that may be written in a "humble, kindly, moral, unassuming" way—and thus within the American heart, and that writing in a way that shows English-speaking readers a different use of their own language can reveal their capacity for "mestiza" consciousness. Writing within a form of stylistic and syntactic crossing of the "border land," Sui Sin Far helps the reader to "hear" the Chinese frame of reference, just as Mrs. Spring Fragrance is able to soften the heart and change the mind of Mary Carman.

Austin and the Limits of Story

Austin's writing emerges from an intense relation with a particular and extreme landscape, and, like Thaxter's, her work asserts an intimate connection between topography and form. As the title of her first book of sketches expresses it, the desert is above all "the land of little rain"; Austin thus identifies the driving force of desert life as the search for water and she offers her stories to readers as themselves a form of water. In reflecting on why people are drawn to the desert, to a land so barren, desolate, even "villainous" (*AWR* 567), she observes that here you find "the pulse and beat of a life laid bare to its thews and sinews" (591) for "go as far as you dare . . . you cannot go so far that life and death are not before you" (570). Like Thaxter on her bit of rock in the north Atlantic, in the desert one "gets close to the heart of these things" (*AWR* 166) and in one's attraction to the desert and its ways of knowing one comes face to face with one's desire, one's thirst. In the land of little rain, Austin realizes herself as one who both desires and knows, for if she wants water, she must become expert in the ways of water, must learn to read water and its trails, must learn to trust both trails and her reading of them "no matter what the maps say, or your memory" (*Stories* 22).

Austin connects the desire that leads one to the desert and that the desert reveals to the desire to tell and write stories: "A land of lost rivers, with little in it to love; yet a land that once visited must be come back to inevitably. If it were not so there would be little told of it" (*AWR* 568). Through telling stories people try to explain why the desert "lays such a hold on the affections" (570–71), for only stories can express this desire. Austin recognizes how conventions shape the construction of desert stories and how these conventions in turn stem from a particular understanding of desert desire that itself becomes a kind of convention. She writes that "in that country, you can get anybody to believe any sort of tale that has gold in it" (590), anybody, that is, who accepts these conventions. Hills "strewn with nuggets" and "virgin silver" find a ready audience: "Old miners drifting about the desert edges, weathered into the semblance of the tawny hills, will tell you tales like these convincingly. After a little sojourn in that land you will believe them on your own account. It is a question whether it is not better to be bitten by the little horned snake of the desert that goes sidewise and strikes without coiling, than by the tradition of a lost mine" (571). Austin herself neither believes nor tells "fables, chiefly of lost treasure" (571), and in "The Land" she recounts how she once made up such a tale simply to prove her point about gold and story and belief. Such beliefs, however, prove inimical to the ways of knowing Austin finds in the desert and the desire she wishes to honor in her own sketches, for they create expectations that constrain one to write of the desert in a certain way and as a result to "lose much of pleasantness" (572). In a land of "lost borders," the title she gave to her second collection of regionalist fiction, where no boundaries exist, where convention, law, even form itself become meaningless, "for law runs with the boundary, not beyond it" (588), stories will both look and be different. Still Austin recognizes that even in the context of a land of lost borders where conventional understandings of plot and character and form are already disrupted, other conventions can nevertheless emerge and she places her desire to tell stories more different still in tension with these other conventions. Urged by Long Tom Basset to "make a story" of his account of a dead woman perfectly preserved in a salt lake that had collapsed under the weight of a wagon train, she tries once, "at a dinner, but I never got through with it" for "about the time the candles began to burn their shades and red track of the light on the wine-glasses barred the cloth, . . . it had a garish sound" (590).

At times, however, Austin shows herself to be as much in the grip of the desire to tell a "garish" desert story as any Long Tom she knows. In "The Woman at the Eighteen-Mile," she acknowledges her obsession with a story about Death Valley that she is sure, if she can ever get it, will be "the biggest story of the desert ever written" (*Stories* 210) and that will be of the kind you can get "anybody" to believe, for "there was a mine in it, a murder, a mystery, great sacrifice, Shoshones, dark and incredibly discreet, and the magnetic will of a man" (205). She pursues the trail of the story as if it were gold and when she believes she has gotten it she experiences "the full-throated satisfaction of old prospectors over the feel of pay dirt" (207). The story she actually writes, however, is not this story at all but is rather the story of why she never will write the "biggest" of all desert stories. In "The Woman at the Eighteen-Mile," Austin implicitly critiques her desire to write such a story and exposes the ethical complications of such a conventional ambition, for she gets the story she is after from the woman who knows it only by agreeing "not to write that story" (206). In listening to the woman tell her story, the woman who has "no more pertinence to the plot than most women have to desert affairs" (205), Austin discovers a knowledge far more important than the solution of a mystery; she discovers how this woman has against all odds "been able to keep a soul alive and glowing in the wilderness," how she has been able to be "warmed and nourished from within," how she found water (205). Although Austin cannot tell the story she has tried to get for seven years and has already half-constructed as "a story of Death Valley that should be its final word" (203), and though she cannot tell the woman's story either as "she kept it so against the heart of my story" (205), she can tell the story of what and how stories mean and that may be the biggest story of all: "Every now and then arises some city-surfeited demand for a great primitive love-story; it is usually a Professor in the English Department or some young man on the Daily News at fifteen per who dreams of writing it. Only those who have learned it at firsthand understand that there is no such thing" (210). Such a story, threading its way through "Society . . . Respectability . . . the Church and Property," must accommodate itself to those conventions that dictate what constitutes "the fascinating intricacy of story" and that make it impossible to characterize her own writing as "story": "but here in the borders, where the warp runs loose and wide, the pattern has not that richness it should show in the close fabric of civilization. If it lived next door to you, you probably wouldn't have anything to do with it" (210).

A second story, "The Walking Woman," presents itself as even more self-reflexive than "The Woman at the Eighteen-Mile" and gives further insight into Austin's relation to story. If Austin sees desert stories as a series of trails to water, the story of the Walking Woman whom she meets by "Warm Spring in the Little Antelope" (*AWR* 579) offers the water of self-knowledge, what the narrator calls "wisdom and information" (578). Like the Walking Woman, Austin's narrator, too, "came and went," moves "hurriedly" (577) across the desert landscape, and so for a long time they miss each other. And like the Walking Woman, Austin's narrator does things that by "no canon" could be considered ladylike (578). As sheepherders and cowboys tell the narrator "as much of her way of life as they could understand," so, she reflects, "like enough they told her as much of mine" (577). Such tellings are, however, partial, distorted by the notion of story these men bring to the situation ("a mine . . . , a murder, a mystery" [*Stories* 204–5]). Thus the narrator comes to "wish for a personal encounter with the Walking Woman," the chance to test "the contradiction of reports of her" against "her own account" (*AWR* 578–79), and to be herself so tested. For, "like enough," the Walking Woman recognizes the distortions in the reports she hears of Austin's narrator and this may be why, when they finally meet, the narrator writes, at a certain point "the walking woman touched me, . . . put out her hand and laid it on my arm" (582).

The narrator's wish for a personal encounter with the Walking Woman differs from the ambition that drives Austin's desire for a story in "The Woman at the Eighteen-Mile." She does not seek out the Walking Woman but lets the encounter happen, if it will, by accident, taking an approach that alerts her to opportunity, makes her ready to be there and to listen. Although the narrator recognizes that because she has been at places where "some rare happenings" occurred, the Walking Woman could provide material for many a "garish" desert story—could tell, for example, "whether DeBorba killed Mariana for spite or for defense"—"it was not for such things I was wishful to meet her" (578). Perhaps having learned something from her encounter with the Woman at the Eighteen-Mile, she looks to the Walking Woman for a different kind of story, a story that occasions an "unconscious throb of sympathy" or "the unpremeditated way of her heart" (582), even though—or perhaps because—the story, like the Walking Woman herself, has no conventional form. Austin's narrator learns from the Walking Woman that "*any* way you get it, a child is good to have" and we read this as her recognition that, any way you get it, a different kind of story is good to have.

Still Austin recognizes that one's ability to hear such a story depends upon how one approaches the teller and how one understands the act of listening. In this story Austin, like Cary and Jewett, models what Morton calls "organic listening," a listening out of the "wholeness" of one's own being that enables another to speak out of the wholeness of his or her own being (30). Although she has some "things I wished to know" that increase her desire for a personal encounter, "when the occasion came we talked altogether of different things" (*AWR* 579). If such stories cannot be hunted down but must happen by accident, to get them requires as well a profound openness and a readiness to hear what the other has to say despite the pressure of what one wants to know and one's own sense of what matters. Such a mode of listening depends on and produces an empathic response that the narrator believes led the Walking Woman to touch her. We may also read that touch as the Walking Woman's recognition that the narrator's mode of listening has been "organic"; in acknowledging the intimate connection between talking and listening, the Walking Woman realizes as well that by listening to her the narrator has touched her as much as she has touched the narrator by speaking. We are free to read this moment, to which Austin draws our attention by emphasizing its openness to interpretation, as Austin's vision of the way her own stories work upon her reader. In a land of lost borders where a woman becomes able to walk off "all sense of society-made values," and, "knowing the best when the best came to her, was able to take it," there can be an exchange of essential, life-giving knowledge; the good of the place, "the best," can be given and taken. The narrator's wish for a personal encounter with the Walking Woman has been particularly "pointed" by the contradictory reports of her—"as to whether she was comely for example" (578). At the end of her encounter the narrator observes the Walking Woman as she departs: "She had a queer, sidelong gait, as if in fact she had a twist all through her. Recollecting suddenly that people called her lame, I ran down to the open place below the spring where she had passed. There in the bare hot sand the track of her two feet bore evenly and white" (583). To get the Walking Woman "straight" requires a different kind of story from those embedded in the "reports" of her.

In "The Basket Maker," Austin describes Seyavi's bowls as "wonders of technical precision" but declares that "the subtlest appeal is in the sense that warns us of humanness in the way the design spreads into the flare of the bowl" (574). According to Austin, "Seyavi made baskets for the satisfaction of desire,—for that is a house-bred theory of art that makes anything more of it" (575), and the desire Seyavi satisfies in making her bowls touches the desire in those who see, buy, and use them. Form gives Seyavi a container for her desire, and in linking desire, design, and humanness, Austin proposes "humanness" as the desire for form. Yet as Austin suggests, this form may not be one that readers conventionally recognize as such. Defining the form that humanness in regionalism takes as the way "the design spreads into the flare of the bowl," Austin proposes for regionalism a version of "organic" form, one constituted out of a desire to "listen into speech," a desire that extends to "listening" to the topography of the "land of little rain" and the "country of lost borders." Identifying a relation between the land, nature, the elements, and the material of art, Austin writes, "whenever Seyavi cut willows was always a golden time, and the soul of the weather went into the wood" (574); in the form of her art, Seyavi's bowls reflect her desire. In regionalist fiction we do not find form in its conventional sense, for "not the law, but the land sets the limit" (567).

In *Conflicting Stories,* Ammons includes a number of regionalist writers—

Jewett, Dunbar-Nelson, Chopin, Austin, and Sui Sin Far—in her assertion that "what stands out about a significant number of the writers that I am talking about is their relative failure with conventional form, even if they professed to admire it, compared with their greater success at experimental structures or at radical adaptations of existing high-culture narrative patterns. . . . Their experiments with form and language emphatically assert their originality and independence—their desire, even, to explode or circumvent fundamental structures of white patriarchal consciousness itself" (87). In their choice of the sketch form in particular, regionalist writers do assert their desire to write beyond conventions of gender that dominate traditional narratives. In calling attention to issues of plot, narrative interruption, techniques of framing, uses of dialect, narration as dialogue, self-reflexive concepts of story itself, stylistics as cultural intervention, and what lies beyond the "limits" of story, regionalist writers work, like Austin's Walking Woman, in a literary terrain that "by no canon" can be considered "ladylike" (*AWR* 578). Austin's insistence that the Walking Woman has "walked off all sense of society-made values" (582) characterizes regionalism as a textual region within which gender itself as a form of constraint ceases to be fully operative. She writes, "if there were ever any truth in the exemption from offense residing in a frame of behavior called ladylike, it should have been inoperative here. What this really means is that you get no affront as long as your behavior in the estimate of the particular audience invites none. In the estimate of the immediate audience—conduct which affords protection in Mayfair [a fashionable district of London] gets you no consideration in Maverick [a Western mining town]" (578). Austin inverts the usual priorities; in the world of Maverick, unlike the world of Mayfair (which we read as a metonym for conventional literary culture), "ladylike" behavior would "affront" the Walking Woman's "particular audience." In their "maverick" constructions of form and their choice of the sketch as the mode of writing which allows for the greatest deviation from "a frame of behavior called ladylike," regionalist writers create out of their "country of lost borders" a literary terrain that perhaps no one else wanted where readers would be free from the "affront" of gender.

Regionalism and the "Minor"

As we noted at the beginning of this chapter, the association of the sketch form with regionalist fiction has served as evidence of its minority status and has justified its relegation to the margins of American literary history. Yet, as we have also noted, regionalist writers chose the sketch form in order to gain a discursive freedom unavailable to them in those modes perceived as major. As we observed in chapter 2, *Ethan Frome* constitutes Wharton's critique of the "sentimentality" of her regionalist predecessors; in writing *Ethan Frome* Wharton sought to distance herself from a tradition she perceived as hopelessly minor and to align herself instead with the major tradition of American fiction exemplified by Hawthorne. *Ethan Frome,* then, reveals Wharton's anxiety about her own status as a woman writer seeking to be a major American author. In her effort to manage this anxiety, however, Wharton found it necessary to construct a text that is rather virulently misogynist and which in effect argues against the very claim she seeks to make in writing it. Despite Wharton's intentions, *Ethan Frome* complicates rather than clarifies the definition of major and minor; indeed, it reveals the crisis that regionalism creates for these categories.

As we have seen, Wharton's critique of her regionalist predecessors includes issues of subject matter as well as form; she charges that the texts of her predecessors failed to include significant dimensions of human experience, a charge she relates to their choice of form. According to Wolff, Wharton views regionalism as purchasing "peace . . . at the price of passion. There is no rage, and the climax of sexual fulfillment has been indefinitely suspended" (182). Indeed, we have observed how Cary's "The Wildermings," in a signature statement of regionalist theory and practice, relegates the material of the "seduced and abandoned," of sexuality, shame, and guilt, to the sidelines, making it a minor event within a larger story that has other issues as its focus. In *The Awakening,* as we will discuss further in chapter 10, Chopin reverses this emphasis; she foregrounds issues of sexuality and relegates the material of regionalism to a region within her fiction, the garret apartment occupied by Mlle. Reisz. Indeed, we may read *The Awakening,* as we read *The Pearl of Orr's Island,* as a text that theorizes the form of regionalism from within the tradition itself. Recognizing that she occupies a different historical moment from that of her predecessors, Chopin proposes that by the end of the nineteenth century a woman could write differently about sexuality and that, after publishing two successful collections of regionalist fiction (*Bayou Folk* and *A Night in Acadie*), she could return to the novel form without the limitations earlier writers had encountered (she was, of course, mistaken in her belief). Chopin, like Wharton, presumes certain forms and certain subjects to be "major," and she further presumes that only the novel can treat such major subjects as "passion, . . . rage, . . . the climax of sexual fulfillment."

Yet when Cary relegates the content of the "seduced and abandoned" woman to the status of an inset story in "The Wildermings," she is in part raising questions concerning dominant definitions of major and minor and suggesting that the plot of sexuality may play a far less prominent role in the lives of women than novels would have readers believe. Far from occupying a position in women's lives definitive of adulthood, sexual passion as conventionally understood locks women into the story of arrested development, an enclosure reflected in the novel's obsession with the late adolescent woman. Moreover, by typically ending with the young woman's marriage, as if her life were at so young an age already effectively over, the novel reveals that its ultimate "plot" is to tell her so. Indeed, we might read "The Wildermings" as proposing that to write about heterosexual romantic passion is to write the story of women's death and that to write the story of women's lives requires the ability to imagine a different form. When Mara in Stowe's *The Pearl of Orr's Island* asks the minister, "Are there any lives of women," regionalist writers would answer, not if one has to write romances, for these are the stories of women's death, literally if they are "seduced and abandoned," metaphorically if they result in marriage and hence coverture. Murfree says as much in "The Star in the Valley" when she associates Celia Shaw's death with her love for the seductive and abandoning Chevis.

In contrast, regionalism suggests that in the lives of women sexual passion as conventionally understood may play a minor role or none at all, and furthermore that the passions of women's adult lives may lie elsewhere—in, for example, their relations with "mother," or in their desire to write "a book about Americans," or in a woman's efforts to become "a guest to her own self." Moreover, as the last example should remind us, this challenge to the definition of major and minor extends to questioning what constitutes sexuality for women, a point to which we shall return, from a slightly different angle, in chapter 10. While Wharton might read Louisa's gentle acquiescence to Joe's original proposal of marriage as signaling the absence of sexual passion in regionalist fiction and thus as reaffirming its "evocation of childhood" (Wolff 182), we read Freeman as challenging the conventional understanding of women's sexuality and the formal requirements for its expression. Contrasting the prospect of marriage to Joe with Louisa's passionate commitment to the sensuality of her solitary daily life (the "greatest happening of all" [*AWR* 359], Freeman calls our attention to a formula for sexual behavior devised by men and imposed on women that allows for the expression of male sexuality even when such expression actually prevents the autonomous development of women's own sexuality. What some writers and critics have read as a sign of regionalism's limitations instead offers a provocative challenge to what constitutes the major and the minor in the world of fictional forms and subjects. Even in "The Walking Woman," where "maverick" constructions of form actually do allow for unconventional narratives of heterosexual passion—"'to work together, to love together'"—Austin also insists on other powerful forms of sexuality—a child's "'mouth at the breast,'" "'the lips and the hands, . . . the little, pushing hands and the small cry'" (*AWR* 582).

In choosing the sketch form over the novel, then, regionalist writers sought to escape the conventions of plot so that they might be free to say something other than "the old, old story" of heterosexual romance. While Wharton and others have read this choice as regressive, as indicative of a failure of ambition and of a desire to be minor, it can also be seen as containing ambitions of its own, in particular and most significantly the ambition not only to problematize the definition of what constitutes the major and the minor but also to destabilize the critical landscape secured by these terms. In a certain sense, as we have indicated, writing in the mode of the regionalist sketch or short story did constitute a decision to opt for minority status. In the moment of its production, both the sketch form itself and the regional sketch in particular, despite the attention accorded to it, occupied the place of a minor mode of writing. As such, regionalism provided an entrance to literary activity for numerous women who might have recoiled from the ambition explicit in the pursuit of more major modes of writing, for whom the anxiety of influence might have registered as the fear of having influence at all. Given the parameters set by its location as a minor mode of writing, women could accept whatever recognition they realized from writing regionalism since the mode itself operated to contain their achievement. To be sure, other American writers such as Irving, Edgar Allan Poe, and Hawthorne had worked extensively in short forms and had arguably made a case for the sketch as a major mode of *American* writing. However, Irving's status possessed a certain ambiguity precisely because his greatest success occurred in the form of the sketch; Poe gained his reputation as much through poetry, criticism, and the invention of genres as through his short fiction; and Hawthorne's sketches gained significance from the attention paid to his novels. Moreover, despite the case the short work of these male writers may have made for the importance of the sketch, it was their longer work and their contributions to the development of the American novel that informed the cultural context within which the women regionalists wrote. It would appear, then, that if and when regionalist writers had ambitions to be major, they would have located these ambitions elsewhere than in their sketches, as many in fact did; they would have tried to write novels and poetry. Still it would be a mistake to overlook the fact that many of the sketches anthologized in *American Women Regionalists* initially appeared in prominent national literary magazines such as the *Atlantic Monthly, Harper's Monthly, Harper's Bazar,* and *Century,* so that to attribute to regionalist writers innocence of literary hierarchy and even of ambition would be inaccurate. How then might we begin to think about the ambitions of regionalism?

If we begin again with Cary as the first writer of regionalism, we find that she is already using the regional sketch to explore questions of ambition. Although her preface accommodates itself to the narrative of limited or no ambition ("without a thought of making a book," "for myself, I confess that I have no invention," "they may perhaps interest if they do not instruct" [*AWR* 60–61]), many of her fictions present characters who do express the ambition to be recognized as different and special, as more talented than their circumstances would suggest, and whose ambitions are either frustrated or, if realized, prove not to provide the anticipated satisfaction. Given Cary's own history, her unwavering pursuit of a literary career and her unabashed desire to make a name for herself in poetry, one of the nineteenth century's "major" genres, we might reasonably assume that she is using regionalist fiction to explore the implications of her own ambitions to be a major writer. We might further assume that her perception of the minority status of regionalist fiction makes it available to her for such explorations, allowing her to construct regionalism as a quasi-private space within which she can deal with issues she does not want to treat "in public." Yet one might also see in her placement of this conversation an exploration of the complex relation of ambition to region and to empathy and particularly of her fear that her own ambition constituted a betrayal of both the region and the capacity for empathic narration that it represents. In "Charlotte Ryan," for example, when Charlotte finally achieves a position that enables her to humiliate the minor poet who earlier humiliated her, instead of glorying in her majority she wishes only that she had never left the region, as if in achieving her ambition she has lost what really matters—her minority regional status and its attendant empathic stance. In this story we locate an early version of the paradox of major as "minor" and minor as "major" that informs our own reading of regionalism and the work of regionalist writers as well. Leaving Ohio and moving to New York, Cary writes regionalist sketches to teach those who live in what is called the world to see as Clovernook sees, to become empathic, and thus to challenge and change their attitudes about world and region, major and minor. To the degree that this desire to "instruct" stems from a chafing resentment against being read as minor, it reveals an implicit desire to attain majority status. However, if achieving this status tempts one to treat others as minor, then it replicates the very "world" being critiqued and creates the desire to regain one's minority. In *The Power of Empathy,* Ciaramicoli proposes a connection between empathy and humility and associates the empathic stance with that of humility. He writes, "Whenever we put ourselves in a privileged place, assuming our situation is unique or the rules don't apply to us or we're somehow 'above it all,' we diminish the power of empathy. Presenting ourselves as different or better or smarter than others, we create a distance that can only lead to misunderstandings. Empathy always seeks to bring us closer together, reminding us that we need each other and, in fact, cannot get by without each other" (167). In this context, we might conclude that empathy itself represents a commitment to one's "minority" even as it requires the recognition that "when people are in pain or trouble, their deepest longing is to be understood as exceptions rather than rules" (80). Empathy itself, then, comes entangled with the paradoxes of major and minor.

Other regionalist texts explore the question of the minor in less paradoxical ways. We may read Candace Whitcomb's collapse at the end of "A Village Singer," for example, as Freeman's way of marking the limitations of regionalism as a site from which to launch a critique of authority. Furthermore, in allowing her to be so quickly defeated, Freeman not only suggests that the form of the regionalist sketch cannot do justice to a character like Candace; she also reveals her fear that regionalism would not provide a large enough canvas for her own talents and ambitions. She makes a similar revelation in "A Poetess." When Betsey Dole capitulates so quickly to the judgment of the minister and burns her poems, she reveals the fragility of her belief in the value of her work and exposes her vulnerability to the judgments of "authority." Despite Freeman's obvious dissociation of her own art from Betsey's, we still recognize the parallels between the "village art" of regionalism and the village art of the poetess (Campbell 28). While Freeman published her own fiction in a magazine, an act that links her to the minister, we observe in her identification with Betsey the kind of self-doubt that never troubles the minister and that might lead Freeman to disavow her own work just as it did Betsey.[14] Even as it mourns the death of an art that met the emotional and spiritual needs of the village, "of feminine sensibilities and community at the hands of a dispassionate masculinist aesthetic" (28), "A Poetess" does not seem to challenge the validity of this aesthetic or its right to dominate (28). In such stories Freeman seems to propose regionalist fiction as minor writing. In *Being a Minor Writer,* Gail Gilliland defines the minor writer as one who "could stop writing tomorrow and no one would notice" (2). When Freeman lost the encouragement of Mary Louise Booth after Booth's death and stopped writing regionalist fiction, did anyone notice or care?[15] Or if someone did implore her to return to the regionalist sketch, were the terms and tenor those Henry James employed in writing to Jewett after receiving a copy of her one historical novel, *The Tory Lover* (1901), a work he described in a letter to Howells as "a thing to make the angels weep": "Go back to the dear country of the *Pointed Firs, come* back to the palpable *present-intimate* that throbs responsive, and that wants, misses, needs you, God knows, and that suffers woefully in your absence" (qtd. in Campbell 56)?

On the other hand, Austin's sketches exude a seriousness about their enterprise that clearly stakes out a claim for majority status. Indeed, Austin's sketches evince the sense of self-importance that Austin claimed for herself and that made her an object of ridicule to so many of her contemporaries.[16] For Austin the regional sketch is not a way into writing nor is it a minefield of ambition, betrayal, and guilt. It is not an ambivalent arena where success can actually mean failure. Instead with every sentence Austin claims that only through the regional sketch can she get "you" to understand the "land" and every word in its intensity speaks to this purpose and its seriousness. Austin does not participate in the narrative of her own minority; hers is no "little noiseless life." Rather she insists on the significance of the desert, her writing about it, and herself, figuring all together in the image of the desert as a woman, indifferent to the pressures of others, and utterly sure of her own majority: "If the desert were a woman I know well what like she would be: deep-breasted, broad in the hips, tawny, with tawny hair, great masses of it lying smooth along her perfect curves, full lipped like a sphinx . . . eyes sane and steady as the polished jewel of her skies, such a countenance as should make men serve without desiring her. . . . and you could not move her, no, not if you had all the earth to give, so much as one tawny hair's breadth beyond her own desires" (*AWR* 592).

Still more interesting perhaps are those writers and fictions that seem to occupy a position outside the context of "major" and "minor." Those of us in the business of literature, whose livelihood depends upon our ability to manipulate "major" and "minor," become obsessed with issues of distinction and forget that most of what gets written at any given moment in time does not claim attention even as minor literature. If we simply consign all this writing to the category of "minor," the category ceases to have meaning. Inevitably, then, there exists a space outside these categories where the questions can be different from those critics usually ask. Even as we struggle with the issue of regionalism's relation to "major" and "minor" and our own relation to these terms, we wonder whether it is this other place we really wish to inhabit. Just as King's "The Balcony" situates her sketches as a series of transitory and impermanent stories women tell each other on summer evenings, we might view regionalism as a mode of writing profoundly uninterested in the entire debate around major and minor and willing to leave the determination of its significance to any given reader at any given moment. However, even this desire cannot avoid the question of ambition, as Louis Renza makes clear in his book on Jewett, *"A White Heron" and the Question of Minor Literature.*

Renza argues that Jewett systematically deconstructs the possibility of reading "A White Heron" within any of the codes and conventions that might appear to frame it; indeed he argues that the story reveals her desire to have written a text "completely outside the socioliterary setting of her times" (71). Nevertheless he sees this desire itself as framed by the question of major and minor and as expressive of Jewett's "ambition" to create the category of "minor minor" literature, a category other than the "major" and the "minor" and one that embodies "an unregenerate desire for literary finitude" (38). Although we put "ambition" in quotation marks to indicate that the meaning of Jewett's act is precisely what is under question, we pointedly use the term to indicate as well our recognition that, within the current academic intellectual climate, it would be hard to imagine anything more ambitious than the desire to escape binary thinking. Renza claims for Jewett the accomplishment of—or at least the discovery of the ambition to accomplish—this extraordinary desire; "Jewett's 'A White Heron' dreams the possibility of a nondialectical species of minor literature" that has as its motive "to secure a literarily untrammeled space, so to speak, wherein she can produce texts somehow excused from the question of their literary value" (Renza 167, 172). How, then, do we read Jewett's relation to ambition?

More than any other regionalist writer, Jewett based her career on the writing of the regional sketch. While for some writers regionalist fiction proved a byway off the main road, for Jewett regionalism was the "Maine" road. Indeed she frequently presents herself as incapable of writing otherwise, as in her oft-quoted letter of 1873 to Horace Scudder:

> But I don't believe I could write a long story as he [William Dean Howells] suggested, and you advise me in this last letter. In the first place, I have no dramatic talent. The story would have no plot. I should have to fill it out with

> descriptions of character and meditations. It seems to me I can furnish the theatre, and show you the actors, and the scenery, and the audience, but there never is any play! I could write you entertaining letters perhaps, from some desirable house where I was in most charming company, but I couldn't make a story about it. I seem to get very much bewildered when I try to make these come in for secondary parts. And what shall be done with such a girl? For I wish to keep on writing, and to do the very best I can. (*Sarah Orne Jewett Letters* 29)

For Jewett, then, regionalism did not provide a way into print, a space to try out her potential for success before committing to the ambitions of novel writing, as was perhaps the case with Murfree; nor did it represent a mode whose limitations she wished to overcome, as perhaps it did for Chopin and Cather; nor did it create a quasi-private space, as it seems to have done for Cary, within which she could explore the implications of her struggle to achieve a name and a reputation in another genre. Rather regionalism gave her the "way" she chose to write.[17]

In his extensive discussion of the ambivalence and contradictions of this self-presentation, Brodhead writes that "Jewett presents a single historical exhibit. Whether taken as leading a progress into art or a shrinkage into 'Art,' Jewett embodies a historical renegotiation of the relation of American women to literary careers" (*Cultures of Letters* 173–74). She wrote to make art, not money, and while on occasion she theorized a social purpose for her work, she did not write to change the world; "she became more dedicated to her art at the price of having that art give up larger functions of social edification and political address embraced by the less 'artistic' domestic-sentimental generation" (173). At the same time, however, she frequently presented herself in the discourse of self-diminution, leading Brodhead to label her letters the "diary of a self-belittler" (163). It would be easy to read this posture as protective, as deflecting attention away from the presumptuousness of her claim to the status of artist and as covering an ambition still unacceptable in a woman. Further, we could read her decision to devote herself to regionalist fiction as similarly self-protective. By consciously choosing a minor mode of writing within which to express her ambition to be an artist, she chose as well a safe space since, as we have suggested, regionalism by definition set limitations on any literary ambition realized within its form. Brodhead, however, concludes that Jewett's "limitations are the product neither of mere personal lack of 'power' nor of a general disablement of women's relation to writing but of Jewett's adherence to structures of literary self-conception specific to her cultural situation—structures built into her genre through its institutional articulation in her time" (167). In other words, because Jewett embraced the elitist values of "high art," because those values required subservience to the "cult of the master," and because she could not be a "master," she could do nothing but aspire to the category of "minor" writer, even if we read *The Country of the Pointed Firs* as "her well-disguised bid to become 'big' and do a 'big thing'" (167). For Brodhead, then, Jewett's ambition takes the form of trying to find her place in a major-minor conceptual structure, not of locating herself outside this binary; and if Henry James can "powerfully" identify with the idea of the major, Jewett "identifies instead with the idea of the minor, and so embraces a literary self projected on a more circumscribed plan" (166).

But should we accept this placement of Jewett or should we further explore the reading laid out by Renza who, at the very least, convinces us that Jewett was absorbed by the larger questions surrounding the conceptual structures of major and minor and perhaps possessed by the dream of a "minor" writing capable of standing outside those structures? As he comes to elaborate this dream in the process of deconstructing other possible readings of "A White Heron," Renza ends by considering the story a "pre-text," with all puns intended. Viewing the story as one that "procrastinates all possible definite readings which phenomenologically would situate it as a public text," the "sketchy story" allows Jewett to forget that she "ever wrote the story with such a 'minor' desire—the desire to produce a minor literature outside the context of the public and 'publishing' world" (Renza 162). The story "desires to become a quiescent instance of a nonideological as well as non-'literary' minor literature"; it "both traces and seeks to withdraw from the marketplace and honorific literary codes of success subtending its production"; and it projects an "endlessly self-determining preliminary or pre-text to serious literary activity" (162, 163). While Brodhead understands Jewett's relation to the minor as one that accepted "the major-to-minor gradient" (*Cultures of Letters* 174), Renza, in his survey of critical conceptions of minor literature from Northrop Frye to Gilles Deleuze and Félix Guattari, reads the position of critics like Brodhead as "criticism's self-disguised or, in the case of Harold Bloom, openly professed 'power' relation to such literature" (*"A White Heron"* 39). In its attempt "to define minor literature as a datum of literary experience, criticism is condemned to interpret it in canonical terms" (39). Thus, "minor literature" becomes "an undeconstructed critical category" (3), and to accomplish that deconstruction perhaps becomes Renza's own ambition in writing on Jewett, as his "small" critical question ironically and self-reflexively manifests its own grandiosity: "In the end, 'minor literature,' the conception of minor literary texts, comes down to a questioning of—as well as permanent question for—the act of criticism" (42).

In a certain sense, reading Jewett for Renza becomes a "pretext" for "reading" criticism itself, and in his text we find a critical pre-text for our own interest in the kind of "close" relationship with readers that regionalism postulates, one that we will take up in more detail in chapter 11, and that itself "comes down to a questioning of—as well as permanent question for—the act of criticism." In articulating Jewett's dream of "the possibility of a nondialectical species of minor literature" (167), Renza also connects her "admission about her nonheterosexual imagination" (95) to the possibility of a "nondialectical" and "nonheterosexual" form of criticism itself. Using Renza as a pre-text, we might extend this connection to include the possibility that a text's relation with a reader might be that of a "friend" and that such a relation might contain at least the dream of a community of readers in which literary critics and critical interpretations do not have to dominate in some binary "heterosexual" way the reading practices and interpretive responses of the entire community.

While we consider all of the writers anthologized in *American Women Regionalists* to have anticipated their own readers, Jewett more than any other has explored both in her own "private" writing and in her "constant determination to imagine an ideal private reading of her sketchy stories" (Renza 160) the possibility that readers might also be friends. Pryse traces the source of Jewett's impulse to write fiction to her inability, otherwise, to sustain female friendship when she was a young woman. Jewett found in writing her diaries a way to keep friends "with" her even though they were geographically distant, and even though, as she comes to recognize with sadness, she is capable of "outgrowing" them. (See also Jewett, "Outgrown Friends.")

> The textual dialogues between friendship and fiction in "Outgrown Friends," between the archival materials [esp. the diaries] and the sketches she would publish in the *Atlantic Monthly* . . . and would later revise for *Deephaven* (1877), and between *Deephaven* and *The Country of the Pointed Firs* (1896) provide new evidence for asserting Jewett's awareness of the generative and rhythmic reciprocity between love for her friends and love for her work. Indeed, the "way" she chose to write required her to create fiction out of friendship and to teach her reader, also a potential friend, how to make friends with her characters . . . for Jewett wished to write fiction that her readers would not outgrow the way she had outgrown most of the books of her childhood. (Pryse, "Archives of Female Friendship" 47–48)

As Renza expresses the relation, "writing in terms of such 'friends,' *structured* in turn on friends with whom she frequently corresponds, she can write literature as if it were letterature, i.e., as if it were exempt from the 'highly critical' codes of literary evaluation" (158). Perhaps where we differ with Renza is simply a matter of emphasis; for we understand Jewett's relation to her readers as always involving "an anticipation of loss or separation from friends—yet the process of writing offers some consolation, for it has the potential of preserving, at least archivally, lost human connections," and we have "returned" all these years to regionalism, like Jewett's narrator to Dunnet Landing, because we have found in regionalism as well as in Jewett's particular work "a fiction of friendship we do not outgrow" (Pryse, "Archives of Female Friendship" 61, 66).

Jewett does, of course, write for persons who are not her intimate friends; as early as her first diary entry she already writes for some reader a "hundred years" from now, a reader she envisions as a "young woman." While she may indeed dream of exempting her work from the "'highly critical' codes of literary evaluation," she nevertheless imagines her work as surviving for a century or longer. When the narrator of *The Country of the Pointed Firs* resists the temptation to become Mrs. Todd's literal apprentice and chooses instead her own writing, despite the fact that "literary employments are so vexed with uncertainties at best" (*The Country of the Pointed Firs* 7), we can interpret this as her recognition, one eventually shared by Mrs. Todd, that she can better pass on Mrs. Todd's knowledge and wisdom through writing than through the gathering and dispensing of herbs. In this textual moment we can also read Jewett's recognition of the capacity of writing to reach an audience wider than the local and to last longer than its own historical moment. However, the narrator's recognition that she can keep Mrs. Todd "alive" far longer through writing than if she simply took over her business articulates Jewett's dream as ambition. "Letterature" becomes literature within the context of a fiction in which Jewett has figured out how to make a book-length text out of the regionalist sketch and thus to secure for herself a permanent place in American literary history, however minor that place may be. James would not have taken Jewett seriously had it not been for *The Country of the Pointed Firs;* and his praise, however patronizing, has gained her an entrance to American literary history denied most other regionalist writers. Ironically, as we observed in chapter 1, Jewett's foothold in American literature has positioned her to receive the sharpest critique from contemporary critics; her visibility, however slight, makes her the focal point for efforts to recover or dismiss the larger textual body for which she serves as a synecdoche. Not a novel, *The Country of the Pointed Firs* is nevertheless more than a collection of sketches. While it is a mark of Jewett's genius that she managed to figure out how to write a novel-length work of regionalist fiction without betraying or abandoning the poetics of regionalism and thus gained for at least one work of regionalism the recognition that a culture of letters obsessed with gendered hierarchies is willing to accord to texts that look like novels, the question still remains: what exactly has she managed to figure out?

At the end of his book on Jewett, Renza quotes a comment she made in a letter of 1885: "I often think that the literary work which takes the least prominent place nowadays is that belonging to the middle ground. Scholars and so-called intellectual persons have a wealth of literature in the splendid accumulation of books that belong to all times, and now and then a new volume is added to the great list. Then there is the lowest level of literature, the trashy newspapers and sensational novels, but how seldom a book comes that stirs the minds and hearts of the good men and women of such a village as this" (178; *Sarah Orne Jewett Letters* 51). While this comment operates within the hierarchical frame of high and low, of major and minor, we might still see in it Jewett's desire to identify a space outside such hierarchies, for in effect she proposes here that for most people the meaning of writing and reading does not occur within the context of major and minor. Most people do not turn for their reading to the "classics" that occupy the attention of scholars, nor are they nourished by what Jewett refers to as "trash." Rather, what feeds them are those unrecognized texts of the "middle ground," the ground on which we would locate regionalism, that can stir the hearts and minds of "such a village as this." Such texts will last just so long as there are readers whose minds and hearts they stir and no longer. Expressing perhaps "an unregenerate desire for literary finitude" and profoundly uninterested in the economy of major and minor, they understandably go unrecognized as "literature."

In calling attention to such texts, however, we, like Jewett, inevitably reengage the question of ambition and its attendant discourse of major and minor. Finally we must confront our own ambitions for regionalism and for ourselves, and the extent to which we, like Renza, also want to raise the question of "minor criticism." It would be disingenuous to claim that we do not seek for regionalism a major place in American literature or that we do not seek to elevate our own critical reputations by attempting such a task in a book that may seem to be our own not-so-well-disguised "bid to become 'big' and do a 'big thing'" (Brodhead 167). As Robyn Wiegman has remarked, "minoritization is the language of being major today."[18] Yet we persist in believing that regionalism has the potential to rearrange our understanding of American literature, not simply in order that the old minor may become the new major but so that we might reunderstand what these terms could mean. In "A White Heron," Jewett's Sylvia is nine years old, the same age Jewett claimed "always" to be (*Letters of Sarah Orne Jewett* 125). Yet if Jewett remains a "minor," it is because her work reflects a "nonheterosexual" imagination of what might allow a girl like Sylvia to achieve her adult "majority" unaccosted by "the great red-faced boy," the hunter/ornithologist, her grandmother's expectations for her conformity, or the assumptions readers conventionally bring to their understanding of what constitutes development for girls. As we have tried to demonstrate, regionalism views women as adults and expects boys also to grow up. In this way we can make a critical claim for regionalism as "major": it becomes the literature of women writers' "majority." No longer "always nine years old," regionalist writers become "free to say" that women do not need to marry in order to achieve maturity; that their "whoop of the heart" leads to emotional fulfillment; that a woman who works for suffrage is the "superior" woman; that friendship "restores" an old woman to her fortune; and that boys need not be "boys."

While we may find in Jewett's reiteration of her own minority a dream of readers who desire to remain "outside" the power relations that constitute "literature" or "criticism," readers from the "middle ground," it is only by reading Jewett in the context of the larger group of regionalist writers that we can even begin to interpret that dream. And while she may not have been able to articulate it herself, just as she never used the word "lesbian" to describe her "Boston marriage" with Annie Fields, her work reflects her ambition to create the first discursive region in which women might claim their own majority, and at the same time might displace models of adult development constructed in the service of masculinism and designed to keep them "always nine years old."

CHAPTER 7

Regionalism and the Question of the American

The revolutionary impulse . . . has been turned against the nationalist ideal itself.

—Peter Carafiol, "Commentary: After American Literature"

"I am enjoying a most agreeable visit, and American friends, as also our own, strive benevolently for the accomplishment of my pleasure. Mrs. Samuel Smith, an American lady, known to my cousin, asked for my accompaniment to a magniloquent lecture the other evening. The subject was 'America, the Protector of China'!"

—Sui Sin Far, "Mrs. Spring Fragrance"

Reflections on the Idea of American Literature

Since the 1970s the field of American literature has undergone an extraordinary change. Challenges to the perceived hegemony of the field's canon, enabling assumptions, and intellectual foundations have emerged from numerous quarters and have produced for many Americanists the paradoxical position of being defined by a term they no longer believe can be itself defined.[1] As Carolyn Porter puts it, referring to the persistence of "the contempt for American literature traditionally held by those Anglophile literary scholars for whom, as a Renaissance specialist once remarked to me, American literature is the cultural equivalent of 'military band music,' . . . Americanists these days have little time to worry about such old quarrels; they are too busy trying to keep up with developments in a field bearing an increasingly remote resemblance to the one in which many of them were trained" (467). Indeed, William Spengemann, in his "reflections . . . on the idea of American literature" (1), has offered a daunting map of this "new world," one calculated to convince those graduate students who currently turn to American literature because they "find the Renaissance or Victorian period too large to manage" that they cannot so easily escape their woes (15). While he acknowledges that his redefinition of the field "will not necessarily assuage our pangs of cultural inadequacy" (23) nor, we might add, convince our colleagues in British literature that we have not simply increased the number of trombones in the band, Spengemann presents his map with the same sense of wonder traditionally associated with England's first glimpse of the new world:

> When the phrase "American literature" is stripped of its acquired qualifications, the word "American" signifies everything having to do with civilization in the New World since the European discovery, and "literature" includes every written document that will respond to literary analysis. Here is a vast landscape indeed—one fully commensurate to our capacity for belief in the nobility, complexity, and uniqueness of American literature. The American literature embraced by this definition is nearly five hundred years old. It is written in many languages, and it comes from many places scattered throughout a world whose size, shape, and meaning have changed continually since 1500 because America was discovered. (24)

While Spengemann's proposed redefinition of the field has received little "official" notice in Americanist circles, its contours can certainly be observed in the changing shape of the field. The Norton and Heath anthologies of American literature, to cite just two, now begin with the literature of encounter and with American Indian poetry, song, and legend. The point of origin for American literature has changed, extending the history of its existence. In addition, American literature is now understood as multicultural and multilinguistic; it includes the writings of Spanish and French Europeans as well as those of British Europeans and the texts of a wide range of American Indian cultures.[2] Finally, while both the Norton and the Heath remain essentially within the traditional understanding of the geographical identity of America, the fourth edition of the Heath has opted to include selections from the writings of early Spanish and French explorers; the Haitian revolutionary Toussaint L'Ouverture; the Spanish and Mexican *californios;* and the Cuban writer José Martí, and thus to at least mark the question of geography as well as those of history, language, and culture; through this fissure a whole new wave of materials may soon "pour in upon our attention" as well (Spengemann 23).

This expansion of the textual base of American literature may produce exhilaration, in part because by so doing we may have saved our field "in a time of shrinking budgets and withdrawing professional opportunities" (15), but it has also generated concern. Those groups organized around "identity politics," whose challenge to the perceived hegemony of American literature developed along the axes of race, gender, class, and ethnicity, may now find themselves in the position of having achieved inclusion only to discover that the value of the field has declined by virtue of their success in gaining entrance to it, just as housing values typically drop in a neighborhood that becomes "integrated" and salaries cease to rise in a profession finally opened to women. Scholars who may have hoped to gain attention for minority and women writers by claiming them as "American" now find themselves told that the term has no meaning and hence no rhetorical power; in effect they are told that the members of the country club have decided to go out of business rather than admit women or blacks, even as they suspect that the club has simply moved elsewhere and is operating under a different name. Certainly stress characterizes the experience of those Americanists who continue to do business under the old name even as they recognize that, as Peter Carafiol puts it, "a historicist perspective . . . deprives us of the certainty that the category 'American literature' refers to anything in particular, much less anything special, that it serves any useful purpose in criticism other than keeping a particular set of institutional wheels turning" ("Commentary" 543). Moreover, the sense of acting in bad faith, as Carafiol also points out, is further aggravated by the fact that "for the first time, the revolutionary impulse that has always been the orthodoxy of American literary scholarship has been turned against the nationalist ideal itself, rather than merely its imperfect institutional manifestation" (539). Thus those engaged in the critique of American literature as reifying and reinforcing a politically suspect concept of nation, suspect in good part because of its connection to empire, cannot help but be troubled by the possibility that their "very willingness to expand the territory of American literature recalls a long history of previous territorial expansionism in politics and literature" (542).

However, anxiety also attends those engaged in the critique of the foundational assumptions of American literature as they realize their critique is itself enabled by institutional positions dependent upon the very category they seek to dismantle. In Spengemann's "time of shrinking budgets and withdrawing professional opportunities," only the most resolute and dedicated of the "new" Americanists actually desire a disintegration that would put them out of a job, especially when they take into account how out of touch such a posture is with a larger American public substantially conservative and often stridently nationalist. Moreover, as Nina Baym, among others, has observed, many of these "new Americanist" critiques occur within a framework that participates in the very assumptions they purportedly seek to disable. In a comment that echoes Bercovitch's perception that even the most ardent critiques of America are undertaken under the aegis of the American, "recalling the country to its sacred mission" and "reaffirming the American dream" (29), she writes,

> Scholars considering how the field might be revised are not considering alternatives to America as the field's subject; rather most revisionary hypotheses are offered as improvements in our understanding of America. . . . To the extent that American literature teaching is practiced for the ultimate aims of forming student character and producing better citizens it incorporates familiar nationalistic aims. The much touted revisionary Heath anthology of Amer-

ican literature, for example, is a passionately nationalistic, patriotic document. No matter how radical or revolutionary the teachers' aims may be, and no matter how deeply teachers feel these aims, if they hope to produce better Americans, a better America, or even just a better understanding of the *real* America, then the supposedly suppressed or overturned Whig project continues in full force. (*Feminism* 100–101)

In the atmosphere of fatigue and even despair created by these dilemmas and represented by Lawrence Buell in the final interchange of his imaginary dialogue on the state of American literature, "Circling the Spheres," we might be glad of a reprieve offered by the bell that tells us it is time for our 2:30 class on "American Literature: 1815–1860," or, if we have taken Gregory Jay's words to heart, on "Writing in the United States: 1815–1860" (see his "The End of 'American' Literature"). Buell writes:

B: "Such as it is"—precisely so. An identity in perpetual quotation marks, shifting about with history, with authorial impetus, with critical vantage point.
A: With the hour, you mean. All this sounds mighty nebulous to me. Those who keep shifting their identity, lose their identity. Or never had it.
B: Foundationalist nostalgia isn't the problem for me that it is for you. But I agree that it's part of the story, part of the critical mix.
C: Yes. On the one hand, there's obviously no such thing on the current critical scene as *the* "Americanist community," maybe never really was, even though we sometimes wish for it and thereby make that wishfulness a part of our artifacts. On the other hand, to the extent that the icon of "negotiation" becomes more or less consensual, as it now is, that reestablishes something like a common coinage, or at least the hope of such.
A: For how long, though? Will it outlast the present conversation?
B: But what else is there? (484)

As Carolyn Porter reminds us, in concluding her reading of Carafiol, current revisionary efforts above all else "testify to the extraordinary difficulty entailed in resisting the virtually gravitational force of 'America' as a foundational assumption. . . . We can try, that is, 'simply to ignore' the issue of 'America,' but it is not going to go away" (478).

Proposals for solving these dilemmas, though critiqued as inadequate or complicit as soon as they appear, seem not to be wanting, however. Donald Pease calls for a new "field-Imaginary" for American studies that will reestablish "the relationship between the cultural and political spheres" denied and repressed by the field-Imaginary of the "old" Americanists (15), one "predicated upon the linkage between the cultural and the public" (31), capable of connecting "repressed sociopolitical contexts *within* literary works to the sociopolitical issues *external* to the academic field," and thus ultimately capable of changing "the hegemonic self-representation of the United States' culture" (32).[3] Carafiol suggests as a model those essays "that appear to give up long-cherished essentials of American literary scholarship without a murmur" since "they make no particular disciplinary claims, describe no particular field of study, and display no need to import interest from debates about the boundaries or characteristics of a national literature" and since they "show both the bankruptcy of the old 'project' of demonstrating the 'Americanness' of texts and the increasing willingness, especially among younger scholars, simply to ignore it" ("Commentary" 545). Additional proposals include, for example, Bercovitch's attempt to use "ideology to get a purchase on American literary history" (Porter 475) and Philip Fisher's attempt to replace "myth"—"always singular" and always "a fixed, satisfying, and stable story"—as the foundational assumption of American literature with "rhetorics"—always "plural because they are part of what is uncertain or potential within society" (232). For Fisher, replacing "myth" with "rhetorics" reveals "interests and exclusions" (232) and thus enables us to recover "the pervasive, continuously unsettled, open struggle within American culture" that makes our cultural history "the history of civil wars" (245).

Among book-length proposals we might note Eric Sundquist's massive effort in *To Wake the Nations* to require "readers to overcome their fundamental conception of 'American' literature as solely Anglo-European in inspiration and authorship" (7). In contrast, Sundquist offers "a redefinition of the premises and inherent significance of the central literary documents of American culture" (7) that begins from the recognition "that the mainstream of American culture" has "always been significantly black and southern, bearing the clear inflection of African American language and creativity in popular as well as high culture" (3). We also note Lora Romero's effort in *Home Fronts* to complicate the conversation around nineteenth-century domesticity by releasing it from the binary that has constructed domesticity as either complicit, powerful, and corrupt, or resistant, alternative, and pure, and by reading it instead as multiple and conflicted, traversed at once by "antipatriarchal motivations" (20) and "always on the verge of reproducing patriarchal culture's male gaze" (22). Recognizing at the outset that "the available paradigms for thinking about mid-nineteenth-century culture were insufficiently interpretive, being themselves unable to represent power—and resistance to it—in a manner fundamentally different from that informing the materials and practices under consideration" (1), Romero provides a model for contemporary Americanists, whatever their area of special interest, who find themselves caught in the dilemma of trying to redefine their field by means of "insufficiently interpretive" paradigms. Most significantly, however, Romero's work provides a salutary reminder of the degree to which current debates over the question of the American are profoundly shaped by the impulse toward "exceptionalism." This impulse pushes critics to locate their definition of the American in texts that can be claimed as purely oppositional, alternative, and resistant, and thus to create the category of the American by identifying as un-American the texts they see as complicit in whatever it is they wish to resist. In arguing for the necessity of "a method of analysis responsive to privileges that do not amount to dominance and disenfranchisements that do not constitute powerlessness" (10), Romero models an alternative to "exceptionalism," though following her model may prove American literature to be ultimately not distinctive from British or continental literature.

Finally, we might note the remapping of the field of American literature offered by those current writers and scholars who can be said to comprise the "School of Caliban," who take as a key originary text José Martí's 1891 essay "Nuestra America," and who propose that we reconfigure American literary history by placing it "in relation to a cultural politics centered in 'the extended Caribbean'" which has "its center in postrevolutionary Havana" (Porter 504). In *The Dialectics of Our America* José Saldívar articulates the goal of this "school" as reading "the literary history of the Americas . . . in transgeographical terms" (qtd. in Porter 504). Such a project crosses the boundaries of both nation and language and "goes a long way toward overcoming the parochialism of traditional, and even not so traditional, American literary studies" (Porter 506). Additionally, it proposes that "the specific 'politics of location' at work here must be rearticulated in relation to a history that encompasses the entire post-Columbian period, including European colonialism, from a Calibanic perspective" (506). Such a project

> might enable the more complex geopolitical relations between Europe and both Americas . . . to come into view as a field-imaginary whose "political unconscious" is colonialism itself. Such a framework would necessarily include Africa and the triangular trade route joining its east coast to Europe and the Americas. . . . The aim here would not be to expand American studies so as to incorporate the larger territory of the hemisphere, but rather to grasp how the cultural, political, and economic relations between and within the Americas might work to reconstellate the field itself, reinflecting its questions in accord with a larger frame. (510)

While Porter is well aware of the difficulties facing any effort to reimagine American literature, she concludes her essay by insisting that the work of those who comprise the "school of Caliban" at the very least "invites us to join in developing a field-imaginary that might enable us and our students to see beyond 'Our America' to that other America 'which is not ours'" and "offers the promise of approaching America's literatures as the very opposite of parochial or insulated or exceptional, without thereby assuming a global or imperialist perspective" (521).

As feminist Americanists we have ourselves participated in the challenges to the hegemony of the field of American literature perceived to be the legacy of the 1940s, 50s, and 60s, and we have in various ways sought to contribute our own modest proposals for reimagining the field. Our current project, which began as a work of textual recovery, also engages both explicitly and implicitly with the question of the American. Indeed, the frequent appearance of regionalism in the current debates over the question of the American suggests that the work of textual recovery has achieved its purpose; it has at least placed regionalist writers on the map in such a way that their work and critical writing about their work has become part of the dialogue. For example, Fisher describes regionalism as the force "which tore apart the previous unifying and singular myths of America" and thus enables a new foundational assumption for American literature, namely "rhetorics" (243). For another, we note how quickly the term "regionalism" emerges in Buell's "Circling the Spheres" as a site for conversation. Regionalism, it would seem, has gained a certain currency, and while we might take satisfaction from this fact, we more typically experience distress as we chart the fate of regionalism in the current debates over the question of the American and note the frequency with which it is attacked as complicit in a variety of politically suspect projects. Moreover, we note as well a certain animus in these attacks that seems to derive from our own and others' suggestion that regionalism contains a discourse of opposition and resistance specifically gender-inflected, or, to use Buell's more cautious phrase, "roughly gender-tilted" (467).

This approach to regionalism has received its most extensive articulation in Richard Brodhead's *Cultures of Letters,* but it appears as well in the recent work of scholars such as Amy Kaplan, Sandra Zagarell, and Elizabeth Ammons, and it informs in part June Howard's collection *New Essays on The Country of the Pointed Firs.*[4] While we appreciate Romero's approach and might well have adopted it ourselves, pointing out with respect to regionalism the ways in which "privileges . . . do not amount to dominance and disenfranchisements . . . do not constitute powerlessness," in the context of the current critical climate we hesitate to do so. Despite Brodhead's breezy assertion that "the feminist rehabilitation of regionalism" is "nearly consolidated" (*Cultures of Letters* 144), we would argue that it has barely begun and that those of us committed to a reading of regionalism as a feminist tradition within American literature need to continue to make that case, allowing readers to explore the complexities of privilege and disenfranchisement by reading dialogically our work and that of critics such as Brodhead.

Such complexities seem all too often absent from the critiques of regionalism as we observe, for example, the differential treatment accorded Chesnutt and the women writers who constitute the basis of our study, particularly Jewett. For example, in an essay that we will discuss more fully later in this chapter, Kaplan observes parenthetically that it was "The Goophered Grapevine" "which launched Chesnutt's career in the *Atlantic Monthly*" (245), as if to be so launched was both good for Chesnutt and a measure of the *Atlantic*'s literary taste; yet when she refers to "the conditions of literary production for regionalist writers," she describes them as "published by a highly centralized industry located in Boston and New York that appealed to an urban middle-class readership," an industry that obviously included the *Atlantic Monthly* (251). She further observes that "this readership was solidified as an imagined community by consuming images of rural 'others' as both a nostalgic point of origin and a measure of cosmopolitan development" (251). While Chesnutt, writing in the same tradition in the same magazines and to the same audience, manages to "subvert the plantation tradition," undo "the Northern romance of the Southern garden," rechart "the projection of an exotic and romantic Southern landscape as a palimpsest of destruction," and expose "the broader national allegory of reconciliation through marriage" (245), white women regionalists work to contain "the threatening conflicts of social difference," to efface through region "the more explosive social conflicts of class, race, and gender," and to render "regional inhabitants . . . more familiar and less threatening than the feared flood of immigrants whose foreignness lay too close for comfort in an urban context" (251).

If we ask what produces such different descriptions and judgments, particularly in light of our own analysis in chapter 1 of the similarities between some of Chesnutt's work and that of the women regionalists, we will not find an answer within Kaplan's essay any more than we will find one within *Cultures of Letters,* where Brodhead exaggerates still further the distinction between Jewett and Chesnutt. We might note that in his "Introduction" to *The Conjure Woman and Other Conjure Tales,* Brodhead raises the possibility that the editorial protocol that allowed Houghton Mifflin to select some tales and reject others for the 1899 text of *The Conjure Woman* "may have censored some of Chesnutt's more overtly subversive visions, but it is arguable that it also kept Chesnutt from a racial self-caricaturing that he was too willing to engage in. All we can say here is that any simple reading of the case is likely to be a wrong one" (19). When Brodhead reads Chesnutt alone, he rightly suggests that "simple" reading, whether of Chesnutt or any other recently recovered writer, is likely to be "wrong," but when he reads Chesnutt against Jewett, he relies on simplicities of privilege and disenfranchisement to set the black male writer against the white female writer in a critical "contest" whose outcome is predetermined by the antifeminism of the larger culture.

While we do not offer *Writing out of Place* as a proposal for a new "field-Imaginary" for American literature, we do see it as providing a vantage point from which to reflect on the recent debates in the field. In this chapter, then, we bring the narrative of chapter 2 into the present. While we acknowledge the need to continue to do the work of feminist analytics and to continue to make the case for regionalism as a feminist tradition within American literature, we seek here as well to position regionalism as a "third" term, one that creates a crisis for the categories that continue to structure the field.

"Roughly Gender-Tilted"

From the outset Brodhead alerts the reader of *Cultures of Letters* to the fact that his emphasis on culture and "working conditions" has a self-conscious political dimension absent from the old approaches to American literary history; like Pease's "new" Americanists, he too seeks to reconnect the cultural and the political spheres. Yet the actual politics of *Cultures of Letters* remain unarticulated even as they are depressingly familiar. This is particularly unfortunate in a book that promises on the surface to provide a model for the integration of male and female writers within a single literary history and so to move genuinely beyond "separate spheres." Responding to feminist challenges to the canon and feminist efforts to incorporate women writers into American literary history, Brodhead includes women in his study of nineteenth-century cultures of letters but in such a way as to orchestrate the terms of their re-dismissal. In a pattern similar to Kaplan's, Brodhead concludes his book with a chapter on Chesnutt that presents him as a decisive self-fashioner who seized "the idea that if the forms of literary expression must be found in a dominant culture, they can still be used in the interest of subordinated peoples" (195) and whose "long-enforced constraint within regionalist formulas" did not "set absolute limits to his creativity" despite their toll upon it. Moreover, he claims him as a writer whose work in the "prolific years . . . deserves full consideration on another occasion" (209). In contrast, in his penultimate chapter, Brodhead presents Jewett as a writer without agency, whose fiction both wittingly and unwittingly served only to further the interests of social, cultural, political, and economic elites, and whose absolute commitment to regionalism signals how "profoundly" she "embraced the conceptual structures aligned with regionalism—the religion of art, the autonomization of the aesthetic, the stratification of high and low, the major-to-minor gradient" (174), even if it meant she herself would always be understood to be minor. Brodhead's relentless attack on her as passive, complicit, and compromised has the effect of writing "case closed" over the file marked Jewett and of discouraging any further consideration of her work.

Brodhead's hostility toward Jewett can be explained in part by the fact that, among nineteenth-century women writers, Jewett presents one of the strongest cases for inclusion as a major figure in American literary history. In the past the devaluation of the mode of writing with which she is associated—regionalism/local color—has been sufficient to keep her marginal. But, as Brodhead acknowledges, more recently feminist scholars have called for a re-vision of regionalism that, if successful, would also entail a re-vision of Jewett. In order to dismiss Jewett, then, Brodhead must first dismiss regionalism. Since feminists have proposed regionalism as an alternative and oppositional tradition, one that worked against the construction of nation and empire and that challenged the constructions of masculine and feminine that underwrote the projects of nation and empire, Brodhead directs his energies to demonstrating that in fact regionalism served as the all-too-willing handmaid to such projects. Thus in *Cultures of Letters* "The Reading of Regions" precedes the reading of Jewett.

According to Brodhead, regionalism set the competence required for its production so "unusually low" that virtually anyone, including women, could participate (116). Requiring only the knowledge one might have from living in "some cultural backwater," regionalism turned marginality into literary capital and so "provided the door into literary careers for women" (117). Once marginality has been re-understood as advantage rather than disadvantage, regionalism can be reread as complicit rather than as oppositional, as engaged in the cultural work of composing "a certain version of modern history" that "tell[s] local cultures into a history of their supersession by a modern order now risen to national dominance" (121). Linking the production of regional fiction with that of the international-theme novel, Brodhead argues that, just as the international novel produced a "visitable 'Europe,'" so too regionalism produced an "inhabitable backwardness"; both provided upper- and middle-class readers the opportunity to rehearse the "habit of mental acquisitiveness" essential to imperialism (133).

Brodhead situates his reading of Jewett in the context of his reading of regions. Asserting that "few authors of any time or condition have clung to a single genre more tightly than Jewett," he acknowledges that the feminist "revisionary gambit in Jewett's case has been to claim that the genre itself has been read 'unfairly,' and to correct this 'injustice' by making the seemingly minor regionalist form the site of major cultural transactions" (143). Referring to the "blurb" on the jacket of Sarah Way Sherman's *An American Persephone,* he argues that "feminist criticism has supplied Jewett with her most successful rescue plan to date" (143).[5] To challenge the results of this rescue operation, Brodhead must call into question the value of a feminist approach to Jewett and the legitimacy of gender as a category of analysis. Thus he writes that "with the success of the feminist rehabilitation of regionalism so nearly consolidated, it is time to remember" that "no culture is ever specified by its gender dimension alone" (144). While we would applaud any reading that actually enlarged our understanding of the complex operations of privilege and disadvantage as articulated in the intersections of gender, race, and class identities, *Cultures of Letters,* unlike Romero's *Home Fronts,* does not in fact do such work. Rather, where white women are concerned, Brodhead asks us to accept that class—a category of analysis that makes no appearance in his treatment of men be they white (Hawthorne) or black (Chesnutt)—constitutes not simply another "dimension" but the only dimension worth considering. While Brodhead does not ask his readers to consider, in relation to Chesnutt, that no culture is ever specified by its racial dimension alone, nor to examine how the privilege of gender may for Chesnutt have complicated the disadvantage of race, he does ask readers to accept that Jewett's class privilege, and by implication that of other white women regionalists, did not simply complicate their gender disadvantage but rather made it irrelevant. In effect, Brodhead uses class as a category of analysis to cancel out rather than complicate gender as a category of analysis. Moreover, he does so in order to further what is in fact a gender-based agenda—namely the production of a "new" American literary history that continues to take seriously only the work of male writers, though "male" may now be more racially inclusive.

Within *Cultures of Letters,* white men inhabit a space magically exempt from critique. Brodhead never turns on Hawthorne the analysis that proves so devastating in the cases of Stowe, Louisa May Alcott, and Jewett. He devotes an entire chapter to *The Blithedale Romance* in order to show us a Hawthorne "meditating" upon "the new social conditions of literary production" (55), not a Hawthorne written by these social conditions or complicit in their questionable projects even though we might reasonably assume that these conditions offered him the opportunity to promote his own class and gender interests. Nor does he invoke class as a category of analysis in his reading of James, who makes only a fleeting appearance in *Cultures of Letters.* Yet, as the most powerful architect of the religion of art and as the writer whose insistence upon the role of "master" had much to do with creating the context in which Jewett came to be seen as minor, James would seem to be central to Brodhead's goal of understanding the role of the literary in the production of postwar ruling-class subjectivity.[6] Brodhead's model of selective analysis proves attractive as it allows "new" Americanists to engage in their critiques without doing damage to the reputations of canonical writers (consider here Sundquist's need to assure readers that "my intention is certainly not to depose canonical figures" [*To Wake* 7]). While white men constitute a protected class in the pages of *Cultures of Letters,* and white women constitute a legitimate object of attack for their preposterous claims at once to disadvantage and to agency, African American women make no appearance at all, presumably because they would disrupt the simplistic but familiar binaries that structure the book.

Brodhead's hostility to Jewett derives not simply from the claims feminists have put forward with respect to her significance, claims we can only assume strike Brodhead as presumptuous even though we might see them as posing on behalf of women the same question (why could not a woman?) he finds so compelling when asked by Chesnutt ("why could not a colored man . . . if he possessed the same ability, write a far better book about the South than Judge Tourgee or Mrs. Stowe has written?" [qtd. in Brodhead, *Cultures of Letters* 192]). It derives as well from the fact that once Jewett begins to attract critical attention, it becomes less easy to minoritize her. Indeed, Brodhead himself acknowledges that Jewett marks a moment of "immense historical resonance: the moment when a publishing American woman author first claims the duty (hence the right) to take her art seriously, and to define her proper self as the maker of her art" (169). Once she is taken seriously by critics, Jewett becomes a strong contender for a significant place in American literary history not only by virtue of her artistic accomplishments but also by virtue of her self-consciousness as to her own historical moment and her consequent "right" to see herself as a "maker." Thus to dismiss Jewett, Brodhead must find a way to undercut her sense of agency. He does so by portraying her as in effect an automatic writer, one who "by chance of birth" (151) found "her lived world presented to her as a literary subject" at precisely the moment she "came to her literary ambition" (152). Possessing "literary capital" simply by virtue of this accident of birth and by the experience of merely living, Jewett needed to do nothing more than reproduce "her known world in the contours of this genre." By this easy, natural, almost automatic process of "taking regionalism as her work," Jewett also acquired "an access to readership and recognition as unobstructed as any American literary history has to show" (152).

However, "taking regionalism as her work" means for Brodhead that Jewett constructed an alignment between regionalism and "high culture." Kaplan associates this alignment with the production of fiction "that appealed to an urban middle-class readership" whose relations to the regions took the form of tourism (251). Both Brodhead and Kaplan see regionalism as complicit in "the stratification of high and low" (*Cultures of Letters* 174) and assume that regionalist writers align themselves with urban and middle-class readers over against their purportedly nonliterate and nonliterary regional subjects. Referring to Garland's claim that "the tourist could not write the local novel," Kaplan comments, "tourists did and could read local color fiction, which, after all, could not be read by the people it depicted" (252). In a similar vein, Brodhead, in commenting on a letter Jewett wrote to Cather, observes how Jewett's text is "shot through with markers" of the "class outlook" of a group who "adopted high culture as their project and group ideal," an ideal that included "hostility in particular to the McClurean or mass media world of writing." Such writing formed the "continual object, at the turn of the century, of the elite fear of a new popular culture's threatened 'debasements' of the 'best'" (*Cultures of Letters* 171).

Kaplan offers no support for her claim that local-color fiction "could not be read by the people it depicted" (252), and Brodhead is clearly unaware of the complexities of Jewett's publishing history. In his work on the nineteenth-century newspaper syndicates, Charles Johanningsmeier notes that both Jewett and Freeman managed to reach mass local audiences by selling stories to the syndicates as well as to magazines like *Atlantic* and *Harper's*, and consequently that regionalism could be, and was, "read by the people it depicted."[7] Johanningsmeier disputes Brodhead's claim that regionalist authors "found their literary roles bound together with the high zone in a steeply hierarchized plan of culture, with correlative class prerogatives of leisure and consumption, with a certain socially based appetite for underdevelopment, and with a related will to renew the dominance of culturally dominant groups" (*Cultures of Letters* 137–

38, qtd. in Johanningsmeier 61). Johanningsmeier points out that Jewett and Freeman "also contributed to a number of less prestigious magazines . . . as well as to a widely dispersed newspaper market that tended to transcend geographical, class, and gender boundaries" (61–62). "By the 1880s," Johanningsmeier writes, "most daily journals in larger cities were already selling throughout their entire regions, not just within city limits" (62–63). Johanningsmeier argues that Jewett in particular was aware of the opportunity the syndicates offered. Writing to McClure in 1888, Jewett said, "I have grown more and more interested from the first in your syndicate plans and wish that I could oftener see my way to reaching exactly the wide range of readers with which these plans are concerned" (qtd. in Johanningsmeier 70). This wide range of readers "included the humble as well as the elite" (70). Johanningsmeier offers as an example Jewett's "Stolen Pleasures," published in the *New England Homestead* of Springfield, Massachusetts, "a paper with a wide circulation throughout the rural Connecticut River Valley," as well as in at least four other journals, including the *Detroit Free Press* with circulation "almost double the *Atlantic's*" (71). Furthermore, "given the breadth and depth of its penetration, syndication, it appears, tended to dissolve the usual boundaries between [Freeman's] rural subjects and her urban readers. Now rural inhabitants—who from the urban reader's point of view apparently existed to provide material for recreational distraction—were empowered to become consumers, and thus proprietors, of their own fictional currency" (72).

Realism, Regionalism, and Naturalism

Writing from a position similar to Brodhead's, Kaplan, in "Nation, Region, and Empire," extends the argument concerning the political complicity of regionalism in the production of empire.[8] Instead of viewing region as the "margin" to some national "center," Kaplan argues that, in their literary representations in the work of regionalist writers, regions served "the national agenda of reunion" (251) after the Civil War and thereby created the context for American imperialism. Regionalism "performs a kind of literary tourism in a period that saw the tourist abroad and at home as a growing middle-class phenomenon; tourism was no longer limited to the grand tours of the upper class" (252). Regionalism, Kaplan appears to be arguing, naturalizes empire by associating an urban reader's nostalgia for his or her regional roots with travels to bring back souvenirs from other far-away places, and conversely by creating a context within which imperial excursions to dominate and expropriate resources and labor from exotically "other" cultures may be viewed as just another form of the domestic tourist's desire, in Brodhead's words, to carry "the good of the place *out* of the place" (*Cultures of Letters* 148). "Regionalists," Kaplan writes, "share with tourists and anthropologists the perspective of the modern urban outsider who projects onto the native a pristine authentic space immune to historical changes shaping their own lives." Such projection, dramatized "most often in the narrator who comments on, interprets, and translates the life of the natives to an urban audience," habituates readers to acts of imperialist appropriation (252).

"Nation, Region, and Empire" is one of the most significant essays to date to address regionalism within the framework of American literary history; indeed, it appears in the prestigious 1991 *Columbia History of the American Novel.* Kaplan's essay legitimizes the critical study of regionalism even though she refers to such fiction at several points as "local color" and disparages it as a limitation from which certain writers have deservedly been rescued, writing, for example, that "Kate Chopin has rightfully been removed by feminist critics from the confines of local color in which she made her career" (254). Yet, in a move similar to Brodhead's, Kaplan's attention to regionalism only serves to devalue it once again as regionalism must take on the burden of the complicity of the literary in the political and ideological work of nation and empire.

From its influence on such critics as Zagarell, Ammons, and Howard, Kaplan's essay appears to be one of those provocative texts that, while not having the space to fully develop its argument, nevertheless creates a paradigm of reference for others. However, even granting the limits of space, we find problematic the essay's unanalyzed and almost effaced conflations of nation and realism, region and regionalism, and empire and naturalism, with region and regionalism the middle terms that elide realism's own agency in the formation of nation.[9] As a close analysis of the essay demonstrates, such an argument can allow Kaplan to engage in critique without really destabilizing the major contours of the field. Thus her conflations create a typology of fictional modes of the late nineteenth and early twentieth centuries that, instead of challenging traditional hierarchies of critical value, in effect replicates these hierarchies. Kaplan wants to introduce empire into our thinking about America and American literature but not at the expense of calling into question the status of William Dean Howells, Mark Twain, and James. Kaplan's positioning of regionalism serves as a way of displacing critique from realism and its canonical exemplars. Regionalism becomes a convenient surrogate, in effect the term that enables her to do the work of critique without destabilizing literary history's construction of realism as the dominant mode in the period.

The rhetorical structure of Kaplan's argument turns not only on a foregrounding of regionalism but also on the near-elision of the category of realism. We can read as symptomatic of this elision the absence of any extended treatment of two of the major writers of the period, Howells and James. Similarly, while Kaplan occasionally refers to "naturalists," she uses the term "naturalism" only once. She writes that "the ending of *The Octopus* suggests an important but overlooked historical context for American literary naturalism: America's shift from continental expansion to an overseas empire at the turn of the century" (263). While she repeatedly invokes the concepts of "regionalist" fiction and "regionalism," she allows the categories of "realism" and "naturalism" to remain unexamined, indeed almost unmentioned, even though the pervasiveness of nation, nation building, nationality, the nationalist project, and things national throughout the essay creates "nation" as a metonym for realism. Howells and James become included by virtue of this metonymic effect, even as the omission of any direct reference to their work allows Kaplan to elide the extent of their own and realism's complicity in the move from nation to empire, as well as to avoid considering either of these canonical figures in the same critical context as Jewett. In effect they stand above this essay, just as realism itself stands above those "lesser" modes of regionalism and naturalism, inhabiting a space apparently exempt from critique.

Kaplan's essay traces the plot of "national reunification, the cultural project that would inform a diversity of American fiction" from the end of the Civil War to the end of the nineteenth century (240). She argues that American fiction writers engaged in this project as part of nation building in the aftermath of sectional division, that regionalism in particular "contributes to solidifying national centrality by reimagining a distended industrial nation as an extended clan sharing a 'common inheritance' in its imagined rural origins" (251), and that naturalism, with its glorification of American manhood, "forges the bond that transcends social conflict and turns a former divided nation into a reunited global power" (249), identifying the project of "national reunification" as one of "empire building" (258). Kaplan's panoramic review of the period tells a convincing story of the uses of American fiction in the service of larger political agendas of overseas expansion and influence.

In this story, regionalism becomes the agent that prepared readers for the U.S. move to empire. While Kaplan's argument for "national reunification" as "the cultural project that would inform a diversity of American fiction" in the decades after the Civil War rests on the acknowledgment of sectional difference before the war and the continued existence of sociopolitical differences among disparate geographical regions after the war, she suggests at the same time that writers like Jewett also created "regions" to express and fulfill their own projected needs. Kaplan variously identifies these needs as "the projection of a desire for a space outside of history, untouched by change" (252) and "the projection of the outsider's desire to view his or her life as less confining, more sophisticated and 'adult'" (253). Kaplan's reading of regionalism not only removes realism from critique, maintaining realism itself in some "space outside of history, untouched by change," but also neutralizes the critical challenge regionalism poses to our understanding of the ideology of realism, thereby creating a comfort zone—"less confining, more sophisticated and 'adult'"—within which critics can continue to read realism canonically. Kaplan's move to center regionalism so that it may bear the brunt of the critique that traces the complicity of the literary in the nation's move to empire seems particularly ironic in light of the fact that it is the almost metonymic association of realism with nation that makes realism the dominant category in the literary history of the late nineteenth- and early twentieth-century United States. Were regionalism in fact to have been as instrumental in empire building as Kaplan argues, we might legitimately expect to find it occupying a far more prominent place in our national literary history than it currently does or ever has.

In *Vested Interests,* as we noted in chapter 1, Marjorie Garber discusses the role of what she calls the "third term" to introduce and indicate a "category crisis." "Category crisis" is her term for "a failure of definitional distinction, a borderline that becomes permeable, that permits of border crossings from one (apparently distinct) category to another: black/white, Jew/Christian, noble/bourgeois, master/servant, master/slave" (16). She argues that the transvestite challenges binary thinking about gender, "putting into question the categories of 'female' and 'male,' whether they are considered essential or constructed, biological or cultural" (10), and so becomes "what looks like a third term. . . . But what is crucial here is that the 'third term' is *not a term.* Much less is it a sex. . . . The 'third' is a mode of articulation, a way of describing a space of possibility" (11). For Garber, the "third" is something "that challenges the possibility of harmonious and stable binary symmetry" (12) and that "puts in question identities previously conceived as stable, unchallengeable, grounded, and 'known'" (13). The addition of regionalism to the map of late nineteenth- and early twentieth-century American literary history has produced a crisis for the category of realism, a crisis that, as we have noted, critics such as Kaplan try to manage by deflecting the challenge regionalism poses to both the definition and the status of realism back onto regionalism itself. Our reading of regionalism, however, leads us to position it as a "third term" that "puts in question identities previously conceived as stable, unchallengeable, grounded, and 'known.'"

When we first began our work on the writers we have called regionalists, we were aware that "regionalism" did not exist as an acknowledged critical category. Indeed, when the Vanderbilt Agrarians in the 1930s chose the term "regionalism" to describe their particular conservative literary politics, they could do so because the term had no prior agreed-upon cultural or literary meaning despite the fact that Mary Austin, in "Regionalism in American Fiction," used the term to describe what she saw as a literary tradition.[10] One of the challenges we faced in the early 1980s when we first began to contemplate a series of editorial and critical projects designed to recover these writers involved identifying a new category for their work that would distinguish it not only from local color but also from realism. In so doing, we were aware that we might thus unsettle critical certainties. The operative categories in 1980 were those of realism and naturalism, and naturalism then as now offered no real challenge to the canonical status of either realism or the writers associated with it. Naturalism hyperdeveloped certain features of realist texts, and though Norris, Stephen Crane, London, and Theodore Dreiser produced a substantial body of work, none of it challenged the primacy of either realism or the realists. The writers and texts in *American Women Regionalists,* however, do create an alternative set of texts that call into question the assumptions we make when we call realism, understood as the work of Howells, James, and Mark Twain, the most significant achievement of American writers in the second half of the nineteenth century. Indeed, our reading of regionalism leads us to engage in the same kind of critique of realism and naturalism that Kaplan and others have deployed in their reading and writing about regionalism.

Although the logic of Kaplan's argument would seem to imply a different order for the terms of her title, since in her view region allowed nation to become empire, when she conflates "nation, region, and empire" with realism, regionalism, and naturalism and places "region" and "regionalism" in the middle, she in effect reveals "metaphoric resonances" (see Katrak) of the radical origins of these terms that make them, like Garber's "third term," capable of unsettling what lies on either side. For indeed, regionalism requires us to rearrange our understanding of both realism and naturalism and it unsettles the comfortable paradigm within which realism dominates naturalism and within which Howells, James, and Mark Twain achieve prominence by virtue of their difference from Norris, Crane, London, and Dreiser.

In *Resisting Regionalism,* Donna Campbell argues that "naturalism grew in part as a gender-based countertradition not only to realism but to female-dominated local color writing" (5).[11] Thus, for Campbell, "the naturalists' response to women's local color fiction was shaped not only by literary generation or by genre, but by gender as well" (7). The addition of regionalism to late nineteenth- and early twentieth-century American literary history allows Campbell to propose a re-understanding of both realism and naturalism; realism, she writes, "was not all local color, of course, and yet a continual thread of feeling runs through the works of Norris and other naturalists: that 'real life,' the stuff of literature, was not the same as the realists' teacup tragedies, and that the fit ones to write about real life were men (naturalists), not women (local color writers)" (5). She writes further:

> Through their endless descriptions of accumulated objects and their ambivalent but frequently admiring portraits of buccaneer capitalists, naturalistic authors . . . celebrated reportorial immediacy and a kind of experiential excess in behavior, an excess that led to brutishness. Yet even the danger of degeneration into brutishness seemed preferable to intense self-denial and endurance, for these virtues represented the almost suffocatingly insular and feminine outdated world of local color fiction. Indeed, the sheer number of words that they showered on an increasingly receptive public suggests a commitment to overthrowing the small, careful, and limited sketches of the local colorists. (10–11)

While we would not necessarily agree with Campbell's reading of regionalism (for example, as "small, careful, and limited"), her work indicates that the category has introduced a disturbance in our understanding of the relation of realism and naturalism, one that includes issues of gender as well as issues of nation and empire. In proposing that naturalism in effect rescues realism from women, even at the cost of "degeneration into brutishness," Campbell implicitly suggests that realism, as practiced by Mark Twain, James, and Howells, included a gender-based agenda. Moreover, given Kaplan's demonstration of the relation of "manliness" to the nation's aspirations to empire, we can see how realism could more accurately than regionalism be called the enabler of empire.

Robert Shulman begins his essay on "Realism" for *The Columbia History of the American Novel* by quoting the opening passage of Rebecca Harding Davis's story "At the Station," one she collected in *Silhouettes of American Life* in 1892. We find his approach symptomatic of the crisis regionalism produces for critics' reading of the category of realism. Shulman quotes Davis:

> "Nothing could well be more commonplace or ignoble than the corner of the world in which Miss Dilly now spent her life. A wayside inn, near a station on the railway which runs from Salisbury, in North Carolina, up into the great Appalachian range of mountains; two or three unpainted boxes of houses scattered along the track by the inn; not a tree nor blade of grass in the 'clarin'; a few gaunt, long-legged pigs and chickens grunting and cackling in the muddy clay yards; beyond, swampy tobacco fields stretching to the encircling pine woods." (qtd. in Shulman 160)

As we read this passage, we concur with Sharon Harris who writes that "Davis's work aligns itself best with that of writers we typically term regional realists" (8). Numerous features of Davis's language identify the story's opening in strongly regionalist terms: it takes place in a "corner of the world"; the protagonist is an unmarried older woman; though this corner includes a "wayside inn, near a station on the railway," that railway runs not from rural village to city, but rather from one rural (Southern) village to another (Appalachian mountain) village; except for the railroad, the village reflects no other sign of modernity—its houses are "unpainted boxes," its "gaunt" animals convey a lack of prosperity, its tobacco fields are "swampy"; and Davis includes a touch of dialect in her reference to the "'clarin.'" Shulman sees all of these features of the passage but identifies them as realism:

> The emphasis on the commonplace, on the ignored or despised; the attention to the unpainted houses, the muddy clay yards, and the gaunt pigs and chickens—or their human equivalents; the possibility of sympathy and satire; the awareness of regions and regional differences; the sensitivity to American dialects and their class and racial implications; the conversational middle—and middle-class—style, vocabulary, and syntax; the focus on Miss Dilly not on Captain Ahab or Leatherstocking—here is a preliminary list of the traits of American realism. (160)

It is only because Davis "is not working at the height of her powers" as she did earlier in her 1861 novella *Life in the Iron Mills* that, according to Shulman, this story "does not take us deep into the unexplored territory of America's emerging industrial capitalism or make us see the complex realities of money and power that were affecting women and men in the new America" (160). Implicitly offering these complexities as more compelling features of realism, Shulman moves quickly to a second definition: "The corrosive, vital power of an expanding market society undermined moral, religious, and social stabilities. No wonder that a questioning of conventions and the conventional is perhaps the central unifying convention of American realism" (161). If we ask why Shulman chooses to begin his presentation of realism with a passage from a story he dismisses as insufficiently realist, we might find one answer in the difficulties regionalism has created for realism and we might understand his choice, so similar to the moves we discussed in chapter 2 as characterizing the history of American literary history, as one way to handle these difficulties. By beginning with a text that others might see as regionalist he acknowledges, however indirectly, the existence of the category of regionalism. However, by subsuming Davis's story under the category of realism and by quickly moving to discredit it as an instance of failed realism, he at once effectively eliminates regionalism as a separate and potentially oppositional category, recovers it as a subset of realism, and reclaims the ground of the radical, the "questioning of conventions and the conventional," for the realism of James, Howells, and Mark Twain, and for Davis and Chesnutt to the extent that they wrote like James, Howells, and Twain. It is this work, then, not something called regionalism, that will "take us deep into the unexplored territory of America's emerging industrial capitalism" as his essay moves to focus on single works by these "representative post–Civil War realists" (188).

While in response to challenges to a realist canon represented primarily by Mark Twain, James, and Howells Shulman adds discussions of a short work by a white woman (Davis) and a novel by a black man (Chesnutt), these additions, designed to give the appearance of enlarging the category, do not in fact significantly alter his understanding of realism or challenge the traditional view of it. Indeed, Shulman goes to some lengths to undercut the assignment of *Life in the Iron Mills* to the category of realism, thereby suggesting that its current inclusion is politically motivated. Concluding his reading of Davis, he observes that "part of what is missing from the narrator's story, however, is any sense of the kind of working-class consciousness and cohesion Herbert Gutman finds among actual nineteenth-century American workers" and he proposes that "the story also negates the prospect of radical change" (177). While he acknowledges that "in these respects Rebecca Harding Davis and her narrator are at one with almost every other writer in the American canon," it is only in reference to Davis that he raises the question of "why some works are and other works are not entering the canon" and whether or not it is now "a condition for entry into the canon that a work should be open to subversive interpretation and at the same time reinforce the sense both of the need for and the near impossibility of fundamental change" (177–78). Leaving us, like Brodhead, with an injunction to "keep our eyes open" for something better even as we continue to read Davis, Shulman also demonstrates how an enforced attention can become a subtle form of dismissal. Nevertheless, it is crucial to Shulman's larger purpose to include a discussion of *Life in the Iron Mills* in his treatment of realism. Because Davis wrote this now recognized realist text, she can be categorized as a realist and her more regionalist fiction can then be read as a failed form of realism. Moreover, since Shulman does not mention any other nineteenth-century regionalist writer in his essay, his readers might legitimately conclude that any other writer who wrote as Davis does in the opening of "At the Station" might also not be working at the "height of her powers," indeed might not have any power to begin with, and is thus not fully a realist but only a failure. We might suggest, then, that the perspective Shulman offers is neither "fresh" nor "contemporary" (a claim the editor makes for the essays included in *The Columbia History of the American Novel* [Elliott xviii]) but is rather fairly familiar and traditional. Between Shulman's essay that implicitly devalues "regional realism" and Kaplan's essay that focuses on the political complicity of regionalist texts, *The Columbia History of the American Novel* succeeds in marginalizing regionalism once again.

But if it is so evident that regionalism is realism not working up to its powers, it seems ironic to us that Shulman begins his essay with Davis's regionalist prose and that the analytic weight of Kaplan's argument should rest on the reading of one scene in a regionalist writer, the Bowden reunion scene from Jewett's *The Country of the Pointed Firs.* We read this irony as further evidence of the crisis regionalism has created for critics, indeed as evidence even of a certain attraction to regionalism that must itself be resisted. What the plot of national reunification elides, then, is more than the ongoing articulation of regional differences in the fictions themselves; it elides as well the critical "plot" of the reunification of American literary realism. As we noted in chapter 1 and will discuss further in chapter 8, "plot," according to Lennard Davis, involves literary property, who may claim ownership, and who may enjoy occupancy. Drawing on our analysis of form in chapter 6, we might argue that the crisis regionalism creates for American literary history is a crisis of "plot."

Jewett's Bowden Reunion

Carolyn Porter writes, "if we are to believe the talking heads, the 'global economy' is destined to relocate the relation between 'development' and 'underdevelopment' on a plane where the 'politics of location' will be registered with decreasing reference to nations. According to Miyoshi, 'unencumbered with nationalist baggage,' transnational corporations 'represent neither their home countries nor their host regions but simply their own corporate selves'" (511). She quotes Alvin and Heidi Toffler: "'By the middle of the next century, such nation-states as Germany, Italy, the United States or Japan will no longer be the most relevant socioeconomic entities and the ultimate political configuration. Instead, areas like Orange County, Calif.; Osaka, Japan; the Lyon region of France, or Germany's Ruhrebiete will acquire predominant socio-economic status. The real decision-making powers of the future . . . will be transnational companies in alliance with city-regional governments'" (qtd. in Porter 512). As regions increasingly supplant nations as the point of contact between transnational corporations and the locations they require for their operations in the global economy of the twenty-first century, they also become understood as potential sites of resistance to the postcolonial encroachments of globalization. In turn, this understanding provides a frame for reading the fictions of nineteenth-century regionalism.

While we recognize the difficulties of reading nineteenth-century writers through a postcolonial lens, we nevertheless find useful the intricacies of complicity and resistance that Ketu Katrak explores in his examination of the postcolonial. Even further expanding the textual base of American literature in an essay included in the 1991 *Columbia History of the American Novel,* Katrak considers "a genre that may be called the immigrant novel or the cosmopolitan novel" written in English by postcolonial subjects in exile (653), some of whom have taken up residence in the United states. Taking as his subject both external colonizations, "such as invasions by colonizing powers as well as continuing imperialist dominations" and "internal, that is, mental colonizations, such as through education," he identifies what he calls "metaphoric resonances of colonization—for instance, of women within patriarchal cultures, of 'minority' groups who must struggle to make spaces for themselves within hegemonic white academic institutions and literary marketplaces" (650). To the extent that both white women writers and members of "minority" groups in the United States now and then may reflect "internal, that is, mental colonizations" (650), their fictions may provide textual moments that express lingering colonial effects, even as they articulate resistance to colonial domination. Thus, such writers may reinscribe hierarchies of gender, race, or class even while they may be resisting colonialism or regionalization. At the very least, Katrak reminds us that both external colonization and the internal colonization of mental and psychological states produce "multiplicities of identities that are necessarily negotiated in terms of 'choices' of language or of location, the search for belonging and for an audience" (678). We are interested in Katrak's formulation of "internal, that is, mental colonizations," for in some sense regions themselves have always been colonies and the inhabitants of those regions have both offered resistance to their own regionalization and revealed "metaphoric resonances of colonization" in which they have internalized some of the values of the concept of nation to which they have been subordinated.

Understanding the complexities of lingering colonial effects that emerge alongside resistance and the resulting "multiplicities of identities that are necessarily negotiated" can help us reread moments like the Bowden reunion in Jewett's *The Country of the Pointed Firs,* the scene that provides Kaplan with her argument concerning regionalism's complicity in the nation's move toward empire. We will argue on the contrary that Jewett's text proposes region as a site of resistance to empire and offers the region's values as alternatives to those of the nation but that her narrator, an urban visitor, and Mrs. Todd, the regional character, occupy different positions with respect to the relationship between nation and region. Jewett's narrator appreciates the values she finds in the region she visits and translates between region and urban reader in order to make "nation" more like "region." Still, Jewett's portrait of her narrator represents a regionalist variation on Katrak's "metaphoric resonances of colonization." Jewett encourages her own reader to sympathize with the narrator, and at the same time makes it clear that her narrator overstates her success at becoming integrated into the Bowden family. It is not the narrator, whom both Mrs. Todd and Jewett recognize as in need of and capable of development, who serves as Jewett's measure of regional resistance to exploitation and colonization.

Mrs. Todd sets limits on the extent to which either summer visitors, urban readers, or national life can expect to transform themselves at the expense of the region. Although on the one hand Mrs. Todd is willing to make the narrator her apprentice, and to develop a relationship in which the urban visitor learns from the region, on the other she also makes it clear that the urban visitor cannot become an adopted Bowden and that regional subjectivity cannot be appropriated. Ultimately Jewett identifies the region and her text's values with Mrs. Todd rather than with her narrator. Jewett makes it clear that the growth that results from the narrator's development may take from but may not take away from the region. However, the narrator is free to work to change the values of the world she inhabits, and thus Jewett makes the narrator, not Mrs. Todd, responsible for creating an alternative model of nation and seeking to gain a hearing for this model by writing the text that becomes *The Country of the Pointed Firs.* Jewett wishes, then, to change the nation rather than to appropriate the region.

From the beginning of the chapter titled "The Bowden Reunion," Jewett's narrator articulates her resistance to prevailing concepts of nation at the turn of the twentieth century, thereby expressing her desire to serve as translator between the region's "country" and the allegiances of urban life. The chapter begins:

> It is very rare in country life, where high days and holidays are few, that any occasion of general interest proves to be less than great. Such is the hidden fire of enthusiasm in the New England nature that, once given an outlet, it shines forth with almost volcanic light and heat. In quiet neighborhoods such inward

> force does not waste itself upon those petty excitements of every day that belong to cities, but when, at long intervals, the altars to patriotism, to friendship, to the ties of kindred, are reared in our familiar fields, then the fires glow, the flames come up as if from the inexhaustible burning heart of the earth; the primal fires break through the granite dust in which our souls are set. Each heart is warm and every face shines with the ancient light. Such a day as this has transfiguring powers, and easily makes friends of those who have been cold-hearted, and gives to those who are dumb their chance to speak, and lends some beauty to the plainest face. (*The Country of the Pointed Firs* 95–96)

Prematurely claiming her own inclusion in the scene ("our familiar fields" and "our souls"), she describes her enthusiasm for "country life" as different from the "petty excitements of every day that belong to cities." Jewett's narrator seems clearly to be addressing urban readers. She wishes to translate "altars to patriotism" into models of friendship for her readers, and if "such a day as this has transfiguring powers," then perhaps her writing as well "makes friends of those who have been cold-hearted, and gives to those who are dumb their chance to speak, and lends some beauty to the plainest face."

At the same time she suggests that such a narrative as the Bowden reunion will present ways to "transfigure" the nation itself. She offers the theory that "perhaps it is the great national anniversaries which our country has lately kept, and the soldiers' meetings that take place everywhere, which have made reunions of every sort the fashion" (*The Country of the Pointed Firs* 110); in this one, however, she "fancied that old feuds had been overlooked" and "lesser rights [to the Bowden name] were forgotten in the claim to a common inheritance" (110). In describing the Bowden reunion as the regional equivalent to the "great national anniversaries," she seems to hope that perhaps her urban readers will be able to see it as "the fashion." However, despite what may appear to be the lingering colonial effects of the narrator's choice to work within the trope of "national anniversary," if the Bowden family does come to represent the nation, as Kaplan suggests, then the nation will be a very different kind of political organization than the one more familiar to those readers who "belong to cities."

For example, if this kind of nation has a military dimension, it does not exist to display military power or masculine potency. Santin Bowden, who manages to line all the Bowdens up and march them in military formation, hardly offers an example of the virility Theodore Roosevelt called for in "The Strenuous Life," the 1905 speech that summarized his political philosophy of the previous decade. Roosevelt wrote that "we do not admire the man of timid peace" but rather "the man who embodies victorious effort," one "who has those virile qualities necessary to win in the stern strife of actual life" (13). Roosevelt's nation is not comprised of "weaklings" (18) like Sant Bowden, who was unable to enlist in the Civil War; as Mrs. Todd explains, "'he ain't a sound man, an' they wouldn't have him'" (*The Country of the Pointed Firs* 101). Furthermore, as a woman named Mrs. Caplin adds, "'All he thinks of, when he sees a crowd, is how to march 'em. 'Tis all very well when he don't 'tempt too much. He never did act like other folks'" (103). If Jewett here "links two public arenas often considered separate or even antagonistic, the national and the local" (Kaplan 250), she does so in order to parody Roosevelt's conception of nation as virile, military, and poised for the work of empire. Furthermore, in Roosevelt's version of nation, women hold no political role other than that of "the house-wife, the helpmeet of the homemaker, the wise and fearless mother of many healthy children" (*The Strenuous Life* 16). Yet the most important person at the Bowden reunion is not a man at all but rather Mrs. Blackett, Mrs. Todd's mother; in the narrator's version of nation the most honored persons become "Mrs. Blackett and a few distinguished companions, the ministers and those who were very old" (*The Country of the Pointed Firs* 99). Jewett's narrator values old age and wisdom, not those "virile qualities necessary to win in the stern strife of actual life" that Roosevelt admires (*The Strenuous Life* 13). If the nation were to reflect Mrs. Blackett's values, we would be living in a different country, the "country" of the pointed firs.

However, the narrator does not herself live in this "country" and Mrs. Todd lets her know it, even though Jewett's narrator does not understand as much as Jewett reveals to her own reader through Mrs. Todd. Earlier in the novel, while attempting to separate herself from Mrs. Todd and to find a place to write in the schoolhouse, the narrator has discovered that her decision "made myself and my friends remember that I did not really belong to Dunnet Landing" (15), and *The Country of the Pointed Firs* shows her trying to negotiate what Katrak calls "the search for belonging and for an audience" (678). Although she claims in describing the Bowden reunion that "I came near to feeling like a true Bowden" (110), ironically the reunion also underscores her distance from the community. The language of "national anniversaries" and of "old feuds . . . overlooked," the overlay of military parade and rank-order among the family members, the narrator's description of the family as doing "all these things in a finer way than most country people would have done them" (105), and her reference to their ancestral origin "in the great hall of some old French house in the Middle Ages" (105) may serve to elevate the significance of the reunion for urban readers and may even enhance her own feelings of being "adopted" by the family (99). Nevertheless, the narrator's view of the scene remains incongruent with that of the regional participants' experience of the event.

This incongruence suggests that the narrator's desires and her observations are frequently at odds with each other. The narrator seeks a sense of belonging; what she observes is the evidence of old feuds not overlooked. For example, at one point Mrs. Todd and Mrs. Caplin appear embarked on an increasingly tense conversation until Mrs. Blackett appears, "to see, as she insisted, that we were out of mischief" (103). Then, when Mrs. Todd calls Mari' Harris "'a sordid creature,'" Mrs. Blackett interjects, "'Live and let live'" (103).[12] When a cousin goes by whom Mrs. Todd dislikes, the narrator reports that Mrs. Todd moved "with an alarming transition from general opinions to particular animosities" (104). Here the narrator is reporting her own alarm, not that of Mrs. Todd. Her desire for reunion is so great that she discounts Mrs. Todd's response, reporting that "[t]his was so different from Mrs. Todd's usual largeness of mind that I had a moment's uneasiness; but the cloud passed quickly over her spirit, and was gone with the offender" (104). Yet Mrs. Todd continues to contradict the narrator's assessment of her "spirit." Although she is referring to a stranger they had met earlier and not to the narrator, Mrs. Todd dismisses the woman "with but scant interest or approval. 'She ain't a member o' our family,'" she says (111). Her final comment on the reunion takes the form of laughing at one of the singers in the family chorus: "'Yes, there was excellent singers, . . . but I chanced to drift alongside Mis' Peter Bowden o' Great Bay, an' I couldn't help thinkin' if she was as far out o' town as she was out o' tune, she wouldn't get back in a day'" (112). For all of the narrator's desire to participate in reunion, if Mrs. Todd is the arbiter of who's in and who's out, we may legitimately wonder how well she accomplishes her desire since Mrs. Todd chooses to emphasize not-belonging and being "out o' tune." We can read this emphasis as Jewett's insertion of regional subjectivity into the urban narrator's construction of the reunion. The narrator is not Jewett and Jewett offers Mrs. Todd's reading as divergent from the narrator's; her account underscores animosities rather than harmonies, points to the difficulties of the attempt to communicate across urban/rural lines, problematizes the narrator's desire to minimize difference, and insists that the text reflect Mrs. Todd's own resistance to reunion.

By the end of her book, the narrator recognizes that she can only visit Dunnet Landing but does not "belong" there. She must return to "the world in which I feared to find myself a foreigner" (129), a comment reflecting something of the condition of exile of which Katrak writes. When the summer season ends and the narrator makes plans to return to the unnamed city that is probably Boston, what the narrator describes as but the "natural end" of "some chapters of our lives" (131) seems less than "natural" to Mrs. Todd and more a chosen separation marked by the limits of the narrator's own growth: "Mrs. Todd had hardly spoken all day except in the briefest and most disapproving way; it was as if we were on the edge of a quarrel" (130). Perhaps it is by way of acknowledging that the narrator's return to urban life cuts her off from the values she seemed to find in Dunnet Landing that Mrs. Todd leaves her a gift fit for an exile—"the coral pin that Nathan Todd brought home to give to poor Joanna" (131), the woman who chose to live as a recluse in self-imposed isolation on Shell-heap Island.

In Mrs. Todd's gift, she marks the limits of the region's responsibility to nation. Jewett's narrator and the urban world of "nation" that she represents have to discover for themselves how to find again a sense of belonging. In the contrast between her narrator's "natural" departure from Dunnet Landing and Mrs. Todd's lingering sense of injury, Jewett creates a narrative effect of resistance to appropriation of the region. The ending of *The Country of the Pointed Firs* as Jewett published it in 1896 records not what Kaplan terms the "measure of cosmopolitan development" (251) but rather the enormity of the distance between regional and urban life. It is no wonder that the narrator and Mrs. Todd ultimately understand the meaning of the Bowden reunion differently; their desires diverge. In the narrator's ability to feel the loss of separation and in her awareness that she has caused Mrs. Todd pain—"I glanced at my friend's face, and saw a look that touched me to the heart. I had been sorry enough before to go away" (*Country of the Pointed Firs* 130)—Jewett records the complexity of cross-class and cross-border relationships. Jewett presents her own narrator as caught in Katrak's "metaphoric resonances of colonization." Mrs. Todd rather than the narrator occupies the site of resistance, both to the values of nation and to any attempts, even those by a narrator misled by good intentions, to exploit the region.

This portrait of the complex Mrs. Todd as the center of the text's regional sensibility represents Jewett's own view of the significance of resistance in spite of what we might call, following Katrak, her own internalized regionalization. Critics following Brodhead and Kaplan have argued that in publishing her text, Jewett nevertheless invites tourists to come to "Dunnet Landing" and see it for themselves, thereby setting up the region for exploitation. Still, Mrs. Todd's "animosities" and unspoken "quarrel" with the narrator at the end of the text reflect Jewett's own self-consciousness of "internal colonizations." *The Country of the Pointed Firs* in part documents this awareness.

Regionalist Alternatives to Cultural Imperialism

Previously we have indicated our sense of the differences between what American literary history has termed "local-color writing" and the texts we have identified as regionalist. Central to this distinction is the resistance regionalist texts make to imperialist incursions. Indeed, literary regionalism in the nineteenth-century United States critiqued imperialist aggression and in the process called into question nationalist visions of an "American" literature. Writers do not have to write explicitly about empire in order to critique imperialist attitudes, though some regionalists did so. In an earlier version of this argument, "'Not in the Least American': Nineteenth-Century Literary Regionalism," Fetterley writes that the texts of regionalism "have been systematically excluded from the definition of American literature precisely because they do not reproduce the national narrative of violence or the definitions of masculine and feminine, American and foreign, which such a narrative presents as our national interest" (893). In this section we want to extend this argument in order to characterize the "not in the least American" subjectivity regionalist writing creates as an approach to entering another's home, village, or region, one that includes anti-imperialist practice. Such an approach does more than critique; it constructs an alternative model. In the process, it establishes limits on the extent to which outsiders may enter a village, region, or culture with the intent to appropriate whatever might be marketable in urban centers. The region becomes a site of cultural encounter but equally the site of resistance to exploitation.

In one of the defining moments of literary regionalism as a pedagogy of cultural encounter, Zitkala-Ša, in "Impressions of an Indian Childhood," writes about the instructions she received from her mother when entering the wigwams of neighbors. She recalls her own excitement when her mother would send her out to offer invitations to the old men and women to join her family for the evening meal, which as a young girl she associated with "the time old legends were told" (*AWR* 537). Zitkala-Ša writes, "Running all the way to the wigwams, I halted shyly at the entrances. Sometimes I stood long moments without saying a word. It was not any fear that made me so dumb when out upon such a happy errand; nor was it that I wished to withhold the invitation, for it was all I could do to observe this very proper silence. But it was a sensing of the atmosphere, to assure myself that I should not hinder other plans" (537). In her "sensing of the atmosphere," she takes care not to intrude herself or her message; and in the space of restraint, while she pauses to listen, she learns to "read" her neighbors and to remember what she has seen: "All out of breath, I told my mother almost the exact words of the answers to my invitation. Frequently she asked, 'What were they doing when you entered their tepee?' This taught me to remember all I saw at a single glance. Often I told my mother my impressions without being questioned" (537). Zitkala-Ša's mother asks her this question in order to make certain that her daughter has shown self-restraint. But Zitkala-Ša associates this "sensing of the atmosphere" with intense listening, "reading," that allows the neighbors inside the wigwams to inscribe their own impressions on her that she can then relate "without being questioned."

The approach she has learned from her mother, however, does not prepare her for an encounter with persons whose approach is quite different. She is beguiled by the promises of the missionaries who come to her village to persuade her and other children to attend their school in the East, and in her own eagerness and lack of experience with such "others," she does not perceive that they do not observe toward her the kind of restraint and respect she has been taught to show on entering the wigwams of others. Almost immediately she discovers that she has put herself "in the hands of strangers whom my mother did not fully trust" (547), and in her second narrative, "The School Days of an Indian Girl," she describes the intrusiveness of the "throngs of staring palefaces" on the train as she travels East with the other Indian children and the missionaries. She describes the women who "scrutinized the children of absent mothers" and the men who "riveted their glassy blue eyes upon us": "I sank deep into the corner of my seat, for I resented being watched. Directly in front of me, children who were no larger than I hung themselves upon the backs of their seats, with their bold white faces toward me. Sometimes they took their forefingers out of their mouths and pointed at my moccasined feet. Their mothers, instead of reproving such rude curiosity, looked closely at me, and attracted their children's further notice to my blanket. This embarrassed me, and kept me constantly on the verge of tears" (548). Zitkala-Ša finds that she has entered into a contract that removes her subjectivity. She has become an object of scrutiny, a child whose hair and identity may be shorn, "one of many little animals driven by a herder" (551), "neither a wild Indian nor a tame one" (555) who loses her ability to communicate with her mother and who feels she has betrayed her origins.

Zitkala-Ša's autobiographical narratives reflect the contradictions of assimilation when she tries to use English to reflect what has been taken from her, what she has lost by remaining in the East to enter college instead of returning home to "find my living upon wild roots" (558). Like her later English-speaking postcolonial counterparts, Zitkala-Ša has been influenced by those who initially colonized her in the name of Christianity and by the time she comes to write her autobiographical narratives for the *Atlantic Monthly* in 1900, she recalls the process of her acculturation as a series of "sad memories" that "rise above those of smoothly grinding school days" (555). Yet the colonizer's language does not make it easier for her to express the "melancholy of those black days" and "sad memories" (555). She writes, "Perhaps my Indian nature is the moaning wind which stirs them now for their present record. But, however tempestuous this is within me, it comes out as the low voice of a curiously colored seashell, which is only for those ears that are bent with compassion to hear it" (555). Once Zitkala-Ša leaves behind the world that valued "sensing of the atmosphere" at the moment of encounter and in which impressions become the source of speech, she can no longer expect to find listeners or readers capable of hearing her speak in her native language. Her American Indian identity has become a relic, a hardly audible voice, out of place in an English-speaking world in which the "white man's papers" do not console her (557). The language Zitkala-Ša has learned is inextricably bound up with the attitudes of imperialism that, like the invasiveness of the children's "rude curiosity" on the train, have made their impression *on* her, but that do not allow her to relate such impressions "without being questioned." The language she has learned is not capable of recording her own "low voice" that survives, if at all, "only for those ears that are bent with compassion to hear it." Zitkala-Ša writes her story in part for the readers who possess those ears, but more often her text, like those of other regionalists, has seemed only as "a curiously colored seashell," out of place in the larger context of American narrative.

In "A Gentleman of Bayou Têche," Chopin also differentiates between cultural encounter and exploitation and in the process creates a narrative of resistance to imperialism. The story opens as a visiting "artist" named Mr. Sublet, "looking for bits of 'local color'" on the bayou (*AWR* 421), proposes to make a picture of Evariste, a poor Acadian, to sell to a magazine. When Evariste's daughter Martinette proudly reports this proposal to Aunt Dicey, a Negro woman who also works on the Hallet plantation, Aunt Dicey becomes angry and explains to Martinette that Mr. Sublet intends to exploit Evariste, not to honor him, with his picture. She describes her own response the previous day to Mr. Sublet's son:

> "I knows dem kine o' folks," continued Aunt Dicey, resuming her interrupted ironing. "Dat stranger he got a li'le boy w'at ain't none too big to spank. Dat li'le imp he come a hoppin' in heah yestiddy wid a kine o' box on'neaf his arm. He say 'Good mo'nin', madam. Will you be so kine an' stan' jis like you is dah at you' i'onin', an' lef me take yo' picture? I 'lowed I gwine make a picture outen him wid dis heah flati'on, ef he don' cl'ar hisse'f quick. An' he say he baig my pardon fo' his intrudement. All dat kine o' talk to a old nigga 'oman! Dat plainly sho' he don' know his place." (423)

Aunt Dicey objects to the boy's assumption that she and her ironing board exist as subjects for "local color," which she understands as cultural imperialism; she associates the boy's desire to take her photograph for his own potential gain as "intrudement," a word that conveys both the intrusion of exploitation by outsiders and the rudeness of his lack of respect for her personhood. Martinette, in distress, asks, "'W'at you want 'im to say, Aunt Dice?'" and Aunt Dicey replies: "'I wants 'im to come in heah an' say: "Howdy, Aunt Dicey! will you be so kine and go put on yo' noo calker dress an' yo' bonnit w'at you w'ars to meetin', an' stan' 'side f'om dat i'onin'-boa'd w'ilse I gwine take yo' photygraph." Dat de way fo' a boy to talk w'at had good raisin''" (423). Aunt Dicey expresses no objection to being photographed as long as the act of representation allows her to dress for "meetin'," a word that conveys Aunt Dicey's sense that cultural representation can construct a site of encounter between subject and potential viewer as long as the representation itself is based on respect. If she were allowed to put on what she "w'ars to meetin'," she would be able to prepare herself to meet an "other's" gaze. For the boy to take her photograph at the ironing board, however, would confirm the stereotype of the Negro laundress for Northern viewers rather than present her as a person dressed for "meetin'" who might signify by that dress that she remains the autonomous subject of her own universe and not merely a servant in someone else's.

Other regionalist texts translate imperialism into the power relations of gender and create resistance effects as an aspect of gendered interactions. In "Uncle Christopher's" Cary delineates imperialism in the relation of Uncle Christopher to his wife and six daughters, each of whom has been rendered useful, silent, and indistinguishable through the colonizing effects of the regime of Uncle Christopher, who cannot tolerate speech from or discern individuality among his subjects; only the colonized mother can acknowledge difference, remarking that her youngest daughter, Lucinda, "had the 'liveliest turn' of any of the girls" (*AWR* 65). In his relation to his grandson Mark, Uncle Christopher also exhibits imperialist assumptions as he takes from Mark the dollar he has earned from selling potatoes, arrogating to himself whatever wealth his colonials produce. In the narrator's description of how "soon" she "tired of Uncle Christopher's conversation" (67) and of how "as the hours went by I grew restless, and then wretched" (71), she articulates her resistance to what King later called "the monotonous tone of supremacy" (*AWR* 384). In her declaration that "I did not then, nor can I to this day, agree" (68) with Aunt Rachel in regarding Uncle Christopher "as not only the man of the house, but also as the man of all the world" (67), she registers her refusal to be appropriated. Noting how dominance in the household leads to dominance in the world, Cary's narrator links domestic arrangements with imperialist assumptions and attitudes and in resisting Uncle Christopher she models an anti-imperialist stance.

Jewett's "A White Heron" dramatizes a similar resistance as Sylvia refuses to turn over the wealth of her region to the hunter who has entered it with a gun and ten dollars, even though to do so she must overcome her own attraction to the hunter, his expectations, her grandmother's desire for the money, and her own anticipation of "the splendid moment" when she can give the hunter the information he wants and cannot get without her help. Unlike Chopin's story, in which Aunt Dicey articulates her objection to the outsider's exploitation, in "A White Heron" Sylvia does not explain her refusal to reveal the bird's secret. The narrator says only that Sylvia "cannot tell the heron's secret and give its life away" (*AWR* 205), an enigmatic ending that has inspired numerous and conflicting interpretations. We read this story in part as Jewett's expression of her own effort to resist imperialism, her struggle to avoid colonizing her subject(s) and to find a way to portray the lives of regional persons without "selling" them. Sylvia's refusal to speak establishes for Jewett the limits of representation. That such limits should lead to a problematic, possibly even flawed, story is understandable, but for Jewett this is preferable to telling her character's secret and giving its life away.

Freeman's "A New England Nun" provides a final and perhaps still more interesting example of regionalism's recognition that the relations of gender can be understood as a form of imperialism. Joe Dagget will not marry Louisa Ellis until he has made his fortune and he "would have stayed fifty years if it had taken so long, and come home feeble and tottering, or never come home at all, to marry Louisa" (*AWR* 359). Making his fortune gives Joe the right to establish toward Louisa a relation of dominance. To make his fortune, however, Joe must go to Australia, a colonial entity designed precisely to allow those men from dominant nations who cannot make their fortune at home to make it there. Thus Freeman links the global operations of imperialism with the domestic arrangements of home. A man who has made his fortune has the right to demand that his wife leave her home and her ways and follow his ways and him to the "old homestead" to which he had lately made "some extensive and quite magnificent alterations" (360); he has the right to expect that she will leave her books as he has placed them, that he can do as he wishes with her dog, and that she will willingly submit to "sterner tasks than these graceful but half needless ones" of "distilling . . . essences" (360, 361). In refusing marriage to Joe, then, Louisa resists a domestic imperialism grounded in a global imperialism. Her success depends upon a "diplomacy" she did not know she had, the "meek" diplomacy that constitutes one of the "little . . . weapons" of the colonized, and in her success we find another example of regionalism's resistance effects.

The writer who most explicitly considers regionalist alternatives to imperialism is Sui Sin Far, whose title story in *Mrs. Spring Fragrance* and its companion story, "The Inferior Woman," as we discussed in chapter 6, create a Chinese-American woman who explores the question of American empire and who creates an empathic model for translating between cultures and promoting communication across the lines of class, tradition, and ethnicity. In "The Inferior Woman," Mrs. Spring Fragrance explains that she intends to write "'a book about Americans, an immortal book,'" and expresses her opinion that "'The American woman writes books about the Chinese. Why not a Chinese woman write books about the Americans?'" (*AWR* 524), a question that uncannily both echoes Chesnutt and challenges Brodhead. Sui Sin Far's stories constitute her book "about the Americans" in which she carefully constructs a respectful yet ironic critique of American imperialism. Just as Mrs. Spring Fragrance's own empathy inspires a change of heart in Mrs. Carman, leading her to accept her son's chosen sweetheart, Sui Sin Far's fiction, in the context of the Chinese exclusion laws, allowed her contemporary readers to explore and possibly to change their attitudes toward the Chinese.

Mrs. Spring Fragrance demonstrates a remarkable combination of successful assimilation to American life and a desire to bring together the best of Chinese and American cultures. Thus, when she is constructing her critique of American attitudes toward the Chinese, she brings to bear on this critique a language replete with respect and apparently lacking in anger; and when she insists on making her own decisions, demonstrating a broad view of the possibilities for women in American life, both in love and in politics, she demonstrates how advanced she is in her thinking, ahead both of her Chinese husband and of the American woman in her acquaintance, Mrs. Carman. She alternately finds wisdom in Tennyson, whom she calls an American poet, and in Confucius, depending on the situation and depending on the particular teaching she is trying to effect. She concludes with a great deal of respect for the American suffragist character, whose example she implies she would like any daughter of her own to follow.

While it is love interest and the words of Tennyson that dominate the plots of both stories, American politics and prejudices constitute the thematic counterpoint. American empire enters the fiction first through a letter Mrs. Spring Fragrance writes to her husband while she is visiting her cousin in the Chinese community in San Francisco. She writes:

> I am enjoying a most agreeable visit, and American friends, as also our own, strive benevolently for the accomplishment of my pleasure. Mrs. Samuel Smith,

> an American lady, known to my cousin, asked for my accompaniment to a magniloquent lecture the other evening. The subject was "America, the Protector of China!" It was most exhilarating, and the effect of so much expression of benevolence leads me to beg of you to forget to remember that the barber charges you one dollar for a shave while he humbly submits to the American man a bill of fifteen cents. And murmur no more because your honored elder brother, on a visit to this country, is detained under the rooftree of this great Government instead of under your own humble roof. Console him with the reflection that he is protected under the wing of the Eagle, the Emblem of Liberty. What is the loss of ten hundred years or ten thousand times ten dollars compared with the happiness of knowing oneself so securely sheltered? All of this I have learned from Mrs. Samuel Smith, who is as brilliant and great of mind as one of your own superior sex. (509)

The politics that both the lecture and Mrs. Smith support require Mrs. Spring Fragrance to ignore the imperialist and racist implications of the U.S. "protection" of China and the more local expression of these attitudes that resulted in suspicion and exclusion of ordinary Chinese, even as visitors. Mrs. Spring Fragrance, however, critiques American imperialism by extending the metaphor of "protectorate" to include her husband's brother's stay in the "Detention Pen" for Chinese laborers on Angel Island in San Francisco Bay. At the same time, she keeps alive the reminder, despite her urging that her husband "remember to forget," that the government's policies extend to the level of ethnic prejudices and discriminatory practices, as in the case of the American barber.

Will Carman, the son of Mrs. Spring Fragrance's American friend in Seattle and the Spring Fragrances' neighbor, views himself as above the common prejudices. Still, as a reporter for the local newspaper, he asks Mr. Spring Fragrance for an invitation to a party with other Chinese men so that he will have a "scoop" and he proposes to title the article, "A high-class Chinese stag party," suggesting his own affinity with local-color writers and his contrast to Mrs. Spring Fragrance as a regionalist writer (510). Moreover, like Mrs. Smith, he minimizes Mr. Spring Fragrance's objection to his brother's detention. Will tells Mr. Spring Fragrance that "'all Americans are princes and princesses, and just as soon as a foreigner puts his foot upon our shores, he also becomes of the nobility—I mean the royal family'" (510). He asserts that "'we that are real Americans'" are against the detention of the Chinese as "'it is against our principles'" (511). When Mr. Spring Fragrance offers "'the real Americans my consolations that they should be compelled to do that which is against their principles,'" Will Carman replies that "'we're not a bad sort, you know. Think of the indemnity money returned to the Dragon by Uncle Sam'" (511). During the Boxer Uprising of 1898–1901, a protest against increasing foreign imperialism in China, foreign lives and property were destroyed. Later the Qing government agreed to pay foreign governments $333 million in gold as compensation for the damage (Spence 235). In an action Will Carman cites as benevolence but that actually reflects America's interest in protecting its investments in China, the United States government returned much of the money due it according to the terms of the Boxer indemnity to establish scholarships to educate Chinese students in American colleges (283). Mr. Spring Fragrance, who has supported the education of his own younger brother and worked as well to increase trade between Seattle and Canton, complains to his wife about the attention given to these students in the American press and the failure of the press to mention the accomplishments of Chinese merchants. By dint of "painstaking study" he has himself "worked his way up" in America and "acquired the Western language and Western business ideas" (*AWR* 519). In response, Mrs. Spring Fragrance quotes Confucius, which does not provide her husband with the "wifely sympathy" he wants but does offer a Chinese cultural perspective as an alternative to condemning the Americans and as a model for Americans as well: "'Be not concerned that men do not know you; be only concerned that you do not know them'" (520). Despite her critique, Mrs. Spring Fragrance wishes not to reinforce cultural differences but to transform American attitudes by making Americans more Chinese.

Mrs. Spring Fragrance's relationship with Mrs. Carman expresses the pedagogical aesthetic of Sui Sin Far's fictions. The narrator writes, "Having lived in China while her late husband was in the custom service there, Mrs. Carman's prejudices did not extend to the Chinese" and so "there had been social good feeling between the American and Chinese families" (523). In this context Sui Sin Far can focus her attention on Mrs. Spring Fragrance's project of changing Mrs. Carman's mind and heart regarding her son's lover without appearing to write an explicitly political fiction. However, as Alice Winthrop thinks about Mrs. Carman's attitude toward her, a young working-class woman whom Mrs. Carman's son Will loves but whom his mother considers "unworthy," she evokes the political implications of Sui Sin Far's fiction: "When a gulf of prejudice lies between the wife and mother of a man, that man's life is not what it should be. . . . Prejudices are prejudices. They are like diseases" (525). Using her writing, Mrs. Spring Fragrance convinces Mrs. Carman to leave behind her prejudices. Sui Sin Far's fiction, while apparently dealing with romance—by the end of both stories, sets of Chinese lovers and American lovers are united—also constructs a critique of American imperialism, reflected in the story as "prejudices," and reconstructs what it means for either a Chinese or an American to confront the prejudices of American empire. Like Zitkala-Ša, whose own voice survives "only for those ears that are bent with compassion to hear it," and like Thaxter, who writes about "ears made delicate by listening," Sui Sin Far establishes her own mode of fiction as one in which a Chinese woman might write books about the Americans in order to change minds and hearts. In these examples, regionalism presents narrators and characters who urge readers to take a "different approach" than either "rude curiosity" or "intrudement," than either prurience at the local level (Will Carman's desire for a "scoop") or imperialism at the national level (Mr. Spring Fragrance's brother in the "detention pen").

If we transpose "nation" and "region" in Kaplan's triad and understand "nation" instead of "region" as the mediating middle term, we bring to visibility the way nation-states have become complicit with neo-imperialist forces in subjugating regions and regional peoples for capitalist exploitation. While nation-states have decreased in power under globalization, regions have increased in economic value as potential sites of profit making and thus we can imagine regions as socioeconomic and cultural entities autonomous from "nation." At the turn of the twenty-first century, "region" and "empire" have become the sites of conflict, and "nation" the enabler for empire's expansion. Thus regional subjects, and their histories of resistance as recorded in literary texts, become potential sources for models of alternatives to corporate transformation of the world. We envision not a new "field-Imaginary" for American literary studies but rather a new regionalism. Such a regionalism allows us to reconceive the inherent cultural, political, and economic value of regions that derive their identity less from their political subordination to nation-states and more from their rejection of imperialism.

While the public reputation of the humanities has declined along with government funding in an era of critique in which, as Carafiol observes, "the revolutionary impulse . . . has been turned against the nationalist ideal itself" ("Commentary" 539), rather than lament this consequence we can understand it as a productive unmooring of American literary history from a nationalist concept of "America." Thus, writers, texts, and literary modes that might have remained on the margin of our concerns as scholars, critics, and literary historians when we thought our field was "American literature" now become free to help us understand the present moment. Without question, one of the places to turn for understanding the continual reemergence of empire at the turn of the twenty-first century and its relation to U.S. political and cultural struggles is to look just outside our borders, to Central America, Latin America, and the Caribbean, to the "Caliban" school of "New Americanist" criticism and theory. Yet because we must bring to bear on our understanding of the new imperialism a multiplicity of sites of investigation and even more interdisciplinarity than we have traditionally understood as part of American literary and cultural studies, our collective project must be larger than any one site of investigation. American literary regionalism, we propose, remains an under-read and insufficiently theorized site of struggle at the end of the nineteenth century that can offer us in the twenty-first century one set of texts to study for their resistance effects.

CHAPTER 8

Feminist Epistemology and the Regionalist Standpoint

When one is hard pressed, one, however simple, gets wisdom as to vantage-points.

—Mary E. Wilkins Freeman, "A Church Mouse"

Each island, every isolated rock, has its own peculiar rote, and ears made delicate by listening, in great and frequent peril, can distinguish the bearings of each in a dense fog.

—Celia Thaxter, *Among the Isles of Shoals*

Vantage Points

The interested but presumably small audience for minor literature lacks the political power to claim for it the status of major, and the size of its audience seems to provide evidence that such literature has little to offer in the way of knowledge of the human condition, does not possess "universality." Critics deem its intended audience narrow, possibly marked by race, gender, or some other "special interest," and view its characters as incapable of knowing anything worth passing on to future generations. In this chapter we want to challenge the assumption that regionalist characters in particular know very little by exploring what it is they know, how they know it, and how their knowing calls into question the kinds of knowledge construction practiced and valued by members of dominant cultural groups. In effect, we want to consider the epistemology of regionalism and regionalism as epistemology. In order to do so, we will focus on specific fictions as central to the construction of regionalist knowledge and will explore the concepts of feminist standpoint theory for their relevance to our understanding of the epistemology of regionalism.

As we noted in chapter 1, in 1905 Roosevelt exhorted Americans to "grasp the points of vantage which will enable us to have our say in deciding the destiny of the oceans of the East and the West" (*The Strenuous Life* 28). For Roosevelt, grasping "points of vantage" supports the politics of imperialism. Moreover, Roosevelt obscures the connection between "points of vantage" and the location of power by his appeal to "us" as metonymic for the United States and by his implication that if we do not actively "grasp the points of vantage," we will not have "our say," an implication that links U.S. imperialism with protecting "our" freedom to speak. For Hetty Fifield in Freeman's "A Church Mouse," grasping "points of vantage" becomes a politics of resistance to the imperialism of gender, age, and class. Moreover, "A Church Mouse" explicitly links what Freeman calls "vantage-points" to Hetty's social position, which in turn is defined by her poverty, gender, age, and unmarried status. Indeed, we can trace our interest in feminist standpoint theory to that moment in Freeman's "A Church Mouse" when Hetty Fifield discovers a "vantage-point." Freeman writes, "When one is hard pressed, one, however simple, gets wisdom as to vantage-points. Hetty comprehended hers perfectly. She was the propounder of a problem; as long as it was unguessed, she was sure of her foothold as propounder. This little village in which she had lived all her life had removed the shelter from her head; she being penniless, it was beholden to provide her another; she asked it what" (*AWR* 349).

As a homeless woman daring to ask the deacons for a job as sexton ("'I never heard of a woman's bein' saxton,'" Caleb Gale asserts in the story's opening line [344]), Hetty translates standpoint into "vantage-point": she discovers that she does have a certain power in a situation which would appear to render her entirely powerless—she owns no property, has worked her entire life as a live-in servant for room and board, and has "not laid up a cent" because "for the most of the time she had received no wages" (349). As the "propounder of a problem" who raises questions about women's lives that men in power would prefer to ignore, Hetty in effect gains a "foothold," for she has observed the men around her much more closely than they have cared to know her: "This little settlement of narrow-minded, prosperous farmers, however hard a task charity might be to them, could not turn an old woman out into the fields and highways to seek for food as they would a Jersey cow. They had their Puritan consciences, and her note of distress would sound louder in their ears than the Jersey's bell echoing down the valley in the stillest night" (349). Hetty understands that their having "Puritan consciences" means they have constructed a particular image of themselves that provides her with a point of leverage she can use to ameliorate her situation. Thus her question is not an appeal to their "consciences"; rather it constitutes her recognition that, having based both their identities and their civic power on the assertion of conscience, they will now be forced to solve a problem they would have preferred her not to raise.

Although Hetty has used her vantage point to gain a foothold, and has moved her few belongings into the meetinghouse, Freeman, as we noted in chapter 4, recognizes the fragility of her negotiated settlement. The deacons have not changed; they are simply waiting for her to make a mistake that will give them the opening they need to reassert their control over her. Luxuriating in the sense of having secured a home for herself, Hetty makes the mistake of cooking cabbage and turnips for her Saturday night dinner and "the next day the odors of turnip and cabbage were strong in the senses of the worshippers" (350). Freeman writes further, "This superseding the legitimate savor of the sanctuary . . . by the homely week-day odors of kitchen vegetables, was too much for the sensibilities of the people" (350–51), and public sentiment shifts to the side of the deacons as they prepare to remove Hetty from the meetinghouse. Having gained her foothold, however, Hetty forces into the open the violence that structures gender and class relations in this small New England community, and by making it visible, makes it also subject to critique and resistance. Anticipating the deacons' move, Hetty locks the doors and windows of the meetinghouse. To remove her now will require an act of forced entry that Freeman, as we also noted in chapter 4, associates with sexual assault: "the windows were fast. Hetty had made her sacred castle impregnable except to violence. Either the door would have to be forced or a window broken to gain an entrance" (353). As the deacons attempt to reassert masculine dominance, they fall back on age-old strategies for controlling women, namely, violation. Yet when the men approach the door with a crowbar and the intention to force it open, their wives, whose adolescent daughters are watching from a distance, suddenly come to Hetty's defense. When Hetty peers out of a window and says, "'Jest let me say one word,'" Mrs. Gale replies, "'Say all you want to, Hetty, an' don't be afraid'" (354). While Freeman does not explicitly tell us what produces the change in Mrs. Gale's understanding of the situation or the shift in her allegiance, we can speculate that she comes to Hetty's defense in part because she sees a violence heretofore invisible. Breaking into the church evokes violation of Hetty's own body. Because the men cannot figure out how to solve the problem she propounds in any other way than penetration, the women, who cannot sanction what looks like rape as social control, shift their allegiance and Hetty emerges triumphant. Indeed, when Hetty speaks to the assembled crowd through the meetinghouse window, in spite of the fact that her voice shakes and "the magnitude of her last act of defiance had caused it to react upon herself like an overloaded gun" (354), she takes a position of authority. Her vantage point creates a pulpit of sorts, and the village responds by giving her "that little room side of the pulpit, where the minister hangs his hat" (355) for her permanent home and allowing her to become the church's sexton. We can assume that from now on Hetty will be able to occupy her home with full freedom, even to the cooking of cabbage and turnips, because a genuine change in understanding has taken place and with it a shift of power; the hard-pressed women in this story have indeed gained "wisdom as to vantage-points."

In *Toward a Feminist Theory of the State,* Catharine MacKinnon writes, "The feminist theory of knowledge is inextricable from the feminist critique of power because the male point of view forces itself upon the world as its way of apprehending it" (114). Because the men have no real desire to solve the problem Hetty raises, they plan to force her to accept their "solution." Here power substitutes for knowledge, for the men neither have nor wish to have any knowledge of her ethical claims, which emerge from the way the labor system has exploited her throughout her working life and from the limitations of her position as a woman to find work for wages. MacKinnon's analysis provides a lens for interpreting "A Church Mouse." Writing that "the perspective from the male standpoint enforces woman's definition," MacKinnon offers in a footnote the following elaboration on the concept of "male standpoint":

> Male is a social and political concept, not a biological attribute. As I use it it has *nothing whatever* to do with inherency, preexistence, nature, inevitability, or body as such. It is more epistemological than ontological, undercutting the distinction itself, given male power to conform being with perspective. The perspective from the male standpoint is not always each man's opinion, although most men adhere to it, nonconsciously and without considering it a point of view, as much because it makes sense of their experience (the male experience) as because it is in their interest. It is rational for them. A few men reject it; they pay. Because it is the dominant point of view and defines rationality, women are pushed to see reality in its terms, although this denies their vantage point as women in that it contradicts (at least some of) their lived experience. Women who adopt the male standpoint are passing, epistemologically speaking.[1]

When Hetty "gets wisdom as to vantage-points," she ceases to pass epistemologically and gains access to a reality outside the terms of men's perspective and men's definition of rationality. And when Mrs. Gale, who earlier in the story objects to Hetty's presence in the meetinghouse ("passing, epistemologically speaking" at this point in the story), finally refuses to see reality in her husband's terms, she emerges from behind her husband's perspective and occupies the vantage point defined by the contradictions of her role as a woman who is also his wife; she cannot countenance acts of violation, but she is also supposed to "obey" the man who presses forward with the crowbar.

While the men in the story wish to force Hetty to see reality the way they do, Hetty recognizes sex inequality, and thus her vantage point, like Mrs. Gale's, is feminist: it brings into consciousness the contradictions in her situation and in her community and thus enables her to critique what passes for objectivity and rationality. As MacKinnon observes, "objectivity—the nonsituated, universal standpoint, whether claimed or aspired to—is a denial of the existence or potency of sex inequality that tacitly participates in constructing reality from the dominant point of view" (*Toward a Feminist Theory* 114). When Caleb Gale begins to "reason" with Hetty by declaring, "'I never heard of a woman's bein' saxton,'" Hetty replies, "'I dun' know what difference that makes; I don't see why they shouldn't have women saxtons as well as men saxtons, for my part, nor nobody else neither. They'd keep dusted 'nough sight cleaner'" (*AWR* 344). At each point in their interchange, Hetty counters Caleb's "rationality" with her own. Indeed, it is her access to an alternative reality that enables her to discover her own power as propounder. MacKinnon tells us why: "Objectivity, as the epistemological stance of which objectification is the social process, creates the reality it apprehends by defining as knowledge the reality it creates through its way of apprehending it" (*Toward a Feminist Theory* 114). Thus when Hetty Fifield refuses her own objectification she also challenges the epistemological stance of objectivity, thereby making it impossible for Caleb and the other deacons to recreate their definition of reality. "A Church Mouse" is concerned with epistemology of a very particular kind: a feminist standpoint epistemology. Without the feminism, Hetty would have neither knowledge nor the "foothold" that gives her the power to survive.

"A Church Mouse" serves not only as a point of origin for our interest in epistemology; it also grounds us in questions of theory by emphasizing the connection between feminism and our own attempts to reconstruct regionalism. Without the feminist lens, we might not have "seen" the value of regionalist fiction. But a feminist lens is present in Freeman's story; without Freeman's story, we might not have "seen" feminist standpoint theory. Even further, "A Church Mouse" emphasizes the relationship between the "feminist lens" and the ability to perceive the way in which dominant ideologies carry with them the narratives of masculinism, imperialism, and classism "forced" onto others, especially onto women's bodies and minds. To the extent that narratives of masculinist ideology encourage readers to "naturalize" the way they have learned to see and read the world (recall MacKinnon's analysis of the way the dominant point of view defines rationality and pushes women to see their experience in its terms), they produce an experience of "recognition." But the word "recognition" carries with it some of the history of "common-sense" quasi-epistemology, the kind of false knowledge that is merely a reprocessed ideology. Fictions become re-cognized, thought "again" but not newly thought. Readers who recognize the familiar in fiction have only the illusion of cognition; by reassuring them that the world is as they thought it to be, dominant fiction actually prevents a genuine pursuit of knowing, ideology serving as a mediator or gatekeeper between the eager would-be knower that most lovers of reading might acknowledge in themselves and what is available for them to "know" when the only texts they are encouraged to read or have access to merely replicate the limitations of the ideology they have internalized. Feminist standpoint theory postulates, through its discovery of "gap" knowledge, that there is an alternative to the epistemology of re-cognition. Epistemology begins for marginalized people when they discover that they live within a gap created by the contrast between their own lives and the dominant conceptual schemes, cultural frameworks, and discourse, and when they begin to theorize about that gap. It is through such an alternative epistemology that feminist standpoint theory poses a challenge to the postmodern insistence that subjects cannot escape their discursive construction within ideology. To the extent that minor literatures expose the epistemology of re-cognition, they can offer alternative ways of knowing that "take place," become located or regionalized, in the gaps within ideology. Our story of the relation of feminist standpoint theory to regionalism thus begins with the concept of Hetty Fifield's "vantage-points"; indeed, we would argue that standpoint and regionalism are interchangeable terms, for both feminist standpoint theory and feminist standpoint fiction discursively represent the world as regionalized. In order to understand this relationship, however, we offer an overview of the concepts that ground feminist standpoint theory.

Feminist Standpoint Theory

In the same year that Foucault's *The Archaeology of Knowledge* was published in English translation (1972), Dorothy Smith presented "Women's Perspective as a Radical Critique of Sociology," a paper that marks one point of origin for feminist standpoint epistemology. Smith proposed that feminist knowledge and theory originate in what she called women's "direct experience of the everyday world" (91). Rather than serving as an application of theory constructed by male philosophers and social theorists, feminist standpoint theory begins by "thinking from women's lives."[2] Although Smith focuses her 1972 essay on a critique of the discipline of sociology, her work has influenced feminist thinkers in their analysis of structures of knowledge more generally. Within sociology, Smith argues, "There is a difficulty first then of a disjunction between how women find and experience the world beginning (though not necessarily ending up) from their place and the concepts and theoretical schemes available to think about it in" (86). Other theorists have developed this idea and express it in different terms. For example, for Sandra Harding, feminist epistemology constructs a way of knowing that emerges from "the gap between women's experiences and the dominant conceptual schemes," and she argues that "powerful critical theories *can be developed*" out of this gap (*Whose Science?* 70–71). Alison Jaggar describes Smith's "disjunction" and Harding's "gap" as an experience of "outlaw emotions" that "may provide the first indications that something is wrong with the way alleged facts have been constructed, with accepted understandings of how things are" ("Love and Knowledge" 161). Since knowledge is organized, or as Smith alternately terms it "managed" and "administered," "in terms of a perspective on the world which is a view from the top and which takes for granted the pragmatic procedures of governing as those which frame and identify its subject matter" (87), members of a discipline "learn to discard our experienced world as a source of reliable information or suggestions" and "to confine and focus our insights within the conceptual frameworks and relevances which are given in the discipline" (87). Because feminist standpoint theory emerges from the perspective of persons who live "within the gap," or what Donna Haraway has described as the view from "below" ("Situated Knowledges" 584), the questions that emerge from such standpoints are also about how to do research because, as Sandra Harding has said, they are about "thinking differently" (qtd. in Hirsh and Olson 22).

Recognizing the existence of disjunctions, gaps, and outlaw emotions leads Harding to develop the question of methodology as a significant feature of feminist standpoint epistemology. Such a methodology makes an argument for "starting off research projects, starting off our thought about any particular phenomenon, from outside the dominant conceptual framework" (qtd. in Hirsh and Olson 16), and focuses attention on the "context of discovery" rather than limiting method, as the sciences and positivist social science have done, to the "context of justification" (see Harding, *Whose Science?;* also Ewick). The problem with sociology, Smith argued in 1972, was that its practice required sociologists, if they were women, to subsume their own experience in a procedure that she describes as "a sort of conceptual imperialism" (88). The methodology of traditional knowledge-systems thus sets "boundaries of inquiry . . . within the framework of what is already established" (88); feminist standpoint theory offers a way for researchers to move beyond those boundaries, those established and exclusionary frameworks.

Beginning research—or writing narratives—by asking questions from women's lives not only determines methodology but also, according to feminist standpoint theorists, leads to an increased objectivity. Because "women's perspective . . . discredits sociology's claim to constitute an objective knowledge independent of the sociologist's situation," Smith argues, "if sociology cannot avoid being situated, then sociology should take that as its beginning and build it into its methodological and theoretical strategies" (91). Harding considers the social situatedness of science and proposes the idea of "strong objectivity" as a corrective to the exclusions of scientific method. For Harding, research that moves outside the dominant conceptual framework reveals conventional notions of "objectivity" to be weak because such objectivity, when practiced as scientific method, is restricted to "those processes controllable by methodological rules." Because the processes by which research questions are generated are not themselves governed by the rules of scientific method, the political and social issues that influence the selection of research topics remain invisible. Harding's "strong objectivity" would allow individuals and cultures to detect the assumptions and agendas that govern the research questions we are allowed to ask (*Whose Science?* 149). Or as Donna Haraway writes, "Feminist objectivity means quite simply *situated knowledges*" (581), and she adds that "it is precisely in the politics and epistemology of partial perspectives that the possibility of sustained, rational, objective inquiry rests" (584).

For standpoint theorists, thinking from the lives of women and nondominant men increases objectivity in part by strengthening the "reflexivity" of the observer, researcher, or narrator. Harding states, "the fact that the observer changes, interacts with the object of observation, with what he or she's looking at, . . . can be used in a positive way" (qtd. in Hirsh and Olson 17) to strengthen the social, political, and historical context within which we might be able to develop a less biased objectivity. Researchers who begin their work from the standpoint of the oppressed, as Alison Jaggar has written, gain methodological access to a "perspective that offers a less partial and distorted and therefore more reliable view," namely the "epistemological privilege" of oppressed people (162). When researchers interact with the researched and are themselves willing to change in that interaction, they gain access to a "less partial and distorted" view of themselves as well as of the biases in their own research methods. As Harding writes, "to enact or operationalize the directive of strong objectivity is to value the Other's perspective and to pass over in thought into the social condition that creates it—not in order to stay there, to 'go native' or merge the self with the Other, but in order to look back at the self in all its cultural particularity from a more distant, critical, objectifying location" (*Whose Science?* 151).

Central to the postulates of feminist standpoint theory with respect to methodology, objectivity, and knowledge is the proposal that disenfranchised, marginalized persons have the potential for what Alison Jaggar calls "epistemological privilege." Jaggar writes, "the perspective on reality available from the standpoint of the oppressed, which in part at least is the standpoint of women, is a perspective that offers a less partial and distorted and therefore more reliable view. Oppressed people have a kind of epistemological privilege insofar as they have easier access to this standpoint. That is, they are more likely to incorporate reliable appraisals of situations" (162). The concept of "epistemological" or, as it is sometimes called, "epistemic privilege" is an important corollary to Harding's "strong objectivity," though Harding cautions that "while both 'women's experiences' and 'what women say' certainly are good places to begin generating research projects . . . , they would not seem to be reliable grounds for deciding just which claims to knowledge are preferable," and she argues that it is the subsequently articulated *theory* starting from the perspective of women's lives that provides the grounds for feminist claims (*Whose Science?* 123–24). For Harding, women's stories are necessary but not sufficient generators of feminist epistemology. Uma Narayan, however, observes that "'nonanalytic' and 'nonrational' forms of discourse, like fiction or poetry, may be better able than other forms to convey the complex life experiences of one group to members of another" (264), though she cautions that persons from dominant groups who may not share the oppressions of a marginalized group often fail to understand the complexities of that experience of oppression. Nevertheless, she points out, "The view that we can understand much about the perspectives of those whose oppression we do not share allows us the space to criticize dominant groups for their blindness to the facts of oppression" (265).

In these observations we can distinguish the complex interrelation of story and theory and we can further observe how it is that certain stories create a perspective that enables them to function as theory. It is the combination of being "hard pressed" *and* getting "wisdom as to vantage-points" that produces feminist epistemology. Indeed, we must emphasize here that the concept of epistemic "privilege" does not mean that members of oppressed groups must or even will "get wisdom as to vantage-points," only that they may; nor does it mean that members of oppressed groups will always have better knowledge than those who are not oppressed. The concept of epistemic "privilege" implies a necessary but not a sufficient condition, a capacity that may but need not inevitably be activated. For this reason, theory and access to theory, whether in narrative or discursive form, becomes significant in determining whether or not oppressed persons will develop epistemological privilege. Stories matter in enabling members of oppressed groups to develop the social and structural knowledge required to theorize from the base of their experience. In a striking example of the relation between storytelling and epistemology, MacKinnon invokes the consciousness-raising of the 1970s women's movement as methodology, suggesting that epistemic "privilege" and social locations derive from individual experience but that it is the collective thinking of a group that makes it possible to construct theory. Understanding epistemology to "establish an account of how knowing connects with what one purports to know" (*Toward a Feminist Theory* 96), she argues that feminist method, "taken as a theory of knowing about social being," pursues an epistemology that does not insist on distance and aperspectivity, two tests science and social science have erected in order to claim "objectivity" for the results of their research methods (97).

> Women are presumed able to have access to society and its structure because they live in it and have been formed by it, not in spite of those facts. Women can know society because consciousness is part of it, not because of any capacity to stand outside it or oneself. This stance locates the position of consciousness, from which one knows, in the standpoint and time frame of that attempting to be known. . . . [I]t redefines the epistemological issue from being the scientific one, the relation between knowledge and objective reality, to a problem of the relation of consciousness to social being. (98–99)

In light of these observations, and as an example of the intercommunicative relation of theory and story, we might propose the following revision to Freeman's "A Church Mouse": "When one is hard pressed, one, however simple, *may* get wisdom as to vantage-points."

Nancy Hartsock first developed the idea of a feminist standpoint in her 1984 attempt to critique the inadequacy of Marxist analysis for women and to develop "the ground for a specifically feminist historical materialism" (158). Crucial to feminist standpoint theory is an understanding of the way material life and practical activity directly structure epistemology (160). Critiquing the narrowness of Marx's understanding of labor, Hartsock identifies women's labor as "contact with material necessity" (165) and thus women make a dual contribution to subsistence in capitalism—the institutionalized sexual division of labor makes women "responsible for both housework and wage work" (166). It is precisely women's "doubled" contact with material necessity that leads standpoint theorists to view women's experience as a key structural component of epistemology. Although feminist standpoint theory has remained only tangentially connected to Marx's construction of a "proletarian standpoint" and its role in capitalist production, standpoint theorists continue to insist on the relationship between the material conditions and tasks allotted to women and nondominant men and the development of a way of thinking, an epistemology, that derives from the experience of these material conditions. Hartsock considers what would be involved in a "redefining and restructuring of society as a whole on the basis of women's activity" (175) and writes, "Generalizing the activity of women to the social system as a whole would raise, for the first time in human history, the possibility of a fully human community, a community structured by connection rather than separation and opposition. One can conclude then that women's life activity does form the basis of a specifically feminist materialism, a materialism which can provide a point from which both to critique and to work against phallocentric ideology and institutions" (175–76).

Situating the Regionalist Standpoint

We would argue that regionalism anticipates a "specifically feminist materialism" and a creative vision of what it might mean to "generalize the activity of women to the social system as a whole." In the section that follows, we explore what is materialist about the spatial component of regionalism. Many of the concepts that ground feminist standpoint theory (Smith's "perspective from women's lives," Adrienne Rich's "politics of location," Patricia Hill Collins's "outsider within," Haraway's "situated knowledges," Harding's "gap," and even Anzaldúa's positioning of feminist epistemology in the "borderlands" of *mestizaje*)[3] work from a spatial, even geographical metaphor, a viewpoint that is situated in some material location, whether that location exists in the specific institutional sites of the discipline of sociology, in the way perspective is connected to materialist position, or in the way geographical borders create psychic and epistemic structures for the person who straddles worlds on both sides of the border and is more than and different from their sum. Standpoint above all is connected to place, position, situation—indeed, standpoint as used in the context of feminism may be understood as a late twentieth-century reclaiming both of Marx's mid-nineteenth-century concept and of a nineteenth-century literary regionalism that did not neatly "fit" either the literary genres or the cultural frameworks of the mid-to-late nineteenth-century United States.

One of the more curious features of regionalism as a literary genre emerges when we consider that, while the specific fictions may generally be located by the author's birthplace or region of residence and while regionalist narrators offer readers highly specific and materialist descriptions of the houses, villages, farms, and coastal sites their characters inhabit, these descriptions frequently lack correlatives to particular geographical places—or if they do establish such correlatives, as in the case of Jewett and Murfree, it is not the reference to place that establishes the regionalist perspective but rather all of those formal and descriptive features we discussed in chapter 4. Furthermore, as we observed in chapter 1, space in regionalism is both a discursive construction and a cultural location grounded in the everyday lives of women and other nondominant regional persons (see Pryse, "Reading Regionalism" 50). Another way of understanding the difference between regionalism and actual place, and the similarity between regionalism and standpoint, is to note that "even though the literal topography of place matters for some of these writers, especially Celia Thaxter and Mary Austin, the texts are not 'about' place in a literal sense. Rather, 'geographical region' stands in the same relation to 'regionalism' as 'female' stands to 'feminism': 'region' and 'female' are naturalizing terms, but they do not serve as the 'essences' of regionalism or feminism" (Pryse, "'Distilling Essences'" 9). Just as not all women achieve a feminist standpoint, not all regional persons, characters, and writers achieve the rhetorical awareness of difference as critique that we have, throughout our work, defined as regionalism and distinguished from local-color writing. Thus regionalism and standpoint come close to being interchangeable concepts, at least within literary and cultural study.

Patricia Hill Collins's work is particularly important for making the connection between literary regionalism and feminist standpoint epistemology. In outlining what she describes as the contours of an alternative black feminist epistemology in chapter 11 of *Black Feminist Thought,* she includes the following four characteristics: (1) lived experience as a criterion of meaning; (2) the use of dialogue; (3) the ethic of caring; and (4) the ethic of personal accountability. In articulating the significance of "lived experience as a criterion of meaning," Collins makes a distinction between "knowledge and wisdom" and sees "experience as the cutting edge dividing them" (257). She writes, "In the context of intersecting oppressions, the distinction is essential. Knowledge without wisdom is adequate for the powerful, but wisdom is essential to the survival of the subordinate" (257). We are reminded here, of course, of the passage from Freeman's "A Church Mouse" with which we began our discussion of regionalist epistemology as it specifically invokes the concept of "wisdom." In elaborating further the connection between the condition of being "hard pressed" and the getting of "wisdom," Collins observes, "For most African-American women those individuals who have lived through the experiences about which they claim to be experts are more believable and credible than those who have merely read or thought about such experiences. . . . Even after substantial mastery of dominant epistemologies, many Black women scholars invoke our own lived experiences and those of other African-American women in selecting topics for investigation and methodologies used" (257–58). She refers specifically to Lorraine Hansberry who wrote, "'In certain peculiar ways, we have been conditioned to think not small—but tiny. And the thing, I think which has strangled us most is the tendency to turn away from the world in search of the universe.'"[4] In the context of Hansberry's observation, regionalism's focus on the "tiny" and the local becomes a mode of "free to think."

Collins makes another point that is helpful in enabling us to make the connection between nineteenth-century literary regionalism and twentieth-century feminist standpoint epistemology. She explains that "practical images" are the "symbolic vehicles" through which "experience as a criterion of meaning" is conveyed. Her point directs our attention to the emphasis on the details of women's day-to-day lives that we find in regionalist fiction and to the ways in which those details become "symbolic vehicles" for conveying the knowledge derived from "lived experience" (258). We might recall here once again the language of Cary's "Preface"—"incidents for the most part of so little apparent moment or significance that they who live in what is called the world would scarcely have marked them had they been detained with me while they were passing"—as an instance of what we have elsewhere called the "poetics of detail" (Fetterley, "Introduction" and "Entitled"). This describes the regionalist text's ability to mark the infinite particularity of experience that from another perspective, that of "what is called the world," appears, like Thaxter's Isles when seen from the mainland, an undifferentiated mass. In regionalist fiction, the infinite particularity of women's lived experience becomes "practical images" that serve as "symbolic vehicles." For example, when Joe Daggett, returning after a fourteen-year absence to fulfill his promise to marry Louisa Ellis, enters her "solitary home," Freeman writes, "He seemed to fill up the whole room. A little yellow canary that had been asleep in his green cage at the south window woke up and fluttered wildly, beating his little yellow wings against the wires" (*AWR* 357). In the canary's terror Freeman conveys Louisa's own misgivings about marriage, misgivings based on her lived experience of the pleasures she finds in controlling her own environment; when, at the end of the story, she tells Joe that she does not want to marry him, Freeman writes: "Now the little canary might turn itself into a peaceful yellow ball night after night, and have no need to wake and flutter with wild terror against its bars" (365).

In discussing "the use of dialogue in assessing knowledge claims," Collins observes that for "Black women new knowledge claims are rarely worked out in isolation from other individuals and are usually developed through dialogues with other members of a community. A primary epistemological assumption underlying the use of dialogue in assessing knowledge claims is that connectedness rather than separation is an essential component of the knowledge validation process" (260). She later observes, "when African-American women use dialogues in assessing knowledge claims, we might be invoking ways of knowing that are also more likely to be used by women" (262). We have previously drawn attention to the emphasis on dialogue in regionalist texts, both as a way of structuring the fictions themselves and as a way of signaling regionalism's dialogic relation with "what is called the world." Collins's discussion enables us to see the connection between this feature of regionalist fiction and feminist standpoint theory, and to see dialogue as a form of regionalist epistemology, the way in which characters, and writers, test and validate their claims to knowledge. For example, when Mary Jane Beers in Cooke's "Miss Beulah's Bonnet" explains and defends Miss Beulah's refusal to attend church, her claim that Miss Beulah's "'ben a real home-made kind of a saint'" even though "'I know she don't look it'" gains immediate validation from the other women present because "they could appreciate Miss Beulah's self-sacrifice better than the deacons could," having lived through such experiences themselves (*AWR* 135). Similarly, in Chopin's "A Gentleman of Bayou Têche," Martinette's "knowledge" ("'You know, Aunt Dicey,' she began a little complacently . . .") that the visiting artist appreciates her "popa" and wants to "make" his picture out of respect collapses in dialogue with Aunt Dicey, who has observed the behavior of the artist's son and who has listened to her own son's report of "'how the folks they talk, yonda up to Mr. Hallet's'" (*AWR* 422, 423). Finally, we might point to the example of Mrs. Spring Fragrance in Sui Sin Far's story "The Inferior Woman," whose knowledge of the value of the working-class woman her neighbor's son wishes to marry against the objections of his upper-middle-class mother gains validation from dialogue with a representative "Superior Woman." Armed with this validated knowledge, Mrs. Spring Fragrance can in conversation with Mrs. Carman effect a change of mind and heart because Mrs. Carman is herself in dialogue with the "Superior Woman": "There was eagerness in Mrs. Carman's voice. What could Ethel Evebrook have to say about that girl!" (*AWR* 524). Regionalism's emphasis on dialogue is intimately connected to issues of epistemology—to how one knows, to what constitutes useful knowledge, and to how knowledge may be communicated and shared.

In addition, Collins identifies "the ethic of caring" as an element of standpoint epistemology, writing that "the convergence of African-influenced and feminist principles in the ethic of caring seems particularly acute" (264). Her reference to the "emphasis placed on individual uniqueness" (263) as a component of the ethic of caring connects regionalism's concern with particularity, what we call the "poetics of detail," to epistemology. Collins further characterizes the ethic of caring as "developing the capacity for empathy" (263). We have previously identified empathic narration as a key feature of regionalist poetics and we will return to the crucial role of empathy in regionalist fiction in chapter 11. As with dialogue, what we observe here is the overlap between those elements Collins proposes as definitive of feminist standpoint epistemology and those elements we see as definitive of regionalism, an observation that supports our proposal that regionalism and standpoint are almost interchangeable concepts.

Collins also offers "an ethic of personal accountability" as an aspect of black feminist epistemology (265). Derivative from the first characteristic, "lived experience as a criterion of meaning," and related to the "connectedness" associated with dialogue, the ethic of personal accountability asserts "that every idea has an owner and that the owner's identity matters" since "[k]nowledge claims made by individuals respected for their moral and ethical connections to their ideas will carry more weight than those offered by less respected figures" (265). Regionalist fiction is replete with situations in which knowledge is evaluated by its relation to personal accountability. For example, when Celia Barnes at the conclusion of "How Celia Changed Her Mind" gives thanks for having been restored to the condition of an "old maid," her conviction that she now knows the truth of her assertions, whereas before she spoke in "ignorance," gains conclusive weight from her personal experience with marriage (*AWR* 153). Similarly, the narrator's perception that "[t]here in the bare, hot sand the track of her two feet bore evenly and white" can be trusted to provide more accurate knowledge of the Walking Woman than the reports of those who "called her lame" since the narrator has established a deep and empathic connection to her (*AWR* 583). And Zitkala-Ša, who leaves her community to attend school in the East, wishes her mother could appreciate her triumph in winning an oratory contest but feels the weight of her mother's judgment for she knows her mother has knowledge that she fears she herself may be in danger of losing (*AWR* 559). Finally, we recall Freeman's scathing critique in "A Mistaken Charity" of those who propose ideas for the lives of others without any knowledge of their "lived experience" as an illustration of Collins's assertion that from the perspective of standpoint epistemology "every idea has an owner and that the identity of the owner matters."

In concluding her discussion, Collins writes:

> Alternative knowledge claims in and of themselves are rarely threatening to conventional knowledge. Such claims are routinely ignored, discredited, or simply absorbed and marginalized in existing paradigms. Much more threatening is the challenge that alternative epistemologies offer to the basic process used by the powerful to legitimate knowledge claims that in turn justify their right to rule. If the epistemology used to validate knowledge comes into question, then all prior knowledge claims validated under the dominant model

> become suspect. Alternative epistemologies challenge all certified knowledge and open up the question of whether what has been taken to be true can stand the test of alternative ways of validating truth. (271)

As an alternative epistemology, regionalism opens up a wide range of questions about the validity of "what has been taken to be true," in terms of story, in terms of the "question of the American" and of American literary history, and in terms of knowledge derived from dominant ideological frameworks.

Playing in the Dark

Theorists such as Collins, Smith, Harding, Haraway, and others have argued extensively for the usefulness of feminist standpoint theory in understanding the limitations of both epistemology and methodology in science and social science, but it has been more difficult to imagine extending their arguments to literary study. Questions of "strong objectivity" and "reflexivity" directly address the researcher whose subjects inhabit either the human social world or conform in some way to the "laws of nature."[5] It is more difficult to trace the signature of the writer in the text, leading some critics to psychoanalytic and "symptomatic" reading practices and others to saturate the text with historical and biographical contexts and/or theoretical models. However, as our opening discussion of "A Church Mouse" indicates, questions of standpoint are complexly interwoven with questions of region and regional life, and making qualitative or narrative space for the regional voice reduces the distance of "objectivity" and at the same time requires some degree of self-reflexivity on the part of the writer if not the narrator in order for readers to "hear" that voice. The most useful literary argument we have found for extending questions of feminist standpoint theory to regionalist fiction is Toni Morrison's *Playing in the Dark.*

In *Playing in the Dark,* Morrison constructs an alternative epistemology of American literature from the standpoint of the minority writer; she thus also makes feminist standpoint theory available for understanding literary texts as well as for examining the science and social science studies in which it has primarily been deployed. *Playing in the Dark* investigates "American Africanism," the ways in which "a nonwhite, Africanlike (or Africanist) presence or persona was constructed in the U.S." (6), and suggests that this construction tells us more about how white identity came to define itself than about the black persons who provided the imagery of blackness. Suggesting that "black slavery enriched the country's creative possibilities," Morrison writes, "in that construction of blackness AND enslavement could be found not only the not-free but also, with the dramatic polarity created by skin color, the projection of the not-me. The result was a playground for the imagination. What rose up out of collective needs to allay internal fears and to rationalize external exploitation was an American Africanism—a fabricated brew of darkness, otherness, alarm, and desire that is uniquely American" (38). Morrison suggests that "this Africanist presence may be something the United States cannot do without" because "American means white" (47); a dismantling of white projections onto African Americans would radically alter the foundations of American white identity itself. In "thinking about the validity or vulnerability of a certain set of assumptions conventionally accepted among literary historians and critics and circulated as 'knowledge,'" Morrison is also offering an alternative epistemology in Collins's terms, one capable of challenging in particular the assumption that "the characteristics of our national literature emanate from a particular 'Americanness' that is separate from and unaccountable to this [Africanist] presence" (4–5). Thus Morrison links the imaginative construction of an American Africanism with the social construction of knowledge, for, as she writes, "knowledge, however mundane and utilitarian, plays about in linguistic images and forms cultural practice" (49).

In Morrison's exploration of Africanist presence, "playing in the dark" becomes a meditation on writing out of Harding's gap. Morrison writes, "As a writer reading, I came to realize the obvious: the subject of the dream is the dreamer. The fabrication of an Africanist persona is reflexive; an extraordinary meditation on the self; a powerful exploration of the fears and desires that reside in the writerly conscious. It is an astonishing revelation of longing, of terror, of perplexity, of shame, of magnanimity. It requires hard work not to see this" (17). Indeed, Morrison writes her own variation on Harding's central concepts. First, she indicates that the subject of research is at least in part the researcher, with the researcher's own "objectivity" constructed as a way of creating distance from those "fears and desires" that reside in the "writerly conscious"; in Morrison's terms, we might understand both "objectivity" and "rationality" as precisely that "hard work" required "*not* to see" the researcher's biases. As she writes, "It is important to see how inextricable Africanism is or ought to be from the deliberations of literary criticism and the wanton, elaborate strategies undertaken to erase its presence from view," leading to "startling displays of scholarly lapses in objectivity" (8). "What is fascinating," she writes, "is to observe how [the critics'] lavish exploration of literature manages *not* to see meaning in the thunderous, theatrical presence of black surrogacy—an informing, destabilizing, and disturbing element—in the literature they do study" (13). This "willful critical blindness" has itself produced weak objectivity in the study of American literature and culture, "a blindness that, if it had not existed, could have made these insights part of our routine literary heritage" (18).

Second, methodology for Morrison involves a shift in critical perspective that occurred when she "stopped reading as a reader and began to read as a writer" (15). Her formulation becomes most interesting when we realize that she is not saying that the act of writing itself led to her "shift in critical perspective"; rather, she claims she made the choice to *read* differently, as if from the perspective of the person making the choices that produced the fictions. We might see this as an act of reading from the inside out, an effort at what we have called in chapter 4 "shifting the center of perception" (see also *AWR* xvii–xviii). Following Morrison, we would argue that writers, whatever their positioning with respect to concepts of "major" and "minor" literature, must choose either to reflect the ideology that produces conventional expectations in their readers or to work against that ideology and those expectations in some way. Reading "as a writer," and reading as a writer situated in a complex set of cultural, critical, and historical contexts, allows Morrison to understand how language and literature project and reflect the structures of the social: "I began to see how the literature I revered, the literature I loathed, behaved in its encounter with racial ideology" (16). Using the metaphor of a fishbowl, she describes herself as suddenly seeing "the bowl, the structure that transparently (and invisibly) permits the ordered life it contains to exist in the larger world" (17). If it "takes hard work *not* to see this," then what is "hard" is that literary critics have also, in MacKinnon's terms, been "epistemologically passing"—as white and as male. "Objectivity" and "rationality" become values that express a particular standpoint and may also demonstrate efforts at "willful critical blindness," a resistance to the interpolation of the researcher/writer in the construction of knowledge.

Furthermore, as a writer contemplating her own readers, Morrison realizes that "until very recently . . . the readers of virtually all of American fiction have been positioned as white" (xii), and that therefore writers like Poe and Herman Melville had access to what she calls "metaphoric shortcuts" that are unavailable to her: "Neither blackness nor 'people of color' stimulates in me notions of excessive, limitless love, anarchy, or routine dread. I cannot rely on these metaphorical shortcuts because I am a black writer struggling with and through a language that can powerfully evoke and enforce hidden signs of racial superiority, cultural hegemony, and dismissive 'othering' of people and language which are by no means marginal or already and completely known and knowable in my work" (x). Thinking as a (black) writer rather than as a (white) reader gives her epistemic "privilege"; in beginning to read as a writer instead of as a reader, she becomes able to think from a standpoint in which blackness does not evoke metaphor but rather very material social being. However, it also means that she has no "shortcuts"; she must struggle "with and through" a language that itself may "evoke and enforce hidden signs" despite her own efforts to avoid such "metaphoric resonances of colonization" (Katrak 650).[6]

Finally, if the "fabrication of an Africanist persona is reflexive; an extraordinary meditation on the self," then coming to terms with such fabrication—the actual making of Africanist, and we would also argue, of female and of regional personae who can carry the fabricators' "fears and desires"—requires incorporating "self-reflexivity" into both research and critical practices. Morrison thus describes her project as "an effort to avert the critical gaze from the racial object to the racial subject; from the described and imagined to the describers and imaginers; from the serving to the served" (90). Shifting the center of perception is itself an attempt to encourage "self-reflexivity" in the reader. "Playing in the dark," writing out of the "gap," gaining "wisdom from vantage-points" and "thinking from women's lives" all share a common paradigm. Black and feminist standpoint theorists, as well as regionalist storytellers, all emphasize the need for situated knowledge and a shift in the critical gaze. Whether or not we may always already be discursively constructed as subjects within dominant forms, the existence of gaps gives marginalized persons standpoints within which to imagine maneuvering.

Location, Property, and Place

Playing in the Dark demonstrates how feminist standpoint theory can work in the context of literary texts, and for our purposes it provides an alternative way to think about regionalist epistemology. Just as Morrison discovered that as a black writer she could not use blackness as a metaphorical "shortcut" to literary authority or productivity or even subjectivity because "black" for her is not metaphoric but a feature of her lived material experience, regionalist writers could not use place as a metaphorical "shortcut" to ownership, either of property ("the plot of the novel is property" [Davis 201]) or authority or of their own subjectivity. Similar to Morrison's revelation in *Playing in the Dark* of her discovery that metaphors of blackness were unavailable to her, the regionalist writers discovered that, whatever their own personal access to wealth, they did not have access to metaphors of place and of location without coming up against their characters' dispossession.

In a literature that by virtue of its very interest in region leads many readers to expect place to be one of its salient organizing features, the lack of specific reference to place in many regionalist writers and the corollary focus on specific places that have remained generally uninhabited (Thaxter's Isles of Shoals, Austin's California desert) suggest that regionalist writers had a different relationship to place and to what Lennard Davis calls "location" as a convention of fictional narrative than did their realist contemporaries. Indeed, reading regionalist texts from the standpoint of the writer allows us to identify features of ideology that inform narrative strategies in realist fiction but that are missing from regionalist texts. Davis is quite helpful here in moving from Morrison's alternative epistemology to an analysis of regionalist literary and epistemological strategies. He argues: "Novelistic space as I will show is involved in a series of more or less hidden, ideological presuppositions about the nature of property and lands, foreign and domestic, the relationship of various races and classes to those lands, and the ways Europeans at various times found it necessary to represent, describe, and control terrains and property—their own as well as others. . . . In the simplest terms, locations are intertwined with ideological explanations for the possession of property" (54).

One of the most startling features of many regionalist texts is that characters do not derive their identity from the ownership of property and thus that their "locations" are not "intertwined with ideological explanations for the possession of property." This feature is particularly striking in light of the fact that the right of unmarried women to hold property had been established in the United States well before the nineteenth century, and, after 1848, this right began to extend to married women through the Married Women's Property Act, first in New York, and subsequently in other states. Yet despite the predominance of unmarried and widowed women in regionalist fiction, women do not appear in these texts as property owners, or, if they do, they own modest rural houses which they have inherited through the death of parents or husbands. In "A Mistaken Charity," for example, Freeman describes the house which Harriet and Charlotte Shattuck inhabit as "settling down and mouldering into the grass as into its own grave." With their parents dead, Harriet deaf and rheumatic, and Charlotte blind, "it was a small and trifling charity for the rich man who held a mortgage on the little house in which they had been born and lived all their lives to give them the use of it, rent and interest free. He might as well have taken credit to himself for not charging a squirrel for his tenement in some old decaying tree in his woods" (*AWR* 315). Freeman elaborates on the description of the house—it has holes in its roof, is overgrown with moss, and provides a haven for birds—but she emphasizes that the Shattuck sisters' ability to have their "own" house has nothing to do with the kind of power associated with property ownership. When the sisters are moved out of this house in an act of "mistaken charity" and taken to an "'Old Ladies' Home' in a neighboring city" (319), Freeman describes them as the victims of others' power. However, Harriet and Charlotte rebel, run away from the home, hang the "new white lace caps with which [they] had been so pestered" (321) on the bed posts, hitch a ride in a covered wagon, and manage to get back into the dilapidated house where they feel truly at home. Harriet's understanding of their behavior as a declaration of independence—"'I guess they'll see as folks ain't goin' to be made to wear caps agin their will in a free kentry'" (321)—has nothing to do with property ownership and everything to do with even propertyless persons' right to define and inhabit home.

Among the most intriguing stories about wealth, property, and dispossession is King's "The Old Lady's Restoration," in which the old lady is mysteriously "restored to her fortune" after having been deprived of it "so long ago that the real manner of her dispossession had become lost" (*AWR* 394). When the newspaper publishes the news of her restoration, those who had known her in a previous unspecified time ("so long ago") refurbish their affections for her and begin to anticipate sharing in her wealth. While it seems likely that King is using the theme of dispossession as a historical reference to plantations ruined and fortunes lost in the Civil War, her interest in this story lies in the knowledge one gains when one loses property. When "two of the clever-heads" become "determined to seek her out" to congratulate the old lady on her fortune's restoration, they discover the old lady in a space on the margins, at the "very extreme end" of an old, old—and apparently valueless—house:

> Provided with congratulatory bouquets, they set forth. It is very hard to find a dweller on the very sea-bottom of poverty. Perhaps that is why the effort is so seldom made. One has to ask at grocers' shops, groggeries, market-stalls, Chinese restaurants; interview corner cobblers, ragpickers, gutter children. But nothing is impossible to the determined. The two ladies overcame all obstacles, and needled their way along, where under other circumstances they would not have glanced, would have thought it improper to glance.
>
> They were directed through an old, old house, out on an old, old gallery, to a room at the very extreme end. (398)

As King's description reveals, the old lady lives within what feminist standpoint theorists identify as the gap between marginalized lives and the dominant conceptual frameworks. The "clever-heads," motivated by the chance of proximity to fortune and power, enter a world at which "under other circumstances they would not have glanced" because as upper-middle-class persons they need not and often literally do not see such places. But the old lady has apparently learned a great deal from her years of dispossession and abandonment by her former friends. The ending of the story defines regionalism as a propertyless condition and region itself as a location, space, and place that is disconnected from ownership. Indeed, King's story offers a critique of the way location functions in more conventional narratives that assume a connection between subjectivity and property ownership. Regionalism thus marks out its own territory, its own category of fictions that call attention to place, location, and implicitly the power of property, by writing out of the gap between the apparent connection of regionals to place and their lack of ownership or control of property in that place.

Regionalist writers appear to provide what Davis terms "a complex rendering of space" (53) but they do so in a way that represents the relationship between character and land as different from that of either owner or colonizer. As Davis elaborates the relationship between novelistic space and property, he writes, "the seemingly neutral idea that novels must take place in locations was actually part of a collective structure of defenses that gave eighteenth-century society a way to justify the ownership of certain kinds of property" (54). In the following discussion of Thaxter and Austin, we will examine the relationship between location and property in regionalist fictions. At the same time we are also exploring the degree to which regionalism offers an alternative standard for evaluating knowledge claims.

Questions of Knowledge and Ownership

Thaxter in *Among the Isles of Shoals* and Austin in *The Land of Little Rain* and *Lost Borders* do represent specific places in their work, and therefore we have chosen to examine the relationship between property, place, and home for these writers. *Among the Isles of Shoals* is a particularly interesting text to consider in the context of property ownership because Thaxter can be viewed as providing support for the claims of some recent critics who have argued that, instead of resisting imperialism, regionalism has been complicit in it. As we discussed in chapter 7, the idea that "regionalism performs a kind of literary tourism in a period that saw the tourist abroad and at home as a growing middle-class phenomenon" serves as an indictment of regionalists who "invent places as allegories of desire generated by urban centers" (A. Kaplan 252). Although Kaplan does not discuss Thaxter, Brodhead does, providing in brief the terms of what we assume to be Kaplan's critique:

> Celia Thaxter's 1873 serial *Among the Isles of Shoals* similarly memorializes the death of shipping activity in these islands off the coast of New Hampshire but then produces a second life for them through its prose, in which they are notable for their wind and light conditions, their austere landscape, and their superb birds and flowers. The fact that there was a tourist hotel on the Isle [*sic*] of Shoals founded by Thaxter's father and now largely run by her, and that in "naturalizing" the islands she has been covertly creating touristic desire to visit them, is concealed until Thaxter's last page. (*Cultures of Letters* 151)

Even though Thaxter's book does not focus on what she refers to there as the "house of entertainment" on the islands that her brothers owned and operated, with Celia's help in the summer months, its serial publication in the *Atlantic Monthly* in 1869–70 certainly would have introduced readers to the possibility of travel and stay in the Appledore Hotel, the first summer resort hotel on the New England coast (*AWR* 155). *Among the Isles of Shoals* probably did contribute to making the islands "suitable for a second-growth industry of aesthetic 'appreciation'" (Brodhead 151). Yet what Brodhead fails to point out is that Thaxter's relationship to the Isles of Shoals was not primarily or even secondarily economic. She did not own the business that may have benefited from her book nor was it her ownership of the islands that brought her there in the first place. She may not even have owned the cottage in which she lived during the summer and her relative poverty was always a determinant factor in her life decisions, leading her, for example, to undertake china painting as a means of support. When Thaxter wrote about the Isles of Shoals, she wrote not about a place she owned but about the place where she grew up and to which she continued to return.

Among the Isles of Shoals articulates an epistemology informed by Thaxter's childhood and lifelong experience on the Shoals for it constructs the way a female child can come to know the world when she is in some sense removed from the social constraints of gender. That is not to say that the young Celia Laighton escaped conventional female socialization. As we noted in chapter 6, Hawthorne described her as the "Miranda of the islands" for her early betrothal and marriage (in effect at age twelve, though she did not marry until sixteen) to the first male "creature" (of her own class) she had ever met, her Harvard-educated tutor, Levi Thaxter. However, she was not subject to restrictions on her activity or on what was appropriate for her to study other than the physical and cultural limitations of growing up in an environment the size of a small laboratory. On White Island she became a researcher in the natural world; later as the narrator of *Among the Isles of Shoals* she produced a text from the results of this research and what she learned in the process. As one who has studied the islands for most of her life, Thaxter claims knowledge rather than ownership. If "standpoint" and "location" are synonymous terms in feminist standpoint theory, they become so because, like Marx's proletariat, regionalist characters come to "own" their places only epistemologically, not as emerging capitalists.

One of the significant contributions Thaxter makes in *Among the Isles of Shoals* is to delineate research methods that work against the "conceptual imperialism" (D. Smith 88) of much sociological and scientific research. Thaxter's narrative anticipates, a century earlier, the language and concerns of the feminist standpoint theorists, for whom "thinking from women's lives" and from the perspective of the objects of research articulates a methodology informed by "strong objectivity" and "self-reflexivity" that researchers across a myriad of disciplines can implement. Thaxter's research leads her to ask questions that appear to emerge from the objects of her own study. In the following passage she describes how she engaged in her research: "I remember in the spring kneeling on the ground to seek the first blades of grass that pricked through the soil, and bringing them into the house to study and wonder over. Better than a shop full of toys they were to me! Whence came their color? How did they draw their sweet, refreshing tint from the brown earth, or the limpid air, or the white light? Chemistry was not at hand to answer me, and all her wisdom would not have dispelled the wonder" (*AWR* 178). Later in the passage she notices that the scarlet pimpernel, which she knew "by its homely name of poor-man's weather-glass," seems to know that rain is coming before she can detect a cloud in the sky and she writes, "How could it know so much? Here is a question science cannot answer" (178).

Thaxter's primary research method involves meticulous observation from the perspective of the objects of her research. She describes "ears made delicate by listening" (162) to the birds and to the sound of the waves on the island; and she writes of the weather, the northern lights, and the constellations that "all are noted with a love and careful scrutiny that is seldom given by people living in populous places" (165). In such observation, she developed an interest in particularity that connects her research method to the aesthetics we have described as the poetics of detail: "Each island has its particular characteristics" (161) and "I was led to consider every blade where there were so few" (179). Indeed, Thaxter situates her text at the intersection of scientific and artistic observation, writing from the perspective of the naturalist as she maps the topography, geology, botany, and marine biology of the islands; yet *Shoals* is foremost a literary creation.

As we noted in chapter 4, Thaxter brings her reader into her writing as if she is trying to teach the reader how to approach a text in the same way that the careful observer approaches research. "Sailing out from Portsmouth Harbor" the Isles of Shoals "lie straight before you, nine miles away,—ill-defined and cloudy shapes, faintly discernible in the distance." Yet "as you approach they separate, and show each its own peculiar characteristics, and you perceive that there are six islands if the tide is low; but if it is high, there are eight, and would be nine, but that a breakwater connects two of them" (157). She seems to be urging her reader, like the naturalistic researcher, to begin reading/research without any hypothesis concerning what he or she will find; and she notes that persons who visit the islands often reject their first impressions, making a distinction between first readings/observations and later ones: "At first sight nothing can be more rough and inhospitable than they appear" (159) but "[l]et him wait till evening comes, . . . and he will find himself slowly succumbing to the subtile charm of that sea atmosphere" (159). Yet she is also aware of the potential loneliness of both art and research—"Landing for the first time, the stranger is struck only by the sadness of the place,—the vast loneliness" (159)—and she also observes the cost of human intervention to the natural world—for example, she writes that "the lighthouse, so beneficent to mankind, is the destroyer of birds" (170).

In addition to observing what she is studying from the perspective of the object, she also develops a relationship with the objects of her study. For example, she describes her interest in the snowy owls that "haunt the islands the whole winter long." One March night she watches a particular owl, "his curious outline drawn black against the redness of the sky, his large head bent forward, and the whole aspect meditative and most human in its expression." She writes, "I longed to go out and sit beside him and talk to him in the twilight, to ask of him the story of his life, or, if he would have permitted it, to watch him without a word" (169). Thaxter's method resembles that of the geneticist Barbara McClintock, who learned by "listening" to the corn plants she was studying and by developing a "feeling for the organism" that enhanced her research results (see Keller, *Feeling*). Using other words for this kind of reflexivity, Haraway describes "the loving care people might take to learn how to see faithfully from another's point of view" (583). Thaxter writes that "all flowers had for me such human interest, they were so dear and precious" (*AWR* 180) and she develops "perpetual anxiety" that the family's cow might eat "one single root of fern, the only one within the circle of my little world" (180).

Thaxter engaged in what we might call qualitative naturalistic research: "We picked out from the kelp-roots a kind of star-fish which we called sea-spider; the moment we touched it an extraordinary process began. One by one it disjointed all its sections,—whether from fear or anger we knew not; but it threw itself away, bit by bit, until nothing was left of it save the little, round body whence the legs had sprung!" (177). Although she interacts with the marine creatures and the insects whom she calls her "friends and neighbors," she does not own the objects of her research: "we were never tired of watching the land-spiders that possessed the place" (177). The land-spiders, not the people, own the island. She tries to learn the language of the loon: "At one time the loon language was so familiar that I could almost always summon a considerable flock by going down to the water and assuming the neighborly and conversational tone which they generally use" (171).

In the arts and humanities, women's lives shape research in part through the writing of fictional and autobiographical narratives. Joan Hartman writes, "we construct ourselves as agents by piecing together our telling stories, by *emplotting* the events of our lives (to use Hayden White's term) in narratives that have explanatory power" (12). In narrating, marginalized storytellers speak from a subjugated standpoint, write "out of the gap," and thus discover agency in creating their own discursive authority. As bell hooks writes, "To make my voice, I had to speak, to hear myself talk" (5). Thaxter's text is autobiographical but she subsumes the story of her life in the process of studying the islands and discovering her own relationship to them. Within that world she finds her voice. But because her world is not a particularly social world, *Shoals* demonstrates what one female child can produce when she has not been taught that women cannot "do" science. As she merges feminist science with artistic expression she discovers her own voice, in language not unlike that which bell hooks uses a century later. She recalls a storm that produced a rainbow:

> I hid my face from the glory,—it was too much to bear. Ever I longed to *speak* these things that made life so sweet, to speak the wind, the cloud, the bird's flight, the sea's murmur. A vain longing! I might as well have sighed for the mighty pencil of Michael Angelo to wield in my impotent child's hand. Better to "hush and bless one's self with silence"; but ever the wish grew. . . . [B]y day or night, the manifold aspects of Nature held me and swayed all my thoughts until it was impossible to be silent any longer, and I was fain to mingle my voice with her myriad voices, only aspiring to be in accord with the Infinite harmony, however feeble and broken the notes might be. (*AWR* 183–84)

Thaxter's writing suggests a different relationship to place than that of ownership, a relationship connected to the inquisitive rather than the acquisitive, to epistemology and methodology rather than imperialism.

Like Thaxter, Austin also locates epistemology in the place she studies in her writing, but unlike Thaxter, who humanizes her relationship with the islands and their nonhuman plants and animals, Austin is interested in the California desert because it marks the limits of human and social habitation. Indeed, Austin's desert defies the colonizing impulse, inverts what scientists have called the natural order of things, and disrupts conventional expectations. Her writing throughout *The Land of Little Rain* and the stories in *Lost Borders* portrays whites as out of their element and beyond their knowledge in the desert and American Indians as knowing enough to keep a respectful distance or to be extremely careful in crossing the desert. Austin's desert thus represents her attempt to explore a land that will not be settled in a narrative that directly "unsettles" the relationship Davis describes as operative in realism between the novel, "plot," colonization, and property ownership.

The desert's ability to throw off human control even as it elicits a lust for ownership among the prospectors is a repeated theme in many of Austin's stories, as men's desire for gold and their belief in "lost mines" brings them to dehydration, death, and failure. In "The Return of Mr. Wills," for example, Austin portrays the West as far removed from "the church, public opinion, the social note" of life in the East, and she observes that "without these there are a good many ways of going to pieces. Mr. Wills's way was Lost Mines" (*AWR* 583). Life in the West, by which she means the California desert, underscores the obsession with getting rich off the land that also serves as "the baldest of excuses merely to be out and away from everything that savored of definiteness and responsibility" (585). Like a Western turn-of-the-century Rip Van Winkle, or more aptly, an ordinary man infected with the kind of desire turn-of-the-century American imperialism represented on a larger scale, Mr. Wills is motivated in a vulgar way by the gold-rush fever. Austin writes:

> To go out into the unmapped hills on the mere chance of coming across something was, on the face of it, a risky business; but to look for a mine once located, sampled and proved, definitely situated in a particular mountain range or a certain cañon, had a smack of plausibility. Besides that, an ordinary prospect might or might not prove workable, but the lost mines were always amazingly rich. Of all the ways in the West for a man to go to pieces this is the most insidious. Out there beyond the towns the long Wilderness lies brooding, imperturbable; she puts out to adventurous minds glittering fragments of fortune or romance, like the lures men use to catch antelopes—clip! then she has them. (583–84)

Austin's gold mines, especially the "lost mines," hold the lure that an explorer has already been there, the mine is "definitely situated," and the riches are there for the taking. But in Austin, men only succeed in getting rich in legends told at second and third hand. Mr. Wills, for example, leaves home for three years in a search for lost mines that proves futile. However, his absence gives his wife an opportunity to become self-reliant and to think hopefully about a future without her husband and his obsession. Austin invokes the language of the desert to describe Mrs. Wills's transformation from dependent to provider: "All up and down the wash of Salt Creek there were lean coyote mothers, and wild folk of every sort could have taught her that nature never makes the mistake of neglecting to make the child-bearer competent to provide" (586). But the lesson Mrs. Wills learns is lost on her husband. When Mr. Wills returns unexpectedly after his long absence, without gold, and "settled on his family like a blight" (587), he insists on taking up his position as head of household again, to his wife's dismay. As the story ends, Mrs. Wills takes up novel-reading and, "with something like hope in her eye," waits for her husband to become obsessed with another lost mine and to leave home again. "And this time, if I know Mrs. Wills," Austin's narrator writes, "he will not come back" (588). It is as if Mrs. Wills has read Davis and learned to take consolation from the novel's association between land and property—as if the novels themselves give her hope that her husband will not be able to continue inhabiting the land without locating again his desire to own it, a desire that, in the desert, can kill a man and leave a woman a relieved widow.

In *The Land of Little Rain,* Austin writes, "Not the law, but the land sets the limit. Desert is the name it wears upon the maps, but the Indian's is the better word. Desert is a loose term to indicate land that supports no man; whether the land can be bitted and broken to that purpose is not proven" (*AWR* 567). The desert, for Austin, represents a place where the usual rules do not apply. In the language of feminist standpoint theory, it is a "gap" location, a place in which it is possible to ask questions and develop a way of knowing that contradicts assumed sureties. Austin addresses her reader in the second person, as someone with a thirst for the desert's knowledge that recalls but is more authentic than Mr. Wills's gold fever. The gold mines are "often pure fakes" (584), but the person who goes to the desert to learn whatever lessons it has to teach will not be disappointed: "A land of lost rivers, with little in it to love; yet a land that once visited must be come back to inevitably. If it were not so there would be little told of it" (568).

One of the attractions of the desert for Austin is the way it humbles what passes for human control and contradicts what people believe they know. For example, she writes, "It is related that the final breakdown of that hapless party that gave Death Valley its forbidding name occurred in a locality where shallow wells would have saved them. But how were they to know that?" (568). What passes for knowledge elsewhere makes no sense in the desert: "There are hints to be had here of the way in which a land forces new habits on its dwellers. The quick increase of suns at the end of spring sometimes overtakes birds in their nesting and effects a reversal of the ordinary manner of incubation. It becomes necessary to keep eggs cool rather than warm" (570). The only way of surviving in the desert is to acquire local knowledge, primarily by studying the animals and plants that grow there. "The angle of the slope, the frontage of a hill, the structure of the soil determines the plant" and by learning to read the plants, "the best index the voiceless land can give the traveler of his whereabouts," it is possible "to go safely across that ghastly sink" (569).

Austin's sparsely populated landscape in *The Land of Little Rain* (1903) becomes more directly entangled with human life in her collection of stories, *Lost Borders* (1909). The opening essay of that collection, "The Land," further explores the relationship between land, property, and epistemology. She associates Indian habitation with land that whites would consider uninhabitable:

> The boundaries between the tribes and between the clans within the tribe were plainly established by natural landmarks—peaks, hillcrests, creeks, and chains of water-holes—beginning at the foot of the Sierra and continuing eastward past the limit of endurable existence. Out there, a week's journey from everywhere, the land was not worth parceling off, and the boundaries which should logically have been continued until they met the cañon of the Colorado ran out in foolish wastes of sand and inextricable disordered ranges. (*AWR* 588)

In this land of "lost borders," Austin terms the human inhabitants the "borderers," and much of her writing in this collection tests the limits of life and law for these persons.

Fundamentally what interests Austin is the way the white men who are attracted to the desert—"mind you, it is men who go mostly into the desert. . . . Their women hate with implicitness the life like the land" (591)—cannot achieve dominion over it, much less "own" it as property; she has already informed her reader that "out there, a week's journey from everywhere, the land was not worth parceling off." Since what passes for knowledge of the desert is frequently illusory, to explore the limits of the land's ability to sustain life is to discover the epistemology of human limitations. Austin's narrative takes "place" in the gap between what a man can know and what he can desire to know. She writes,

> First and last, accept no man's statement that he knows this Country of Lost Borders well. A great number having lost their lives in the process of proving where it is not safe to go, it is now possible to pass through much of the district by guide-posts and well-known water-holes, but the best part of it remains locked, inviolate, or at best known only to some far-straying Indian, sheepherder, or pocket hunter, whose account of it does not get into the reports of the Geological Survey. But a boast of knowledge is likely to prove as hollow as the little yellow gourds called apples of Death Valley. (591)

However, it is not just men's relationship with the desert that intrigues Austin. In one of her finest short narratives, "The Walking Woman," she explores the relationship between her apparently female and self-reflexive narrator and the woman known on the desert and in the mining camps only as "Mrs. Walker." The narrator traces her encounters with Walking Woman from "the first time of my hearing of her" (*AWR* 577) and, as we discussed in chapter 6, seems to find in the Walking Woman's story something that ratifies her own version of herself. Like the narrator, whose wanderings through the desert recall Austin's own, the Walking Woman "came and went about our western world on no discoverable errand, and whether she had some place of refuge where she lay by in the interim, or whether between her seldom, unaccountable appearances in our quarter she went on steadily walking, we never learned" (577). Unlike the men in Austin's tales, the Walking Woman is not looking for a lost mine; she is not a pocket hunter or a sheepherder—though she has had some experience with sheep, as she relates to the narrator; and she is in every way unconventional by Austin's reader's standards. Because she does not share any of the men's goals or conventional women's values, she seems to partake of epistemic "privilege." Living truly not only in the gap between "Mayfair" and "Maverick" (578) but surviving as one of the borderers in the uninhabitable land of little rain, she seems to possess a knowledge that the narrator is drawn to discover in her own encounters. Austin describes the Walking Woman as coming and going in "a kind of muse of travel which the untrammeled space begets, or at rare intervals flooding wondrously with talk, never of herself, but of things she had known and seen" (577). The Walking Woman has apparently witnessed a great deal and "if she had cared for it could have known most desirable things of the ways of trail-making, burrow-inhabiting small things" (578).

However, for the narrator "it was not, in fact, for such things I was wishful to meet her; and as it turned out, it was not of these things we talked when at last we came together" (578). What intrigues the narrator is that the Walking Woman has "gone about alone in a country where the number of women is as one in fifteen" and yet "through all this she passed unarmed and unoffended" (578). As an "unoffended" woman in a world of men, the Walking Woman generates conflicting reports: some say she is comely, others call her "plain to the point of deformity" (578). Above all, the Walking Woman does not fit any of the conventional categories by which women are judged: "On the mere evidence of her way of life she was cracked; not quite broken, but unserviceable. Yet in her talk there was both wisdom and information, and the word she brought about trails and water-holes was as reliable as an Indian's" (578).

When the narrator does have an opportunity to have a conversation with her, she asserts that though the "genius of talk" flowed smoothly, her narrative goes beyond report: "You are not to suppose that in my report of a Borderer I give you the words only, but the full meaning of the speech. Very often the words are merely the punctuation of thought; rather, the crests of the long waves of intercommunicative silences. Yet the speech of the Walking Woman was fuller than most" (579). What the narrator takes from the Walking Woman is her philosophy of life, what she has learned by living outside of convention. She tells the story of working side by side with a sheepherder named Filon, of Filon's departure in the fall, of the birth of a child, and of the child's early death. She is able to tell of the child at a moment when the narrator expresses what she calls an "unconscious throb of sympathy," uttering "'Ah-ah—!'" (582). The Walking Woman puts out her hand and touches the narrator: "'To work together, to love together,' said the Walking Woman, withdrawing her hand again; 'there you have two of the things; the other you know.' 'The mouth at the breast,' said I" (582). The Walking Woman has been able to experience what they agree are the three essential things in life without remaining restricted by convention. In effect, the story is about a woman who, refusing both bounds and bonds, removes herself as a candidate for colonization. She rejects the concept of herself as property: "She had walked off all sense of society-made values, and, knowing the best when the best came to her, was able to take it. Work—as I believed; love—as the Walking Woman had proved it; a child—as you subscribe to it" (582).

The Walking Woman turns epistemology into ontology, and the narrator concludes, "At least one of us is wrong. To work and to love and to bear children. *That* sounds easy enough. But the way we live establishes so many things of much more importance" (583). For the true borderers, the way of living becomes the way of knowing, and the best of both ontology and epistemology takes place in the gap, the space of contradictions. In the narrative's closing lines, the Walking Woman remains in that indeterminate space. As the narrator watches her walk away, "she had a queer, sidelong gait, as if in fact she had a twist all through her," but when the narrator runs down to the place where she had passed, "there in the bare, hot sand the track of her two feet bore evenly and white" (583). Long before Anzaldúa would identify the "borderlands" as "la frontera" of knowledge, what she calls the possibility of a "*mestiza* consciousness," Austin and her narrator traverse a country inhabited by "borderers" like the Walking Woman and find it a place in which it is possible to walk off "all sense of society-made values" and to discover how ways of living and ways of knowing complement each other. The country of lost borders is a place where neither land nor women can be forced to become property. In writing about this country, Austin eschews the conventions Davis describes as preconditions for the novel—"known unknown" place, character, dialogue, and plot. Instead Austin gives us an unknowable place, "borderers" that unsettle conventions of character, dialogue that at its best becomes "intercommunicative silences," and no plot at all in the usual sense.

In the gaps between readers' expectations of what they will encounter in fiction and the kinds of narratives regionalist writers tell instead, regionalism can be said to "take place," not as an assumed ownership but rather as the construction of an epistemological and ontological "home" for women, borderers, and other socially disenfranchised beings. Thus, though Thaxter and Austin present very different understandings of the relationship between the places in their narratives and the epistemology that inhabiting those places educes, both the Isles of Shoals and the California desert, locations that can be visited and viewed on a map, serve to dislocate the conventions of reading that Davis associates with the novel. Because they come as close as any regionalist narratives to taking place in a real location, Thaxter's and Austin's texts best illustrate what the representation of place means for regionalist writers. Since regions can only be locally known, they exist in a borderland, a gap between the dominant conceptual frameworks for ruling and ordering—whether the object of colonization is other people's land or other people's stories—and the lived experience of regional people. While in the ordered world of the nineteenth-century realist novel, as Davis observes, "these places, that pretend to be open spaces of the real, are actually claustrophobic encampments of the ideological" and "as such they are not ancillary to but the absolute concomitant of the novel's discourse" (101), in the borderlands of regionalist narrative characters, narrators—and readers—can briefly move around in a space which is not owned.

Transitivity and the Transversal

Although we have argued that regionalism disrupts the connection between place and property and thus to some extent can be said to represent a world prior to capitalism and therefore premodern in the historical materialist meaning of that term, we do not thus conclude that "'region' first appears as a projection of a desire for a space outside of history, untouched by change" (A. Kaplan 252), or, for the "tourist" reader, a "projection of the outsider's desire to view his or her life as less confining, more sophisticated and 'adult'" (253). That the late nineteenth-century urban reader may have desired such a space and projected that desire onto "region" is not itself an idea we would contest; what we find in our readings of the texts, however, is that regionalist writers knew that regions exist in relation to urban centers and, as we discussed in chapter 7, to concepts of "nation," and that regionalist writers wrote against the tendency of urban readers to create regions as a "space outside of history" and to project their desires onto regional persons and places.

Kaplan chooses Jewett's *The Country of the Pointed Firs* as her primary example of the text that constructs a tourist-narrator who can always "go home" to Boston. However, we believe it is reductive to read Jewett's unnamed narrator simply as an urban dweller in search of escape, "a quiet retreat where she can meet her publishing deadline" (252). As we have argued elsewhere (see Pryse, "Sex, Class"), Jewett, herself a hybrid who lived seasonally in her native village of South Berwick, Maine, and her adopted urban Boston, where she shared Annie Fields's house and life, is interested in what Eve Sedgwick has called "transitivity," which in Jewett becomes the ability of her narrators and characters to move back and forth across the borders that separate not only regions but also economic classes (*Epistemology* 88). Jewett's narrator inhabits a space that cannot be mapped, for it is a psychological space. In effect, Jewett's narrator develops a *mestiza* standpoint, not unlike Jewett's own, which makes her much more than a tourist in either of her worlds but always an outsider as well. In a letter to Charles Miner Thompson dated October 12, 1904, Jewett responds to an essay he has written about her work in the *Atlantic.* She writes, "It was hard for this person (made of Berwick dust) to think of herself as a 'summer visitor,' but I quite understand your point of view; one may be away from one's neighborhood long enough to see it quite or almost from the outside, though as I make this concession I remember that it was hardly true at the time of 'Deephaven'" (*Sarah Orne Jewett Letters* 196–97). It is "hard" for Jewett to "think of herself as a 'summer visitor'" even though she was "away from [her] neighborhood" in South Berwick, Maine, for long periods of time, spending much of the year with Annie Fields in Boston; it is equally difficult for Jewett's narrator in *The Country of the Pointed Firs* to negotiate the complexities of moving between region and urban center. While in Dunnet Landing, the narrator believes she can throw off her "outsider" status and become "near to feeling like a true Bowden" (*Country of the Pointed Firs* 110), but upon her departure from Dunnet Landing, she discovers that she is returning home "to the world in which I feared to find myself a foreigner" (129). In *A Country Doctor,* the only fiction in which Jewett constructs a character who moves in the reverse pattern, that is, who leaves the rural region where she grew up in order to spend time with wealthier urban-connected relatives as a "tourist" from rural life, her main character, Nan Prince, chooses to return to her region and to imagine herself becoming, like her mentor, a "country" doctor. In this novel, Nan Prince explores what it means to be an outsider in a more cosmopolitan setting and, while Nan's movement seems more recognizable than that of Jewett's narrator in *The Country of the Pointed Firs,* as an earlier exploration of the problem of movement across class and regional lines it suggests that "tourism" is a complex phenomenon and that "transitivity" is one of Jewett's most complex thematic explorations (see Pryse, "'I was country'").

While Jewett herself was aware of the limitations of regional life, writing in the essay "Outgrown Friends" of her sadness and confusion that books, persons, and by implication places were all subject to being "outgrown," she returned in her fiction to her Maine region as if, as she expresses it in the opening passages of *The Country of the Pointed Firs,* knowing a village "is like becoming acquainted with a single person. The process of falling in love at first sight is as final as it is swift in such a case, but the growth of true friendship may be a lifelong affair" (1–2). For Jewett, the "lifelong affair" requires ongoing dialogue, which she represents in her fiction as movement across class and regional borders. Jewett's transitivity, or what Nira Yuval-Davis, building on work by Patricia Hill Collins and the Italian feminists Raphaela Lambertini and Elizabetta Dominini, terms "transversal" movement, is an approach "based on the epistemological recognition that each positioning produces specific situated knowledge which cannot be but an unfinished knowledge, and therefore dialogue among those differentially positioned should take place in order to reach a common perspective" (88). Transitivity is Jewett's solution to her grief at the phenomenon of "outgrown friends"; her movement across geographical and emotional borders during the more than quarter of a century in which she and Annie Fields lived in relation to each other recognized the standpoint epistemology of situated or "local" positioning, and recognized it as well as always unfinished, developing, in process. Long before modernists would celebrate "nomadic" writing, Jewett took her inspiration from always being in transit.

Yuval-Davis's description of "transversal dialogue" further clarifies the meaning of Jewett's transitivity—indeed, establishes Jewett quite literally as a "pivotal" figure at the turn of the twentieth century in terms of her exploration of the multiple meanings of female subjectivity. Yuval-Davis writes, "Transversal dialogue should be based on the principles of rooting and shifting—that is, being centred in one's own experiences while being empathetic to the differential positionings of the partners in the dialogue, thus enabling the participants to arrive at a different perspective from that of hegemonic tunnel vision" (88). These techniques of "rooting and shifting," or of pivoting between alternate and sometimes contradictory standpoints in recognition of the multiplicity of one's subject position, promote dialogue, and "dialogue, rather than fixity of location, becomes the basis of empowered knowledge" (129). When critics expose Jewett for her upper-class elitism and describe Jewett's narrator in *The Country of the Pointed Firs* as a "tourist," they fail to move with Jewett beyond "fixity of location" as the basis for a feminist subjectivity. Jewett's interest, and the interest of other regionalist writers, in the premodern, the preindustrial, the precapitalist, the prenational formations that regional characters often appear to inhabit does much more than provide for urban readers an escape from the "claustrophobic encampments of the ideological," to recall Davis's phrase; it keeps open the possibility of multiple subjectivities and the concomitant necessity of learning transitivity, the transversal "rooting," "shifting," and pivoting that moves beyond the ruling and ordering of the realist novel's narration and, like Austin's Walking Woman, walks off "all sense of society-made values" (*AWR* 582).

CHAPTER 9

Race, Class, and Questions of Region

It was no wonder Mr. Sublet, who was staying at the Hallet plantation, wanted to make a picture of Evariste. The 'Cadian was rather a picturesque subject in his way, and a tempting one to an artist looking for bits of "local color" along the Têche.

—Kate Chopin, "A Gentleman of Bayou Têche"

Intersections

When we have given presentations from the material in this book, we have often been asked whether or not the women of color we have termed regionalist would have accepted that term and to what extent the category "region" complicates or obscures the work these women did to bring race into visibility as a concern for their readers. For each of the three women of color we included in *American Women Regionalists,* external evidence suggests that they did recognize the value of writing from their regions, a recognition they shared with the white writers in the tradition. For example, Paul Laurence Dunbar first encouraged Alice Ruth Moore (later Dunbar-Nelson) to write by invoking the example of Grace King (Metcalf 80). Dunbar-Nelson's collection of stories, *The Goodness of St. Rocque,* was published as a "companion volume" to Dunbar's *Poems of Cabin and Field* and in it, according to Gloria Hull, she is "exploiting the local-color literary tradition popular at the time" (49, 50), a tradition that Hull identifies as "associated with women" and that includes writers we label regionalists (Hull refers specifically to Chopin and Jewett). Zitkala-Ša chose to write for the *Atlantic Monthly* and *Harper's,* both magazines that published numerous regional writers. Sui Sin Far published her earliest Chinese stories in *The Land of Sunshine,* a California magazine edited by Charles Lummis, who became her literary mentor. In advertisements and articles he himself wrote for his magazine, Lummis expressed his interest in publishing "'the best Western literature'" as well as unknown "'writers of promise,'" including both Sui Sin Far and Mary Austin, and the journal emphasized local-color writing (White-Parks 86–87).[1] Whether or not the three writers of color we anthologize in *American Women Regionalists* would have accepted the term, it seems evident that without the interest in local-color and regional writing at the end of the nineteenth century, editors would not have published their work.[2] Writing under the sign of region, then, gave these writers an opportunity, however limited, to bring issues of importance to them to the attention of readers, issues that included race.

The question concerning the extent to which writing as a regionalist complicates or obscures efforts to write about race is a question we have asked about the white women in our study as well as the women of color. As Ruth Frankenberg observes in an early contribution to "whiteness" studies, "it has . . . for the most part been Other, marked subjects rather than white/Western, unmarked subjects whose racial and cultural identities have been the focus of study" (17). Yet regionalism portrays hardly any subjects that are not "other" and "marked"; as we will discuss in chapter 10, the cultural, linguistic, and regional differences that characterize these subjects render them "queer" to urban readers. Regionalism therefore calls attention to the way regional identities themselves complicate racial identity for white characters as well as for characters of color. In chapter 1, we suggested regionalism itself as a productive site of inquiry for "whiteness" studies to the extent that regionalist writers, unlike local-color writers, set up conditions for empathy to cross lines of race, class, gender, and region. Although as Frankenberg discovered, "interviews [with a group of thirty white women] did *not,* for example, suggest that one experience of marginality—Jewishness, lesbianism—led white women automatically toward empathy with other oppressed communities" (20), we will conclude our discussion by arguing in chapter 11 that regionalism attempts to "teach" its readers such empathy, necessary in order for white urban readers to begin to engage in white critique.

Given our analysis of nation, region, and empire in chapter 7, we can speculate further that the kind of white nationalism that emerged in the second half of the nineteenth century may also have led urban readers to use the "queer" characters they found in local color to construct themselves as "white." Frankenberg, outlining the dimensions that give shape to whiteness, observes that whiteness "is a 'standpoint,' a place from which white people look at ourselves, at others, and at society" (1). To the extent, as we have argued in chapter 8, that regionalism constructs a "standpoint" epistemology located in the subject position of the "queer," it also reveals whiteness itself to be a standpoint constructed against the "otherness" of characters a late nineteenth-century white reader would have found in both local-color and regional fiction. In a post–Civil War climate of social and legal pressure to enforce essentialist binaries, culminating in the 1896 *Plessy v. Ferguson* Supreme Court decision, however, regionalism's empathic representations of characters who are elsewhere "othered" and who also resist various kinds of binary categorization kept open a space of critique in which constructions of the "other" and of the process of "othering" could be questioned. In so doing, it may have offered certain writers of color, including Chesnutt, as well as certain of the white women writers anthologized in *American Women Regionalists,* a sense of a possible literary site for explorations of race, and of the way racial identity intersects with class, that also included white critique.

Indeed, in regionalist fiction race becomes inextricably intertwined with class, and various critics have become aware of this intertwining. For example, Hull reads Dunbar-Nelson as interested in class issues as well as race issues, though Hull also suggests that attention to class differences may in some texts stand in for attention to race. She writes, "Dunbar-Nelson's continued attention to class and class conflict makes one wonder whether she used class as a psychological metaphor to replace race in her writings. Since she was not always able, for a variety of internal and external reasons, to express buried racial feeling, portraying opposing classes may have been her way—perhaps unconsciously—of hinting at group differences and hierarchical oppression" (55). While we are not suggesting that "buried racial feeling" occupies white writers to the extent that Hull suggests it does for Dunbar-Nelson, we do find in their work some of the same uses of class analysis to analyze "group differences and hierarchical oppression" across racial lines.

While the categories of race and class are not interchangeable, they complicate each other for both white writers and writers of color in ways that we have not found in local-color writing. In this chapter, we begin by discussing the work of those writers from a region, New Orleans, arguably more aware of issues of race than class. We then turn to writers for whom class constitutes a primary category of concern. As readers will discover, however, these distinctions are more relative than absolute; in regionalist fictions questions of race and class are complexly intertwined and it is difficult to discuss the one without discussing the other. Thus our discussion of issues of race leads inevitably to our discussion of issues of class, which in turn leads us back to issues of race.

Race and Class in New Orleans Regionalists

Although it may well be the case, as we suggested in chapter 1, that African American women wrote regionalist fiction for the numerous African American periodicals that developed after the war, the only African American woman to publish such fiction in book form and to gain a reputation from it was Dunbar-Nelson. We might infer from this that African Americans did not perceive in regionalism a particularly effective form for doing the work either of racial uplift or of anti-racism. Indeed, while Dunbar-Nelson embeds issues of race in her fiction to a far greater extent than do white writers of regionalist fiction, she does so with an indirection and subtlety that distinguishes her work from that of writers such as Frances Harper or Pauline Hopkins who are her contemporaries. In part she was constrained by the views of Northern editors like Bliss Perry of the *Atlantic Monthly* who, in response to her proposal to expand "The Stones of the Village" into a novel, "offered his opinion that at present the American public had a 'dislike' for treatment of 'the color-line'" (Hull 57). Yet what made regionalism attractive to Dunbar-Nelson may well have been the possibility it offered of a space to be "free to say" a great deal about race but not only about race, and about race unconstrained by any particular political agenda. We find evidence in the first letter she wrote to Dunbar that she associated writing fiction about "folk characters" with a certain discursive freedom. She declared that she hadn't "much liking for those writers that wedge the Negro problem and social equality and long dissertations on the Negro in general into their stories. . . . Somehow when I start a story I always think of my folk characters as simple human beings, not as types of a race or an idea, and I seem to be on more friendly terms with them" (Metcalf 38). However, though she may have viewed regionalist fiction as a space in which she was free to write about subjects other than race and to write about race indirectly, Dunbar-Nelson nevertheless uses regionalist fiction to do the work of racial analysis and to encode her own sympathies.

The title story of her major collection of regionalist fiction suggests how one can read a story lacking obvious markers of race, whose characters might perhaps be seen as "white," as in fact a story about racial hierarchies. Indeed, unless read in this way, "The Goodness of St. Rocque" might well seem incoherent, for both the tall dark Manuela and the petite blonde Claralie pray to the same saint and invoke his power on their behalf; the triumph of the former and the defeat of the latter render "goodness" meaningless unless we accord a positive value to favoring the dark over the light. Although both Manuela and Claralie belong to the same Creole culture and thus most readers will presume them to be white, Theophilé's sudden preference for the blonde Claralie, whose name underscores her racialization, reflects the degree to which whiteness is conventionally understood and here marked as making women more desirable. Manuela's own racialization as "black" emerges from the fact that she does not pray solely to St. Rocque; she also has recourse to "the Wizened One," an old woman whose relation to voodoo and whose own yellow color associate her with African peoples and culture. Thus Manuela finally triumphs because she has access to "black" arts, and the goodness of St. Rocque rests in his being, unbeknown to Claralie, also a "black" god whose power is greater than the racism that leads Theophilé to defect, temporarily, from the dark woman to the blonde one.

We can also read "Mr. Baptiste" as a story in which a secret sympathy for, even identification with, the "black" emerges in a moment of crisis. Although presumably Creole, given the Irishman's reference to him as "'that damned fruit-eatin' Frinchman'" (*AWR* 474), Mr. Baptiste has no easily identifiable cultural or racial location. He comes from nowhere and goes nowhere and no one even knows his "real" name. He makes a living picking up fruit too spoiled for commercial use but not too spoiled to bring to the back door of some woman who will fix him a meal in exchange. When the Irish longshoremen go out on strike to protest being asked to work with "niggers," Mr. Baptiste is unwittingly caught up in a race war. Perhaps because the strike cuts off his source of food, Mr. Baptiste expresses antipathy to the Irishmen. Yet the act of identification that costs him his life seems to come from a deeper source. Hearing the sound of the Negro workers unloading the boats, the Irish strikers roar, "'Niggers! niggers! Kill 'em, scabs!'" (473). In choosing to cheer on the Negroes in an environment of such overt racial hostility, Mr. Baptiste may be acknowledging a secret racial identity elicited only in response to and in defiance of such hatred. Struck in the head by a brickbat hurled by an enraged Irish striker, Mr. Baptiste is surely killed for being "black," one "nigger" they can easily reach.

In the context of "Sister Josepha," however, such a racially marked and racially located death may be preferable to a life lived without even a despised identity, for what possibilities exist for one with "'no name but Camille'" (*AWR* 479)? Planning her escape from the suffocating environment of the convent, Sister Josepha pauses when she overhears the others discussing "'how hard it would be for her in the world, with no name but Camille, no friends, and her beauty'" (*AWR* 479). In this context "beauty" can be read as a racial mark for it points to the stereotype of the beautiful quadroon or octoroon, but with no name or history to give her even that social location, she has no choice but to remain in the convent. To be in the "world," one must be "raced," and in a world where so much depends upon race, not having a specific racial identity may be the worst oppression of all.[3]

In her longest fiction, "The Stones of the Village," Dunbar-Nelson explores this oppression in depth. For Victor Grabért, the lack of any recognized racial or cultural identity produces a state of total isolation. Prohibited from playing with "niggers," yet despised by the boys "whose faces were white like his own," he suffers abuse from all the boys, white, black, and yellow, who follow him with jeers of "white nigger" (*AWR* 483). Knowing nothing of his origins, Victor does not know who he is. His grandmother refuses to let him play with "niggers" but she offers no explanation for her refusal or for the question he is too afraid to ask as he looks up into her brown face surrounded by "a wealth of curly black hair" (483). "No one ever spoke to him of a father" (482), nor of the mother who died a few months after his birth. Although such ignorance may seem unrealistic, we understand it as a rhetorical strategy designed to provoke the reader into recognizing the arbitrariness of race. By refusing to participate in the fixing of race, Dunbar-Nelson proposes that, while race determines everything, it does not in fact exist. Although Victor lives in constant fear of exposure, a fear so intense it finally kills him, we do not know any more than he what there is to expose. In this sense Victor serves as a symbol for Americans in general, a reminder that given the history of racial mixing in the South and in the North as well, Americans may know less than they think about their own origins. The family Victor marries into shows a remarkable, and again unrealistic, willingness to accept him without any knowledge of his background. Equally provocative, their behavior suggests a secret acknowledgment of the wisdom of not inquiring too closely into anyone's background, including their own. Indeed Victor's terror in Dunbar-Nelson's story comes to mirror a terror at the heart of post-*Plessy* America, a terror not so much of the possibility that white might turn out to be black or black white, but of the possibility that the categories themselves are an illusion, the ultimate social fiction. If Victor Grabért's way of dealing with this terror is to develop a racism so severe that nothing escapes it, to become a judge who spends his days implementing laws that reinforce this fiction—"The law was very explicit about the matter. The only question lay in proving the child's affinity to the Negro race" (495)—then in Dunbar-Nelson's analysis racism itself becomes a defensive reaction to the arbitrariness of racial identity. Anticipating Morrison's argument in *Playing in the Dark,* Dunbar-Nelson recognizes blackness as the product of a whiteness that does not itself exist.

In the regionalist fiction of Kate Chopin, questions of race become inseparable from questions of class in those stories that include Cajun characters. Significantly, these complications enable Chopin to move beyond an otherwise uncritical approach to representations of African Americans that characterize those fictions that do not include Cajun characters. For example, Chopin does not problematize her portrait of Aunt Pinky in "Odalie Misses Mass." In this story, a white child refuses to abandon her "old friend and protegée" (*AWR* 426) who has been left alone on the morning of the Assumption mass and who dies by the end of the white child's visit. Although Aunt Pinky confuses Odalie with Paulette, another white child whose kindness once kept her from being sold and "who seemed to have held her place in old Pinky's heart and imagination through all the years of her suffering life" (429), the story focuses on a relationship informed by empathy, which we have identified as central to the poetics of regionalism. Yet Chopin does not question the politics of such empathy when it occurs in the context of race and class power, nor does she question the degree to which such empathy is a luxury of skin and class privilege. Despite Chopin's inattention to the lives of the mostly nameless women of color who move in and out of the pages of *The Awakening,* the novel's radical position on gender, its relentless critique of the "mother-woman" as a social role in Southern society, and its representation of female sexuality have led Chopin's critics to evade the "full implications" of her racism (H. Taylor 155). While we are not interested in contributing to such evasion, we do find, in her exploration of Cajun life, that Chopin reveals an interest in the ways class and race intersect to create social categories that are far from distinct and rigid. Moreover, Chopin openly acknowledges that African Americans are part of the drama of her region and she frequently gives them voice as well as name in her Cajun stories if not in *The Awakening.*

In Chopin's representation, the class position of Cajuns seems inextricably connected to their brownness. When the upper-class Creole Alcée Laballière in "At the 'Cadian Ball" tells Bruce, his Negro servant, that he needs a "'li'le fling'" after a hurricane has destroyed his entire crop of rice, he goes for his fling across what can be construed as race as well as class lines. Although Calixta, the Cajun woman he would like to seduce (and later does, in the story "The Storm"), is presumably white—indeed only "whites" are allowed at the ball—the narrative makes reference to her kinky hair and suggests that this racial mark forms part of her erotic appeal: "He caught a wisp of her kinky hair that had escaped its fastening, and rubbed the ends of it against his shaven cheek" (*AWR* 415). When his cousin Clarisse, whom he later marries, shows up to "save" him from himself and for her, she does so armed with the power of class understood as white. Her name associates her with whiteness and so does her appearance, as Bruce believes he is seeing a ghost when she first accosts him to find out where Alcée has gone. Moreover, Clarisse carefully refers to Calixta as "mon enfant," while Calixta addresses her as "mam'zelle," a distinction operative in contexts of race as well as class (417). Indeed in this story Chopin recognizes the powerful roles class and race play in shaping the emotions associated with gender, or, to put it slightly differently, she recognizes the role race and class play in the construction of the erotic: Alcée desires Clarisse, Calixta desires Alcée, and Bobinôt desires Calixta, whose desire for Alcée marks her off from others of her class and race. Only Bobinôt, among the darkest of those men allowed to attend the dance, seems excluded from the erotics energized by hierarchies of race and class.

Chopin's exploration of race and class in the figure of the Cajun allows her to experiment as well with the figure of the white woman. In most regionalist fiction white women represent those values we can summarize as empathic caring; in Chopin's fiction, however, Cajun men primarily represent these values. Because Chopin writes about a culture obviously structured by class as well as race hierarchies, one that cannot, like New England, be even imaginatively projected as classless, she can identify gender privilege with class and race privilege and thus can construct Cajun men as different from upper-class white men. We see this quite clearly in "Ozème's Holiday" as Ozème puts aside his own long-anticipated holiday to stay with Aunt Tildy and Sandy until both are well and the cotton crop picked. Similarly, though Bobinôt loves Calixta, his attitude toward her in "At the 'Cadian Ball" seems more maternal than erotic, and in "The Storm" he acts the part of a mother to his son.

Given the existence of Cajun men willing to do the work of empathic caring, certain women in Chopin's fiction become free to explore regions of the self not accessible to women in other regionalist fictions. In both "Lilacs" and "The

Storm," as well as in *The Awakening,* women express a sexuality absent from most regionalist writing. In "The Storm" Bobinôt's obvious and maternal care for Bibi allows Calixta to discover her sexuality with Alcée free from worry about her child; free to be sexual because not solely maternal, Calixta can enjoy the masculinity Alcée possesses by virtue of the privilege of his class and race without having to suffer from his demands. Clarisse, for whom "the first free breath since her marriage seemed to restore the pleasant liberty of her maiden days," becomes only too happy to forgo for awhile "their intimate conjugal life" (*AWR* 451). As for Bobinôt, his tenderness earns him those domestic pleasures that seem to matter most to him, for when he and Calixta and Bibi sit down to enjoy the feast she has made from the food he has brought, "they laughed much and so loud that anyone might have heard them as far away as Laballière's" (451). Chopin takes advantage of a rich and intricate mix of race, class, and gender constructs to blur conventional distinctions and create alternate possibilities.

In "A Gentleman of Bayou Têche," Chopin locates knowledge of the way class operates in the figure of a black woman and indicates how race crosses and complicates structures of class and how class traverses and equally complicates structures of race. Although Martinette may occupy a higher social position than Aunt Dicey by virtue of her race, despite the latter's better economic position, and may feel herself superior to Aunt Dicey, Aunt Dicey knows herself to be superior to Martinette in understanding. Declaring Martinette and her father to be "'bof de simplest somebody I eva come 'crost'" (*AWR* 422), Aunt Dicey explains that the artist Sublet wishes to make a picture of Martinette's father as a bit of "local color" picked up in his wanderings along the Têche, an example of the "queer" and simple sort of folks one finds when one goes to an out-of-the-way place. While Sublet probably does not intend to put the words "'Dis heah is one dem low-down 'Cajuns o' Bayeh Têche'" underneath the picture, that is only because he does not need to, since the picture he wants of Evariste, "'like I come out de swamp,'" and the magazine in which he intends to place it will say it for him (422). How does Aunt Dicey know this? She knows this because Mr. Sublet's son has treated her disrespectfully, coming into her cabin and wanting to take her picture at the ironing board instead of asking for her portrait in her new dress and the good bonnet she wears to "meetin'." In rejecting his request, Aunt Dicey insists upon her own right to be seen as occupying a respectable class position, superior perhaps to Martinette and Evariste, and refuses to be constructed as lower class simply because of her race. In this boy, too little to be safe alone in a boat, Aunt Dicey recognizes the sense of entitlement, the belief in the power and right to place that comes when male gender, white race, and superior class privilege are conjoined. While she claims that his behavior shows he doesn't know his place, we can read in it evidence that he knows his place only too well. Given this fact, there is no guarantee that the boy's father will honor Evariste's desire to be represented as a "gentleman" no matter what he wears for his picture since it is Sublet who finally controls the technology of representation. Chopin, however, chooses to use her own access to publication to critique those modes of representation that serve the ideology of local color, that reinforce and simplify class and race hierarchies, and that seek to fix people in their place.

King's New Orleans: Race, Class, and "Whiteness"

In adopting a strategy for publishing fiction in the North that opens a space for her to write critically of both the South and the North, King is not unlike Dunbar-Nelson, who, in order to write about race in Northern periodicals, had to write about Creoles. Yet King's strategy has often led critics to assume that her work reinscribes a conservative Southern racial agenda. In an essay critiquing King, for example, Lori Robison alludes to the problematic origins of King's career as a writer of regionalist fiction. Asked by Richard Watson Gilder, editor of the *Century,* "one of the literary journals that was responsible for encouraging and sustaining the late-nineteenth-century local color movement" (Robison 54), to explain "the inimical stand taken by the people of New Orleans against George [Washington] Cable and his works" (King, *Memories* 60), King replied, "I hastened to enlighten him to the effect that Cable proclaimed his preference for colored people over white and assumed the inevitable superiority—according to his theories—of the quadroons over the Creoles. He was a native of New Orleans and had been well treated by its people, and yet he stabbed the city in the back, as we felt, in a dastardly way to please the Northern press" (60). In response, Gilder asks King, "'Why, if Cable is so false to you, why do not some of you write better?'" and King recalls that after a sleepless night in which she asked herself, "Why, why, do we not write our side?" she began "Monsieur Motte" in the morning (60–61). According to Robison, "writing 'our side' is finally a hegemonic project" that "implicitly represent[s] a white, upper-middle-class retelling of regional politics that serves to reinscribe harmful stereotypes of African Americans" (55).

In light of the fact that both Chesnutt in *Paul Marchand, F.M.C.* and Dunbar-Nelson in "The Praline Woman" appear to rely on King's 1895 *New Orleans: The Place and the People,* we propose a reconsideration and a rereading of King's treatment of race. King's book includes extensive descriptions of the life of the *gens de couleur,* or persons of color, and offers what Chesnutt calls one of the "careful studies of life in the old Creole city" (*Paul Marchand* 3).[4] Although King is commonly understood, even by the editor of *Paul Marchand, F.M.C.,* to *mis*understand race relations in the South,[5] it is significant that *New Orleans* was reprinted in 1968 by Negro Universities Press. Of particular interest to us, as we have mentioned in chapters 1 and 4, is the fact that both *Paul Marchand, F.M.C.* and "The Praline Woman" include a character based on the historical figure King describes at length. Because King's work has clearly served as a specific source for both Chesnutt and Dunbar-Nelson, we can only assume that at least for some

African American writers early in the twentieth century, King's portraits of the complexity of racial definition and mixed-race relations in New Orleans at the turn of the nineteenth century have been considered accurate.

King's description of the "praline woman" is worth quoting at length and comparing with Dunbar-Nelson's in "The Praline Woman," which we discussed in chapter 4:

> No relation of the city in the first quarter of the century is complete without Elizabeth, or "Zabet Philosophe," who was as much a part of the *vieux carré* as the Cabildo [the town hall] was. She always maintained her age at the current standard of a hundred. She was born in the house of the widow of an officer who had served under Bienville; and, a pet of her mistress, had been freed by will, and since then had made her living as hairdresser to the aristocratic ladies in the city, her last patron being Madame Laussat. No Frenchman in the community suffered more than she did when the French flag was lowered to the American. She wept bitterly. Being told that the new government had proclaimed that all white men were free and equal, she ceased to be a menial, and took to selling pralines on the steps of the cathedral, or under the porch of the Cabildo, where she could see her friends, the judges and lawyers, as they passed on their way to court; and they seldom failed to loiter around her tray to provoke from her the shrewd comments, piquante stories and picturesque tales which won her the surname of Philosophe. She could neither read nor write, but she spoke pure, elegant French, as the court of the Grand Monarque did, by ear, and to her blue-blooded patrons she used her best language and all the high-flown courtesy of the old regime, and was profuse in well-set phrases of thanks when their silver pieces fell in her tray; common customers she treated with careless indifference. When court and cathedral closed, she would take up her place in the Place d'Armes, and pass the evening promenaders in review, recalling aloud this about their parents and grandparents, reminding them of one story and another, complimenting the ladies and petting the children of her old people, as she called them. General Jackson, in 1815, shook hands with her and gave her a dollar. (341–42)

Dunbar-Nelson excludes Zabet Philosophe's ancestry—and name—from her sketch and revises the praline woman's relation to her customers but includes her deference to her social superiors, King's "blue-blooded patrons." Chesnutt adds a Haitian lineage for Zabet Philosophe in *Paul Marchand, F.M.C.,* as we noted in chapter 4, and expands the character in his novel. Moreover, Chesnutt draws on King's descriptions for his chapter "The Quadroon Ball," makes use of her extensive history of the "old duelling ground" called the Oaks (*New Orleans* 292–99) for his chapter "The Duel," and echoes her treatment of *gens de couleur* in the *ancien régime,* suggesting that he, like Dunbar-Nelson, found King's work to be more the product of the dispassionate historian than that of the Southern apologist.[6]

Thus, while we find Robison's analysis to be thought-provoking, and while even Helen Taylor, who attempts the most complex reading of the ways gender, race, and region intersect in King's work, suggests that King as well as Chopin held conservative views that did not challenge dominant Southern ideology, we find King's approach to race to be more complicated. For example, in her description of the Sisters of the Holy Family in *New Orleans,* King writes that "in their renunciation, they at least, of their race, found the road to social equality. No white woman could do more; none have done better" (352). She appears to sympathize with the desire of the sisters to achieve "social equality," a phrase that would have brought criticism had King expressed it in some other form than her history. Furthermore, while some of King's stories may contain problematic representations of African American characters, in her best fictions King chooses to resist the binary of race that she observed in the work of Cable and that she felt misrepresented the complex intersections of race and class—Creole, slave, European, and free mulatto—that constituted New Orleans before and after the war.[7] In presenting our analysis of King, we seek to reexamine race in her fiction, noting that she also racializes white women and, among white women writers, seems to be the most conscious of "whiteness." In particular, we are interested in the ways in which little Mammy in "A Crippled Hope" serves as a mirror for white women, as King explores their recognition that they themselves have been racialized by the Northern soldiers who occupied New Orleans during the Civil War—"soldiers whose tone and accent reminded [one] of the negro-trader" (*Balcony Stories* 122).

Among all the fictions produced by regionalist writers, "A Crippled Hope" seems on a first reading to rely most on racist representations, to confirm stereotypes about the paternalism of the institution of slavery, and to allow Northern readers to avoid recognizing the reality of black experience in the Reconstruction South. We are not the only readers who have had initial difficulty with this story. Although King's biographer Robert Bush offers the most benign reading, writing that "A Crippled Hope" "suggests Flaubert's 'Un coeur simple' in that it is a portrait of a commonplace servant woman whose life story is unified by the spirit of caring for others" ("Introduction" 21), feminist critics have been more severe. Linda Coleman terms the story a "highly romanticized and distorted picture of the slave's world" (38) in which its protagonist, little Mammy, denied the pleasures and the romance of plantation life, must first settle for nursing black slave infants damaged, like herself, by careless mothers, and then for nursing a sick white woman, "the victim of a war that destroyed her 'lover,'" even though, as Coleman further observes, "historical records suggest [this role] was seldom actually accepted by black women after the war" (41, 39). Robison writes that "though the story very explicitly condemns slavery and uses a discourse of femininity, motherhood, and story to redeem the young African American woman who is its main character, these same discourses also support the story's inherent racism" (65–66). Focusing on the contrast between the security the sleeping white children in King's prefatory sketch "The Balcony" enjoy and the precarious position of the slave infants in "A Crippled Hope" in danger of "being overlaid and smothered, or what was worse, maimed and crippled" by the fact that "negro mothers are so careless and such heavy sleepers" (*Balcony Stories* 113), Robison argues that King's strategy for making little Mammy sympathetic not only leads her to distinguish between little Mammy as a good mother and other African American women as bad mothers; it also leads her to reinforce the very "stereotypes used in the defense of slavery and in the disenfranchisement of African Americans; the very characteristics that are used to redeem little Mammy make her want to remain enslaved" (67).

In "The Literature of Impoverishment," Ann Douglas Wood claims that "'The [*sic*] Crippled Hope' could serve as the title for many of the finest stories of the women" whom she terms "Local Colorists" (30–31). "They themselves," she writes, "had much in common with Little [*sic*] Mammy. Existing in the past, left in the forgotten reaches of their society, they . . . too took their stand in the 'little town[s],' which, no matter how narrow or poor, were the places of 'refuge' for women like themselves" (31). While we do not accept Wood's reading of regionalism, as we noted in chapter 2, and particularly her view that regionalist writers "drew their artistic life, if not from nursing diseased women, at least from examining their sicknesses" (31), we follow her lead in recognizing little Mammy as an act of self-representation on the part of King's "balcony sitters." We may criticize this strategy as appropriative, but we recognize as well that King's strategy opens up a space for the inclusion of African American women within regionalism, suggesting that regionalism need not be, like the "vague, loose . . . garments" of the balcony sitters, also "white." King's narrator alludes frequently to her desire for this inclusion: "She can tell it; no one else can for her"; "It would be tedious to relate, although it was not tedious to hear her relate it, the desperations and hopes of her life then"; "But one should hear her tell it herself, as has been said" (*Balcony Stories* 117, 123).

That little Mammy does not in fact "tell it herself" reflects at once the limitations of King's balcony and of her perspective; yet this should not keep us from examining the implications of this story for the one who does tell it and for those who listen to it. The story locates King's white narrator as herself a "maimed and crippled" creature, dropped, like little Mammy, by a culture careless of the damage it has done and desirous only of concealing it "until the dislocation became irremediable" (106). Dislocated irremediably by the war that such carelessness and concealment brought into being, Southern white women must now confront not only their current dislocation; they must also re-understand their location before the war. If little Mammy's hands are the only thing that soothes such "wakeful, restless, thought-driven" (105) women, if "the poor, poor women of that stricken region say that little Mammy was the only alleviation God left them after Sheridan passed through" (123), then they must recognize that their current woe has some profound connection to little Mammy's. Her story alone can provide a "balm" for their woe because her story helps them understand their own. For King, such understanding also includes what it means to be "white women."

King explicitly indicts the negro-trader—"like hangmen, negro-traders are fitted by nature for their profession" (*Balcony Stories* 118)—and the slave trade; she writes that the "negro-trader's auction-mart" is "so plain, so matter-of-fact an edifice that emotion only comes afterward in thinking about it, and then in the reflection that such an edifice could be, then as now, plain and matter-of-fact" (107, 108). Yet her story constructs little Mammy as very curiously enslaved. She is born in the "great room, caravansary, stable, behind a negro-trader's auction mart" (107) to a mother who drops her "when a baby," then, "for fear of punishment," conceals the injury she has done to her child "until the dislocation became irremediable" (106). While initially "some doctoring was done, . . . some effort made to get her marketable," what seems strange, in this story apparently about a slave, is King's premise that legally little Mammy never really belongs to anyone. The slave trader seems to own her by default, but because he never allows her to climb the auction block, she never has any other master or mistress. Out of "animosity" for her biological mother she develops her own love for children and an inability not to respond whenever some woman or baby falls into "some emergency of pain and illness" (119). As a child, she becomes an expert sick-nurse and therefore priceless to the negro-trader, for whom "there was no capital so valuable as the physical soundness of his stock" (108); he repeatedly refuses to sell her and even begins to seclude her from view whenever white "ladies, pale from illnesses that she might have nursed, and overburdened with children whom she might have reared" visit the caravansary on "shopping visits, so to speak" (118–19).

Moreover, the language King uses to describe little Mammy's hopes and their "crippling" evokes that of an aging child always passed over for adoption rather than that of a slave afraid of being sold: "The others came and went, but she was always there" (112); "[b]abies of her babyhood—the toddlers she, a toddler, had nursed—were having babies themselves now; . . . [a]ll were marketable, all were bought and sold, all passed in one door and out the other—all except her, little Mammy" (115). When Emancipation finally arrives and the negro-trader vanishes, little Mammy becomes a "runaway" who follows "a railroad track . . . until she came to the one familiar landmark in life to her—a sick woman, but a white one" (123). She never travels further, for "[a]lways, as in the pen, some emergency of pain and illness held her" (123).

Southern white women after the war also find themselves caught in an "emergency of pain and illness," women not unlike King's own mother, who courageously managed to escape Northern-occupied New Orleans with her family of seven children and five servants in 1862. "After this," King writes, "the long years rose and spread over us like the waters of the Deluge in Noah's time" (*Memories* 23). Little Mammy's story gives King a rhetorical frame for expressing the sudden change of world and position many Southern white women experienced and allows her to indict, however indirectly, both the Northern occupation she herself experienced as the end of the world she had once known and the slave trade that, as she writes of the trader, has "not been entirely guiltless of producing" the war itself. She writes a story of solidarity between white women and little Mammy, not so that "gender seems to transcend race" (Coleman 38) but in order to mark the moment when Southern white women were forced out of their ideological construction as Southern belles in a patriarchal society and thereby became both raced and gendered differently than before. In this new racialization, "after Sheridan passed through," the town that serves as a "refuge for soldiers' wives and widows" more closely resembles the caravansary than the plantation, and little Mammy's story is retold by a white narrator who identifies with the perspective of the sick woman to whom little Mammy has told her own story. Positioning her listeners as well alongside this woman, the narrator suggests that the balm little Mammy's story offers is the opportunity to reinvent "white woman" and so to address, if not heal, their sickness. For a white mother now, even in her convalescence, becomes "wakeful, restless, thought-driven, as a mother must be, unfortunately, nowadays, particularly in that parish, where cotton worms and overflows have acquired such a monopoly of one's future" (105).

Reinventing the present in order to survive the future, however, requires re-understanding the past. Little Mammy's situation before the war—the slave who never leaves the auction house—indirectly, but eerily, represents that of white upper-class women enslaved not literally by slavery but by ideologies of white femininity that rendered them effectively motherless and unadopted. While late twentieth-century feminist theory has critiqued the nineteenth-century feminist equation of white women's position with slavery, Helen Taylor argues that the "desire on the part of bourgeois white women to compare their conditions with those of black slaves should not simply be dismissed as false consciousness" (14–15). She writes, "In terms of their emotional loyalties and ties to blacks, especially black women, the juxtaposition of their own kinds of bondage with slavery inevitably led to an unconscious or conscious identification with black women that could perhaps only emerge in the contradictions, curious absences or eruptions, and unsatisfactory closures of women's postbellum fiction" (15). In "A Crippled Hope," King avoids equating white women's situation with that of slavery; rather she creates a liminal black character whose "curious" relation to slavery comments on the curiousness of white women's own situation. We can read this as appropriative and hence racist, as a way in which King positions black women in service to white women. Yet in so doing we should not overlook the implication of King's use, for it includes not only reinventing whiteness and re-understanding the past; it also makes space in fiction for African American women. Coleman invokes Eugene Genovese's recognition that the "woman behind the Mammy mask . . . was a 'worldly-wise, enormously resourceful' person" (Coleman 42). So too is little Mammy, who as a child studied the legs of other children in order to invent a solution to her problem of "locomotion"—a broom-handle walking stick that allows her a "three-footed step"; who gains a knowledge of medicine from the doctors occasionally called in "to furbish up some piece of damaged goods" (*Balcony Stories* 114); who becomes a superior healer through her aptitude for "picking up, remembering, and inventing remedies" (113); and who manages to survive the second dislocation of her life just as she has the first. From her story, those who hear it can find a model for their own capacity for survival and can discover as well that their world, however much it has dropped them, still contains resources to provide some balm to their woe. Those who listen to her story can become as if a new kind of child, listening to the "mother voices" that, in however limited and problematic a fashion, still include little Mammy. "But one should hear her tell it herself, as has been said," King writes (*Balcony Stories* 123).

In addition to exploring the relationship between black and white women "dropped" by the North and by Reconstruction, and the consequent need for white women to understand their social position and racial identity differently, "writing our side," for King, seems also to have involved an analysis of class that further complicates her representation of race and gender. King's fiction includes a critique of the class structures of the prewar South and an implication that the South's defeat derived in part from these structures. While King's fiction may include the perspective of what she perceives to be the disestablished upper class, that perspective is far more complex than Robison's characterization of it as a "white, upper-middle-class retelling of regional politics" (55). Indeed, in various stories King explicitly dissociates herself from "the identification of the southern woman with the southern white man in mutual grief over the destruction and loss of the war" that Anne Goodwyn Jones sees as complicating Southern feminism (qtd. in Coleman 37).

When we turn to a story like "La Grande Demoiselle," an example of those fictions in which King chooses to emphasize issues of class, we discover as well another instance of her project of re-understanding the past. In the figure of the heiress, Idalie Sainte Foy Mortemart des Islets, King represents the prewar South, for "one could find heiresses then as one finds type-writing girls now" (*AWR* 386). Invoking Southern excess, King writes that the plantation Reine Sainte Foy is "really well described in those perfervid pictures of tropical life, at one time the passion of philanthropic imaginations, excited and exciting over the horrors of slavery," pictures that though they "were then often accused of being purposely exaggerated, . . . seem now to fall short of, instead of surpassing, the truth" (386). Conspicuous consumption and the personality that attends it form the substance of King's characterization of Idalie Sainte Foy Mortemart des Islets. With "a mouth that, even in prayer, talked nothing but commands," with a disregard for cost so thorough that she never lowered herself to provide her dressmaker with a budget, with habits of self-indulgence so extreme that she would have a new dress cut off her rather than exert herself to turn over and be unlaced, "la grande demoiselle" represents now inconceivable waste and self-indulgence (387). While King's representation of the "grande demoiselle" might suggest the North's construction of the South before the war as a woman out of control, King's critique focuses on class and on the ways in which gender serves to construct class; upper-class men require the conspicuous consumption of "their" women—along with the "slaves, slaves, slaves everywhere, whole villages of Negro cabins" (386)—to manifest their status.

King takes up the grande demoiselle's story after the war, after she has lost everything, and at a time when her poverty has led her to take a job as "the teacher of the colored public school" (389). One morning "old Champigny," who "also belonged to the great majority of the *nouveaux pauvres,*" encounters the grande demoiselle while taking a walk (389). Earlier King makes the point that "it is almost impossible to appreciate properly the beauty of the rich, the very rich," since the "limitless" opportunity for development, dress, and self-esteem produce "a certain effect of beauty" that makes ordinary assessment impossible, and therefore, when the grande demoiselle was wealthy, "there was nothing in her that positively contradicted any assumption of beauty on her part" (386–76). In the woman whom he sees approaching—head "hidden by a green barege veil," figure "like a finger or a post," feet "like waffle-irons or frying-pans"—old Champigny cannot possibly imagine the former grande demoiselle. Through this transformation King identifies the role class plays in the construction of gender, female beauty being the product of class privilege, just as she also understands the role gender plays in the construction of class. More significantly still, through this transformation King reveals the ugly truth behind the effect of beauty; the grande demoiselle serves as metonym for King's portrait of antebellum plantation life, with its "ease, idleness, extravagance, self-indulgence, pomp, pride, arrogance, in short the whole enumeration . . . of the wealthy slaveholder of aristocratic descent and tastes" now revealed to be "horrors" (386). When Champigny, himself old and impoverished and a man who does not care for women, learns that she is not "some Northern lady on a mission" (390) but is in fact "la grande demoiselle," he marries her.

Although King avers that "only the good God himself knows what passed in Champigny's mind" (390), she provides her readers with a framework for interpretation. Champigny, we can infer, wishes to reconstruct the old South and to recover the grande demoiselle, grown significantly darker from her years of poverty, as "white." More important to him than his "uncomplimentary attitude toward women" is his outrage that the grande demoiselle should be in such a position, "teaching a public colored school for—it makes one blush to name it—seven dollars and a half a month" (390). Reading race as the North's tool for destabilizing previous arrangements of class, Champigny does whatever he can to restore those arrangements. Yet King's narrator hardly shares his commitments. Nothing in the story suggests that the narrator desires to see the grande demoiselle restored to her former position, and, as the story's closing lines make clear, marriage has decidedly *not* restored the "assumption of beauty" that depends upon race and class privilege. When the grande demoiselle lifts the veil over her face in order to catch a glimpse of her old plantation outside the train window, King's narrator writes, "What a face! Thin, long, sallow, petrified! And the neck! If she would only tie something around the neck! And her plain, coarse cottonade gown! The Negro women about her were better dressed than she" (390). In the ending of "La Grande Demoiselle" we might well read King's attitudes toward the old South and the possibility of its restoration. "Poor old Champignon! It was not an act of charity to himself, no doubt cross and disagreeable, besides being ugly. And as for love, gratitude!" (390). Champignon manages to restore only everything "cross and disagreeable, besides being ugly." In the context of this story, a world of type-writing girls seems preferable to a world of heiresses.[8]

In "A Drama of Three," King openly argues for class as the primary "drama" of Southern culture. Journel, son of the former overseer on the old General's plantation, sends an anonymous letter to the General every month containing the amount the General owes him in rent just for the pleasure of having power over one who formerly had power over him. Journel keeps his contribution a secret (only the reader learns his identity) because this allows him to draw the General into elaborate displays of presumed superiority. Although King is not necessarily promoting Journel as a model for the new South, she is certainly acknowledging that class antagonism formed the basis of the old South, and that the new South will be shaped to a considerable degree by the history of that antagonism. "A Drama of Three" reveals no sympathy for the old General, whose false sense of superiority in the present moment seems to reflect retroactively on the past, implying that, like the grande demoiselle's, his sense of superiority before the war was equally false. Yet King recognizes how difficult it may be to prevent a "restoration" of the old ways, for the habit of superiority persists long after its economic basis erodes, and in the General's case his old habits construct his present reality. For example, he retains the habit of choosing what he will or will not acknowledge that he knows. No matter how many times his wife reminds him that Pompey fetches the mail "'to oblige us, out of his kindness'" (*AWR* 383), the General refuses to recognize that he does not hire Pompey and uses his wife's reminder to launch into an attack: "'Oblige us! Oblige me! Kindness! A Negro oblige me! Kind to me! That is it; that is it. That is the way to talk under the new régime. It is favor, and oblige, and education, and monsieur, and madame, now'" (383).

In this story King distances herself from the old General even as she recognizes the obstacle he presents to any significant rearrangement of class and race hierarchies in the South. Yet she suggests there is another obstacle, perhaps deeper still, that will make such rearrangements difficult. For Honorine, despite her efforts to instruct the General in the realities of their situation, is deeply invested in maintaining his sense of superiority as it forms the source of her own erotic identity. Although she suffers bitterly from the mystery of the monthly donation, for her husband "had been irresistible in excess" and who knows what infidelity to her may have produced such fidelity in another, her erotic life has been defined by her sacrifice to the General in marriage; and while shaving him with cologne, preparing him to receive the anonymous sheet of paper ("From one who owes you much" [384]) and the bank-notes which will then enable him to pay the rent, she feels the "faintness" she once felt as a bride and "thinks thoughts to which it must be confessed she looked forward from month to month" (382). As long as Honorines exist so will generals and if Journel knew of her role in the drama he might consider himself an even more successful "*farceur*" (385).

However, "A Drama of Three" actually includes four; there would be no drama if the general had to get his own mail. Pompey's kindness, like Honorine's adoration, allows the General to go on believing that nothing has changed and so creates the basis for Journel's monthly farce. Yet while King creates a space to explore Honorine's role in the drama and its cost to her, she opens no similar space for Pompey. The reader is not invited to speculate, as we are with Honorine, why Pompey continues to be kind to one who abuses him, whether he too enjoys the farce, whether his motive may be compassion for the white woman or contempt for the white man, even whether the "drama" that delivering the General's mail underscores serves to remind him that he is free. Given this omission on her part, it is possible to conclude that King sees blacks as only too willing to return to the old arrangements of master and servant and as decisively different from the poor whites who relish the changes brought about by the war and take full advantage of them. Still, Pompey remains in King's text as unaccounted for and therefore invites analysis. We may view King's inclusion of Pompey without "counting" him into her title as a rhetorical strategy that allows her to foreground class and gender in her critique of the South and to resist the privileging of race as the primary axis of social organization and regional difference, a privileging that would align her with the occupying Union army she had despised as a child.

Class and Race in Writers outside the South

While the regionalist writers who locate their fictions in or near New Orleans are the writers who include African American characters in their work and who take up questions of race with a much clearer sense that the topic is not congenial to Northern editors and readers, they also, as we have indicated, write about race in ways that intersect with questions of white women's identity and of class structures. When we turn to examine regionalist texts by writers outside the South, we find an emphasis on class that nevertheless at various points also raises questions of race. Moreover, when we look at other regionalist writers through the lens the New Orleans writers construct, we become aware of references to race that we might otherwise have missed. For example, we begin to notice apparently unproblematized uses of the word "white." We recall Austin's final description of the Walking Woman—"the track of her two feet bore evenly and white" (*AWR* 583)—and we must ask if Austin uses white as a shortcut to counter the negative reports of the Walking Woman's deviance. On the other hand, Austin describes the desert as a woman with "tawny" hair and a "largeness" to her mind and her desires that comes close to being her own self-portrait, and we wonder whether Austin is racializing herself or the Walking Woman. For another example, Jewett in writing about a rare bird chooses a white heron, not a blue or green one. Does it make a difference to the ornithologist that the rare bird is white—or to Sylvia, who saves the bird from the hunter? Is this an instance of unexamined racism or does it accurately reflect the relative rarity of the white heron in southern Maine?[9]

Certainly there are unmistakable instances of unexamined racism in regionalist writing. For example, in "Freedom Wheeler's Controversy with Providence," we can note Cooke's presentation of Moll Thunder, the "half-breed Indian" woman who comes to nurse Freedom during his long illness. Moll speaks the crudest form of "injun" English; her relation to Native American medicine is parodied as a knowledge of "yarbs" that produces potions as likely to kill as to cure; and she is described as finally dismissed with "a jug of cider-brandy" for pay, "a professional fee she much preferred to money" (*AWR* 111). Similarly, in "How Celia Changed Her Mind," Cooke refers stereotypically to the "slatternly negress" whom Parson Stearns finds washing some clothes in Rosabel's kitchen when he goes to bring her home from the "west" (*AWR* 150). Jewett's least successful stories are those in which she moves outside of New England and into South Carolina (in "The Mistress of Sydenham Plantation") and Virginia (in "The War Debt") and adopts what she must have understood as "Southern" attitudes toward black characters.[10] To what extent are regionalist writers, to recall Morrison's analysis, relying as much on "metaphorical shortcuts . . . that can powerfully evoke and enforce hidden signs of racial superiority" (x) as the local colorists and realists whose work we have asserted they critique? Alternatively, to what extent does regionalism distinguish itself from local color and serve as a corrective to the impulse to project the "fears and desires that reside in the writerly conscious" onto persons of color (17)?

To be sure, regionalist fiction contains few instances of such overt racism. Since for many regionalist writers region becomes a space within which to critique operations of class, more typical is the racism that comes from relegating persons of color to the background. For example, in "About the Tompkinses" Cary, like King, recognizes the role race plays in the construction of class and in creating the sense of injury that accompanies class hierarchies in America. Mrs. Tompkins believes that the Haywoods think themselves "big bugs" and above everyone else because Mrs. Haywood "kept a negro woman in her kitchen" (*Clovernook Sketches* 40). In Cary's fiction black characters appear primarily as pawns in the operations of class, and while she is quick to sympathize with those whom such operations injure she shows little interest in exploring in her fiction the interior of the racially other, in wondering what kind of noise such a life might make or in considering that a "negro woman" might also be a poet.

The association of the regional with the perspective of a subordinate class can be seen in Stowe's introduction of Roxy and Ruey in *The Pearl of Orr's Island.* These characters, who speak in dialect, not standard English, are effectively a version of "serving women," Faye Dudden's term for a certain mid-nineteenth-century class,[11] and when Captain Pennel goes to the sea chest that stands in the corner of his kitchen and declares that he will give Aunt Roxy "all there is in my old chest yonder" if she will only make the child Mara live, his possession of the chest as well as the gold within it articulates significant distinctions of class. The use of region to foreground issues of class begins, however, with Cary. In her "Preface" to *Clovernook,* she expresses the hope that her sketches may have the merit at least of interesting "if they do not instruct, readers who have regarded the farming class as essentially different and inferior" (*AWR* 61). Speaking from inside the region, Cary articulates the difference between region and world as one of class, for Cary, perhaps more than any other regionalist writer, posits class as the primary hierarchy of American society. Indeed, one might convincingly argue that class displaces, or at least overshadows, gender as a category of analysis in Cary's fiction. Cary's fiction is remarkably free of what we might call "genderlect," that nineteenth-century discourse practiced by both male and female writers that had as its goal the construction of gender as the primary axis of social difference. Although her fiction contains radical gender thematics, as we have seen in our discussion of "Uncle Christopher's" in chapter 2, gender is not the organizing category in her fiction. While it is true that in Clovernook only women are seduced and abandoned and that mothers, when they indulge, indulge only sons, Cary makes little distinction between men and women in general and does not link character traits, behaviors, or possibilities for development to gender. In Clovernook, mothers can be good or bad and boys can want something pretty, for class constitutes the primary distinction and parents form one class and children another.

"About the Tompkinses" provides an excellent example of Cary's understanding of class and its operations. "In every neighborhood," her narrator declares, "there must be one family more fashionable, more aristocratic, than the rest. In Clovernook, this family was the Haywoods" (*Clovernook Sketches* 40). Still finer distinctions exist for "the Tompkinses were not quite so respectable as the deacon's folks; they were not so well-to-do in the world, and were by no means regular in their attendance at meeting; and their relations, generally, were of a lower level" (37). Clovernook, as Cary presents it, is structured by minute and subtle gradations of class; moreover, these gradations structure the psychology of her characters and provide the material for her story. Susan desires to go to the Haywoods' party because they are "big bugs" and her mother resists her desire for the same reason. Yet in her own family Mrs. Tompkins plays the part of a "big bug" while her children occupy the position of inferiors: "Mrs. Tompkins always talked to her children as if they were greatly to blame for wanting anything, or, in fact, for being in the world at all," and she addresses her little boy "as though he belonged to quite a different order of beings" (42–43). The boy learns to associate his inferior class position with being a child, and "at length he asked his mother when he should grow big" (43). Mrs. Tompkins also relishes the opportunity to place others lower than herself. While Cary's own understanding of class is quite nuanced, Mrs. Tompkins holds to the cruder distinction between "big bugs" and "nobodies." Returning home with a story about a robbery, she reflects on the fact that "'There has a family lately moved into Mr. Hill's old house, that people think are no better than they should be. . . . They don't work, they say, and no body knows how they live; but we all know they must eat, and some think they get it between two days'" (44).

In Mrs. Tompkins, Cary analyzes and exposes the particular form that class injury takes in supposedly democratic America, for the ideology of equality when combined with the reality of class hierarchy produces citizens who resent those presumably above them but find no contradiction in creating or accepting categories that place others below them. Not surprisingly, Cary's narrator participates in this psychology for her consciousness has been shaped by being part of that "farming class" considered inferior by the "world" and by the subtle operations of class within the region itself. Thus we find Cary's narrator frequently more willing to challenge the pretensions of those above her than to critique her own pretensions to superiority. In the autobiographical sketch, "The Sisters," Ellie Hadley feels justified in rebuffing the overtures of the farmer William Martin; and she feels equally justified in interpreting her own rejection by a "gentleman" as an insult, for "Ellie Hadley, plain, obscure, and depreciated, had in her soul creative energies which entitled her to be regarded as of a more elevated order of nature" (*Clovernook* 329). Distinctions based on money or heritage are spurious and capable of challenge; distinctions created by intellect, by "poetry," are "natural." For Cary, then, regionalism creates a space for a truly striking analysis of the operations of class, but we might legitimately wonder to what extent she identifies the perspective of regionalism with the class position of those who recognize the superiority of "poetry."

Like Cary, Freeman offers a complex analysis of class, and, like Cary, she also identifies with those defined as lower class. Yet, unlike Cary, her identification does not cover the assumption that she deserves to be located differently; nor does she present class as an experience of personal injury. Rather she uses regionalism to stage a variety of challenges to the hegemony of middle-class values and perspectives. In "A Church Mouse," for example, the crisis that threatens to bring about Hetty's expulsion from the meetinghouse is precipitated by her having cooked a Saturday dinner of cabbage and turnips and "the next day the odors of turnip and cabbage were strong in the senses of the worshippers" (*AWR* 350). The smell of these homely vegetables, indicative not only of Hetty's poverty but of her taste, for to her the boiled dinner "had been a banquet" (351), creates an offense sufficient to rouse the village to action. And when Mrs. Gale rallies the women to stop their husbands from breaking down the door and dragging Hetty out by force, her empathy extends across class difference. In this story regionalist values are located within the lower-class figure and regionalism becomes a space for the articulation of what one learns from being "hard pressed" by the operations of class as well as those of gender and age. Indeed, Hetty, with her worsted work of wool flowers that she hangs throughout the meetinghouse, serves for Freeman as a figure of the regionalist writer as artist, even though the narrator acknowledges that the taste that creates and responds to such work is "crude" (350).

In "A Gala Dress," Freeman articulates still more sharply her perception of the significance of class in supposedly classless New England and writes with great sympathy and understanding of a variety of class perspectives, fashioning a story in which some meaningful negotiation across differences can take place. Although just as poor as their neighbor, Matilda Jennings, the Babcock sisters consider themselves superior for they have seen better days and they come from better "stock": "There had been in their lives a faint savor of gentility and aristocracy. Their father had been college-educated and a doctor. Matilda's antecedents had been humble, even in this humble community" (*Selected Stories* 151). The Babcock sisters devote themselves to maintaining the signs of their class status. They do not sit in front of their house, even though that would be more comfortable, for they view such publicity as inappropriate to their class. They guard "nothing more jealously than the privacy of their meals" (148), and while their neighbors assume they do so to hide their poverty, the narrator assures us they would have done so no matter how much they had to eat. In particular they retain one relic of their better days that most particularly signals status, a black silk dress which they take turns wearing to church, changing the trim every week in order to create the illusion that they have two dresses rather than one. With this detail Freeman records the significance of class to the sense of identity in this New England village, for these women would rather miss church than wear to meeting a dress inappropriate to their class. Matilda Jennings, who has never known better days and has never owned even one black silk dress, resents the Babcocks for their continual performance of class superiority and she strongly suspects their ruse around the dress. Accompanying Emily to the Fourth of July picnic, she allows the nearsighted Emily to step on some firecrackers that she has seen and avoided. The firecrackers scorch holes in the dress, making it impossible for the sisters any longer to pretend that one dress is two. They narrowly avoid exposure by the unexpected arrival of a trunk full of the clothes of their dead aunt with "two black silk dresses among the other gowns" (157). When

Emily and Elizabeth decide to offer Matilda their old dress and when she accepts the offer, class antagonism seems resolved as the sisters recognize the motive that has produced Matilda's animosity and as Matilda acknowledges that she too would like a black silk dress. While we might sense a privileging of middle-class values in the prominence accorded to the dress and in the hint that, in acknowledging that she saw the firecrackers and purposely let Emily step on them, Matilda rises above her class, Freeman achieves a delicate balance in this story. She enters into the perspective of both the Babcock sisters and Matilda Jennings, recognizing the differences between them and recording how they see these differences, yet without participating in their own often invidious valuations. She contrasts the sisters' obsessive desire for privacy with Matilda's pushiness, the delicacy and slightness of their tea of bread and butter with Matilda's coarse but ample meals of brown bread, cheese, and cold pork; and she registers the physical distinctions of class through a detail as subtle as her description of Matilda's "broad foot" which "just cleared a yellow portulaca which had straggled into the path, but she did not notice it" (160). Freeman offers no sense that such distinctions can or should disappear but rather suggests the possibility of a perspective that can encompass and relish both sweet cake and brown bread, that can find room for both flowers and broad feet, and that can imagine positive exchanges across such differences capable of transcending class antagonism.

In "A Mistaken Charity," Freeman analyzes the way middle- and upper-class women gain their sense of identity by taking a charitable interest in their lower-class neighbors, and suggests that the sense of moral superiority, the fineness of feeling that supposedly distinguishes the middle class from the lower class, is in fact a kind of imperialism since it is purchased at the expense of others: "Mrs. Simonds . . . was a smart, energetic person, bent on doing good, and she did a great deal. To be sure, she always did it in her own way. If she chose to give hot doughnuts, she gave hot doughnuts; it made not the slightest difference to her if the recipients of her charity would infinitely have preferred ginger cookies" (*AWR* 319). Harriet and Charlotte Shattuck live in a house that barely deserves the name and they survive by gifts of food from neighbors. Fiercely independent, they live in terror of going to the poorhouse. Mrs. Simonds sees in their poverty an opportunity to "do good" and she arranges for them to be taken to "the Old Ladies Home" in a neighboring city where, ominously, there has been "an unusual mortality among the inmates" (319). It does not occur to Mrs. Simonds to ask Harriet and Charlotte whether and how they might wish to be helped, for her interests lie in constructing herself as one who knows what is best for others; she uses her economic advantage to reinforce her belief that Charlotte and Harriet would like to become "ladies," like Mrs. Simonds and her partner in charity. The "Old Ladies Home" provides the context for reconstructing Charlotte and Harriet as "ladies," though without of course providing the resources that would make such a reconstruction possible, even if it were desired or desirable.

Charlotte and Harriet, however, refuse to be so reconstructed: "But nothing could transform these two unpolished old women into two nice old ladies. They did not take kindly to white lace caps and delicate neckerchiefs . . . and they wanted to twist up their scanty gray locks into little knots at the back of their heads and go without caps, just as they always had done" (320). They consider themselves to be in prison, even though "'they don't lock us in, nor nothin'" (321), and when they finally leave they do so with a conscious sense of making a prison break, hanging "the new white lace caps with which [they] had been so pestered, one on each post at the head of the bedstead, so they would meet the eyes of the first person who opened the door" (321). Reclaiming their old clothes, they triumphantly return to their own home, their own food, and their own ways, and to the miracle for blind Charlotte of glimpses of light, "'so many chinks they air all runnin' together'" (323). As in "A Church Mouse," Freeman locates value in the position of those who resist the hegemony of the middle class and who speak from a different perspective.

More complex still is the treatment of class in Thaxter, for Thaxter in effect racializes the class differences that distinguish her own middle-class family from the residents of the fishing village of Gosport on Star Island. *Among the Isles of Shoals* intertwines more than one narrative. In one, from which we have drawn our excerpt in *American Women Regionalists* and which served as the basis for our analysis of her epistemology in chapter 8 of the present book, Thaxter tells the story of growing up on White Island from age five to age eleven and then on Appledore after her father built a hotel and moved the family to that island. In this narrative, in which Thaxter describes her relationship to the islands—to their topography, their weather, the sea fowl and other birds, the flowers, insects, and bats who served as "friends" and "neighbors" to the small child—she writes as a regionalist, telling the story of her own development within the region, and even writing as if White Island and, later, Appledore were their own "regions" within the Shoals themselves. However, even in this narrative Thaxter duplicates the inaugurating gesture of America and its literature in which the land is emptied of previous inhabitants in order to be settled imaginatively. While Thaxter asserts that no one but her own family lived on White Island, Star Island was still peopled by the descendants of seventeenth-century settlers, and some lived scattered on other islands as well, as her own narrative acknowledges. Yet Thaxter's relation to her region depends upon its being empty and her being solitary. To what extent, then, is her relation to region class-inflected, the product of a class consciousness that leads her to see herself as solitary simply because she was the only female child of her own class and ethnicity on the islands, not literally alone but uncompanioned by others of her class? In posing this question, we must ask as well to what extent Thaxter, like Cary, proposes regionalism as a perspective available only to one whose subjectivity has been formed by a particular class consciousness and a particular consciousness of class.

Issues of class structured Thaxter's relationship to the inhabitants of Gosport on Star Island and to the families on Hog and Smuttynose. Thaxter moved to the Isles of Shoals because her father had just purchased three of them and he took the job of lighthouse keeper in order to be on hand to attend to his business interests.[12] Her relation to many of those already on the islands was that of owning class to working class, as they became her father's tenants and employees. Moreover, from the start her father's resort on Hog (later named Appledore, the name Thaxter uses in her text) depended on class for its success; it was designed to fulfill the desires of those wealthy enough to travel to the islands for vacation and it distinguished itself from competitors through its claim to attract a higher-class clientele. *Among the Isles of Shoals,* as we observed in chapter 8, functioned in part to generate publicity for the family business, though Thaxter herself worked long hours without pay and most likely was not a financial partner. Her history of human habitation on the islands and her anecdotes about natives must be read in the context of this frame.

Thaxter saw capital in quaintness and queerness, for we can identify a recognizable local-color narrative intertwined with her regionalist text.[13] Her descriptions of the "Shoalers" frequently partake of the grotesque and have the effect of distancing herself and her readers from these queer figures. No reader would identify with old Peter, "said to be a hundred years old; and anything more grisly in the shape of humanity it has never been my lot to behold" (*Among the Isles of Shoals* 74), or Old Nabbaye, whose beard "gave her a most grim and terrible aspect . . . like one of the Furies" (75). Another old Shoaler "had the largest, most misshapen cheek-bones ever constructed, an illimitable upper lip, teeth that should not be mentioned, and small watery eyes. Skin and hair and eyes and mouth were of the same pasty yellow, and that grotesque head was set on a little, thin, and shambling body" (79). In her treatment of the Shoals' dialect Thaxter becomes most recognizably a local-color writer, for she distinguishes this dialect not only from "Yankee drawl or sailor-talk," but also from the language she herself uses. The pronunciation of the local Shoalers she describes as "peculiar," "something not to be described," even though she tries to give her reader something of its flavor (68–69). She offers further examples of their idiosyncratic diction as expressed through nicknames and idioms, but she carefully refrains from providing any instances of their "genius" for swearing, defining such speech as beyond the bounds of what her own middle-class dialect can record, despite the fact that it has power enough to chill the blood of the listener. Summarizing her response, and by implication that of her readers, to the Shoalers' speech, she declares that "the prevailing sentiment was likely to be one of amazement mingled with intense amusement—the whole thing was so grotesque and monstrous, and their choice and arrangement of words so comical, and generally so very much to the point" (68–69).

In the local-color narrative that characterizes a significant portion of her text, Thaxter includes the history of the Shoals, copies a few segments from the old town records that she finds "quaint and interesting," with "spelling and modes of expression so peculiar" (55), and describes the "color and the picturesque effect of the general aspect of the natives in their element" (61) for her *Atlantic Monthly* readers. Moreover, it is in her role as local-color narrator that she racializes the inhabitants of the Shoals; the fisherman are "brown and swarthy" and she remembers childhood glimpses of the old women, "their lean brown shapes crouching over the fire, with black pipes in their sunken mouths, and hollow eyes" (66). The inhabitants of the Shoals, however, are all descended from Europeans; Thaxter cites a 1623 text she identifies as "Christopher Leavitt's Voyage into New England," in which Leavitt describes his first arrival upon the Isles of Shoals and writes, "No savages at all" (25). As Thaxter relates it, the original settlers were "decent, God-fearing folk" but "in later years they fell into evil ways, and drank 'fire-water,' and came to grief" (31), and depending on whether she is lauding the settlers or whether she is lamenting their fall, she describes them alternately as "principally Swedes and Norwegians, . . . a fine, self-respecting race" (184) or as people "beyond the bounds of civilization" (78), whom she likens at one point to Caliban (52).[14]

While it might be possible to separate out and distinguish between the commercial impulses that produce the local-color text and the aesthetic and gendered imperatives that produce the regionalist text, *Among the Isles of Shoals* poses the question of the difference between these texts. There is an instability in Thaxter's use of the term "native" and in her relation to the "native" that complicates this question still further. Near the beginning of her narrative, Thaxter uses the word "native" in such a way as to raise the question of her own relation to the term: "The natives, or persons who have been brought up here, find it almost as difficult to tear themselves away from the islands as do the Swiss to leave their mountains. From a civilized race's point of view, this is a curious instance of human perversity, since it is not good for men to live their whole lives through in such remote and solitary places" (16). Is she a "native" by virtue of having been brought up on the islands or a member of "a civilized race" because she was not born there and has lived elsewhere? Is she a native because she finds it difficult to tear herself away, or civilized because she finds such clinging unhealthy? In leaving open the possibility that she might be native rather than civilized, Thaxter leaves open as well the possibility that regionalism may also be native rather than civilized.

Thaxter's ability to see herself as "native" complicates both her racialization of the Star Islanders and her references to race in general. As she associates growing up on the islands with her own claim to being "native," she engages in a kind of cross-racial identification that for some readers may verge on appropriation, but at the very least suggests that Thaxter, like King, could imagine someone of African descent as her own mirrored reflection.[15] Early in the narrative, Thaxter describes various treasure hunters on the islands, including

> old black Dinah, an inhabitant of Portsmouth [who] came out to Appledore, then entirely divested of human abodes, and alone, with only a divining-rod for company, passed several days and nights wandering over the island, muttering to herself, with her divining-rod carefully balanced in her skinny hands. . . . [T]he old negress returned empty-handed; but what a picture she must have made wandering there in the loneliness, by sunlight, or moonlight, with her weird figure, her dark face, her garments fluttering in the wind, and the awful rod in her hand! (34–35)

Later in her text she writes, "I had a scrap of garden, literally not more than a yard square, wherein grew only African marigolds, rich in color as barbaric gold. I knew nothing of John Keats at that time . . . but I am sure he never felt their beauty more devoutly than the little, half-savage being who knelt, like a fire-worshipper, to watch the unfolding of those golden disks" (133). We sense a connection between the figure of black Dinah seeking literal gold on Appledore and the child Thaxter responding so passionately to the "barbaric gold" of African marigolds.[16] Moreover, Thaxter locates her origins as a poet, not in reading Keats—in another reference to *The Tempest,* she writes that "later, the 'brave new world' of poets was opened to me (133)—but rather in an experience of beauty "half-savage."

What moves Thaxter's identification as "native" and her interest in "barbaric gold" beyond appropriation is the fact that she herself becomes interested in a certain kind of buried treasure on the island and becomes a strange figure to the Shoalers. She writes, near the end of the book, that some young people camping on Appledore one summer dug up a skeleton. Although the bones crumbled, "the skull remained intact, and I kept it for a long time. The Shoalers shook their heads. 'Hog Island would have no "luck" while that skull remained above ground'" (175). Thaxter keeps the skull on her desk as a way of understanding the "nameless dread invested" in it; thinking back through what she imagines as the primitive and the savage, she struggles to unravel "the riddle that has troubled every thoughtful soul since the beginning of time" (176). We read Thaxter's fascination with old Dinah, the African marigolds, and the skull "thick as an Ethiop's" as her desire not to project onto the African an aspect of herself she does not want to own but rather as her way to recognize the primitive and the savage within herself and so to construct an identity outside the bounds of acceptable middle-class female sensibility. Elizabeth Stuart Phelps recalls the experience of watching with Thaxter a midwinter shipwreck in which the members of the crew, flung from their boat onto a rock, hung on for hours before they gave up and drowned: "'Fools to cling!' she cried. 'They were fools—*fools* to cling'" (178). Thaxter's refusal to take Phelps's own conventional Christian view of the scene ("While there is hope of life eternal, the saddest mortal life is worth the living" [178]) defines her as distinctively different from Phelps, indeed as savage. We read this savagery as central to Thaxter's construction of herself and to the subjectivity from which she writes. It is a quality she associates with what it means to grow up on a bit of rock in the north Atlantic Ocean and it fully informs her writing of *Among the Isles of Shoals*, allowing her to create a text that does not draw back from horror even as it describes ecstasy. Thaxter's association of Africa with her sense of her own primitiveness and her belief that growing up on the islands as a "native" has given her the ability to cross over in imagination into a world in which she herself becomes a "little, half-savage being" shape the subjectivity that has given us *Among the Isles of Shoals* and opens up a space in regionalism for the presence of blackness seen as powerful and positive.

One of the most interesting approaches to class occurs in the work of Sui Sin Far, whose sketch "The Inferior Woman" presents a striking reading of the ways in which perceptions of class are shaped by assumptions about gender. In seeking to reconcile her American neighbor Mrs. Carman to her son's desire to marry an "inferior" woman, the Americanized Chinese Mrs. Spring Fragrance points out, as we have observed in chapter 6, that were the "inferior woman" a man, Mrs. Carman would admire him for having overcome his class disadvantage and for being "a man who has made himself" (*AWR* 524). While Mrs. Carman supports upward mobility in men, she finds it threatening to imagine class as equally negotiable for women. Mrs. Carman's insistence on female stratification could be seen as the logical consequence of her commitment to male mobility, since possession of an upper-class woman often serves as the sign of a man's success, as we noted above in our discussion of King's "La Grande Demoiselle." However, there seems to be more at issue for her here. Mrs. Carman objects to Alice Winthrop as a wife for her son in part because Alice has secured "the position of private secretary to the most influential man in Washington—a position which by rights belongs only to a well-educated young woman of good family" (*AWR* 521). Implicitly recognizing the economy of scarcity that is the driving force of capitalism and that makes sexism so important to its operations, Mrs. Carman knows that feminist efforts will at best open only a few doors for women, will allow only a few women to experience what might be called gender mobility, and she has recourse to the concept of class as a "natural" principle for determining which women should get access to this limited privilege. We may imagine that she also believes those who have done the work of opening doors—women such as her friend's educated suffragist daughter, Ethel Evebrook—should receive the fruits of that work rather than those who, like Alice, have specifically rejected the label of suffragist. Indeed, in this context, Mrs. Carman's commitment to disregarding class as a significant category for men requires her to reinforce its significance for women since the prioritizing of self-made men will presumably restrict still further the opportunities for women. Mrs. Spring Fragrance recognizes that Mrs. Carman's conservative analysis will not produce social change, and it may be for this reason that she hopes her own daughter, should she have one, will walk in the way of the "superior" woman, the feminist.

Hybridity

Unlike Dunbar-Nelson, for whom writing about race invoked two centuries of social structures based on white dominance, Sui Sin Far regarded the experience of the mixed-race person as opening up a space rich in possibility for creative self-fashioning and communication across cultural lines.[17] In "The Sing Song Woman," for example, though Mag-gee is introduced by the narrator as "half-white," a construction that would make "Chinese" racially marked, she describes herself as American, a construction that would make "Chinese" a mark of culture (*AWR* 503). Thus she can declare that she is not in effect Chinese: "'I'm not Chinese in looks nor in any other way. See! My eyes are blue, and there is gold in my hair; and I love potatoes and beef, and everytime I eat rice it makes me sick, and so does chopped up food'" (503).

This sense of race as fluid rather than fixed allows Sui Sin Far to create characters who combine elements of different cultures in order to produce a new set of possibilities for themselves. Ah Oi, the Chinese actress who is accustomed to hearing the Chinese reviled "by the white and half white denizens of Chinatown" (*AWR* 503), participates in destabilizing the relation between race, culture, and identity. She encourages her friend to elope with her American boyfriend while she herself takes her friend's place in the wedding that has been arranged for her. She explains to Mag-gee's father, when he realizes that an "imposter" has stood in for his daughter, "'Mag-gee has gone to eat beef and potatoes with a white man. Oh, we had such a merry time making this play!'" (504). Ah Oi's "rippling, amused laugh," as we observed in chapter 5, signals her consciousness of her role as a trickster who actively subverts her own culture's assumptions about the meaning of race, particularly as they relate to gender. In this story Ah Oi's subversion has the effect of creating a space for others as well to escape the fixed definition of race and culture. The tricked husband, instead of joining in the general abuse of Ah Oi, appreciates her kindness to both her friend and himself, and from this we can infer that he appreciates as well both her qualities of resistance and critique, and her hybridity. In accepting her as his wife, he changes his own identity.

Sui Sin Far intentionally accords this response to a Chinese man for she recognizes the unlikelihood of a white man's finding value in anything not defined as white, a point she demonstrates in another of her stories, "'Its Wavering

Image.'" In contrast to Mag-gee, introduced as "half-white" and as looking "strange" and "odd" when forced by her father to put on Chinese makeup and dress in Chinese clothes, Pan in "'Its Wavering Image'" is introduced as "a half-white, half-Chinese girl" (526). Sui Sin Far emphasizes Pan's hybridity and implies that Pan's distinction derives from it. Exempt by virtue of being "born a Bohemian" from "the conventional restrictions imposed upon either the white or Chinese woman," Pan is, according to Mark Carson's editor, "'unusually bright'" and "'could tell more stories about the Chinese than any other person in this city—if she would'"; and the narrator adds that while "a white woman might pass over an insult" and "a Chinese woman fail to see one," Pan both sees and responds (527). Although more comfortable with her father's Chinese culture than her mother's white one—she shrinks "from their curious scrutiny as she would from the sharp edge of a sword" (527)—Pan can still see how Chinese culture appears when viewed from a white perspective. Yet she has no wish to choose between these worlds and "if she were different in any sense from those around her, she gave little thought to it" (526); her difference is not to her a source of difficulty but of possibility.

Mark Carson, however, finds her ambiguity intolerable. He returns from his first encounter with her "puzzled. . . . What was she? Chinese or white?" (527). Although his editor refuses to participate in Carson's insistence on racial and cultural distinctions, Carson himself is determined to find out what she "really" is; he intends to get both his story and his girl. With an arrogance Sui Sin Far reserves primarily for white males, he sets out to give Pan a lesson that will teach her her true identity and put an end once and for all to her "wavering image." Publishing in his paper all he has learned of the "sacred and secret" (529) from his association with her and her trust in him, he intends to separate her from the Chinese part of herself and to force her to come out as white. His betrayal, however, has the opposite effect, for from it she learns what it means to be white: "'Betrayed! Betrayed! Betrayed to be a betrayer!'" (529). Given this knowledge, she chooses to be Chinese: "'I would not be a white woman for all the world. You are a white man. And *what* is a promise to a white man!'" (531). The tragedy of this story lies not only in the betrayal of a "half-white, half-Chinese" girl by a white man; it lies also, and perhaps more so, in the betrayal of the possibility of hybridity, for in response to Carson's actions, Pan chooses to identify as only Chinese. In this story Sui Sin Far delivers a scathing critique of the dominant ideology of assimilation, even as she works in many of her fictions to counter the claim, used to support anti-Chinese sentiment, that the Chinese "'did not assimilate with whites and never could become an integral and homogeneous part of the population'" (qtd. in Ling 23). Mark Carson assumes Pan's capacity for assimilation, since her mixed-race background poses no obstacle to his desire if she will only act American—that is, white—and he assumes as well her desire to assimilate. While understanding race as in effect a function of culture would have saved Dunbar-Nelson's Victor Grabért, for Sui Sin Far such an understanding, as it enforces assimilation, proves to be not only arrogant but self-destructive; in forcing Pan to choose, Carson destroys the very qualities that made her attractive to him.

In the context of "'Its Wavering Image,'" a story that exposes the deep-seated hostility of America to the hybrid, Mrs. Spring Fragrance emerges as an even more significant figure, one who, as we have noted in chapter 6, represents the incarnation in turn-of-the-century American fiction of the *mestiza* consciousness described by Gloria Anzaldúa. Anzaldúa argues in *Borderlands/La Frontera* for the emergence of a new "race," one that is inclusive rather than exclusive, "wavering" rather than fixed, and by virtue of its mixture producing not the bastard of racial degeneration but a new and indeed superior kind of human. Such persons would have a tolerance for ambiguity and the mental flexibility to shift out of habitual ways of thinking, away from rigidity and toward ambiguity, fluidity, indeterminateness; such persons would not inherit culture so much as creatively construct its meaning from the perspective of the border.

The figure of Mrs. Spring Fragrance gains even further significance when we consider the number of stories Sui Sin Far wrote representing the immense difficulties presented to those "caught," as Ling puts it, "in the between-world condition" (44). Among these stories is "The Wisdom of the New," in which a Chinese wife brought to the United States by an Americanized husband whom she has not seen for ten years kills her son the night before he is to start American school, believing that death is preferable to either assimilation or hybridity. Similarly in "Her Chinese Husband, Sequel to The Story of the White Woman Who Married A Chinese," another mother speculates on the fate of her child, wondering what will happen to him as he grows up caught between two worlds with "no kindliness nor understanding between them" (45). Yet in accord with her belief that the Chinese man was more open to difference than the white man, Sui Sin Far presents the father's perspective in language that anticipates Anzaldúa: "'What is there to weep about? The child is beautiful: the feeling heart, the understanding mind is his. And we will bring him up to be proud that he is of Chinese blood; he will fear none and, after him, the name of half-breed will no longer be one of contempt'" (Sui Sin Far 82). Since the man is later murdered by other Chinese "opposed to all progress, and who hate with a bitter hatred all who would enlighten or be enlightened" (83), we might read this story as indicative of Sui Sin Far's despair at ever achieving such "progress"; but we can also read it as her effort to make such progress possible by presenting the senselessness of the resistance to it. Indeed, Sui Sin Far felt that in her own person as well as in her writing she embodied in the present moment the possibility of that desired future; she saw herself as a pioneer, believing that "some day a great part of the world will be Eurasian," and as the "connecting link" between East and West that could make this dream a reality (Ling 49).

When Sui Sin Far describes Mrs. Spring Fragrance as "Americanized," she puts the term in quotation marks, thus indicating that Mrs. Spring Fragrance's relation to the American is not to be read as an instance of assimilation. Indeed, Mrs. Spring Fragrance is not white in the way Mark Carson wishes Pan to be, for she rejects the ideology he represents. As we discussed in more detail in chapter 7, hearing a lecture while in San Francisco on "America, The Protector of China," she writes to her husband ironically urging him "to forget to remember that the barber charges you one dollar for a shave while he humbly submits to the American man a bill of fifteen cents" (*AWR* 509). Americanization for Mrs. Spring Fragrance does not mean forgetting that she is Chinese; and Mr. Spring Fragrance eventually comes to appreciate that she is "Americanized" rather than American and to realize that her appreciation of the "American" poetry of Tennyson does not make her, despite his business colleague's comment, "just like an American woman" (511). More than Pan, Mrs. Spring Fragrance moves comfortably between both Chinese and white American cultures; she expresses in a single sentence the wish to remain in San Francisco "for the celebration of the Fifth Moon Festival and the making of American 'fudge'" (509), and she concludes her declaration to her husband that she intends to write a book as the American women do with a request that he bring her her parasol and fan (520). Although she delights in addressing her husband in traditional Chinese phrases, she also delights in informing him that there are women in America "'as brilliant and great of mind as one of your own superior sex'" (509). Her comment has, of course, a double edge since the woman she refers to, Mrs. Samuel Smith, has taken her to hear the lecture on "America, the Protector of China." In critiquing this lecture Mrs. Spring Fragrance defines herself as superior to both the white woman and the Chinese man. Her comment serves not only to ironize her assertion of the superiority of men's minds; it serves as well to suggest that the conventions of male superiority may inhibit men in their ability to develop a cross-gendered *mestiza* consciousness just as the conventions of American superiority stifle the development of "whites." Mrs. Smith is an intelligent woman, yet she becomes stupid in her belief that such a lecture would be "edifying" to her Chinese friend. Mr. Spring Fragrance is an intelligent man but he becomes stupid when he tells his neighbor Will Carman that Mrs. Spring Fragrance remains in San Francisco by his "bidding" because he wishes to give a "smoking party" in her absence. Although initially Mr. Spring Fragrance declares himself uninterested in "the secret talk of women" (506), by the end of the story he acknowledges himself more interested in such talk than in business (514). For Sui Sin Far, hybridity includes a mixing of the cultures of gender as well as those of race, and in drawing on multiple cultures she makes for herself a culture richer than any one of her sources.

Mrs. Spring Fragrance demonstrates considerable tolerance for ambiguity; she possesses the ability to change habitual ways of thinking and to do that which she has previously declared she never would do: "'When I first came to America . . . my husband desired me to wear the American dress. I protested and declared that never would I so appear. But one day he brought home a gown fit for a fairy, and ever since then I have worn and adored the American dress'" (517). These "Leaves from the Mental Portfolio of an Eurasian," the title Sui Sin Far gave to her autobiographical sketch, give her the flexibility to respond to situations as they arise, to treat issues locally and contextually, and to model this behavior for others. When she discovers that her neighbor's son is in love with the "inferior woman," she ceases instantly to argue the case of the "superior woman," much to her husband's surprise and bewilderment. Such transformations of perspective in response to new information are the very essence of Mrs. Spring Fragrance's *mestiza* consciousness, and in response to her husband's confusion she declares that "'yesterday, O Great Man, I was a caterpillar'" (516). Similarly, when confronted with her friend Laura's resistance to her arranged marriage, she intervenes to prevent the marriage. While her intervention leads her husband to believe she may be rejecting her own arranged marriage to him, Mrs. Spring Fragrance possesses the flexibility to know that, while an arranged marriage would be a tragedy for her friend, in her own case it has proved to be the source of her greatest happiness. For Sui Sin Far such flexibility makes Mrs. Spring Fragrance the truly superior woman.

While hybridity constitutes a creative possibility for Mrs. Spring Fragrance, despite the fact that she is by birth fully Chinese, for Zitkala-Ša hybridity means deracination without assimilation, the *mestiza* seen as neither fish nor fowl and totally queer and despised as a result. Zitkala-Ša can neither pass as white nor creatively fashion herself as a hybrid; she can neither lose her racial and cultural identity nor remain within it, nor can she find a way in America to become more than either white or red by becoming a mixture of both. Although assimilation is the putative goal of removing her from the reservation and sending her east to school, even those who run the school do not believe that assimilation is really possible. No matter how educated she becomes, she will always be a "squaw," the label that confronts her when she begins to win contests in oratory (*AWR* 559). But once so educated, she can never go home again, nor can she imagine how to put her various identities together to make a new culture hospitable to her. If she wears shoes instead of moccasins she will be denying her Indian heritage, but if she wears moccasins instead of shoes she will be masquerading as something she no longer is, impersonating her former self. When she decides to return east to college, she does so against her mother's express wishes and in so doing she irrevocably separates from her mother. Thus she ends her second sketch with a scene in her room following her triumph in the oratorical contest: "I laughed no more in triumph when thus alone. The little taste of victory did not satisfy a hunger in my heart. In my mind I saw my mother far away on the Western plains, and she was holding a charge against me" (559).

Recognizing that in her "deliberate disobedience" (558) to her mother she has elicited a "charge" against her, we return to her first sketch with the realization that it seeks to lay to rest that charge. Written after her separation from her mother and in an apparent effort to prove that "'mother' lives," it presents her mother's world as uncomplicatedly positive. Writing to answer her mother's charge, however, she cannot answer the key question her sketch raises—if this world was so wonderful why did she leave it? In the absence of any possibility of hybridity, a possibility that might have provided an answer to this question, Zitkala-Ša throws her readers back on old fables and stereotypes, on the biblical story of the temptation and fall, reinforced by her reference to apples, and on the white man's favorite image of the Indian as easily seduced into giving up everything for a handful of glass beads. This gap in her ability to explain herself mirrors the one she feels between her culture of origin and her current position. The world of her mother as she recreates it was good but it is gone, and she has no model for how she might carry the values of her mother and the lessons that she learns from her into a world that cannot hear Iktomi stories. When she returns to school for her second term she takes with her a "tiny bunch of magic roots" (557) to ward off the evil she feels in the environment to which she has chosen to return. But she loses the bag containing the roots and then she loses her faith in them, and so she signals the impossibility of bridging the culture of home and the culture of school. Unable to pass and therefore to use passing as a way of critiquing concepts of race, yet unable as well to remain Indian, with no model of hybridity or of an America that might be made to mean the space in which a new race could emerge, Zitkala-Ša lacks a rhetorical foothold for negotiation. Although she has oratorical power sufficient to win contests, in her writing we find mostly silence.

Ironically and inadvertently, of course, this very silence seems to reproduce the attitude toward Indians that has effectively silenced her. Even the praline woman in Dunbar-Nelson's story feels affronted by Tonita, "'dat lazy Indien squaw'" (*AWR* 480), who sits wrapped in her blanket, saying nothing, and we might explain her response by recalling the passage from *Feminism Unmodified* that we chose as the epigraph for chapter 2. As MacKinnon points out, "If certain experiences are never spoken about, if certain people or issues are seldom heard from, it is supposed that silence has been chosen" (168), and the praline woman, who has managed to insert her voice into the speech of her customers, assumes Tonita has chosen silence to affront her. Austin, however, as we have noted in chapter 4, understands this silence differently, seeing it as a sign of the difficulties that beset attempts at cross-cultural communication and interpreting it as a limit beyond which she may not go in her attempt to understand the "other." She writes, "But suppose you find Seyavi retired into the privacy of her blanket, you will get nothing for that day. There is no other privacy possible in a campoodie. . . . Something to wrap around him is as necessary to the Paiute as to you your closet to pray in" (577). Similarly, the narrator of King's "A Crippled Hope" ends by marking little Mammy's silence. Although the convalescent white woman finds it balm "to have another's story given her" (*Balcony Stories* 166), and though the narrator who tells little Mammy's story urges at the end that "one should hear her tell it herself" (123), the narrator's own story, like that of Austin's "The Basket Maker," ends with silence: "the ear drops words, sentences; one gets confused—one sleeps—one dreams" (123).

Austin's reticence to intrude her own interpretation of Seyavi's silence and King's suggestion that little Mammy's auditors drop her "words, sentences" and therefore cannot do justice to her story both mark the white female narrators' own choice of silence as a form of cross-cultural and cross-racial liminality. In that middle space, where neither the racialized other nor the racially self-conscious white narrator feels "free to say," chosen silence marks a space of indeterminacy. Within that space, narrators demonstrate restraint. Unlike the white mothers on the train Zitkala-Ša recalls, whose children "took their forefingers out of their mouths and pointed at my moccasined feet," and who, "instead of reproving such rude curiosity, looked closely at me, and attracted their children's further notice to my blanket" (*AWR* 548), the narrators in "The Basket Maker" and "A Crippled Hope" recognize the limits of their desire or ability to tell someone else's story, especially across racial lines. In this way, the respectful silence that marks regionalism's careful approach reflects its own *mestiza* consciousness; hybridity becomes a feature of narrative as well as a condition of social identity. Whether it is chosen silence that wraps Seyavi in her blanket or a culturally enforced silencing of persons of color that only allows King's narrator in 1893 to wish that little Mammy could tell her own story, when a white writer makes such silence visible in the text, she is in effect marking her own "whiteness" and its narrative privilege, thereby approaching something akin to *mestiza* consciousness. Wherever white regionalist narrators demonstrate reticence, they thereby recognize hybrid textual space. Leaving such space unoccupied, they mark openings for regionalist writers and characters of color to enter unaffronted, free either to tell their stories or to keep silence. Regionalism becomes "free to say" hybridity. Of course, to the extent that such hybridity reflects the full range of Anzaldúa's "*mestiza* consciousness," it is also very much a "queer" space, as we will discuss in chapter 10.

CHAPTER 10

Regionalism as "Queer" Theory

"She is the Queen's Twin," and Mrs. Todd looked steadily to see how I might bear the great surprise.
"The Queen's Twin?" I repeated.

—Sarah Orne Jewett, "The Queen's Twin"

Even when coupled with a toleration of minority sexualities, heteronormativity can be overcome only by actively imagining a necessarily and desirably queer world.

—Michael Warner, "Introduction," *Fear of a Queer Planet*

Difference and the Odd

In our story, regionalism enters fiction by way of the queer. Choosing in *The Pearl of Orr's Island* to introduce Aunts Roxy and Ruey after her "main" story has begun, Stowe places these "singular" women (*AWR* 26) outside of the main. Yet, as we have observed in chapter 6 and argued elsewhere (Fetterley, "Only a Story"), Stowe's desire to write a "Maine" story stemmed in large part from her desire to introduce the figures of Roxy and Ruey. Aware as Stowe must have been of the homonymic relation of main and Maine, yet also of the difference between a region and the national norm, we can argue as well that Stowe intends us to see these women as at once queering the region and destabilizing the certainties that accompany assertions of normalcy: "Miss Roxy sometimes, in her brusque way, popped out observations on life and things, with a droll, hard quaintness that took one's breath a little, yet never failed to have a sharp crystallization of truth,—frosty though it were" (*AWR* 28).

Initially we were attracted to regionalism because of its difference from what we had come to know as American literature. Indeed, in a certain sense we have long thought of regionalism as "queer" fiction. The emergence of queer theory, however, creates a context within which our use of the term becomes at once more problematic and more resonant. In particular, it may seem queer to use the term "queer" in a context in which sexual orientation is not clearly identified as the origin of stigma, in which the queer is not read specifically in relation to the categories of lesbian and gay, and in which a focus on "mismatches between sex, gender, and desire" does not seem obviously operational (Jagose 2). Yet within queer theory there is a recognition that "the preference for 'queer' represents, among other things, an aggressive impulse of generalization . . . a more thorough resistance to regimes of the normal," a recognition that "'queer' gets a critical edge by defining itself against the normal rather than the heterosexual" (Warner, "Introduction" xxvi). While the impulse toward generalization carries with it the danger of overextension and overuse to the point of meaninglessness, it also "has the effect of pointing out a wide field of normalization, rather than simple intolerance, as the site of violence" and allows us to place regionalism within this understanding of queer theory as it challenges a "wide field" of "regimes of the normal" (xxvi).

In *The Trouble with Normal,* however, Warner emphasizes the pervasive and deep connection between regimes of the normal and regimes of the (hetero)sexual. Critiquing the contemporary gay and lesbian movement for its belief "that to have dignity gay people must be seen as normal" (52) and that to be "normal" requires repudiating the very "sex for which it stands" (48), Warner proposes that we

> [t]ry imagining, by contrast, that heterosexuality might be irrelevant to the normative organization of the world. People are constantly encouraged to believe that heterosexual desire, dating, marriage, reproduction, childrearing, and home life are not only valuable to themselves, but the bedrock on which every other value in the world rests. Heterosexual desire and romance are thought to be the very core of humanity. It is the threshold of maturity that separates the men from the boys (though it is also projected onto all boys and girls). It is both nature and culture. It is the one thing celebrated in every film plot, every sitcom, every advertisement. It is the one thing to which every politician pays obeisance, couching every dispute over guns and butter as an effort to protect family, home, and children. What would a world look like in which all these links between sexuality and people's ideals were suddenly severed? (47)

As we have indicated in chapter 6, regionalist fiction resists the plot of plot, "the old, old story" whose "bewitching power" Cooke acknowledges even as she seeks to subvert it and whose "desire and romance," as Warner observes, "are thought to be the very core of humanity." It thus resists as well the circuits of heterosexuality and heteronormativity that such plots embody and enforce. In this sense, the very form of regionalist fiction is queer and queer in a way that touches on issues of sexuality.[1] Further, regionalism's insistence on foregrounding characters who do not participate in heterosexual plots and who thus do not participate actively in the reproduction of heterosexuality—characters who are old women with beard hairs rather than heroines falling in love—challenges the link between heterosexuality and humanity and locates regionalism as participating in the construction of a queer planet (see Warner, "Introduction").

In this context we might also consider the point Douglas Crimp makes when he observes that "in many circumstances the mark of one's heterosexuality is the open expression of hatred towards queers" (305). If hating queers provides the surest proof of heterosexuality, then the term "queer" is never very far removed from the realm of the sexual. Moreover, it also follows that refusing to participate in the hatred of queers creates the ground for a suspicion of sexual deviance. By its refusal to participate in the hatred of queers, regionalist fiction becomes suspect as sexually deviant. At the very least, it self-identifies as non-heteronormative and as resisting regimes of the normal that include the regimes of sexuality. For example, in Freeman's "A New England Nun," we might read Louisa's queerness, those behaviors that make her an oddity in her culture and would make her even more odd were she to fully reveal them as having a sexual dimension, for her "path" seems less that of celibacy than of auto-eroticism. The language Freeman uses to describe Louisa's treatment of herself—the sensual delight she takes in preparing her food, distilling her essences, and sewing her seams—partakes of the erotic even though no specifically erotic language is used. In this context we might also return to Jagose's concept of "mismatch" and read Louisa's queerness as an example of the kind of "mismatch" that dramatizes "incoherencies in the allegedly stable relations between chromosomal sex, gender, and sexual desire" (2). Louisa's delight in performing femininity alerts us to locate a "mismatch" not in the relation of sex and gender but in the relation of gender and desire. Louisa desires to love herself and she accurately perceives a mismatch between her desire and her gender whose cultural script requires her to want marriage. In articulating this mismatch and in connecting it to Louisa's queerness, Freeman destabilizes the supposedly stable relations of sex, gender, and desire, raising the profoundly provocative and deeply disturbing possibility that any woman who retains the birthright of self-love may indeed be labeled sexually "queer." Such a reading serves to remind us as well of the historic connection between feminism and the "queer" and of the possibility that feminism may be the queerest theory of all. Indeed, the current stigma attached to the label "feminist" enables it to be mobilized as a mode of social control in much the same way as the term "queer" is mobilized.

One could argue that the term "lesbian" remains potentially more radical for feminist analytics than the term "queer," given that the virtue of queer's range of reference can all too easily become the danger of a diluted specificity in which the challenge to male privilege and to patriarchal regimes of power becomes obscured, insignificant, or even nonexistent. Nonetheless, it would be inaccurate for us to seek to recuperate regionalist fiction as part of a tradition of nineteenth-century lesbian literature, even though certain texts, and certain writers, may usefully be so understood.[2] The difficulty here goes well beyond the problematics of terminology, made so spectacularly apparent by Foucault in his *History of Sexuality, Volume I.*[3] It includes as well the discursive conventions governing women's writing in the second half of the nineteenth century and the conventions governing magazine publication in the post–Civil War era, neither of which were hospitable to explicit discussions of female sexuality. More significantly, however, such an attempt threatens the term "lesbian" with the same danger that accompanies the term "queer"; it threatens to dissolve the specificity of lesbian identity, lesbian experience, and lesbian erotics into the less specified category of women's culture and into a post-bellum version of "the female world of love and ritual."[4] Nevertheless, in *The Girls Next Door,* Lindsy Van Gelder and Pamela Brandt, in their effort to define what constitutes lesbian identity and what predicts that a woman will come to call herself a lesbian, conclude: "The embrace of weirdness is actually a pretty good predictor of which women are going to find lesbianism an easy fit. The two of us like to say that we were queer years before we were gay. To be a lesbian is, by definition, to flout social conventions. Bookworm? Tomboy? Rule-breaker? Felt like a changeling in your family? Women who answer yes to any of the above may feel instantly comfortable with the outsider status that more readily comes with the lesbian territory" (111). In their construction of the personal history of those women who in the late twentieth century might at some point define themselves as lesbian, Van Gelder and Brandt posit "queer" as a prior identity that can serve as a predictor of lesbianism. In a similar vein we might argue that in terms of cultural history, queer is an identity that precedes, as well as succeeds, lesbian, and in the latter part of the nineteenth century the word "queer" indicates the presence of anxiety and conflict specifically related to issues of gender and sexuality that might later be labeled lesbian. As Lindemann notes, in her discussion of a "pivotal moment in Cather's life—the 1890's," her "primary goal was to contribute to the historiography of the 'queer' by demonstrating that it was a name for sexual deviance—and specifically for female sexual deviance—well before World War I and in a region far removed from the eastern, urban enclaves of long-haired men and short-haired women analyzed by Chauncey and others" (77).[5]

Earlier in her study of Cather, in an effort to articulate her own particular relation to queer theory, Lindemann explains:

> In certain contexts—i.e. the context of the contemporary struggle for civil equality—I believe it is important and even urgent to use names that insist upon what Sedgwick has called the legal and "the epistemological distinctiveness of gay identity and gay situation in our culture." In terms of the present study, however, what really matters is that "queer" *is* a name Willa Cather called *her*self, and she did so in the only documents we have that speak directly to her sexual self-identification, the letters of the 1890's that are either to or about her college crush, Louise Pound. Beyond these private, terrified acts of self-nam-

ing and -unnaming, the word "queer" resonates throughout Cather's fiction with the snap, crackle, and pop of acute anxiety and ideological work. (12)[6]

In describing the essays included in *Fear of a Queer Planet,* Michael Warner writes that they "suggest that political struggles over sexuality ramify in an unimaginably large number of directions. . . . Every person who comes to a queer self-understanding knows in one way or another that her stigmatization is connected with gender, the family, notions of individual freedom, the state, public speech, consumption and desire" (xii). Similarly, we might argue that areas apparently disconnected to issues of sexuality—areas such as "notions of individual freedom, the state, public speech"—are in fact so connected and we might propose a model of working backward, exemplified by our reading of "A New England Nun," to complement Warner's model of working forward. Indeed, both Lindemann's understanding of the operations of the term "queer" in the late nineteenth-century United States and Warner's understanding of its operations in the late twentieth-century United States provide frames that allow us to suggest that stigmatization as queer in areas apparently disconnected with sexuality may in fact be so connected. Given this context we can legitimately attend to the ways in which the term "queer" as it appears in regionalist fiction resonates "with the snap, crackle, and pop of acute anxiety and ideological work" around issues of gender and sexuality as they affect women's experience, identities, and erotics, and, in certain instances, see it as a precursor to what could legitimately be called lesbian literature.

Invoking queer theory as a frame for reading regionalism, then, allows us to attend to the presence of sexuality in texts that at first glance seem remote from such concerns. In addition, it allows us to sharpen our argument for regionalism as a fiction of resistance by connecting "the preference for 'queer'" to "a more thorough resistance to regimes of the normal" understood as encompassing a "wide field" that goes well beyond the sexual (Warner, "Introduction" xxvi). Queer theorists seem to agree that the "essence" of the term lies in its "fundamental indeterminacy" (Jagose 96). "Queer is by definition whatever is at odds with the normal, the legitimate, the dominant. *There is nothing in particular to which it refers,*" writes David Halperin; "it is an identity without an essence" (62). Jagose proposes that queer is "less an identity than a *critique* of identity" (131). She extends this proposal to argue that the term is "necessarily relational rather than oppositional. . . . By refusing to crystallize in any specific form, queer maintains a relation of resistance to whatever constitutes the normal" (98, 99). These various formulations point to the fact that "queer" is a shifting signifier, capable of being self-consciously adopted and deployed as a mode of critique against what in any given moment gets constructed as the "normal."

When used to refer to someone else, however, "queer" can be deployed as a fear-inducing tactic designed to establish the normativity of a wide range of behaviors. Warner notes that queer is "a term initially generated in the context of terror" (xxvi), and Lindemann observes that queer "is generally a judgment rendered in a context of terror and threat" (47). Such recognitions enable us to attend to the terrorism that accompanies the operations of the term "queer" in fictions where the presence of terror and terrorism, like the presence of sexuality, may not be obvious. Moreover, they enable us to conceptualize regionalist fiction as engaging in the cultural work of anti-terrorism. In its recognition that queer is not so much a fixed identity as it is a shifting signifier used to do the work of constructing the normal, regionalism both exposes and opposes that work, using the perspective of the so-called queer to suggest the oddity of the so-called normal and offering empathy as an alternative to terrorism in the approach to difference. By so doing, regionalism participates in what Eve Sedgwick has termed "epistemology of the closet" and becomes a form of what Berlant and Warner call "queer commentary," a term they develop in recognition of the fact that texts may provide insight as to the operations of the "queer" without being what could legitimately be called theory (343).

As we consider the extraordinary array of queerness that regionalist fiction presents in terms both of character and of form, we might argue that regionalism merits the definition of queer simply for the energy it devotes "just in finding ways of being queer" and for the "kind of practical social reflection" it engages in as a result of this activity (Warner xiii). More significantly, however, regionalism merits the label "queer" for its willingness to engage in the social reproduction of queers. In "How to Bring Your Kids Up Gay," Sedgwick exposes the homophobic wish at the heart of Western culture "that gay people *not be,*" and articulates "the overarching, hygienic Western fantasy of a world without any more homosexuals in it" (79, 78). In his comments on Sedgwick's essay, Warner argues that because "[t]he idea that the emergence of more queers might be a desirable outcome remains unthinkable," we must engage in "actively imagining a necessarily and desirably queer world" (xvi). Regionalism, we would propose, engages in actively imagining a queer world as both necessary and desirable. It does so explicitly in stories like Cooke's "How Celia Changed Her Mind," which dramatizes the social reproduction of the queer when Celia holds a Thanksgiving dinner to celebrate the existence of old maids and declares that she intends "'to adopt Rosy Barker's two children, and fetch 'em up to be dyed-in-the-wool old maids'" (*AWR* 153); and it does so implicitly by presenting as unthinkable a world *without* queers, for little would be left if queers were removed from regionalist fiction. In discussing Cather's account of the Jewett-Fields establishment at "148 Charles Street," Lindemann notes that the Annie Fields who appears in Cather's memoir "laughingly greets the 'queer' as a signifier of aesthetic originality, a boldness and newness that are clearly welcome at her tea table" (84).[7] Similarly, in her analysis of *The Song of the Lark*, she observes that "[a]s with so many of the spinster-story-tellers of Jewett's fiction, Tillie's eccentricity is not coded as pathology, and the instability she brings to her community is viewed as productive rather than destructive" (48). Writing that "[t]he narrator of *The Song of the Lark* literally smiles on Tillie, insisting that the 'wildest conceits' of this queer 'romancer,' far from threatening the prairie, are essential to its imaginative and economic life," she argues that "here the queer is a tonic presence, for Tillie's stories make Moonstone 'habitable and wholesome'" (48).[8] Through the links that connect Jewett, Fields, and Cather we can theorize regionalism as a fiction that also asserts the queer as "a tonic presence" and commits itself to "actively imagining a . . . *desirably* queer world" (emphasis added). For we should not forget that the person most "welcome at [Fields's] tea table" was none other than Jewett herself, whose "aesthetic originality" is profoundly tied to the queer. If we wish, we can think of regionalist fiction in its entirety as a version of Celia's Thanksgiving dinner dedicated to welcoming and reproducing queers.

Queer theory in a certain sense is a recent development; in another sense it has been around a long time. Perhaps part of the reason for the increasing interest it has generated at the turn of the twenty-first century stems from the fact that it articulates and frames thinking that has itself been waiting to "come out." In this context we might profitably adapt Berlant and Warner's question, "What Does Queer Theory Teach Us about X?" to ask, what can regionalism teach us about queer theory? For just as queer theory enables a more complicated reading of regionalism, so regionalism enables a more complicated understanding of what constitutes queer theory, particularly through its emphasis on approach and its choice of form.

Queer Consciousness

A sense of being queer shapes the consciousness that produces our historically first set of regionalist texts. In Cary's "My Grandfather," the narrator, already on the outside of the family circle and observing through the window the daily activities of "normal" life, listens as her brother reads from the paper the story of a wild man recently discovered whose "nails are grown like claws" and whose "hair, in rough and matted strings, hangs to his knees." He flees in terror from his "discoverers" uttering hideous screams and they suspect that there are others like him more terrible still (*Clovernook Sketches* 11). The narrator's father rebukes his son for reading such "foolish" stories, but, as we suggested in chapter 6, we are invited to speculate on the attraction of this story to the narrator and to see in this attraction her perception of her own wildness and the terror that accompanies this sense of being different. For in this brief account Cary analyzes the operations of terror in the context of difference. The wild man is terrorized by his discoverers because they construct his difference as terrible and terrifying. Cary's narrator comes to consciousness then in a context of the queer, recognizing that it is possible to be so "wild" that one becomes a source of terror to others and is thus terrorized herself. Yet this perspective also enables her to see the terrorism in so-called normal daily life—in the rebuke of a father, for example, and in his teasing behavior that reduces another child to tears. The queer child sees things differently and Cary's fiction seeks to articulate what the world looks like from this perspective.

Like Cary, Zitkala-Ša presents directly and rawly the emotions that accompany being seen as wild, and, as with Cary, we come to realize that the subjectivity speaking to us in her work has been formed in the crucible of the queer, that we are reading the words of one who has been labeled a freak and who has had to negotiate life from within and around that label: "Directly in front of me, children who were no larger than I hung themselves upon the backs of their seats, with their bold white faces toward me. Sometimes they took their forefingers out of their mouths and pointed at my moccasined feet. Their mothers, instead of reproving such rude curiosity, looked closely at me, and attracted their children's further notice to my blanket. This embarrassed me, and kept me constantly on the verge of tears" (*AWR* 548). Yet when she returns home during "four strange summers," she discovers that her mother can no longer understand her and "was not capable of comforting her daughter who could read and write. Even nature seemed to have no place for me. I was neither a wee girl nor a tall one; neither a wild Indian nor a tame one" (555). In both contexts, her identity becomes that of a person who is queer.

Although consciousness of the self as queer is not directly present in their fiction, Murfree, Austin, and Sui Sin Far struggled with such perceptions and labels throughout their lives—Murfree because of the illness she suffered at the age of four that left her permanently lame; Austin because as a child she experienced rejection from her mother and then from her schoolmates for her "difference"; Sui Sin Far for being mixed-race in a race-stratified social world. We might reasonably surmise that Murfree's attraction to mountain culture stemmed from her sense of its difference and we might further conclude that she found a way to negotiate her own sense of difference through writing about mountain culture. Similarly, we might argue that Austin found herself attracted to the desert because in this region all conventional understandings of the normal and the queer become suspended; writing about the desert, where what is ordinarily seen as different becomes natural and accepted, permitted the unimpeded expression of her own genius. In particular, the desert allowed Austin to imagine a woman like herself as something other than a freak, for in her description of what the desert would be like if it were a woman we see transformed all those features that led Austin to be labeled queer—her size, her looks, her aggressive sexuality, and even her arrogance (see *AWR* 591–92). As we discussed in the previous chapter, Sui Sin Far found a way to explore what she called "Leaves from the Mental Portfolio of an Eurasian" by writing fiction about the experience of mixed-race and hybrid Chinese in the United States.

In some ways Cooke's narrator presents herself as more resolutely normal than the narrators of most regionalist texts—she seems determinedly cheerful, occupies more space than most narrators, seems to have no end or limit to the words she can produce, and addresses her readers with breezy self-confidence. Yet we might understand this as compensatory behavior, symptomatic in the psychoanalytic sense of reaction formation, if we consider an early Cooke story to be a coded form of self-representation. "Maya, the Princess," a story that can be read as Cooke's narrative of her own origins, offers an extended fable of what it means to grow up queer, to feel "like a changeling in your family" (Van Gelder and Brandt 111). At the birth of her daughter, Maya, Queen Lura invites all the fairies of her realm to come and bestow gifts upon the child, but she neglects to invite the fairy Anima, whose night-black hair, lurid glow, and palpable power mark her as different. Enraged by her rejection and coming now in anger, she bestows upon the child despite her mother's protestations the "gift" of the Spark, the gift of intelligence, desire, and power that will render her different from other women and queer. Although the child will be no ordinary woman and lead no ordinary woman's life, the Spark will not exempt her from the desires of ordinary women (or, perhaps better, will not protect her from the pressure to have those desires) for love, home, and family. Thus it will prove a curse because she will not, like other women, be able to accept illusion for reality.[9] Although she arrives too late to prevent the "gift" of the Spark—in this story good mothers definitely do not want to bring their kids up gay and Queen Lura is delighted when she has another daughter "who was just like all the other children" (*"How Celia Changed Her Mind"* 7)—the fairy Cordis, "her deep gray eyes brimming with motherhood" (5), offers a "countercharm" that if used correctly will allow the princess to distinguish the true from the false and will enable her to lead the "perfect life" in which heart and head are one (5, 6). In holding out the hope that this queer child might be normalized, the countercharm becomes an even greater curse; encouraging her to seek only love, home, and family, it leads her inevitably to the most bitter of all disillusions and to the self-hatred that attends one intelligent enough to realize she has been tricked by appearance and has pursued an illusion. Although Maya becomes a successful artist, known throughout the world for "the stinging arrows of her wit" and her "mad and rapt music" (11), she can find no peace from the bitterness of her discovery that all is illusion, is "maya," and for the hopeless division she acknowledges between mind and heart. And so she willingly accepts the way out offered at last by her "mother" Anima, taking up life as the humblest of beggars, concealing rank, intelligence, passion, and power in the guise of one who has and is nothing, "songless, discrowned, desolate" (13).

In this devastating story of the fate of a woman singled out as different we may read Cooke's own desire not to be queer and we may understand even more the determined performance of the normal by which she veils her difference.[10] However, we might see in this story as well her acknowledgment that, despite her desire to be ordinary, she is not, and so we might infer that her fictions emerge, like those of Cary and Zitkala-Ša, from queer consciousness. Queerness is a curse that cannot be evaded no matter what programs of normalization one might attempt. In her fiction, then, Cooke continues to speak those truths that are the "gift" of the Spark; in particular she exposes those illusions that form the fabric of the ordinary—those illusions of love, home, and family—by which women lead their lives and are cheated of their lives, even as she finds herself drawn to those illusions and even as she recognizes that the world offers little welcome to the truths she must speak. Cooke offers scant hope for the reconciliation of mind and heart for women, and while it would be better not to be cursed with the Spark, if one is so cursed one has no alternative save to continue to tell the truth, in full recognition of the fact that telling the truth will be seen as the queerest behavior of all.[11]

Queering the Region

If we turn from what might be called the formation of queer consciousness to the presentation of queer characters, we can extend our analysis of how regionalism deploys the term "queer" and how it understands and approaches difference. In light of Cooke's "autobiographical" Maya, we are not surprised to find the term "queer" appearing in her fiction "with the snap, crackle, and pop of acute anxiety and ideological work." She titles one of her stories "Odd Miss Todd" and in it specifically refers to her main character as "queer" (*Huckleberries* 90). Through her title Cooke links the term "queer" to the category of "old maid," thus providing a context for understanding the terror that drives Celia Barnes in "How Celia Changed Her Mind" to marry anyone at any cost simply to escape being stigmatized and despised. In "Odd Miss Todd," however, Cooke performs the yet odder act of creating a character who, while seeming odd to others, does not see herself as odd but rather finds odd those behaviors others label normal.

Hermione Todd is "odd" because she has been raised by an odd father in an odd fashion, isolated and without formal education. When her father dies, she inherits enough money to move to town and to commence her project of learning to know her own "kind."[12] Once there, she discovers behaviors that are anything but kind and that suggest she has no kin; these behaviors puzzle and disturb her, for they seem odd indeed: "Their gossip grated on her charity of soul, their little meannesses seemed to her unworthy of beings who had an eternity at stake, and her heart raged at the cruelties of domestic life which she could not but see among those about her" (91). Miss Todd finds equally odd the discrepancy between what people say and what they do, and she finds odd the failure of others to notice or comment on this discrepancy. Confronting one of the worst gossips in Dorset, who prefaces every mean remark with "'I wish her well'" and "'well, I don't want to say nothin,'" but continues to accuse a "'poor homeless cretur'" of lying, Miss Todd snaps back, "'What in the world do you keep doing it for, then?'" (97–98). Similarly, when a visiting minister delivers a sermon that everyone agrees to be "a most be-a-utiful discourse," Miss Todd confronts him with the question of how he can preach such "stuff" to persons whose souls he has but this one chance to save (93–94). Miss Todd survives, avoiding outright rejection and abuse, because she speaks from the heart and out of charity and because she delivers her truths with a disarming sense of humility. Moreover, she is rich and "when Dorset knew that Miss Todd owned thirty thousand dollars besides her fifty-acre farm, it tacitly agreed that she could do and say what she pleased" (92). However, the village contains her truths by calling her "odd." When the visiting minister, aghast at her comment, asks "who the woman was who had stopped him," he is told, "'Oh, that is odd Miss Todd'" (94). As Cooke realizes, to be labeled queer severely circumscribes one's ability to be heard.

By the end of the story, however, we can understand still more fully why Cooke's own narrator wants to be seen as normal. The narrator needs to be heard as Cooke begins her most complex treatment of the odd. In the final incident Miss Todd does the most "normal" thing in the world—she falls in love with a man who is not what she thinks him to be and who abandons her despite the allure of her thirty thousand dollars. Although Miss Todd is protected from exposure because no one in Dorset can imagine that odd Miss Todd would be experiencing something so ordinary as a woman's affection for a worthless man and a man's exploitation and then rejection of that affection, if we have accepted the narrator's perspective Miss Todd's behavior seems now to be odd. How, we ask, could such a clear-seeing and clear-hearted woman be so deluded? We find odder still the revulsion and self-hatred that this previously self-loving woman feels when the man in question proves his worthlessness. From the narrator's perspective Miss Todd becomes truly odd only when she acts most "normal." Or to put it another way, when Miss Todd begins to act "normal," Cooke's narrator begins to emerge as "odd."

When Miss Todd recovers from the illness she suffers on account of the young man's marriage and begins to act like herself again, Cooke's analysis takes another turn. More odd than ever in the eyes of Dorset, in the eyes of the narrator she makes a reasonable and intelligible response. "Toward men she became pitiless and almost fierce" but toward women she expresses a "deeper, tenderer charity," sympathizing "with their pains and follies more than women often do with each other" (118). She establishes a private school for the education of local girls and makes a new will in which all her money will go to found a "female college" (119). In effect Hermione Todd becomes that queerest of all creatures, a feminist, who reasserts her sense of her own worth, and, refusing to blame the victim, devotes her love, energy, and resources to women rather than to the worthless man who still believes he will inherit the money that attracted him in the first place. In "Odd Miss Todd," Miss Todd finds a way of being queer that calls into question conventional understandings of the normal and that makes clear that such terms as "odd" and "normal" have no inherent, fixed, or stable meanings but are shifting signifiers, deployed in the service of various interests.

In *Deephaven* Jewett gives us "real" freaks in real freak shows ("The Circus at Denby"), but Sylvia from "A White Heron" is a queer child and Jewett's work contains many queers.[13] To name only a few, these include Captain Littlepage, Poor Joanna, William Blackett, and Sant Bowden from *The Country of the Pointed Firs;* Mrs. Bonny from *Deephaven;* Abby Martin from "The Queen's Twin"; Nan Prince, the feminist protagonist of her novel *A Country Doctor;* and the transvestite Captain Dan'l Gunn in "An Autumn Holiday" (for an extended discussion of this story, see Pryse, "Sex, Class, and 'Category Crisis'"). By filling her fiction with queers, by so thoroughly queering the region, Jewett questions the existence of the "normal" and indeed thoroughly destabilizes the concept of normal. Yet this does not prevent her from recognizing how the concept functions as a form of social control. In fact, Jewett's work gains much of its energy from negotiating the tension that comes from at once recognizing the meaninglessness of the term "normal" and being drawn to participate in its operations. When her Boston narrators arrive in Deephaven or Dunnet Landing, how do they keep from laughing at all the quaint queer folks they find there, even as Jewett allows us to see that her narrators are also queer and see themselves as such? One might say that Jewett bends her art entirely to this challenge and it may not be accidental that her prime negotiator in this business is a Mrs. Todd—Cooke's story was originally published in *Harper's Monthly* in 1882, almost fifteen years before *The Country of the Pointed Firs.* "The Queen's Twin" exemplifies how Mrs. Todd negotiates the challenges posed by the queer and the normal.

Even Mrs. Todd acknowledges that Abby Martin "'might be called a little peculiar'" (*AWR* 225). She lives alone in a remote part of the country and "'she never was a great hand to go about visitin'"; even her visits to her children seem more "ceremonious" than familiar and one of her son's wives declares that Abby would "'much rather have the Queen to spend the day if she could choose between the two'" (225). She has turned her parlor into a shrine to Queen Victoria, covering the walls with pictures clipped from newspapers, and she lives a life of such ritual and regularity that Mrs. Todd can tell exactly what she is doing at any given moment of the day. Yet while all of this might indeed be called peculiar, what marks Abby Martin as truly different and queer is her belief that she is the Queen's "twin"—"'[s]he is the Queen's Twin,' and Mrs. Todd looked steadily to see how I might bear the great surprise" (222). "'There's all sorts o' folks in the country, same's there is in the city,'" says Mrs. Todd, and she further observes that Abby Martin is perfectly "'pleasant and sprightly if you had sense enough to treat her her own way'" (225). Mrs. Todd's willingness to enter into Abby's way of seeing things is itself odd, given that most people, including Mrs. Todd herself, see Abby as a "little peculiar." Yet her understated approach destabilizes the "peculiar," for it points out how little seems queer when viewed from the perspective of the peculiar person. If we ask why Mrs. Todd is so interested in Abby Martin, we might answer that she finds in her a model for approaching the challenges of loneliness, survival, and self-esteem, even if it leads one to be considered eccentric, queer, or even delusional by others. In the most unlikely of circumstances, Abby Martin has found a way to think of herself as a queen, and, as Mrs. Todd acknowledges, "'I expect this business about the Queen has buoyed her over many a shoal place in life'" (227). Meeting the challenge of survival by finding ways of being queer seems preferable to constructing oneself as normal and others as queer—so Mrs. Todd observes that Abby has always been "'high above makin' mean complaints of other folks'" (227)—and if one cannot or will not engage in the business of defining the self as norm and the other as queer, then perhaps there is only the option of finding creative ways of being queer.

All summer long (in *The Country of the Pointed Firs,* which preceded Jewett's writing of "The Queen's Twin") Mrs. Todd has been teaching the narrator how to adopt her approach to difference and the visit to Abby Martin serves as a test of what the narrator has learned. Will she approach Abby with the same respect Mrs. Todd does? Will she communicate this respect to Abby so that Abby will ask her "'into her best room where she keeps all the Queen's pictures'" (227)? Mrs. Todd takes a risk in introducing the narrator to Abby, for from Abby's perspective the narrator is "normal" and she might bring the judgment of the "normal" into the visit. But the story reveals that Mrs. Todd's trust in the narrator is not misplaced: "'I think likely she will ask you; but 'tain't everybody she deems worthy to visit 'em, I can tell you!' said Mrs. Todd warningly" (227). When Abby judges that the narrator does show "genuine interest in the most interesting person in the world"—Queen Victoria—she begins to tell her story, and "Mrs. Todd gave a satisfied nod and glance, as if to say that things were going on as well as possible in this anxious moment" (229). When Mrs. Todd encourages Abby to tell about the time she caught a glimpse of the queen, both listeners are moved to silence by her story: "''twas a moment o' heaven to me. I saw her plain, and she looked right at me so pleasant and happy, just as if she knew there was somethin' different between us from other folks'" (231). The narrator writes, "One could not say much—only listen" (231). At the end of Abby's story, Mrs. Todd says "gently" to Abby: "'Don't it show that for folks that have any fancy in 'em, such beautiful dreams is the real part o' life? But to most folks the common things that happens outside 'em is all in all'" (233). Abby responds by inviting both Mrs. Todd and the narrator into her best room to look at her pictures of the queen. The narrator's success in passing this test proves that one can teach and learn an empathic approach, even though it may require a very long walk to a most out-of-the-way place. Furthermore, "The Queen's Twin," as we observed in chapter 4, suggests that empathic and respectful listening work against conventions of the "normal" that might otherwise silence the stories of those who are unlike "most folks" but who, Mrs. Todd implies, are more connected to "the real part o' life." Queering the region, as we have come to characterize this approach, is Jewett's way of bringing her readers to the same point Mrs. Todd has brought the narrator. Indeed, there are all sorts of folks in the city as well as in the country, and urban readers who read for local color in order to construct their own normality will miss all of life but the "common things."

Jewett is also the writer who brings same-sex desire between women into regionalism in texts that could legitimately be recovered as part of a lesbian literary tradition (Lillian Faderman, for example, includes "Martha's Lady" in her anthology of lesbian literature, *Chloe Plus Olivia*),[14] and who, in one fiction, introduces what in the 1990s came to be named "transgender" into the question of the queer. As we have indicated elsewhere (Fetterley, "Reading *Deephaven* as a Lesbian Text," and Pryse, "Archives of Female Friendship and the 'Way' Jewett Wrote"), we read the relationship between Helen Denis and Kate Lancaster as an erotic one and *Deephaven* as the narrator Helen's retrospective reconstruction of what might be possible in a world in which women like Kate might find "freedom from the pressure to marry" and thereby become available to women like Helen (Fetterley, "Reading 'Deephaven' as a Lesbian Text" 171).[15] In "Martha's Lady" Jewett also explores same-sex desire and its intersection with structures of class; and in "An Autumn Holiday," her narrator explores a community's response to Captain Dan'l Gunn when he begins to wear his dead sister's clothes.[16] In her regional novel, *A Country Doctor,* Jewett implicitly acknowledges her awareness of the medicalization of homosexuality and presents the possibility that her protagonist in that novel, Nan Prince, refuses to marry because she is herself sexually attracted to women (see Donovan, "Nan Prince and the Golden Apples"). However, like most regionalist writers, Jewett has an interest in the queer that derives primarily from her desire to critique the social dynamics by which the odd becomes deviant in order for "most folks" to view themselves as normal. Like Mrs. Todd, Jewett finds ways of being queer far more creative than constructing the self as normal, and by queering the region she provides readers with ways of "actively imagining a necessarily and desirably queer world."

In "The 'Harnt' That Walks Chilhowee," Murfree presents a character whose life has been shaped by the terror that deformity, difference, and queerness elicit in others and that leads them in turn to terrorize those so stigmatized. Reuben Crabb, born with only one arm, a "porely, sickly little critter" (*AWR* 291) who all seem to agree should never have been raised to adulthood, has been subjected all his days to ridicule, abuse, and violence. Supposedly shot dead by the sheriff for killing another man, Reuben is rescued by his brother Joel, who devotes his life to protecting him. When Joel dies, Reuben begins to walk Chilhowee Mountain, for without Joel to get him food he is starving to death. Considered a "harnt" by some, those who have figured it out—"'town folks'" who "'don't think nobody in the mountings hev got good sense'" (299)—have set a two hundred dollar reward for catching him and so he is hunted in "death" as well as in life.

In this story Murfree does not particularly concern herself with destabilizing the definition of queer; though she does not present Reuben Crabb as a freak, neither does she challenge the view others have of him as "deformed" (293). Rather she is concerned with approaches to difference and with exploring approaches that engage difference as something to respond to with empathy rather than abuse. Here queering the region takes the form of locating queer knowledge in those who treat the "harnt" with compassion—in a brother's decision to save him; in Clarsie Giles's insistence that she cannot help feeding him no matter what the law says; in Simon Burney's decision to "catch" him, help him stand trial, and then take him home to live with him for the rest of his miserable life. For Murfree recognizes that living life as a freak does not necessarily develop queer knowledge and indeed may work against doing so: "The cruel gibes of his burly mockers that had beset his feeble life from his childhood up, the deprivation and loneliness and despair and fear that had filled those days when he walked Chilhowee, had not improved the harnt's temper" (302). What Murfree does "queer," however, is the law of the town folks, who believe the mountaineers do not have good sense. In Clarsie's brief encounter with the "party of horsemen" who have come into the mountains to try to collect the reward for the "harnt," she presents Clarsie herself as stigmatized and vulnerable. Here is the passage: "They reined in suddenly as their eyes fell upon her, and their leader, an eager, authoritative man, was asking her a question. Why could she not understand him? With her nerveless hands feebly catching at the shrubs for support, she listened vaguely to his impatient, meaningless words, and saw with helpless deprecation the rising anger in his face. But there was no time to be lost. With a curse upon the stupidity of the mountaineer, who couldn't speak when she was spoken to, the party sped on in a sweeping gallop" (297). It is to Clarsie that Murfree turns for the model of approach to someone in need. Like King's little Mammy, who cannot turn her back on any "emergency of pain and illness" (*Balcony Stories* 124), Murfree writes about Clarsie, "She wondered that she did not fall dead in the road. But while those beseeching eyes were fastened in piteous appeal on hers, she could not leave him" (*AWR* 298).

When Simon Burney, himself marked as queer for his courting of Clarsie, challenges the norms of terrorism by becoming a "powerful ally" for Reuben in court (302), he is also in effect defending Clarsie's "law" against that of the "party of horsemen" for whom the value of a man's life has become commodified in the bounty on his head. In so doing, Simon represents queer knowledge in the story. Out early in the morning on his way to fish, he witnesses Clarsie feeding the starving man and tries to dissuade her: "'Ye air a-doin' wrongful, Clarsie,'" he tells her. "'It air agin the law fur folks ter feed an' shelter them ez is a-runnin' from jestice.'" But Clarsie, who Simon Burney has earlier described as "'a merciful critter,'" "'mighty savin' of the feelin's of everything'" (288), replies, "'I can't holp it. . . . I can't gin my consent ter starvin' of folks, even ef they air a-hidin' an' a-runnin' from jestice'" (301). Clarsie's "merciful" nature does not extend to marrying old widowers, but Simon prevents the sheriff from criminalizing Clarsie's act of charity by becoming Reuben Crabb's advocate. Although he tells Reuben, "'I ain't a-goin' ter holp no man ter break the law an' hender jestice'" (302), he ends by embracing Clarsie's "law" as he commits himself to providing a home for Reuben "'till ye die'" (302). With "no possibility of a recompense" for himself, "ungrudgingly he gave of his best" (303). Clarsie cannot "understand" the "party of horsemen" because they do not speak her language, and their own speech when applied to the mountaineers becomes "meaningless." In Murfree's fiction it is the mountaineers' perspective, as "queer" as it may seem to an urban reader, that becomes "normal" and it is the "impatient" men of the law who can only "curse . . . the stupidity of the mountaineer" who become "queer" in their meanness.

Freeman also creates figures who remain recognizably eccentric and strange but she writes from inside a queer perspective more than do most other regionalist writers. In Freeman's fictions queer consciousness and queer knowledge come together to offer a powerful instance of queering the region. In "Christmas Jenny," for example, included in *Selected Stories,* Freeman explicitly analyzes the horror that the eccentric produces in many New Englanders. The villagers seek to normalize Christmas Jenny's queerness—a queerness that consists in turning her house into a hospital for sick and wounded creatures and bringing the woods inside to make Christmas wreaths—by calling her "love-cracked" (207). Still the pressure of her difference, her "eccentricity, her possibly uncanny deviation from the ordinary ways of life," grows upon the village, for "everything out of the broad, common track was a horror to these men and to many of their village fellows. Strange shadows, that their eyes could not pierce, lay upon such, and they were suspicious" (213–14), and so the minister and the deacon make their way up the mountain to Jenny's house in what Freeman declares "in actual meaning . . . was a witch hunt" (214). The investigation is turned back by the spirited defense of Mrs. Carey, who follows them up the road determined that there be someone there who can speak for Jenny even if, in the process, she too becomes "so abnormal that she was frightful" to the men (213). As far as Mrs. Carey is concerned, Jenny "'ain't love-cracked no more'n other folks'" (213) and she has good reason to know how "cracked" most love is, for she is married to old Jonas who prefers to sit outside on a stone wall in a tantrum when his shoelace comes untied rather than ask for help. Embedding in her story the figure of old Jonas, whose behavior could be said to follow conventional definitions of normal masculinity, yet who from the narrator's perspective is decidedly odd, Freeman makes the point that constructions of the queer are relative and derive more from who has power to impose the label on others than from any absolute standard. Indeed, in the way she tells the story, Freeman makes the point that everything can look queer if viewed a certain way, just as Jewett's Mrs. Todd makes the point that very little looks queer when viewed from the perspective of the "peculiar." Even the behavior of two young lovers, participants in the "heterosexual desire and romance [that] are thought to be the very core of humanity" (Warner, *The Trouble with Normal* 47), seems queer in the context set by the narrator, for the young man never looks directly at the girl, has "little idea as to what she was saying," and the girl herself appears embarrassed to be seen in public with a man to whom she has just become engaged (Freeman 208).

Following up rumors that Jenny has caged and starved wild birds and rabbits and is mistreating a deaf and dumb boy at her cabin in the woods, the minister and the deacon determine to pay her a visit, and when they find her not at home, they feel free to enter her hut uninvited. What they find there, however, alters their perception and subdues their voices, for Jenny has brought nature inside her hut; its walls are lined with the cages of injured animals, its floor is heaped with evergreens, and a little boy "dressed like a girl, in a long blue gingham pinafore" is twining boughs into wreaths (209). As if the boy, queer in the transvestite sense as well, represents Jenny, the men speak in "hushed tones" for "it was hard for them to realize that the boy could not hear, the more so because every time their lips moved his smile deepened. He was not in the least afraid" (210). As the men survey the room "half guiltily" and "did not say what they thought, on account of the little deaf-and-dumb boy," the boy begins a "wild and inarticulate" cry that "seemed to have a meaning of its own" (210). The men have entered a world in which they do not have authority and whose meaning they cannot fathom. The boy's cry "united with the cries of the little caged wild creatures, and it was all like a soft clamor of eloquent appeal to the two visitors, but they could not understand it" (210). Upon the arrival of Mrs. Carey, any lingering authority the men might have retained ends, leaving the deacon speechless and the minister apologetic. Mrs. Carey, on the other hand, finds her voice to criticize at length these self-appointed guardians of the normal: "'I knowed she wa'n't to home, an' there wa'n't nothin' here that could speak, an' I told Jonas I was comin'. . . . I ain't goin' to have you comin' up here to spy on Jenny, an' nobody to home that's got any tongue to speak for her'" (211). Concluding that there is no need for "interference" (214), the deacon and the minister resort to redefining Jenny as someone in need of charity, and the story ends, as do several of Freeman's stories, in a Christmas mood, Jenny and the Careys feasting on a dinner the deacon has sent, the two lovers out walking, and the minister's daughter identifying a light on the mountain as "'Christmas Jenny's candle.'"

However, despite the conventional overtones of the story's ending, its power lies in the portrait of Jenny herself and the capacity of her queerness to disempower the deacon and the minister. If the deacon could be less "severe and grave" (213), then he and the minister might themselves seem less alien from the perspective of the little boy, the animals, and Mrs. Carey, who speak the language of compassion, the one language the villagers seem unable to understand. Thus Freeman leaves her readers with the conviction that the only standard worth embracing is that represented by the wild but utterly sane and compassionate Jenny, and that the story's wisdom is not to be found in the deacons but in the mountain woman who "made one think of those sylvan faces with features composed of bark-wrinkles and knot-holes, that one can fancy looking out of the trunks of trees" (204). The power of Jenny's hut, even in her absence, forces the men who represent "parish discipline" (213) to choose between carrying out their "witch hunt" or normalizing her as an object of charity. When they choose the latter, their Christmas charity allows them to rationalize her power. For Freeman's close readers, however, Jenny retains her eccentricity and a queer knowledge that will not be so rationalized. She remains unruly, unregulated—a regional queer within her own world.

We can understand further what it means to say that Freeman writes from inside the perspective of the queer if we examine "Sister Liddy," a story that takes place in an almshouse. As Freeman notes, "[t]he almshouse stood upon rising ground, so one could see it for a long distance" and she describes the town's pride in the facility for "no town far or near had such a house for the poor" (*AWR* 323). Although Freeman does not specifically place the almshouse with respect to the rest of the town, we may infer that it is on the outskirts as it is surrounded by the town fields and can be seen from a distance. Both isolation and visibility indicate how nineteenth-century communities dealt with those whom they considered different and at the same time normalized themselves. In the almshouse the town creates a reference point, for every time the townspeople look at the almshouse they see evidence both of their own normalcy and of their own generosity in building such a fine facility for their undesirables—the poor, the old, and the insane. However, to the narrator, the almshouse "seemed like the folks it sheltered, out in the full glare of day, without any little kindly shade between itself and the dull, unfeeling stare of curiosity" (323). Raising questions about the goodness of normalcy, the narrator suggests that the almshouse functions as a permanent freak show, putting the queers on view so that those who see them can define themselves as normal. The almshouse, then, is queer space inhabited by those who understand themselves to be defined as queer and who are negotiating their differences from those both inside and outside the almshouse.

The story opens with an image of gazing out and potentially back, as Freeman hints at another reason why the townspeople have set the almshouse so far apart from themselves. Polly Moss stands at the window of the women's sitting room and, looking out at the woods beyond the fields, remarks, "'It's cur'us how them oak leaves hang on arter the others have all fell off'" (324). Difference appears natural and curiosity about it can come without the need to mark one thing normal and another queer. Yet Freeman understands just how queer such an approach to difference is. In the conversation that takes place in the women's sitting room each woman, already defined as queer by being in the almshouse, seeks to find another still more queer who can make herself seem normal. One woman rebukes Polly for her stupidity in not knowing about oak leaves and warns, "'When the oak leaves fall off an' the others hang on, then you can be lookin' for the end of the world; that's goin' to be one of the signs'" (324). Yet she herself is immediately labeled crazy by another woman for "'Allers a-harpin' on the end of the world . . . I've got jest about sick on't. Seems as if I should go crazy myself, hearin' on't the whole time'" (324). However, all these women can agree on one thing—that Polly Moss is "'a dretful-lookin' cretur,'" "'the wust-lookin' objeck,'" a real queer (325). With her twisting limp, bent figure, and a face that "seemed to look from the middle of her flat chest" (325), Polly Moss, old, poor, female, and deformed, seems about as marginalized as one can get. Yet Freeman gives us Sally, who tears up her bed and runs up and down the hall in her petticoats, and the still more isolated Agnes, whom we do not see but only hear shrieking as she is dragged off to "the cell" (327).

With such "companions" Polly could seek to try to make herself normal by comparing herself to Sally or Agnes. Instead, she engages in an extraordinary form of "actively imagining . . . a queer world"; she invents a "sister Liddy." Drawing on the stories she has heard these women tell and gathering up the bits and pieces of their happier past, she allows her listeners to recollect their normalcy at the same time that she destabilizes their quest by her parodic exaggeration of their behavior. As the women begin their daily ritual of remembering a past when they were not as they now are and of competing with each other over who was most normal, Polly Moss suddenly pipes up, "'You'd orter have seen my sister Liddy'" (331). Since Polly has never spoken before and no one expects her to participate in the ritual, the women are temporarily stunned into silence. Taking advantage of this silence to get started, Polly adds detail upon detail until Liddy becomes the embodiment, indeed the caricature, of all these women ever hoped to be or thought they were. Although at some level they suspect that sister Liddy is a fiction, they encourage Polly's performance because they recognize it as superior to their own and because they sense in it a mirror that enables them to see themselves: "Every day Polly Moss was questioned and cross-examined concerning her sister Liddy. She rose to the occasion; she did not often contradict herself, and the glories of her sister were increased daily. . . . [A]nd the old women listened with ever-increasing bewilderment and awe" (332). Listening to Polly talk about her sister Liddy, they refrain from their usual competitive behaviors; and even after Polly's death and her confession that there never was a sister Liddy, we can imagine that they will think twice before returning to their old ways, for they will hear Polly's voice saying, "'You'd orter have seen my sister Liddy'" (331). At the opening of the story, the label "queer" serves as a convenient way to salvage one's self-esteem at the expense of others, but by the end of the story, after the queer has finally spoken, it becomes "a signifier of aesthetic originality, a boldness and newness that are clearly welcome" (Lindemann 84) at the collective table.

Queer Commentary

Dunbar-Nelson's fiction does not present characters so clearly marked as queer as those we find in the fictions of Cooke, Jewett, and Freeman. Rather, her fiction returns us to those larger questions with which we began this chapter and to the ways in which regionalism as a whole can be understood as "queer commentary." In chapter 4, we discussed regionalism's emphasis on the insignificant, its habit of bringing into the foreground that which usually forms the background. In Dunbar-Nelson's work, we find an exploration of the connection between this emphasis on the insignificant and the concept of the queer. In stories like "Mr. Baptiste" and "M'sieu Fortier's Violin," Dunbar-Nelson poses the question of whether one becomes insignificant because one is queer or whether one becomes queer by being insignificant, and suggests that however one answers this question, insignificance itself is a queer position. Her insight invites us to complicate further our understanding of the cultural work of regionalism. If one becomes insignificant because queer or queer because insignificant, does paying attention to the insignificant serve the purposes of normalization or does it have the effect of making queerness visible and hence of exposing and destabilizing the operations of the normal? Mr. Baptiste, we will recall from our discussion in chapter 9, is killed when he draws attention to himself and elicits the rage of the Irish strikers for his support of the Negro "scabs." Yet Dunbar-Nelson implies that they are equally enraged by the phenomenon of someone so insignificant challenging their right to refuse to work with "niggers." The moment that he cheers for the Negroes, he becomes visibly queer and in this sense he is killed as much for being queer as for being black.

Like so many regionalist figures, M'sieu Fortier is little, old, solitary and poor, living in a house that is like himself "little and old and queer" (*AWR* 466). For companionship he has his violin and a cat to whom he talks because his landlady is deaf; his life revolves around his job with the orchestra and the music he can make with his superb instrument. We know nothing of what has brought him to this place, but when the new "American" management chooses not to rehire him, we infer that he must be too queer for a company interested only in business and profit. Of his musical ability there can be no doubt, so the difficulty must lie in the image he projects. Perhaps in a world where making money is the norm, to love music too much makes one queer. M'sieu Fortier, however, has attracted the attention of at least one person, the upper-class Courcey, who has "'picked him up in my French-town rambles'" (467). Young, rich, and companioned, Courcey engages in "slumming" to indulge his appetite for the quaint and the queer, categories constructed by their very difference from and insignificance to himself. Although he cannot play the instrument, Courcey wishes to purchase M'sieu Fortier's violin presumably for reasons similar to those that motivate him to "collect" M'sieu Fortier. When M'sieu Fortier is driven by poverty to sell his violin, Courcey gladly gives him fifty dollars for it and just as gladly returns it when the musician declares a week later that he cannot live without his violin; Courcey declares that "'it was worth a hundred dollars to have possessed such an instrument even for six days'" (470). If M'sieu Fortier were rich like Courcey, or a famous violinist, would his passion for his violin seem normal rather than queer? And if Courcey were poor and old and solitary would his passion to possess an instrument he cannot play seem queer? By raising such questions, Dunbar-Nelson probes the relation between the insignificant and the queer and indicates that in focusing on the insignificant regionalism engages in a form of "queer commentary."

As we indicated briefly in the preceding discussion of Jewett, there are occasional references in regionalist fiction, particularly in the 1880s and later, to characters readers in the twenty-first century would associate with queer politics and queer theory, namely, women who manifest same-sex attraction and persons who challenge presumably stable binaries of gender by dressing as transvestites. While such characters are most prominent in Jewett's work, there are other stories that raise questions concerning the increasing visibility of the sexually queer at the turn of the twentieth century. Freeman portrays same-sex jealousy in the murder mystery "The Long Arm"; and in her regionalist story "Up Primrose Hill," included in *Selected Stories,* a character repeatedly asks the question, "'What's the harm, I'd like to know,'" as she draws her friend deeper and deeper into an act that can be read as homoerotic (257–73, and see Pryse, "Afterword" 323–24).[17] Chopin's story "Lilacs," as we discussed in chapter 5, portrays Sister Agathe as infatuated with the annual visitor to the convent, Mme. Adrienne Farival. In Sui Sin Far's "The Smuggling of Tie Co" and "Tian Shan's Kindred Spirit," women dress as men in order to evade or deceive immigration authorities, and in "A Chinese Boy-Girl," a father dresses his son as a girl in order to protect him from what he sees as an evil spirit that has caused the death of his other four sons: "'Evil spirit think him one girl, and go away; no want girl'" (159). Curiously the teacher who has objected to Ku Yum's behavior when she believed him to be a girl is no longer interested in reporting Ku Yum's father when she finds out he is "really" a boy. A "girl's" apparent queerness and deviation from norms of prescribed gender behavior matter a great deal to the teacher, but transvestism never occurs to her as a possibility, for what Chinese boy would "really" want to be a girl? As we noted in the beginning of this chapter, however, it is in the pervasive but implied contrast throughout regionalist fiction between the standards of heteronormativity and the characters it foregrounds, characters who do not actively participate in the reproduction of heterosexuality and heteronormativity, that makes it queer in the contemporary sense. We end our discussion of the queer, then, with Kate Chopin's *The Awakening,* a novel that like Stowe's *The Pearl of Orr's Island* embeds within it a regionalist text and associates that text and its protagonist with the queer, now understood to be connected to the sexual.

In her novel, Chopin locates regionalism in the figure of the minor character, Mlle. Reisz. Mlle. Reisz first appears after Saturday night dinner in the Lebrun boarding house, and Chopin describes her as a queer figure in the community of upper-class white heterosexual Creoles and their black and quadroon servants: "She was a disagreeable little woman, no longer young, who had quarreled with almost every one, owing to a temper which was self-assertive and a disposition to trample upon the rights of others" (26). As she enters the hall, Chopin writes further, "She was a homely woman, with a small weazened face and body and eyes that glowed. She had absolutely no taste in dress, and wore a batch of rusty black lace with a bunch of artificial violets pinned to the side of her hair" (26). In her person, Mlle. Reisz is disagreeable, the very incarnation of the stereotypical old maid, but at the piano, her playing arouses passion, agitation, a "fever of enthusiasm" (27). Among the audience, she singles out Edna Pontellier as "'the only one worth playing for'" (27), suggesting some commonality between them. Later, Edna reports to others gathered at the beach, "'I wonder if I shall ever be stirred again as Mademoiselle Reisz's playing moved me to-night'" (30). After Robert leaves unexpectedly for Mexico and Edna discovers her infatuation for him, Mlle. Reisz seeks her out on the beach for a conversation about Robert. During this encounter, Chopin continues to characterize the single woman as eccentric: she wears false hair, she has an aversion to water "sometimes believed to accompany the artistic temperament," she mostly eats chocolates, either not liking Madame Lebrun's food or not wanting to pay for it, and she laughs "maliciously" as she gossips about the Lebrun family to Edna (48–49). She then invites Edna to visit her in the city after they have all left Grand Isle. Back in New Orleans, Edna finds herself in a mood to hear Mlle. Reisz's piano playing and tries to find her. But the woman has moved, and the neighboring grocer calls her "the most disagreeable and unpopular woman who ever lived in Bienville Street" (59). Nevertheless, Edna remembers that the Lebruns would have her address and thus manages to locate Mlle. Reisz's apartment.

Chapter 21, in which Edna pays Mlle. Reisz an impromptu visit, takes place entirely within Mlle. Reisz's apartment, three rooms up under the roof with dingy windows that let in smoke and soot along with the light and air, and in which the "magnificent piano crowded the apartment" (61; 445).[18] Mlle. Reisz seems just as taken with Edna Pontellier as Robert and, later, Alcée Arobin. The woman who is disagreeable to others "laughed all over when she saw Edna." She has thought about Edna: "'So you remembered me at last,' said Mademoiselle. 'I had said to myself, "Ah, bah! she will never come"'" (62; 445). And she presses Edna: "'I sometimes thought: "She will never come. She promised as those women in society always do, without meaning it. She will not come." For I really don't believe you like me, Mrs. Pontellier'" (62; 445). When Edna replies,

"'I don't know whether I like you or not,'" Chopin writes, "[t]he candor of Mrs. Pontellier's admission greatly pleased Mademoiselle Reisz. She expressed her gratification by repairing forthwith to the region of the gasoline stove and rewarding her guest with the promised cup of coffee" (62; 445).

We read Chopin's reference to the "region of the gasoline stove" as her way of placing Mlle. Reisz within her understanding of regionalism and of locating regionalism as the source of Mlle. Reisz's strength; coffee, passion, and art all emerge from the region. Mlle. Reisz fits the profile of the queer regionalist character but she is also knowledgeable about sexual passion; her attraction to Edna, though indirectly expressed, seems as obvious as her awareness of Edna's attraction to Robert ("'Ah! here comes the sunlight,'" Mlle. Reisz says when Edna arrives for a later visit [78]; and when Edna drags herself on her knees to her, Mlle. Reisz "took the glowing face between her two hands" [81]). While initially refusing to show Edna the letter she has from Robert, she promises to do so when Edna asks her to play an impromptu by Chopin. Yet Mlle. Reisz stalls: "'But you have told me nothing of yourself. What are you doing?'" (63; 446). When Edna tells her that she is becoming an artist, Mlle. Reisz replies, "'You have pretensions, Madame.'" When Edna asks, "'Why pretensions? Do you think I could not become an artist?'" Mlle. Reisz proceeds to define what she understands art to require: "'I do not know you well enough to say. I do not know your talent or your temperament. To be an artist includes much; one must possess many gifts—absolute gifts—which have not been acquired by one's own effort. And, moreover, to succeed, the artist must possess the courageous soul. . . . The brave soul. The soul that dares and defies'" (63; 446). While Edna does not admit to any of these gifts, she begs again to see the letter and to hear the impromptu, and asks whether persistence counts for anything in art. Mlle. Reisz replies, "'It counts with a foolish old woman whom you have captivated'" (63; 446).

Edna, of course, is intrigued by Mlle. Reisz but only as the older woman manages to elicit in Edna through her music "strange, new voices" of feeling and emotional agitation. While we recognize the erotic dimension of Mlle. Reisz's performance for Edna, Chopin makes clear that her captivation is one-sided. In her description of the musician at her piano, she creates a figure who repels rather than attracts: "She sat low at the instrument, and the lines of her body settled into ungraceful curves and angles that gave it an appearance of deformity" (64; 447). Later in the novel, in their only other sustained interchange, Chopin reveals the ambivalence with which Edna approaches the eccentric musician, writing, "[t]here was nothing which so quieted the turmoil of Edna's senses as a visit to Mademoiselle Reisz. It was then, in the presence of that personality which was offensive to her, that the woman, by her divine art, seemed to reach Edna's spirit and set it free" (78). Much later, discussing the woman with Alcée Arobin, Edna tells him, "'She says queer things sometimes in a bantering way that you don't notice at the time and you find yourself thinking about afterward.'" She reports that Mlle. Reisz has told her, "'"The bird that would soar above the level plain of tradition and prejudice must have strong wings. It is a sad spectacle to see the weaklings bruised, exhausted, fluttering back to earth"'" (82). When Arobin replies, "'I've heard she's partially demented,'" Edna replies, "'She seems to me wonderfully sane'" (83).

If Edna herself were stronger, or if she were less focused on heterosexual passion, she might have taken Mlle. Reisz as her mentor, if not her lover. But in Mlle. Reisz's words to Edna, Chopin foreshadows the novel's end, when Edna at least avoids the "sad spectacle" of a failure to "soar above the level plain of tradition and prejudice" in her final swim. While Mlle. Reisz cannot directly express her erotic attraction to Edna, she can attempt to assess her soul and to discover whether or not Edna can survive in the path she chooses, for what Edna seems to mean by "artist" becomes a code of sorts for the woman who wishes to define herself and not be bound by the conventions the roles "wife" and "mother" impose on a woman of her social class. In these interchanges Mlle. Reisz recognizes in Edna a kindred soul, if not a responsive lover, just as Edna recognizes this kinship in her reference to Mlle. Reisz as "wonderfully sane."

In *The Awakening,* Chopin is not writing regionalism, though she sets her novel in the regions of New Orleans and Grand Isle. In Mlle. Reisz and her "region of the gasoline stove," however, she constructs a regionalist character to carry the burden of the queer, the unconventional, and the sexually radical. Otherwise Edna herself would surely merit these labels, as numerous conversations with her disapproving husband elsewhere in the novel imply. Chopin queers Mlle. Reisz, or more accurately, includes a regionalist character in her novel in order to "normalize" Edna's sexuality, which might otherwise seem deviant rather than legitimate. Indeed, in correcting Arobin, Edna recognizes how easily she might occupy the position of the queer, a point Madame Ratignolle brings home to her when she tells her that, given the rumors of Arobin's visiting Edna in her "pigeon-house," "'I shan't be able to come back and see you; it was very, very imprudent today'" (95). Mlle. Reisz, so unremittingly queer except to Edna at the end, provides Edna herself with a cover, for Edna seems conventional by contrast. By making Edna so resolutely heterosexual and by locating an alternative erotics in a figure so offensive and asexual to her and others, Chopin tries to take the queer out of the sexual; in that sense, *The Awakening* is neither regionalism nor queer fiction. Still, Chopin makes a "region" for regionalism in her novel, and it is Mlle. Reisz's apartment. In so doing, she also suggests that odd, deformed, and older women are themselves capable of sexual interest, even captivation, if only vicariously, and that their objects can be young women. Edna allows Chopin to avoid queering the sexual but Mlle. Reisz allows her to sexualize the queer.

CHAPTER 11

"Close" Reading and Empathy

> I do so long to read it with you.
>
> —Sarah Orne Jewett, Letter to Annie Fields

> As our world undergoes what some consider to be the birth pangs of its first truly "global civilization," in which national, ethnic, religious, gender, and class boundaries are shifting on unprecedented scales, all of us will need new postmodern psychologies with which to navigate. The ability to empathize with other individuals and other groups may become the most important interpersonal and even political competence.
>
> —Maureen O'Hara, "Relational Empathy"

The Politics of Emotion

In her "Preface" to the "No More Separate Spheres!" issue of *American Literature,* Cathy N. Davidson cites Lora Romero and Eve Sedgwick as examples of writers who are calling for criticism to move beyond "implausible and unhealthy" binaries. Significantly, from our perspective, both of these critics introduce the language of emotion into their attempts to ameliorate critical oppositionality. In *Home Fronts,* calling for readers to "perhaps temper our disappointment when we realize that authors have not done the impossible, that is, discovered the one key for the liberation of all humankind" (5), Romero writes what Davidson terms a "version of sympathetic critique" (457). Sedgwick, in her introduction to *Novel Gazing,* borrows a term from the British object relations psychoanalyst Melanie Klein to describe "reparative criticism." Sedgwick cites the Kleinian idea of "positions" rather than "fixation points" in psychological development and writes, "The flexible to-and-fro movement implicit in Kleinian *positions* will be useful for my purpose of discussing paranoid and reparative critical *practices,* not as theoretical ideologies (and certainly not as stable personality types of critics), but as changing and heterogeneous relational stances" ("Paranoid Reading and Reparative Reading" 8). In choosing to cite

Romero and Sedgwick as models, Davidson is teasing out these critics' concern with an affective dimension in criticism. Indeed, as Sedgwick notes, "Among Klein's names for the reparative process is love" (8). What constitutes "working across the gender divide" for Davidson (460) is in part the use of these adjectives—"sympathetic" and "reparative"—to modify "critique" and "criticism," terms that constitute the methodology of literary and cultural studies in the academy. While not in itself a gendered term, methodology is associated with science, positivist objectivity, and rationality. Because emotion in the context of rational inquiry is believed to contaminate objectivity, to introduce emotion into critical discourse is to risk having one's work dismissed. Thus we find it even more compelling that Davidson implicitly credits both Romero and Sedgwick for taking this risk.

Although Davidson does not explicitly discuss the "separate spheres" of gendered emotional development, she does note "how often sentimentality is wielded as a weapon to control the expression of emotion" (265). In an essay entitled "In Defense of Sentimentality," Robert C. Solomon traces Western culture's "disdain for sentimentality" (305) to the work of Emmanuel Kant and patriarchal politics. Defining sentimentalism as "nothing more nor less than the 'appeal to tender feelings'" (305), and further defining tender feelings as "pity, sympathy, fondness, adoration, compassion" (310), to which we might add empathy, he writes:

> But Kant's unprecedented attack on sentiment and sentimentalism was at least in part a reaction, perhaps a visceral reaction, not only against the philosophical moral-sentiment theorists (whom he at least admired) but against the flood of popular women writers in Europe and America who were then turning out thousands of widely read pot-boilers and romances which did indeed equate virtue and goodness with gushing sentiment. It is no secret that the charge of sentimentalism has long had sexist implications as a weakness which is both more common (even "natural") and more forgivable in women than in men, and one might plausibly defend the thesis that the moralist's attack on sentimentality cannot be separated from the more general Victorian campaign in pseudoscience and politics against the rising demand for sexual equality. But in the purportedly nonpolitical, genderless world of philosophy, sentimentalism was forced into a confrontation with logic and became the fallacy of appealing to emotion instead of argument (now standard in almost every ethics or logic textbook). (320)

Throughout his essay Solomon raises the question, "why is it only the tender sentiments that come in for such criticism and abuse" (314), and he observes that "we find few similar objections in either art or ethics, we might note, to one-dimensional cynicism, to that gloomy view of the world that commonly co-opts the name 'realism'" (320). Concluding that "it is discomfort with the tender affections, I am convinced, that is the ultimate reason for the stylish attack on sentimentality," he suggests that such discomfort has to do generally with the ways in which emotions make one vulnerable and in particular with the ways in which more powerful members of Western societies manipulate the discourse of reason and feeling to serve their own interests. Extrapolating from Solomon's essay, we might argue, then, that "logic" or "reason" is just another name for patriarchal sentiments, particularly those of fear and anger.

Alison M. Jaggar provides an additional context for understanding how the discourse of emotions can be manipulated to serve the interests of patriarchal politics. Sharing the premises of Solomon's argument but writing from an explicitly feminist perspective, she observes, "Within the western philosophical tradition, emotions usually have been considered as potentially or actually subversive of knowledge" (145). Emotion and reason have been "separated from each other" (165), viewed as unequal terms of a binary locked in opposition, with emotion (not reason) requiring restraint. However, not everyone in the Western tradition is considered equally emotional. Members of dominant political, social, and cultural groups view themselves as reasonable and associate emotion with members of subordinate groups, such as men of color and women. Jaggar argues that emotion itself is socially constructed and culturally variable; she challenges the stereotype of the emotionality of women, suggesting that women may appear more emotional "because they, along with some groups of people of color, are permitted and even required to express emotion more openly" in contrast to men, for whom the free expression of any other emotion but anger calls into question their masculinity (157). As we have discussed at length in chapter 8, the myth of the objective inquirer functions ideologically to reinforce the epistemological authority of dominant groups and to discredit the knowledge base of subordinate groups, including many people of color and white women. As Jaggar writes, "The more forcefully and vehemently the latter groups express their observations and claims, the more emotional they appear and so the more easily they are discredited. The alleged epistemic authority of the dominant groups then justifies their political authority" (158). The myth of dispassionate inquiry and the separation of reason from emotion that underpins that myth therefore "promotes a conception of epistemological justification vindicating the silencing of those, especially women, who are defined culturally as the bearers of emotion and so are perceived as more 'subjective,' biased, and irrational" (158).

The historical and critical reception of regionalism that we have discussed at length in this book reveals a politics of reading that has done more than construct "American literature" as a field of study and identify texts that are "not in the least American" (Jewett, *Deephaven* 84; see Fetterley, "'Not in the Least American'"). It has also socialized an "American" reader to identify the national literature with those texts that present white male characters estranged from home, community, and "tender feelings"; men who prefer the company of other men to making any but sexual connections with women; and protagonists who prove their masculinity and dominance by hunting and killing large animals or Indians or black men. The values that emerge from such texts are clear: the "American" hero is an individualist, separated from home, on a quest to establish his dominance, sometimes in the company of other men. In effect, then, the construction of American literature has also been the construction of an emotional register for readers. In contrasting "classic" American literature with the tradition she refers to as literary sentimentalism, Joanne Dobson observes,

> In many of the classic men's texts of the era, the ultimate threat to individual existence is contamination of the self by social bonds; in the sentimental vision, the greatest threat is the tragedy of separation, of severed human ties: the death of a child, lost love, failed or disrupted family connections, distorted or unsympathetic community, or the loss of the hope of reunion and/or reconciliation in the hereafter. "Orphaned as we are," says the narrator of Alice Cary's regional tale "The Sisters," "we have need to be kind to each other—ready with loving and helping hands and encouraging words, for the darkness and the silence are hard by where no sweet care can do us any good." It is a collective "we" Cary uses here, and an existential orphanhood to which she refers. The sentimental crisis of consciousness is not so much an anxiety regarding the ultimate nonbeing of the self as it is the certain knowledge of inevitable separation—whether temporal or eternal—from the others who constitute the meaning of one's life. (267)

While regionalism does not in general employ the themes, stylistic features, or figurative conventions of sentimentalism, it does share its emotional and philosophical ethos, an ethos "that celebrates human connection, both personal and communal, and acknowledges the shared devastation of affectional loss" (266).

However, most regionalist fictions emphasize strategies and models for establishing and maintaining connection rather than "the shared devastation of affectional loss." In so doing, they demonstrate their interest in establishing a connection with their readers that has at its heart a commitment to what the journalist and psychologist Daniel Goleman has called "emotional intelligence" and to the development in their readers of an alternative emotional register.[1] By reflecting the value of empathy for their own readers, regionalist writers, like Goleman, also reveal themselves to be writing about emotional development for a "popular" audience. In our own time, reading regionalism can bring readers "close" to the experience of empathy for others. While the effects of such textual interest may be difficult to determine outside of the classroom (see Pryse, "Reading Regionalism"), analysis of the fictions does offer evidence that they invite what we have elsewhere described as "close" or "relational" reading (see Pryse, "Writing Out of the Gap"). In this chapter we want to extend the discussion of empathy that we began in chapter 4. In particular we want to examine the relationship between "close" reading and the development of empathy to suggest the uses these texts may have for readers in our own time—both women and men—who find the canonical values of patriarchal culture to be emotionally repressive, even pathological. While literary critics have not adopted the scientific method per se, many have accepted the positivism of the claim to "unbiased" approaches to texts and have participated in the exclusion of emotion from critical reading. In focusing on emotion and on empathy in particular, we too, like the critics Davidson cites, are proposing the integration of emotion into criticism and other forms of analysis. Understanding the western positivist conception of reason as a patriarchal panic against emotion, we are interested in how regionalist writers' construction of the "close" relationship between text and reader relocates the value of "tender feelings" and challenges a patriarchal masculinism that contains women's development and narrowly channels men's identities and range of acceptable emotional response.[2]

The "as if" Condition

The commercial success enjoyed by Goleman's *Emotional Intelligence* (1995) suggests that many contemporary readers feel a need to engage in the kind of reexamination of feeling that we are proposing as the project of regionalism. Indeed, while we might see a trace of the anxiety associated with the sentimental in Goleman's need to tie his case for the emotions to readers' commitment to rationality, in discussing the concept of emotional intelligence Goleman invokes phrases similar to those we have used to describe the transactions regionalist fictions seek to engage in with their readers, phrases such as "to soften and open their hearts" (x). Central to Goleman's definition of emotional intelligence is what he refers to as "recognizing emotions in others," or empathy, and he emphasizes the significance of this aspect of emotional intelligence when he observes that the "failure to register another's feelings is a major deficit in emotional intelligence, and a tragic failing in what it means to be human" (96).

As one aspect of "emotional intelligence," empathy can be taught and learned. While Goleman stresses the importance of teaching emotional intelligence to children, concluding his book with a chapter entitled "Schooling the Emotions" in which he describes various instances of such instruction within the context of schools, he also emphasizes that "[e]motional learning is life long" (214) and that such learning can occur at any time in a person's life through what he refers to as reparative relationships. For Goleman, of course, psychotherapy constitutes the most obvious example of such a reparative relationship as it provides a location within which adults can experience the kind of attunement so crucial to the emotional development of infants and young children, and at one point he refers to psychotherapy as "an emotional tutorial" (213). Through various techniques, the therapeutic relation provides "an emotional corrective, a reparative experience of attunement" (101).

Melanie Klein, whom Sedgwick explicitly references and whose language Goleman appears to be borrowing here, can help us understand empathy as a reparative process that readers can learn from "close" relation with regionalist texts and subsequently use as a guide to improving the quality of their own everyday relationships with real, not fictional, people. Emerging out of what psychoanalytic theorists call an "object relation," empathy itself begins when one person makes a connection with another while remaining separate and becomes willing to hold the other in attention long enough to hear and feel "as if" that other. We understand regionalism's relationship to the reader as a form of object relation, one in which a reader can develop a "healing connection" (Miller and Stiver) and one that allows us to theorize the "close" relationship to a reader that many regionalist texts assume to be part of the interchange between writer and reader. Both Klein and the American ego psychologist Margaret Mahler give us additional language to describe the relational reading process that regionalism elicits. Klein's healthy infant, in its earliest relation to the mother or caretaker who feeds it, develops feelings of reparative empathy when it recognizes its earlier murderous rage at its inability to control the mother's disappearance and desires to comfort the mother for its own hostile feelings.[3] It develops this empathy in emerging relationship with an adult caretaker who has the capacity to "read" the infant's world in what Mahler calls "attunement," a learned mutuality and reciprocity between infant and caretaker.[4] Empathy in Klein results from this learned attunement in which one becomes capable of recognizing reparative feelings. For therapists who work with Klein's model, the growing child and adult continue to learn and relearn empathy, since anger and the opportunity for reparative emotions recur throughout life.

From the perspective of persons taught to read through the cultural filters of dominant ideologies about gender, race, class, and region but who have felt stunted and alienated rather than mothered by stories that reinforce those ideologies, reading itself may lead to a kind of rage that seems to confirm the exclusion and powerlessness reminiscent of Klein's model of early infancy. To the extent that regionalist narratives attempt to resist dominant ideologies, we may interpret regionalism as an intentional attempt to "take care" of such stunted and alienated readers and we may see such "intentions" as reparative, reconstructive, and empowering. Recalling that the etymology of the word "intention" derives from the Latin *intendere,* "to stretch toward," we can view regionalist narratives as "intending" or "stretching" or empathic toward those whose cultural expressions have remained unheard, who have what Zitkala-Ša describes as the "low voice of a curiously colored seashell" (*AWR* 555). Moreover, in regionalism's construction of the reader as its "second person," whether she or he be from Clovernook or the world, and in its willingness to postulate attunement with this person, writing out of the regional perspective becomes a model of empathic connection that can transform as well as comfort.

Such a relationship allows us as readers to reconnect with what object relations theorists term the "good object," an internalized image of a caring parent, as the first step in the work of emotional healing. Region becomes the "good object" in a cultural application of object relations. In the way in which the texts themselves "reach out" to culturally deprived and dispossessed subjects, readers can learn to resist internalizing narrators and narratives that abuse or ignore certain characters or groups of persons. Such writing practices allow readers to move beyond the paranoia of murderous rage and toward reparation, to imagine and to work to create a society constructed out of critique, but also attuned to the needs of its human members. In this attunement and move toward reparation, regionalism enables its twenty-first-century readers to do the emotional work of becoming empathic toward "regionals" and many "others" as well. Regionalism as a mode of writing provides readers with a model of "healing connection."

In their work on empathic psychotherapy, the feminist therapists Jean Baker Miller and Irene Pierce Stiver propose that one of the most basic needs humans have is "to participate in connection with others" and that this need even supersedes the drive to gain gratification from others. They define "disconnection," on the other hand, as the "psychological experience of rupture that occurs when a child or adult is prevented from participating in a mutually empathic and mutually empowering situation," and they assert that it constitutes the most basic source of psychological problems pervading Western culture. Similarly, Arthur C. Bohart and Leslie S. Greenberg write, "Most of our psychological models of the genesis of psychopathology emphasize relationship deficits" ("Empathy and Psychotherapy" 4). Disconnection flourishes in cultures built on hierarchies of dominance and subordination because "situations in which one person or group has more power than another . . . create and enforce disconnections and violations" (Miller and Stiver 50). Maureen O'Hara makes a similar argument that she frames as a contribution "to the fast-growing discussion of the limits of the indigenous psychology of the Western world in addressing the relational needs of its members" (295). Given what she calls "the West's current disproportionate impact on global realities," the limitations of "indigenous" Western psychology become still more significant as we may export not only our psychopathology but a psychology that actually aggravates the problems it supposedly seeks to solve. In this context, those local practices that challenge the assumptions of Western psychology have global implications. As she puts it: "As our world undergoes what some consider to be the birth pangs of its first truly 'global civilization,' in which national, ethnic, religious, gender, and class boundaries are shifting on unprecedented scales, all of us will need new postmodern psychologies with which to navigate. The ability to empathize with other individuals and other groups may become the most important interpersonal and even political competence" (295). Empathy and particularly mutual empathy provide the remedy for the ills of disconnection; as O'Hara writes, "The experience of being known and accepted deeply by another, being aware of another being aware of you, . . . is among the most psychologically important human experiences" (314). For these writers, developing the capacity for empathy is essential to the transformation of culture as well as to human well-being.

Bohart and Greenberg stress empathy as a "multi-dimensional construct" but agree that all definitions of empathy "involve trying to sense, perceive, share or conceptualize how another person is experiencing the world" ("Empathy" 419). Even more directly applicable to regionalism, Greenberg and Robert Elliott assert that empathy "first and foremost is an attitude and is implemented by the taking of a specific type of vantage point or stance toward another. . . . Empathy involves listening from the inside as if 'I am the other,' as opposed to occupying an outside vantage point" (167–68), the distinction, we might note, that we make between regionalism and local color. Indeed, in translating psychological concepts for his general readership, Goleman equates listening and empathy, writing that "[t]he most powerful form of non-defensive listening, of course, is empathy: actually hearing the feeling *behind* what is being said" (145). In *The Power of Empathy,* Ciaramicoli distinguishes listening as a skill required for empathy but identifies it as the most difficult to master. He writes, "Yet of all the skills involved in empathy, listening requires the greatest concentration and focus, for there are so many ways we can be distracted" (65; here we might recall the narrator of "'One of Us'"), and he quotes Carl Rogers's observation that if you try empathic listening "'you will discover that it is one of the most difficult things you have ever tried to do'" (85).[5]

Greenberg and Elliott further observe that "empathy is not simply friendly rapport, sympathetic encouraging, listening, or being warm and supportive" but is rather "the process of deeply contacting the inner world of the other" (168). Indeed, Morris Eagle and David L. Wolitzky emphasize the distinction between empathy and sympathy, arguing that sympathy does not have the cognitive dimension required for empathy as "one can feel sympathy for another without a deep understanding of that person's subjective reality" (218; see also Ciaramicoli 38, 54). However, while something that we might call sympathy may be a required component of therapeutic empathy, therapists who write on empathy return again and again to the definition formulated by Carl Rogers in 1959: "The state of empathy or being empathic, is to perceive the internal frame of reference of another with accuracy, and with the emotional components and meanings which pertain thereto, as if one were the other person, but without ever losing the 'as if' condition" (qtd. in O'Hara 299). The distinction here is crucial for it prevents therapeutic empathy from collapsing into "egocentric empathy" (Eagle and Wolitzky 218) in which one simply imagines how *we* would feel if *we* were in another's shoes. More significantly, the condition of "as if" provides a cognitive dimension to empathy for it requires that one retain an awareness of the distinction between self and other and thus of the process one is engaged in. In other words, empathy requires an other-centered connection while maintaining an awareness of separateness from the other. While, as O'Hara points out, the tendency to label empathy regressive and the tendency to defend empathy by insisting on its distinction from "merging" stem from a suspicion "of any psychic organization not based on the modernist idea of individuation" (301), the distinction between empathy and "merging" is central to empathy's operations. As Greet Vanaerschot makes the point, "therapy would be impossible" if the therapist's experience is simply identical to the client's (147).

How then does empathy heal? According to Miller and Stiver, empathy in the therapeutic context works to heal the damage done by a culture of disconnection. It does so by offering an experience of relating to a therapist that can replace past negative "relational images" and provide clients with the skills and the motivation needed to engage in relationships of mutual empathy and connection. This model of therapy challenges the conventional assumption, derived from Freud, that the therapist must remain a neutral observer, a "blank screen," distanced and disconnected in order to remain objective and to allow for transference. Indeed, Miller and Stiver argue that such a stance can actually reinforce and aggravate the client's problem by impeding the ability of therapy to "provide a new and different experience" (138). Instead they argue that "change occurs when the therapist can feel *with* a person, that is, when the therapist can be moved emotionally by the person and the person can be moved by the therapist" (129).

Margaret Warner elaborates further on how the process of empathy promotes healing, writing that the "communication of empathy tends to facilitate change because it generates a particular sense of experiential recognition within the receiver—both the sense of being recognized in one's own experience of the moment by another human being and the sense of recognizing one's own experience in the moment" (130). She continues by observing that "this kind of recognition is often accompanied with a sense of . . . relief at being seen" especially as it is "in the absence of a sense of threat or judgment about the experience" (130). We might hypothesize that for women who are so often the object of the male gaze this relief is particularly keen as it in effect recognizes them as subjects. Some therapists choose to dramatize this shift from object to subject characteristic of empathic interaction by placing their chair alongside that of the client. We are here reminded of that moment in *The Country of the Pointed Firs* when Mrs. Blackett invites the narrator to sit in her chair: "'Come right in, dear,' she said. 'I want you to set down in my old quilted rockin'-chair there by the window; you'll say it's the prettiest view in the house. . . . I shall like to think o' your settin' here today,' said Mrs. Blackett" (54; *AWR* 219).

One of the primary disconnections identified by Miller and Stiver occurs in women who do not feel "they have a right to their own experience" (134). "Not allowing women to acknowledge their own experience makes sense in a patriarchally derived culture: women being able to know and speak their own experience would profoundly disrupt the social structure" (134). Empathy-based therapy offers women the opportunity to make a connection with themselves and to heal this primary form of disconnection. As Margaret Warner puts it, clients in therapy are often asking, implicitly or explicitly, "if their way of experiencing themselves has a right to exist in the world" (138). Empathic therapy provides a positive answer to this question and thus produces healing. In the empathic therapeutic relationship, Judith V. Jordan writes, "the client begins to feel an appreciation for his or her inner world and its evolution, and thus, the client begins to take an empathic attitude toward his or her own feelings, thoughts, and context. The observing, often judging self then makes empathic contact with some experiencing aspect of the self" (345). Jordan has labeled this process "self-empathy." For mutual empathy to occur, self-empathy must also be present, for one cannot feel truly empathic toward another if one does not feel empathic toward the self and one cannot feel empathic toward the self if one is not capable of empathy toward another. Indeed, self-empathy could be said to be the art of treating oneself as if one were another, and here we might be reminded of Freeman's description of Louisa Ellis preparing her meal "as if she had been a veritable guest to her own self" (*AWR* 356). As Jordan writes, "when empathy and concern flow both ways, there is an intense affirmation of the self and paradoxically a transcendence of the self, a sense of self as part of a larger relational unit" (347). The development in the client of the capacity for mutual empathy constitutes the primary goal of empathic therapy.

Bohart and Greenberg suggest that "empathic responding can be used to facilitate the challenging of dysfunctional beliefs" ("Empathy and Psychotherapy" 12). While they refer here to the beliefs clients may have about themselves and their relations to others, Miller and Stiver argue that these beliefs tend to reflect the larger social structures in which they are embedded. Thus we might extend empathic responding to include a challenge to the dysfunctional beliefs of patriarchal culture and particularly its model of power as hierarchical rather than mutual. To the degree that empathy succeeds in challenging the dysfunctional beliefs that result in racism, classism, sexism, and homophobia, it produces a particularly deep form of healing, one that has major transformative potential. Moreover, in valorizing empathy, regionalism in its entirety works against the pathologizing of empathy as sentimental, soft, and counter to the needs of the separating, individuated self, a position that disconnects individuals from their own experience and feelings and is part of a larger cultural illness. All human beings are born with the capacity for empathy, for what Miller and Stiver refer to as "that great unsung human gift" (29), and, as Goleman and others have stressed, like any other cognitive and emotional potential, the capacity for empathy can either be developed or inhibited. It is within this context that we now turn to an examination of regionalist fiction as a form of "emotional tutorial" that provides its readers with the opportunity to do the emotional and cognitive work of developing their capacity for empathy. It does this by emphasizing its own relation with readers, what we call "activating the 'second person'"; by modeling an empathic stance that readers may learn from their reading of regionalist fiction and take up elsewhere in their lives; by challenging individuation as the desired model of emotional development; and by proposing instead a model of separating while staying connected, a model both conducive to and the product of empathic relation.

Activating the "Second Person"

When, on the occasion of Stowe's death, Jewett rereads *The Pearl of Orr's Island,* the text she identifies as the source of her own inspiration, she writes to Annie Fields to share with her the thoughts and feelings produced by this reencounter and at one point exclaims, "I do so long to read it with you" (*Letters of Sarah Orne Jewett* 47).[6] Her comment can serve to mark the impulse in regionalist fiction to foreground the experience of reading, its desire to make those who are literally reading the text aware of the fact that they are reading and that the writing they are reading seeks to produce a certain experience for them. While any text written for publication presupposes some reader, different texts place variable emphasis on the imagination that has written the work and that required to read it. Regionalism draws less attention to itself as something someone has composed than as something someone will read. This may in part explain its lack of critical reputation, for in placing its emphasis thus, it may appear to be easy, even automatic writing, writing that required little art or even skill. In this section, then, we seek to explore regionalism's interest in the reader and in the "close" relation it makes possible between reader and text, and we seek as well to emphasize the art required to realize this possibility. Jewett's comment to Fields suggests that the relational dimension of reading regionalist fiction extends to creating connections between and among readers, and thus we might speculate that regionalist fiction also imagines a community of readers for whom the meaning of any individual act of reading cannot be realized until it is shared with others.

In only a few instances do regionalist writers directly address their readers, but in those instances the invitation to relationship with a reader emerges quite clearly. In her "Preface" to *Clovernook,* Cary expresses concern that her material "will fail to interest the inhabitants of cities, where, however much there may be of pity there is surely little of sympathy for the poor and humble, and perhaps still less of faith in their capacity for those finer feelings which are too often deemed the blossoms of a high and fashionable culture" (*AWR* 60–61). In her effort to engage such readers in an empathic relation to Clovernook and to teach them to see as Clovernook sees, Cary invokes a second category of readers whom she calls "competent witnesses" (61). The "testimony" of these readers, from within the region and presumed to be already sympathetic, to the fidelity of her sketches will, she hopes, persuade urban readers to find her material of "interest," even if it does not "instruct" (61). In effect, Cary constructs two sets of readers, one from within the region and one from outside the region, and she draws on the experience of the first set to shape the experience of the second set, thus establishing her writing as a transaction not simply between herself and her readers but between multiple communities of readers.

Cooke addresses her "Dear reader" (*AWR* 115) perhaps more in keeping with nineteenth-century conventions of narrative than out of a desire for intimacy, but nevertheless reserves for that reader metaphysical questions that appear to emerge from her narrator's private reflections. For example, she writes, "Why is it that 'the curse of a granted prayer' comes sometimes immediately? Why do we pant and thirst, and find the draught poisonous? or, after long exile, come home, only to find home gone? Alas! these are the conditions of humanity, the questions we all ask, the thwarting and despair we all endure" (117). Thaxter invokes engagement with the reader, making liberal use of the "second person" in her text: "Sailing out . . . before you"; "As you approach" (*AWR* 157). By such locutions she engages the reader in making the journey from mainland to island and prepares her reader to engage in a shift of perspective. Thaxter seeks to bring her "second person" with her to the islands so that she or he can experience how one sees, thinks, and knows, as well as how the mainland, the "world," looks, from an island perspective. Jewett interrupts her own narrative in "A White Heron" and, while not directly addressing the reader, writes as if someone else is within hearing: "Alas, if the great wave of human interest which flooded for the first time this dull little life should sweep away the satisfaction of an existence heart to heart with nature and the dumb life of the forest!" (*AWR* 202). King asks a rhetorical question, but a question nevertheless, which implies a listener: "For do we not gather what we have not, and is not our own lacking our one motive?" (*AWR* 381). Dunbar-Nelson's "The Praline Woman" carries on one part of a dialogue, with the "second person" implied; in trying to follow the very short sketch, the reader becomes one of the praline woman's addressees.

Austin's invocation of the "second person" is one of the most intriguing. Unlike Thaxter, whose "you" can frequently be translated into "one" or even "I," Austin's "you" seems always distinctly specified and separate from herself.[7] It would be difficult to substitute "I" or "one" for "you" in the following quotation from *The Land of Little Rain* without substantial loss of meaning: "The poet may have 'named all the birds without a gun,' but not the fairy-footed, ground-inhabiting, furtive, small folk of the rainless regions. They are too many and too swift; how many you would not believe without seeing the footprint tracings in the sand. . . . In mid-desert where there are no cattle, there are no birds of carrion, but if you go far in that direction the chances are that you will find yourself shadowed by their tilted wings" (*AWR* 570).[8] Austin here makes a distinction between her own knowledge of the desert and that of her reader just as she imagines that reader as an embodied person who she wishes could "read [the desert] with" her. Perhaps more than any other regionalist writer Austin constructs her material as removed from anything the reader might be familiar with or able to imagine. She is acutely aware of the imaginative and cognitive leap required for the reader to enter her region and of her own role as a translator of her region to the reader. Austin's attunement to the situation of her readers creates an empathic relation between herself and her readers.

Regionalism addresses its readers as much through scenes of misreading as through direct address and uses scenes of misreading to encourage the reader to read differently. For example, the reader of Chopin's "Madame Célestin's Divorce" witnesses the misreading of lawyer Paxton. An outsider to the conventions of Creole culture, the lawyer misreads Madame Célestin's complaints about her long-absent husband and her affability toward himself as agreement with his view of her situation and his solution to it, namely that she get a divorce so that she will be free to marry him. However, when, at the end of the story, Célestin returns home and in the morning Madame Célestin's "face seemed to the lawyer to be unusually rosy" (*AWR* 421), the reader discovers the extent of the lawyer's misreading. Chopin suggests that, while Madame Célestin has enjoyed her flirtation with the lawyer and his sympathy for her situation, she remains unpersuaded about divorce, especially when Célestin's return seems to involve, like much of Chopin's fiction, sexual passion. In lawyer Paxton the reader encounters the person who fails to read empathically and whose failure is linked to his own acquisitive desires. Through this scene of misreading Chopin seeks to construct her own reader as someone who understands that acquisition is not the appropriate stance to take toward the regionalist subject, even if it emerges from a "benevolent" desire to rescue. Indeed, "Madame Célestin's Divorce" proposes that the regionalist subject does not in fact need to be rescued and that such fantasies derive from the self-referential and self-gratifying conventions of those who live in "what is called the world." Similarly, in "A Mistaken Charity," as we have seen, the charitable impulses of Mrs. Simonds and her wealthy "worthy coadjutor" (*AWR* 319) fail to take into account the actual feelings, desires, and values of those they seek to help and so eventuate in acts that are in fact self-promoting. As Sylvia demonstrates in Jewett's "A White Heron," the appropriate stance for the reader of regionalist fiction to take toward the regionalist subject is the one Sylvia takes toward the bird. One can only have this experience if one witnesses the subject from its own perspective in the full complexity of its environment, respects the integrity of its existence, and leaves it unmolested.

Another example will underscore these points. Sui Sin Far's "'Its Wavering Image'" offers one of the most powerful instances of misreading in regionalist fiction. Although Mark Carson initially develops Pan's trust in order to get a good story and to make his name by gaining access to places and rituals no white man has seen before, he comes to have a significant personal investment in Pan and in "Americanizing" her. Like that of lawyer Paxton, his misreading is fueled by his own erotic desires for he seeks to "rescue" Pan from the Chinese half of herself and convert her into a white woman whom he can possess sexually. Mark Carson's misreading of Pan has extraordinarily negative consequences, and, in demonstrating this, Sui Sin Far places her readers differently. She constructs her reader as one who does not use reading as a form of erotic imperialism through which to colonize the regionalist subject for one's own desires, who does not read to indulge a fantasy of the exotic "other" who can be familiarized and thus possessed. Instead she positions reading as a way of enlarging one's capacity to value that which is different from the self and to approach difference without desiring to assimilate it. The reader presumed by the fiction of Sui Sin Far is one who can move between worlds without prioritizing one over the other, one who engages "in that process of becoming, enlarging, and expanding" that Ciaramicoli equates with empathy and that contrasts so sharply with the stance adopted by Mark Carson—"an expansion of your life into the lives of others, the act of putting your ear to another person's soul and listening intently to its urgent whisperings. *Who are you? What do you feel? What do you think? What means the most to you?*" (Ciaramicoli 11).

Interestingly enough in a body of literature that emphasizes reading, there are very few scenes of actual reading; in contrast to the novels women wrote during this period, many of which compulsively iterate the scene of women reading, in regionalist fiction women occasionally get a letter but they rarely, if ever, read printed matter of any kind. Instead, regionalist fiction presents scenes of talking and listening—dialogue, storytelling, rehearsal of stories already told. By such devices regionalism sustains the illusion that we as readers are actually listening to someone tell a story. This illusion in turn creates a compelling intimacy that has the effect of emphasizing the presence and engagement of the reader. The orality of regionalism makes its fictions a form of direct address; it locates the "second person" as the position of the reader and constructs reading as a form of active listening. To hear the story the regionalist subject has to tell, one must be willing to do work. "A White Heron" illustrates the demands regionalist fiction makes of its readers and indicates that regionalist writers recognize the difficulty of what they are asking readers to do. In order to see the white heron in its nest, to get as it were to "Clovernook," Sylvia must make a long and arduous journey, for one cannot easily inhabit another's perspective.

Regionalist fiction, then, activates the "second person." Through the illusion of orality, it constructs itself as a dialogic and dynamic interaction between "writer" and "reader," as if writer and reader stand in the same relation to each other as speaker and listener do. Moreover, this relation assumes a certain parity, possibly even an exchange of roles. In "The Balcony," King theorizes this aspect of regionalist fiction as she describes how the women gathered together on the balcony move from being listeners to the stories of others to tellers of their own stories. Story elicits story so that every speaker becomes a listener and every listener a potential speaker. Thus we might argue that regionalist fiction constructs the reader as "herself" potentially a regionalist writer and we might argue as well that the emotional work regionalism invites the reader to undertake involves realizing that potential. Above all, we can say that regionalist fiction constructs the reader empathically. It imagines a reader willing to engage in the dialogue between writer and reader; it imagines a reader capable of development and change, a reader in need of and interested in what regionalism has to offer; and it presents the transaction between writer and reader as the opportunity to do significant, necessary, and desired emotional work.

Regionalism as an "Emotional Tutorial"

The development of empathy involves mirroring from the "good-enough" mother-caretaker in such a way that the infant—and client in psychotherapy—feels attunement. Winnicott writes in "Ego-Integration in Child Development" (1962) that the "I" develops in part through such empathy: "Add to this: 'I am seen or understood to exist by someone'; and, further, add to this: 'I get back (as a face seen in a mirror) the evidence I need that I have been recognized as a being'" (61). Ciaramicoli also comments on the role of mirroring in the practice of empathic therapy: "When we are treated with empathy—when people accurately understand and sensitively respond to our thoughts and feelings—we learn that we are worthy of such tender care. Our empathy for ourselves grows by leaps and bounds as we mirror inside what the outside world has revealed to us about our self-worth" (34). He notes further that the end result of this process is that "[w]e feel the need to give back what we have been given, mirroring to the world the trust, faith, and love that we have taken into ourselves" (34). We recall here our discussion in chapter 5 of the ways in which writers such as Thaxter and Austin construct the landscape as a mirror and find their relationship to such a landscape reparative. In presenting narrators who have experienced such mirroring from their respective landscapes, Thaxter and Austin reflect as well regionalism's desire to "give back" to readers a similar experience. While the act of reading fiction is obviously not the same as the experience of therapy, in the various resonances we observe between empathic psychotherapy and regionalist fiction we find evidence of regionalism's intention to provide readers with a reparative relationship that, like psychotherapy, can increase their capacity for empathy. Thus we would propose regionalist fiction as itself an instance of an "emotional tutorial" designed to offer readers the opportunity to engage in the kinds of emotional work that therapists have identified as part of the "lifelong" process of emotional development.

As we have demonstrated in chapter 4, regionalist narrators adopt an empathic stance toward the region, one that "involves listening from the inside 'as if I am the other,' as opposed to occupying an outside vantage point" (Greenberg and Elliott 167–68). Thus regionalist fictions model the stance of empathy for readers, and to the degree that readers emotionally and cognitively participate in the narrator's perspective, they may achieve the experience of empathic response. Regionalist fictions frequently make explicit use of the language of attunement. For example, we might think of Mrs. Blackett in "The Foreigner"—

"'Think if 'twas you in a foreign land!'" (*AWR* 242)—or Charlotte in "A Mistaken Charity"—"'if you was me, Harriét, you would know there was chinks'" (*AWR* 319). Such comments express the hope that one person will be able to attend to the experience of another as that other thinks and feels it, as when the narrator in "The Walking Woman" writes, "There ensued a pause of fullest understanding" (*AWR* 582). While writers cannot know their readers' response, at least the directive in these texts cannot be mistaken or misread. Regionalist writers further strengthen this directive by building into their fictions, as we have discussed above, examples of disconnection and non-empathic responses, and critiquing them so that readers at least know, for example, that Betsey Carey's approach to Freeman's Christmas Jenny is preferable, from the narrator's perspective, to the witch hunt of the deacons, or that Chevis's approach to Celia Shaw in Murfree's "The Star in the Valley," however superficially sympathetic it may be, falls far short of the requirements for empathic attunement just as does the minister's approach to poor Joanna in *The Country of the Pointed Firs.* Indeed, the efforts of Jewett's narrator, inspired by the example of Mrs. Todd, to understand the situation of Joanna from the inside out provides a good example in regionalist fiction of the modeling of empathy, as does Sui Sin Far's Mrs. Spring Fragrance in her attempt to help Mrs. Carman understand the "inferior woman." Thus regionalism insistently models empathic attunement and provides readers with a vision of an alternative to disconnection and of the value to be derived from such an alternative. To those readers who respond empathically to both narrator and character it offers an experience of connection that develops and expands readers' capacity for empathy even while the act of reading remains an "as if" experience of another "as if" experience, the empathic interaction itself.

In an observation that recalls regionalism's emphasis on approach, Ciaramicoli points to the need to "slow things down" (48) if one wishes to be truly empathic. "Timing," he writes, "is everything" (58) and empathic approach depends for its success on one's ability "to let the story unfold. . . . We express empathy by immersing ourselves in the story" (60). We are reminded once again of the emphasis Cary places in her "Preface" to *Clovernook* on "detaining" her readers in Clovernook long enough to see as Clovernook sees, and of the strategies of narration she employs in her fiction to allow a story simply to unfold so that we may become immersed in it. In further detailing what is required to be empathic and to express empathy, Ciaramicoli connects the need to slow down with that "focus on the moment-to-moment experience" which constitutes the real "power of empathy" (52) and the real work of being empathic. "Empathy," he writes, "always focuses on the present, on what is happening right now, at this very moment" (80) and by so doing it creates the conditions for that "real trust" which can only be "developed by moment-to-moment empathic interaction" (62). As we recall the narrator of King's "'One of Us,'" whose "thoughts, also as usual, distracted me from listening" (*AWR* 391), we recognize that her ability to be empathic begins with that "inspiration of the moment" (406) when she first pays attention to "what is happening right now, at this very moment" and realizes that the woman before her does not in fact accord with her preconceptions of her. As Ciaramicoli puts it, "[r]eal life often doesn't follow our well-laid plans; we have to think on our feet and always be prepared to take off in some unexpected direction" (73), a comment that connects empathic approach with the fragment as form. For King's narrator this "thinking on our feet" means a new understanding of the woman speaking to her; for Aaron Stow of "Dely's Cow" it means imagining the relationship that is possible between human and animal companions; for Kate and Helen of *Deephaven* it means a change in their perception of who qualifies to be "somebody's neighbor"; for the reader of Dunbar-Nelson's "The Praline Woman" it means recognizing the revolutionary potential of empathy.

Most significantly, for readers who like women have historically been denied "a right to their own experience" (Miller and Stiver 134), regionalist fictions model self-empathy. They often do so, however, in ways that may seem indirect, as for example when Jewett in "The Foreigner" records Mrs. Todd's response to the narrator's suggestion that she "must have felt very tired": "'I was 'most beat out, with watchin' an' tendin' and all,' answered Mrs. Todd, with as much sympathy in her voice as if she were speaking of another person" (*AWR* 247–48). In so doing they acknowledge the difficulties that women in particular encounter in developing the capacity for self-empathy. Indeed, the very rarity of a story like Freeman's "A New England Nun" suggests the degree to which regionalism is still bound by a cultural narrative that marks self-empathy in women as selfish and therefore makes its case for the value of empathy through the more culturally acceptable model of empathy toward others. Even those contemporary critiques of regionalism that charge it with complicity and elitism seem to operate from an assumption that if women, whether as characters, narrators, or authors, engage in any behavior that can be calculated as self-promoting or self-interested, such charges are thereby legitimated. In the context of a culture that separates women from the birthright of survival and self-love, that values women's selflessness and finds selfish their empathy for themselves, that values women's advocacy only on behalf of the (preferably male) other, women may be able to advocate for themselves only indirectly. Thus when women in regionalist fiction stand up and advocate for other women, we can also understand them as engaging in a form of self-empathy. When Mrs. Carey climbs the hill to advocate for Christmas Jenny, she speaks up for herself as well, since Jenny is the only person capable of handling her perversely difficult husband, Jonas, and curtailing his tormenting behavior. When Cary's narrator in "Uncle Christopher's" befriends the little boy sent to his grandfather for "straightening" (*AWR* 74), she is also extending empathy to herself as she too has been delivered to Uncle Christopher presumably for correction. When Sylvia in "A White Heron" chooses not to give away the bird's secret to the hunter, we also interpret her decision in light of her identification with the bird. Indeed, a brief look at "A White Heron" will help clarify the connection in regionalist fiction between empathy for the other and self-empathy.

When Sylvia's grandmother rescues her from the city and brings her to live in the country, Sylvia moves from an antipathetic environment to an empathic one and we could read the region here as a version of the empathic therapist. This move has allowed her to develop empathy for herself as someone whose "way of experiencing themselves has a right to exist in the world" (Warner, "Does Empathy Cure?" 138), as someone capable of knowledge (how to find the heron's nest) and of deciding what to do with that knowledge. It has also allowed her to develop empathy for the little girl overwhelmed by the city, terrified by the red-faced boy, and compassionate toward "the wretched dry geranium" (*AWR* 198). Sylvia's development of this capacity for self-empathy leads her to make the decision not to betray the bird and give its life away; like the wretched geranium, the bird is at once an entity in and of itself and a subject with which she can identify, so that in saving the bird she expresses both empathy for another and empathy toward the self. We might see this particular form of mutual empathy reiterated in the narrator's relation to Sylvia, which is a version of Sylvia's relation to the heron; that is, we might read Sylvia as both an independent character and as a version of the narrator and thus we might read the narrator's empathic stance toward Sylvia as a form of self-empathy as well as empathy for another. To the extent that the reader participates in Sylvia's experience as well as the narrator's, regionalism provides an occasion for the development of the reader's own capacity for self-empathy. Indeed, once we have understood regionalism as "activating the 'second person,'" we can postulate the development of empathy for the self as a key component of the regionalist transaction. As we have noted above, the difficulty women have in feeling they have a right to their own experience constitutes one of the primary disconnections that feminist-based empathic therapy is designed to heal. When regionalist fiction validates this right, the reader who responds empathically may be said to be developing a form of self-empathy.

As Jordan has indicated, however, self-empathy matters finally because it is necessary for developing the capacity for mutual empathy. In the instances we have noted above, identification with the other does not preclude recognition of the other's separateness, her or his "otherness," and regionalist fiction's emphasis lies in the modeling of mutual empathy. We might return to Dunbar-Nelson's "The Praline Woman" as a text that makes visible the relation between empathy for the self and empathy for the other. In engaging her customers in empathic exchange Tante Marie feeds both herself and her customers. While her use of empathy to persuade passersby to become customers might make her vulnerable to the charge of self-interest so often lodged against women who advocate for their own right to life, if we focus for a moment on what she is selling—food that is sweet, delicious, and a treat—we might complicate our understanding of this exchange. For the pralines themselves mark the site of empathy, the means by which Tante Marie can encourage someone not used to eating to treat herself, like Louisa Ellis, "with as much grace as if she had been a veritable guest to her own self" (*AWR* 356). To give back something in return for this encouragement does not corrupt but rather completes the exchange. In this reading, the making, selling, buying, and eating of Tante Marie's pralines become transactions of mutual empathy just as regionalist fiction offers its readers the opportunity to "eat" the "sweet care" of "soft interpretation" not only of others but also of the self. Such transactions become regionalism's version of a sacrament (pralines, we would note, are also wafers), and Tante Marie thus becomes Dunbar-Nelson's alternative source of spirituality, replacing the Holy Father himself to whom Tante Marie gives a praline. Yet in Dunbar-Nelson's version, the "holy" woman—and the truly empathic listener or reader—would also attend to the material as well as the spiritual and emotional needs of the poor.

In addition, regionalism models the possibility and process of re-narration, what Margaret Warner terms "a continuing revision of one's life narrative and the 'scripts' by which experiences are organized and interpreted" (134) and what psychologists refer to as "seeing things differently, or cognitive reframing" (Goleman 74). Building on our discussion in chapter 6 of framing and form in regionalism, we can also understand regionalist fiction as "cognitive reframing." Warner suggests that in the context of establishing a relationship with an empathic therapist, clients can begin to contact aspects of their past experience repressed by relationships of disconnection and previously unavailable to them as narrative, and that these "less integrated and articulated aspects" of one's experience are often also most "'alive'" (Warner, "Does Empathy Cure?" 134). Being able to hold "these 'alive' aspects of experience in attention" allows clients to reorganize their understanding of themselves and to re-narrate their lives (134). As we have indicated in our discussion of King's "'One of Us'" in chapter 4, regionalism also moves into the foreground and holds "in attention" as significant that which others have previously assigned to insignificance, and in chapter 10 we explored the connection between the "insignificant" and the "queer," proposing in effect that the construction of "insignificance" constitutes a form of cultural psychopathology marked by disconnection.

In attending to the insignificant, regionalist fiction models the use of what Ciaramicoli refers to as "peripheral vision," a way of seeing that "[i]n therapy and life I am always reminding myself to rely on. . . . What is it that I haven't noticed? What am I missing?" (132). The "poetics of detail" evident in the work of Cary and Thaxter and discussed in chapter 8 also reflects a reliance on peripheral vision. When Cary engages our interest in details "of so little apparent moment or significance that they who live in what is called the world would scarcely have marked them had they been detained with me while they were passing" (*AWR* 60), she dramatizes the process of bringing "in attention" that which usually goes without notice. When Thaxter separates each island from the others, she breaks up what has previously been an undifferentiated blur on the horizon and brings into the foreground that which is usually consigned to the backdrop. This feature of regionalist fiction models for the reader the importance of attending to those aspects of one's own or another's less-articulated experience and, as it makes this material the source of its narrative, it also implicitly accords it "aliveness." While regionalist writers cannot guarantee that their readers will recognize the value of this process, they can demonstrate how such a process changes the story one becomes able to tell.

Few regionalist narratives actually portray characters in the act of re-narrating their stories of themselves. A rare exception is Cooke's "Dely's Cow," discussed in chapter 4, in which Aaron Stow contacts his "experiencing" self and, in telling the story of the consequences of his actions in buying the cow, comes to see himself differently and therefore chooses to re-narrate himself as empathic rather than hard. However, we might also understand certain regionalist fictions as acts of re-narration if we consider that in these fictions characters tell their own story to counter the stories told about them by others. In Sui Sin Far's "The Inferior Woman," Ethel Evebrook reads aloud the letter in which Alice Winthrop tells her own story. It is overheard by Mrs. Spring Fragrance, who then uses it to counter the narrative she has been given by Mrs. Carman. When Austin's "Woman at the Eighteen-Mile" finally tells her story, it counters the many narratives her listener has previously heard about her. In recognizing the impossibility of telling her story to anyone else but Austin's narrator, this woman acknowledges as well how difficult the act of re-narration can be when the story one has to tell goes so counter to the narratives told about one. In other texts, re-narration occurs when characters tell stories different from those in general circulation—for example, when Mary Jane Beers explains Miss Beulah's decision not to attend church, or when Betsey Carey describes the scene in Christmas Jenny's cabin. Regionalism also engages in re-narration in those fictions that embed a more conventional narrative within stories it chooses to tell differently. For example, we might point to "A New England Nun," which includes within it Joe Daggett's "common sense" understanding of Louisa's story and counters it with a different reading of Louisa's character and choices; or "A White Heron," which gives full play to a reading of Sylvia's behavior as regressive, even pathological, but counters this reading with a different approach to her decision. In the tension we have discussed throughout this book between regionalism's awareness of an "external" pathological reading that might be accorded to its material and an "internal" empathic reading that it is seeking to assert, we might see a version of the tension that empathic therapists identify within individuals and within the culture at large between "the observing, often judging self" and the "experiencing" self (Jordan 345). Such stories provide readers with a model of how the judging self of the conventional narrative can make empathic contact with the experiencing self of the counter narrative so that previously "split off experiences" can "flow back into connection" producing new narratives that perform the work of healing (345).

The entire archive of regionalist fiction may be considered a re-narration to the extent that it seeks to tell a different story about U.S. culture than dominant ideologies do. In so doing, regionalism becomes a change agent and the larger culture a "client"; the empathic stance of the narrators creates a relationship within which readers can contact those "less-integrated and articulated aspects" (Warner, "Does Empathy Cure?" 134) of the American experience and can hear those stories that have not been told. However, as we noted in chapter 4, regionalist fictions acknowledge the difficulties involved in trying to tell these stories, the rarity of "ears made delicate by listening." In this context we might read Chopin's "Ozème's Holiday" as a story about the difficulty of telling a story of empathy as opposed to a story of holiday, or, perhaps more accurately, a story about the difficulty of convincing listeners that a story of empathy is in fact a story of holiday. Ozème cannot tell the story of what he actually did on his holiday because it goes so counter to the image of himself that he has carefully built up for his audience. But Ozème has constructed this image of self and holiday in conformity with his audience's expectations of story and with the values that inform this expectation. While "Ozème's Holiday" might initially seem an instance of the impossibility of re-narration, Chopin tells us the story Ozème cannot tell his audience so that we have access to "these 'alive' aspects of experience" and can make them the basis of our own re-narrations. To the extent that this happens throughout regionalist fiction, we might see the mode in its entirety as a model for cultural therapy; it provides an opportunity for the culture as a whole to engage in an act of re-narration, allowing it to tell a different story of itself, one that counters the dominant narrative of individuation and violence with a narrative of empathy, relation, and connection. A major example of regionalism's work of re-narration occurs in the context of models of emotional development, and it is to this aspect of the uses of empathy in regionalist fiction that we now turn.

Regionalism and Masculinity

At the conclusion of her study of fraternity rape culture on American college campuses at the end of the twentieth century, Peggy Reeves Sanday implies that gang rape results in part from the persistent reinforcement of cultural myths about men and that it depends upon constructing men as "incapable of feeling anything for anyone outside their organization," as incapable of "display[ing] empathy" (73). She writes, "The popular Western view that man (i.e., the male) is basically an animal who evolved by virtue of his dominance over women and nature rationalizes the 'boys will be boys' mentality" (193). We share Sanday's interest in asking why the "image of the cooperative, tender male," who appears frequently in regionalist fiction as an alternative, even a corrective for the patriarchal masculinism of other characters, "does not occupy the same mythical status in American culture as the image of the heroic sadist" (193).

In our discussion of Stowe's proto-regionalist "Uncle Lot" in chapter 3, we described the sketch as a narrative of conversion designed to open the "chestnut burr" of Uncle Lot's heart, a heart Stowe describes as "abounding with briers without and with substantial goodness within" (*AWR* 8). Uncle Lot prides himself on living in an emotional state similar to the topography of his region—hard, rocky, granite. His refusal to engage emotionally, to display empathy, becomes a spiritual liability at the death of his son when Uncle Lot can neither express his grief nor accept God's will. Through the efforts of his surrogate son, James, Uncle Lot is finally able to open his heart and become a somewhat different man. Stowe's interest in this "conversion" provides humor as well as theme in "Uncle Lot," and in later works she continues to make a narrative joke at the expense of conventional understandings of masculinity.

For example, though she presents the male privilege Moses receives in *The Pearl of Orr's Island* (1862) and the masculine subjectivity created by that privilege as a tragedy for his "sister" Mara, in "The Minister's Housekeeper" (1872) the serious and authoritative minister becomes the butt of humor. In this story, Huldy, the housekeeper, stays on to take care of things after the minister's wife dies. Sam Lawson, who is telling the story, describes the minister who is "great on texts" as helpless without a woman's care: "'Lordy massy! he didn't know nothin' about where anything he eat or drunk or wore come from or went to: his wife jest led him 'round in temporal things and took care on him like a baby'" (*AWR* 49, 48).[9] When the good women of the church suggest to the minister that he really needs "an experienced woman" to do his work (and one of them has an interest in replacing his wife), he rejects their advice but tries to lighten Huldy's load. His first instruction to her is to "'be sure to save the turkey-eggs, so that we can have a lot of turkeys for Thanksgiving,'" but when his hen-turkey is found killed, and Huldy expresses regret because she had been planning to "set" the turkey on the eggs, the minister has a solution—use the tom turkey. "'But,' says Huldy, 'you know *he* can't set on eggs.' 'He can't? I'd like to know why,' says the parson. 'He *shall* set on eggs, and hatch 'em too.' 'O doctor!' says Huldy, all in a tremble; 'cause, you know, she didn't want to contradict the minister, and she was afraid she should laugh,—'I never heard that a tom-turkey would set on eggs'" (51). The minister himself is "set" on his idea, however, and there ensues a scene in which, since he is "used to carryin' his p'ints o' doctrine," as Sam Lawson tells his audience of listening boys, he "skirmishes" with the turkey, and after several attempts, including putting a "long, thin, flat stone" on the turkey, he finally manages to get the tom to sit on the eggs. While the minister remains, the turkey sits; but when he returns to the house, the tom gets up and the stone proceeds to smash the eggs. For a mild-mannered man, the minister's response is rather shocking: "'I'll have him killed,' said the parson: 'we won't have such a critter 'round'" (53). Although he relents and spares the turkey's life, the tom's obstinacy merely reflects the minister's own; ironically self-reflexive, his statement about the turkey allows Stowe, through the cover of her male narrator, Sam, to offer a humorous critique of the "setness" of masculinity and allows Sam to instruct his audience of boys in different ways of being men.

After a second disastrous attempt to handle the arrival of a pig—which the nearsighted minister mistakenly throws into the well—he yields his authority to Huldy, who then demonstrates her faculty for managing, gardening, and baking, and instead of coming to give her advice, he begins to ask for her opinions. His ability to give up his own authority enables him to discover that he loves Huldy and so, after the ladies and deacons of the church begin to object that instead of treating her as a "hired gal," he is treating her as an "equal" (55), he asks her to marry him. In the story's final scene, the minister achieves his own sense of humor: "'I thought,' says he, 'as folks wanted to talk about Huldy and me, I'd give 'em somethin' wuth talkin' about'" (57). Like "Uncle Lot," then, "The Minister's Housekeeper" is also about the conversion of men. Indeed, many other characters in Stowe's fiction, including Uncle Tom from *Uncle Tom's Cabin* (1852), Horace Holyoke of *Oldtown Folks* (1869), and Sam Lawson, who narrates "The Minister's Housekeeper" and others in *Oldtown Fireside Stories* (1872), all represent variations on the "cooperative, tender male" whose rarity Sanday laments.

We have discussed at various points in this book other male characters who represent patriarchal authority and its chilling effect on those around them, characters such as Cary's Uncle Christopher, who punishes his grandson so severely that he ends by killing him; the ministers and deacons in Freeman, who seem intent on policing women who live independent lives or hold unorthodox opinions; King's old General in "A Drama of Three" or Old Champigny in "La Grande Demoiselle," formerly wealthy Southerners now dispossessed of their wealth but holding firm to patriarchal authority. If Cary shows the fatal consequences of patriarchal authority, Cooke examines more closely how such authority manifests itself. "Freedom Wheeler's Controversy with Providence," Cooke's novella-length story, depicts the kinds of damage such masculinity is capable of doing to women and children.

Cooke's story sets in context with its title character two wives, one of whom dies in the service of producing a first-born son his father names "Shearjashub," and several daughters whose births make Freedom more and more determined to keep trying for a second son to be named for him ("'there's allus ben a Shearjashub 'nd a Freedom amongst our folks'" [*AWR* 99]). Allied with the women and children are Aunts Huldah and Hannah, who raised Freedom from the time he was six but who become concerned with his obstinacy and domineering sway over the household after he gets married. Cooke describes his first wife, Lowly, as a woman with a "simple, tender heart" that "went out to her husband like a vine feeling after a trellis; and, even when she found it was only a boulder that chilled and repelled her slight ardors and timid caresses, she did still what the vine does,—flung herself across and along the granite faces of the rock, and turned her trembling blossoms sunward, where life and light were free and sure" (98). The "boulder" that is Freedom not only works this wife in his effort to produce sons; he also requires her to take care of a large dairy herd, and two weeks after she gives birth to her first baby, a boy, he wants her back with the herd. Lowly, however, is used to obeying; as she tells Aunt Huldah, "'you know Scripter says wives must be subject to husbands'" (100). In response, Huldah, "who was lost to the strong-minded party of her sex by being born before its creation," pounces upon the nearest hen and plunges her into a barrel to set on thirteen eggs. In a curious moment of both self- and historical reflection, Cooke intrudes on her narrative to remark that the "hen"—a stand-in for Lowly—"evidently represented a suffering and abject sex to Aunt Huldah, and exasperated her accordingly" (100).

Huldah clearly represents Cooke's own position, and throughout the story, as Freedom's behavior becomes more and more stubborn, she becomes increasingly "free to say" her mind. When Lowly gives birth to a second child and it proves to be a girl, Huldah says in response to Freedom's "silent rage at the disappointment": "'Imperdent, ain't it? . . . To think it darst to be a girl when ye was so sot on its turnin' out a boy!'" (101). At the birth of a third child, another girl, Freedom "grimly remarked, ''Tain't nothin' to me what ye call her: gals ain't worth namin' anyhow!'" (102). A fourth child is also born—another girl. While Lowly is busy giving birth to daughters, Freedom is working hard "'to make a man'" of Bub: "the boy learned, among other manly ways, a sublime contempt for 'gals,' and a use of all the forcible words permitted to masculine tongues" (104). When at last Lowly's fifth baby is a boy and Freedom brings the parson in right away to baptize him "Freedom," the child "quivered suddenly all over, gasped, opened its half-shut eyes glazed with a fatal film, and then closed the pallid, violet-shadowed lids forever" (105). In response to comments by Aunt Huldah, Freedom finally allows Lowly to rest; he realizes that if she works less, she might be able to produce another healthy child. And indeed, her sixth baby is another boy. "The old parson was brought in haste to baptize it. The pallid mother grew more white all through the ceremony, but nobody noticed her. She took the child in her arms with a wan smile, and tried to call it by name: 'Free,' was all she said. Her arms closed about it with a quick shudder and stringent grasp; her lips parted wide. Lowly and her baby were both 'free,' for its last breath fluttered upward with its mother's" (106–7).

Freedom's response to the deaths of his wife and infant is to become more defiant still "toward the divine will that had overset his intentions and desires" (107), and within six months he has married again, this time to a "strapping, buxom, rosy-faced girl . . . that would have furnished forth at least five feeble pieces like Lowly" (108). However, shortly after his new marriage, Freedom contracts typhus fever and is therefore delirious the morning his new wife, Melinda, gives birth to a boy whom she names Tyagustus. Freedom, she says, "'sounds like Fourth o' July oh-rations, 'nd Hail Columby, 'nd fire-crackers, 'nd root-beer, 'nd Yankee Doodle thrown in'" (111). The parson who comes to minister to Freedom tells the aunts, "'There seems to be a root of bitterness. . . . His speritooal frame is cold and hard. There is a want of tenderness'" (112). Freedom continues to want a namesake, and the narrator reports, "he was a terror to the children; and, had there been any keen observer at hand, it would have been painful to see how 'father' was a dreadful word, instead of a synonym for loving protection and wise guidance" (113). Aunt Hannah is shocked when Marah refuses to say the Lord's Prayer one night: "'Me won't! Me don't want Father in heaven: fathers is awful cross'" (113).

The following year Melinda has a second child, a girl. Freedom's first greeting to that child is "'Keep that brat out o' my sight. . . . Don't fetch it 'round here: it's nothin' but a noosance'" (114). However, when her third child proves to be a healthy boy, Freedom once again brings in the parson, has the child baptized "Freedom," but, unaccustomed to carrying babies, he trips over a stool and "fell full-length upon the floor, with the child under him" (117). The child dies; he has killed him, and Melinda feels free to tell him so. "Melinda's accusations were the first sermon that ever awoke his consciousness" (119), and as a result he begins to change. When Melinda's fourth child is born, a healthy boy, Freedom takes two months to name the child, and tells Melinda it is "'for you to say'" (122). Although it has taken the death of his first wife and several of his children, for whose deaths he has been both directly and indirectly responsible, Freedom at last, in the language of Cooke, has "'gin up his controversy'" (122), but of course, he has also given up his claim to patriarchal authority. In one sense the story ends happily, but in another it represents Cooke's protracted indictment of what today we would call masculinism. Although Cooke explicitly gives the credit to God for Freedom's change, it is really Melinda who finally wears him down by refusing, unlike Lowly, to be an "obedient" wife.

In *The Country of the Pointed Firs,* Jewett comprehensively explores the spectrum of male identity and proposes alternatives to masculinism. In the figure of Captain Littlepage, Jewett seems to be setting up a model of the man's man of her century in her region—the sea captain who survives all his voyages, lives long enough to reflect on them, and tells the only "action" story in the narrative—even though he is no longer at the peak of his authority. She quotes Darwin to reinforce Captain Littlepage's importance: "'there is no such king as a sea-captain; he is greater even than a king or a schoolmaster!'" (17–18). Littlepage describes the life of the sea captain and his crew: "'It was a dog's life . . . but it made men of those who followed it'" (20). In the chapter titled "The Waiting Place," he tells the narrator the story of his last voyage on the *Minerva,* when he is blown off course and ends up on an island with a group of Moravian missionaries somewhere near the North Pole. The captain's narrative has all the elements of a boys' adventure story, including leaving home and going as far away as possible, battling the elements, and encountering men like Gaffett who have gone even further. Shipwrecked off the Greenland coast, Gaffett is the only survivor left who can report what he saw: "'There is a strange sort of a country 'way up north beyond the ice, and strange folks living in it'" (24). Gaffett's is a "'tale of dogs and sledges, and cold and wind and snow,'" then "'rotten'" ice; a "'current flowing north,'" "'scant of provisions and out of water'"; arrival at a "'place where there was neither living nor dead,'" inhabited by "'blowing gray figures,'" "'fog-shaped men'"; and finally conflict: when Gaffett and the other men decide to leave the strange town, "'Those folks, or whatever they were, come about 'em like bats; all at once they raised incessant armies, and come as if to drive 'em back to sea. They stood thick at the edge o' the water like the ridges o' grim war; no thought o' flight, none of retreat'" (24–26). The captain finds metaphysical meaning at the edge of male adventure: "'Say what you might, they all believed 'twas a kind of waiting-place between this world an' the next'" (26). Despite Captain Littlepage's advanced age, he tells what Mrs. Todd later calls "great narratives," interspersed with references to Milton and Shakespeare. "'Some o' them tales hangs together toler'ble well. . . . An' he's been a great reader all his seafarin' days. Some thinks he overdid, and affected his head, but for a man o' his years he's amazin' now when he's at his best. Oh, he used to be a beautiful man!'" (29). What Mrs. Todd admires in the captain is not the exploits themselves but their narrative; she views adventure stories, and the images of men they construct, as fictions. It is not the captain's masculinity or authority that she finds attractive but his ability to tell a tale that "'hangs together toler'ble well.'" However, Jewett's narrator has difficulty becoming interested in the captain's narrative.

The only other male character in *The Country of the Pointed Firs* who might be considered to value gendered masculine interests, the "straight, soldierly little figure" (99) Sant Bowden, who leads the procession at the Bowden family reunion, is, as we observed in chapter 7, discredited by Mrs. Todd who transforms his military formation at the reunion into a charade of masculine occupation. Mrs. Todd explains: "'No, Santin never was in the war. . . . It was a cause of real distress to him. He kep' enlistin', and traveled far an' wide about here, an' even took the bo't and went to Boston to volunteer; but he ain't a sound man, an' they wouldn't have him. They say he knows all their tactics, an' can tell all about the battle o' Waterloo well's he can Bunker Hill. I told him once the country'd lost a great general, an' I meant it, too. . . . 'Twas most too bad to cramp him down to his peaceful trade, but he's a most excellent shoemaker at his best'" (101). The most likely candidate to claim masculine authority "some thinks he overdid," and the other "ain't a sound man." Readers looking for men who engage in what Roosevelt called the "strenuous life" will not find them in Jewett.

The men who interest Jewett's narrator the most—Mrs. Todd's brother William Blackett and Elijah Tilley—have done much to work, in Cathy Davidson's words, "across the gender divide" (460). Indeed, though Jewett does not identify William and Elijah as "queer," both challenge conventional models of masculinity. Jewett's narrator first meets William when she sails with Mrs. Todd out to Green Island, where Mrs. Todd's mother and brother live. Before William enters the narrative, the reader learns that he is very shy. Mrs. Todd reports that he would not come inside the house the day she got married: "'He was always odd about seein' folks, just's he is now. I run to meet 'em from a child, an' William, he'd take an' run away'" (41). Mrs. Blackett, Mrs. Todd's mother, identifies him as a person who crosses conventional gender lines: "'William has been son an' daughter both since you was married off the island. He's been 'most too satisfied to stop at home 'long o' his old mother, but I always tell 'em I'm the gainer'" (41). She hints that others—perhaps in Dunnet Landing—have talked about William, for she has defended him against "'em." Even Mrs. Todd expresses irritation with William's behavior in keeping his distance since their arrival, and announces that she will both go to look for him and "'blow the horn for William. . . . He needn't break his spirit so far's to come in. . . . I won't put him to no pain'" (43). The narrator writes, "Mrs. Blackett's old face, for the first time, wore a look of trouble, and I found it necessary to counteract the teasing spirit of Almira" (43). Almira's teasing, however affectionate, reflects a certain intolerance of William's difference, one that creates an evident anxiety in her mother. The narrator, however, declares that "I became possessed of a sudden unwonted curiosity in regard to William, and felt that half the pleasure of my visit would be lost if I could not make his interesting acquaintance" (42). While Mrs. Todd is looking for her brother, the narrator takes the hoe and goes out to dig potatoes for Mrs. Blackett's fish chowder. As she lifts her basket, a "pleasant anxious voice" belonging to an "elderly man, bent in the shoulders as fishermen often are, gray-headed and clean-shaven, and with a timid air," asks to carry her basket (43–44). The narrator understands that "it was the first step that cost, and that, having once joined in social interests, he was able to pursue them with more or less pleasure" (44). Thus, when he invites her to see the "great ledge" after dinner, surprising both Mrs. Blackett and Mrs. Todd, she accompanies William to the highest point on the island, from which they can see "the ocean that circled this and a hundred other bits of island ground, the mainland shore and all the far horizons." Although the narrator demonstrates the difference between her own world and William's, writing that "it was impossible not to feel as if an untraveled boy had spoken, and yet one loved to have him value his native heath," she seems to share his valuation of the "great prospect" from the island's high point: "'There ain't no such view in the world, I expect,' said William proudly" (45).

If William is the book's "high point" in terms of its male characters, Elijah Tilley, whom the narrator has a chance to meet at the end of *The Country of the Pointed Firs*, occupies the place of final significance. Elijah, an old fisherman who is now a widower, keeps his house as neat as if his dead wife, whom he addresses as "poor dear," might at any moment step back into her kitchen. He has refused help because, as he explains, "'I was the only one knew just how she liked to have things set,'" and even though she has been dead eight years, "'I miss her just the same every day'" (121). Spending much of his time knitting he has space to think: "'I keep a-lookin' off an' droppin' o' my stitches; that's just how it seems. I can't git over losin' of her no way nor no how'" (121). Most of all, he has learned to see the world as his wife once saw it: "'I used to laugh at her, poor dear. . . . She used to be fearful when I was out in bad weather or baffled about gittin' ashore. She used to say the time seemed long to her, but I've found out all about it now. I used to be dreadful thoughtless when I was a young man and the fish was bitin' well'" (123). Elijah demonstrates that men can learn to empathize with women and that they do not need to distance themselves from expressing the emotions of grief and empathy.

Departure and Return

In Freeman's "On the Walpole Road," two women driving home from market see a dark cloud on the horizon and it reminds one of them of a story: "'That cloud makes me think of Aunt Rebecca's funeral,' she broke out, suddenly. 'Did I ever tell you about it, Almiry?' 'No; I don't think you ever did, Mis' Green'" (*AWR* 308). By the end of Freeman's story, however, Almira recollects that she has indeed heard Mis' Green's story before: "'The last time I took you to Walpole, I guess, you told it'" (314). "On the Walpole Road" draws attention to the importance of telling and listening to a certain story. When we recall that the story is initiated by the prospect of a storm and concludes when the two women arrive safely home and the storm has blown over, we might speculate that telling and listening to this story has helped them to manage the anxiety induced by the possibility of bad weather. If we think of "bad weather" as a metaphor, we might conclude that this ritual helps them manage a certain kind of emotional weather and to do a certain kind of emotional work. As we have suggested in our previous discussion of this story in chapter 5, this emotional work includes making connections in a "motherless" world in which one must seek "mother" beyond the biological relation. The story suggests the resolution of that anxiety through the projected possibility of the return of "mother" in the form of mutual telling and listening. In this way, Freeman extends her frame to include the reader; noting that the two women have told and listened to the same story before, she directs her own readers to the possibility that they might want to read this story more than once or at least that they might want to become more cognizant of and reflective about those stories they also seek ritually to retell or rehear. The emotional work this story both requires of the reader and enables her or him to do is clearly ongoing; hence the willingness of Almira to hear the story every time she and Mis' Green take the road to Walpole. It is also work that cannot be rushed. Confronted by the possibility of a storm, Almira tries to make the horse go faster but to no avail. The work of getting "home" to "mother" requires a slow and steady pace; it cannot respond to the impulses of anxiety and it will have to be undertaken again and again. It is this rhythm that Jewett articulates in *The Country of the Pointed Firs.*

Jewett creates a space for both men and women readers to explore their relation to "mother." In the preceding section we discussed William Blackett and his choice as a son to remain with his mother (later bringing his middle-aged bride to live with them in the story "William's Wedding"). But Mrs. Almira Todd, the daughter, also struggles with her relation to "mother." In the way Mrs. Todd avoids the direct expression of emotion in her interactions with the elderly woman, we might find evidence that she experiences conflict in having chosen to move to the mainland instead of fulfilling a daughter's prescribed role of caring for her biological mother. Yet Mrs. Blackett responds as if she were reading her daughter's mind, a form of empathy Jewett's narrator has earlier identified as "tact" (46) and an example of William Ickes's definition of empathy as "everyday mind reading" (qtd. in Ciaramicoli 10): "'But here's Almiry; I always think Providence was kind to plot an' have her husband leave her a good house where she really belonged. She'd been very restless if she'd had to continue here on Green Island. You wanted more scope, didn't you, Almiry, an' to live in a large place where more things grew? Sometimes folks wonders that we don't live together; perhaps we shall some time,' and a shadow of sadness and apprehension flitted across her face" (*The Country of the Pointed Firs* 52; *AWR* 218).[10] Honoring the daughter's need for separation, she creates the possibility for that daughter to return. Although separated, Mrs. Todd remains connected to her mother; attuned to Green Island, she watches for signs that might tell her of her mother's movements and she studies the weather for the possibilities it offers of making or receiving a visit.

When earlier in the text the narrator decides she can no longer caretake Mrs. Todd's herb business but must retire to an old schoolhouse to do her summer writing project, Mrs. Todd expresses regret: "'Well, dear,' she said sorrowfully, 'I've took great advantage o' your bein' here. I ain't had such a season for years, but I have never had nobody I could so trust. All you lack is a few qualities, but with time you'd gain judgment an' experience, an' be very able in the business. I'd stand right here an' say it to anybody'" (*The Country of the Pointed Firs* 7). Although the narrator will not become Mrs. Todd's apprentice in the business of herbs, she will learn from the older woman how to stay connected while also separating, and in that way she becomes Mrs. Todd's apprentice in the "business" of emotional work. In constructing her narrator as a person in need of learning how to continue emotional growth as an adult, a topic we introduced in chapter 7, Jewett seeks to articulate a model of development that contrasts with the dominant paradigm, based on what is presumed to be good for boys. This paradigm proposes development as requiring a separation from and a rejection of home and mother and understands home and mother as oppositional and potentially damaging to men's developmental needs and to their independence and masculinity.

Instead, Jewett proposes a model of development based on a rhythm of departure and return that acknowledges both the need to individuate and the need to stay connected, a model similar to that which feminist psychologists in the mid-1970s began to articulate. Jean Baker Miller, for example, called in 1976 for a "new psychology of women." She writes, "One central feature is that women stay with, build on, and develop in a context of attachment and affiliation with others. Indeed, women's sense of self becomes very much organized around being able to make and then to maintain affiliations and relationships" (Miller 83). A few years later, Carol Gilligan's *In a Different Voice* (1982) explored developmental models in classical literary as well as psychological texts and concluded that "there seems to be a line of development missing from current depictions of adult development, a failure to describe the progression of relationships toward a maturity of interdependence. Though the truth of separation is recognized in most developmental texts, the reality of continuing connection is lost or relegated to the background where the figures of women appear. In this way, the emerging conception of adult development casts a familiar shadow on women's lives, pointing again toward the incompleteness of their separation, depicting them as mired in relationships" (155–56). Gilligan's object in her research has been "to restore in part the missing text of women's development" and to include "the perspectives of both of the sexes" in understanding human development (156). Resembling the models of Miller and Gilligan, the rhythm of departure and return that pervades Jewett's text provides its structural, thematic, and emotional dynamics. Readers can see this most clearly in the doubled relation of the narrator to Mrs. Todd and of Mrs. Todd to her mother. When Mrs. Todd takes the narrator to visit her mother, she does so in part to signal her honoring of the narrator's decision to separate and to model how to stay connected.

Jewett signals her intent to foreground this pattern and to provide a space for readers to rethink what it means to develop by titling her first chapter "The Return." This title indicates that the narrator is coming back to a place she already knows and suggests that she does so because she finds something of value in it and wishes to stay connected to it. Upon her return, the narrator locates her access to that value in the person of Mrs. Todd and the meaning of the pattern of departure and return becomes most fully articulated through their relationship. In a way similar to that of Freeman in "On the Walpole Road," Jewett extends the definition of mother and daughter beyond the biological, allowing it to encompass significant cross-generational relationships characterized by nurturance and the mutual transmission of knowledge; by so doing she emphasizes the importance even for adults of finding "mothers" and "daughters" regardless of biological relation. Mrs. Todd needs a "daughter," someone to whom she can pass on her collective, and ancient, knowledge and wisdom.

While she would like that daughter to be her literal apprentice, she can recognize the daughter's need to use what she learns in her own way. Indeed, the potentially painful and divisive act of individuation that occurs when the narrator begins spending her days in the schoolhouse leads neither to separation nor estrangement; "on the contrary," as the narrator puts it, "a deeper intimacy seemed to begin" (*The Country of the Pointed Firs* 7; *AWR* 208). Similarly, the narrator needs a "mother" to whom she can return as well as from whom she can separate in order to learn how to write the sentences that do not fail "to catch these lovely summer cadences" (*The Country of the Pointed Firs* 14–15). While the need to write such sentences reminds the narrator that "I had now made myself and my friends remember that I did not really belong to Dunnet Landing" (15), once written, these sentences have the capacity to dispense a textual healing equivalent to Mrs. Todd's herbal remedies.

Jewett recognizes that the process of separating while remaining connected is not easy. When the narrator leaves Dunnet Landing, even though the text signals the expectation of her return, Mrs. Todd cannot bring herself to say goodbye. Instead she leaves the house abruptly and rejects the narrator's effort to part differently. The narrator herself acknowledges that "it seemed impossible to take my departure with anything like composure" (130), and she must live with the recognition of the pain she has caused Mrs. Todd: "So we die before our own eyes; so we see some chapters of our lives come to their natural end" (131). Separation can feel like death; remaining connected brings with it the necessity of learning how to endure separating again and again, emotional work that requires a great deal of inner strength. Indeed, the model of development that defines adult masculinity as separation produces a core fragility, an adult who fleeing the pain of separation becomes incapable of tolerating connection. In this context, William's choice to remain at home seems preferable. While waiting for the boat the narrator catches a glimpse of Mrs. Todd in the distance; then, watching as she slowly disappears from view, she registers the pain of separation, especially for the one who is left behind. Through her narrator's empathic connection to Mrs. Todd's pain, Jewett underscores the point that the same person can occupy more than one position. Mrs. Todd is "daughter" in her relation to Mrs. Blackett, but "mother" in her relation to Jewett's narrator. Since daughters (and those sons who choose to do so) may themselves become "mothers" or mentors, they have an investment in a model that accommodates both positions. For the reader for whom her text provides the occasion for learning how to do the emotional work of separation and continual reconnection, Jewett provides sites of multiple identification. *The Country of the Pointed Firs* does not simply valorize the position of the child/daughter, which is common, or of the parent/mother, which is rare; rather it allows the reader to inhabit both positions equally, to engage the challenge involved in recognizing that one inhabits more than one position, to undertake the emotional work involved in each, and to acknowledge the pain that accompanies this work.

Although to our own readers, to move a morning's sail away to the mainland when that "large place where more things grew" is only Dunnet Landing may not seem significant, Green Island is a discrete region from Dunnet, demonstrating in part that no place is too small to have its own regions. In the relation of Green Island to Dunnet Landing and of Mrs. Blackett to Mrs. Todd, however, Jewett also sets up regions as "home" and suggests that we separate forever from "home" at our peril. Even if "home" is only an image of the way our parents' and grandparents' generations lived, it is good to go there, if only in imagination, and to maintain a connection to that place. Regionalism allows readers to make that connection, not in order to confirm the superiority of their own way of life but rather to honor and to try to keep alive the perspectives region represents, even if it does so only by being somewhat removed from that "large place where more things grew." Still, though regionalism in Cary begins with the assumption that much can be learned by being detained in Clovernook long enough to learn to see as Clovernook sees, she does not propose that one should remain forever in Clovernook. Indeed, Cary assumes that some of the readers of her Clovernook sketches live outside her region and that the value of Clovernook lies in its providing an alternate space that one can "inhabit" and return to, at least in reading, even though one lives elsewhere. Thus at the outset regionalism proposes that there is something of value in the place that can and should be brought from the place, and a "close" reading practice makes this process possible.

In a sense, this reading of regionalism defines it as exchange, but, as we observed in our discussion of *Deephaven* in chapter 4, instead of destroying the region, this exchange is a necessary component of its vision. Indeed, this reading illuminates a particular feature of Jewett's text that may seem puzzling at first glance—namely, the willingness, even avidity, with which the inhabitants of Dunnet Landing seek to share their stories with the narrator. Perhaps they recognize in this outsider who is also a writer not only someone who will listen to their stories but someone who will pass on those stories to others. In this context, stories become a form of export and we might argue that, far from engaging in a nostalgic lament for the former glories of Maine, Jewett positions Maine as in the present day a major exporter of "goods." Indeed, Captain Littlepage, who most laments the loss of the exchange involved in shipping, is the first to recognize in the narrator someone who might pass his story on and thus reactivate the exchange. He makes the point that with the loss of the shipping industry in Maine, people became disconnected from the rest of the world:

> "I view it . . . that a community narrows down and grows dreadful ignorant when it is shut up to its own affairs, and gets no knowledge of the outside world except from a cheap, unprincipled newspaper. In the old days, a good part o' the best men here knew a hundred ports and something of the way folks lived

> in them. They saw the world for themselves, and like's not their wives and children saw it with them. They may not have had the best of knowledge to carry with 'em sight-seein', but they were some acquainted with foreign lands an' their laws, an' could see outside the battle for town clerk here in Dunnet; they got some sense o' proportion. Yes, they lived more dignified, and their houses were better within an' without. Shipping's a terrible loss to this part o' New England from a social point o' view, ma'am. . . . No: when folks left home in the old days they left it to some purpose, and when they got home they stayed there and had some pride in it." (20–21)

While Captain Littlepage places his emphasis on what might be called the import side of the exchange, the value one gets from leaving home, he nevertheless describes not only the process of separation and return, repeated with each shipping voyage, but a kind of "sight-seein'" that is more than tourism. For Captain Littlepage, shipping represents an exchange—of goods, and also of the "good" to be brought back to one place from another. Indeed, he explicitly distinguishes the kind of leaving home he is talking about from late nineteenth-century tourism: "when folks left home in the old days they left it to some purpose." But the point is that they both left home and returned to it. Rather than viewing the region as a self-contained unit which has achieved its identity through isolation and separation, Jewett perceives region as exchange. The exchange involved in import and export reflects the dynamics of taking in and sending away, of connecting and separating. It is this exchange, this pattern of leaving "to some purpose" and then returning, that Jewett seeks to replicate in her narrator's life and to model for readers who may then learn how to do this emotional work themselves.

We have derived our explication of this model of development from *The Country of the Pointed Firs*, but we have come to recognize its prominence in other writers as well. Indeed, it gives us a particularly interesting way to approach the regionalist fictions written by women of color. For when the regionalist writer is a woman of color, the model of separating while staying connected addresses not only the uncertain gains to be achieved by learning English and/or assimilating into white society but also the difficulties of retaining ties to ethnic and regional traditions when one becomes a writer. While the model may seem inadequate to describe the complexity of racial identity in the United States, all three writers of color included in *American Women Regionalists* demonstrate this complexity textually as a psychological as well as a social struggle. For example, in "The Stones of the Village," Dunbar-Nelson explores the psychology of a man who believes he must separate completely from his grandmother, a woman with a "brown face surmounted by a wealth of curly black hair" (*AWR* 483). While more typically read as a story about the perils of "passing," from the perspective of regionalism "The Stones of the Village" also reflects a block in emotional development that mirrors a developmental pathology in the larger culture. When at the end of the story Grabért dies while preparing to give a speech, the vision that unsettles him and "kills" him is that of his grandmother demanding of him an account of his life: "He had expected to address the chairman; not Grandmére Grabért" (499). In Dunbar-Nelson's account, Grabért "dies" of his failure to stay connected with the grandmother who raised him; he dies of having held to the belief that, through his own vigilance and defense mechanisms, he can manage to define his identity exclusively through separation. His panic at the vision of his grandmother is a product of his commitment to this patriarchal model, but ironically, dying, he seeks to "run away to Grandmére who would soothe him and comfort him" (499).

Sui Sin Far, on the other hand, through the vision of her most fully developed character, Mrs. Spring Fragrance, presents a more successful model of separating while staying connected in a context that includes the complexities of racial and ethnic identity in the United States. The model Mrs. Spring Fragrance provides is one in which Americans can learn from the Chinese; in which her husband can learn from her; and in which, by becoming "Americanized," she is not forced to separate from her own culture and she feels free to critique U.S. imperialism. In those stories of Sui Sin Far that end tragically, Sui Sin Far presents Americanization as a threat to remaining Chinese for many immigrants.[11] But in the stories that include Mrs. Spring Fragrance, she proposes hybridity as a response to the clash of cultures and suggests, especially in "The Inferior Woman," that the Chinese woman can teach the white woman empathy. For Sui Sin Far, the solution to the challenge of separating from China while staying connected is to make the Americans more like the Chinese even while she herself is adopting parts of American culture as her own.

We can see the complexity of this model for writers of color most clearly in the work of Zitkala-Ša. The three essays Zitkala-Ša published in the *Atlantic Monthly* in 1900 (and later collected in *American Indian Stories*) take the form of separation from her biological mother ("Impressions of an Indian Childhood"), estrangement from her mother ("The School Days of an Indian Girl"), witness to her mother's rage and subsequent disillusionment with the charity offered as education to Indian children by the "Christian palefaces" ("An Indian Teacher among Indians," *American Indian Stories* 98), and ultimately a "return" to her Indian identity.

In the first of the three sketches, Zitkala-Ša portrays a childhood spent closely connected to her mother. As we observed in chapter 7, she learns how to approach others with respect and a "sensing of the atmosphere" (*American Indian Stories* 13; *AWR* 537);[12] she associates listening to the "talk of the old people" with pillowing her head "in my mother's lap" (15; 537); and she receives from her mother "practical observation lessons in the art of beadwork" (19; 539). From the perspective of her community, Zitkala-Ša reveals an alternative model of psychological development to that of individuation achieved by separation from mother. She writes of her own mother's guidance: "The quietness of her oversight made me feel strongly responsible and dependent upon my own judgment. She treated me as a dignified little individual as long as I was on my good behavior; and how humiliated I was when some boldness of mine drew forth a rebuke from her!" (20; 539). Zitkala-Ša is already an "individual" from her mother's perspective; yet her connection to her mother gives her mother a great deal of power over her nevertheless, and in this connection she will discover the source of her own sorrow, ambivalence, and ambition. Until her eighth year, as she recalls, "I knew but one language, and that was my mother's native tongue" (39; 545). However, other Indian children, including her own brother Dawée, have had a chance to become educated in the East, and when the missionaries invite her to come with them, she chooses to go despite her mother's resistance. In the language she uses to describe her own feelings in the retrospective narration, she characterizes herself as empowered by her decision:

> This was the first time I had ever been so unwilling to give up my own desire that I refused to hearken to my mother's voice. . . . I begged the Great Spirit to make my mother willing I should go with the missionaries.
>
> The next morning came, and my mother called me to her side. "My daughter, do you still persist in wishing to leave your mother?" she asked.
>
> "Oh, mother, it is not that I wish to leave you, but I want to see the wonderful Eastern land," I answered. (44; 547)

In the morning her brother comes for her mother's decision. The child creeps close to her aunt and listens. Her mother predicts the outcome of her separation: "'Yes, Dawée, my daughter, though she does not understand what it all means, is anxious to go. She will need an education when she is grown, for then there will be fewer real Dakotas, and many more palefaces. This tearing her away, so young, from her mother is necessary, if I would have her an educated woman. The palefaces, who owe us a large debt for stolen lands, have begun to pay a tardy justice in offering some education to our children. But I know my daughter must suffer keenly in this experiment'" (44; 547). Momentarily, when her mother walks her to the "carriage that was to take us to the iron horse," Zitkala-Ša writes, "I was happy." However, apprehension and fear soon follow: "When I saw the lonely figure of my mother vanish in the distance, a sense of regret settled heavily upon me. I felt suddenly weak, as if I might fall limp to the ground. I was in the hands of strangers whom my mother did not fully trust. I no longer felt free to be myself, or to voice my own feelings. The tears trickled down my cheeks, and I buried my face in the folds of my blanket. Now the first step, parting me from my mother, was taken, and all my belated tears availed nothing. . . . I was as frightened and bewildered as the captured young of a wild creature" (44–45; 547). In effect, in giving herself over to the missionaries, she also replaces a psychology that allows her to be an individual while remaining close to her mother with one that insists she separate completely from her mother in order to become "civilized." At a cultural level, assimilation requires separating from all that is Dakota, but for the child Zitkala-Ša remembers it meant leaving her mother with no possibility of "return," a realization she begins to explore in "The School Days of an Indian Girl."

Three years pass before she sees her mother again except in her dreams. Although she receives an education and learns English, she takes no comfort from the "white man's Bible," and among the white missionaries, she experiences inward rebellion. Describing some of the small ways in which she enacts that rebellion, she ironically suggests that her separation from her mother has not led to individuation after all but has only separated her from her own development: "Within a week I was again actively testing the chains which tightly bound my individuality like a mummy for burial" (67; 555). When she returns home, hoping to reconnect with her mother and her Indian identity, she finds herself sadly estranged: "During this time I seemed to hang in the heart of chaos, beyond the touch or voice of human aid. . . . My mother had never gone inside of a schoolhouse, and so she was not capable of comforting her daughter who could read and write" (69; 555). Returning east with the hope still that the "white man's iron steed . . . would bring me back to my mother in a few winters," she brings with her a "tiny bunch of magic roots" from "one of our best medicine men," but despite her attempt to carry her childhood identity with her, "the following autumn I ventured upon a college career against my mother's will" (75; 557). Following the white man's ways leads her to continue down the path of ongoing and eventually total separation from her mother: "Often I wept in secret, wishing I had gone West, to be nourished by my mother's love, instead of remaining among a cold race whose hearts were frozen hard with prejudice" (76; 558).

But memories do not allow her to reconnect with her mother. As she writes in "An Indian Teacher among Indians," "Though an illness left me unable to continue my college course, my pride kept me from returning to my mother" (81). Instead she begins to look for ways "to spend my energies in a work for the Indian race" (81). She chooses to take a job in an eastern Indian school and eventually is sent west to recruit Indian pupils for the school. As part of her trip, she hopes to see her mother. When she arrives, she discovers that her mother's situation has worsened. A white man sent to the reservation by the government has taken her brother's job and therefore the family's only income; her mother's log cabin has gaps in the walls; poverty-stricken white settlers have begun to claim Dakota lands; and her mother is filled with hatred: "She sprang to her feet, and, standing firm beside her wigwam, she sent a curse upon those who sat around the hated white man's light. . . . Long she held her outstretched fingers toward the settler's lodge, as if an invisible power passed from them to the evil at which she aimed" (94).

When Zitkala-Ša returns east, she implies that her mother's anger gives her a new view of the "large army of white teachers in Indian schools" who have a "larger missionary creed than I had suspected;" it is one that "included self-preservation quite as much as Indian education" (95). She arrives at a new view of the whites and a new mission for herself: "For the white man's papers I had given up my faith in the Great Spirit. For these same papers I had forgotten the healing in trees and brooks. On account of my mother's simple view of life, and my lack of any, I gave her up, also. I made no friends among the race of people I loathed. Like a slender tree, I had been uprooted from my mother, nature, and God. . . . At last, one weary day in the schoolroom, a new idea presented itself to me. It was a new way of solving the problem of my inner self" (97). She does not tell us what this idea is, but from what biographers have been able to learn of the writer's history we can conclude that though "she was never reconciled with her mother" (D. Fisher xiii), she engaged in a series of activities which eventually led to her life's work in Indian reform. She seems to have resolved her inability to reconnect personally with her mother by giving up her individuation as author and making a "return" to her Indian heritage. As Dexter Fisher assesses her choices, "Her career . . . exemplifies the tremendous difficulty confronting minority people who would become writers but who are constantly under pressure from their own groups to use literature toward socio-political ends. For American Indian writers, this dilemma has been further compounded by the heritage of an oral tradition that has its own aesthetic imperatives. It is not surprising at all that Zitkala-Ša subsumed her creative energy into a life work of progressive reform for Indians. The wonder is that she wrote at all" (xvii–xviii). We can understand this redirection of her creative energy as a way of staying connected to her mother, but in the compromises Fisher describes, we can also detect the price Zitkala-Ša paid. At one point, in a letter dated 1901, she writes, "As for my plans—I do not mean to give up my literary work—but while the old people last I want to get from them their treasured ideas of life. This I can do by living among them. Thus I mean to divide my time between teaching and getting story material" (qtd. in Fisher vi). That she did not in fact manage to continue her "literary work" makes the autobiographical sketches and her few stories even more valuable. They allow her to record "the moaning wind" of her "Indian nature" (*American Indian Stories* 67; *AWR* 555) and textually, in "Impressions of an Indian Childhood," to use an autobiographical variation on the regionalist sketch as a way to stay connected.

Although the work of Zitkala-Ša may, to some readers, make more sense when read in the context of American Indian literature and history, we read Zitkala-Ša as regionalist for several reasons. In growing up on a reservation, she learned first-hand what it is like to be "regionalized," that is, to be marked off from the United States by physical borders as well as to be "ruled" by the Bureau of Indian Affairs. In addition, as an assimilated Indian, she witnessed the investment white society has in defining Indians as "wild" and itself as "civilized." Even when she is hired to teach in the Indian school, her employer talks to her as if she is not present: "'Ah ha! so you are the little Indian girl who created the excitement among the college orators,' he said, more to himself than to me" (83). She is aware of herself throughout her autobiographical essays as the object of the white gaze, the person on display, a version of the Kentucky giantess in Jewett's "The Circus at Denby" from *Deephaven.* Further, writing for a white audience, she attempts to speak from the subject position of the regionalized, the queer, the "colored." However, in 1900, the size of the white audience capable of reading her work as anything but that of the "curiously colored seashell" (68; 555) would probably have been limited to a few ethnologists (and perhaps Austin). Still, even though embedded in the "curiously colored," her voice constructs another reader, one with "ears bent with compassion" (68; 555) to hear her. In order to continue her own emotional work, that of "staying connected" with her "mother," she committed her energies to Indian reform oratory and advocacy writing. "Close" reading, however, puts readers a century later back in touch with the voice Zitkala-Šа wanted her readers then to hear. Her essays constitute a text that brings into view the patriarchal imperialism of a developmental model that values only individuation through separation, that restricts even this limited form of development to those in power (whether "men" or "man"-like women), and that constructs rigid boundaries as defenses against compassion.

"The Foreigner"

Jewett published "The Foreigner" in 1900, a year after "The Queen's Twin" and four years after the publication of *The Country of the Pointed Firs.* In both of these late stories, she returns to explore further the relationship she created in *The Country of the Pointed Firs* between her narrator and her narrator's "friend and hostess" (*AWR* 234), Mrs. Todd. From the perspective of the writer, then, these stories reflect Jewett's own model of separating while staying connected and demonstrate as well that an author can come to know her own characters "better" over time (Pryse, "Women 'At Sea'"). In terms of the model of empathic therapy we have discussed above, we may consider these stories to be Jewett's own acts of re-narration. But what exactly do the stories suggest Jewett has learned since the 1896 text? Or even more to the point, what is different about these stories that suggests ongoing attempts on Jewett's part to get right the relationship between her narrator and Mrs. Todd? What use does that relationship continue to have for Jewett and for her readers?

In both stories, and especially in "The Foreigner," Jewett proposes empathy as one of the ways of remaining separate from another person but also staying connected. Empathy, then, becomes the emotion that Jewett associates with growth and development. It is empathy that seems to have replaced the tension between the narrator and Mrs. Todd apparent at the end of the earlier book and that we analyzed at length in chapter 7, just as it is the achievement of empathy that suggests the narrator's development of emotional maturity. By the time

Jewett "returns" to Dunnet Landing in "The Queen's Twin," her narrator appears to have served a successful apprenticeship with Mrs. Todd in the art of listening and to have made several "returns" of her own to visit Mrs. Todd. As we discussed in chapter 4, "The Queen's Twin" emphasizes the importance of careful approach in Jewett. Indeed, it is the narrator's ability to listen reflectively, respectfully, nonintrusively, and empathically that creates the opening for Abby Martin to tell her story. When Abby tests the narrator, "looking straight in my eyes to see if I showed any genuine interest," and when she is satisfied that the interest is there, "she . . . smiled as she had not smiled before" (229). Mrs. Todd watches the narrator closely, as if she is also testing her apprentice, and when the narrator listens well, "Mrs. Todd gave a satisfied nod and glance, as if to say that things were going on as well as possible in this anxious moment" (229). In "The Queen's Twin," Jewett returns to the theme of reflective listening and suggests that her narrator has grown in this skill since her abrupt separation from Mrs. Todd at the end of *The Country of the Pointed Firs.*

In taking up again the question of listening in "The Foreigner," Jewett suggests, as she does in "The Queen's Twin," that empathy creates the condition for narration, and that mutual storytelling and listening in the context of an empathic relationship is conducive to emotional growth. Perhaps even more than *The Country of the Pointed Firs,* "The Foreigner" reveals the workings of empathic interaction; indeed, as the narrator, whom Mrs. Todd has herself taught to become more empathic, becomes the listener for her own mentor, it is "as if" she has learned empathy-based therapy. When Mrs. Todd finds herself unable to sleep from worrying about her mother out on Green Island during "the first cold northeasterly storm of the season," she knocks on the narrator's door and tells her, "'Yes, I thought I'd come in and set with you if you wa'n't busy'" (*AWR* 234). The narrator is attuned to Mrs. Todd's distress: "I thought as I had never thought before of such anxieties" (235), and as Mrs. Todd sits in a rocking chair the narrator has drawn up to the fire and begins to tell the story of Mrs. Captain Tolland, the "foreigner," the narrator listens and Jewett records that listening: "I kept silence now, a poor and insufficient question being worse than none" (237). During a break in her story, the narrator does ask a question that reflects her "deepest interest" (243), and thereafter speaks as little as possible, only to further encourage Mrs. Todd to continue: "'You said that she lived alone some time after the news came,' I reminded Mrs. Todd then" and "'What was that?' I asked softly" (245). Near the end of the story, "Mrs. Todd drew her chair closer to mine" and "began to speak almost in a whisper. 'I ain't told you all,' she continued, 'no, I haven't spoken of all to but very few'" (251).

The narrator's experience of listening to Mrs. Todd is deeply satisfying. Indeed, perhaps more than any other work of regionalist fiction, "The Foreigner" allows us as readers to witness and participate in the experience of deep and focused listening, "of heightened awareness and patient attentiveness—an attitude that the psychologist William James called 'the strenuous mood'" (Ciaramicoli 45) and that Jewett proposes as a healing alternative to Roosevelt's "strenuous life." The narrator listens but she listens actively. At one point she encourages Mrs. Todd to continue speaking by observing, "'You have never told me any ghost stories,'" but sensing that her request is out of tune with Mrs. Todd's mood and realizing that "I had not chosen the best of moments," she hastens to reassure: "'Never mind now; tell me tomorrow by daylight'" (*AWR* 236). In telling the narrator of her efforts to befriend the foreigner, Mrs. Todd remarks that "'I got interested watchin' her an' findin' out what she had to say'" (244), but she acknowledges that, unlike her mother, she did not succeed in really listening to the foreigner and her failure haunts her—"'I used to blame me sometimes'" (244). Through listening to Mrs. Todd as she navigates her own emotional storm, the narrator arrives with her friend at a point of deep calm where "[w]e sat together in silence in the warm little room; . . . the sea still roared, but the high wind had done blowing." "'Sometimes,'" says Mrs. Todd, "'these late August storms'll sound a good deal worse than they really be. . . . [T]hey'll find it rough at sea, but the storm's all over'" (253).

Although Mrs. Todd, listening to the "great breakers," speculates "that the sea knows anger these nights and gets full of fight" (235), it is anxiety and fear that apparently bring her to the narrator's door. Her initial worries about the danger the sea's anger poses for her mother and brother out on Green Island seem easily calmed by the narrator's ready assurance "that Johnny Bowden and the Captain were out at Green Island" (234–35). Yet despite her apparent acceptance of the narrator's reassurance ("'yes, they'll have a beautiful evenin' all together, and like's not the sea'll be flat as a doorstep come morning'" [235]), Mrs. Todd nevertheless moves into the deeper territory of an underlying fear that goes well beyond the anxieties raised by this particular August storm, whose "tidal waves occur sometimes down to the West Indies" (234), and pursues the long reach of her own emotional wave back to its source.

Appearing to the narrator as "absent-minded," Mrs. Todd enters this territory during a pause "so long . . . that I was afraid she and the cat were growing drowsy together before the fire, and I should have no reminiscences at all" (237). But reminiscences follow upon the narrator's gentle encouragement ("Who was Mrs. Captain Tolland?"), and through the rather jolly story of four captains "three sheets in the wind" (237) Mrs. Todd approaches her real subject—the ongoing anxiety produced by her fear of a rift between her mother and herself that has its roots, like those tidal waves, in the West Indies. She has experienced such a rift in connection with Mrs. Tolland, and as the storm reminds her of the night the foreigner died, so the foreigner reminds her of this most terrifying of possibilities. Mrs. Blackett alone has been able to comfort Mrs. Tolland upon the departure of her husband and she returns from her visit with a charge to her daughter: "'I want you to neighbor with that poor lonesome creatur',' says mother to me, lookin' reproachful. 'She's a stranger in a strange land,' says mother. 'I want you to make her have a sense that somebody feels kind to her'"

(242). Implicitly accused by her mother of insufficient empathy, and perhaps slightly jealous of her mother's affection for another "daughter" and a foreigner at that, Mrs. Todd responds defensively and with anger: "'Why, since that time she flaunted out o' meetin', folks have felt she liked other ways better'n our'n,' says I. I was provoked because I'd had a nice supper ready, an' mother'd let it wait so long 'twas spoiled. 'I hope you'll like your supper!' I told her" (242). Although Mrs. Todd admits "'I was dreadful ashamed afterward of speakin' so to mother'" (242), and though she does in fact fulfill her mother's charge, the foreigner remains associated with Mrs. Todd's failure to be sufficiently empathic and with her fear of conflict between her mother and herself, even of her own hostile feelings. It is this fear and its attendant anxiety—fear of a deeper loss of "mother" than even that of her mother's own death—that leads Mrs. Todd to seek out the narrator on this particular evening.

Throughout her narrative Mrs. Todd gives ample evidence of possessing that "sense of ongoing attention to one's internal states" in which "mind observes and investigates experience itself, including the emotions" (Goleman 46). She recalls, for example, being upset with the foreigner for not having "'stayed through'" the long prayer and for "'kind o' declar[ing] war'" (*AWR* 241), and she acknowledges being still more upset that she "'couldn't get to no affectionateness with her'" (244). Describing the moment when she sees the ghost of the foreigner's mother in the room as her daughter is dying, she observes that she tried to act calm but "'I was a-shakin' as I done it'" (252). As she thinks through the feelings elicited by that moment in which she saw "'all I could bear,'" she notes, "'No, I wa'n't alarmed afterwards; 'twas just that one moment I couldn't live under'" (253). Waiting for her uncle to return from the funeral, Mrs. Todd finds herself agitated by the sound "'o' them black spruces a-beatin' an' scratchin' at the front windows'" but knows that her real "'discomfort was I thought I'd ought to feel worse at losin' her than I did'" (247).

At the heart of Mrs. Todd's emotional storm lies the fear of losing her mother and the anxiety produced by that fear, the same fear and anxiety that Mis' Green in "On the Walpole Road" manages through her narrative of "'mother' lives" and that we have identified as central to the thematics of regionalism, the fear that through insufficient empathy she might become a foreigner to her mother or her mother a foreigner to her. Yet a failure of empathy is also symptomatic of hostile feelings on the daughter's part. In a Kleinian reading of her anxiety, Mrs. Todd's recognition of her failure to be sufficiently empathic toward the foreigner elicits more than concern for her mother's physical safety; it also leads to anxiety that her own feelings of hostility and anger toward her mother as she expresses them in relating, "'I hope you'll like your supper!' I told her" (242), will lead to the loss of her own internalized "mother," Klein's "good object," and therefore to fears of "danger offshore" that threaten her sense of her own well-being and her very identity.[13]

In the moment of the foreigner's greatest need, however, Mrs. Todd manages to achieve both empathy and reparative connection. Worried that she might fall asleep from being so tired out by watching over the dying woman, but aware that "'If you give way, there ain't no support for the sick person,'" Mrs. Todd is glad when Mrs. Tolland shows signs of movement, for "'I forgot me quick enough, an' begun to hum out a little part of a hymn tune just to make her feel everything was as usual an' not wake up into a poor uncertainty'" (*AWR* 252). Suddenly, however, Mrs. Tolland sat up in bed "'with her eyes wide open'" and Mrs. Todd "'stood an' put my arm behind her. . . . And she reached out both her arms toward the door, an' I looked the way she was lookin', an' I see someone was standin' there against the dark'" (252). Aligning herself with the foreigner's perspective and seeing as if through her eyes, Mrs. Todd confirms for Mrs. Tolland the presence in the room of the foreigner's (dead) mother and gives her "that great unsung human gift" (Miller and Stiver 24) of attuned empathy: "'You saw her, didn't you?' she said the second time, an' I says, 'Yes, dear, I did; *you ain't never goin' to feel strange an' lonesome no more*'" (*AWR* 253). Mrs. Todd's empathy for the foreigner has allowed Mrs. Tolland to ask her question; it has also given Mrs. Todd a strategy for coping with her own deepest fear and so has become a form of self-empathy. Speaking of herself "with as much sympathy in her voice as if she were speaking of another person" (248) as she relates the story of returning to Mrs. Tolland's house after her death, Mrs. Todd comes to know through the foreigner that staying connected to her mother even when separated can happen after death as well as in life and that acts of "reparation," of even belated empathy—"'I set close by the bed; there was times she looked to find somebody when she was awake. . . . I did think what a world it was that her an' me should have come together so'" (251)—allow her to experience this connection. The narrator writes, "I could see that the recollection [of Mrs. Tolland's mother's face] moved her in the deepest way," and Mrs. Todd describes her feeling then that "'they'd gone away together'" (252, 253). Mrs. Todd invokes spiritual language to explain an experience so beyond the ordinary but not "'beyond reason'" that she can tell it "'to but very few.'" "'You know plain enough,'" Mrs. Todd tells the narrator, "'there's something beyond this world; the doors stand wide open'" (253). Mrs. Todd seems to be saying to the narrator that this experience has shown her that "mothers" even after death stay with their children, that she will be able to remain connected to her mother even when separated by death, and that she too can enter the place she has promised Mrs. Tolland, one where "'*you ain't never goin' to feel strange an' lonesome no more.*'"

In "The Foreigner," Jewett manages to hold in tension both the absence of the mother and her presence. The opening "anger" of the sea in the story makes visible the child's lifelong ambivalence toward the mother; but in repetitive and developmental acts of empathy the developing child and adult make Kleinian "reparations" to the mother. Indeed, what we internalize as "mother," Jewett suggests, is in part the reparative emotions and actions we find ourselves capable of feeling and taking. But we can experience reparative emotion only when we are capable of acknowledging ambivalence, hostility, and the "absence" of mother. At the same time, when we act empathically, we manage to become reconnected to "mother," here understood as at once an internalized object, an actual living person, and a remembered presence, a "ghost." Mrs. Todd's own failures at empathy in the past reemerge in the present as deeply troubling material that she becomes capable of revisiting in the presence of an empathic listener. In listening to Mrs. Todd, the narrator also encounters anxieties that may have to do with her relation to "mother," as she observes, "I thought as I had never before of such anxieties" (235). Mrs. Todd and the narrator thus engage in mutual empathy for their existential condition, understanding the need to remain connected even in their separation.

When we read "closely," we become open to empathy with both narrator and characters. "Close" reading, our conscious allusion to and deliberate revision of the rejected methodology of New Criticism, serves as a critical representation of the "ghost" we have found in regionalism; it is like the apparition of Mrs. Tolland that nevertheless brings Mrs. Todd back into reparative relation with her mother. Reading "closely"—both in the sense of allowing ourselves as readers to become emotionally engaged as part of our critical analysis and also of insisting on the need for careful textual analysis, "close reading" in the methodological sense—requires us to improve our abilities to listen and to pay attention. In so doing, we become capable of intimacy with texts and their representations. Gilligan writes that "intimacy becomes the critical experience that brings the self back into connection with others" and that "the experience of relationship brings an end to isolation" (163). Intimacy itself may be the ultimate goal of empathy. And yet, in Jewett's model of separating while staying connected, there is no permanent reunion, only a sense that art as re-narration, as ongoing reparative "returns" to "mother," can at least promote emotional development in human beings.[14] "The Foreigner" demonstrates that Jewett connected storytelling with an appeal for empathy and suggests that when the "close" or relational reader listens carefully, the act of reading can produce empathic response. The "foreigner" is "foreign" no longer; the "'poor lonesome creature'" has become "free to say."

"I Do So Long to Read It with You"

Throughout this book we have moved between what we might call the local and the global, understanding the local as the "close" reading of individual texts and the global at least in part as the myriad of theoretical problems and questions a reader can bring to an individual text or texts. Bringing these questions to bear on the tradition of regionalism has been our attempt to listen to regional writers and to the very idea of region, and we would describe our "close" reading of regionalist texts as our own expression of empathy as well as our recognition that regionalism is a fictional archive of immense contemporary value, one capable of being put to everyday use by everyday readers interested in emotional and cultural work. In attending to these texts, in trying to listen "deeply to both what is said (content) and how it is said (manner)" (Greenberg and Elliott 173), and in listening as well to what is not said but implied, we draw on our own capacity for empathy, developed in part from reading this fiction, to respond to and interpret it. "Close" reading is itself a form of empathy and thus a particularly appropriate approach to regionalist fiction.

As we have earlier observed, empathy has a cognitive as well as an emotional dimension. This dimension provides the distinction between sympathy and empathy for it is possible to sympathize with another's situation without understanding it. Empathy on the other hand requires one not only to experience what a person feels but to understand why the person feels that way. In asking readers to see how Clovernook sees, regionalism invites readers not only to feel but to think—how does it happen that certain persons are marginalized and what are the mechanisms that create and reinforce these hierarchies? It is this aspect of regionalist fiction, its critique of the "world," that provides its primary and most powerful cognitive dimension. For when regionalist fictions invite us to engage in the empathic act of shifting the center of perception from the one who gazes to the one gazed at and when we see how things look from the vantage point of the "peculiar," we are forced to ask how it happens that "somebody's neighbor" becomes a circus freak. In answering that question we reintegrate reason and emotion into our own reading and critical practices, perhaps enabling us finally to move beyond the "separate spheres" that have been foundational to Western understandings of knowledge as well as gender. As Jaggar writes,

> Time spent in analyzing emotions and uncovering their sources should be viewed . . . neither as irrelevant to theoretical investigation nor . . . a clearing of the emotional decks, "dealing with" our emotions so that they not influence our thinking. Instead, we must recognize that our efforts to reinterpret and refine our emotions are necessary to our theoretical investigation, just as our efforts to reeducate our emotions are necessary to our political activity. Critical reflection on emotion is not a self-indulgent substitute for political analysis and political action. It is itself a kind of political theory and political practice, indispensable for an adequate social theory and social transformation. (164)

The "close" relationship regionalism invites challenges readers to reintegrate analysis and empathy, even to imagine that one cannot happen without the other. Yet it is not only in the "soft" fields of the humanities and philosophy that we find renewed interest in relational reading. For example, Evelyn Fox Keller imagines "the ways in which science might be different" (*Reflections* 158) and writes about the geneticist Barbara McClintock, whose work for most of her career was marginalized, viewed as eccentric, and finally, and belatedly, awarded the Nobel Prize. What distinguishes McClintock from other scientists is what Keller calls, in her biography by the same title, "a feeling for the organism." In a series of interviews with McClintock, Keller heard a model of a science in which a recognition of the difference between organisms "provides a starting point for relatedness" rather than reinforcing "hard and fast divisions in nature, or in mind, or in the relation between mind and nature" (*Reflections* 163). For what McClintock described as her own scientific method included close observation of each of the corn plants she used in her genetics research: "'I start with the seedling, and I don't want to leave it. I don't feel I really know the story if I don't watch the plant all the way along. So I know every plant in the field. I know them intimately, and I find it a great pleasure to know them'" (164). Keller's description of McClintock's relationship to her plants presents it as similar to what we might understand as a relationship of human connection. Keller writes:

> In the relationship she describes with plants, as in human relations, respect for difference constitutes a claim not only on our interest but on our capacity for empathy—in short on the highest form of love: love that allows for intimacy without the annihilation of difference. I use the word *love* neither loosely nor sentimentally, but out of fidelity to the language McClintock herself uses to describe a form of attention, indeed a form of thought. . . . The crucial point for us is that McClintock can risk the suspension of boundaries between subject and object without jeopardy to science precisely because, to her, science is not premised on that division. Indeed, the intimacy she experiences with the objects she studies—intimacy born of a lifetime of cultivated attentiveness—is a wellspring of her powers as a scientist. (164)

"Close" reading is our attempt to replicate McClintock's method when she says, "'I start with the seedling, and I don't want to leave it.'"

We began our relationship with regionalism through "close" reading, and the empathic connection we have experienced with these texts over the years has allowed us to stay with this project from its seedling stage to its completion. In one sense we "don't want to leave it." We think of regionalism, however, the way Cather once reflected on *The Country of the Pointed Firs,* as having "a long, joyous future," one that we hope this book will help make possible. We also think of that future as existing here and now, for we have entered those "far distant years to come" ("Preface" 11) that Cather predicted would bring recognition to Jewett and that Jewett needed to imagine in order to begin writing. In her 1896 letter to Annie Fields (see note 6), Jewett reported rereading Stowe's *The Pearl of Orr's Island.* She had read the book for the first time at the age of thirteen or fourteen, and while she had long recognized it as an early influence on her own work, it was not until she returned to read it again as a mature writer that she discovered its power. Jewett's letter conveys as well her desire to share her discovery by reading the book with Fields. In seeking to place regionalism for ourselves and for our readers, we have tried to articulate the power of these texts and to propose the beginnings of another rereading. We end our work by extending Jewett's words about a single text to the much larger archive of regionalism itself and we now say to our own readers, "I do so long to read it with you."

Notes

Chapter 1: Redefinitions

Jewett's unpublished diaries (1867–71) are housed in the Houghton Library, Harvard University. The 1867 diary is catalogued as bMS Am 1743.26(3) and is quoted with permission.

1. See Pryse, "Archives of Female Friendship and the 'Way' Jewett Wrote," for a full discussion of the relationship between writing and friendship in Jewett's diaries and other published and unpublished early work.

2. See Cary, *Clovernook Sketches and Other Stories,* ed. Fetterley; Cooke, *"How Celia Changed Her Mind" and Selected Stories,* ed. Ammons; and Austin, *Stories from the Country of Lost Borders,* ed. Pryse. In *Provisions: A Reader from Nineteenth-Century American Women,* Fetterley also attempted to make available writings by women between 1830 and 1865 and to revise our understanding of the American Renaissance period in American literature.

3. Because we view *American Women Regionalists* as a companion volume, when we cite a text or writer included in the anthology, we will generally include parenthetical page references to *AWR* rather than to the original publication, occasionally adding the title of a text if it is not clear in the context of our discussion. In some instances, where we will be discussing entire texts for which we have included only excerpts in *AWR,* we will present double citations in parentheses when referring specifically to excerpted materials. We expect *AWR* to make it easier for readers unfamiliar with these literary texts to gain access to many if not all of the primary works we will be discussing in *Writing out of Place.*

4. See Donald Davidson, *The Attack on Leviathan: Regionalism and Nationalism in the United States* (Chapel Hill: University of North Carolina Press, 1938).

5. In her recent introduction to a collection of fiction by Mary Wilkins Freeman, Sandra Zagarell adds a new element to the study of regionalism. She writes, "While recognizably a part of the literary movement now known as regionalism, Freeman's short fiction questions the common regionalist premise that rural New England was cut off from modernity and modernization. In a host of ways, some direct, some implied, her work portrays rural New England and 'modern' America as dynamically connected. Freeman often suggests that modernization is ubiquitous throughout city and country, although not the same in one as in the other" ("Introduction," *New England Nun* xvii–xviii).

6. Davey argues that in Canada, the myth of geographic determinism allows the nation-state to "deter or limit the growth of transregional ideologies, playing regionalism, for example, against native rights, or against feminism"; it also allows "centralizing critics . . . to produce regionalisms as being too specific to be mainstream, and to select for national canonicity—usually on human-

ist or internationalist grounds—only regional artists who can be constructed as exceptions to this regional specificity" (5). In American literary history, regional writers like Mark Twain and William Faulkner serve as examples of this phenomenon; they do not become local-color writers but rather "exceptions" to regional specificity.

7. In an intriguing article, for example, Christine Gerhardt suggests teaching Southern (U.S.) literature in tandem with German literature in order to understand the former East Germany as a region with its own perspective. See "Exploring Unexpected Regions: Teaching Southern Literature from an (East) German Perspective," *Profession* (1999): 68–78.

8. See, for example, Donovan, *New England Local Color Literature: A Women's Tradition,* or the more recent Ammons and Rohy, *American Local Color Writing, 1880–1920.*

9. For earlier collections, see Harry R. Warfel and G. Harrison Orians, eds., *American Local-Color Stories* (New York: American Book Company, 1941); Wallace Stegner, ed., *Selected American Prose, 1841–1900* (New York: Holt Rinehart, 1958); and Claude M. Simpson, ed., *The Local Colorists: American Short Stories, 1857–1900* (New York: Harper and Brothers, 1960).

10. See Van Wyck Brooks, *The Flowering of New England, 1815–1865,* rev. ed. (New York: E. P. Dutton, 1940).

11. We are referring here in particular to Brodhead, *Cultures of Letters;* A. Kaplan, "Nation, Region, and Empire"; and Howard, ed., *New Essays on The Country of the Pointed Firs,* all of which have created the critical impression that Jewett epitomizes regionalism itself. The recent essay by Zagarell on Freeman ("Introduction," *A New England Nun*) offers evidence that critics are beginning to focus attention on regionalist writers other than Jewett.

12. For a fuller discussion of this argument, as well as discussions of other regionalist texts in which writers position their characters within the contradictions inherent in "woman's sphere," see Pryse, "'Distilling Essences.'"

13. Stephanie Foote's recently published *Regional Fictions* provides an instance of recent work on regionalism that deals extensively with male writers, including Garland, Frederic, and Cable.

14. Although we have no evidence to indicate that either Chesnutt or Murfree read the other's work, we do find it an intriguing coincidence that among all the names possible for an infant who might play a significant role in a text, both Chesnutt in "Sis' Becky's Pickaninny" and Murfree in *In the "Stranger People's" Country*—roughly coterminous both in their writing and their publication in the 1890s—would choose "little [or, in Murfree, leetle] Mose," though Moses was, for obvious reasons, a very common slave name.

15. For a discussion of the way Chesnutt reworks white plantation literature, see William L. Andrews, *The Literary Career of Charles W. Chesnutt* (Baton Rouge: Louisiana State University Press, 1980) and Houston A. Baker Jr., *Modernism and the Harlem Renaissance* (Chicago: University of Chicago Press, 1987).

16. In Annie's response to this particular story, we may read Chesnutt's attempt to address the pragmatic fact that, in order to be successful, his work in the 1890s had to appeal to white women readers. Julius's response to Annie's statement here appears to speak to this point: "The old man looked puzzled as well as pained. He had not pleased the lady, and he did not seem to understand why" (*The Conjure Woman* 79). Although we read *The Conjure Woman* in part as a story of Annie's growth in relationship with Julius, Chesnutt here also seems to be recording his own ambivalence toward the power white women (as readers) have over him. At the same time, we might read Annie's response as Chesnutt's recognition of her legitimate claim to be in some way included in the stories Julius tells her. Singular among the stories included in *The Conjure Woman,* "The Conjurer's Revenge" deals only with one man's revenge upon another for stealing his "shote."

17. For an excellent discussion of the evidence from the historical record concerning sexual relationships between white women and black men, the politics of such illicit liaisons, and the relation between rape accusations and lynching in the post-Reconstruction South, see Martha Hodes,

White Women, Black Men: Illicit Sex in the Nineteenth-Century South (New Haven: Yale University Press, 1997), especially chapters 7 and 8.

18. The 1921 Chesnutt novel *Paul Marchand, F.M.C.*, recently published for the first time, offers a further intriguing glimpse into the relationship between Chesnutt and the women regionalists, as well as into the emphasis on property that distinguishes them. In Chesnutt's "Foreword" to this novel in which a "free man of colour" becomes white overnight as the result of a dead man's will, and therefore must come to terms with a white man's relationship to property, including chattel slaves, he writes that "the author has made free reference" (*Paul Marchand* 3) to the work of Grace King and George W. Cable, and indeed, at numerous points, he paraphrases quite extensively from King's *New Orleans: The Place and the People.* King's book, a history, itself draws heavily on the early nineteenth-century New Orleans historian Charles Gayarré and was clearly known not only to Chesnutt but in all likelihood to Alice Dunbar-Nelson.

19. Frances Smith Foster's discovery of the texts of three novels by Frances E. W. Harper previously unknown to literary critics and historians in the late twentieth century offers hope in this area. Following up on bibliographic work by Jean Fagan Yellin, Foster describes how she turned to the archives of the Afro-Protestant press, and in particular to the *Christian Recorder,* the journal of the African Methodist Episcopal Church, to locate the texts of *Minnie's Sacrifice* (1869), *Sowing and Reaping* (1876–77), and *Trial and Triumph* (1888–89). She attributes the fact that "until 1991, no published bibliography of Frances Harper and no discussion of the African American novel that I have seen has mentioned the existence of these three novels" to the speculation that "few literary scholars or social historians thought to look in the Afro-Protestant press or to read the research of theologians and church historians and vice versa." Urging increased efforts to see "our ancestors, our neighbors, and ourselves in the complexity and multiplicity of real life," she suggests that "not only does the examination of the Afro-Protestant press demonstrate that some of our received knowledge about African American literary heritage is misinformed and incomplete, but it also offers the potential to reinterpret, to understand in new ways the literature that we have" (xxxv–xxxvi).

20. Foster lists a number of these periodicals, including the *Provincial Freeman, Frederick Douglass's Paper,* the *New York Independent,* the *Weekly Anglo-African,* the *Women's Era,*the *African Methodist Episcopal Church Review,* and the *Anglo-African Magazine,* "a periodical founded in New York in 1859 and generally assumed to be the first literary journal for, by, and about African Americans" (xv).

21. McWilliams describes *Paul Marchand, F.M.C.* as a "historical romance set in New Orleans," and notes that "the manuscript was returned by three separate publishers in late 1921" (ix, x). McWilliams speculates concerning the reasons for these rejections. "Chesnutt, who had enjoyed only modest commercial success with his previous publications, had been off the literary scene for fifteen years. The Harlem Renaissance would stimulate interest in Negro writers later in the decade, but this movement was just getting under way and could do Chesnutt little good in 1921. There was an additional obstacle in that *Paul Marchand, F.M.C.,* on one level at least, is a local-color romance. The vogue for this type of fiction, pioneered by Chesnutt's friend George Washington Cable, had crested and receded in the late nineteenth century; it would not have seemed a promising genre to market-conscious publishers in the 1920s" (x).

22. Ammons and Rohy are quoting James Herbert Morse, "The Native Element in American Fiction," *Century Magazine* 26 (1883): 362–75.

23. A full discussion of "whiteness" studies falls outside the scope and purpose of this book. However, see Mike Hill's "Introduction" to *Whiteness: A Critical Reader* for an analysis of the ways in which any attempt to engage in white critique must also recognize "a certain plurality that adds to race matters the mediating presence of gender and class" (7). In other words, white men cannot critique race privilege without also taking up questions of gender and class positioning. See also and especially E. Ann Kaplan, "The 'Look' Returned," for a discussion of her observation that

"in the 1990s, most of the books by whites on issues of whiteness have been by male scholars" (323). However, white women have certainly contributed to "whiteness" studies, as well as to race critique in the United States in numerous fields of study as well as in feminist theory and discourse. See, for example, Ruth Frankenberg, *White Women, Race Matters: The Social Construction of Whiteness* (Minneapolis: University of Minnesota Press, 1993); Marilyn Frye, "On Being White: Thinking toward a Feminist Understanding of Race and Race Supremacy," in *The Politics of Reality: Essays in Feminist Theory* (Trumansburg, N.Y.: Crossing Press, 1983); and Mab Segrest, *Memoirs of a Race Traitor* (Boston: South End Press, 1994).

24. Two essays that have contributed to our thinking in this introduction are Amy Kaplan, "Black and Blue on San Juan Hill," and Donna Haraway, "Teddy Bear Patriarchy: Taxidermy in the Garden of Eden, New York City, 1908–1936," both of which call attention to the central role Theodore Roosevelt played in articulating imperialist manhood. Both essays are included in Amy Kaplan and Donald E. Pease, eds., *Cultures of United States Imperialism* (Durham, N.C.: Duke University Press, 1993).

25. For an analysis of the similarities between Jewett's herbalist, Mrs. Todd, and healers in Toni Morrison, see Marilyn Sanders Mobley, *Folk Roots and Mythic Wings in Sarah Orne Jewett and Toni Morrison* (Baton Rouge: Louisiana State University Press, 1991).

Chapter 2: Locating Regionalism in American Literary History

1. Foote's recent *Regional Fictions* addresses the question of "regional" writing, primarily as novels written between 1870 and 1900 take up questions of the representations of difference. She explains that she is "less interested" in the development of regionalism as a form than in "how the regional fiction that was marketed in national venues represented various sections of the consolidating nation to an audience that was conscious of itself as a national elite" (4). Thus in her discussion of Garland, she does not differentiate between his work and that of the women regionalists.

2. The phrase is Mary Poovey's, from the title of her book *Uneven Developments: The Ideological Work of Gender in Mid-Victorian England* (Chicago: University of Chicago Press, 1988).

3. For a discussion of the role of anthologies in shaping the American literary canon during the 1920s, see Lauter, esp. 22–47.

4. Edited by William Peterfield Trent et al.; citations in the text will refer to *CHAL*.

5. See Werner Sollors, ed., *Multilingual America: Transnationalism, Ethnicity, and the Languages of American Literature* (New York: New York University Press, 1998), for his edited collection of essays on the non-English literature of the United States.

6. In addition to Austin, three other women contributed chapters to the four-volume, thirty-two-chapter enterprise. Elizabeth Christine Cook contributed "Colonial Newspapers and Magazines, 1704–1775" to volume 1; Ruth Putnam contributed "Prescott and Motley" to volume 2; and Louise Pound contributed "Oral Literature" to volume 4.

7. Lauter identifies this as an article on James Weldon Johnson. See Robert E. Fleming, "Irony as a Key to Johnson's *The Autobiography of an Ex-Coloured Man*," *American Literature* 43:1 (March 1971): 83–96.

8. Edited by Robert E. Spiller et al.; citations in the text will refer to *LHUS*.

9. Shumway (306) is quoting Robert E. Spiller, "History of a History: A Study in Cooperative Scholarship," *PMLA* 89 (May 1974): 604.

10. Edited by Emory Elliott; citations in the text will refer to *CLHUS*.

11. Although Schmitz does not credit James M. Cox for an earlier version of this reading of Stowe's impact on the humorists of the Old Southwest, he seems clearly to have read Cox's essay "Humor and America: The Southwestern Bear Hunt, Mrs. Stowe, and Mark Twain," in which Cox writes that "it was Harriet Beecher Stowe, coming right out of Connecticut, who killed them" (591).

12. Although he does not mention Robert Frost's sonnet "The Oven Bird," Cox is certainly referring to the poem's last lines, which read, "The question that he frames in all but words / Is what to make of a diminished thing."

13. In his discussion of these forces, Lauter notes that "the strenuous nationalism of even the most professional scholars, the masculinist attitudes of otherwise refined novelists, defined the issues for the art of the time as fundamentally distinct from the concerns of the domestic sphere which, it was insisted, were to occupy most women, including most female writers" (34).

14. According to Susan Stanford Friedman, Showalter first used the term "gynocriticism" in 1979 in "Toward a Feminist Poetics," reprinted in Showalter, ed., *The New Feminist Criticism: Essays on Women, Literature, and Theory* (New York: Pantheon, 1985), 125–43. For an interesting discussion of Showalter, and of the differences between the terms "gynocriticism" and "gynesis," see Friedman, "'Beyond' Gynocriticism and Gynesis," including her note 1 (33).

Chapter 3: Origins

A version of the section "Irving, Stowe, and Longstreet" appeared as Pryse, "Origins of Literary Regionalism," and is reprinted here with permission.

1. For further discussion of Edgeworth's influence, see Watson, "Introduction"; Butler, *Maria Edgeworth;* Baym, *Woman's Fiction;* and Buell, *New England.*

2. It is interesting that Stowe in a sense sent Sam Lawson out to do battle for her literary reputation, choosing an "Ichabod Crane" over a "Brom Bones" for this task. In the wake of negative reviews of *Oldtown Folks,* including one by Bret Harte, she vigorously promoted "her new series of Sam Lawson stories, eventually published under the title *Oldtown Fireside Stories,*" which she predicted "'will make a book that will sell immensely on the cars and every where & combined with authentic New England traditions will make quite a rush—Moreover it will keep "Old Town folks" afloat & going'" (Hedrick 347). Stowe's battle for her own literary reputation, particularly given the negative review in *The Nation,* clearly involved an understanding of assumptions about gender and literature; thus we find even more remarkable her courage in refusing to write in the "Brom Bones" way: "Like many of the prestigious journals emerging in post–Civil War America, the *Nation* was an institution of male literary power. The first issue contained no articles by women, prompting Henry Clapp of the *Saturday Press,* whose contributors included Harriet Prescott and Mary S. Gove Nichols of water-cure fame, to suggest that 'for this and other reasons its name be changed to the Stag-Nation.' In fact, the *Nation* took the lead in the backlash against women's cultural power" (Hedrick 348).

Chapter 4: The Poetics of Empathic Narration

1. See, for example, Janet Sternburg, *The Writer on Her Work,* vols. 1 and 2 (New York: Norton, 1980, 1991).

2. Both of us have had numerous opportunities during the twenty years we have been interested in regionalist writers and their work to have conversations with nonprofessional readers of American literature. During that time we have separately done lectures and workshops for both the Vermont and New York Councils on the Humanities, have been invited to informal community and campus-based "reading groups" to talk about regionalism, and in addition, have sometimes separately, more often together, presented various phases and stages of our work at conferences. It is based on these conversations, as well as those we have had with our own students, that we recognize some of what we will analyze in this chapter as "narrative effects" to be reading experiences we share with others. Some of our most surprising encounters over these decades have been with older readers who read Jewett's "A White Heron" or Freeman's "The 'Revolt' of Moth-

er" in school textbooks (now) seventy or more years ago. One man said that his mother had kept a copy of Jewett's *The Country of the Pointed Firs* in her bedside table and had read a chapter each night, as if it were a kind of bible. During the summer of 1996 we joined the "general public" for a Celia Thaxter weekend sponsored by Cornell University's Marine Biology lab on Appledore Island. The excursion, which allowed us to bunk in the lab dormitories for two nights, was titled "A Garden Is a Sea of Flowers." Among the forty or fifty men and women who had signed up for the excursion in order to see the historically reconstructed Thaxter garden as well as the graves of Celia and her family on the island, there were two Thaxter descendants. Others, including a couple of poets inspired by Thaxter's work, had clearly found out about her through means other than that of the "discipline of American literature." In fact, we were the only "professional" readers in the group—awed into silence by a phenomenon of interest and respect among "general readers," which the lack of critical interest in Thaxter had not prepared us to find.

3. Cooke later collected the story in *Somebody's Neighbors* (1881). Our own page references are to Ammons's edition of Cooke's *"How Celia Changed Her Mind" and Selected Stories.*

4. Consider, for example, the way Thaxter needed to educate James T. Fields, editor of the *Atlantic Monthly.* Rosamond Thaxter relates an incident in which Thaxter wrote to Fields after he had accepted her poem "Off Shore" but had edited one of the lines in that poem, "Sweet sounds on rocky shores the distant rote," to read "distant note." Thaxter wrote to Fields, "Did you really mean to mark out the r in rote and substitute n, making the word note? Then I think you are not familiar with the word rote. It means the sound of the sea on the rocks, it is very sweet and suggestive, that word, I cannot possibly spare that. It is all right, you will find it in Worcester's Dictionary. I find many people are unfamiliar with it, but it is much used at sea. The islanders at the Shoals can tell their whereabouts in the densest fog or the darkest night by the rote of the different islands and the mainland, so nicely educated is their sense of hearing. . . . Please let it remain rote, if anybody should chance to read it, and reading, understand it not, there is the Dictionary with a full and pleasant explanation of its meaning" (*Sandpiper* 62–63).

5. We take this phrase from the title Cooke gave to her 1881 collection of regionalist fiction, *Somebody's Neighbors.*

6. Due to the brevity of "The Praline Woman," entirely contained in *AWR* 480–81, we have not provided parenthetical citations to individual page numbers in our commentary on this sketch in this section.

7. See McWilliams for the history of Chesnutt's inability to publish this novel in his lifetime.

8. While *Paul Marchand, F.M.C.* has been available only for a short time as we write, and while no one else to our knowledge has made the connection between Chesnutt's praline woman and Dunbar-Nelson's, we find it inconceivable that Chesnutt would not have read *The Goodness of St. Rocque,* in which "The Praline Woman" appeared. In addition, though more work needs to be done on Dunbar-Nelson, she appears to have remained active as a cultural figure as well as a journalist and activist in the years following her separation from Paul Laurence Dunbar in 1902 and his subsequent death in 1906. According to Ann Allen Shockley, Dunbar-Nelson became "more of a public figure in her own right" and "much in demand as a lecturer" in subsequent years (264, 265), published a book of speeches entitled *Masterpieces of Negro Eloquence: The Best Speeches Delivered by the Negro from the Days of Slavery to the Present Time* (1914), edited *The Dunbar Speaker and Entertainer: Containing the Best Prose and Poetic Selections by and about the Negro Race* (1920), and of particular interest to Chesnutt in the years before he attempted publication of *Paul Marchand,* wrote a two-part article, "People of Color in Louisiana," that appeared in the *Journal of Negro History* (1916–17) (264–65).

9. For educating us in general concerning the significance of frequently overlooked references to Haiti in American literature, we are indebted to Eiko Owada, who completed her Ph.D. dissertation, "Faulkner, Haiti, and Questions of Imperialism," at the University at Albany, SUNY, in December 1999.

Chapter 5: "Free to Say"

1. In her discussion of Willa Cather's relation to "the culture wars of the 1920s," Lindemann refers to "Cather's fantasy that 'girls' books' could attain the same cultural power as 'boys' books,'" and she argues that Cather's editing of *The Best Stories of Sarah Orne Jewett* emerged from her "stubborn" commitment to that fantasy (99). Pointing to a series of issues that made writing "the preface to *Jewett* a difficult piece of work" for Cather despite her commitment, she suggests, interestingly enough, a link between the problem that the actual dominance of "boys' books" over "girls' books" posed to Cather and the dominance of nationalism over regionalism (97). She writes, "The greater difficulties arise from the complex of issues that had 'teased' her mind for years and would emerge as central preoccupations of both *The Professor's House* and *Death Comes for the Archbishop:* the relationship of 'boys' books' to 'girls' books,' the relationship of 'regionalism' to 'nationalism' (or whether, indeed, a meaningful distinction could be made between the two), the power of the 'masterpiece' and the terms that define it to shape American cultural history and critical debate" (97). For the full discussion of this subject, see Lindemann, chapter 3, "'In Prohibition Country': The Culture Wars of the 1920s."

2. For example, Cooke writes in "Polly Mariner, Tailoress," "'Firstly I hate damp boys: they're always gettin' damp and steamin', and I'd as lieve be choked to once'" (*Somebody's Neighbors* 232) and in "A Town Mouse and a Country Mouse," "'I s'pose there is a puppus in boys, but I've wished frequent that men growed out o' somethin' more pleasant'" (*Huckleberries* 333). For additional examples, see "Amandar," *Somebody's Neighbors,* 203; "Love," *Huckleberries,* 83; and "Salathiel Bump's Stocking," *The Sphinx's Children,* 396.

3. We are only vaguely invoking Jacques Lacan in this discussion, though we acknowledge that without a reading of Lacan, we might not have marked King's use of the word "lacking" in the way we do. However, we understand the regionalist construction of "mother" to supply the relationality we find "lacking" in Lacan's concept of the infant's origins as expressed in "The Mirror-Stage as Formation of the Function of the I" (*Écrits* 1–7).

4. For a full discussion of this novel, see Fetterley, "Only a Story, Not a Romance."

Chapter 6: The Sketch Form and Conventions of Story

The epigraph is from Cooke, *"How Celia Changed Her Mind,"* ed. Ammons, 184.

1. Critical controversy has centered on ideological questions rather than form, though as we have indicated in chapter 2 and examine further in this chapter questions of form are also ideological. To enter the often acrimonious critical debates concerning Jewett, with an emphasis on *The Country of the Pointed Firs* but in a discussion that includes other works as well, see Elizabeth Ammons, "Going in Circles: The Female Geography of Jewett's 'Country of the Pointed Firs,'" *Studies in the Literary Imagination* 16.2 (Fall 1983): 83–92; idem, "Material Culture, Empire, and Jewett's 'Country of the Pointed Firs,'" in Howard, ed., 81–100; Brodhead, *Cultures of Letters;* Judith Fetterley, "Commentary: Nineteenth-Century American Women Writers and the Politics of Recovery," *American Literary History* 6.3 (Fall 1994): 600–11; idem, "'Not in the Least American'"; Judith Fetterley and Marjorie Pryse, "On 'Reading New Readings of Regionalism,'" *Legacy* 15.1 (1998): 45–52; Susan Gillman, "Regionalism and Nationalism in Jewett's 'Country of the Pointed Firs,'" in Howard, ed., 101–18; June Howard, "Introduction: Sarah Orne Jewett and the Traffic in Words," in Howard, ed., 1–38; idem, "Unraveling Regions, Unsettling Periods: Sarah Orne Jewett and American Literary History," *American Literature* 68.2 (June 1996): 365–84; Karen L. Kilcup and Thomas S. Edwards, "Confronting Time and Change: Jewett, Her Contemporaries, and Her Critics," *Jewett and Her Contemporaries: Reshaping the Canon,* ed. Kilcup and Edwards (Gainesville:

University Press of Florida, 1999), 1–30; McCullough, *Regions of Identity;* Pryse, "Sex, Class, and 'Category Crisis'"; Renza, *"A White Heron";* Sandra A. Zagarell, "*Country*'s Portrayal of Community and the Exclusion of Difference," in Howard, ed. 39–60; idem, "Crosscurrents: Registers of Nordicism, Community, and Culture in Jewett's 'Country of the Pointed Firs,'" *Yale Journal of Criticism* 10.2 (1997): 355–70; idem, "Troubling Regionalism."

2. We take this phrase from Jane Tompkins, *Sensational Designs: The Cultural Work of American Fiction, 1790–1860* (New York: Oxford University Press, 1985).

3. Jewett's *A Country Doctor* (1884) may offer an example of an exception to this point, for in this novel Jewett writes the plot of a young woman who rejects marriage, despite a romantic courtship and much social pressure from her aunt's community, in order to become a doctor. However, the novel's lack of critical recognition may also confirm the general point concerning the conventions of plot for women. In a letter to Charles Miner Thompson dated October 12, 1904, Jewett offers her own disclaimer, writing, "Indeed, I understand that 'The Country Doctor' is of no value as a novel, but it has many excellent ideas" (*Letters of Sarah Orne Jewett* 195). See Pryse, "'I was country when country wasn't cool,'" for commentary on this novel.

4. In a letter to Annie Fields (for discussion of the date of this letter, see chapter 11, n. 6), Jewett describes rereading *The Pearl of Orr's Island* for the first time since she had first read it at the age of thirteen or fourteen, praises it as "original and strong," but writes, "Alas, that she couldn't finish it in the same noble key of simplicity and harmony; but a poor writer is at the mercy of much unconscious opposition" (*Letters of Sarah Orne Jewett,* 46–47). We propose a greater consciousness of her dilemma on Stowe's part than Jewett accords her.

5. Chapter 4 of Stowe's text, in which she introduces Roxy and Ruey, is included in *AWR* (24–30).

6. Even in Cooke's "Dely's Cow," from which we take the epigraph to this chapter, the real love story turns out not to be the one between Dely and her husband but between Dely and her cow.

7. When Cary writes novels, however, she moves this conventional material into the center and the resulting texts and their implied author seem quite different from what we find in her regionalist fiction. For a full discussion of Cary's novels and their differences from her sketches, see Fetterley, "Introduction."

8. In *The Journey Is Home,* Morton cites Amos Wilder's use of the term in *Theopoetics* (Philadelphia: Fortress Press, 1976).

9. See, for example, the Eagle Island sequence in chapter 16 of *Pearl,* in which Moses climbs a hemlock to raid the eggs from an eagle's nest, then expresses his wish that he had a gun so that he could stop the eagles' screeching after the violation of their nest. Mara replies, "'But the poor birds,—do hear 'em scream. Moses, don't you suppose they feel bad?'" (Stowe 176).

10. Other examples include King's "Pupasse" (*AWR* 399–407) and Chopin's "Odalie Misses Mass" (*AWR* 426–429) and "A Little Country Girl" (*AWR* 451–457).

11. See, for example, "Miss Lucinda" in *"How Celia Changed Her Mind" and Selected Stories.*

12. For example, at the end of "A Chinese Boy-Girl," Mr. Ten Suie speaks in a Chinese-inflected English dialect. He begins speaking as follows: "'Perhaps you speak too much about Ku Yum alleady,' he said. 'Ku Yum be my child. I bling him up as I please'" (Sui Sin Far 159).

13. We take this phrase from the title of her autobiographical essay "Leaves From the Mental Portfolio of an Eurasian" that was published in the January 21, 1909, issue of the *Independent.* The essay is included in *Mrs. Spring Fragrance and Other Writings.*

14. In this context we might usefully consider the significance of Freeman's 1917 retraction of the "truth" of "The Revolt of 'Mother'"; see Westbrook 64.

15. For an analysis of Freeman's relationship with Booth, see Pryse, "Mary E. Wilkins Freeman."

16. The title of Austin's 1912 semi-autobiographical novel, *A Woman of Genius,* reflects her own self-valuation in spite of her rejection by her mother, her inability to attain an equal sexual relationship with a man, and a feminism that "rattled even the liberal critics" (N. Porter 307). For further discussion, see Porter's "Afterword" to the novel.

17. In placing the word "way" in quotation marks, we are invoking Jewett's own use of the word as a "calling" in some of her early personal writing. See Pryse, "Archives of Female Friendship and the 'Way' Jewett Wrote."

18. In open discussion at the Dartmouth Futures of American Studies Summer Institute, June 2000.

Chapter 7: Regionalism and the Question of the American

1. We use the term "perceived" advisedly, recalling Peter Carafiol's observation in "The New Orthodoxy" that the "myth of genesis" invoked by what he calls the "New Orthodoxy" to "legitimate its project . . . is not about 'America' but about American literary studies" (627). He writes, "the myth of American literary scholarship that underwrites the New Orthodoxy can seem so neat only by excluding more than half of the history it aims to describe and thus necessarily oversimplifying the critical debates that have enlivened scholarship in American literature over the past one hundred years" (629).

2. See also Sollors, *Multilingual America.*

3. Pease is considering the "norms, working assumptions, and self-understanding of the field" of American Studies that "constitute what might be called a disciplinary unconscious: an Americanist cannot at once act upon these assumptions and be conscious of them" (3). He then writes, "By the term field-Imaginary I mean to designate a location for the disciplinary unconscious mentioned earlier. Here abides the field's fundamental syntax—its tacit assumptions, convictions, primal words, and the charged relations binding them together. A field specialist depends upon this field-Imaginary for the construction of her primal identity within the field" (11).

4. See chapter 6, note 1.

5. The jacket copy Brodhead is quoting reads as follows: "Sarah Orne Jewett, best known for her book *The Country of the Pointed Firs,* has been unfairly considered a minor regional writer of vivid descriptions of the simple life of rural Maine in the late nineteenth century. Sarah Sherman has taken steps toward correcting this injustice by enabling us to see Jewett as an artist whose stories, focusing on women's lives and relationships, contain the prevalent symbols and myths of a culture struggling to find expression" (qtd. in *Cultures of Letters,* 142). See Sarah Way Sherman, *Sarah Orne Jewett: An American Persephone* (Hanover, N.H.: University Press of New England, 1989).

6. In an earlier essay written for *Columbia Literary History of the United States,* Brodhead traces the "high-cultural organization of literature of the mid-nineteenth century" that "did make the great mass of readers defer to it as the realm of 'literature' proper" ("Literature and Culture" 472), portrays "literary institutions under gentry control in the later nineteenth century" (472), and identifies James as "another product of these same arrangements" (473). In this essay, as in *Cultures of Letters,* Brodhead characterizes Jewett and Constance Fenimore Woolson as "enabled . . . by the support they derived from the gentry establishment of a 'serious' literary realm," and writes, "in terms of its cultural production the literature of regionalism is a product more particularly of the high-cultural literary establishment" ("Literature and Culture" 474). The point that interests us is that for Brodhead, James manages to occupy "his own" artistic creed even as he is a "product of these same arrangements," whereas the literature of regionalism is simply a "product" of the establishment. Brodhead writes, "Less interested than Howells in what might be called the administrative aspect of literary creation (he was never an editor), James nevertheless published virtually all of his work in the *Atlantic.* . . . And while his supporting artistic creed is in one sense his own creation, in another sense he derives this support too from the gentry literary culture of the 1860s, 1870s, and 1880s. James brings to the intensity of an authentic personal faith the group ethic that locates the supreme good in the cosmopolitan, aesthetic creation, and the civilizing powers of the artistic imagination" ("Literature and Culture" 473). Although Brodhead omits a critique of James in his 1993 book, it is clear that he might have made the same analysis of James that he later does of Jewett.

7. For further reflections on the question of regionalism's readers, see the discussion of Cary in chapter 11.

8. While it is difficult to trace the origins of the critique of regionalism—Kaplan's essay appeared in the 1991 *Columbia History of the American Novel,* while Brodhead did not publish *Cultures of Letters* until 1993—we understand Brodhead to be the originary point. In "Literature and Culture," published in *Columbia History of the United States* (1988), Brodhead constructs the view of regionalism as embedded in the "high-cultural organization" of the "new literary establishment" (472–73). Then, in chapter 2 of *Cultures and Letters,* he reprints an essay that first appeared in *American Literary History* in 1989 (ix). In this chapter he first cites "touring" as the trope by which readers should understand new "entertainments of the mid-nineteenth century" and their effects on the "mass publics that consumed them" (*Cultures of Letters* 61). His discussion of "touring" and the construction of literary audiences as consumers of the "life" of others lays the groundwork for Kaplan's use of the trope of "tourism" to construct regionalism in "Nation, Region, and Empire" (252). Zagarell also credits Brodhead for this originating trope, identifying him as explaining the "alternative stable, if imaginary, geographic-cultural space made literally accessible by tourism" ("Troubling Regionalism" 641).

9. In making her connection between naturalism and empire, Kaplan notes that both Frank Norris and Jack London "were deeply influenced by Rudyard Kipling, and themselves spent time in contested colonial areas of Europe and the United States (Norris in the Transvaal and Cuba, London in the Pacific, the Klondike, Japan, and Korea)" (263). Moreover, they "took up Kipling's 'white man's burden,' not simply in overt racism against Asians, Mexicans, and all nonwhites, but by reconstructing American identity as a biological category of Anglo-Saxon masculinity" (263). Both of these writers "projected imperial adventures onto imaginary open frontiers of the 'Wilds,' the open seas, arctic exploration, and the primordial beast within modern man" (263). Kaplan associates Norris's endorsement of American imperialism as an "Anglo-Saxon inclination to dominate the world" with the "desire to dominate women" expressed in *McTeague.* In a provocative reading of London's *The Call of the Wild,* Kaplan writes that the book enacts "an allegory of national development" even though it "may seem as far away from a national novel . . . as the Yukon is from United States borders, and as dogs are from men" (264). In another article, she explores Stephen Crane's journalistic reports from the front in the Spanish-American War of 1898, thereby bringing Crane as well into her association of naturalism with imperialism ("Black and Blue on San Juan Hill," *Cultures of United States Imperialism,* ed. Amy Kaplan and Donald A. Pease [Durham, N.C.: Duke University Press, 1993], 219–36). Not only is this association extremely provocative (and one we find compelling), but it also links naturalism as a mode with the third term in her triad, "empire." Nevertheless, this association has the effect as well of emphasizing the critique of naturalism and of locating it negatively—an emphasis and a location that highlight still further Kaplan's elision of realism in her analysis.

10. Austin is the only regionalist who ever used the term, and the only one who also wrote literary criticism. In "Regionalism in American Fiction," Austin writes, "Art, considered as the expression of any people as a whole, is the response they make in various mediums to the impact that the totality of their experience makes upon them, and there is no sort of experience that works so constantly and subtly upon man as his regional environment" (97). She attempts to "discriminate between a genuine regionalism and mistaken presentiments of it" (98) and differentiates between those works which may be "colored" by what she calls "local rather than regional" phases of American life and a "fiction which has come up through the land, shaped by the author's own adjustments to it" (101). Austin further describes one of the "indispensable conditions" of regionalism, namely "that the region must enter constructively into the story, as another character, as the instigator of plot" (105). Following upon her contribution to the *Cambridge History of American Literature,* "Non-English Writings II: Aboriginal," that we discussed in chapter 2, she concludes her discussion of regionalism by describing how difficult it is to tell or write stories that are truly "about the region rather than of it" (106), and she suggests that Indian stories fit her category, citing a collection transcribed by Frank Applegate entitled *Indian Stories from the Pueblos.*

Austin concludes her essay with a warning that, in effect, challenges American readers to avoid the merely picturesque, the superficially local. She writes of regionalism, "Time is the essence of the undertaking, time to live into the land and absorb it; still more time to cure the reading public of its preference for something less than the proverbial bird's-eye view of the American scene, what you might call an automobile eye view, something slithered and blurred, nothing so sharply discriminated that it arrests the speed-numbed mind to understand, characters like garish gas stations picked out with electric lights. The one chance of persuading the young reader to make these distinctions for himself would be to whet his appreciation on the best regional literature of our past so that he may not miss the emerging instance of his own times" (107). While we do not find Austin's words definitive, we read her here as making an attempt to articulate both the existence of regionalist writing and its distinction from local color.

11. Campbell explains that she chooses not to make a distinction between "local color" and "regionalism" (180–81 n. 20).

12. Later, in her 1900 story "The Foreigner," which we discuss at length in chapter 11, Jewett reveals the source of Mrs. Todd's animosity toward Mari' Harris. In "The Foreigner," when Mrs. Todd's mother invites the "foreigner" Mrs. Tolland to a "social circle" at the meetinghouse, Mrs. Tolland, who has a good ear for music, tries to help Mari' Harris and others find the right notes their singing has "flatted." Then, eliciting excitement in the group, the "foreigner" picks up a tambourine and begins to dance. As Mrs. Todd later tells the narrator in "The Foreigner," "'You couldn't help seein' how pretty 'twas; we all got to trottin' a foot. . . . There wa'n't one of 'em but enjoyed it'" (*AWR* 240). However, the next day "'there was an awful scandal goin' in the parish, an' Mari' Harris reproached my mother to her face, an' I never wanted to see her since, but I've had to a good many times'" (241). In "The Foreigner," it appears that the source of Mrs. Todd's animosity toward Mari' Harris lies in her treatment of Mrs. Blackett and in the role she has played in getting up a "'sight o' prejudice'" (240) toward Mrs. Tolland and contributing to her remaining a "foreigner" in their community.

Chapter 8: Feminist Epistemology and the Regionalist Standpoint

1. MacKinnon includes this footnote in an earlier version of work that she would revise for *Toward a Feminist Theory of the State,* though it does not appear in the revision. See "Feminism, Marxism, Method, and the State," in Sandra Harding, ed., *Feminism and Methodology* (Bloomington: Indiana University Press, 1987), 150 n. 3.

2. We are referring here to the subtitle of Sandra Harding's book, *Whose Science? Whose Knowledge?*

3. We are referring here to Adrienne Rich, "Notes toward a Politics of Location," in *Blood, Bread, and Poetry* (New York: Norton, 1986), 210–31; and to Patricia Hill Collins, "Learning from the Outsider Within: The Sociological Significance of Black Feminist Thought," *Social Problems* 33.6 (1986): 14–32.

4. Although we have followed Collins's 2000 revision of her 1990 text throughout most of our discussion here, in this case we have reinserted into the text the quote by Lorraine Hansberry that Collins cut for the second edition but which we still find relevant for our understanding of regionalism. The quote appears in *Black Feminist Thought: Knowledge, Consciousness, and the Politics of Empowerment* (Boston: Unwin, 1990), 209.

5. Evelyn Fox Keller takes up the concept of the "laws of nature" from a feminist standpoint in *Reflections on Gender and Science.*

6. In teaching this material to a class that included a physically disabled student sensitive to the language of disability used in the way Morrison describes American language and literature as constructing an "American Africanism," we became aware of the way Morrison herself uses the language of "blindness" as a metaphor for an unwillingness or inability to "see" or understand, thereby committing the same lapse she is criticizing, and perhaps in the process demonstrating her point concerning how difficult it is to work "with and through" a language that

already encodes social hierarchies and ideologies. We are indebted to Constance Laymon for this insight.

Chapter 9: Race, Class, and Questions of Region

1. Annette White-Parks discusses at length Sui Sin Far's interest in being "accepted by editors without racialization," quoting an undated letter in which she wrote, "'Though I myself prefer to branch out, so many friends prefer to think that the Chinese should be my only theme'" (45). Lummis was probably one of these "friends," with his interest in "exotic ethnics." Here and throughout her discussion, White-Parks is taking her information concerning Lummis from Edwin R. Bingham, *Charles F. Lummis, Editor of the Southwest* (San Marino, Calif.: Huntington Library, 1955), "who argues that it was Sui Sin Far's concern with the 'Oriental in the West' that qualified her as a *Land of Sunshine* contributor" (86). Sui Sin Far would certainly have been aware of Lummis's regionalist interests, and there is no doubt that without Lummis's editorial acceptance and active encouragement, we would not have Sui Sin Far's stories (see White-Parks for a discussion of her brief writing career and short life). However, Lummis also apparently revealed a contradiction between his editorial interest and his political allegiances. White-Parks writes, "Though popularly seen as a crusader against imperialism and a champion of racial tolerance, Lummis did not carry this stand to the point of promoting social or political equality for Chinese Americans in the United States. In 1901 he warned of 'the danger that the Exclusion Act, now about to expire, may not be renewed,' and he supported popular racist stereotypes about the Chinese as 'non-assimilable'" (86–87).

2. In the case of Dunbar-Nelson, it was perhaps more accurately her association with Dunbar himself that enabled her publication. After her break with Dunbar in 1902, creative writing took "second place" in her life and though "her major achievements occurred in short fiction," this was a form that "never again occupied her so totally" (Hull 59).

3. Violet Harrington Bryan notes that "refuge in the convent when in doubt of one's identity or the evils that await one is a resolution of many Creole tales," and recalls the historical personage Henriette Delille, "who not only fled into the convent because of her reluctance to go the way of the rest of her relatives—Creoles of color—and attend the quadroon balls, be selected by a white man, and spend the rest of her life as his faithful mistress, but actually went much further and established an order for women of color, the Sisters of the Holy Family" (129).

4. Chesnutt also credits Cable for his portraits and acknowledges that he has made "free reference" to both King and Cable (*Paul Marchand* 3).

5. In his "Introduction" to *Paul Marchand, F.M.C.*, Dean McWilliams writes, "Cable's literary rival Grace King made it clear that, for her part, the ideal mulatto was distinguished by his 'humble acquiescence in the exigencies of his social position'" (xiii). However, McWilliams is actually misquoting King. In King's *New Orleans,* she quotes at length from the historian Charles Gayarré on the subject of "free coloured men." It is from this long quote that McWilliams draws his misattribution to King. Furthermore, Gayarré himself is hardly being disrespectful to men of mixed race. He writes about them that "it is always to be remembered that in their contact with white men, they did not assume that creeping posture of debasement—nor did the whites expect it—which has more or less been forced upon them in fiction" (qtd. in King 347). It is unfortunate that, in a reprint of Chesnutt's novel that is certain to attract a wide readership, the editor includes a careless citation and does not take seriously the extent to which Chesnutt, throughout the novel, paraphrases from King's *New Orleans,* though to his credit, he does include footnotes that alert the reader to Chesnutt's sources in King.

6. As Chesnutt's source for "The Quadroon Ball," King quotes one of the Sisters of the Holy Family as reporting that their chapel had once been the "'old Orleans ball-room; they say it is the best dancing floor in the world. It is made of three thicknesses of cypress'" (*New Orleans* 355). Chesnutt writes that the building in which the quadroon ball is held was "later occupied by a con-

vent of colored nuns" (*Paul Marchand* 70) and that "the floor was of solid oak, three inches thick, said to be the best dancing floor in New Orleans" (72).

In echoing King, Chesnutt paraphrases so closely as almost to quote directly from Charles Gayarré as quoted in King. In fact, he cites the same passage McWilliams uses to misrepresent King. Gayarré writes, concerning the relations between men of color and white men, that "'nevertheless it must not be imagined that the amenities were not observed when the men of the races met, for business or otherwise'" (qtd. in King, *New Orleans* 348). Chesnutt writes that men of color "were denied civil and social equality, including the right of intermarriage, and they were not admitted to the professions, but beyond these limits the amenities were as a general thing fairly well observed when the men of the races met for business or otherwise" (*Paul Marchand* 164).

7. Taylor describes a New Orleans that falls into anything but binary categories in the years before the Civil War. For example, she writes that "for decades there had been an unusually large community of free blacks with a sophisticated and economically and culturally varied lifestyle," that the population of New Orleans "had the highest percentage of mixed-race ancestry of any American city," that because of the "heterogeneous citizenry comprising Italians, Spaniards, and French as well as blacks and people of mixed race, it was impossible to differentiate people simply by color or language," and that by 1860, "New Orleans had adopted a fairly liberal attitude toward black-white relations, which was soon to be eroded [by the War]" (4).

8. As an interesting footnote, Dunbar-Nelson by the age of nineteen was described in a newspaper of an artistic-fraternal organization for which she wrote a column as follows: "She has the honor of being the only colored female stenographer and type-writer in this city ['employed as bookkeeper and type-writer for the Paragon Printing Company, the largest colored establishment in the country']" (Hull 35–36).

9. Pondering this question, we consulted Peterson's *A Field Guide to the Birds*. In Jewett's story, the hunter-ornithologist describes the bird he is looking for as "rare," one that has "'never been found in this district at all. The little white heron, it is" (*AWR* 201). According to Peterson, the most likely candidate for this bird is the American egret, "a large Heron of snowy-white plumage" that breeds in the southern United States and "wanders in summer to Ontario and Maine" (*Field Guide* 20). When the hunter describes it as "little," he seems to be differentiating the bird he is tracking from that other white heron, the great white, described by Peterson as the "largest American heron, inhabiting the most restricted range of any. . . . Never abundant, persecution and natural disasters reduced it to about 150 birds in 1935. . . . Range:—Extreme south Florida and the Keys. Almost unknown north of Miami" (17, 20). We read "A White Heron" as in part Jewett's attempt to encode in her text Celia Thaxter, Jewett's closest friend outside of her connection to Annie Fields. Thaxter, known as Sandpiper to her friends, loved birds, was a member of the Audubon Society, and at the end of her life dressed only in the colors of the sandpiper. Her husband, Levi, did not work, abandoned the care of their mentally handicapped son Karl to his wife, and spent his time hunting and killing rare birds. In particular, he made a series of "ornithological expeditions to Florida and to the West Indies" (Vallier 83), where indeed he might have hunted the great white heron and contributed to its endangered status. Frequently separated from her husband by her own choice, Thaxter told Annie Fields of her marriage in despairing tones; Levi clearly enraged and even emotionally abused her. Vallier speculates that Celia must have wondered whether her father had engaged her to marry Levi "just to get money to finance the hotel scheme" he had in mind for Appledore, and that despite her outward demeanor, Celia must have lived in a state of "internal rage" that "would not be stilled until Levi's death in 1884" (85–86). In writing "A White Heron" two years later, Jewett seems to be allowing Celia/Sylvia to rewrite her own history, to reject the attentions of the hunter-ornithologist, and to choose instead the birds who might have been "better friends" (*AWR* 205).

10. Her portrait of Caesar, the black servant in her historical novel, *The Tory Lover*, published at the end of her career as a writer (1901), somewhat ameliorates the racist representations in her two "Southern" short fictions. At the beginning of this novel set during the Revolutionary era,

during a conversation between Captain Paul Jones and a group Jewett's narrator terms "a simple senate of New England" (7), Jones recalls "'the worst of my boyish days when I sailed in the Two Friends, slaver.'" When the minister defends slavery as "'some manifestation of a kind Providence in bringing so many heathen souls to the influence of a Christian country,'" Jewett's narrator writes: "The fierce temper of the captain flamed to his face; he looked up at old Caesar who well remembered the passage from his native land, and saw that black countenance set like an iron mask. 'I must beg your reverence's kind pardon if I contradict you,' said Paul Jones, with scornful bitterness. There was a murmur of protest about the table; the captain's reply was not counted to be in the best of taste. Society resents being disturbed at its pleasures, and the man who had offended was now made conscious of his rudeness" (12–13). While *The Tory Lover* is considered Jewett's least successful work and an unfortunate deviation from the regionalism that characterized almost everything else she wrote, it nevertheless presents a more complex representation of black characters, though Caesar "speaks" only through Paul Jones and is characterized by his devotion to the upper-class Hamilton family. However, Jewett's representation of Caesar does not challenge class hierarchies in the way her presentation of the Civil War does in her two "Southern" stories.

11. In Faye E. Dudden, *Serving Women: Household Service in Nineteenth-Century America* (Hanover, N.H.: University Press of New England, 1983).

12. For a discussion of Celia's father Thomas Laighton's purchase of Appledore (then named Hog), Smuttynose, and Malaga Islands, his subsequent position as keeper of the light on White Island, and the family's moves back and forth between White and Smuttynose (especially during the two-year period in which Thomas Laighton was elected to the New Hampshire legislature), see Rosamond Thaxter.

13. Thaxter published most of the book as a series of four essays in the *Atlantic Monthly* during 1869–70. When she later collected the essays, she added significantly to them. In particular, she adds the long autobiographical description of her own arrival and much of what we are calling here the "regionalist" narrative.

14. In light of Hawthorne's description of Thaxter as the Miranda of the Isles of Shoals in his *American Notebooks* (537), as we mentioned in chapters 6 and 8, it is even more interesting to find Thaxter making reference to Caliban in her text.

15. Local history of the Isles of Shoals further suggests that Indians never inhabited the islands, though they may have landed on them. Lyman Rutledge quotes John Smith as writing in 1614 that the isles were "not inhabited" (12), though the fishermen who "frequented the Shoals harbor before the time of John Smith" (15) likely included American Indians. However, Thaxter clearly does not have Indians in mind when she uses the word "native."

16. In researching African marigolds, we chose to consult Norman Taylor's *A Garden Dictionary* (in part because Mary Wilsdon Fetterley, the mother of one of us, worked as an unacknowledged editorial assistant on this massive book in the 1930s). African marigolds are "better called Aztec or big marigold" because they are native to Mexico and have large yellow or orange flower heads, two to four inches wide, on foliage eighteen to twenty-four inches high. They are called African marigolds because they were "long thought to be native there" (482). In Thaxter's reference, it appears that she also considers them native to Africa.

17. In "Leaves from the Mental Portfolio of an Eurasian," included in *Mrs. Spring Fragrance and Other Writings,* Sui Sin Far relates her own experience with prejudice as a mixed-race person, including the way she overcame her own class prejudice against working-class Chinese. When forced to choose, she claims her mother's Chinese identity, but she loves her father as well, and she writes that neither her mother nor her father would understand her own condition as Eurasian. On the subject of race, she writes, "Fundamentally, I muse, all people are the same. My mother's race is as prejudiced as my father's" (223). Despite her report of numerous incidents in which she has experienced and witnessed acts of discrimination against both Chinese and black persons, she writes, "People, however, are not all alike. I meet white men, and women, too, who are proud to mate with those who have Chinese blood in their veins and think it a great honor to be distinguished by the

friendship of such" (228). She concludes her essay by writing, "My experiences as an Eurasian never cease; but people are not now as prejudiced as they have been. In the West, too, my friends are more advanced in all lines of thought" (230).

Chapter 10: Regionalism as "Queer" Theory

1. In thinking about the relation of form to the queer, we find illuminating Lindemann's reflections on Cather's relation to form. Describing "a vital pattern that shapes Cather's first decades as a novelist," she writes: "That pattern, which has not been sufficiently explored, may be stated in the form of a proposition: *The further Cather moves away from realism as the structuring principle of her narratives, the more likely it is that white heteronormativity will be challenged by a 'queerness' marked not as individual pathology but as forceful oppositionality.*" As part of her definition of realism she includes "plots driven by conflicts and the rhythms of heterosexual desire" (49).

2. Here, of course, we think specifically of such texts as Jewett's *Deephaven* and "Martha's Lady," and generally of such writers as Jewett, Freeman, and Dunbar-Nelson.

3. Foucault's model of distinguishing between homosexual behavior and gay identity and his claim that the latter emerged only at the end of the nineteenth century have become fairly standard assumptions in much of contemporary gay and lesbian history. For example, in *Boots of Leather, Slippers of Gold,* Kennedy and Davis introduce their study of working-class lesbian bar culture in mid-twentieth-century Buffalo with the following observations: "Fourth and finally, there were the women like those who are the center of this book, who socialized together because of their explicit romantic and sexual interest in other women. These communities mark the beginning of modern lesbian identity. Those who participated in these communities experienced themselves as different and this difference was a core part of their identity. . . . Homosexual behavior certainly existed in earlier times and in other cultures, but it was a discrete part of a person's life, not something around which an individual constructed his or her identity. In the twentieth century, however, being lesbian or gay became a core identity around which people came together with others like themselves and built their lives" (8). Similarly, John D'Emilio writes in *Sexual Politics, Sexual Communities* that "[i]n America's cities from the 1870s through the 1930s, there emerged a class of people who recognized their erotic interest in members of their own sex, interpreted this interest as a significant characteristic that distinguished them from the majority, and sought others like themselves" (11). Before this time, "the existence of lesbians and gay men was inconceivable" (10). Certain other historians have, however, posed challenges to these assumptions. In *Passions between Women,* for example, Emma Donoghue speculates that "the change from a concept of sex acts between women to a concept of lesbian identity was very gradual," and "that these ideas overlapped for several centuries" (20), and she argues more specifically that certain "seventeenth- and eighteenth-century words do not seem to refer only to isolated sexual acts, as is often claimed, but to the emotions, desires, styles, tastes and behavioural tendencies that can make up an identity" (3). For further insight into the complexities of this debate, see the introduction to and the first three sections of Martin Duberman, Martha Vicinus, and George Chauncey Jr., eds., *Hidden from History: Reclaiming the Gay and Lesbian Past* (New York: Penguin, 1989).

4. The phrase refers to the title of Carroll Smith-Rosenberg's essay "The Female World of Love and Ritual: Relations between Women in Nineteenth-Century America," *Signs* 1.1 (1975): 1–29.

5. See also her discussion of the use of the term "queer" during the period in question (Lindemann 2–3).

6. The quotation Lindemann gives from Eve Kosofsky Sedgwick is found in Sedgwick's *Epistemology of the Closet* (75).

7. Cather's essay, "148 Charles Street," is collected in *Not Under Forty* (New York: Knopf, 1936).

8. Lindemann is citing Willa Cather, *The Song of the Lark* (Boston: Houghton Mifflin, 1983), 580 and 581, in these passages.

9. As did Freeman, Cooke also married late in life, at age forty-six, as if succumbing, like Celia

Barnes in "How Celia Changed Her Mind," to the pressures on an "old maid." However, this marriage to a man sixteen years younger brought economic hardship, as her husband worked only infrequently and her father-in-law used Cooke's money unwisely in his business ventures. If she had hoped to achieve love, home, and family without the loss of self and her own independence, she must have been bitterly disappointed.

10. In one reading of the story, Cooke, like Thaxter and Austin, also derives her creative power from what she considers the "black"; however, in another reading, Cooke, like Maya, views her own "anima" "with accusing eyes" (*"How Celia Changed Her Mind"* 12) and turns against the very source of anger that in many ways "animates" her own best fiction. Thus, in fiction that more often critiques structures of dominance, the few but marked negative references to women of color may also be symptomatic of Cooke's struggle against her own queerness, for, as Anima tells Maya, "'the Spark abides no other fate but shining'" (12).

11. In "Some Account of Thomas Tucker," Cooke creates a character who possesses an "aggressive" and "ghastly honesty" (*"How Celia Changed Her Mind"* 253, 256) that cuts him off from human relationship, destroys his ability to work, and ends by killing him.

12. That Cooke is consciously working with questions of "kind" in a way that has resonance for the queer is established at the beginning of the story when she writes, of "Miny" Todd's father, "The trees were his congeners" (*Huckleberries* 85), a word that derives from *genus*, the same kind or group.

13. In this context we might give a slightly queer turn to Jewett's comment to Annie Fields that while "A White Heron," rejected by the *Atlantic Monthly*, "isn't a very good magazine story, I love her and mean to keep her for the beginning of my next book" (*Letters of Sarah Orne Jewett* 60; qtd. in Lindemann, 89). Not only did Jewett "keep her"; she named the collection after her as if to insist on her preference for the queer child, her willingness to stand by her despite her rejection by the normalizing *Atlantic Monthly*, and her determination to create a space for her public appearance.

14. Lillian Faderman, *Chloe Plus Olivia: An Anthology of Lesbian Literature from the Seventeenth Century to the Present* (New York: Viking, 1994).

15. As Pryse discusses, Kate Lancaster is modeled on Jewett's friend Kate Birckhead, and her diaries and early writing about friendship suggest archival links between the real friend and the fictional one. See also Jewett, "Outgrown Friends," ed. Marjorie Pryse, *New England Quarterly* 69.3 (Sept. 1996): 461–72.

16. See Pryse, "Sex, Class, and 'Category Crisis,'" for a discussion of both of these stories, and see this essay and Fetterley, "Reading *Deephaven* as a Lesbian Text," for the contexts surrounding critics' understanding of lesbianism in Jewett and her work.

17. "The Long Arm" is included in Faderman, *Chloe Plus Olivia* (see note 14).

18. We have provided parenthetical double pagination at several points throughout this section. The first number will refer to *The Awakening;* the second to *AWR,* where we include only chapter 21 from the novel, but do so in order to call attention to Mlle. Reisz and her connections with characters in regionalist fiction. Where we indicate only one page number, we are referring to chapters in *The Awakening* not included in *AWR.*

Chapter 11: "Close" Reading and Empathy

1. In his book *Emotional Intelligence,* Goleman develops the concepts of numerous other psychologists, most notably the Yale psychologist Peter Salovey. In a footnote, Goleman directs his own reader to Peter Salovey and John D. Mayer, "Emotional Intelligence," *Imagination, Cognition, and Personality* 9 (1990): 185–211.

2. We are consciously echoing Eve Sedgwick's exploration of the phrase "homosexual panic" from both psychiatric and legal discourse in *Epistemology of the Closet* and her earlier book, *Between Men: English Literature and Male Homosocial Desire* (New York: Columbia University Press,

1985). Lindemann cites the work of Jonathan Ned Katz (*Gay/Lesbian Almanac: A New Documentary* [New York: Harper, 1983]), who "traced the origins of the phrase 'homosexual panic' to the work of Dr. Edward J. Kempf, a psychiatrist at a U.S. government mental hospital in Washington, D.C., who relied heavily on case histories of World War I soldiers and sailors to document the type of anxiety attack that occurs 'due to the pressure of uncontrollable perverse sexual cravings' arising 'wherever men or women must be grouped alone for prolonged periods' (quoted in *Almanac* 391–92)" (Lindemann 75).

3. The major essays in which Klein develops these ideas and related concepts of "paranoid" and "depressive" "positions" are "Envy and Gratitude" (1957) and "Notes on Some Schizoid Mechanisms" (1946), both in Melanie Klein, *Envy and Gratitude and Other Works* (New York: Delacorte Press, 1975). For readers skeptical of Klein's ability to "know" how infants feel, as Winnicott writes in "The Theory of the Parent-Infant Relationship" (1960), "it is not from direct observation of infants so much as from the study of the transference in the analytic setting that it is possible to gain a clear view of what takes place in infancy itself" (54).

4. See Margaret Mahler, F. Pine, and A. Bergman, *The Psychological Birth of the Human Infant* (New York: Basic, 1975).

5. Ciaramicoli is quoting Rogers, *On Becoming a Person: A Therapist's View of Psychotherapy* (Boston: Houghton Mifflin, 1961), 332–33.

6. In editing the letters Jewett had sent her over the years for the volume *Letters of Sarah Orne Jewett* that she compiled after Jewett's death, Annie Fields was working with pages that included only partial dates, which may explain the following discrepancy. The letter we are quoting is dated "Sunday, 5th July," and Fields places it among other letters dated 1889. However, it is in this letter that Jewett reports rereading Stowe's *The Pearl of Orr's Island,* and she writes, "I felt at the funeral that none of us could really know and feel the greatness of the moment, but it has seemed to grow more great to me ever since. I love to think of the purple flowers you laid on the coffin" (47). Stowe died July 1, 1896. Given the content of this letter, with its unmistakable reference to Stowe's funeral, we believe it must have been written July 5, 1896, not in 1889.

7. That Austin was self-conscious concerning her use of pronouns is evident from her autobiography, *Earth Horizon* (Boston: Houghton, 1932), in which she refers to herself throughout in the third person as "I-Mary."

8. The poet Austin is referring to here is Ralph Waldo Emerson and the poem she is quoting is "Forbearance" (1842).

9. Almost all of "The Minister's Housekeeper" is included in quotations, as it is told by Stowe's narrator, Sam Lawson. In order to avoid the excessive use of quotation marks within quotation marks, we have chosen to disregard the second, and on occasion, third, set of marks that would technically be required.

10. For an early essay on "tact" and empathy in Jewett, see Marcia McClintock Folsom, "'Tact Is a Kind of Mind-Reading': Empathic Style in Sarah Orne Jewett's 'The Country of the Pointed Firs,'" *Critical Essays on Sarah Orne Jewett,* ed. Gwen L. Nagel (Boston: G. K. Hall, 1984), 76–88.

11. See, for example, "In the Land of the Free," in which by the time Lae Choo wins the right to take her own child out of detention with the missionaries who have raised and "Americanized" him, he no longer recognizes her; or "The Wisdom of the New," in which Wou Sankwei's wife, newly arrived from China, decides to murder her own beloved son in order to prevent him from going to the American school, both included in *Mrs. Spring Fragrance and Other Stories.*

12. In citing Zitkala-Ša in this section, our first reference will be to *American Indian Stories.* For those sketches reprinted in *American Women Regionalists,* the second page number will refer parenthetically to *AWR.*

13. For another and more detailed Kleinian reading of "The Foreigner," see Church. Church invokes Klein's theory of mourning, rather than her concept of reparation, suggesting that the story "involves a difficult coming to terms with guilt and anxiety that result from conscious but mostly unconscious feelings of hostility toward the lost loved one" (53), namely Mrs. Todd's mother.

Church's reading here supports our understanding of Mrs. Todd's anxiety. Church sees "surfacing impulses" in Mrs. Todd's language of the "great breakers" that "pound" on the shore, evoking the sea's "anger" and "fight"; "that this imagined force comes from impossibly far below associates it with Mrs. Todd's unconscious impulses, ones that in a Kleinian sense have in fact persisted 'since [her] world began' in infancy" (57).

14. Klein also saw art as reparative, and thereby as an extension of the empathy the infant learns in the earliest attempt to modify its rage at the absent mother. See, for example, her essay "Love, Guilt, and Reparation" (1937), *Love, Guilt and Reparation and Other Works, 1921–1945* (New York: Delacorte, 1975), 309–43.

Works Cited

Adams, John. *Harriet Beecher Stowe.* New York: Twayne, 1963.

Alcoff, Linda. "Cultural Feminism versus Post-Structuralism: The Identity Crisis in Feminist Theory." *The Second Wave: A Reader in Feminist Theory.* Ed. Linda Nicholson. New York: Routledge, 1997. 330–55.

Allen, Walter. *The Short Story in English.* Oxford: Oxford University Press, 1981.

Ammons, Elizabeth. *Conflicting Stories: American Women Writers at the Turn into the Twentieth Century.* New York: Oxford University Press, 1991.

———. *Edith Wharton's Argument with America.* Athens: University of Georgia Press, 1980.

Ammons, Elizabeth, and Valerie Rohy, eds. *American Local Color Writing, 1880–1920.* New York: Penguin, 1998.

Anzaldúa, Gloria. *Borderlands/La Frontera: The New Mestiza.* San Francisco: Aunt Lute Books, 1987.

Aristotle. Trans. Philip Wheelwright. New York: Odyssey Press, 1951.

Armstrong, Nancy. "A Brief Genealogy of 'Theme.'" *The Return of Thematic Criticism.* Ed. Werner Sollors. Cambridge, Mass.: Harvard University Press, 1993. 38–45.

Austin, Mary. *Earth Horizon: An Autobiography.* Boston: Houghton, 1932.

———. "Non-English Writings II: Aboriginal." *The Cambridge History of American Literature.* Ed. William Peterfield Trent et al. Vol. 4. New York: G. P. Putnam's Sons, 1921. 610–34.

———. "Regionalism in American Fiction." *English Journal* 21 (Feb. 1932): 97–107.

———. *Stories from the Country of Lost Borders.* 1903, 1909. American Women Writers Series. Ed. Marjorie Pryse. New Brunswick, N.J.: Rutgers University Press, 1987.

Baker, Carlos. "Delineation of Life and Character." *Literary History of the United States.* Ed. Robert E. Spiller et al. Vol. 2. New York: Macmillan, 1948. 843–61.

Baym, Nina. *Feminism and American Literary History.* New Brunswick, N.J.: Rutgers University Press, 1992.

———. *Novels, Readers, and Reviewers: Responses to Fiction in Antebellum America.* Ithaca: Cornell University Press, 1984.

———. *Woman's Fiction: A Guide to Novels by and about Women in America, 1820–1870.* Ithaca: Cornell University Press, 1978.

Benjamin, Jessica. "A Desire of One's Own: Psychoanalytic Feminism and Intersubjective Space." *Feminist Studies/Critical Studies.* Ed. Teresa de Lauretis. Bloomington: Indiana University Press, 1986. 78–101.

Bercovitch, Sacvan. *Rites of Assent: Transformations in the Symbolic Construction of America.* New York: Routledge, 1993.

Berlant, Lauren, and Michael Warner. "What Does Queer Theory Teach Us about X?" *PMLA* 110.3 (1995): 343–49.

Blair, Walter. *Native American Humor.* San Francisco: Chandler, 1960.

Bohart, Arthur C., and Leslie S. Greenberg. "Empathy: Where Are We and Where Do We Go from Here?" *Empathy Reconsidered: New Directions in Psychotherapy.* Ed. Arthur C. Bohart and Leslie S. Greenberg. Washington, D.C.: APA, 1997. 419–49.

———. "Empathy and Psychotherapy: An Introductory Overview." *Empathy Reconsidered: New Directions in Psychotherapy.* Ed. Arthur C. Bohart and Leslie S. Greenberg. Washington, D.C.: APA, 1997. 3–31.

Brinker, Menachem. "Theme and Interpretation." *The Return of Thematic Criticism.* Ed. Werner Sollors. Cambridge, Mass.: Harvard University Press, 1993. 21–37.

Brodhead, Richard H. *Cultures of Letters: Scenes of Reading and Writing in Nineteenth-Century America.* Chicago: University of Chicago Press, 1993.

———. "Introduction." *The Conjure Woman and Other Conjure Tales.* By Charles Chesnutt. Durham, N.C.: Duke University Press, 1993. 1–21.

———. "Literature and Culture." *Columbia Literary History of the United States.* Ed. Emory Elliott. New York: Columbia University Press, 1988. 467–81.

Bryan, Violet Harrington. "Race and Gender in the Early Works of Alice Dunbar-Nelson." *Louisiana Women Writers.* Ed. Dorothy H. Brown and Barbara C. Ewell. Baton Rouge: Louisiana State University Press, 1992. 121–38.

Buell, Lawrence. "Circling the Spheres: A Dialogue." *American Literature* 70.3 (1998): 465–90.

———. *New England Literary Culture: From Revolution Through Renaissance.* Cambridge: Cambridge University Press, 1986.

Bush, Robert. "Introduction." *Grace King of New Orleans: A Selection of Her Writings.* Ed. Robert Bush. Baton Rouge: Louisiana State University Press, 1973. 3–31.

Butler, Marilyn. *Maria Edgeworth: A Literary Biography.* Oxford: Clarendon Press, 1972.

Campbell, Donna M. *Resisting Regionalism: Gender and Naturalism in American Fiction, 1885–1915.* Athens: Ohio University Press, 1997.

Carafiol, Peter. "Commentary: After American Literature." *American Literature* 6.3 (1992): 539–49.

———. "The New Orthodoxy: Ideology and the Institution of American Literary History." *American Literature* 59.4 (1987): 626–38.

Cary, Alice. *Clovernook.* New York: Redfield, 1852.

———. *Clovernook, Second Series.* New York: Redfield, 1853.

———. *Clovernook Sketches and Other Stories.* Ed. Judith Fetterley. American Women Writers Series. New Brunswick, N.J.: Rutgers University Press, 1987.

Cather, Willa. "Preface." *The Country of the Pointed Firs and Other Stories.* By Sarah Orne Jewett. 1925. Garden City, N.Y.: Doubleday, 1956. 6–11.

Chesnutt, Charles. *The Conjure Woman and Other Conjure Tales.* 1899. Ed. Richard H. Brodhead. Durham, N.C.: Duke University Press, 1993.

———. *Paul Marchand, F.M.C.* Ed. Dean McWilliams. Princeton: Princeton University Press, 1997.

Chopin, Kate. *The Awakening.* 1899. Norton Critical Edition. Ed. Margot Culley. New York: W. W. Norton, 1976.

Chubbuck, Emily, pseud. Fanny Forester; aka Mrs. Emily Judson. *Alderbrook: A Collection of Fanny Forester's Village Sketches, Poems, Etc.* 2 vols. Boston: Ticknor, 1847.

Church, Joseph. "Absent Mothers and Anxious Daughters: Facing Ambivalence in Jewett's 'The Foreigner.'" *Essays in Literature* 17.1 (1990): 52–68.

Ciaramicoli, Arthur. *The Power of Empathy.* New York: Penguin Putnam, 2001.

Cohen, Hennig, and William B. Dillingham, eds. *Humor of the Old Southwest.* Boston: Houghton Mifflin, 1964.

Coleman, Linda S. "Race and Gender in Grace King's Short Fiction." *Louisiana Women Writers.*

Ed. Dorothy H. Brown and Barbara C. Ewell. Baton Rouge: Louisiana State University Press, 1992. 33–55.

Collins, Patricia Hill. *Black Feminist Thought: Knowledge, Consciousness, and the Politics of Empowerment.* 2d ed. New York: Routledge, 2000.

Cooke, Rose Terry. *"How Celia Changed Her Mind" and Selected Stories.* Ed. Elizabeth Ammons. American Women Writers Series. New Brunswick, N.J.: Rutgers University Press, 1986.

———. *Huckleberries Gathered from New England Hills.* Boston: Houghton Mifflin, 1891.

———. *Somebody's Neighbors.* Boston: Osgood, 1881.

———. *The Sphinx's Children and Other People's.* Boston: Ticknor, 1886.

Cox, James M. "Humor and America: The Southwestern Bear Hunt, Mrs. Stowe, and Mark Twain." *Sewanee Review* 83 (1975): 573–601.

———. "Regionalism: A Diminished Thing." *Columbia Literary History of the United States.* Ed. Emory Elliott. New York: Columbia University Press, 1988. 761–84.

Crimp, Douglas. "Right on, Girlfriend!" *Fear of a Queer Planet: Queer Politics and Social Theory.* Ed. Michael Warner. Minneapolis: University of Minnesota Press, 1993. 300–20.

Daigrepont, Lloyd M. "Ichabod Crane: Inglorious Man of Letters." *Early American Literature* 19.1 (1984): 68–81.

Davey, Frank. "Towards the Ends of Regionalism." *A Sense of Place: Re-Evaluating Regionalism in Canadian and American Writing.* Ed. Christian Riegel and Herb Wyile. Edmonton, Alberta, Can.: University of Alberta Press, 1997. 1–18.

Davidson, Cathy N. "Preface: No More Separate Spheres!" *American Literature* 70.3 (Sept. 1998): 443–63.

Davis, Lennard. *Resisting Novels: Ideology and Fiction.* New York: Methuen, 1987.

D'Emilio, John. *Sexual Politics, Sexual Communities: The Making of a Homosexual Minority in the United States, 1940–1970.* Chicago: University of Chicago Press, 1983.

Dobson, Joanne. "Reclaiming Sentimental Literature." *American Literature* 69.2 (1997): 263–88.

Donoghue, Emma. *Passions between Women: British Lesbian Culture, 1668–1801.* New York: Harper Perennial, 1996.

Donovan, Josephine. "Nan Prince and the Golden Apples." *Colby Library Quarterly* 22.1 (1986): 17–27.

———. *New England Local Color Literature: A Women's Tradition.* New York: Frederick Ungar, 1983.

Eagle, Morris, and David L. Wolitzky. "Empathy: A Psychoanalytic Perspective." *Empathy Reconsidered: New Directions in Psychotherapy.* Ed. Arthur C. Bohart and Leslie S. Greenberg. Washington, D.C.: APA, 1997. 217–44.

Eagleton, Terry. *Literary Theory: An Introduction.* 1983. Minneapolis: University of Minneapolis Press, 1996.

Edgeworth, Maria. *Castle Rackrent.* 1800. Ed. George Watson. New York: Oxford University Press, 1964.

Elliott, Emory, ed. *The Columbia History of the American Novel.* New York: Columbia University Press, 1991.

———, ed. *Columbia Literary History of the United States.* New York: Columbia University Press, 1988.

Fetterley, Judith. "Entitled to More Than 'Peculiar Praise': The Extravagance of Alice Cary's 'Clovernook.'" *Legacy* 10.2 (1993): 103–19.

———. "Introduction." *Clovernook Sketches and Other Stories.* By Alice Cary. Ed. Judith Fetterley. American Women Writers Series. New Brunswick, N.J.: Rutgers University Press, 1987. xi–xliii.

———. "'Not in the Least American': Nineteenth-Century Literary Regionalism." *College English* 56.8 (Dec. 1994): 877–95.

———. "Only a Story, Not a Romance: Harriet Beecher Stowe's 'The Pearl of Orr's Island.'" *The*

(Other) American Traditions: Nineteenth-Century Women Writers. Ed. Joyce W. Warren. New Brunswick, N.J.: Rutgers University Press, 1993. 108–25.

———, ed. *Provisions: A Reader from Nineteenth-Century American Women.* Bloomington: Indiana University Press, 1985.

———. "Reading 'Deephaven' as a Lesbian Text." *Sexual Practice, Textual Theory: Lesbian Cultural Criticism.* Ed. Susan J. Wolfe and Julia Penelope. Cambridge, Mass.: Blackwell, 1993. 164–83.

———. "Theorizing Regionalism: Celia Thaxter's *Among the Isles of Shoals.*" *Breaking Boundaries: New Perspectives on Women's Regional Writing.* Ed. Sherrie A. Inness and Diana Royer. Iowa City: University of Iowa Press, 1997. 38–53.

Fetterley, Judith, and Marjorie Pryse, eds. *American Women Regionalists, 1850–1910: A Norton Anthology.* New York: W. W. Norton, 1992.

Fisher, Dexter. "Foreword: Zitkala-Ša: The Evolution of a Writer." *American Indian Stories.* By Zitkala-Ša. Lincoln: University of Nebraska Press, 1985. v–xx.

Fisher, Philip. "American Literary and Cultural Studies since the Civil War." *Redrawing the Boundaries.* Ed. Stephen Greenblatt and Giles Gunn. New York: MLA, 1992. 232–50.

Flanagan, John T. *James Hall: Literary Pioneer of the Ohio Valley.* Minneapolis: University of Minnesota Press, 1941.

Foote, Stephanie. *Regional Fictions: Culture and Identity in Nineteenth-Century American Literature.* Madison, Wis.: University of Wisconsin Press, 2001.

Foster, Edward Halsey. *Catharine Maria Sedgwick.* New York: Twayne Publishers, 1974.

Foster, Frances Smith. "Introduction." *Minnie's Sacrifice, Sowing and Reaping, Trial and Triumph: Three Rediscovered Novels by Frances E. W. Harper.* Ed. Frances Smith Foster. Boston: Beacon Press, 1994. xi–xliii.

Foucault, Michel. *The History of Sexuality, Volume 1.* Trans. Robert Hurley. 1976. New York: Vintage, 1990.

Freeman, Mary E. Wilkins. *Selected Stories of Mary E. Wilkins Freeman.* Ed. Marjorie Pryse. New York: W. W. Norton, 1983.

Friedman, Susan Stanford. "'Beyond' Gynocriticism and Gynesis: The Geographics of Identity and the Future of Feminist Criticism." *Tulsa Studies in Women's Literature* 15.1 (1996): 13–40.

———. *Mappings: Feminism and the Cultural Geographies of Encounter.* Princeton: Princeton University Press, 1998.

Garber, Marjorie. *Vested Interests: Cross-Dressing and Cultural Anxiety.* New York: Harper Collins, 1992.

Garland, Hamlin. *Crumbling Idols.* 1894. Ed. Jane Johnson. Cambridge, Mass.: Harvard University Press, 1960.

———. "Mrs. Ripley's Trip." 1891. *Main-Travelled Roads.* New York: Signet, 1962. 182–94.

Gebhard, Caroline. "The Spinster in the House of American Criticism." *Tulsa Studies in Women's Literature* 10.1 (1991): 79–91.

Geertz, Clifford. *Local Knowledge.* New York: Basic, 1983.

Gilligan, Carol. *In a Different Voice: Psychological Theory and Women's Development.* Cambridge, Mass.: Harvard University Press, 1982.

Gilliland, Gail. *Being a Minor Writer.* Iowa City: University of Iowa Press, 1994.

Gohdes, Clarence. "Foreword." *Stories of American Life, by American Writers.* 3 vols. Ed. Mary Russell Mitford. 1830. New York: Garrett Press, 1969. iii–ix.

Goleman, Daniel. *Emotional Intelligence.* New York: Bantam Books, 1995.

Greenberg, Leslie S., and Robert Elliott. "Varieties of Empathic Responding." *Empathy Reconsidered: New Directions in Psychotherapy.* Ed. Arthur C. Bohart and Leslie S. Greenberg. Washington, D.C.: APA, 1997. 167–86.

Halperin, David. *Saint Foucault: Towards a Gay Hagiography.* New York: Oxford University Press, 1995.

Haraway, Donna. "Situated Knowledges: The Science Question in Feminism and the Privilege of Partial Perspective." *Feminist Studies* 14.3 (1988): 575–99.

Harden, Elizabeth. *Maria Edgeworth.* Boston: Twayne, 1984.

Harding, Sandra. *Whose Science? Whose Knowledge?: Thinking from Women's Lives.* Ithaca, N.Y.: Cornell University Press, 1991.

Harris, Sharon M. *Rebecca Harding Davis and American Realism.* Philadelphia: University of Pennsylvania Press, 1991.

Hartman, Joan E. "Telling Stories: The Construction of Women's Agency." *(En)Gendering Knowledge: Feminists in Academe.* Ed. Joan Hartman and Ellen Messer-Davidow. Knoxville: University of Tennessee Press, 1991. 11–34.

Hartsock, Nancy C. M. "The Feminist Standpoint: Developing the Ground for a Specifically Feminist Historical Materialism." *Feminism and Methodology.* Ed. Sandra Harding. Bloomington: Indiana University Press, 1987. 157–80.

Hawthorne, Nathaniel. *The American Notebooks.* The centenary edition of the works of Nathaniel Hawthorne. Columbus: Ohio State University Press, 1972.

Hedrick, Joan D. *Harriet Beecher Stowe: A Life.* New York: Oxford University Press, 1994.

Heilbrun, Carolyn G. *Writing a Woman's Life.* New York: W. W. Norton, 1988.

Hill, Mike. "Introduction: Vipers in Shangri-La." *Whiteness: A Critical Reader.* Ed. Mike Hill. New York: New York University Press, 1997. 1–18.

Hirsh, Elizabeth, and Gary A. Olson. "Starting from Marginalized Lives: A Conversation with Sandra Harding." *Women Writing Culture.* Ed. Elizabeth Hirsh and Gary A. Olson. Albany: State University of New York Press, 1995. 3–42.

Hoffman, Daniel. *Form and Fable in American Fiction.* New York: Oxford University Press, 1965.

hooks, bell. *Talking Back: Thinking Feminist, Thinking Black.* Boston: South End Press, 1989.

Hovet, Theodore R. "Chesnutt's 'The Goophered Grapevine' as Social Criticism." *Negro American Literature Forum* 7.3 (1973): 86–88.

Howard, June, ed. *New Essays on The Country of the Pointed Firs.* New York: Cambridge University Press, 1994.

Hull, Gloria T. *Color, Sex, and Poetry: Three Women Writers of the Harlem Renaissance.* Bloomington: Indiana University Press, 1987.

Irving, Washington. *Knickerbocker's History of New York.* 1809. New York: Capricorn Books, 1965.

———. "The Legend of Sleepy Hollow." *The Sketch Book of Geoffrey Crayon, Gent.* 1819. Vol. 8 of *Complete Works of Washington Irving.* Ed. Haskell Springer. Modern Language Association Edition. Boston: Twayne, 1978. 272–97.

———. "Rip Van Winkle." *The Sketch Book of Geoffrey Crayon, Gent.* 1819. Vol. 8 of *Complete Works of Washington Irving.* Ed. Haskell Springer. Modern Language Association Edition. Boston: Twayne, 1978. 29–41.

Jaggar, Alison M. "Love and Knowledge: Emotion in Feminist Epistemology." *Gender/Body/Knowledge: Feminist Reconstructions of Being and Knowing.* Ed. Alison M. Jaggar and Susan R. Bordo. New Brunswick, N.J.: Rutgers University Press, 1989. 145–71.

Jagose, Annamarie. *Queer Theory: An Introduction.* New York: New York University Press, 1996.

Jay, Gregory. "The End of 'American' Literature: Toward a Multicultural Practice." *College English* 53.3 (1991): 264–81.

Jewett, Sarah Orne. *A Country Doctor.* 1884. New York: Meridian, 1986.

———. *The Country of the Pointed Firs and Other Stories.* 1896. New York: W. W. Norton, 1981.

———. *Deephaven and Other Stories.* 1877. New Haven, Conn.: College and University Press, 1966.

———. *Letters of Sarah Orne Jewett.* Ed. Annie Fields. Boston: Houghton Mifflin, 1911.

———. *Sarah Orne Jewett Letters.* Ed. Richard Cary. Waterville, Me.: Colby College Press, 1956.

———. *The Tory Lover.* Boston: Houghton Mifflin, 1901.

Johanningsmeier, Charles. "Sarah Orne Jewett and Mary E. Wilkins (Freeman): Two Shrewd Businesswomen in Search of New Markets." *New England Quarterly* 70.1 (1997): 57–82.

Jordan, Judith V. "Relational Development through Mutual Empathy." *Empathy Reconsidered: New Directions in Psychotherapy.* Ed. Arthur C. Bohart and Leslie S. Greenberg. Washington, D.C.: APA, 1997. 343–51.

Kaplan, Amy. "Nation, Region, and Empire." *The Columbia History of the American Novel.* Ed. Emory Elliott. New York: Columbia University Press, 1991. 240–66.

Kaplan, E. Ann. "The 'Look' Returned: Knowledge Production and Constructions of 'Whiteness' in Humanities Scholarship and Independent Film." *Whiteness: A Critical Reader.* Ed. Mike Hill. New York: New York University Press, 1997. 316–28.

Katrak, Ketu H. "Colonialism, Imperialism, and Imagined Homes." *The Columbia History of the American Novel.* Ed. Emory Elliott. New York: Columbia University Press, 1991. 649–78.

Keller, Evelyn Fox. *A Feeling for the Organism: The Life and Work of Barbara McClintock.* New York: Freeman, 1983.

———. *Reflections on Gender and Science.* New Haven: Yale University Press, 1985.

Kennedy, Elizabeth Lapovsky, and Madeline D. Davis. *Boots of Leather, Slippers of Gold: The History of a Lesbian Community.* New York: Penguin, 1994.

Kerber, Linda. "Separate Spheres, Female Worlds, Woman's Place: The Rhetoric of Women's History." *Journal of American History* 75.1 (1988): 9–39.

King, Grace. *Balcony Stories.* 1892. Rpt. Ridgewood, N.J.: Gregg Press, 1968.

———. *Memories of a Southern Woman of Letters.* New York: Macmillan, 1932.

———. *New Orleans: The Place and the People.* 1895. New York: Negro Universities Press, 1968.

King, Kimball. *Augustus Baldwin Longstreet.* Boston: Twayne, 1984.

Kirkland, Caroline. *A New Home, Who'll Follow?* 1839. American Women Writers Series. Ed. Sandra A. Zagarell. New Brunswick, N.J.: Rutgers University Press, 1990.

Lacan, Jacques. *Écrits: A Selection.* Trans. Alan Sheridan. New York: W. W. Norton, 1977.

Lauter, Paul. *Canons and Contexts.* New York: Oxford University Press, 1991.

Leverenz, David. *Manhood and the American Renaissance.* Ithaca: Cornell University Press, 1989.

Lindemann, Marilee. *Willa Cather: Queering America.* New York: Columbia University Press, 1999.

Ling, Amy. *Between Worlds: Women Writers of Chinese Ancestry.* New York: Pergamon, 1990.

Ling, Amy, and Annette White-Parks. "Introduction." *Mrs. Spring Fragrance and Other Writings.* 1912. By Sui Sin Far. Ed. Amy Ling and Annette White-Parks. Urbana: University of Illinois Press, 1995. 1–8.

Longstreet, Augustus Baldwin. *Georgia Scenes, Characters, Incidents, &C.* 1835. Savannah: Library of Georgia Beehive Press, 1992.

MacKinnon, Catharine A. *Feminism Unmodified.* Cambridge, Mass.: Harvard University Press, 1987.

———. *Toward a Feminist Theory of the State.* Cambridge, Mass.: Harvard University Press, 1989.

Madigan, Mark. "Introduction: The Short Stories of Dorothy Canfield Fisher." *The Bedquilt and Other Stories.* By Dorothy Canfield Fisher. Columbia: University of Missouri Press, 1996. 1–11.

Marx, Leo. *The Machine in the Garden.* London: Oxford University Press, 1964.

McCullough, Kate. *Regions of Identity: The Construction of America in Women's Fiction, 1885–1914.* Stanford: Stanford University Press, 1999.

McWilliams, Dean. "Introduction." *Paul Marchand, F.M.C.* By Charles Chesnutt. Princeton: Princeton University Press, 1997. vii–xix.

Meine, Franklin J. *Tall Tales of the Southwest.* New York: Knopf, 1937.

Meriwether, James B. "Augustus Baldwin Longstreet: Realist and Artist." *Mississippi Quarterly* 35.4 (1982): 351–64.

Metcalf, Eugene Wesley. "The Letters of Paul and Alice Dunbar: A Private History." Diss. University of California, Irvine, 1973.

Miller, Jean Baker. *Toward a New Psychology of Women.* Boston: Beacon Press, 1976.

Miller, Jean Baker, and Irene Pierce Stiver. *The Healing Connection: How Women Form Relationships in Therapy and in Life.* Boston: Beacon Press, 1997.

Mitford, Mary Russell. "Preface." *Stories of American Life, by American Writers.* 3 vols. Ed. Mary Russell Mitford. 1830. New York: Garrett Press, 1969. iii–vii.

Morrison, Toni. *Playing in the Dark: Whiteness and the Literary Imagination.* Cambridge, Mass.: Harvard University Press, 1992.

Morton, Nelle. *The Journey Is Home.* Boston: Beacon Press, 1985.

Nagel, James, and Tom Quirk, eds. *The Portable American Realism Reader.* New York: Penguin, 1997.

Narayan, Uma. "The Project of Feminist Epistemology: Perspectives from a Nonwestern Feminist." *Gender/Body/Knowledge: Feminist Reconstructions of Being and Knowing.* Ed. Alison M. Jaggar and Susan R. Bordo. New Brunswick, N.J.: Rutgers University Press, 1989. 255–69.

O'Hara, Maureen. "Relational Empathy: Beyond Modernist Egocentrism to Postmodern Holistic Contextualism." *Empathy Reconsidered: New Directions in Psychotherapy.* Ed. Arthur C. Bohart and Leslie S. Greenberg. Washington, D.C.: APA, 1997. 295–319.

Oliver, Lawrence J. "Theodore Roosevelt, Brander Matthews, and the Campaign for Literary Americanism." *American Quarterly* 41.1 (1989): 93–111.

Pattee, Fred Lewis. "The Short Story." *The Cambridge History of American Literature.* Ed. William Peterfield Trent et al. Vol. 2. New York: G. P. Putnam's Sons, 1918. 367–95.

Paulding, James Kirke. *The Lion of the West; Retitled the Kentuckian, or a Trip to New York.* 1830. Ed. James N. Tidwell. Stanford: Stanford University Press, 1954.

Pavel, Thomas. "Thematics and Historical Evidence." *The Return of Thematic Criticism.* Ed. Werner Sollors. Cambridge, Mass.: Harvard University Press, 1993. 121–45.

Pease, Donald. "New Americanists: Revisionist Interventions into the Canon." *Revisionary Interventions into the Americanist Canon.* Ed. Donald Pease. Durham, N.C.: Duke University Press, 1994. 1–37.

Peterson, Roger Tory. *A Field Guide to the Birds.* 1934. Boston: Houghton Mifflin, 1947.

Phelps, Elizabeth Stuart. *Chapters from a Life.* Boston: Houghton Mifflin, 1896.

Porter, Carolyn. "What We Know That We Don't Know: Remapping American Literary Studies." *American Literary History* 6.3 (1994): 467–526.

Porter, Nancy. "Afterword." *A Woman of Genius.* 1912. By Mary Austin. Old Westbury, N.Y.: The Feminist Press, 1985. 295–321.

Pratt, Mary Louise. *Imperial Eyes: Travel Writing and Transculturation.* London and New York: Routledge, 1992.

Pryse, Marjorie. "Afterword." *Selected Stories of Mary E. Wilkins Freeman.* By Mary E. Wilkins Freeman. Ed. Marjorie Pryse. New York: W. W. Norton, 1983. 315–44.

———. "Archives of Female Friendship and the 'Way' Jewett Wrote." *New England Quarterly* 66.1 (1993): 47–66.

———. "'Distilling Essences': Regionalism and 'Women's Culture.'" *American Literary Realism* 25.2 (1993): 1–15.

———. "Exploring Contact: Regionalism and the 'Outsider' Standpoint in Mary Noailles Murfree's Appalachia." *Legacy* 17.2 (2000): 199–212.

———. "'I was country when country wasn't cool': Regionalizing the Modern in Jewett's *A Country Doctor.*" *American Literary Realism* 34.3 (2002): 217–32.

———. "Mary E. Wilkins Freeman." *Modern American Women Writers.* Ed. Elaine Showalter. New York: Scribner's, 1990. 141–53.

———. "Origins of Literary Regionalism: Gender in Irving, Stowe, and Longstreet." *Breaking Boundaries: New Perspectives on Regional Writing.* Ed. Sherrie Inness and Diana Royer. Iowa City: University of Iowa Press, 1997. 17–37.

———. "Reading Regionalism: The 'Difference' It Makes." *Regionalism Reconsidered: New Approaches to the Field.* Ed. David Jordan. New York: Garland, 1994. 47–63.

———. "Sex, Class, and 'Category Crisis': Reading Jewett's Transitivity." *American Literature* 70.3 (1998): 517–50.

———. "Women 'at Sea': Sarah Orne Jewett's 'The Foreigner.'" *Critical Essays on Sarah Orne Jewett.* Ed. Gwen L. Nagel. Boston: G. K. Hall, 1984. 89–98.

———. "Writing Out of the Gap: Regionalism, Resistance, and Relational Reading." *A Sense of Place: Re-Evaluating Regionalism in Canadian and American Writing.* Ed. Christian Riegel, Herb Wyile, Karen Overbye, and Don Perkins. Edmonton, Alberta, Can.: University of Alberta Press, 1997. 19–34.

Pulsifer, Janice Goldsmith. "Alice and Phoebe Cary, Whittier's Sweet Singers of the West." *Essex Institute Historical Collections* 109 (Jan. 1973): 9–59.

Railton, Stephen. *Authorship and Audience: Literary Performance in the American Renaissance.* Princeton: Princeton University Press, 1991.

Renza, Louis. *"A White Heron" and the Question of Minor Literature.* Madison: University of Wisconsin Press, 1984.

Rickels, Milton, and Patricia Rickels. *Seba Smith.* Boston: Twayne, 1977.

Robison, Lori. "'Why, Why Do We Not Write Our Side?' Gender and Southern Self-Representation in Grace King's Balcony Stories." *Breaking Boundaries: New Perspectives on Women's Regional Writing.* Ed. Sherrie A. Inness and Diana Royer. Iowa City: University of Iowa Press, 1997. 54–71.

Romero, Lora. *Home Fronts: Domesticity and Its Critics in the Antebellum United States.* Durham, N.C.: Duke University Press, 1997.

Roosevelt, Theodore. *The Strenuous Life.* 1905. Bedford, Mass.: Applewood Books, 1991.

———. "True Americanism." *American Ideals and Other Essays.* New York: G. P. Putnam's Sons, 1897. 46–74.

Rutledge, Lyman V. *Ten Miles Out: Guide Book to the Isles of Shoals.* Boston: Peter E. Randall Publisher for Isles of Shoals Association, 1984.

Sanday, Peggy Reeves. *Fraternity Gang Rape: Sex, Brotherhood, and Privilege on Campus.* New York: New York University Press, 1990.

Schmitz, Neil. "Forms of Regional Humor." *Columbia Literary History of the United States.* Ed. Emory Elliott. New York: Columbia University Press, 1988. 306–23.

Sears, Donald A. *John Neal.* Boston: Twayne Publishers, 1978.

Sedgwick, Catharine M. *A New England Tale.* 1822. New York: Oxford University Press, 1995.

———. *Redwood: A Tale.* 1824. New York: Putnam, 1856.

Sedgwick, Eve Kosofsky. *Epistemology of the Closet.* Berkeley: University of California Press, 1990.

———. "How to Bring Your Kids Up Gay." *Fear of a Queer Planet: Queer Politics and Social Theory.* Ed. Michael Warner. Minneapolis: University of Minnesota Press, 1993. 69–81.

———. "Paranoid Reading and Reparative Reading; or, You're So Paranoid, You Probably Think This Introduction Is about You." *Novel Gazing: Queer Readings in Fiction.* Ed. Eve Kosofsky Sedgwick. Durham, N.C.: Duke University Press, 1997. 1–37.

Seyersted, Per. *Kate Chopin: A Critical Biography.* 1969. Baton Rouge: Louisiana State University Press, 1980.

Shockley, Ann Allen. *Afro-American Women Writers, 1746–1933.* New York: Penguin, 1988.

Shulman, Robert. "Realism." *The Columbia History of the American Novel.* Ed. Emory Elliott. New York: Columbia University Press, 1991. 160–88.

Shumway, David. *Creating American Civilization: A Genealogy of American Literature as an Academic Discipline.* Minneapolis: University of Minnesota Press, 1994.

Sigourney, Lydia Huntley. *Sketch of Connecticut, Forty Years Since.* Hartford: Oliver D. Cooke and Sons, 1824.

Singley, Carol J. *Edith Wharton: Matters of Mind and Spirit.* Cambridge: Cambridge University Press, 1995.

Sklar, Katharine Kish. *Catharine Beecher: A Study in American Domesticity.* New York: W. W. Norton, 1973.

Smith, C. Alphonso. "Dialect Writers." *The Cambridge History of American Literature.* Ed. William Peterfield Trent et al. Vol. 2. New York: G. P. Putnam's Sons, 1918. 347–66.

Smith, Dorothy E. "Women's Perspective as a Radical Critique of Sociology." *Feminism and Methodology.* Ed. Sandra Harding. 1972. Bloomington: Indiana University Press, 1987. 84–96.

Sollors, Werner, ed. *The Return of Thematic Criticism.* Harvard English Studies, No. 18. Cambridge, Mass.: Harvard University Press, 1993.

Solomon, Robert C. "In Defense of Sentimentality." *Philosophy and Literature* 14.2 (1990): 304–23.

Spence, Jonathan. *The Search for Modern China.* New York: W. W. Norton, 1990.

Spengemann, William C. *A Mirror for Americanists: Reflections on the Idea of American Literature.* Hanover, N.H.: University Press of New England, 1989.

Spiller, Robert E., Willard Thorp, Thomas H. Johnson, and Henry Seidel Canby, eds. *Literary History of the United States.* 2 vols. New York: Macmillan, 1948.

Stegner, Wallace. "Western Record and Romance." *Literary History of the United States.* Ed. Robert E. Spiller et al. Vol. 2. New York: Macmillan, 1948. 862–77.

Stowe, Harriet Beecher. *The Pearl of Orr's Island.* 1862. Hartford, Conn.: Stowe-Day Foundation, 1979.

Sui Sin Far. *Mrs. Spring Fragrance and Other Writings.* 1912. Ed. Amy Ling and Annette White-Parks. Urbana: University of Illinois Press, 1995.

Sundquist, Eric. "Realism and Regionalism." *Columbia Literary History of the United States.* Ed. Emory Elliott. New York: Columbia University Press, 1988. 501–24.

———. *To Wake the Nations: Race in the Making of American Literature.* Cambridge, Mass.: Harvard University Press, 1993.

Taylor, Helen. *Gender, Race, and Region in the Writings of Grace King, Ruth McEnery Stuart, and Kate Chopin.* Baton Rouge: Louisiana State University Press, 1989.

Taylor, Norman, ed. *The Garden Dictionary.* Boston: Houghton Mifflin, 1936.

Thaxter, Celia. *Among the Isles of Shoals.* Boston: James R. Osgood, 1873.

———. *Letters of Celia Thaxter.* Ed. Annie Fields and Rose Lamb. Boston: Houghton Mifflin, 1895.

Thaxter, Rosamond. *Sandpiper: The Life and Letters of Celia Thaxter.* Hampton, N.H.: Peter E. Randall, 1963.

Thompson, Ralph. *American Literary Annuals and Gift Books, 1825–1865.* New York: H. W. Wilson, 1936.

Tichi, Cecelia. "Women Writers and the New Woman." *Columbia Literary History of the United States.* Ed. Emory Elliott. New York: Columbia University Press, 1988. 589–606.

Trent, William Peterfield, John Erskine, Stuart P. Sherman, and Carl Van Doren, eds. *The Cambridge History of American Literature.* 4 vols. New York: G. P. Putnam's Sons, 1917–21.

Vallier, Jane E. *Poet on Demand: The Life, Letters and Works of Celia Thaxter.* Camden, Me.: Down East Books, 1982.

Vanaerschot, Greet. "Empathic Resonance as a Source of Experience-Enhancing Interventions." *Empathy Reconsidered: New Directions in Psychotherapy.* Ed. Arthur C. Bohart and Leslie S. Greenberg. Washington, D.C.: APA, 1997. 141–65.

Van Gelder, Lindsy, and Pamela Robin Brandt. *The Girls Next Door: Into the Heart of Lesbian America.* New York: Simon and Schuster, 1996.

Warner, Margaret S. "Does Empathy Cure? A Theoretical Consideration of Empathy, Processing, and Personal Narrative." *Empathy Reconsidered: New Directions in Psychotherapy.* Ed. Arthur C. Bohart and Leslie S. Greenberg. Washington, D.C.: APA, 1997. 125–40.

Warner, Michael. "Introduction." *Fear of a Queer Planet: Queer Politics and Social Theory.* Ed. Michael Warner. Minneapolis: University of Minnesota Press, 1993. vii–xxxi.

———. *The Trouble with Normal: Sex, Politics, and the Ethics of Queer Life.* Cambridge, Mass.: Harvard University Press, 1999.

Watson, George, ed. "Introduction" and "Commentary." *Castle Rackrent.* By Maria Edgeworth. Oxford: Oxford University Press, 1964. vii–xxviii, 118–27.

Westbrook, Perry. *Mary Wilkins Freeman.* New Haven: College and University Press, 1967.

Wharton, Edith. *A Backward Glance.* New York: D. Appleton-Century, 1934.

———. *Ethan Frome.* 1911; rpt. 1922, introd. Edith Wharton. New York: Scribner's, 1970.

White-Parks, Annette. *Sui Sin Far/Edith Maude Eaton: A Literary Biography.* Urbana: University of Illinois Press, 1995.

Wilson, Forrest. *Crusader in Crinoline: The Life of Harriet Beecher Stowe.* Philadelphia: Lippincott, 1941.

Winnicott, D. W. *The Maturational Processes and the Facilitating Environment.* New York: International University Press, 1965.

Wolff, Cynthia Griffin. *A Feast of Words: The Triumph of Edith Wharton.* Oxford: Oxford University Press, 1977.

Wonham, Henry B. "In the Name of Wonder: The Emergence of Tall Narrative in American Writing." *American Quarterly* 41.2 (1989): 284–307.

Wood, Ann Douglas. "The Literature of Impoverishment: The Women Local Colorists in America, 1865–1914." *Women's Studies* 1 (1972): 3–45.

Yates, Norris W. *William T. Porter and the Spirit of the Times: A Study of the Big Bear School of Humor.* Baton Rouge: Louisiana State University Press, 1957.

Yuval-Davis, Nira. *Gender and Nation.* London: Sage, 1997.

Zagarell, Sandra A. "'America' as Community in Three Antebellum Village Sketches." *The (Other) American Traditions: Nineteenth-Century Women Writers.* Ed. Joyce W. Warren. New Brunswick, N.J.: Rutgers University Press, 1993. 143–63.

———. "Introduction." *A New England Nun and Other Stories.* By Mary E. Wilkins Freeman. Ed. Sandra Zagarell. New York: Penguin, 2000.

———. "Narrative of Community: The Identification of a Genre." *Signs* 13.3 (1988): 498–527.

———. "Troubling Regionalism: Rural Life and the Cosmopolitan Eye in Jewett's 'Deephaven.'" *American Literary History* 10.4 (1998): 639–63.

Zitkala-Ša. *American Indian Stories.* 1921. Foreword by Dexter Fisher. Lincoln: University of Nebraska Press, 1985.

Index

JUDITH FETTERLEY is Distinguished Teaching Professor of English and Women's Studies at the University at Albany, State University of New York. She is the author of *The Resisting Reader: A Feminist Approach to American Fiction;* editor of *Provisions: A Reader from Nineteenth-Century American Women;* and coeditor, with Marjorie Pryse, of *American Women Regionalists, 1850–1910: A Norton Anthology.* With Joanne Dobson and Elaine Showalter, she founded the American Women Writers reprint series for Rutgers University Press; for this series, she edited *Clovernook Sketches and Other Stories* by Alice Cary. Her articles have appeared in such journals as *American Literature, American Literary History,* and *College English.*

MARJORIE PRYSE is Professor of English and Women's Studies at the University at Albany, State University of New York. She is the author of *The Mark and the Knowledge: Social Stigma in Classic American Fiction;* editor of Mary Austin's *Stories from the Country of Lost Borders* and *Selected Stories of Mary E. Wilkins Freeman;* coeditor, with Judith Fetterley, of *American Women Regionalists, 1850–1910: A Norton Anthology;* and coeditor, with Hortense Spillers, of *Conjuring: Black Women, Fiction, and Literary Tradition.* Her articles have appeared in *American Literature, Legacy, New England Quarterly,* and *NWSA Journal.*

The University of Illinois Press
is a founding member of the
Association of American University Presses.

University of Illinois Press
1325 South Oak Street
Champaign, IL 61820-6903
www.press.uillinois.edu